AF252069

LEVANT SUPPLEMENTARY SERIES
VOLUME 16

EXCAVATIONS AT TELL NEBI MEND, SYRIA
VOLUME 1

Edited by Peter J. Parr

with contibutions by
E. A. Bettles, L. Copeland†, C. Grigson,
V. T. Mathias, L. Moffett, T. Molleson, M. Moussli,
Y. Nishiaki, P. J. Parr, and W. Smith

Oxbow Books
Oxford & Philadelphia

Published in the United Kingdom in 2015 jointly by
the Council for British Research in the Levant
and
OXBOW BOOKS
10 Hythe Bridge Street, Oxford OX1 2EW

and in the United States by
OXBOW BOOKS
908 Darby Road, Havertown, PA 19083

Hardcover Edition: ISBN 978-1-78297-786-5
Digital Edition: ISBN 978-1-78297-787-2

A CIP record for this book is available from the British Library

Printed in the United Kingdom by Short Run Press, Exeter

For a complete list of Oxbow titles, please contact:

UNITED KINGDOM
Oxbow Books
Telephone (01865) 241249, Fax (01865) 794449
Email: oxbow@oxbowbooks.com
www.oxbowbooks.com

UNITED STATES OF AMERICA
Oxbow Books
Telephone (800) 791-9354, Fax (610) 853-9146
Email: queries@casemateacademic.com
www.casemateacademic.com/oxbow

Oxbow Books is part of the Casemate Group

Front cover: Tell Nebi Mend and the river Orontes. Photo taken by Peter J. Parr.

Contents

List of figures, tables and plates

List of figures

List of tables

List of plates

Preface

This is the first of a series of volumes presenting the final results of excavations at Tell Nebi Mend in central Syria, sponsored by the Institute of Archaeology, University College London, during twelve field seasons between the years 1975 and 1995. It comprises a general Introduction to the site and the excavations, a report on the occupation of the site in the Pottery Neolithic period and an account of the investigation of the enclosure formed by a ditch and embankment situated on the south and west of the main *tell*. Further volumes in this series are in progress, and will deal with the occupation of the site from the Chalcolithic period in the early 4th millennium BC until its abandonment in the Byzantine period in the mid-1st millennium AD.

The Introduction, Part I, describes the location and present configuration of the site, its regional and environmental setting and its archaeological and historical importance. There follows a concise account of earlier visitors to the site and its identification with Qadesh on the Orontes (the location of the famous battle between the Egyptians and Hittites in *c.*1286 BC) and Hellenistic/ Roman Laodicea ad Libanum. A brief review of its history as derived from textual sources is given, as well as some comments on previous excavations there by a French expedition in 1921–22. The reasons for, the aims of and the methodologies adopted by the UCL excavations are presented, and an account is given of the process of obtaining sponsorship, permits and funding, with acknowledgements.

Part II assembles the structural, artefactual and ecological data from the Neolithic settlement, with chapters by individual specialists on the stratigraphy, chronology, ceramics, stone tools, human remains, animal bones and plant remains. These are discussed in relation to comparative data from contemporary archaeological sites in the Levant.

Part III assesses the evidence from a resistivity survey and two trenches designed to establish the date and purpose of the fortified enclosure.

List of contributors

Caroline Grigson
Institute of Archaeology
University College London

Virginia Mathias
Institute of Archaeology
University College London

Theya Molleson
Natural History Museum, London

Lisa Moffett
English Heritage

Peter J. Parr
Institute of Archaeology
University College London

Wendy Smith
Institute of Archaeology and Antiquity
University of Birmingham

PART I:

GENERAL INTRODUCTION

1. The site and the excavations

Peter J. Parr

Geographical setting

The archaeological site of Tell Nebi Mend (more correctly Tell el-Nebi Mendu: تل النبي مندو) is today universally recognised as the location, first, of Qadesh (or Kadesh, the preferred spelling of Egyptologists), where, in about 1286 BC, the armies of Ramesses II of Egypt and Muwatalli II of Great Hatti fought the most famous battle of pre-classical antiquity, recorded in vivid detail in reliefs and texts on the pharaoh's temples at Luxor and Abu Simbel; and, second, of Laodicea ad Libanum, founded most probably in the 3rd century BC as the capital of a district of the Seleucid empire and later becoming an important Roman country town and the seat of a suffragan bishop. It is situated in present day Syria, about 25 km south-west of Homs on the southern edge of the plain which takes its name from that city. At this point the river Orontes (the Nahr el-ᶜAsi) is joined from the west by one of its few perennial tributaries, locally known as the Muqadiyah but often called the Tannur after the name of the spring the ᶜAin et-Tannur, which is its source a few kilometres further south. It is in the fork of the two watercourses that the site stands (Figs 1.1 and 1.2). It comprises three distinct parts. To the north, almost at the apex of the fork, is the *tell* proper (Pls 1.1 and 1.2), called here the Main or Upper Mound, which is some 450 m × 220 m in extent at its base and thus approximately 10 ha in total area, with its highest point about 29 m above the flood plain at its foot. In 1975, when the University of London excavations began, much of its summit was occupied by a village and its cemetery, but since then these have been largely abandoned, apart from a mosque (recently rebuilt) dedicated to the *weli* after whom the village is named. South of the *tell* and separated from it by a modern road – almost certainly on the line of the ancient road into the city – is an area of roughly the same size that can most conveniently be referred to as the Lower Mound, and this can itself be subdivided into two more or less equal parts, the northern one some 8 m high at its highest and the southern one about half that, the two being separated by a distinct depression or waist. In 1975 the northern part showed signs of having been cultivated, although during the course of the excavations it was largely lying fallow, grazed only by sheep and goats, while the southern part was just beginning to be occupied by a new village replacing that on the Upper Mound, where building had recently been prohibited by the Syrian government. The Lower Mound and the new village are bounded on the south by an artificial ditch – clearly visible on the French aerial photograph (Fig. 1.3) published by Mesnil du Buisson in 1938 and on recent Google Earth imagery – some 40 m wide that stretches between the flood plains of the Orontes and the Muqadiyah and then continues westward on the far side of the latter, where in places the remains of an accompanying embankment on its inner edge could once also be plainly seen, although it was largely ploughed away by 2010, when these words were written. The ditch then makes a 90° turn to the north and can be followed for about another 800 m before all trace of it on the ground is lost, although another angle and eastward turn may perhaps be visible on the aerial photograph and is tentatively shown on the French 1:50,000 map of the region made in 1932. The only other surface feature to note is just north of the south-west angle, where the contours swing towards the east to form a kind of depression or 'bay' which may well indicate the site of the original entrance. The ditch and embankment thus form two (or possibly three) sides of a rectilinear enclosure, constituting the third major element in the configuration of the site. (Further discussion of the enclosure will be found in Part III of this volume.)

In his seminal study of the Late Bronze Age battle, J. H. Breasted (1903, 21) referred to Tell Nebi Mend as occupying 'the most important cross-roads in Syria', and

Fig. 1.1. Map of the Levant, showing main sites.

although this is something of an exaggeration it is certainly true that the plain around it is one of the most strategically crucial and environmentally favourable regions of the northern Levant. At about this latitude the Lebanon and Anti-Lebanon mountain ranges and the rift valley which they enclose, the Beqaᶜ, have been disrupted by tectonic forces (Fig. 1.4). The coastal range is terminated by the valley of the Nahr el-Kebir (the classical Eleutherus), forming the plain of ᶜAkkar, before rising again (though to a somewhat lower altitude) and continuing northwards as the Jebel el-Ansariyya (or Jebel el-ᶜAlawiyin). Meanwhile, the inland range, the Anti-Lebanon, bears sharply away to the east as a low range of hills and crosses the Syrian desert to die away as the Jebel el-Bishri, overlooking the Euphrates valley. As for the rift valley, this widens into the Homs plain, a structural basin filled with lacustrine marls, and then continues northwards as the Ghab, flanked on the west by the Jebel el-Ansariyya and on the east by

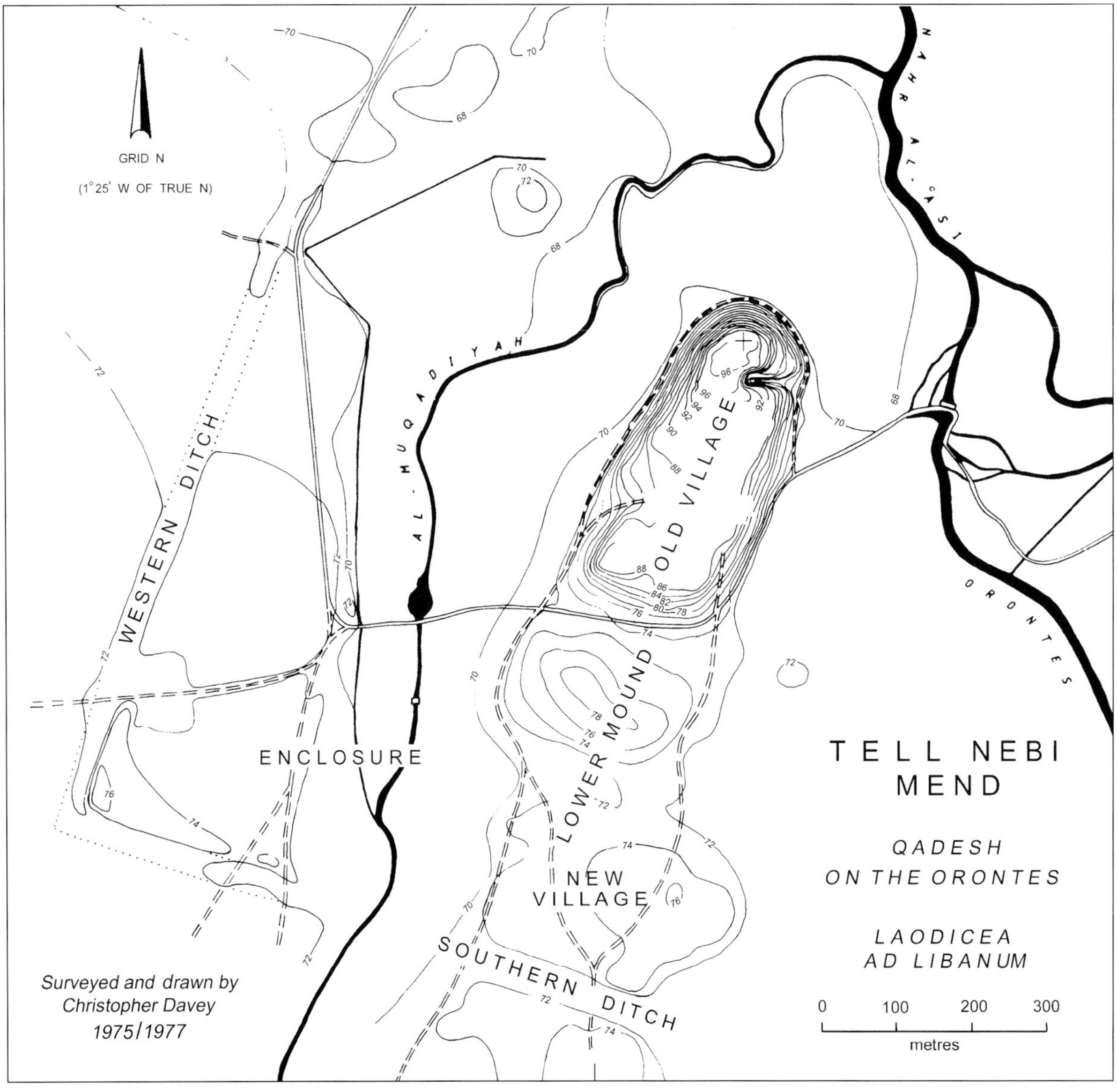

Fig. 1.2. Contour plan of Tell Nebi Mend (surveyed and drawn by C. Davey, 1975–1979).

the Jebel ez-Zawiyah and the poorly defined edge of the Syro-Arabian plateau. Through the rift flow the only two major rivers of the region, the Litani and the Orontes, rising a few kilometres from each other near Ba᷊albek and then flowing in opposite directions, the Litani towards the south and the Orontes towards the north, both discharging eventually into the Mediterranean some 300 km apart.

These mountain ranges and the enclosed rift valley constitute the northern part of the so-called Levantine Corridor, the narrow (never more than 100 km wide) strip of land bordering the eastern end of the Mediterranean, stretching for about 600 km from Anatolia to Sinai and separating the sea from the steppe. Despite the frequent presence until fairly recently of marshy terrain and dense vegetation close to the rivers themselves, the Beqa᷊ and the Ghab provide a comparatively easy north–south route, less constricted and discontinuous than the narrow

coastal plain to the west and better provided with water than the inland route – today roughly the line of the main Aleppo–Damascus highway – along the edge of the steppe further east. It was along this north–south route that, in ancient times, major cultural, ethnic, military and political movements took place between the great Egyptian, Mesopotamian and Anatolian centres of civilisation.

However, for east–west communications the northern part of the Levantine Corridor forms a considerable barrier. The Lebanon mountains, rising in places to over 3000 m, and the Ansariyya to 1600 m, are rugged and are still today largely covered with dense forests which, although formerly a valuable and heavily exploited natural resource, present a serious obstacle to human traffic between the coast and the hinterland, often in the past impeding the flow of trade and of cultural and political influences between the Mediterranean world and Asia. It is no coincidence that,

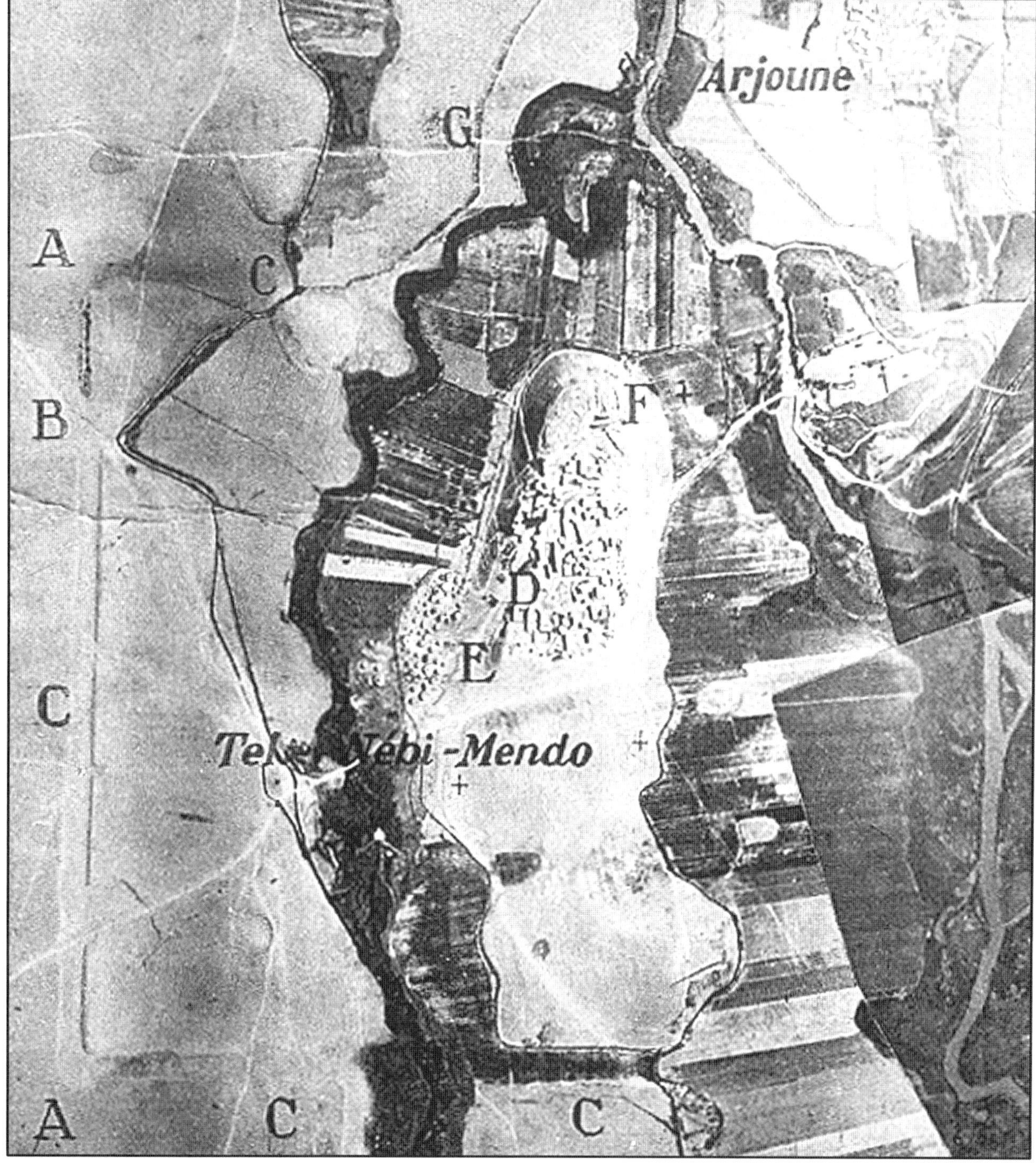

Fig. 1.3. French aerial photograph (reproduced from Mesnil du Buisson 1935–38).

for example, in the 14th and 13th centuries BC relatively few Greek and Cypriot exports found their way beyond the coastal mountains, or that in the 12th century AD the Crusaders never secured a firm footing east of the Orontes. Only in a few places are there breaks in the mountains sufficient to provide reasonably easy natural passage between the coast and the interior. One such is in the far north, where the Orontes turns west to traverse the plain of Antioch (the ʿAmuq) and reach its exit into the sea;

another, much more tortuous, is 300 km further south where the south-flowing Litani also breaks westwards through to the coast; while a third is halfway between the two, and is provided by the valley of the Nahr el-Kebir and the plains of ʿAkkar and Homs – the Homs–Tripoli Gap.

The Homs plain is thus a crossroads and a meeting place for peoples, cultures and ideas. But although great benefits can accrue from such a position so can great dangers. Meeting places are not necessarily peaceful, and

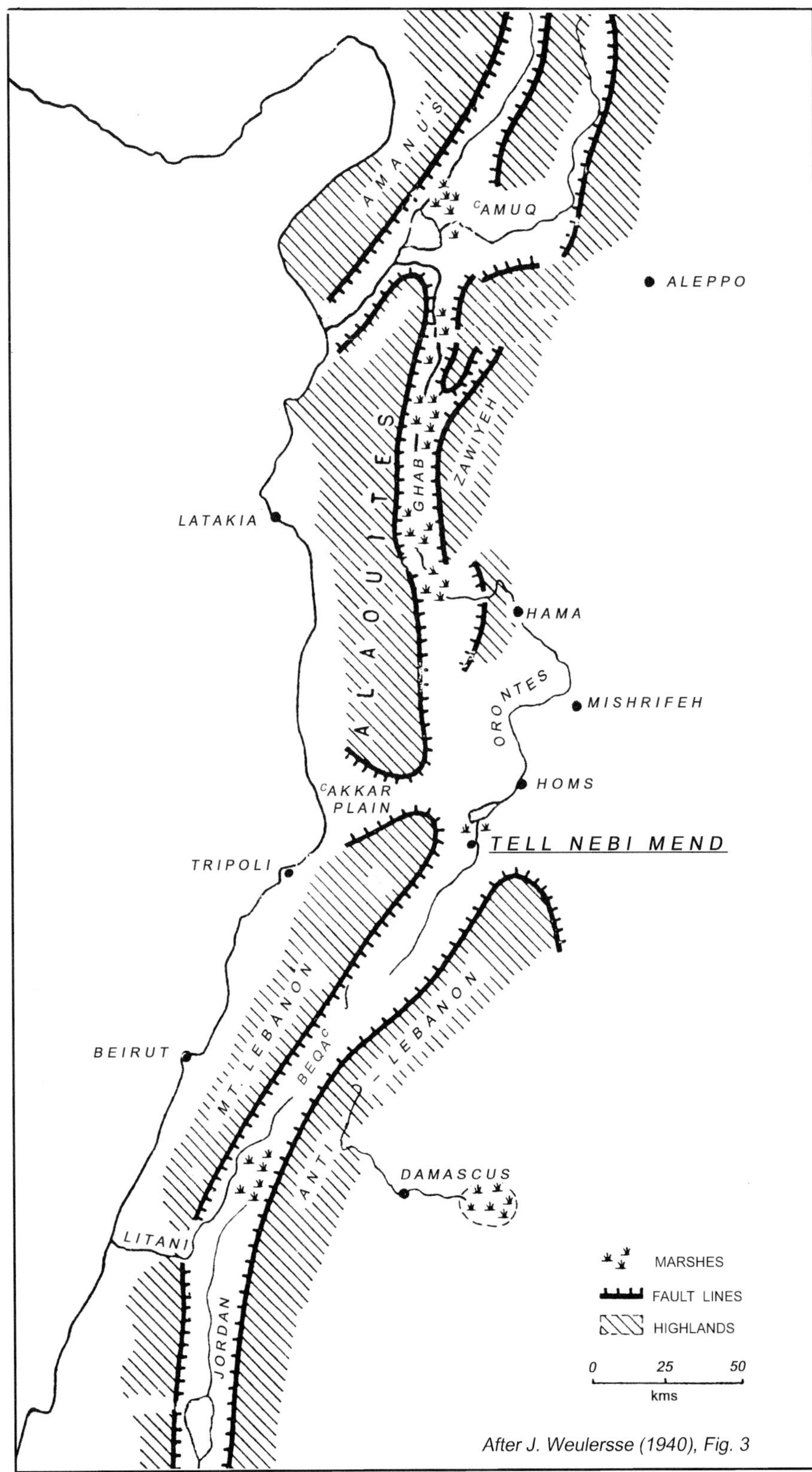

Fig. 1.4. Geomorphology of the northern Levant (after Weulerrse 1940, fig. 3).

the historical information we have suggests that the plain suffered as well as prospered from its strategic position, often forming a disputed frontier between the northern and southern parts of the Corridor and an area of contention between the surrounding powers. The ongoing conflict between Egypt, Mitanni and Hatti during the 15th–13th centuries BC, which affected Tell Nebi Mend directly on a number of occasions, as we shall see below, is the best known but not the only instance of this. For example, it was just a few kilometres away, at Riblah, that in 608 BC the pharaoh Necho II established his headquarters while attempting to defend western Syria from the encroaching Babylonians, and, twenty years later, when the balance of power in the Near East was reversed, Riblah fulfilled the same role for Nebuchadnezzar, at the beginning of the Babylonian invasion which eventually led to the fall of Jerusalem. A few centuries later still, during the wars between the Successors of Alexander the Great, the Eleutherus river – the Nahr el-Kebir – formed the *de facto* boundary between the territory claimed by the Seleucids in the north and that claimed by the Ptolemies in the south; and when, in 221 BC, Antiochus III marshalled his army prior to marching south to confront Ptolemy V it was from Laodicea ad Libanum that he launched his offensive. Nothing is known of the circumstances, military or otherwise, attending the foundation of Homs (Roman Emesa) itself, but it is certain that the town escaped violent destruction by the Muslim Arabs in the 7th century AD only because of the peaceful capitulation of its inhabitants. Four centuries later it was, uncharacteristically, spared by the invading Crusaders, who, despite having gained easy access to the Ghab in the north from Antioch and moved south along the Orontes, turned west when they reached the plain to arrive at the Mediterranean near Tripoli, presumably having decided to secure the coastal cities before moving on to Jerusalem. However, in the following century Homs found itself on the front line between the Muslim rivals Zangi, ruler of Aleppo, and Buri, ruler of Damascus, one episode in the confrontation being the sack of the city itself and the devastation of the surrounding plain in AD 1135. The 13th century AD saw further conflicts here, in 1281 and 1260, when the Ayyubid sultan Baybars defeated the invading Mongols, thus contributing to the eventual expulsion of these Central Asian invaders from the Levant; while in the 19th century AD the events of the 13th century BC around Tell Nebi Mend might have seemed to have been repeating themselves when, just a few kilometres away at Qusair, the Egyptian army of Muhammad Ali Pasha defeated the Ottoman army of Sultan Mahmud II, thus preparing the way for the annexation of Syria. The plain of Homs did indeed form an important crossroads, but was often also a turbulent battlefield.

It cannot, of course, be supposed that the first settlers at the site – who on present evidence were there shortly after 7000 BC (see Part II, below) – had in mind such geo-political considerations as those mentioned above; they would have been more concerned with its more local attractions. Like the Beqaᶜ and the Ghab, it is today well endowed with rich riverine soils, excellent for intensive agriculture, particularly if irrigation is practised, while the higher river terraces are eminently suited to fruit and cereal production. But whereas the Beqaᶜ and the Ghab lie in the rain-shadow of the coastal mountains, here the winter cyclones from the Mediterranean are able to penetrate further inland than they would otherwise, thus ensuring the plain a relatively high average annual rainfall – 460 mm at Homs compared, for example, with 343 mm just 50 km

further north along the Orontes at Hama (Wirth 1911, 92 and Karte 3). The prevailing westerly winds also have the beneficial effect of tempering the summer temperatures, which, while less important for farming, certainly adds to the attraction of the area for human habitation. And with easy access to east and west, unlike the Beqaᶜ and the Ghab, communities on the plain can readily exploit the diverse natural resources of the coast and the mountains, such as fish, timber and minerals, as well as those of the steppe, primarily the products of pastoralism.

The extent to which climatic conditions at Tell Nebi Mend in 7000 BC were different from or similar to those pertaining today is difficult to say; it is a problem on which more local palaeoecological research similar to that carried out recently at the other major site on the Homs plain, Tell Mishrifeh, ancient Qatna (Morandi Bonacossi 2007), needs to be done. There is, of course, no doubt that fluctuations, some of them significant, in temperature and precipitation have occurred across the Near East over the centuries, but it is increasingly being recognised that small sub-regions and even individual localities and communities were not necessarily affected by, or reacted to, such fluctuations in the same way. As Bradbury, in her recent comprehensive review of the palaeoclimate of the Homs region, has stated: 'climate change cannot be seen as an overarching phenomenon which imposes its conditions on human populations, but instead needs to be viewed as a series of reciprocal relationships between the elements of environment, hydrology, geology, climatology, human adaptation and social, economic and political change' (Bradbury 2011, 115). With regard to Tell Nebi Mend, its situation between two perennial watercourses and its proximity to a range of local environments must have shielded it from the worst effects of climatic deterioration. As the climate changed the rivers may well have moved a little closer or further away, the edge of the steppe in the east may have advanced or retreated, and the tree line in the Anti-Lebanon may have moved lower or higher, but the local environment may well have remained essentially the same. If this is so, then the natural vegetation to be expected in the vicinity of the site before human intervention would be open deciduous forest, thinning out eastwards to forest-steppe and savannah, with dense riverine vegetation and gallery forest along the watercourses. It is worth noting in this connection that local forests are several times mentioned in the ancient texts describing Ramesses' battle, and that trees are shown in the representation of the city at the time of its capture by Seti I a generation earlier (Fig. 1.5(a)). Although the analysis of the palaeobotanical data from the recent excavations is not yet complete, remains of cypress, cedar, olive, pistachio, oak, juniper, pine, walnut and zizyphus, as well as of club rushes and sedges, have already been identified from the earliest known levels of occupation dating to the early 7th millennium BC, and are presumably representative of the natural Holocene vegetation (for details see Chapter 8, below). As for the

Fig. 1.5. Representations of Kadesh on the Egyptian reliefs.

fauna, these same early deposits have provided evidence for the presence of wild cattle, pigs, equids, deer and gazelle (Chapter 7, below), while it can be assumed that bears, still extant in the region until a few years ago, and elephants, known to have been hunted by the 18th Dynasty pharaohs in the Ghab, were already to be found.[1] It is noticeable that the water-meadows along the Orontes today support a dense cover of grasses and herbs, in spite of intensive grazing. If this type of vegetation was present in antiquity – and there seems no reason why it should not have been – the area would have had considerable potential for cattle- and, especially, horse-breeding; the latter, in particular, might help to explain its ancient military importance, since areas where mares and foals, essential for armies, can be grazed intensively throughout the year are not at all common in the Levant.

Tell Nebi Mend is not, of course, the only ancient site on the Homs plain; many of the more obvious ones have long been known (Dussaud 1927, 103–15), while others have been discovered more recently by archaeological surveys (Kuschke *et al.* 1976; Kuschke 1979; Philip *et al.* 2002; 2005; Tubb and Dorrell forthcoming). All of them must have benefited from the favourable strategic and environmental features of the region, but it can be safely assumed that the special feature which led to Tell Nebi Mend eventually becoming the site of one of the most important cities in the region was the special degree of protection provided by the two rivers between which it is located. Although by themselves these could never have been a serious barrier to organised armies (as later history shows), they would from the beginning have proved an effective deterrent to small bands of marauders and predatory animals. In later times the distinction they gave to the settlement is shown not only by their prominence in the Egyptian representations of the town of Qadesh at the time of the battle (Fig. 1.5 (b–d)) but also – and perhaps more remarkably – by the fact that as late as the 3rd century AD coins of Caracalla from the Laodicean mint still showed the Tyche of the city flanked by the two rivers, represented by swimmers (Fig. 1.6).[2]

Unfortunately it is difficult today to establish and analyse ancient settlement patterns in the immediate vicinity of Tell Nebi Mend since, even if the climate has not changed very much, the topography has, in small but perhaps locally significant ways. For example, in recent decades irrigation and drainage have removed most of the wide expanses of water just to the east of the site that were shown on the plan made by Koldewey in 1890 (see Fig. 1.10) and on a hitherto unpublished early photograph of the mound taken by Gertrude Bell during her visit 15 years later (Fig. 1.7; see Bell 1907, 175–6); today the river is closely confined to its bed (Fig. 1.8). We may also note the disappearance of the narrow arm of the Homs Lake

which the French map mentioned above shows extending about 3 km upstream from its southern shore to almost the foot of the *tell* (for convenience see Calvet and Geyer 1992, fig. 8), although there is no indication of this on the earlier sketch maps of the region made by Conder in 1881 and Gautier in 1893 (see below and Figs 1.9 and 1.11), and it has disappeared again today. Earlier changes to the landscape were brought about by the lake itself. While this is universally acknowledged to be in origin a natural feature created by a lava outflow blocking the river (Weulersse 1940, 17), and recent geomorphological research suggests that it existed in one form or another as early as the 2nd millennium BC (Philip *et al.* 2002, 14), it is certain that at some time an artificial dam was built on the line of the outflow and was rebuilt and repaired on a number of later occasions (Brossé 1923, 234–40; Calvet and Geyer 1992, 27). Such an artificial dam would clearly have affected the size and shape of the original lake and the topography of the surrounding terrain, and it is therefore unfortunate that its date is unknown (estimates range from the 14th century BC to the 3rd century AD (Calvet and Geyer 1992, 33–8)), as are the dates of any subsequent repairs and alterations, apart from the latest, which took place in 1938 (Calvet and Geyer 1992, 27). It has often been observed that there are five or six small islands in the lake (marked 'tell' on the French) map, which are apparently artificial mounds (Calvet and Geyer 1992, fig. 8). One of these, Tell et-Tin, was investigated at the end of the 19th century and revealed evidence of occupation – though not necessarily continuous

Fig. 1.6. Coin of Caracalla from the Laodicea mint (courtesy of Dr Jack Nurpetlian).

Fig. 1.7. Photograph of Tell Nebi Mend from the east taken in 1905 by Gertrude Bell (courtesy of the Gertrude Bell Archive at Newcastle University).

Fig. 1.8. The Orontes east of Tell Nebi Mend in 1975.

– from the prehistoric to the Roman periods (see below). Nothing is known of the other mounds, nor whether there are additional archaeological sites concealed by the waters, and this possible – indeed, probable – incompleteness of the data must be taken into account when ancient settlement patterns on the plain are considered.

Archaeology in the northern Levantine Corridor: the research context for excavations at Tell Nebi Mend

Despite the important role the Levantine Corridor must have played in the early cultural, economic and political history of Western Asia, much of it was, until fairly recently, largely neglected by archaeologists. Only in the southern third – historic Palestine, the Holy Land – was this not true. Here, right from the beginnings of Near Eastern archaeology in the early 19th century those many scholars whose primary interests lay in biblical antiquities and history rather than in Egyptology or Assyriology flocked in ever increasing numbers to pursue their research. In the north it was different: here it seemed that only the monuments of such classical sites as Ba‘albek and Palmyra could compete with the magnificent ruins of ancient Egypt, Assyria and Babylon for the attention of scholars. This imbalance between north and south was remarked upon as early as 1922 by the French archaeologist Sebastian Ronzevalle, who, in the course of his pioneering investigation of Tell Mishrifeh (ancient Qatna) on the central Orontes, wrote:

> Jusqu'ici, la haute antiquité syrienne est restée à peu près inconnue … tout ce qu'on a trouvé dans la Syrie propre remonte rarement au-delà de la période hellénistique … Et cependant l'on s'acharne à l'envi, durant des années, sur trois ou quatre sites palestiniens, pour l'excavation desquels on engage de grosses sommes, sans qu'on ait jamais pu s'avouer jusqu'ici que le résultat répondait à l'effort. Loin de moi, bien entendu, la pensée de désapprouver ce qui se fait en Palestine; le sentiment particulier, qui préside aux entreprises archéologiques lancées sur ce sol, justifie amplement les sacrifices consentis … Et peut-on oublier, que, si le peuple d'Israël fut moralement très grand, il fut, par contre, très petit et par sa civilisation matérielle et par sa rôle politique? De deux chantiers de fouilles établis, l'un au cœur de la Judée, l'autre dans la Syrie centrale et fonctionnant simultanément, on peut dire, presque sans paradoxe, que c'est le seconde qui est peut-être appelé à fournir le plus de renseignements historiques ou archéologiques sur la Palestine elle-même. (Ronzevalle 1911–21, 123–4)

One does not have to agree with all of Ronzevalle's comments to recognise the essential truth of his observations. They were still valid a generation later when, in 1948, Schaeffer published his monumental *Stratigraphie Comparée et Chronologie de l'Asie Occidentale*, in which he was able to marshal evidence from less than half the number of excavated sites in Lebanon and western Syria that he was from Palestine. Nor did the resumption of archaeological activity in the two decades following the Second World War do much to improve the situation: if anything the imbalance became greater, with the dramatic development of 'national' or 'heritage' archaeology in the new state of Israel. In the north, although work was soon resumed at coastal sites such as Ras Shamra and Byblos, it was some time before major expeditions began to examine new sites, notably Tell Sukas (1958) and Tell

Kazel (1962) on the coastal plain, and Tell Ghasil (1956) and Kamid el-Loz (1963) in the Beqa‵. Further inland – and arguably not strictly speaking in the Corridor itself – work commenced at Tell Rifa‵ at in the far north in 1956 and at Tell Mardikh, south-east of Aleppo, in 1963. The dramatic impetus given to Syrian archaeology later in the 1960s by the international salvage project preceding the construction of the Tabqa dam on the Euphrates had relatively little direct effect on archaeological activity in the west of the country, the newly excavated sites all being on or close to that river, in what can perhaps be termed the 'Mesopotamian Corridor'. Since it naturally took time for the new data provided by this fieldwork to become disseminated, it comes as no surprise that syntheses of western Syrian archaeology in the Bronze and Iron Ages, such as those of Drower and Kenyon in the first volume of the new *Cambridge Ancient History*, published in 1971, still relied entirely on the evidence already assembled by Schaeffer almost a quarter of a century previously, as Kenyon acknowledged (Kenyon 1971a, 583–94; Drower 1971, 333–51). And it is noteworthy that even in a very recent handbook in English entitled *The Archaeology of Syria* (Akkermans and Schwartz 2003) very few of the many sites by then known in the northern Levant other than those already mentioned appear in the index or on the distribution maps.

The Tell Nebi Mend project

It was in the 1960s that the University of London's Tell Nebi Mend Project had its conception. Having recently begun teaching at the Institute of Archaeology on the pre-classical Archaeology of Palestine (shortly to be renamed the Archaeology of the Levant), the writer soon realised not only the difficulty of fully understanding the subject – except perhaps in its narrowest definition as 'Biblical Archaeology' – without taking cognisance of evidence from the region immediately to the north, but also the paucity and unreliability of that evidence. Apart from the main coastal sites, Byblos and Ras Shamra, and Tell Atchana and the other ‵Amuq sites at the far northern end of the Corridor, only Hama on the middle Orontes had produced a long stratified sequence of material such as was necessary to establish a cultural chronology for the interior; and the Danish excavations there (from 1932 until 1938) were not without their problems of interpretation, as witnessed, for example, by the profound disagreements over the dating of the Middle and Late Bronze Age strata between Ingholt, the excavator, Fugmann, the author of the final report, and Schaeffer (Schaeffer 1948, 108–16; Parr 1968, 35 and nn. 108 and 113; Bourke 1993, 263–4).

It was in the hope of helping to rectify this situation by investigating a site in southern or central Syria that the writer, in collaboration with the then Assistant Director of the British School of Archaeology in Jerusalem, Crystal M. Bennett, and with the financial support of the Palestine Exploration Fund, undertook, early in 1964,

a reconnaissance in the region south of Damascus, a region chosen because it was reasonably accessible from the School's base in Jerusalem and because it was considered that a site here would provide a convenient first step towards filling the archaeological lacuna between central and northern Syria and the better-known Israel and Jordan. A methodical systematic survey was not contemplated, since such surveys are useful only if the artefacts collected – mostly potsherds – can be dated with reasonable accuracy, and in a relatively unknown region such accuracy can be achieved only through the prior excavation of a well-stratified site with a clear succession of occupational remains ideally spanning a long period of time – in other words, a multi-period *tell*. It is true that one suitable mound had already been tested by a Swedish expedition in 1953 – Tell es-Salihiyeh, a few kilometres east of central Damascus – where occupation from at least the Middle Bronze Age to the Roman period was found in one restricted area of excavation; but the work here had lasted only four months, there were few finds, and the final report was correspondingly slight and tentative (von der Osten 1956). Moreover, Salihiyeh was rapidly being encroached upon by the suburbs of the city, presenting logistical problems. The Swedish archaeologists had, however, identified another mound, Tell Deir Khabiyeh, about 20 km south-west of the capital, with surface sherds of Middle Bronze and later periods and surface indications of basalt walls probably representing fortifications (von der Osten 1956, 13, 77, 82); most importantly, the site was very accessible and of a size which suggested that useful work could be done even by an expedition with only limited resources, which were all that could be expected while the BSAJ was still primarily engaged in Kenyon's excavations at Jerusalem. With the encouragement of the Department of Antiquities in Damascus an application for a digging permit was therefore made and preparations begun to commence work in the autumn of 1966. However, as is often the case, these preliminaries took longer than expected, and an actual permit had still not been granted by the beginning of 1967.

In June of that year the political situation changed dramatically. War in the Golan Heights broke out, and very soon the town of Quneitra, less than 50 km from Deir Khabiyeh, was largely destroyed and occupied by the Israeli army, and remained inaccessible for years to come. The entire region suffered the effects of an uneasy truce, and all hope of carrying out archaeological research there had to be abandoned. Nor were the prospects of working elsewhere in western Syria now very promising, though for a very different reason. After 1967 the main focus of archaeological activity in the country, by both local and foreign expeditions, was understandably on the salvage operations on the Euphrates already mentioned. These were absorbing most of the time and resources of the authorities, and the chances of obtaining a permit to excavate except on one of the threatened sites were reported to be poor. Nevertheless, enquiries continued to be made and during informal contacts over the next few years it became clear that, in fact, the authorities would consider favourably an application from a British institution for work on a site outside the Euphrates region. Two major sites in the Homs region were suggested: Tell Nebi Mend and Tell Mishrifeh. The offer of the latter was soon withdrawn, however, since the government's intention of moving the modern village from the site prior to any excavation had not yet been achieved. Tell Nebi Mend remained an attractive possibility. It had the advantage over Deir Khabiyeh not only of having a longer sequence of occupation, proved by previous excavations (see below), but also – and more interestingly – of having been often mentioned in written sources and thus providing an opportunity to consider the question of the extent to which political events were, or were not, reflected in the archaeological record. It was, however, a much larger site than Deir Khabiyeh, and its investigation would require considerably more resources. Nevertheless, the opportunity provided by the Syrian authorities seemed too good to be missed, and it was decided to consider the possibility of a joint expedition with another sponsor. Following various unsuccessful approaches to a number of institutions (including the University of Mississippi, at the suggestion of Dr Frances James, an authority on the Egyptian imperial presence in the Levant and the author of an important reanalysis of the early excavations at Beth Shan), a proposal was made to the University of Tübingen, through the good offices of Dr Arnulf Kuschke, who had recently made major contributions to the study of the topography and tactics of the Egyptian–Hittite battle and had conducted archaeological surveys in the nearby northern Lebanese Beqa᷉ (Kuschke 1979; Kuschke *et al.* 1976). Unfortunately this anticipated collaboration did not materialise, leaving the choice of abandoning the project or proceeding alone. The latter course was adopted in full awareness that the funding likely to be available would probably be sufficient for no more than what might at best be called a 'chronological reconnaissance' of the site. (It is appropriate to mention here that from 1990 until 1992 the University of Melbourne became an official co-sponsor of the excavations, while in 1995 a similar arrangement was made with the University of Malta.)

There was only one further obstacle to overcome before a formal application could be made. As a result of the Six Day War the British School of Archaeology in Jerusalem now found itself in that part of the city under Israeli occupation and, while it had scrupulously observed international agreements on the protection of cultural property in occupied territories and although it still maintained cordial relations with the authorities in Jordan, it was clear that the Syrian authorities would prefer a different sponsoring institution to be involved. There was at this time no permanent British archaeological presence in Jordan, the British Institute at Amman for Archaeology and History (BIAAH) – since then amalgamated with the BSAJ to form the Council for British Research in the Levant (CBRL) – not being founded until 1978, and it

was therefore in the name of the University of London, Institute of Archaeology that, in July 1975, permission to excavate at the site was requested and granted.

Tell Nebi Mend: early visitors and identification

Although at least one earlier western traveller had noted a number of 'little hills' along the banks of the Orontes and around the Lake of Homs (Pococke 1745, 140), the first specific mention of Tell Nebi Mend – though not by name – seems to have been made by J. S. Buckingham, who, following the river down from Baᶜalbek towards Homs in April 1816, reached the small village of Arjoune, just east of the site, 'seated beneath an apparently artificial mound of earth, on the summit of which was a sheik's tomb, and a few buildings around it' (Buckingham 1825, 491). Thirty years later the site was examined more closely by the Rev. W. M. Thomson, an American missionary who visited it during the course of a journey from Aleppo to Mount Lebanon in 1846. Thomson wrote little about the mound itself, but observed 'columns and capitals scattered around its base' and noted its location between 'the two main branches of the Orontes [which] glid slily [*sic*] amidst the canes and reeds into yonder pretty lake', and remarked also on the fact that it was 'ditched in such a manner as to convey the water from one branch of the Orontes to the other, thus forming an island like a delta in the fork of the river, including the *tel*' (Thomson 1848, 691–2). These were, he surmised, the ruins of an 'ancient city of Kedes', a name which he knew was that given to the nearby Lake of Homs by medieval Arab historians (whom he cites frequently), and which appeared, in one spelling or another, on at least three available maps of Syria, one accompanying a description of a journey from Aleppo to Damascus (Green 1736), another illustrating an account of journey through western Syria by Lt. Col. Squire (Walpole 1820, 293–352, reproduced by Breasted 1903, 14 and n. 63), and a third in Rennell's *Comparative Geography of Western Asia*, dated 1809 but only published twelve years later (reproduced in Grant 1937). Thomson's mention of the name 'Kedes' has often led authors – for example, Dussaud (1927, 107), Pézard (1931, 24) and Mesnil du Buisson (1935–38, 909–10) – to suppose that it was he who first identified the site with the location of the Egyptian–Hittite battle, but this is not so. It was not to the Late Bronze Age city of the Egyptian reliefs – of which, at this date, he would certainly not have been aware – that he attributed the ruins of Tell Nebi Mend, but to a 'Grecian city called Kedes, also Kudianos', assuming that the lake had been named after it. Although he speculated that Kudianos – a name otherwise completely unattested and which he must have invented – was 'merely the Greek form of Kedes', thus implying (correctly) that Kedes was the original name, he nevertheless ended his account with the lament that he had 'not been able to meet with even the name of this fine city in any old author' (Thomson 1848, 692).

A few years later, in October 1853, another American missionary, the Rev. J. L. Porter, passed near the site and also remarked on the extensive ruins around its base, although he did not have time to make a proper inspection. In the original brief description of his journey he made no attempt at a possible identification (Porter 1854, 675), but in a slightly fuller report published a year later he stated that it was 'evidently a site of considerable antiquity, and a city of importance must at one time have occupied it', suggesting that 'its position answers well to the *Laudicia* of the Itinerary of Antonine' (Porter 1855, 339). This town, Laodicea ad Libanum – of which more will be said below – was one of a number founded by the Seleucids, and had long been known from its appearances in the Roman Itineraries and in the Peutinger Table to be situated in Coele-Syria (the Beqa͜c) somewhere between Emesa (Homs) and Ba͜calbek. All that remained for the 19th-century classically trained and historically minded explorers was to establish its exact location. Thomson (1848, 694) had sited it at Jusiyeh, about 15 km south of Tell Nebi Mend, where substantial classical ruins were also visible, and Edward Robinson, perhaps the most eminent biblical geographer of the time, had, after first agreeing with Thomson, eventually accepted Porter's arguments in favour of Tell Nebi Mend: 'the position, therefore, the vicinity of the lake, and the remains, leave no doubt, but that in Tell Neby Mindau [*sic*] we have the site of the ancient Laodicea of Lebanon' (Robinson *et al.* 1856, 555). Robinson himself never actually visited the *tell*, his journey through the Beqa͜c in 1852 having terminated at Riblah, and he depended entirely on the accounts of Thomson and Porter for his knowledge of the site. It is therefore strange that, given his interest in the Greco-Roman geography of the region, he made no mention of Thomson's speculative reference to a 'Grecian city called Kedes, also Kudianos'. Like his predecessors, Robinson certainly knew the alternative name for the Homs lake, but he was as perplexed by it as were they: 'why it bears the name of Kedes is unknown. No city or village of that name, ancient or modern, is found in the vicinity' (Robinson *et al.* 1856, 549).

In 1861 a comprehensive guide to the Levant published in Paris did not hesitate to record 'Tell Nebi-Mindau' as Laodicea ad Libanum (Joanne and Isambert 1861, 653), and a few years later the *Handbook for Travellers in Syria and Palestine* published in London by John Murray did also – not surprisingly in this case, since the author was Porter himself (Porter 1868, Part II, 544). These guides and others are testimony to the increasing numbers of European and American travellers in the Levant as the century advanced, and although the interests of the majority lay mainly in Palestine – the Holy Land – Syria was also opening up to visitors and it is reasonable to assume that some of the more adventurous of these would have reached Tell Nebi Mend. Two who are known to have done so are Richard Burton and Charles Tyrwhitt Drake, the former being at this time – after a colourful career as explorer and writer – British Consul in Damascus and the latter a young member of the Palestine Exploration Fund's Survey of Western Palestine. Their visit adds little to what the reader of Thomson, Porter or Robinson would already have known, although they can claim credit for being the first to report 'earthwork embankments to the west of the Nahr Tannurin' (the Muqadiyah) – presumably the south-west corner of the Enclosure described above and discussed in more detail in Part III of this volume. They concurred with Porter that, in all probability, the site represented the ancient Laodicea ad Libanum (Burton and Drake 1872, 222–4). A few years later the eminent German orientalist Eduard Sachau followed in their footsteps, although he simply noted the presence of the mound and the obvious ruins, being clearly more impressed by the dam at the north-eastern end of Homs Lake – 'ein gewaltiges Denkmal Orientalischer Wasserbaukunst' – of which he published what is surely its earliest photograph (Sachau 1883, 58–61).

The next explorer to leave a record of his visit was Claude Conder, a former colleague of Tyrwhitt Drake, who was on an expedition in 1881 under the auspices of the Palestine Exploration Fund. By now the reason for the presence in this part of Syria of the name 'Kedes', which had eluded Thomson and Robinson, had become more generally known, with the initial publication in the 1830s and 1840s of the Egyptian reliefs and texts relating to the campaigns of the New Kingdom pharaohs (see Fig. 1.5). Originally printed in large expensive folios accessible only to Egyptologists, in the following decades this information began to be incorporated into semi-popular histories of ancient Egypt by such authors as Maspero, Wilkinson and Brugsch, and would have become available to the educated public.[3] Conder was clearly familiar with this material and in fact declared a special reason for his expedition to Syria to be 'the investigation of a question which is probably of greater antiquarian interest than any other, of those yet unsettled in Northern Syria, namely the recovery and exploration of the sacred capital [*sic*] of the Hittites – the famous city of Kadesh on the Orontes' (Conder 1881b, 135). In preparation for his journey he had, with the assistance of the Rev. H. G. Tomkins, made a careful study of the conflict and its topography as recorded and illustrated on the Egyptian monuments. Although originally inclined to favour one of the islands in the Homs Lake as the location of the ancient city, he soon changed his mind (Conder 1885, 19). Referring in particular to that 'portion of the great battle-piece representing the town ... to be found copied in Sir G. Wilkinson's Ancient Egyptians', he discerned a city with 'a double moat crossed by bridges; on the left a broad stream flows to the lake, but on the right the piece is obliterated, and it is impossible to see whether the moat ran all round, or whether the town lay between the junction of two streams' (Conder 1881a, 164; 1881b,141). Despite this uncertainty of detail, he felt confident that he was seeking 'a fortress surrounded by a river, and situated not far from the borders of a lake', and he eventually had no hesitation in claiming that, at Tell Nebi Mend, he was 'standing on the true site of Kadesh' (Conder 1881a,

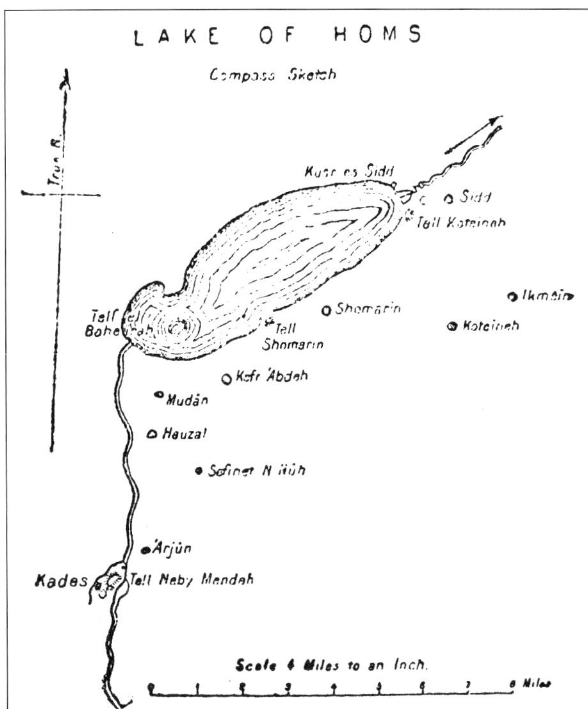

Fig. 1.9. Sketch map of the environs of Tell Nebi Mend made by Conder in 1881 (from Conder 1881a, 165).

164–5; 1881b, 141–2). It is to him that we owe the first comprehensive, even if somewhat confused, description of the site and its environs, accompanied by a simple but nonetheless informative 'compass sketch' map (Fig. 1.9), and it is to him that should thus be given the credit for its identification, which has never been seriously challenged. Ironically, however, it was not accepted by his collaborator Tomkins, who, when he published his own interpretation of the Egyptian evidence in a separate report the same year, preferred to locate the battle at the north-eastern end of the lake (Tomkins 1888, 395).

Conder's enthusiasm for Tell Nebi Mend is manifest and infectious. He wrote that he had 'rarely met with any site which seemed more likely to repay careful examination, and it seems highly probable that, if a mine could be driven through the Tell, Hittite remains might be discovered' (Conder 1881a, 168; 1881b, 145). Whether by coincidence or not, the next reported visit to the site was in fact by one of the most distinguished of contemporary Hittite archaeologists. In September 1890 Robert Koldewey, the director of German excavations at Zinjirli, spent a short time at the site and published, in Volume II of his massive report on that site (Koldewey 1898, 180 and fig. 81), a sketch plan which is commendably accurate, although it does exaggerates the depression or 'waist' between the two halves of the Lower Tell, making it rather closer to the scene on the Egyptian reliefs (to which he refers) than it is in reality (Fig. 1.10). Sixty-five years later this was still the only available plan with which Yadin could illustrate his discussion of the battle in his book on ancient

warfare (Yadin 1963, 106), and it was not superseded until the London expedition's contour survey by C. Davey was published in 1983 (Parr 1983, 112, fig. 1).

Perhaps fortunately for later archaeologists, Koldewey did not feel tempted to drive a 'mine' through Tell Nebi Mend. However, three years after his visit J.-E. Gautier, of the French Institute of Oriental Archaeology at Cairo, apparently unaware of – or unconvinced by – Conder's arguments published fourteen years previously, resolved 'to undertake excavations in the upper valley of the Orontes, to seek to identify the town of Kadesh'. Following a thorough reconnaissance of the region around the lake (Fig. 1.11), the two sites which attracted his interest were Tell et-Tin, the largest of the mounds protruding as an island from the waters of the lake, and Tell Nebi Mend itself (Gautier 1895, 441). He initially favoured Tell et-Tin as the location of the ancient city on the grounds that he considered it corresponded best with its portrayal on the Egyptian representations as being surrounded on all sides by water, although he also acknowledged that, since the lake was largely if not wholly man-made, the topography of the region might have changed since Ramesses' day, making any identification based solely on topographic arguments inconclusive – an astute observation which, of course, strictly speaking, applies to Conder's arguments also. However, Gautier's decision to work at Tell et-Tin seems mainly to have been taken on the practical grounds that the village and cemetery on the summit of Tell Nebi Mend would have restricted his work there, and in 1894 he therefore dug a number of trenches ('galeries') on the mound in the lake. In these he found evidence for occupation in the Hellenistic, Roman and Byzantine periods, and probably also in the Iron Age, while several inhumation burials containing an extensive and important collection of pottery and bronze objects typical of the early 2nd millennium were also excavated. Below these there was a level containing a 'quantity of carefully fashioned flint knives', some of them 'en cristal de roche fumé' – presumably obsidian (Gautier 1895, 462) – indicative of prehistoric occupation at the base of the mound. But the absence of any remains that Gautier recognised as 'Hittite' – that is, Late Bronze Age – persuaded him that this was not the location of Kadesh and that this city was, after all, to be found at Tell Nebi Mend. (Tell et-Tin was one of the sites visited by the London expedition in 1980 as part of its regional survey, and Gautier's excavations and discoveries, never published in detail, are currently being reassessed by Jonathan Tubb.)

The French excavations of 1921–1922

The village and cemetery which had deterred Gautier from excavating Tell Nebi Mend did not appear so daunting to his fellow countryman Maurice Pézard when he arrived at the site in 1921. He was commissioned by the French Mandatory Government of Syria and the Académie des Inscriptons et Belles Lettres to investigate the location

Fig. 1.10. Plan of Tell Nebi Mend made by Koldewey in 1890 (from Koldewey 1898, fig. 81).

of Qadesh, a matter which he also apparently considered still to be a 'problème mystérieux' despite Conder's work, which he did not mention, although he did Gautier's (Pézard 1931, 2). After an initial inspection of the mound Pézard concluded that there were, in fact, sufficient open areas for excavation, especially at the northern end, and it was there that he worked for two seasons, removing an astonishing amount of earth from the eastern slopes of the mound below the cemetery. Pézard died prematurely in 1923, by which time only a preliminary report on the first season had appeared (Pézard 1922). This was reprinted in 1931 together with a summary account of the second season, compiled from the excavator's site records and photographs and illustrated with two plans and a section (Figs 1.12, 1.13 and 1.14), in a volume entitled *Qadesh: Mission Archéologique à Tell Nebi Mend 1921–1922*. Considering that this was not intended to be a final report

and that much of it is posthumous, the volume is not uninformative, and the many photographs of pottery and other objects, including part of stela of Seti I (Pézard 1931, 20, fig. 2 and pl. XXVIII), are still a useful source of information. His observations on the environs of the *tell* and especially on the ditch and embankment noted by Thomson, Burton and Drake are also valuable. But it is clear that the excavator – an Assyriologist by training – lacked the experience and perhaps the temperament required to deal with the complexities of a multi-period site with superimposed mudbrick buildings. He was clearly at a loss when faced with what he called the 'entassement inextricable' of the ruins, as he honestly admitted (Pézard 1931, 29), and he frequently felt obliged to use the terms 'chaos indescriptible', 'état chaotique', and 'redoutable chaos' to characterise the stratigraphy with which he was faced (Pézard 1931, 9, 12, 17). His work should not be

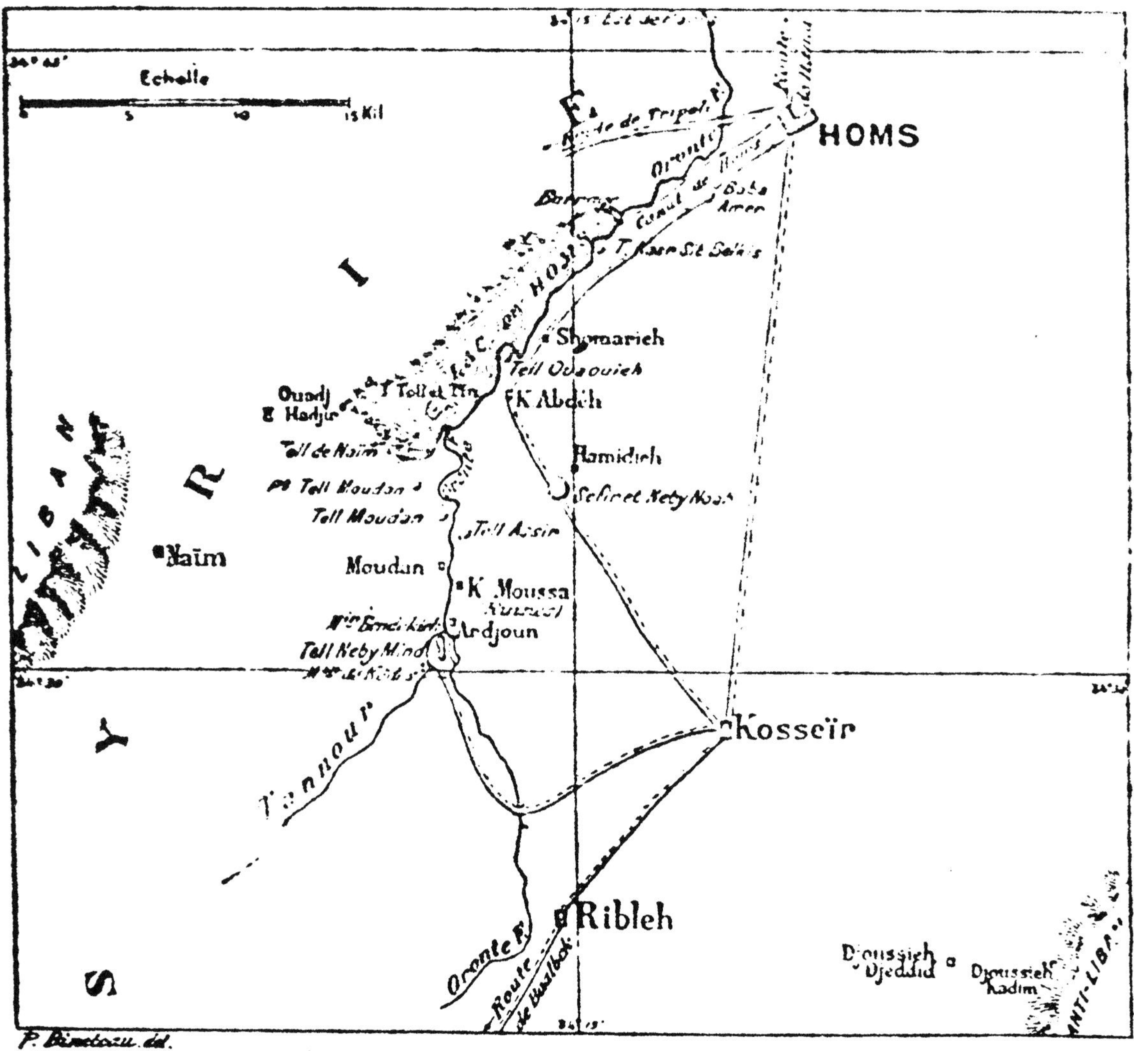

Fig. 1.11. Map of sites around Tell Nebi Mend by Gautier in 1893 (from Gautier 1895, fig. 2).

ignored, however, and a reassessment of it in the light of the results of the London excavations will appear in the relevant future volumes of this report.

Rather surprisingly, in view of the interest which had been shown in the site previously, there seems to have been little thought after Pézard's death of continuing his work under a different director. Whether this was because the difficulties of excavating the site, on which he had laid so much emphasis, acted as a deterrent to other archaeologists, or whether his belief that 'la campagne de 1922 semble bien avoir complété la documentation de 1921, touchant l'identification du Tell Nebi Mend avec Qadesh' (Pézard 1931, 32) was considered by the authorities as sufficient justification for abandoning the project, cannot now be said. Two years after his death W. F. Albright and R. P. Dougherty from the American Schools of Oriental Research in Jerusalem paid a short visit to the site, remarking that 'it had been very partially excavated by the late M. Pézard, but the excavation did not continue long enough to provide very interesting results', although they add that 'thanks to

his trenches we could study his pottery at leisure' (Albright and Dougherty 1926, 6–7). At about the same time a passing reference to the site was made by Dussaud (1927, 105), who, seeking to dismiss Breasted's (1903, 25) argument that during the battle the Hittite army could easily have hidden from the Egyptians behind the city, claimed that 'les fouilles de Pézard ont demontré l'inexistence de cette hauteur à l'époque envisagé' – a claim which, as a result of the recent excavations, is now known not to be true. Pézard's work seems, in fact, to have been largely ignored until 1938, when an analysis of it was published by R. du Mesnil du Buisson, who had recently excavated at Mishrifeh/Qatna. The author of a manual on *La Technique des Fouilles Archéologiques*, Mesnil du Buisson clearly appreciated the complex ways in which the stratification of a *tell* is built up, but his analysis of Tell Nebi Mend, although containing some very sensible observations, is almost completely vitiated by the mechanistic theory of dating which he advocated. Observing that the life of a contemporary Syrian mudbrick house was approximately

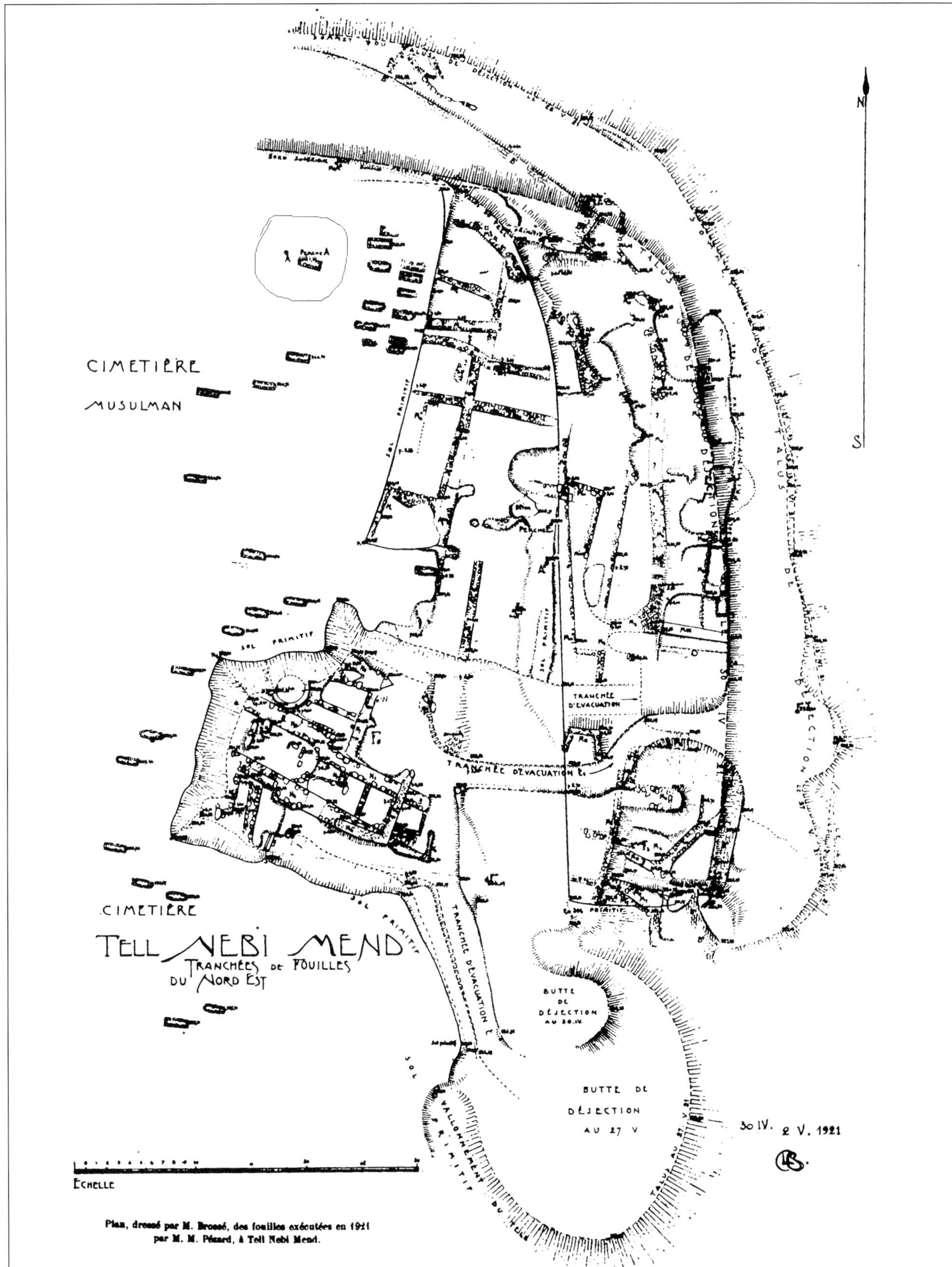

Fig. 1.12. Plan of the French excavations in 1921 (from Pézard 1931, pl. A).

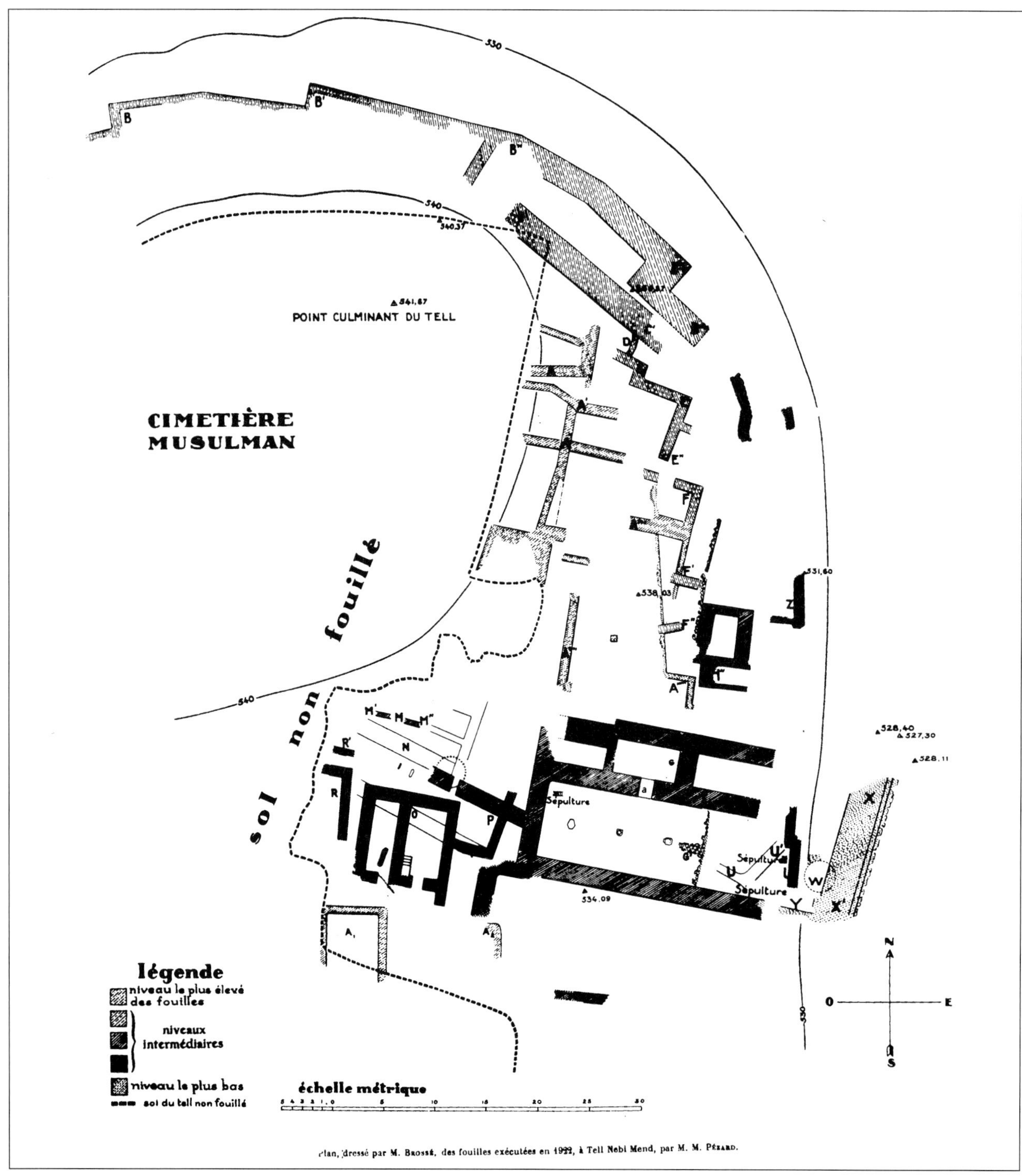

Fig. 1.13. Plan of the French excavations in 1922 (from Pézard 1931, pl. B).

60 years and that such a building produced, when destroyed, approximately 0.6 m of debris, he adopted the rough-and-ready calculation of one metre of archaeological deposit for every century of occupation for a mound continuously occupied by domestic buildings, as he assumed Tell Nebi Mend to have been (Mesnil du Buisson 1935–38, 913–14). Beginning with the obviously Hellenistic/Roman stratum revealed by Pézard just beneath the summit of the *tell*, he applied this formula to the underlying strata, completely ignoring any irregularities, disturbances or possible abandonments that might have affected the rate of accumulation of deposits. By supplementing his argument with reference to a few carefully chosen dated analogies to some of Pézard's pottery finds (for example, imported Cypriot vessels) he arrived at a number of historical conclusions, among them that the site had been largely deserted for half a century following its destruction by Thutmose III and that the lowest defences discovered,

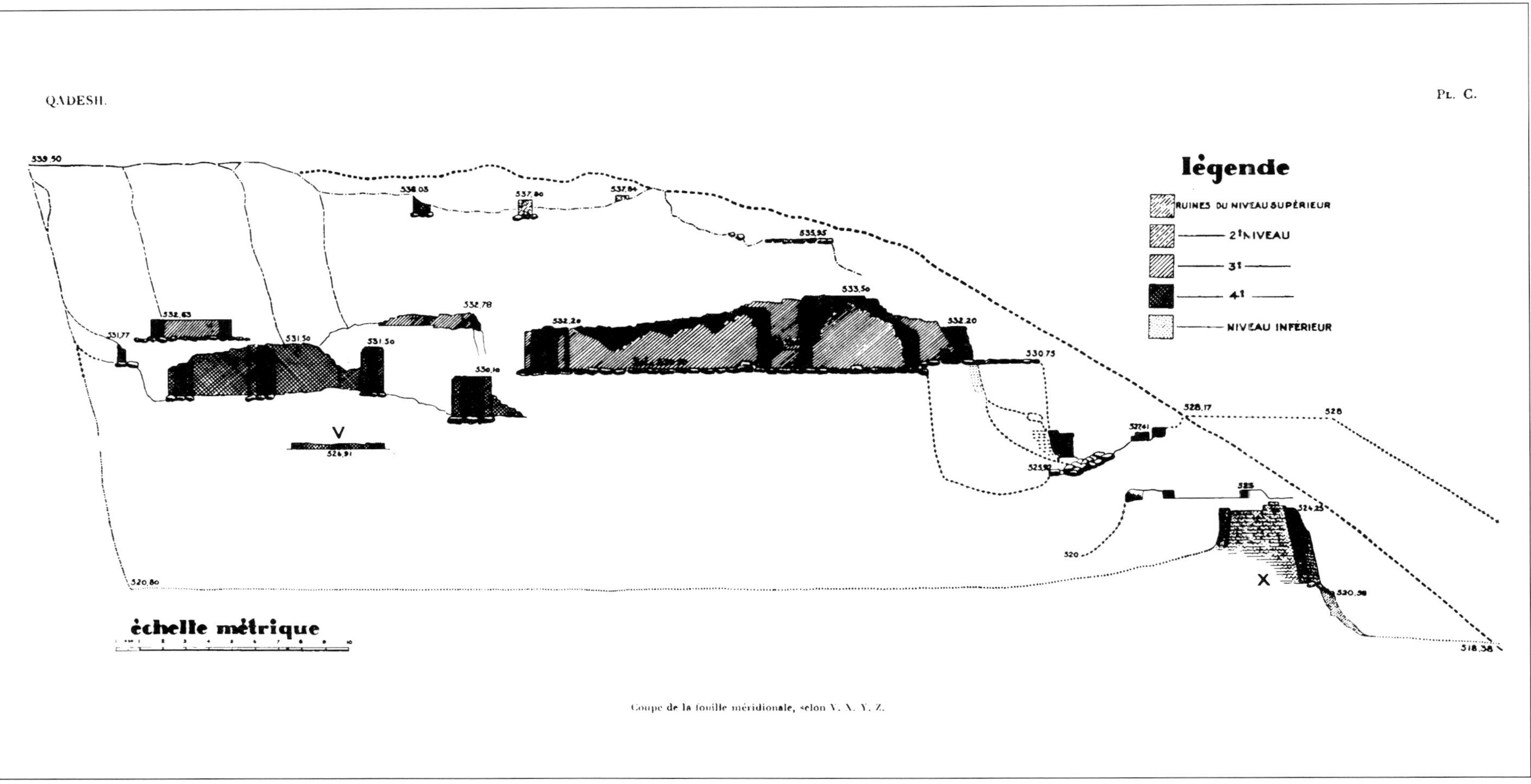

Fig. 1.14. Section through the French excavations in 1922 (from Pézard 1931, pl. C).

'Mur X', had been built *c.*1600 BC and destroyed *c.*1225 BC, and must therefore have been the fortification of the city at the time of Ramesses II's battle. Most of these conclusions are now known to be false, but despite this Mesnil du Buisson's analysis was a valiant attempt to rescue something from Pézard's work, while his concluding sentence – 'La continuité stratigraphique à Tell Nebi Mend est des plus précieuses, car, par une nouvelle fouille de précision, elle permettrait sans doute le classement définitif de tous types de la céramique syrienne pendant deux millénaires' – testifies to a new appreciation of the site as not just the location of a famous battle but also a rich source of archaeological data of far greater significance.

The only fieldwork carried out at Tell Nebi Mend between the cessation of Pézard's work and the beginning of that of the London expedition appears to have been the excavation by the Syrian authorities in 1950 of 71 burials, mostly in simple graves but including four stone sarcophagi, spread over several square kilometres to the west of the Muqadiyah. Only a brief preliminary report has been published, but from the objects found all the burials can be dated to the Roman/Byzantine period (Abdul-ak 1950; HakHak 1950, 121–6).

Tell Nebi Mend in the textual sources

In view of its strategic position Tell Nebi Mend necessarily played an important part in the political history of the Levant, particularly after the emergence and growth of powerful principalities and empires in the 2nd millennium BC. This history has been recounted many times in the standard surveys and textbooks (for example, Klengel 1965–69; Helck 1971; Redford 1992; Grainger 1990; Kuhrt 1995; Cohen 2006), and need not be repeated here. All that is intended is to draw attention to the main occasions on which the site itself – as either Qadesh/Kadesh (or one of its variants in Hittite or Akkadian: Kinza/Kizzu) or Laodicea – appears in the written sources, and any attempt to correlate these occasions with the archaeological discoveries of either the previous French or the present excavations will be postponed until the evidence from these latter have been fully analysed and interpreted.

If the town of *qa-di-sa-a*, mentioned in the account of a military expedition from Qatna going south towards Damascus that is recorded in an 18th-century text from Mari, is Qadesh on the Orontes, as has been proposed (Charpin 1998, 79–92), this would be the first known written reference to the site. Three centuries later its ruler appears, famously, in the Egyptian texts as 'that wretched enemy of Kadesh' who led the coalition of Canaanite princes that assembled at Megiddo in *c.*1468 in an attempt to halt Thutmose III's advance into Syria against the rival kingdom of Mitanni. Whether this ruler was the same as the king named Durusha credited in a somewhat later inventory from Qatna as having made a gift to the temple there, as has been suggested (Epstein 1963), is uncertain,

but whatever his name the Egyptian description of the battle makes it clear that he was a powerful and influential person owning property in Galilee, the north Jordan Valley and perhaps the southern Beqaᶜ, and of at least equal status to the ruler of Megiddo himself, and it must be presumed that his capital, Tell Nebi Mend, was embellished with military, civic and cultic monuments comparable to those which archaeology has shown Megiddo to have possessed. On this occasion Thutmose did not pursue the hostile prince back to his home on the Orontes, which appears to have remained one of the centres of Syrian opposition to Egypt, no doubt supported and encouraged by Mitanni. But it was to be punished a few years later, when Thutmose recorded in his Annals that he 'overthrew it, cut down its groves, and harvested its grain', although whether this implies the actual destruction of the city is unclear. Despite this, Qadesh remained troublesome, and the Egyptian campaigns into Syria continued. In the last of these, a few years before Thutmose's death in *c.*1436, it is reported that he 'arrived at the district of Kadesh [and] captured the cities therein', and it may have been during this assault on Tell Nebi Mend that – as an officer in the Egyptian army, Amen-em-heb, wrote in his diary painted on the wall of his tomb at Thebes – 'His Majesty sent forth every valiant man of his army in order to pierce the wall for the first time, which Kadesh had made', a task which Amen-em-heb himself claimed to have accomplished.

The gradual eclipse of Mitanni and the rise of Hatti in the northern Levant during the course of the following century made little difference to Qadesh's precarious position between Egypt and its rivals. The Amarna letters and the Hittite texts from Boghazköy shed welcome, if brief, light on the vacillating foreign policy of the city's rulers, with Shuttarna, his son Aitakama, and his grandson Niqmadda resisting or submitting to external diplomatic and military pressure from their imperial neighbours. (It is to this period towards the end of the 14th century that the fragmentary cuneiform tablets recovered by the London expedition, including one to Niqmadda from his superior, the king of Aleppo, can be assigned: see Millard 2010). Included in this pressure was the capture of the city from the Hittites by Seti I in *c.*1300, inaugurating a new Egyptian foray into the north and perhaps ending the reign of Niqmadda. Unfortunately there is no written account of the event, but a relief in the hypostyle hall of the Amun temple at Karnak gives a lively impression of the military action (see Fig. 1.5a). It is interesting to note in passing that it was the portrayal of the local terrain on this relief that led some early commentators to deny its association with the city on the Orontes, since it appeared to show it in hilly and wooded country and not on a river (Breasted 1903, 71, note a). However, comparison of the relief with the scene from the same viewpoint in 1978 (see Pl. 1.1) indicates how commendably accurate the Egyptian artist in fact was, while the discovery by the French excavators of part of a monumental stela of Seti, mentioned above, makes it certain that he did take the city and restore its vassalage to Egypt. But not for long: fifteen years later, when Seti's son Ramesses II confronted the army of Muwatalli II on the plain around Qadesh, the soldiers on the battlements depicted on the Luxor reliefs are once more part of the Hittite forces, judging from their distinctive non-Egyptian shields (see Fig. 1.5), and are clearly prepared to defend the city. That they were not called upon to do so was the result of the ambiguous conclusion to the military operation: Ramesses, although in Egypt declaring himself the winner, was left in no condition to repeat Seti's achievement, and his army was forced to leave the battlefield in some disarray. In the years immediately following he was able to regain control of some of the rebellious cities in Palestine, but Qadesh was out of his reach and remained under Hittite control. The peace treaty that was eventually signed in *c.*1280 mentioned no precise boundary between the rival empires, but it seems clear that the Nahr el-Kebir (the Homs–Tripoli gap) was mutually recognised by them as the effective limit of their respective spheres of influence.

References to Ki-in-za and Ki-zu (versions of the Hittite name of the town) in some business documents from Meskene (ancient Emar) on the upper Euphrates, probably dating from shortly before the destruction of that site in the early 12th century BC (Arnaud 1985–87), do no more than testify to its existence at this time. It is generally assumed that, like Emar and many other towns in western Syria, it suffered from the invasion of the Levant by the Sea Peoples, and this is very likely, for although it is never mentioned by name in the literary sources (as perhaps might have been expected given its prominence in earlier records) it is reported that the invaders were active in Amurru, a term which at the time most probably referred to the region around the Nahr el-Kebir, and established a camp there. Nor are there any texts throwing light on the fortunes of the city during the following few centuries, when western Syria was being settled by the Aramaeans and city states being re-established, only to be absorbed into the Neo-Assyrian empire from the 9th century onwards. It is not until the second half of the 8th century that the site is again mentioned, in letters found at Nimrud, one written to the king by the Assyrian governor of Riblah, on the Orontes 12 km further south, concerning the transfer of troops to *Qi-di-si*, and a second containing government orders relating to the same place. It would appear from these that Qadesh, although still playing a military role, had lost its primacy in the northern Beqaᶜ to Riblah, and this seems to be confirmed by the fact that it was at Riblah that in 608 BC the pharaoh Necho II established his headquarters while attempting to defend western Syria from the encroaching Babylonians. Herodotus's mention (*Histories* ii 159) in this context to a battle at 'Kadytis' may be a further reference to the site, although the identification is disputed (Rowton 1951, 128–9; Ahlström 1993, 759, with references). Twenty years later, when the balance of power in the Near East was reversed and the Babylonians were preparing for the invasion which eventually led to the fall of Jerusalem, it was at Riblah that Nebuchadnezzar also

established his base. However, the mention of a district governor residing at *Qi-di-si* in a tablet dated to 564 BC found at Warka (Oded 1964, 273, n.17, citing Wiseman 1956, 31, n.6) must indicate that the place still retained some importance in the mid-6th century.

This is the last known reference to the town of Qadesh in the ancient written records, although – as has already been mentioned – the name or a version of it survived in the vicinity of the Homs Lake into the 19th century. When the site itself is next recorded it is as Laodicea, the place from where in 221 BC – according to the contemporaneous Greek historian Polybius – the Seleucid ruler Antiochus III, on the eve of hostilities against his Egyptian rival in the south, Ptolemy IV, 'took the offensive with his whole army and, crossing the desert, entered the defile known as Marsyas which lies between the chains of Libanus and Antilibanus' (*Histories*: 5: 45.7). Unfortunately there is no evidence to indicate how long before this the town of Laodicea had been founded: Jones (1937, 246) thinks it may have been one of the earliest foundations of Seleucus I Nicator, who is reported to have built five places so named after his mother, although Grainger (1990, 104) and Cohen (2006, 116) are less certain. After this it is mentioned only rarely in the texts, variously termed Laodicea-near-Lebanon (Λαοδίκεια ἡ πρὸς Λιβάνω) by Strabo (*Geography* XVI: 755) and on early 3rd century AD coins; as Laodicea Scabiosa[4] or Kabiosa (Σκαβίωσα/*Kabiosa* Λαοδίκεια) in different editions of Claudius Ptolemy's *Geography* and in the Peutinger Table; or simply as Laudicia in the Antonine Itinerary. Pliny the Elder (*Natural History* V, 19.82) seems to have been the first to use the term 'ad Libanum' to differentiate the inhabitants of the town from those of others named Laodicea, and it is this name which – perhaps because it is in Latin – has survived. These references provide little more than the geographical information on which, as has already been mentioned, Porter based his identification of the classical ruins at the foot of Tell Nebi Mend. Only Ptolemy indicates its importance when he states that it was the head of the administrative district in which he included two other places, Paradisos, generally taken to be modern Jusiyeh some 20 km south of Tell Nebi Mend, and Iabruda, most probably modern Yabrud, a further 50 km south (Robinson *et al.* 1856, 556; Dussaud 1927, 112–13). Robinson's statement (Robinson *et al.*1856, 554) that it became a Roman colony is now considered erroneous,[5] but for a short period during the early 3rd century it minted its own coins (see Fig. 1.6)[6] and later on became the seat of suffragan bishops, several of whom attended the mid-5th century church councils (Le Quien 1740, 841). Urban life at the site must have ceased soon after, although its classical name apparently lived on, if an intriguing record of a certain Paul, a holy man from Asia Minor, establishing himself in the 11th century as a stylite on a column at Laodicea-of-Libanum is to be believed (Peña *et al.* 1975, 74, citing Delehaye 1923, CIX). The more ancient name of Qadesh also survived (as has been mentioned) as Kadas, given locally to a mill on the Orontes which incorporates in its structure a formal Mamluk inscription dated AD 1364, which Sauvaget (1940, 9) suggests came from a caravanserai on one of the major routes of the *barid*, or postal system – a reminder of the continuing strategic location of the site. How long this remained in use is unknown, but Tell Nebi Mend seems to have disappeared from history until its resettlement was noted by Buckingham in the early 19th century. A brief account of its more recent history will be found in Appendix 1.1, below.

The London excavations

Research aims and strategy

As has already been mentioned, the initial stimulus for the Tell Nebi Mend project was the desire to fill the gap in archaeological knowledge between the northern and southern Levant and to develop an understanding of the archaeology and early history of the Levantine Corridor independent of, and supplementing, that based on Palestinian and Biblical research. Once the site had been chosen, the primary aim was to obtain from it as complete a sequence as possible of cultural and environmental data, and this necessitated concentrating on vertical rather than lateral exposure. Kenyon had adopted the same procedure in her excavations at Jericho, which 'consisted of a series of soundings devised to establish the history of the site rather than to provide a large exposure of the structures of any one period' (Kenyon 1981, 3). This sentence, especially the use of the term 'soundings', has led to considerable criticism of Kenyon's strategy: the disadvantages of the necessarily restricted size of such soundings and the difficulties of linking structural phases from individual trenches widely spaced across a large site have been pointed out (Oates 1983, 222). There is truth in these criticisms, and clearly one would not adopt this strategy at a site where the primary objective was to investigate the structural and cultural remains of a particular period and where there was a strong possibility that such remains existed and were easily accessible. But this was not the case at Tell Nebi Mend. Here the French excavations at the north-east corner of the site had indeed demonstrated the presence of monumental architecture, and it was tempting to extend their exposures and study the buildings in greater detail. But they had also shown that many periods of occupation were present, and if the aims of the new excavation were to be fulfilled no single one of these could receive special attention. It was essential to sample all periods of the site's occupation, and it could not be assumed that these would all be located in any one part of the site: over the course of time parts of the settlement might well have been abandoned, either permanently or temporarily, and would thus be missing from a single stratified sequence. Unless the excavator had firm expectations of ample resources of time and funds, in which case wide lateral and deep

vertical excavation might be combined, what has been termed above a 'chronological reconnaissance' of the site, conducted by means of carefully located soundings, was the only strategy possible.

In fact, at Tell Nebi Mend the choice of locations to excavate was largely determined by the presence in 1975 of an occupied village and a functioning cemetery. In 1921 and 1922 these had prompted the French excavators to confine their operations to the north-eastern corner of the site, and by the end of their short-lived expedition this had assumed the appearance of a series of terraces and one deeper trench cut into the slope of the mound, as their plans and section show (see Figs 1.12, 1.13 and 1.14). Although these early excavations had undoubtedly done a great deal of damage to the archaeology of the site, they did provide the new expedition with reasonably easy access to remains of the known different periods of its history, and so – following a laborious and time-consuming clearance of the debris accumulated in the ruins of the previous excavations (Figs 1.15, 1.16 and 1.17) – a number of new trenches were laid out here (Fig. 1.18). An enticing place to begin was at the lowest point reached by the French, at the eastern end of their deep trench (see Figs 1.13 and 1.14), where (as has already been mentioned) part of a substantial fortification, 'Mur X', had been exposed. Trench I of the new excavations was placed against the western, inner, face of this wall (see Figs 1.17 and 1.18), the intention being to investigate eventually a reasonably large area of the contemporary structures. Also in 1975 Trenches II and V were laid out on the higher terraces of the previous excavations, the former revealing mostly Late Bronze Age and the latter Iron Age and Hellenistic/Roman levels. Finally, to complete the re-examination of this previously examined part of the mound, Trench VIII was laid out in 1982 on the eastern side of Mur X where surface indications suggested that there were several metres of deposit pre-dating the wall and undisturbed by previous work. It was intended that in due course the joining up of these separate excavated areas would constitute a kind of broad 'step trench' stretching diagonally from near the summit of the mound to its base, providing a complete stratigraphic profile of this part of the site as well as a not inconsiderable horizontal exposure. However, as noted above, to obtain a reliable sample of the site's archaeology the investigation could not be confined to this one area. Accordingly, areas previously undisturbed by the French archaeologists were chosen for excavation on the western and southern slopes of the mound: Trench III, begun in 1975, on the west and Trenches IV and VII, begun in 1977, on the south-west and south (see Fig. 1.18). Trench III eventually provided a sequence of structures and artefacts spanning the Middle and Late Bronze Ages, supplementing that from Trenches I and II, but Trench VII was unfortunately found to form an obstruction to the local traffic and had to be closed after one season, by which time, however, important information concerning the Middle Bronze Age defences had been recovered. Trench IV, near the bottom of the

Fig. 1.15. North-eastern corner of the mound in 1975, showing a terrace left by the French excavations.

modern vehicle access road into the village, was opened in the hope of finding traces of its ancient predecessors and possibly a gateway, but was soon abandoned when only a shallow deposit of Roman remains was found lying on bedrock. Also in 1977 it was decided to investigate the Lower Mound and the Enclosure, since it was here that major structures of Laodicea – as important a part of the project as was Qadesh – were known to exist and since these were clearly threatened by expanding building and farming activities. To this end Trench VI was opened across the embankment and ditch near the south-western corner of the latter, and was supplemented by Trench IX nearby in 1979 (see Fig. 9.1) and by Trench X on the western edge of the Lower Mound in 1981 (see Fig. 1.18). Also on the Lower Mound, approximately in the centre of its lower southern part, a small sounding, Trench XI, was dug in 1982 in order to investigate two column bases found by villagers excavating for the foundations of a new house. Unfortunately this part of the site was not protected by the Syrian antiquities law and, understandably, the owner of the plot could not be persuaded to halt or delay the work without considerable financial compensation, which the expedition could not afford. Trench XI was therefore also abandoned, though not before interesting information concerning the final days of Laodicea had been recovered. Finally, concurrently with the work mentioned above,

four seasons of excavation were carried out between 1978 and 1982 at the prehistoric site of Arjoune, about a kilometre north-east of Tell Nebi Mend on the eastern side of the Orontes. This site had been discovered in 1975 during a preliminary survey of the environs of Tell Nebi Mend and, in view of the presence on its surface of Halaf pottery – one of the most southerly appearances of the style in western Syria – and the fact that the site was also threatened with destruction by cultivation, it was thought advisable to investigate it further. Table 1.1 gives a list of the above excavated trenches and the years in which they were worked.

When the excavations ended in 1995, after 12 seasons of fieldwork, their principal aim had been largely, though not completely, achieved. They had provided a sampling – not as extensive as had originally been hoped, but nevertheless sufficient to suggest reliability – from almost all the known periods of occupation of the site from the 7th millennium BC to the mid-1st millennium AD. It was now possible to establish not just the 'definitive classification of all types of Syrian pottery over two millennia' that Mesnil du Buisson had anticipated but also a much longer sequence of pottery, stone, metal and bone implements, terracottas and other cultural remains, accompanied by a wealth of environmental data and a series of radiometric dates spanning more than seven millennia. In addition, several areas of excavation, notably Trenches II, III and V, had revealed substantial structural remains which, in combination with those excavated by Pézard, throw light on the architecture of Qadesh in the 2nd and 1st millennia BC. And a few fragmentary inscribed tablets were found that confirm Conders's identification of the site with ancient Qadesh.

But there remained, and remain, gaps, or at least weak links, in the sequence. Two of these, the gap in Trench VIII between the Pottery Neolithic and the Chalcolithic–Early Bronze Age (see Chapter 2, below) and that in Trench V between the Iron Age and the Hellenistic period (Parr 1983, 108), probably represent real abandonments of at least this part of the site. But in Trenches V and II there are several metres of deposit still unexcavated which relate to the end of the Late Bronze Age and the beginning of the Iron Age, a vital and poorly understood transitional period in the history of the Levant, while in Trenches I and VIII the equally controversial transition between the Early and the Middle Bronze Ages at the end of the 3rd millennium BC and the beginning of the 2nd, represented by a depth of about 5 m of structural remains, has been investigated in an area of only a few square metres, providing data from which to draw little more than tentative conclusions. Furthermore, it has to be remembered that the original intention had been to accord Laodicea the same attention as Qadesh, and although the deposits at the summit of the mound excavated in Trench V have told us a little about the Hellenistic occupation, the investigation of the Roman and Byzantine town has hardly begun. Further excavations are clearly needed if these gaps are to be filled.

Fig. 1.16. Location of Trench I in 1977 at the eastern end of the French deep excavation.

Fig. 1.17. The French deep excavation in 1975, with work beginning in Trench I.

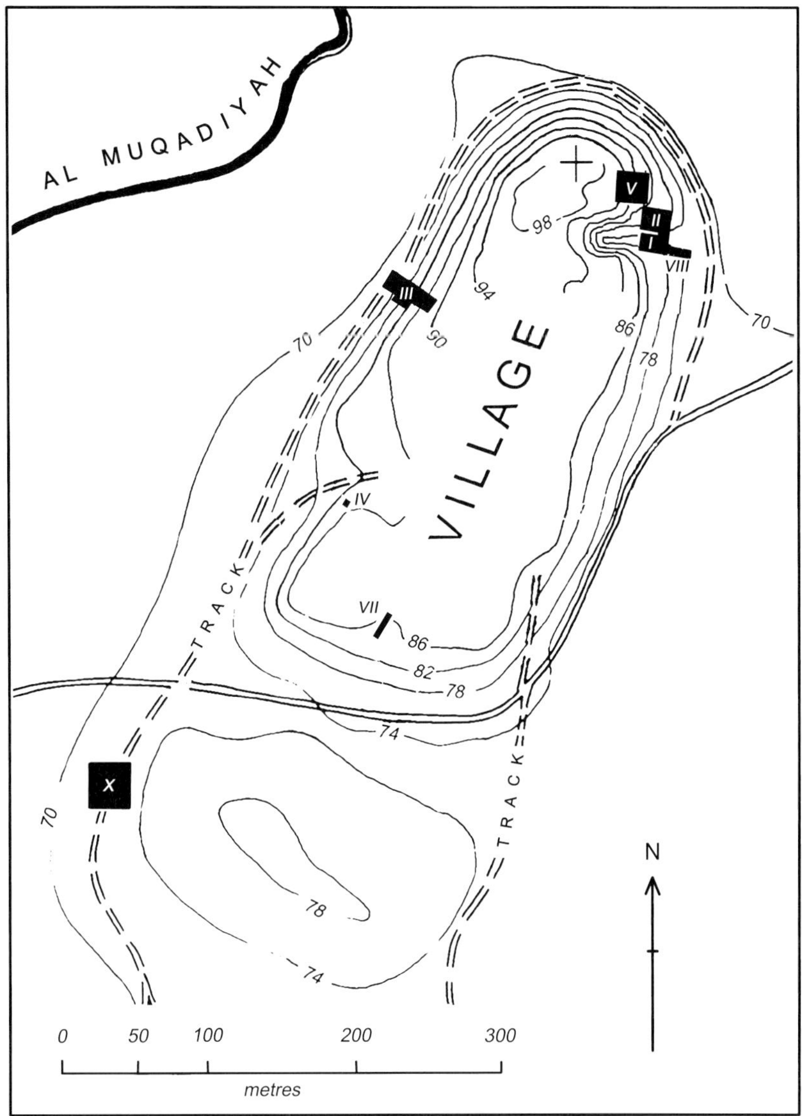

Fig. 1.18. Location of Trenches I–III, V, VII–VIII and X. (Trench IV is not shown as its excavation was abandoned, and Trenches VI and IX, in the Enclosure, are shown on Fig. 9.1.)

Field procedures

For practical reasons, which will be given later, it was judged not feasible to impose a regular grid on the trenches for recording purposes. Instead, individual 'Areas' within each Trench were established as its excavation proceeded, and since the location of these Areas was largely determined by the presence of features such as walls or baulks, they varied in size and shape. The numbers assigned to them were, of course, used for recording purposes. During excavation each discrete archaeological deposit, recognised by composition, colour, texture and so on, was given its own 'Layer' number, the term 'layer' being used in preference to the now more fashionable 'locus', 'deposit' or 'context', since these terms can have several different meanings (according to their context) and therefore often result in ambiguity. Throughout the Tell Nebi Mend reports, therefore, a designation such as 'III.405.16' means Layer

16 in Area 405 of Trench III. During the post-excavation analysis of the stratigraphy these Layers would be grouped into 'Phases', as described by Kenyon (1971b, 274). The completeness with which artefacts and other material were kept varied according to provenance, importance and circumstances, and although no deposits were dry-sieved (again for practical reasons) those which seemed to contain significant quantities of botanical material were sampled for flotation. More details of these procedures, which differed in detail from trench to trench, will be given in the final reports on the individual trenches.

Tell Nebi Mend was not an easy site to excavate. The sides of the Main Mound are steep, making it difficult to dispose of the excavation spoil close to the work, even on the flatter areas left by the French expedition. All too often valuable time and labour needed to be spent on removing stones and earth that had rolled down the slope and were

Peter J. Parr

Table 1.1. Seasons and excavated areas.

TRENCHES

Season	Weeks	I	II	III	IV	V	VI	VII	VIII	IX	X	XI	Arjoune
1975	4	x	x	x									
1977	6	x	x	x	x	x	x	x					
1978	7	x	x			x							x
1979	8	x		x		x	x		x	x			x
1980	5	Study season and regional survey											
1981	8		x								x		x
1982	8	x		x					x		x	x	x
1983	4	Environmental survey											
1984	8	x		x					x		x		
1986	6	x	x	x		x			x		x		
1988	8	x		x					x		x		
1990	8		x	x		x			x				
1992	8	x		x		x			x				
1995	6	x	x			x			x				
1996	4	Study season and closing down											

blocking the track which encircled the base of the mound and was in constant use by the villagers, and this was an operation which had to be repeated at the beginning of each excavation season. It is a windy site also, a feature which, although possibly adding to its original attraction as a place to live, certainly proved detrimental to the conduct of the excavation. In addition to the problems of planning, including (as has been mentioned) the laying out of grids and the taking of elevations in such conditions (in the days before laser instruments and GPS), the sieving of spoil was virtually impossible, while swirling dust also constantly hindered the accurate observation and documentation of the excavation: features such as indistinct but stratigraphically important changes in the colour and texture of deposits were often completely obscured after being exposed for only a short time, making their accurate recording in section and plan by no means straightforward.

It is tempting to think of these and other such local difficulties – children throwing stones, villagers constantly removing survey datum points – as trivial, minor irritants which field archaeologists working in the Near East must accept as part of the job, and therefore not worthy of mention in a scientific report, although they provide material for the 'dig life' type of publication such as Agatha Christie's *Come Tell Me How You Live* or Margaret Wheeler's *The Walls of Jericho*. Nothing could be further from the truth: cumulatively they can have a serious negative impact on the recording of the field data by even the most experienced of site supervisors, and thus on the results of the excavation. It is often forgotten, particularly by non-field archaeologists, that the exact provenance of an excavated object, however humble, is as essential a part of its attributes as are its material, shape, dimensions, colour and so on, and that the most important factor affecting the reliability of the evidence from an excavation is the expertise of those who are responsible for removing that evidence from the ground. Over the course of the 12 excavating seasons at Tell Nebi Mend more than 120 individuals took part in the fieldwork, the majority being involved in the actual digging and most of these being either young professionals or students. The training of such participants was considered to be one of the most important aspects of the work, and not just an obligation to the academic institutions which had helped sponsor and finance it. But it has to be admitted that not all of them had the aptitude, let alone the skills, necessary to make good excavators: the ability to identify the often subtle variations in colour or texture which differentiate the archaeological deposits and the confidence to make the almost instantaneous, even if provisional, interpretations of the stratigraphy necessary for the work to proceed expeditiously. Only if resources had been sufficient to provide close and constant supervision of the novices would this problem have been at least partly solved. As it is, the shortcomings in some of the excavation records, due to the difficulties outlined above, have had to be recognised and taken into consideration when the results of the excavation have been assessed for publication in this and the forthcoming volumes of the final report. Tell Nebi Mend is not unique in this respect, of course. As long ago as 1960 the Braidwoods, in their excellent General Introduction to their ᶜAmuq report, wrote that 'after processing our materials for publication, we are only too conscious of its limitations. What follows [Table I: Relative Reliability of the ᶜAmuq Exposures] is meant merely to give our colleagues the opportunity of benefiting by our mistakes and of arriving at a better understanding of the relative reliability of our materials from the point of view of the factors governing their removal from original context' (Braidwood and Braidwood 1960, 19). In similar vein, the author of the latest volume of the Shechem report has justified 'the candour with which attention is drawn to unnoticed intrusions during excavation' by acknowledging and emphasising 'the vicissitudes of even the most careful excavation work' (Campbell 2002, 5). Unfortunately such candour is rare.

Funding

Tables 1.2 and 1.3 give summary itemised accounts of the income and expenditure of the excavation during the field seasons between 1975 and 1996. It is not usual for this sort of information to be published in excavation reports – the only instances which spring to mind are in Kenyon's preliminary reports on her Jericho campaigns (*e.g.* Kenyon 1955, 96) – but since almost the entire income of the Tell Nebi Mend project came, one way or another, from government funds and so ultimately from the taxpayer, it seems appropriate that the figures should be placed in the public domain. In view of the long period covered and to make comparisons more relevant the actual values have been converted into equivalent 2011 values, using the Bank of England Inflation Calculator.

Perhaps the most important fact to emerge from the accounts is the large proportion of the expenditure devoted to international travel and transportation, primarily of personnel but including also the conveyance by land to the UK of the objects for which the Syrian authorities had granted export permission. This comes as no great surprise, but it suggests that the cost of the excavations could have been substantially reduced and their productivity considerably enhanced had it been possible for them to have taken place over fewer, but more substantially funded and therefore longer, seasons, an arrangement which would also have had the benefit of reducing the total amount of time spent in Syria on necessary but time-consuming tasks such as obtaining residence and vehicle permits. This had, in fact, been the original intention in 1975, when it was hoped that field seasons at Tell Nebi Mend would alternate with those at Tell Brak, also initially sponsored by the Institute of Archaeology, but unfortunately, owing to a number of unforeseen circumstances, this arrangement never became established.

As is usual in the UK with publicly funded archaeological field projects, the Tell Nebi Mend excavations were financed one year at a time, which, although no doubt convenient for accounting procedures, is certainly not the most cost-effective procedure from an academic point of view. The lack of any sort of guarantee, or at least strong commitment, on the part of the sponsoring bodies that adequate funds would be available to pursue the research to an acceptable conclusion over a reasonable period of time made it difficult to plan the annual field operations as effectively as possible. Should the work be concentrated on one area of excavation at a time, hoping that resources for other areas would be available in due course, but taking the risk that if they were not the aims of the excavation would not be achieved? Or should the investigation of several areas be carried out simultaneously, thereby providing a foretaste of the potential of the site as quickly as possible but taking the risk that resources would not be available in future to complete what had been begun, with the same result? The latter option was chosen and in 1995, when funding ceased, the original aims of the excavation had only partly been achieved, as has been recounted above. There can be little doubt that if a different system of funding, on a longer-term basis, had been possible, a more satisfying conclusion to the Tell Nebi Mend project would have ensued.

Publication and presentation

In his stimulating book *What is Archaeology?* Paul Courbin argues that the essential task of the archaeologist is the 'establishment of the facts' – the stratigraphies, sequences, chronologies, identification of artefacts and so on – and that when he or she 'goes further' they become 'something else: a historian, a sociologist, an anthropologist' (Courbin 1988, 159). Irrespective of whether this distinction is entirely acceptable or not, it does have the merit of reminding us that, in the publication of an excavation, the primary task of the archaeologist is the presentation of the retrieved data in as objective a manner as possible, for use by him- or herself and by other scholars as they wish. Objectivity does not, of course, preclude interpretation and speculation; every observed excavated 'fact', be it a thin deposit of clay or a fragment of pottery, needs some basic interpretation before it can make its contribution to the overall understanding of the site, while reasonable speculation often plays an important role in planning the future direction of the work. But it is important that more extensive interpretation, particularly comparisons with other sites and other bodies of material included in

Table 1.2. Excavation income 1975–1995.

	Total Actual values	Total 2011 values	%
British Academy	50,750.00	152,253.80	27.2%
British Institute at Amman	49,827.00	105,222.30	18.8%
British School of Archaeology in Jerusalem	33,000.00	112,244.00	20.0%
University of Melbourne	12,439.23	22,191.20	3.9%
British Museum	9,000.00	44,322.38	7.9%
Palestine Exploration Fund	7,200.00	27,049.84	4.8%
Institute of Archaeology, UCL	6,178.65	18,653.12	3.3%
University of London (CRF)	3,259.00	15,480.08	2.7%
University of Pennsylvania	2,834.09	12,617.76	2.2%
University of Malta	2,475.00	3,903.95	0.7%
Contributions from students etc.	2,449.00	4,028.32	0.7%
University of Mississippi	1,999.96	8,177.07	1.4%
Temple World Tours	1,667.00	2,720.56	0.5%
Birmingham Museum	1,100.00	4,802.89	0.8%
Art Study Tours	538.00	878.02	0.1%
University of London, Hayter Fund	355.00	963.23	0.1%
Ausralian Institute of Archaeology	152.02	715.59	0.1%
University of Liverpool	124.00	853.46	0.1%
Private and Anonymous	4,858.97	21,958.11	4.0%
Total	190,206.92	559,035.68	99.3%

the report should be kept separate from the primary data. This separation is considered to be particularly necessary at Tell Nebi Mend, where, as has been explained, one of chief justifications for the work was the knowledge that evidence from the few other excavated sites in the region, such as Hama, was often of doubtful reliability. This being so, it would clearly be illogical and dangerous to use comparisons with such sites in order to interpret the data from Tell Nebi Mend: the architectural, artefactual, environmental and chronological evidence from the latter site must, at least in the first instance, be allowed to speak for itself. Otherwise, the data from Tell Nebi Mend could easily become infected by a 'dubiety virus' and become part of a chain of comparisons of which all the links were equally weak. In order that the site might make the greatest contribution to the archaeology of a region in which much of the currently available evidence was unreliable, it seems best to assume, initially and temporarily, that there is no other evidence, and to eschew comparative studies until the evidence from Tell Nebi Mend itself had been fully interpreted.

The above observations are equally pertinent to the problems of periodisation and terminology. The confusion

that has resulted in Syrian archaeology from the usage there of terms originating in Palestine or Mesopotamia, and the even greater confusion caused by various attempts to 'simplify' matters by introducing yet new terms, has been remarked upon several times (Akkermans and Schwartz 2003, 13; Parr 2009, 118–19). It is for this reason that it is intended that the presentation of the material from Tell Nebi Mend will initially be by provenance – that is, by Trench and Phase number – and that only later, at the 'interpretation' stage, will labels such as 'EB I' be utilised, accompanied by definitions of what such labels mean in terms of cultural content and chronology.

Acknowledgements

Gratitude must first be expressed to the late Professor John Evans, the then Director of the Institute of Archaeology, for agreeing in 1975 to allow the application for an excavation permit to be submitted in the name of that institution, and to the late Dr Afif Bahnassi, Director-General of Antiquities and Museums for Syria, for granting the permit. In Syria, Dr Adnan Bouni, Director of Excavations, was particularly helpful during the protracted negotiations with

Table 1.3. Summary expenditure 1975–1996.

	Actual values £	Totals Actual values £	2011 values	%
International Travel				
Air fares	39,882.07			
Visas	1,568.00			
Insurance	1,568.10			
Maintenance, tax, etc.	19,058.07			
Petrol	5,977.00			
Hotels, food	5,483.15			
Ferries, etc.	1,835.94			
		75,372.33	206,920.62	37.4
Local Travel				
Petrol	3,173.88			
Vehicle hire	208.81			
Bus, taxis	2,293.24			
		5,675.93	17,501.28	3.2
Maintenance in Syria				
Food	10,578.24			
Electricity, etc.	1,119.53			
Dig House Rent	6,580.82			
Hotels, meals	5,920.16			
		24,198.75	70,838.29	12.8
Wages				
Excavation	30,067.19			
Domestic	5,383.49			
		35,450.68	116,823.42	21.1
Equipment, materials		12,546.92	40,294.60	7.3
Site Guard		8,774.15	25,171.20	4.5
Government Representative		218.14	751.92	0.1
Fees (draughting, etc.)		11,574.36	23,834.81	4.3
Photography, conservation		1,910.04	6,429.08	1.2
Bank Charges etc.		467.68	1,675.37	0.3
Miscellaneous		13,758.91	43,781.84	7.9
Total	554,022.43	189,947.89	554,022.43	100

the Directorate-General between 1966 and 1975, while over the course of the excavations from 1975 to 1996 successive Directors-General – Dr Ali Abu Assaf and Professor Sultan Muhesen – and their colleagues and staff in Damascus and Homs were also invariably welcoming and cooperative. In London, Professor Evans' successors – the late Professors Peter Ucko and David Harris and Professor Stephen Shennan – are to be thanked for providing facilities for the storage and study of artefacts from the excavations, and for general support.

                                              Peter J. Parr

The curator of the Institute's collections, Dr Rachael Sparks, also deserves thanks for looking after those artefacts and providing easy access to them. At University College special mention must be made of the moral and material support given to one of the authors of this volume by Professor Mark Geller of the Department of Hebrew. Particular acknowledgement must be made of the roles played by Professor Antonio Sagona of the University of Melbourne and Professor Anthony Frendo of the University of Malta in obtaining the co-sponsorship of their institutions from 1992 to 1994 and in 1995 respectively.

The excavations could not have been carried out without the financial support of the institutions and individuals listed in Table 1.2, which is gratefully acknowledged. Even more essential was the expertise, hard work and enthusiasm of the members of the excavation teams in Syria, who were drawn from a number of countries: Syria itself, Australia, Canada, Italy, France, Lebanon, Malta, The Netherlands, Pakistan, Portugal, the US and, of course, the UK. All made essential contributions.

In the months following the close of the excavations in 1996 inestimable help was provided by the British Council in Damascus, in collaboration with the British Institute at Amman, with the export of equipment to Amman and of archaeological material to London. Grateful thanks are owed to the then Directors of the BIAAH, Dr Alison McQuitty, and the British Council, Dr Peter Clark, and their staffs for that help.

The preparation of the material for this first volume of the final report has been largely financed by the Leverhulme Trust, with the award to the editor of an Emeritus Fellowship for the services of two of its co-authors, Caroline Grigson and Virginia Mathias, and by the British Academy, with the award of an additional grant to the latter. In 2005 the Council for British Research in the Levant generously assumed responsibility for the production of the final report and its inclusion in its Levant Supplementary Series, and grateful thanks are offered to the Director, Professor Bill Finlayson, the successive editors of that series, Professor Graham Philip and Dr Lindy Crewe, and to Hilary Meeks

and Caroline Middleton of the CBRL Production team, for their encouragement, co-operation and guidance. The comments of the anonymous referee of this first volume have been particularly helpful.

In addition to the above, a large number of colleagues and friends – some sadly now deceased – have, over the course of the decades and in a number of different ways, given counsel and comfort to the editor. Of these, the following merit special mention: Stephen Bourke, Rupert Chapman, Peter Dorrell, Anthony Frendo, Frances James, Leon Marfoe, Carl Phillips, Antonio Sagona and Jonathan Tubb. Finally, the editor would wish to record his personal gratitude to the authors of this volume for their contributions and their patience during the unconscionable length of time it has taken for them to be published.

Notes

1. Although it has been argued that the elephants hunted in Syria by the New Kingdom pharaohs were imported from India specifically for this purpose, there is sufficient evidence in the shape of actual ivory and ivory objects to indicate that the animal was present in the Levant much earlier than this, and that there existed an indigenous Syrian sub-species. See Barnett 1982, 6 and n. 35.
2. These coins have often in the past been described as showing the Tyche flanked by urns representing the rivers (*e.g.* Cohen 2006, 116–7), and I am grateful to Dr Jack Nurpetlian, of the University of Warwick, who has made a special study of the Laodicean mint, for pointing out that this is not so, and that swimmers are always depicted.
3. I am indebted to Professor Kenneth Kitchen of the University of Liverpool for discussing this with me.
4. The meaning of this epithet is not known, although it was long ago suggested that it 'had reference to the leprosy or some cutaneous complaint very prevalent here in time of the Roman power' (Lempriere 1827, 410). It was also sometimes applied to Alexandria ad Issum (modern Alexandretta/Iskanderun), when it is usually interpreted to mean mountainous.
5. Personal communication from Professor Kevin Butcher, University of Warwick.
6. I am grateful to Dr Jack Nurpetlian for this information.

Appendix 1.1

Notes on the ethnography of Tell Nebi Mend

Majed Moussli
Formerly Regional Director, Department of Antiquities, Homs

(*Editor's Note.* The following paragraphs were written by Majed Moussli in 1982 and were based on the observations he made in the village of Tell Nebi Mend during August and September 1978, when he was the official representative of the Syrian Directorate General of Antiquities on the University of London excavations. Mr Moussli, who had recently received an MA in anthropology from the University of Leipzig, readily agreed to the suggestion that he should spend some of his time at the site making an ethnographic study of the village and its inhabitants. He had intended to pursue this in future seasons, and it was unfortunate for the project that he emigrated to Australia shortly afterwards and was unable to carry out his intention. It is also unfortunate that contact with him has subsequently been lost, and that it has therefore not been possible for him to revise and complete these Notes, which are presented here more or less as he left them, apart from some necessary textual editing. The transcription of the Arabic words and names are those adopted by the original author.)

Introduction[1]

Tell Nebi Mend is a locally well-known and important village in the region surrounding the Homs Lake, where it is usually known simply as et-Tell (*the* Mound). Until 1975 the main part of the village was situated on the mound itself, the archaeological site of ancient Qadesh. However, according to the Syrian Antiquities Law it is not permitted to erect new buildings on designated archaeological and historical sites, and since that date extensions to the village have begun to spread outside the main *tell*.[2]

Ethnographic literature on the area where Tell Nebi Mend is situated and on the Orontes valley in general is still very meagre. Such 19th-century scholars and travellers as W. M. Thomson, E. Sachau and J. E. Gautier, who passed through or worked in the area, mentioned the village only very briefly; and although M. Pézard, the first excavator of the archaeological site, did publish in his report many photographs which give a general idea of the village in the 1920s, he did not give any ethnographic information.

1. The history of the village

Archaeological investigation has shown that the ancient settlement on Tell Nebi Mend was more or less abandoned after the Byzantine period, although a few Islamic pottery sherds found during the excavations show that it was not entirely unvisited during the medieval period. According to the information collected during the present field research the re-establishment of the village occurred mainly during the second half of the 19th century, and this receives support from the evidence of early travellers: for whereas Buckingham mentions only a few buildings surrounding the *weli* on the summit of the mound when he observed it in 1816 (Buckingham 1825, 491), in 1879 Sachau referred to it as a large village (Sachau 1883, 58).

According to Mohammed Jameel Abdul-Nebi, a previous *mukhtar* (headman) of the village, around the beginning of the 20th century the settlement consisted of four or five ʿAilat (extended families or lineages).[3] Each of these lineages was a part of a separate clan and each possessed one *hosh* (lineage house), each nuclear family living in just one room. Each lineage house also had only one storeroom and a stable, used mainly for cattle. The houses were separated from one another, but the settlement was concentrated in the middle of the *tell*.

The villagers were always apprehensive of raiding by the bedouin tribe al-Hrouk, who controlled the area east of the Orontes. Before the First World War a considerable part of the population of the village died on account of the spread of a cholera epidemic, and during the war some inhabitants were forced to follow the Turkish army; these did not return.

The ancestor of the lineage Abdul-Nebi was said to have come to the village in the second half of the 19th century, his homeland being the region of Baʿalbek, where the Shiʿite sect dominated the Muslim population. Abdul-Nebi settled beside the sanctified grave of Nebi Mendu (the prophet Mend or Mendu), and one of his sons became *mukhtar* at the end of the 19th century.

Towards the beginning of the 20th century the clan of Juda settled in the village; it was divided into two or three lineages totalling 30 nuclear families, 28 of whom died in the cholera epidemic. The ancestor of the lineage Karan-Dash was reported to have come to the village after the cholera epidemic, but no-one questioned today knew his homeland or why he came to the Tell; it may be noted, however, that Karan-Dash is a Kurdish name. Towards the beginning of the 20th century representatives of bedouin tribes and clans such as the ʿAshirat al-Fawaʿra, ʿGaidat and Al-Hrouk tried to control the area of the village, and it was the conflict between these bedouin and the non-bedouin villagers that prompted the Ottoman government to divide the village agricultural land and pasture between two *pashas* from Homs, whose descendants kept their property until the implementation of the Syrian land reform of 1959.

2. Demography and social structure

At the time of the field research in 1978 71 nuclear families lived in the village, the total population being 600. Twenty families were descendants of Abdul-Nebi and ten families were descendants of the Al-Khaled lineage (of bedouin origin from ʿAshirat Al-Magaldi or Al-Mawali).

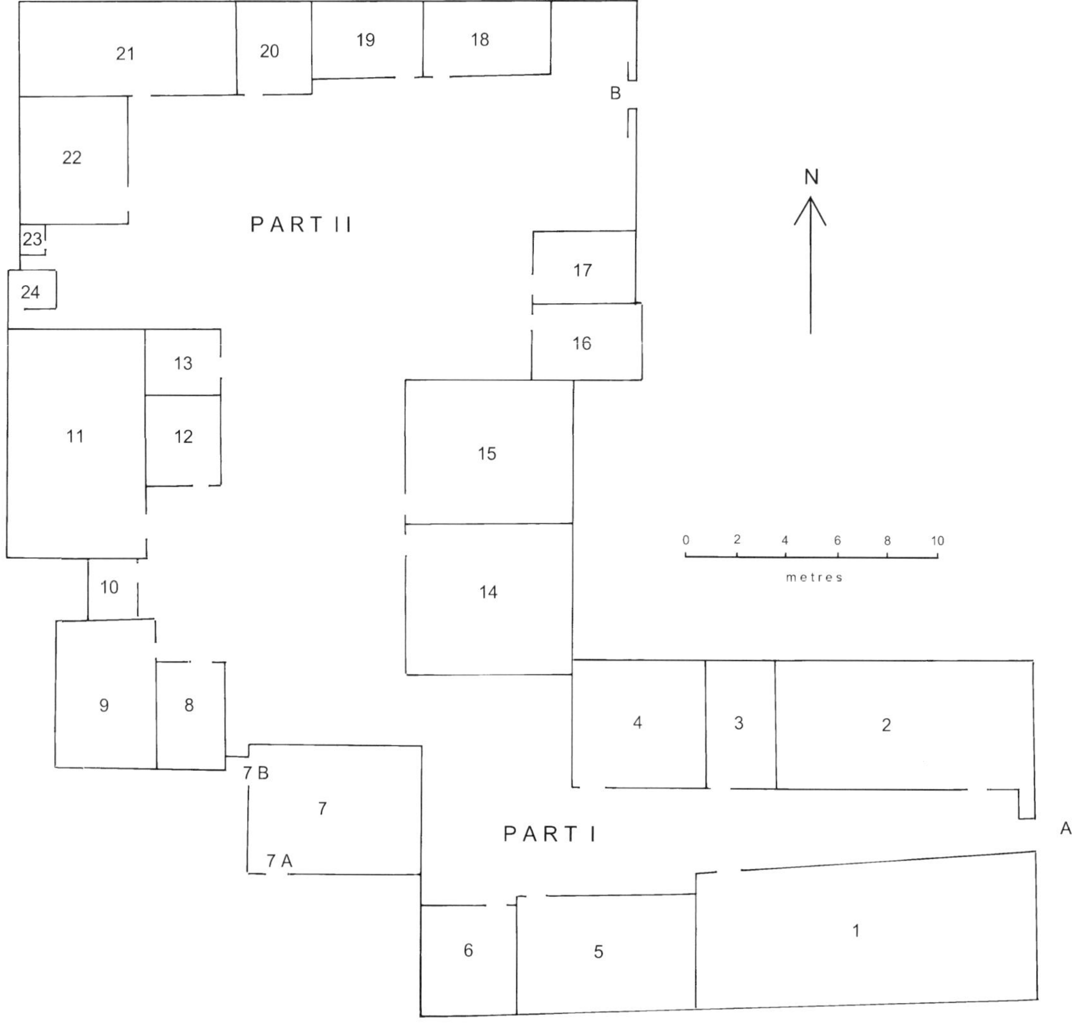

Fig. 1.19. Plan of the lineage house of Karan-Dash in 1978.

From the Juda lineage there were only nine families. Ten families represented the Karan-Dash lineage; six families represented the Khallouff (descendants of the bedouin tribe Al-Naᶜim) lineage; four families represented the Daᶜass lineage (their original name was Al-ᶜOmar). The ᶜOthman lineage and the Ibrahim lineage were each represented by two families, while the bedouin ᶜAshirat Al-Turki was represented by just one family, Al-Khamis.

The population of the village is Sunni Muslim. At the beginning of the 20th century marriage followed the principle of patrilocality but under modern economic circumstances this no longer dominates, and the few examples of patrilocality are exceptional. Lineages of bedouin origin do not seem to have retained any relationship to their previous ᶜAshirat. Blood relationships are remembered no further back than the third generation. The lineage system, which was originally identified with patrilocality, does not exist any more as an economic structure. Patrilinearity by non-bedouin villagers had existed in so far as it was necessary for the preservation of social unity against the strong socially organised bedouin

villagers. During the last 60 or 70 years exogamy in the village has led to an integration in the social life of the village and of the families, with an increasing emphasis on the status of the village as a unit. According to the history of the village lineages endogamy did not exist in a wide sense. The destruction of the lineage as a socio-economic unit was encouraged quickly by the implementation of the 1975 land reform. This destruction strengthened the nuclear family as a socio-economic unit. The new characteristic elements of the nuclear family are reflected mainly in house-building and architecture. However, some survival of the lineage as a socio-economic unit is seen in the unpaid help given during seasonal agricultural work amongst villagers of bedouin origin.

3. Architecture and settlement

Migration to the Tell from outside the area and raiding by local bedouin tribes affected both the character of the settlement and the architecture of the houses. Thus the village is not of uniform character, since there are different traditions of house-building discernible, the result of a historical sequence of settlement by different groups. The occupied area was originally divided into six sections, each occupied by the descendants of one lineage (see above). The destruction of the lineage system has been reflected in the picture of settlement. The extension of occupation or the building of new nuclear family houses has followed approximately the boundaries of the lineage area. In 1978 two complete lineage houses still existed, one belonging to the Karan-Dash lineage and the other to the Abdul-Nebi lineage. Fig. 1.19[4] shows the lineage house of Karan-Dash. At its greatest extent it consisted of 23 rooms and a chicken coop, but in 1978 five rooms of the house were no longer in use. Rooms 1–11 and 14–15 form the older part of the house, but the growth of the lineage as a social and economic unit is reflected in the extension of the house, made first by adding two new rooms, 12 and 13, and later by adding rooms 16–24 around a separate courtyard, with a separate gate, Gate B. Both the original and the new gates faced east. All the rooms of this lineage house are built in rows facing on to the courtyards. The absence of doors between the rooms shows that each nuclear family in the lineage, before the destruction of the lineage as a unit, had its own room. In plan the house has a defensive character, as illustrated by the existence in the original phase of only one gate, Gate A, opening into a long corridor. Room 7 was an exception to the traditional plan of the Karan-Dash house, since its only original door (7A) faced west, opening to the outside. This was later blocked with stones and a new entrance (7B) made, still opening to the exterior. It was not possible to ascertain why room 7 had no door into the courtyard, but it is possible that it was a stable for the cattle that the Karan-Dash lineage owned.

When building their lineage house the Karan-Dash used ancient stones dug up from the *tell*. The roof consisted of horizontal wooden beams covered with straw mats and then a layer of soil and crushed limestone mixed with straw. In the later extension the foundations and the lower parts of the walls were built of stones but the upper parts of mudbrick, perhaps because of the un-availability of stones.

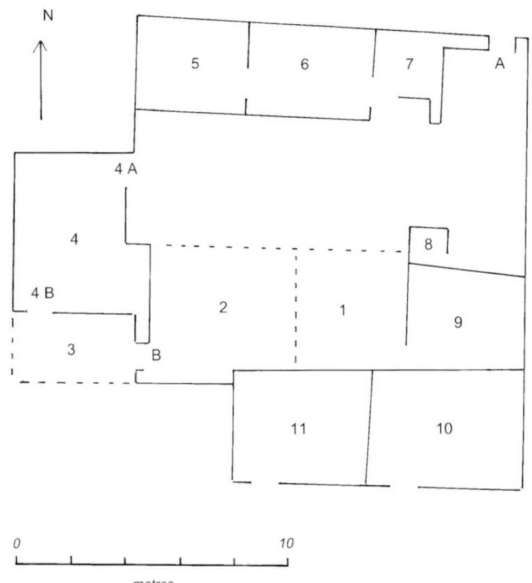

Fig. 1.20. Traditional type of nuclear family house, that of ᶜAwad Ibrahim.

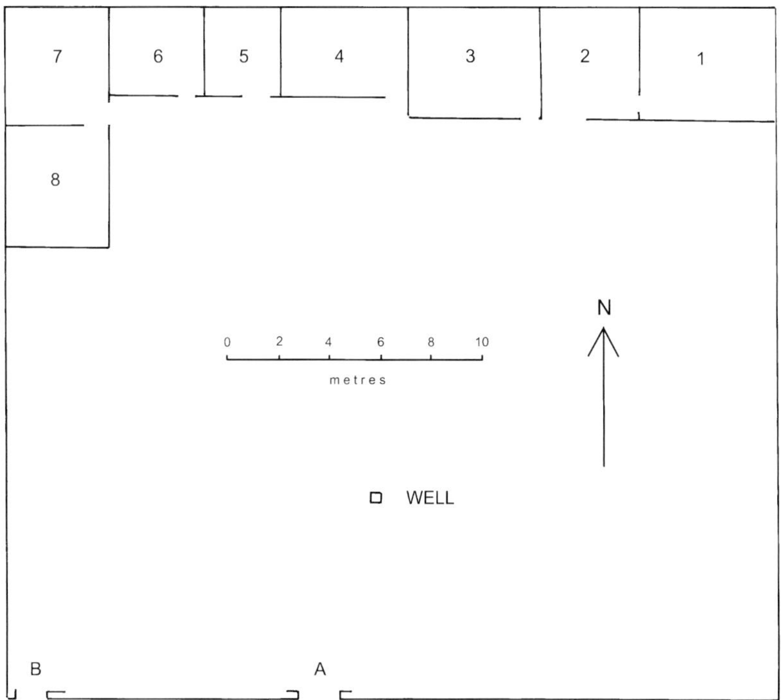

Fig. 1.21. Recent (1978) house of a villager of bedouin origin.

Fig. 1.20 is an example of an old nuclear family house, that of ᶜAwad Ibrahim, built entirely of mudbrick. It originality consisted of four rooms, 1–4, but rooms 1, 2 and 3 were later destroyed and rooms 10 and 11 were added. Also added were two storerooms (5 and 9), the stable (6), the *tannur* room (7), the enclosure wall of the courtyard and Gate A. A chicken coop was added later. Rooms 10 and 11 were used as living rooms and the original living room (4) was reused as a kitchen, with doors 4A and 4B leading into it. The most interesting feature of this house is the fact that the new living rooms, 10 and 11, have their doors opening to the exterior and not to the courtyard. It is a tradition of settled bedouin life that the doors of living rooms face to the south, as protection from wind. However, it is not certain that this arrangement reflects the bedouin origin of ᶜAwad Ibrahim, since specialised craftsmen from outside Tell Nebi Mend were sometimes brought in to build houses.

Fig. 1.21 shows the modern house of a villager of bedouin origin, built in 1973 of mud brick and consisting of three living rooms (1, 2 and 3), a kitchen (4), a *tannur* room (5), a dove cote (6), a stable (7), and a store room for cattle fodder (8). A characteristic traditional feature found in this nuclear family house is a well. There is a large courtyard with two gates – A for people and B for cattle. It will be noted that all the rooms have their doors facing to the south. The doorway connecting rooms 1 and 2 is a recent phenomenon in the village. It is usual for the houses of the villagers of bedouin origin to be built of mudbrick, which is restored every autumn.

4. Economy

The importance of the village derives from a number of factors. These include its rich flora, both of the river banks and the meadow land, providing constant sources of food; its plentiful fauna, especially fish and migratory birds; its ample supply of water, both for irrigation and for the operation of a powerful water-mill; its strategic location on the trade route across the mountains from Tripoli on the coast towards Homs on the edge of the steppe; and, more specifically, its position on a easy ford over the river. All those factors proved an attraction both to settlers and to bedouin raiders, and in turn led, certainly in Ottoman times and most probably in the more distant past, to conflicts over the ownership of land and the consequent intervention by central government in the affairs of the village.

Historically Tell Nebi Mend has been the most productive agricultural area in the region, its pastures being green throughout the year. Agriculture has long been based on a seasonal pattern. The arable land is divided into irrigated and non-irrigated areas. For example, a plot of 50 dunams (50,000 sq m) will be divided into two pieces, one for winter cultivation beginning in early December, and the other for summer cultivation starting in April. The winter crops are lentils, wheat and kidney beans. Following harvesting, the stubble is used for grazing, mainly of cows and horses. This land will then be left fallow until the following December. Summer crops are maize, sugar beet, beans, potatoes, tomatoes and aubergines. The productivity of the land of Tell Nebi Mend is relatively higher than that of neighbouring villages; for example, 1 kg of seed potatoes yields a crop of about 15 kg. The non-irrigated land is mainly dependent on rainfall, the crops being lentils, wheat and barley. If in especially dry years this land does not yield a harvest, agreements will be made with nomads for the grazing of flocks. Fig trees are a traditional source of fruit, although since 1967 the villagers have also been cultivating other fruit trees, such as apricots.

The land between the two rivers, al-ᶜAsi (the Orontes) and et-Tannur (al-Muqadiyah), called ez-Zor, offers permanent pasture throughout the year, mainly for cattle and horses. The richness of the pastures of Tell Nebi Mend have long encouraged the bedouin tribes of the area to change from the nomadic herding of sheep and goat to intensive cattle breeding. The importance of cattle raising in the village is clearly reflected in the domestic architecture in the provision of stables and store rooms for animal feed. This illustrates another change from the traditional life of bedouin nomads in a permanent village.

Although in earlier times Tell Nebi Mend was a well-known source of fish for Homs, the importance of fishing in the Orontes generally has greatly declined in recent years. In the last few years the extensive use of dynamite has superseded more traditional methods of fishing, and industrial fish farming has largely replaced village fishing.

The village has two water-mills, al-Bandjakiya on the Orontes and Kadas on the Tannur. Only al-Bandjakiya, which was always important and well known in both neighbouring and more distant villages, is still working.

In 1963 the dirt track between the village and the larger village of Qusair, 5 km away, was cobbled and in 1967 was asphalted, and this good and quick means of communication with Qusair and thence with Homs has facilitated the growth of trade in Tell Nebi Mend. This is mainly in agricultural products such as sugar beet, maize, potatoes and lentils, and is therefore largely seasonal. Trade in animals and animal products is also important, especially for those villagers who own no land. Those villagers who breed cattle for meat have close contact with traders from Qusair. A daily trade in milk products takes place within the village, although there is also a man who comes to the village and purchases milk and milk products.

5) Material and cultural elements

In the Orient, relationships between peasant settlements and towns were historically founded on the exchange of specialised products. In the Tell Nebi Mend region the town of Homs was always the centre for handicrafts, and the villagers bought their agricultural tools, clothes, furniture, kitchen utensils and so on there or in Qusair. Craftsmen were not to be found in Tell Nebi Mend, although women who knew how to make mudbricks occasionally constructed their own *tannur*. Today, industrial products have replaced the majority of the traditional elements of material culture in the village, although some highly specialised wooden agricultural implements have not been replaced.

The women of the village still wear their traditional costumes, but most of the men have abandoned theirs.

Notes

1. I am indebted to Mr P. J. Parr for suggesting and encouraging my research, and to everyone in the village who gave me help and information. I am grateful especially for the generous help of the Department of Antiquities' guard, Mohamed Tawfik al-Khaled, who acted as my assistant during the interviewing of villagers. This is an initial summary of the ethnographic data I collected; it is hoped that a more detailed publication on the ethnography of Tell Nebi Mend will appear in the near future.

2. Editor's Note. It is unfortunate that since these words were written the new village has spread mainly to the area south of the main tell, which is the location of the Hellenistic–Roman site of Laodiceia-ad-Libanum, and has done much damage to the archaeological remains there.

3. The terms used in this report are those locally used, and include both classical and colloquial Arabic terms.

4. The outline plans are intended to show only the arrangement of rooms and entrances in the houses, details such as the thickness of walls and the position of windows and other fittings being omitted.

PART II:

THE POTTERY NEOLITHIC OCCUPATION

2. Stratigraphy and chronology

Virginia Mathias and Peter J. Parr

Excavation

Neolithic deposits were uncovered at Tell Nebi Mend only in Trench VIII, a limited extension (maximum dimensions 16 m × 7 m) to Trench I at the north-eastern edge of the *tell*, separated from the surrounding alluvial farmland by a dirt track which hindered the continuation of the excavation in this direction (see plan, Fig. 2.1). Judging

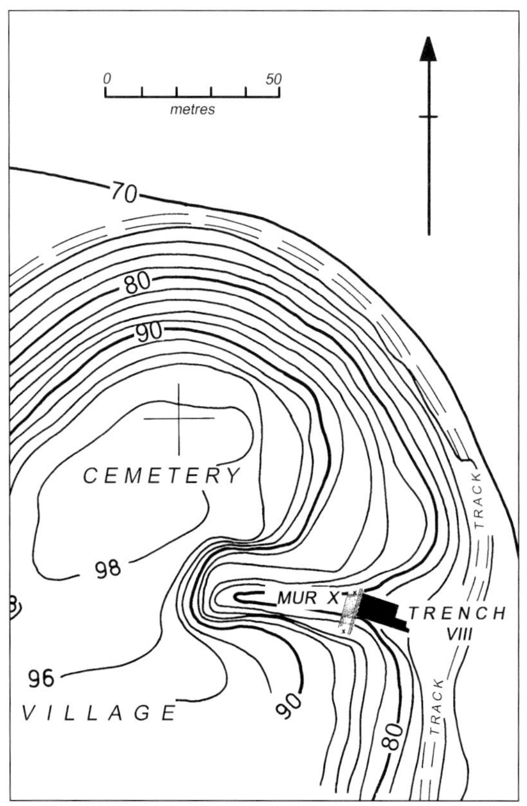

Fig. 2.1. Location of Trench VIII relative to 'Mur X'.

from the cross section published by the French excavators (Pézard 1931, Planche C, partly reproduced here as Fig. 2.2), they had in this part of the site penetrated to about 2 m below the level of the stone foundations of a massive mudbrick town wall ('Mur X': Fig. 2.3) assigned by Pézard tentatively to the 'Amorite' period and dated by Mesnil du Buisson, in his review of the excavations (1935–8, 919), to *c.*1600 BC, but now considered to have been originally built around the middle of the 18th century (Bourke 1993, 163–4). This was the earliest level reached by the French, and it was intended that Trench VIII would make possible the investigation, with minimum effort, of the preceding periods of occupation. The disadvantages of working so close to the edge of the site and – at least at one stage in its history – outside its walls, were, of course, recognised: it was here that disturbances, both ancient and modern, were most likely to occur, that material eroded from higher up the *tell* would have been redeposited and that the previous excavators had dumped spoil from their excavations. On the other hand, it was a relatively flat area, unlike the rest of the site, and was easy of access, and it seemed that, on the whole, the advantages outweighed the disadvantages. In the event the disturbances did create many problems, but, nevertheless, after the removal of the modern rubbish and the French dump there were revealed 3 m or so of substantial 2nd, 3rd and 4th millennium remains (which will be described in forthcoming volumes of this report) overlying some 1.5 m of ceramic Neolithic occupation.

The entire extent of Trench VIII (see Fig. 2.7) was little more than 90 sq m, and of this only about 70 sq m were cleared of the post-Neolithic deposits, while an even smaller area – about 20 sq m – was excavated to bedrock (called thus for convenience: more accurately, the natural lacustrine marlstone), in the two soundings marked B and C on the plan. In a third small sounding, Sounding A, in the south-east corner of the trench, the lowest layer

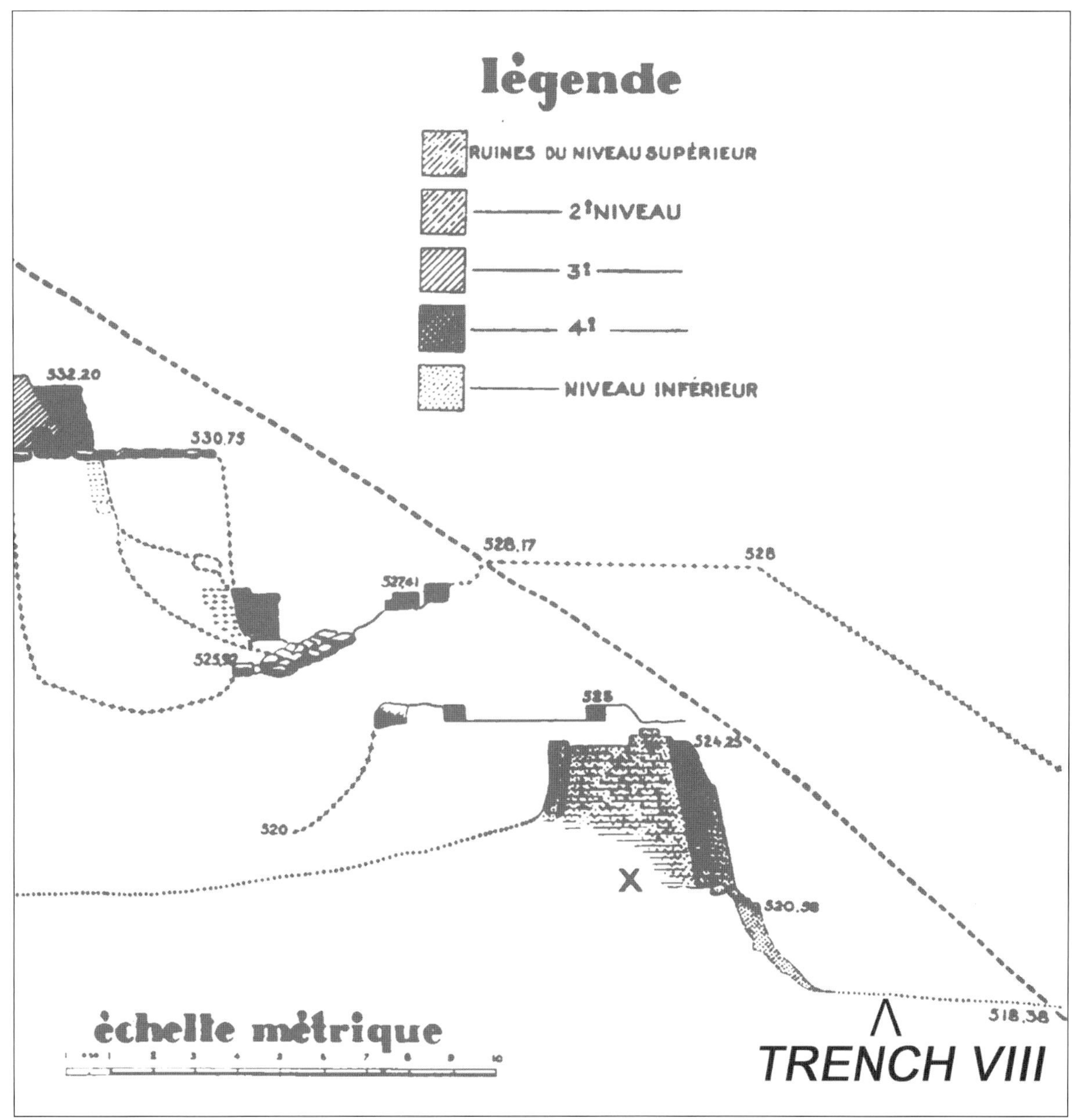

Fig. 2.2. Section through French excavations, showing 'Mur X' and position of Trench VIII (from Pézard 1931, planche C).

reached was of sterile soil and stone rubble, and is almost certainly just above the natural marl. The trench was subdivided as work proceeded into several separate 'Areas', normally delimited by a feature such as a wall or a baulk but irregular in size and shape. The numbers assigned to these Areas were used for recording purposes and their approximate positions are shown on Fig. 2.7, though their actual boundaries are not. (The 2 m grid shown on the plans was added later for ease of reference, and was not used for recording purposes.) As described above, in the Introduction to this volume, excavation was conducted in the conventional way, with each discrete archaeological deposit, recognised by composition, colour, texture and so on, being given its own 'Layer' number; an identification such as VIII.123.6 thus means Layer 6 in Area 123 of Trench VIII. The term 'layer' was used in preference to

the more fashionable 'locus' or 'context', since these terms can, and do, have several meanings (according to their context) and therefore can result in ambiguity. (An index of all the Neolithic layers, with phases, can be found in Table 2.1.) With a very few exceptions all artefacts were kept, as were all animal bones. Although no deposits were dry-sieved (the constant strong winds making this an impractical procedure), a few which seemed to contain significant quantities of botanical material were sampled for flotation (see details in Chapter 8).

The Neolithic levels were first reached in 1982, at the eastern end of the trench, but although work continued on them during five more seasons (1984, 1988, 1990, 1992 and 1995) the total time spent excavating them over the course of this 13-year period amounted to only about 26 weeks. During the later seasons the removal of the post-

Fig. 2.3. Cleaning east face of 'Mur X' in preparation for the excavation of Trench VIII.

Neolithic deposits in Trench VIII and the adjacent Trench I to the west had gone so deep that access to the Neolithic levels had become very difficult, and the disposal of spoil in areas of previous exposure could not be avoided, thus further restricting the area available for examination. Thus, unfortunately, by the end of the actual excavations in 1995 not all of the Neolithic deposits in Trench VIII had been fully excavated, and many problems remained to be resolved. Many of these stemmed from the fact that even those deposits that had been excavated were extensively disturbed by pits, both from late in the Neolithic settlement itself and from later periods, including the Roman; these later pits are shown on Fig. 2.7. Consequently, apart from the substantial wall assigned to Phase 2, the Neolithic structural remains and floor surfaces were in a very fragmentary state, and it was often impossible to correlate with any degree of certainty the isolated areas of stratified deposits in one part of the trench with those in another. Because of this it has been judged misleading to indicate on the published sections (Figs 2.11–2.25) coherent phases valid for the whole trench; instead, attention is drawn to significant groups of layers mentioned in the description of the stratigraphy by numbers enclosed with square brackets, thus [6]. Neither has it been thought necessary to follow the common practice of placing individual layer numbers on the published drawings, since only a proportion of the recorded layers – namely those which are intersected by the sections – appear on them.

Despite these problems and the small area excavated it is possible to identify from the plans and sections five clear major Neolithic stratigraphic phases, which can be summarised thus:

Phase 1. The earliest surviving occupation over bedrock, identified only in exploratory soundings, consisting of ashy layers and clay and/or mudbrick debris, presumably deriving from even earlier occupation, with traces of lime plaster floors but no direct evidence of walls.

Phase 2. One wall of a substantial brick building, with associated clay floors and other deposits.

Phase 3. A succession of lime plaster floors over most of the excavated area, mostly broken and fragmentary but with clear, if sparse, evidence for associated walls. Although there are indications of several episodes of repairs to, and replacement of, the floors, it is not possible, for the reasons stated above, to divide Phase 3 into reliable distinct sub-phases.

Phase 4. A number of small pits and graves over most of the area, with some deeper but amorphous deposits at the western end of the trench but no traces of structures.

Phase 5. A featureless stratum covering the whole area, containing only Neolithic artefacts and probably representing an abandonment of at least this part of the site following the Neolithic occupation.

Stratigraphy

Phase 1: the earliest settlement

Phase 1 consists of all the archaeological deposits between bedrock and the first (and only) substantial surviving Neolithic structure, the mudbrick wall, Wall 1, which defines Phase 2 and is described below. These deposits average about 0.5 m in depth and clearly comprise several sub-phases. As has been stated, bedrock was reached in only a limited area, namely in a narrow (0.7 m wide) sounding (Sounding C) orientated across the middle of the trench from north to south with a small western extension at the northern end, and in a separate small area in the south-west corner of the trench (Sounding B) (plan, Fig. 2.7). From the Sections 1, 9 and 10 (Figs 2.11, 2.24 and 2.25) it can be seen that the surface of the bedrock in this part of the *tell* is more or less level in a north–south direction, but rises gradually from east to west by about 1 m over the 16 m length of the trench. (Unfortunately, the exact height of the outcrop above the present flood plain to the east was not recorded, but an approximate calculation based on the contours shows it to be about 2–3 m.) Traces of the earliest occupation were found either directly on the rock or separated from it by a deposit, varying in thickness from *c*.30 to *c*.150 mm, of reddish-brown stony material, being the original soil overlying the natural marl. These earliest surviving deposits are clearly seen in Sections 9 and 10 (Figs 2.24 and 2.25), where they are numbered [1]; they consist of mixed clayey and bricky material that is apparently the detritus of mud architecture of an earlier stage of occupation. The ashy layers towards the northern end of Section 10, numbered [2], may represent upper occupation surfaces of this Phase, although it is more likely that they are contemporary with Wall 1 of Phase 2; unfortunately the stratigraphy is obscure here because of the later (Phase 4) Pit 1. At the southern end of Section 10 the deposits of Phase 1 are interrupted by a succession of sloping layers of clay and fragmentary plaster, marked [3], which are not easy to interpret, especially since the upper part of the section was unfortunately not completely recorded; however, the presence of the plaster fragments suggest Phase 3 or Phase 4.

Traces of Phase 1 are also visible in the northern part of Sounding C, where Section 4 (Fig. 2.19) has a series of burnt clay surfaces (marked [1]) corresponding with the earliest deposits on Section 10 (Fig. 2.25), which themselves clearly pre-date Wall 1.

These are truncated by a sequence of dipping brick debris, clay surfaces and ashy streaks (marked [2] on Section 4), probably the result of dilapidation and repair still within Phase 1. A patch of white lime plaster, marked [3], at the western end of Section 4, close to bedrock but partly overlying (and therefore later than) the eroded remains of these sloping deposits, appears also in the adjacent Section 6 ([1] on Fig. 2.21), where its absolute level would indicate that it is earlier than Wall 1.

In the south-west corner of Sounding B (Grid B4) a small oval hearth *c*. 0.6 m × 0.7 m in size rested on a deposit of burnt clay associated with the ashy deposit marked [1] on Section 1C (Fig. 2.14), which itself lay on the stony clay immediately above the natural marl. These are the lowest cultural layers in this part of the trench and have been attributed to Phase 1, although strictly speaking this is only an assumption, and it is possible that the remains

of Phase 1 have been completely eroded, as they have been elsewhere in the trench, and that the hearth is of Phase 2. That it is no later, however, is shown by the good-quality plaster floors, typical of Phase 3, which overlie it. Charcoal from oak less than 10 years old yielded from the ash a radiometric date of 7050–6450 cal BC (95.4% probability): BM-2935: see Fig. 2.26 (d).

As can be seen from the above, little has been uncovered of Phase 1, and even this is so fragmentary that it is has been found impossible to establish precise stratigraphic relationships. There is, however, clear evidence for several sub-phases of occupation prior to the construction of Wall 1 in Phase 2, though what length of time these various consecutive episodes represent remains unknown. Relatively little cultural material was recovered from Phase 1, but is clear that, at least in this part of the site, the earliest settlers were utilising structures of mudbrick and/or *terre pisée* with some lime plaster floors, although whether of rectilinear or curvilinear plan cannot be said and no more details of their construction or appearance can be given.

Phase 2: Wall 1 and associated floors and levels (plan Fig. 2.8)

The building of which Wall 1 is the only surviving element introduces a new style and technique of architecture to this part of Tell Nebi Mend. The wall is preserved to a height of some 0.5–0.6 m along the approximately 5 m of its excavated length. It runs from the north-western limit of the Neolithic excavation (Section 6, Fig. 2.21), passes diagonally across the trench through Sections 3 (Fig. 2.18), 7 (Fig. 2.22), 8 (Fig. 2.23), 9 (Fig. 2.24) and 10 (Fig. 2.25), and emerges at an oblique angle in Section 2B (Fig. 2.16). It may have ended here, at a doorway, perhaps, or it may have been destroyed by the ill-defined later pit. Beyond this point there was no definite evidence of any building remains of this phase. The base of the wall was reached only in Sections 9 and 10 (Figs 2.24 and 2.25), on opposite sides of the narrow Sounding C, where it is seen resting on a mixed rubbly or stony layer probably deliberately laid, which in turn overlies clayey and bricky deposits representing the debris of the Phase 1 structures; whether it was built immediately following the destruction of the earlier buildings or only after an interval cannot be said. Despite the lack of proper foundations it was solidly built, although separate bricks – mainly pinkish-yellow, but in one case dark brown – were noticeable in only a few places; mostly it seemed to be formed of thick layers of clay bonded by mortar of fine, clean, grey or orange clay. At the western end, where both faces of the wall were well preserved, they were rendered with two or more layers of similar fine clay, though in this case red or pale yellow, in general 20–30 mm thick but spreading out to more than 0.1 m in depth towards the base; this rendering is clearly visible on Sections 3 (Fig. 2.18) and 6 (Fig. 2.21). The only excavated area where floors definitely associated with the wall were preserved was at the southern end of Section 7

(Fig. 2.22 [1]), where a number of clay surfaces with faint grey deposits run up to it. They probably correspond to the surfaces found in a small sounding some 0.4 m further east (but which were unfortunately not excavated right up to the wall) (visible in Sections 8, Fig. 2.23 [1]), and also perhaps to those in Section 10 (Fig. 2.25 [2]), although these latter, as noted above, could alternatively belong to a late stage in Phase 1. All of these surfaces were composed of light-coloured silty clay similar to the material of Wall 1 itself; there is no evidence for the use of white lime plaster in Phase 2 as there was in Phase 1.

Sections 3 (Fig. 2.18), 9 (Fig. 2.24) and 10 (Fig. 2.25) show that Wall 1 was abutted along its northern side by another brick structure, projecting from the wall by about 0.5 m. Much of it been destroyed by Phase 4 pits, and it can only be traced for some 1.25 m along the wall. It is perhaps a buttress or a bench. It was constructed in the same way as the wall, with courses of brick or layers of clean clay alternating with clay mortar of a different colour. It was not bonded with the main wall and the colours of both the clay and mortar used in the two structures are different, suggesting that the abutment may have been a later addition, although the fact that there was no sign of clay rendering on the wall between it and the abutment argues against this, unless the rendering itself is a later feature. Another similar reinforcement or bench, or perhaps the continuation of that just described, is suggested by the rather weathered and amorphous deposit of bricky material visible in Section 6 adjacent to the north face of the wall and marked [2] on Fig. 2.21. It is about 0.5 m wide and about 0.3 m high, and is bounded by a rough line of stones at its base. Unlike the abutment described above, it lies against the original clay rendering on the face of the wall, and is clearly a later addition.

Also on the north side of the wall and running over the fragmentary remains of Phase 1 is a very mixed deposit containing much pottery, bone, clay and lime plaster fragments, ash with charcoal flecks and small stones which is visible in Section 6 (marked [3] on Fig. 2.21). Although an actual stratigraphic connection with Wall 1 could not be established, the deposit must be close to the level of the base of the wall and probably equates with the early occupation of the building. Over this mixed deposit, grey ashy and greasy layers (marked [4] on Fig. 2.21), with no evidence for proper floors, accumulated against the presumed wall reinforcement or bench described above. They are typical courtyard or alleyway surfaces outside houses where domestic rubbish accumulates.

To the south of the wall, as on the north, Phase 4 pits cut into its face had removed many of the associated deposits. Near the eastern end of the preserved stretch of wall (Grid E3/4; Layer VIII.646.1), was a small circular stone hearth about 0.4 m across made of stones carefully fitted together to form a flattish surface; other stones were set on edge and packed with clay to make a slightly raised rim, perhaps originally in a horseshoe shape (Fig. 2.4). It was resting on the thin grey ashy surface of a light-coloured clay deposit,

presumably a floor, and although, yet again, there was no direct stratigraphic link, this ashy surface is most likely to equate with those visible curving up in the direction of Wall 1 in Section 2B (Fig. 2.16 [1]), which are themselves clearly earlier than a series of Phase 3 plaster floors, marked [2] in the same section. The hearth can therefore almost certainly be ascribed to Phase 2.

Packed against the southern face of the wall at the western limit of excavation (Grid D2) a deposit of very hard orange clay, marked [5] on Section 6 (Fig. 2.21), is perhaps an internal abutment or architectural feature. It rests against the rendering of the wall and may therefore be an addition. Fragments of oak and pistachio charcoal less than 10 years old from this clay yielded a radiocarbon date of 7050–6500 cal BC (95.4% probability): see Fig. 2.26 (c).

The close sequence of clayey, stony and ashy layers, with some apparent surfaces of lime plaster, that appear at the southern end of Section 10 (Fig. 2.25 [3]) curving up in the direction of Wall 1, and which have been mentioned above as truncating deposits of Phase 1, might be taken at first sight to be a succession of floor and occupation levels contemporary with Wall 1. The adjacent Section 1B, where they are marked [1], suggests, however, that they are more likely to be the filling of Pit 10, a large pit of later date one side of which appears also at the southern end of Section 9 (Fig. 2.24), where it cuts the well-preserved sequence of Phase 3 plaster floors.

In the absence of evidence in the area excavated of any other walls contemporary with Wall 1 or of any material indicative of the nature of a superstructure or roof, little more can be said about the size, appearance and function of the building of which it formed part. However, the careful construction of the wall, with clean hard clay or mudbricks, contrasting clay mortar and careful clay rendering, as well as the considerable extent of the structure, may indicate that this was a communal or special building rather than a simple dwelling. There was no evidence of deliberate destruction; the building appears to have simply gone out of use and decayed, the bricky and silty deposits adjacent to the wall on Sections 3 (Fig. 2.18 [1]), 7 (Fig. 2.22 [2]) and 9 (Fig. 2.24 [3]) being the result of this process.

Phase 3: lime plaster floors (plan Fig. 2.9)

Over most of the area of excavation there are remains of lime plaster floors overlying the Phase 2 wall and its associated deposits. They were of fine plaster with a smooth surface (when this was preserved) and had sometimes been covered with one or more additional thin layers of plaster, presumably when the old surface had begun to break up. When excavated the colour of the surfaces varied from white to cream, pale yellow, pink and grey, but this variation almost certainly resulted from natural weathering and staining and not from deliberate decoration. Only in one instance (Floor 7, referred to below) was there possible evidence of an intentional application of red paint or wash, presumably over the whole floor since no pattern was

Fig. 2.4. Phase 2 hearth (VIII.646.1).

discernible. In most cases the plaster was laid on a base of small pebbles, crushed marl or reused plaster debris; there were a few instances where old floors seemed to have been stripped down to the barest traces for reuse in this way. The base and its surface could be several centimetres thick. Often the plaster, with or without this built-up base, was laid on a thick layer of clay, either a deliberate foundation layer or simply mudbrick debris and wash from the walls and roofs of preceding structures.

Unfortunately these remains are fragmentary and disconnected, having been extensively dug into by numerous later pits or simply worn away by use, so that, although several successive episodes of the laying and repair of floors is clearly discernible, it is usually impossible to relate these to one another and so divide the Phase 3 into coherent sub-phases. Only in the southern part of the trench, around Grid Squares D–E 3–4, is the stratigraphic evidence more informative.

Here, in the centre of Section 8 (Fig. 2.23), there is a disturbance with a fill of soft dark earth (perhaps an animal burrow) cutting into a deposit of stiff clay. Although the edges of the clay itself are ill-defined, the succession of lime plaster floors curving up to it from the south sindicates that it is the remains of a wall or kerb, here termed Wall 2 (Fig. 2.5). The floors comprise a lower group of three (Floors 4, 6 and 7), one directly on top of another, and a

higher one (Floor 3) on the same plan but separated from the others by a layer of clay, either a deliberate raising of the level prior to the construction of the uppermost floor or simply the result of erosion from the wall. Charcoal from branches of oak and pistachio, less than about 10–15 years old, from this clay provided a radiocarbon date of 7050–6640 cal BC (95.4% probability): see Fig. 2.26 (b). In section the floors all end in a straight line, and an edge is visible on the plan of Phase 3 (Fig. 2.9, Grid Squares D–E 4), together with another, at right angles to the first, a short distance away, thus forming a corner.

Wall 2 also appears in Section 9, parallel to Section 8 and about 0.35 m to the east, as does the same sequence of plaster floors (marked [2] on Fig. 2.24). The nature of the wall is clearer here, though still indistinct; it comprises a length of yellowish-brown brick or stiff clay furnished on both sides with an orange clay facing. In section, the stiff clay of the wall appears to be the same as that which lies beneath the lowest floor. Unfortunately the upper part of the wall and the levels against its northern face have been removed by a later disturbance. The width of the wall – about 0.3 m – suggests that it could not have risen to any great height and must have been of a fairly insubstantial nature, and possibly no more than a low step or kerb.

The relationship of the plaster floors of Phase 3 with the earlier Phase 2 building is rather ambiguous. In

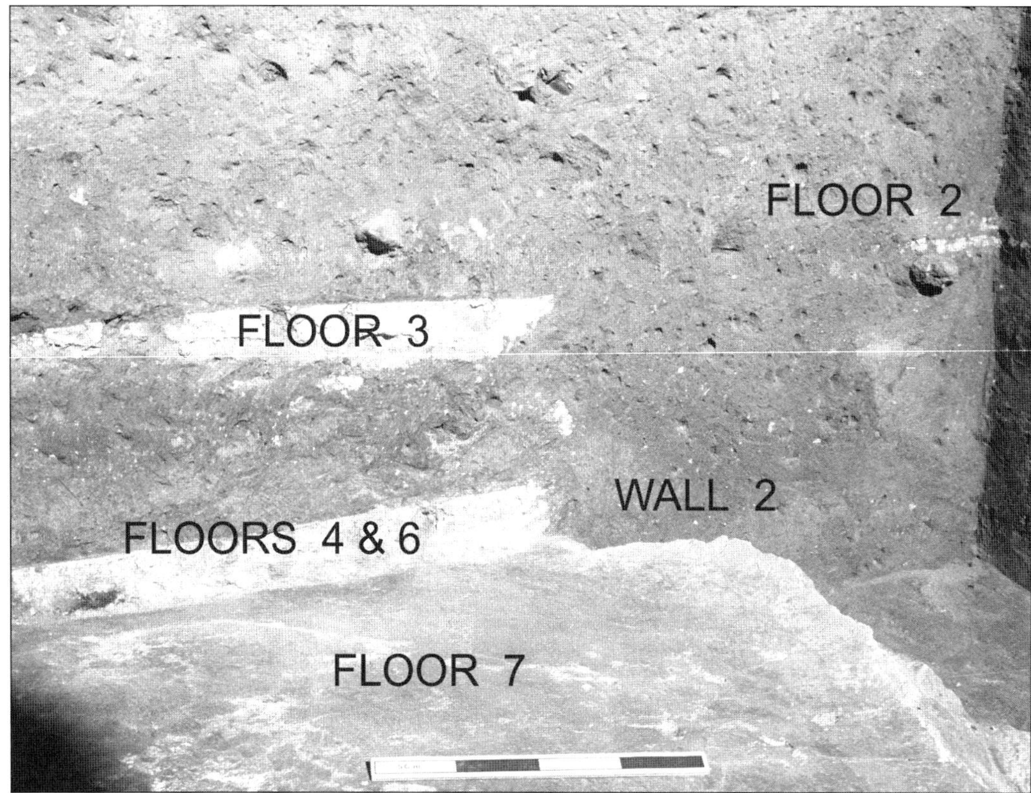

Fig. 2.5. Superimposed Floors 3, 4, 6 and 7 (Phase 3) in Section 8.

several places patches of plaster lie directly across the line of the Phase 2 Wall 1, although only one of these shows in section, namely in Section 3, where a small area, marked [2] on Fig. 2.18, lies directly on top of the Wall 1 abutment, indicating that this, at least, had gone out of use. However, the evidence recorded on Section 8 (Fig. 2.23) seems to indicate that some of the upper part of Wall 1 was still visible when the Phase 3 rooms were built, and that it was incorporated into the new plan. On this section the sequence of floors to the north of Wall 2 clearly corresponds to the sequence of floors to the south, although no exact correlation is possible, since floors on either side of a wall need not necessarily be at the same absolute level. The stratigraphic connections between these floors and Wall 1 to the north has been removed by later activities, but it is clear that the lowest floor, Floor 5, reaches the wall below its highest surviving point. Floor 2 is also lower than that point, while Floor 1, the highest, is about on a level with it. Some of Wall 1 must therefore have been visible when these floors were laid. In fact, if the faint ashy surface shown on Section 8 about 0.15 m below Floor 5 indicates the former presence of yet another floor, whether plastered or not, then it is possible that at least this stretch of Wall 1 remained in use for the entire period during which the floors on either side of Wall 2 were being repaired and replaced; in other words, that there is a chronological overlap between Phases 2 and 3. No useful purpose would be served by giving a detailed description

of each of the other extant patches of plaster flooring; they appear in several of the sections and are shown on the plan of Phase 3 (Fig. 2.9), where an attempt is also made to indicate where several floors are superimposed. Only a few add to our knowledge of the architecture of this phase. At about 1.5 m from the eastern end of Section 2B are fragments of one or possibly two plaster floors (marked [3] on Fig. 2.16) clearly sloping upwards over the remains of Wall 1 (which here is collapsed) and running up to the lower of two large stones set one above the other (Grid E3). No other stones were found aligned with these, and it is doubtful whether they formed part of a wall; if they did they would provide the only evidence for stone architecture in the entire Neolithic at Tell Nebi Mend. Continuations of these floors or others of the same phase are those marked [2] further west in the same section. At the eastern end of Section 4 (Fig. 2.19 [4]) a very fragmentary plaster surface runs up to another large flat stone 0.6 m × 0.25 m in its exposed dimensions, the size and shape of which suggests that it could be some sort of work installation, for food preparation or the like. An association between a floor and a domestic installation is also found in the extreme south-west corner of the trench, in Sounding B (Grid A–B 4), where another sequence of three lime plaster floors is clearly visible in Sections 1C (Fig. 2.14) and 5 (Fig. 2.20). They have no observable stratigraphic connection with the three floors in Sections 2B and 8, some 5 m further east, but the similarity of the two sequences might indicate that they relate to the same three episodes of reconstruction. A small sunken hearth of clay with a prominent raised rim and filled with ashy silt ([1] in Fig. 2.20) seems to be contemporary with the middle floor. The fills between the floors contain much ash and other signs of burning, suggesting that this was a kitchen area, as it had been in Phase 1, when (as noted above) another small hearth had been sited here. The uppermost floor in Section 5 (Fig. 2.20) provides a good example of the use of cobbles as a base for the lime plaster, mentioned above.

These remnants of lime plaster floors found all over Trench VIII seem most likely to represent a dense occupation pattern of small dwellings with thin flimsy walls and insubstantial superstructures. However, in view of the paucity of surviving floor edges and recognisable walls, this cannot be taken as certain, and the quality of the floors and the care with which they were constructed and maintained may rather point to a larger building with internal divisions and with more substantial outer walls beyond the limits of excavation.

Phase 4: pits and burials (plan Fig. 2.10)

In this phase there was a complete change in the use of this part of the site: the earlier structures were abandoned and the area was reused for burials, for open-air activities requiring fires and for rubbish disposal. There are no identifiable structures or floors, and instead the area is honeycombed with pits of various kinds, which had hardly occurred before. These cut through the floors of Phase 3 and often also into Wall 1 and the associated levels of Phase 2; a few penetrated almost to bedrock. Unfortunately there were difficulties in establishing the precise level of origin of many of the pits owing to recutting, subsequent erosion, post-Neolithic disturbances and so on, but on the rare occasions when an individual pit could be traced with some confidence to the level from which it had been originally dug this proved to be a very narrow band of mixed deposits on top of the remains of the Phase 3 structures, separating those remains from the brown soil deposits of Phase 5, to be described below. It seems likely that, before the accumulation of this brown soil, the top of the underlying remains and the original surface (or surfaces) from which the Phase 4 pits originated had been severely eroded. Only at the very western limit of Trench VIII was there a somewhat greater depth of mixed clayey material – for example, in Section 2A (Fig. 2.15 [1]) – later than the Phase 3 floors and possibly earlier than Phase 5. This could have been from the destruction and erosion of the Phase 3 buildings, but is perhaps more likely to be material from structures contemporary with the pits and burials which disintegrated after the site was abandoned and before the final dark brown deposits covered everything. Phase 4 may thus simply testify to a recognition by the inhabitants of the imprudence of building at the outer edges of the site nearest to lower-lying ground adjacent to the flood plain.

There were about 20 pits scattered over the whole area (excluding those of post-Neolithic date). Of these, some were graves (described in Chapter 3). The other pits range between 0.7 m and 1.4 m across and from around 0.2 m to 1 m deep. Some contain mixed fills or rubbish, but the smaller ones seem primarily to have been fire pits or sunken hearths.

Fire pits. Three small pits (Pits 2, 3 and 5) cut through the Phase 3 white plaster floor in this area and into the top of the northern face of the Phase 1 Wall and its outer buttress (see Section 7, Fig. 2.22 [3]). Pit 3 cut into Pit 2 and partially overlay Pit 1, and so was later than both of these. Both Pit 1 and Pit 2 were shallow and contained charcoal, ash and clay, some of which was burnt; neither contained more than a few fragments of bone, flint or pottery. Pit 5 (Section 6 (Fig. 2.21 [6]) also cut into Wall 1 and was deeper, but although its fill was more varied and included large lumps of lime plaster, a piece of basalt and part of a large White Ware bowl (Reg. No. 5333; see Chapter 6), its base was thickly covered with charcoal pieces, suggesting that it too was originally a fire pit. One of these pieces, a short-life sample of willow, provided a radiocarbon date of 7200–6650 cal BC (95.4% probability: see Fig. 2.26 (a)). There are other shallow pits, often irregular in shape, such as Pit 6 (Grid E4: Section 1B, Fig. 2.13) and Pit 7 (Section 2C, Fig. 2.17), which contain mainly ashy deposits and are probably fire pits; all are later than the Phase 3 floors but are sealed by the Phase 5 dark brown soil.

Rubbish pits. The majority of the pits are deeper and contain mixed fills of ash, clay, dark earth, silt and stones, together with pottery, flints, bone and fragments of plaster and charcoal. The quantities of artefacts and bone in the fills varied widely, but were not generally so plentiful as to indicate that pits were dug merely to dispose of such domestic detritus, although other uses are not easy to suggest. The larger pits, such as Pits 1 (Grid E4) and 8 (Grid D3), were mostly round. Pit 8 had some alternating ashy and clayey layers deep down and may have also initially been used as a fire pit (the base was not reached); these were followed by mixed fills of soil, silt, ashy pockets and rubbish. Only a few pits, such as Pit 10 (Grid E4) in Section 1B (Fig. 2.13), showed distinct tip-lines or multi-layered deposits. Many deposits were loose and jumbled, as if from a single deliberate in-filling event after the first use of the pit; occasionally joining potsherds were scattered throughout the fill.

Phase 5: abandonment and erosion

This phase is represented by an almost entirely featureless layer over the whole area exposed, varying in thickness from just a few centimetres to almost 0.4 m. During excavation it was usually described as being comprised of 'chocolate brown' or 'dark brown' soil, and it was often noted that the upper part was generally more gritty or stony than the lower, which was more silty and 'greasy', although with no clear dividing line between the two. Its colour, and the fact that it was rather compact when first dug, contrasted strongly with the mostly light-coloured clayey or ashy layers above and below; the distinction is particularly clear in Sounding A in the south-east corner of the trench (Fig. 2.6). Although no samples were taken, it seemed evident from visual and tactile inspection that the layer was high in humic content, which can only be the result of the decay of vegetation over a period of exposure to the natural elements. It thus seems clear that it was laid down at a time when at least this part of the site was uninhabited and had reverted to its natural state. Neolithic artefacts were plentiful throughout the deposit, all comparable to corresponding material from the preceding phases; there was nothing later. While it is theoretically possible that these artefacts came from occupation levels contemporary with Phase 5 elsewhere on the site but outside the area of excavation, the homogeneity of the 'chocolate brown' deposit makes it more likely that the Phase 5 material originated in the immediately underlying layers, and had been brought up from these by animal or vegetal activity during the period of abandonment. The absence of disturbances (apart from the much later post-Neolithic pits) also strongly suggests that this abandonment affected the entire site, since it seems most unlikely that contemporary inhabitants elsewhere on the site would not have used this peripheral area for such things as rubbish pits, as they had in the preceding phase.

Summary

The earliest settlement so far discovered at Tell Nebi Mend (Phase 1) was built directly on the gently sloping and weathered surface of an outcrop of indurated marl with pockets of red- or orange-brown soil and natural rubble, a short distance away from the western edge of the Orontes flood plain and about 3 m above it. Although no architectural features were identified, the presence of lime plaster fragments and mudbrick or clay debris is clear evidence for the original presence of structures. There are signs of several sub-phases of destruction, erosion and repair, after which the ground may have been cleared for a large building (Phase 2). Of this only a single wall, of mudbrick and clay and with associated structures (possibly strengthening buttresses or benches), and patches of clay flooring were found, but the quality of its construction and its size – at least 5 m × 4 m – suggest that it may have been a communal or special building rather than a simple dwelling, thus indicating a complete change in not only the architecture but also the function of this part of the site. Phase 3 sees a return to the architectural traditions of the earliest settlement, with the use of lime plaster and cobbles for substantial floors but apparently more flimsy walls. Although these remains may possibly represent the internal divisions of a large communal building replacing that of Phase 2, it is more likely that the usage of this part of the site now reverted to domestic occupation. The evidence for at least three successive episodes of replacement of the floors points to an occupation of some

Fig. 2.6. Sounding A, Grid H4, showing distinction between the 'chocolate brown' soil of Phase 5 and the post-Neolithic levels.

duration. Another change of function occurs in Phase 4, when the area is given over to pits – fire pits, rubbish pits and burials – which are not all absolutely contemporary and again are suggestive of utilisation over some time. In the area excavated this phase is little more than a horizon between Phases 3 and 5, but there are some indications in the extreme west of the trench of more substantial deposits, with very indeterminate features perhaps representing the eroded remains of dwellings contemporary with the pits, and it would be therefore be wrong to assume that the entire site was devoid of permanent occupation. However, in Phase 5 a more extensive and now probably total abandonment of the site is indicated. It is represented by an almost featureless homogeneous deposit of dark brown soil that is apparently the result of the degradation by natural causes of the underlying Neolithic deposits and the decay of the vegetation which in the course of time covered over the ruins. It contains exclusively Neolithic artefacts almost certainly derived from the cultural layers below.

Dating

Four calibrated radiometric determinations from well-stratified short-life samples place the Neolithic occupation described above to between the end of the 8th and the middle of the 7th millennium BC (Fig. 2.26; Table 2.2). Unfortunately they are not sufficiently separated to provide an adequate basis for estimating more closely the dates of the individual phases of occupation or their total length. The shallowness of the deposits – little more than a metre where fully exposed – is probably deceptive: with the exception of the building in Phase 2, the materials used would not have produced much debris when destroyed, while the slight but clear evidence for a number of successive episodes of use, destruction, decay and reuse within each of Phases 1–4 suggests that the time covered by the occupation should probably be measured in generations or even centuries rather than in mere decades. However, the calibrated dates show that occupation must have ended by around the middle of the 7th millennium, and it is relevant to note here – in anticipation of a future volume of this excavation report – that two dates of 4045–3960 cal BC (NZA 29431) and 3950–3770 cal BC (NZA 29432), with a 95.4% probability, were obtained from short-life samples (a fruit stone, probably olive, and a fragment of palm stem, *phoenix* sp.) from a hearth contemporary with the first structure built in Trench VIII when the site was reoccupied in Phase 6. An abandonment lasting for some two and a half millennia of at least the area of the *tell* revealed in Trench VIII and – as has been argued above – also probably of the whole site, is thus indicated. In the immediate vicinity of Tell Nebi Mend the gap is partly filled by the evidence from the site of Arjoune, about a kilometre to the north-east on the opposite bank of the Orontes, which was occupied (although perhaps only seasonally) during two, apparently separate, periods between the mid-6th and mid-5th millennia BC by people in contact with the Halaf and Ubaid cultural spheres (Parr 2003). But this still leaves a gap of a thousand years or so between the desertion of Tell Nebi Mend and the arrival of newcomers on the other side of the river, and another gap, perhaps of shorter length, between the desertion of Arjoune and the resettlement of Tell Nebi Mend. New evidence from further archaeological surveys – such as those of Philip (Philip *et al.* 2002; 2005; Philip 2007; Philip and Bradbury 2010) and Haïdar-Boustani and colleagues (2003–4; 2005–6) – and the excavation of known mounds such as Tell et-Tin, where, as we have seen (Chapter 1), levels of prehistoric occupation seem to lie deeply hidden beneath later deposits, may well fill these gaps. But until this research is carried out it would be premature to discuss the fluctuations in the settlement history of the Homs plain and the middle Orontes valley, and particularly whether they were the result of purely local or wider, regional factors.

Table 2.1. Index of Trench VIII (Neolithic) layers.

Layer No.	Description	Phase
AREA 602: SOUNDING B, GRID SQUARE B4		
602.15	Dark brown with stones.	4+5
602.16	Bricky (possible wall?) above top plaster floor 602.26.	4?
602.19	Grey, containing v. dark charcoal patches with ashy lenses and patches of clay and brick.	5
602.20	Banded dark silt and orange clayey, above top plaster floor 602.26 and below 602.19.	4?
602.23	Light clay.	4?
602.24	Very dark charcoal surface.	4?
602.25	Light orange bricky, above 602.19.	4?
602.26	Topmost plaster floor = 605.66, 606.1, 606.66.	3
602.27	Grey-brown.	4?5?
602.28	Very fine grey.	4?
602.29	Black surface.	4?
602.30	Small reddish-brown area.	4?
602.31	Greasy grey clay.	4
602.32	Dirty greasy orange.	4?
602.33	Dirty yellow clay.	4?
602.34	Patchy light clay with stones.	4?
602.36	Mixture of 602.15 and 602.19.	4+5
602.37	Very dark ashy.	4?

AREA 605

605.59–66: Renumbered 606.59–66 because of duplication in field recording.

Layer No.	Description	Phase
AREA 606: SOUNDING B, GRID SQUARE B4		
606.01	Top plaster floor [= 602.26; 605.66 (re-numbered 606.66)].	3
606.02	Pit cutting top plaster floor 606.1, plus probe to south and east.	?4
606.03	Red silty, beneath 606.1.	3
606.04	Dark grey clayey surface.	3
606.05	Dark grey clayey surface, similar to 602.4 but thicker.	3
606.06	Patch of light grey ash, within 602.06.	3
606.07	Pit in NE corner of area.	4
606.08	Reddish-brown silty.	3
606.09	Probe below plaster 606.10.	3 (?+2)
606.10	Plaster patch, below 606.1 (= 606.14?).	3
606.11	Burnt red surface associated with plaster 606.10.	3
606.12	Mudbrick.	3
606.13	Mixed.	Mixed
606.14	Middle plaster floor, below 606.1 (= 606.10).	3
606.14	Re-numbered = 606.24.	
606.15	Mixed clayey with some rubble, above(?) and between lower 2 plaster floors, 606.14 and 18.	3
606.16	Pit, probably hearth = 606.23.	3
606.17	Re-numbered = 606.27.	
606.18	Lowest plaster floor, below 606.14.	3
606.19	Mixed reddish-brown clay, ashy grey soil and plaster flecks. Below 606.18.	2
606.20	Yellowish-brown, very rubbly. Includes ashy grey layer. Below lowest plaster floor 606.18.	1 (?2)
606.21	Mixed yellowish-brown. Probably includes hearth associated with ashy gry surface (= 602.20?) Below lowest plaster floor 606.18. Rubbly deposit beneath, immediately on bedrock.	1(?2)
606.22	Hearth, within 606.21, associated with more extensive ashy deposit near to bedrock.	1(?2)
606.23	Pit/hearth.	3
606.24	Trample/clearance.	Mixed
606.25	Fill/make-up of floor, beneath 606.10/606.14.	3
606.26	Fill/make-up of floor, beneath 606.10/606.14.	3
606.27	Pit cutting plaster floors.	4
606.61–4	Grey-brown, various inclusions, immediately beneath post-Neo. wall.	5
606.65	10 cm of deposits immediately above top plaster floor 606.66 (= 606.1).	4(?3)
606.66	Topmost plaster floor = 606.1.	3
AREA 644: GRID SQUARES D–G 3–4		
644.14	Chocolate brown stony, as 644.29 and 644.34.	5
644.15	Dark greasy surface, patches of clay and plaster.	?4
644.16	Dark brown, with patches of greasy light brown clay and black. Under 644.15 surface, and rests on upper plaster floor 644.39.	4(?3)
644.18	Chocolate brown stony soil, as 644.14 but lower, beneath floor of EB Wall 1 (644.17).	5
644.19	Pit 10 fill ? (= 644.26?) – cuts 644.16?	4
644.20	Dark brown, with patches of greasy light brown clay and black. Under 644.15 surface, and rests on upper plaster floor 644.39.	?4 + EB
644.21	Irregular cobbles, in light brown soil. Over plaster floor 644.22 and 644.23.	4(?3)

644.22	Plaster floor (= 647.1).	3
644.23	Orange-brown soil, below cobbles 644.21, over plaster 644.22.	3
644.24	Greasy black surface/clay/stones, under 644.21.	3
644.25	Loose fill – pit? overlies 644.23.	4(?3)
644.26	Pit 10 fill – same as 644.19.	4
644.27	Pit fill (?) = 647.5).	4
644.29	Brown stony, same as 644.14, 644.34.	5
644.30	Orange-brown soil (= 644.23) on plaster floor 644.22.	3
644.32	Greasy black-brown floor under 644.41.	3
644.34	Chocolate brown stony; beneath floor of post-Neo.wall 3.	5
644.35	Loose grey pit fill, same as 644.26 (Pit 10)	4
644.39	Plaster floor (= 648 Floor no. 3).	3
644.40	Shallow pit cutting plaster floor 644.39.	4
644.41	Clay, plaster, brick destruction material associated with plaster floor 644.39, E of 'broken edge' – pit?	4(?3)
644.42	Red-brown clay, greasy with charcoal flecks, beneath plaster floor 644.39 (Floor 3) and above plaster floors 644.44 and 644. 45.	3
644.43	Hard packed stiff clayey. Robbed-out wall of 644.44/45 or pit?	Mixed
644.44	Plaster Floor 4, beneath 644.42 and directly on top of 644.45).	Mixed
644.45	Plaster floor 6, directly under 644.44.	3
644.46	Same as 644.43.	Mixed
644.47	Same as 644.44.	Mixed

AREA 646: GRID SQUARES D–G 3–4

646.01	Stone hearth, on ashy layer above clay surface against Wall 1.	2
646.02	Pit 6: burnt soil, ash and charcoal fill.	4
646.03	Pit 9, cutting into Wall 1.	4
646.04	Light brown bricky, tightly packed.	
646.05	Orange-brown bricky.	2(?3)
646.10	Brown-grey gritty with plaster and charcoal inclusions. Dug into by post-Neo. terrace wall.	5
646.11	Brown/orange. Under 646.10, above Phase 2 wall extension.	5(?4)
646.12	Part of 706/Wall 1 extension? or above?	2(?3)
646.13	Orange fill or debris against 706/Wall 1.	2
646.14	Grey fill or debris against 706/Wall 1.	2

AREA 647: GRID SQUARE G4

647.01	Plaster floor (= 644.22).	3
647.02	Bricky, hard-packed, under plaster floor 647.1.	3
647.03	Grey/black ash, beneath 647.02, over 647.04.	
647.04	Orange-brown clayey/bricky.	3(?2)
647.05	Pit, cuts floors 647.1 and 647.10.	4
647.06	Fill of pit 647.12.	4
647.07	Bricky patch.	
647.08	Grey/black burnt layer.	
647.07–09	Successive occupation layers below 647.3 and 647.4.	2?
647.10	Plaster in base of pit fill 647.6, or floor below.	3(?4)
647.12	Pit. Cuts 647.03.	4
647.13	Burnt ashy, some fragments of plaster. Occupation level near bedrock, beneath 647.9.	1(?2)
647.14	Light brown pocket of clay on bedrock. Natural?	
647.15	Occupation level on bedrock, beneath 647.13.	1(?2)

AREA 648: GRID SQUARE D4

648.01	Chocolate brown, with broken plaster inclusions.	5
648.03–04	Thin brown/black occupation layers above 648.6	3
648.05	Orange bricky layer above top 648 Floor no.1 (see also 648.3, 4 – Phase 4?).	3(?2)
648.06	Upper plaster – 648 Floor no. 1.	3
648.07	Lower plaster – 648 Floor no. 2.	3
648.08	Dark brown layer, between 648.07 and 648.09.	
648.09	Orange layer, with charcoal and plaster fragments. Beneath 648.7.	3
648.10	Plaster – 648 Floor no. 3.	3
648.11	Stiff orange clay. Under 648 Floors nos 2 and 3	3
648.12	Plaster – 648 Floor no.4.	3
648.13	Stiff orange clay, with flecks of charcoal. Similar to 648.11 but not as clean. Rests on plaster floor (unnumbered).	3
648.14	= 699+. Cleaning Section 2.	Mixed
648.15	Very hard orange clay; possible wall (robbed-out?).	3
648.16	Soft brown, plaster inclusions. Beneath 648.15.	3
648.17	Orange brown, with many plaster inclusions. Lies on top of plaster floor (probably = Floor 2).	3

 Virginia Mathias and Peter J. Parr

648.18	Grey/brown ashy. Beneath 648.16, and above 648.19.	3
648.19	Orange-brown, with plaster inclusions. Below 648.18, and rests on plaster surface.	3
648.20	Black/brown ashy, with few inclusions. Between 648.19 and 648.22. Cut by 648.21.	3
648.21	Soft brown, many plaster fragments. Pit?	3
648.22	Orange-brown. Beneath 648.20, and lying on decayed plaster surface. Cut by 648.21.	
648.25	Thin occupation layer beneath 648.1.	4(?3)

AREA 650; GRID SQUARE H–I 3–4

650.04–05	Unstratified, from deep sounding.	
650.14	Chocolate brown, above 650.16.	5
650.16	Yellow clayey, possibly mudbrick in probe; SW end of Wall 1?	?4
650.17	Orange greasy surface, patches of plaster.	?3

AREA 654: GRID SQUARE H–I 3–4

654.07	Chocolate brown (probably = 650.14).	5
654.09	Chocolate Brown, with clay and brick fragments (? = 650.14).	5
654.10	Dark ashy clay, below 654.09.	4

AREA 655: GRID SQUARE H–I 3–4

655.01	Dark ashy on plaster floor 655.3 (may be bottom of 654.10).	3
655.02	Pit ? (may cut plaster floor 655.3).	4
655.03	Plaster floor.	3
655.04	Burnt plaster, possible lower part of 655.3.	3
655.05	Grey-brown clay, under 655.3, 655.4 and 655.8 and over white/brown pebbly (?decayed bedrock).	?2
655.06	Yellow clay lump/bricks?	?4
655.07	Ashy fill of pit; may cut decayed plaster floor 655.03.	4
655.08	Thin black ash, under part of floor 655.3 and 655. 4.	3

AREA 705: GRID SQUARES D–E 1–2

705.49*	Plaster floor [= 706.8].	3
705.62	Dark soft grey.	5
705.63	Dark bricky below 705.62.	?4
705.64*	Mixed material from probe.	Mixed

705.66	Bricky and dark, below 705.62 and 705.63.	4(?3)
705.67	Grey greasy occupation, against 706/Wall 1, below 705.66.	3(?2)
705.68	Grey greasy, fill against 706/Wall 1; below 705.66 and 705.67.	3(?2)
705.69*	Mixed bricky/ashy/silty; possibly pit/or loose fill against wall/bricky mass?	?3?4
705.70	Dark ashy fill in Pits 2 and 3 (706.13 and 706.9).	4
705.70	Plaster and clay lumps – same as 705.49? Disturbed by pit.	4
705.72	Yellow-grey above 706/Wall 1.	3
705.83	Ashy, below soft dark brown of Phase 5.	4
705.84	Yellow clay.	?4

AREA 706: GRID SQUARES D–E 1–2

706.01–02	Brown gritty.	5
706.03–04	Brown silty.	5
706.05	Mixed gritty/clayey over 706/Wall 1.	3
706.06	Several grey greasy layers below plaster 706.8.	2(?3)
706.07	706/Pit 1 fill (also 706.10, 707.11, and 706.31).	4
706.08	Plaster surface, very broken.	3
706.09	Fill of shallow firepit (706/Pit 3) – cuts 706/Wall 1.	4
706.10	Ashy lower fill of 706/Pit 1.	4
706.11	706/Pit 1 fill, mixture of 706.07 and 706 10.	4
706.12	Light grey greasy, below 706.6.	2
706.13	Hard crumbly yellow clay, with ash. Fill of shallow firepit (706/Pit 2). Cuts into Wall 1.	4
706.14	Loose grey deposit against 706 Wall 1.	2
706.15	Dark grey ashy, below 14. Roughly equivalent to 706.6 and 12?	2
706.16	Soft light grey, below 15. Roughly equivalent to 706.6 and 12?	2
706.17	Surface below 16; equivalent to top of 706.22?	2
706.18	Plaster, clay, charcoal fill of small pit in 706 N section (Pit 5).	4
706.19	Hard grey and burnt orange clay. Upper part of 706/Wall 1.	Unstrat.
706.20	Mixed clayey against outside of 706/Wall 1, or wall itself? (probably same as 706.19).	2(?3)
706.21	Crumbly blackish lower fill of 706/Pit 5 lower fill.	4

706.22	Mixed grey/brown ashy and bricky debris against 706/Wall 1.	2
706.23	Clayey deposit against Wall 706/1 = 706.20.	2
706.24	Loose deposits against 706 Wall 1. Same as 706.14 and 43?	2
706.25	Ashy and broken brick.	2
706.26	Ashy and broken brick.	2
706.27	Mixed yellow and grey.	2
706.28	Small ashy pit.	2
706.29	Stones/silty/mudbrick lumps. Beneath 706.04.	4(?3)
706.30	Orange bricky and grey silty deposit below 706.29.	2(?3)
706.31	Dark ashy, lowest fill of Pit 1 (also 706.7, 706 10, and 706.11).	4
706.32	Crumbly bricky below 706.30. (Has post-Neolithic sherds?)	? Mixed
706.33	Ashy/burnt soil below 706.32.	1
706.34	Bricky, below 706.22.	1
706.40*	Grey greasy fill. (May be mixed with later pit.)	?4
706.41*	Grey greasy fill. (May be mixed with later pit.)	?4
706.42*	Red/orange clayey (=706.30?), mixed with grey and black layers.	2
706.43	Loose fine grey, perhaps fill of Pit 6. (Same as 24 and 14?)	2
706.44	Sticky brown, with charcoal. Below 706.42.	1 (2?)
706.45	Orange clay below 706.44.	1 (2?)
706.46	Clay in N–S channel in bedrock.	1
706.47*	Fill of Pit 1 = 706.7. (Possibly mixed with 706.4.)	5 + 4
706.50	Bricky against south face of Wall 1.	2
706.51	Bricky against north face of Wall 1.	2

AREA 708: GRID SQUARES E 1–2

708.01*	Grey-brown gritty.	5
708.02*	Grey-brown, hard, below 708.01.	4–5?
708.03*	Burial C (pit?), probably mixed with 708.2 (Phase 4) and 708.4 (Phase 1?).	Mixed Neo.
708.04*	Ashy layers, cut by burial pit 708.3 (Burial C).	Mixed Neo.
708.05	Mixed ashy, crumbly brick and small stones, just above bedrock.	1

AREA 709: SOUNDING C

709.01	Brown gritty.	5
709.02	Grey-brown silty.	5
709.03	Soft greyish pit fill. (contained some human bones.	4
709.04	Ashy dark brown earth, above upper crumbled plaster floor (709.05).	3
709.05	Fragmentary plaster levels – in mid-trench baulk.	3
709.06	Possibly decayed wall. ?upper part of Wall 1.	2
709.07	Plaster patch, over 706/Wall 1, under possible wall 709.6.	3
709.08*	Probe to define possible upper wall 709.6 (Phases 2/3)? and burial 709.10 (Phase 4)?	?4
709.09	Burial A, within 710.6 (upper extension of pit 710.6/7/9).	4
709.10	Burial B, cut by pit 709.3.	?4
709.11	Ring of stones, probably associated with burial 709.10.	?4
709.12	Light brown silty, under possible wall 709.6, associated with 709.7 plaster.	3
709.13	Probe to define possible upper wall 709.6 (Phases 2/3)? and burial 709.10 (Phase 4)?	3(?4)
709.14	Probe in bricky fills to define possible upper wall 709.6 (N side).	3
709.15	Probe – ashy layers against W side of baulk 708 (same as 708.4?)	?1
709.16	Upper plaster surface, with clay layer beneath, with some ash.	3
709.17	Lower plaster aurface, clay and ashy patches (E end of mid-trench baulk).	3
709.18	Area below burial 709.10 (Burial B).	4(?3)
709.19	Probe into upper fills against 706/Wall 1; mixed with pit 709.11 – Phase 4?	4(?2)
709.20	Lower part of probe 709.15. Mixed grey-brown, hard pale pinkish brown, clumpy, with stony rubble on bedrock.	1?
709.21*	Mixed material beneath EB wall/baulk 708. May contain Phase 1 deposits.	Mixed
709.22	Mixed material. lower fill against 706/Wall 1, further E than 19, below 16 and 17.	2
709.23	Bricky, ash/charcoal flecks. Below pit 709.3. (May include material from Phase 2 floors.)	1(?2)
709.24	Deposits of gritty/bricky and brown crumbly soil, below 709.23.	1
709.25	Yellow-brown, bricky, with plaster fragments and charcoal flecks, including several thin ashy levels.	2
709.26	Hard yellow and brown clayey, from beneath post-Neo. wall, below 709.21 (mixed – Phases 5–2).	Mixed
709.27*	Hard yellow/brown clayey/bricky, below 706/Wall 1.	2 (?1)

709.28*	Compacted yellow-brown clayey in probe. Below 709.27.	2 (?1)
709.29*	Reddish and yellowish-brown plaster and below down to bedrock, perhaps mixed with Phase 4 pit.	Mixed
709.30*	Probe by S Section (as 709.29) – came down on burial 709.32.	?4
709.31*	Compact red-brown and rubble, above bedrock.	1
709.32*	Burial D, in probe by S Section, near bedrock – cut from Phase 4? (cut not defined.).	4(?+1/3)
709.33*	Yellow-brown clay, charcoal and plaster frgments. Below burial 709.32. (Probably mixed.)	1(?+3/4)
709.34*	Mixed yellow-brown, rubbly, material above bedrock. (Probably mixed.)	1(?2)

AREA 710: GRID SQUARE D 3

710.02	Brown/grey gritty, with clay/brick.	5
710.03	Silty – light, below 2.	5
710.04	Dark gritty, below 710.3	5
710.05	Bottom of Phase 5? (below 710.4) or top of pit fill above 710.6?	5
710.06	Upper fill/extensn deep Pit 8 (contained Burial A, 709.9 + hearth).	4
710.07	Mixed silty/bricky/ashy fill of Pit 8.	4
710.08	Plaster floor, probably = 648/Floor 3 (also Floor 1 above?)	3

710.09	Upper and lower (earth and ashy) fill of Pit 8, including basal ash layer.	4
710.10	Upper fill against 706/Wall 1.	2
710.11	Lower fills and surfaces against 706/Wall 1.	2

AREA 735: GRID SQUARES F–G 1–3

735.01	Gritty brown.	5
735.02	Gritty and silty (mixed 1 and 3).	5
735.03	Silty brown/grey.	5
735.04	Stiff orange-brown, with much burnished coloured (red + yellow) plaster.	3
735.05	Small pit? by N Section.	?5
735.06	Pit fill?	?5
735.07	Orange/black.	4
735.08	Brown, with much burnt bone, at very edge of mound.	?4
735.09	Thick grey layer below 735.8; much burnt bone.	?4
735.11	Brown gritty.	
735.12	Thick plaster (traces more extensive), beneath 735.03.	3
735.13	Under 735.11 (earliest post-Neo. with Neolithic) and 735.10 (post-Neo. wall.)	5
735.14	Pit fill?	?4
735.15	Very gritty, adjacent to 735.14.	?4
735.16	Thin ashy, lying on top of 735.17.	1
735.17	Clay on bedrock, below 735.16. (?natural)	?1

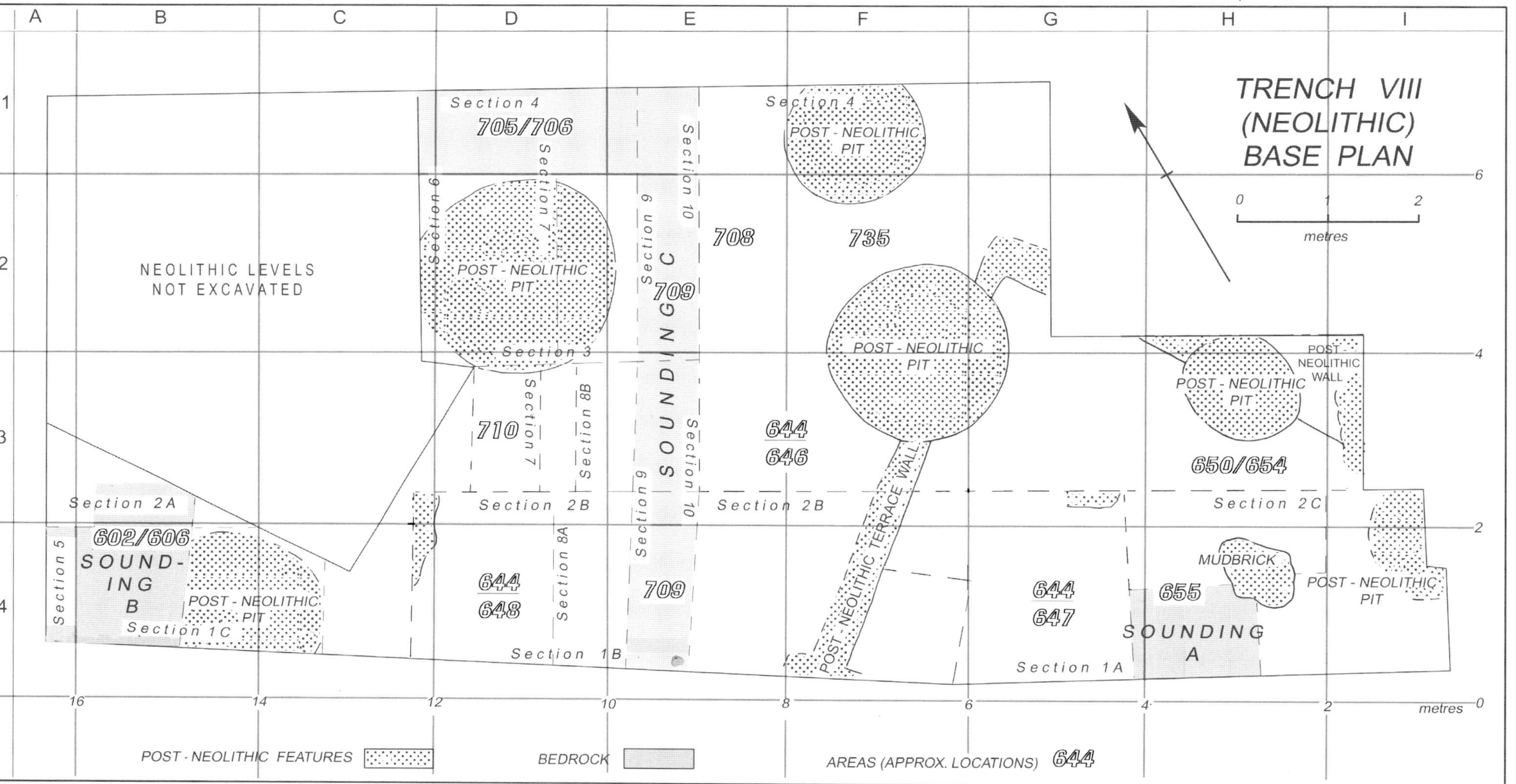

Fig. 2.7. Trench VIII, Neolithic Base Plan, showing Areas, section lines and post-Neolithic disturbances.

Virginia Mathias and Peter J. Parr

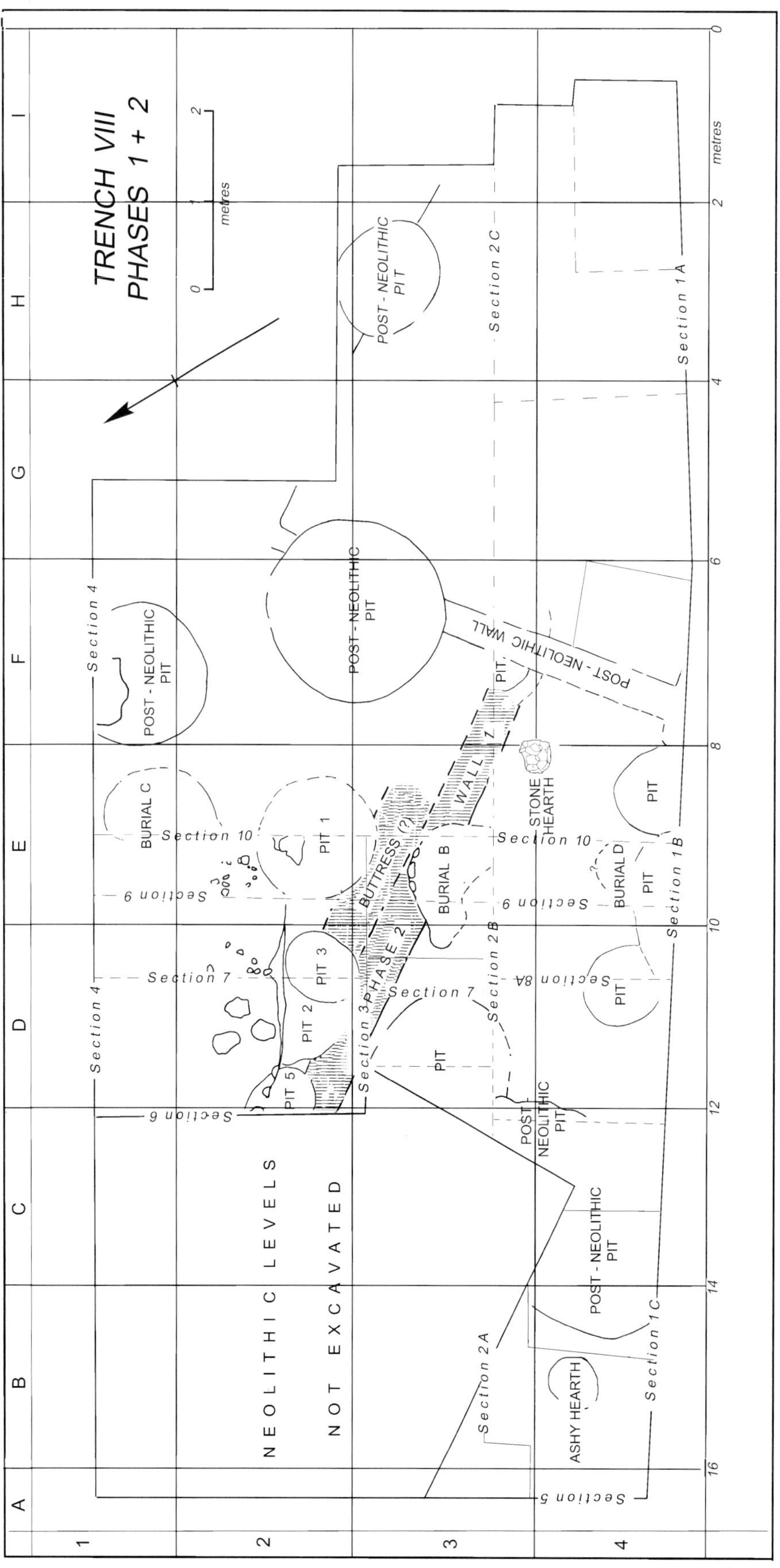

Fig. 2.8. Plan, Phases 1 and 2.

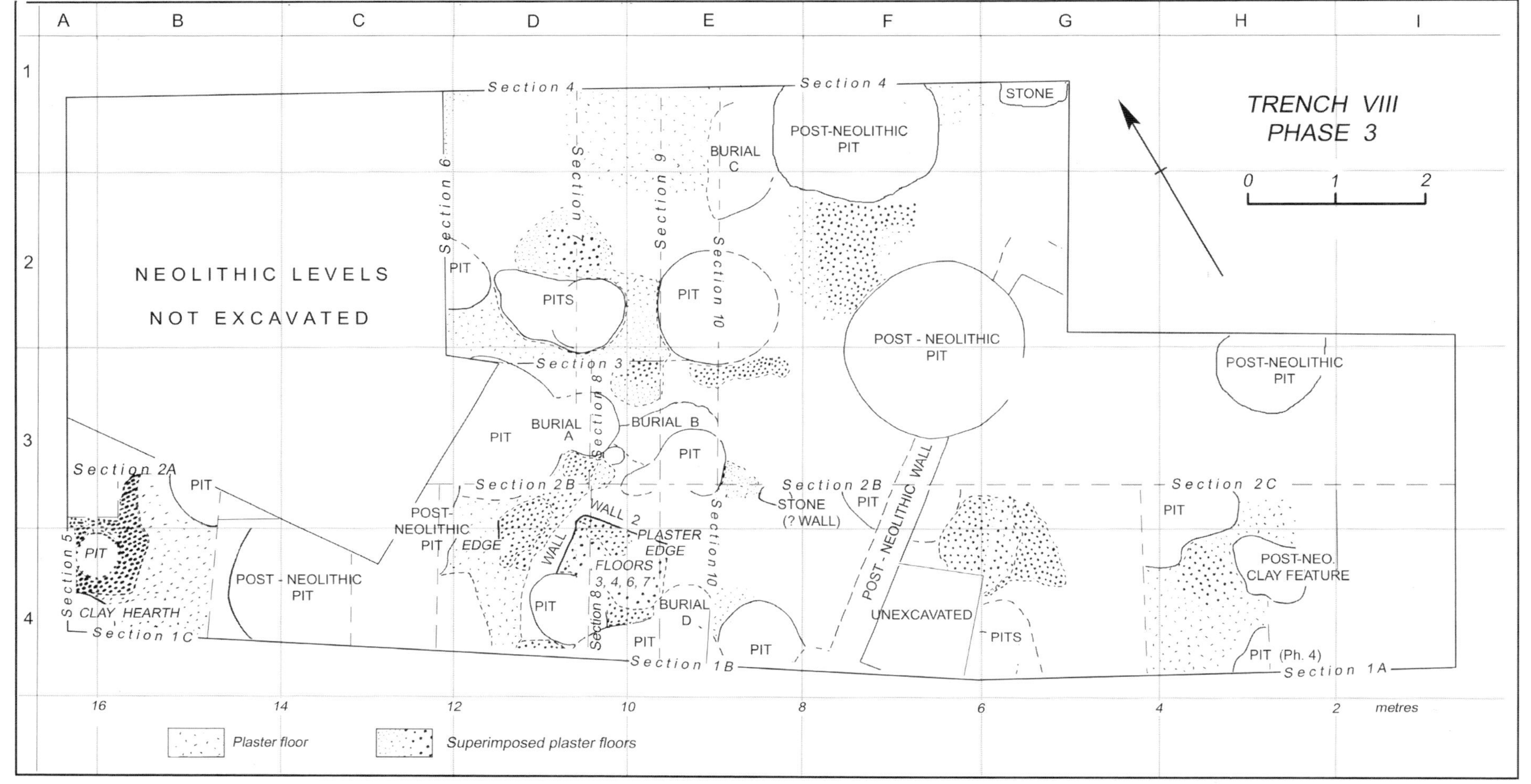

Fig. 2.9. Plan, Phase 3.

 Virginia Mathias and Peter J. Parr

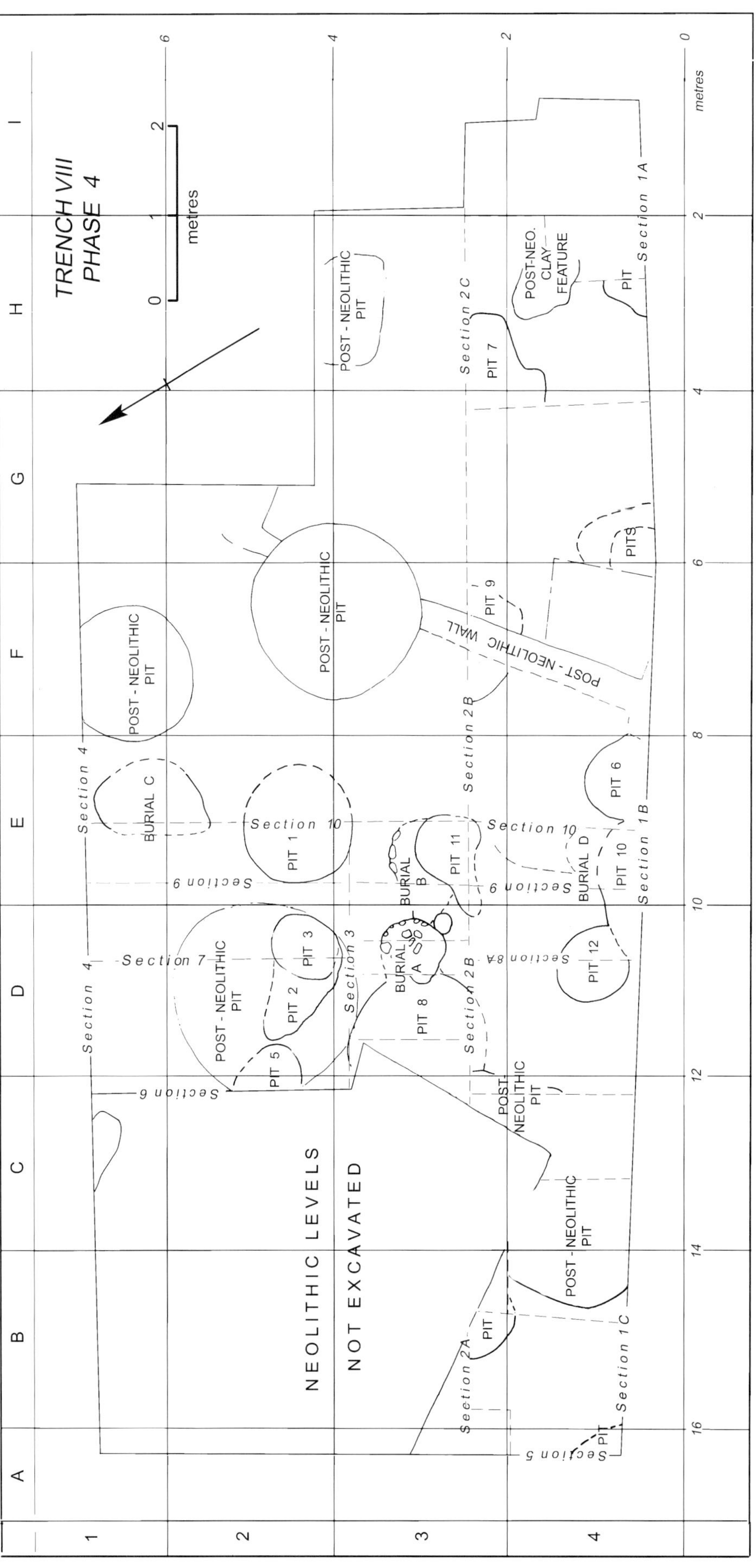

Fig. 2.10. Plan, Phase 4.

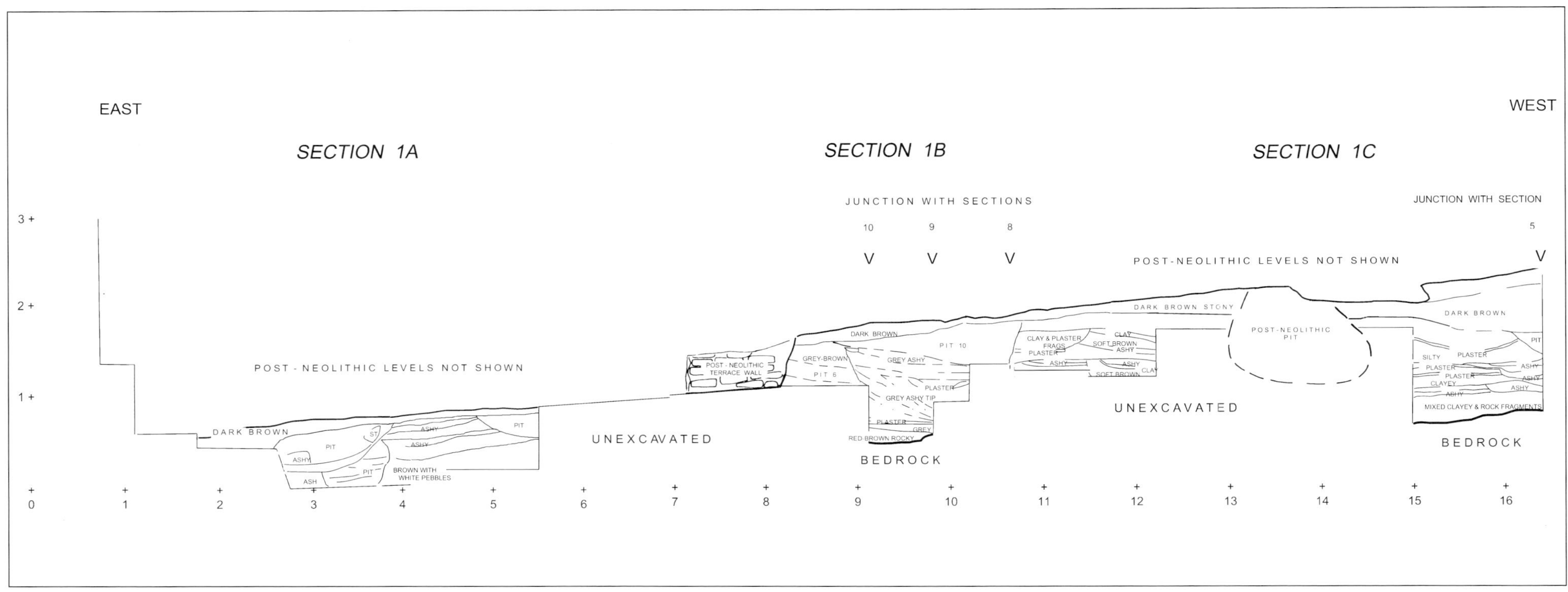

Fig. 2.11. Section 1.

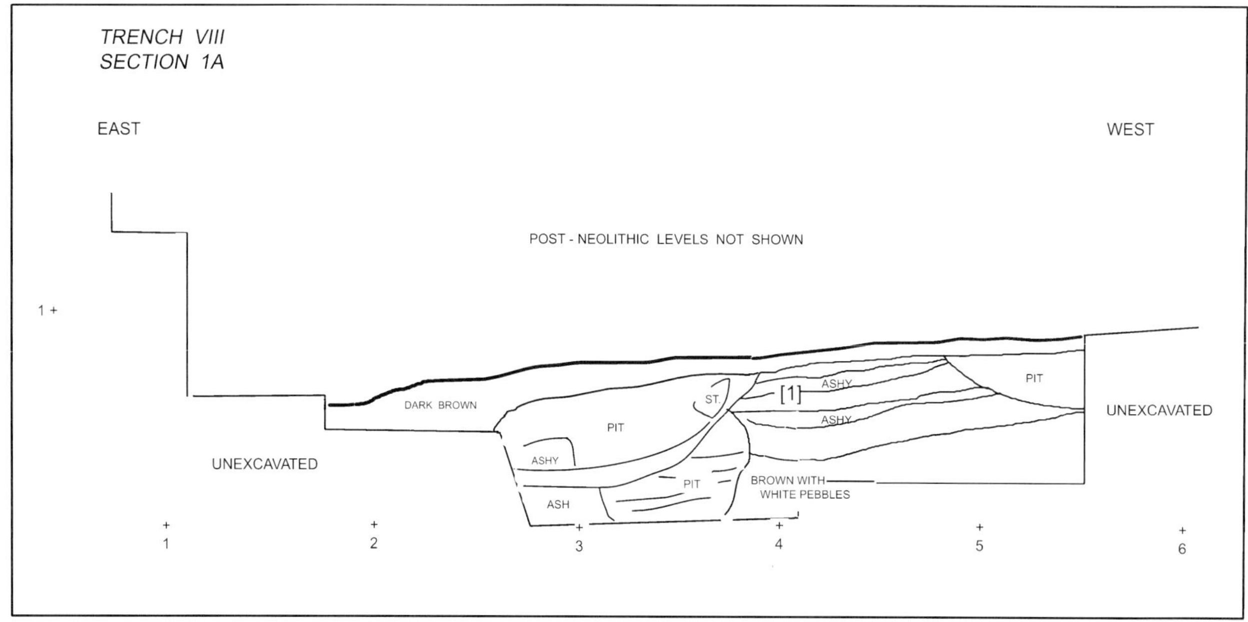

Fig. 2.12. Section 1A.

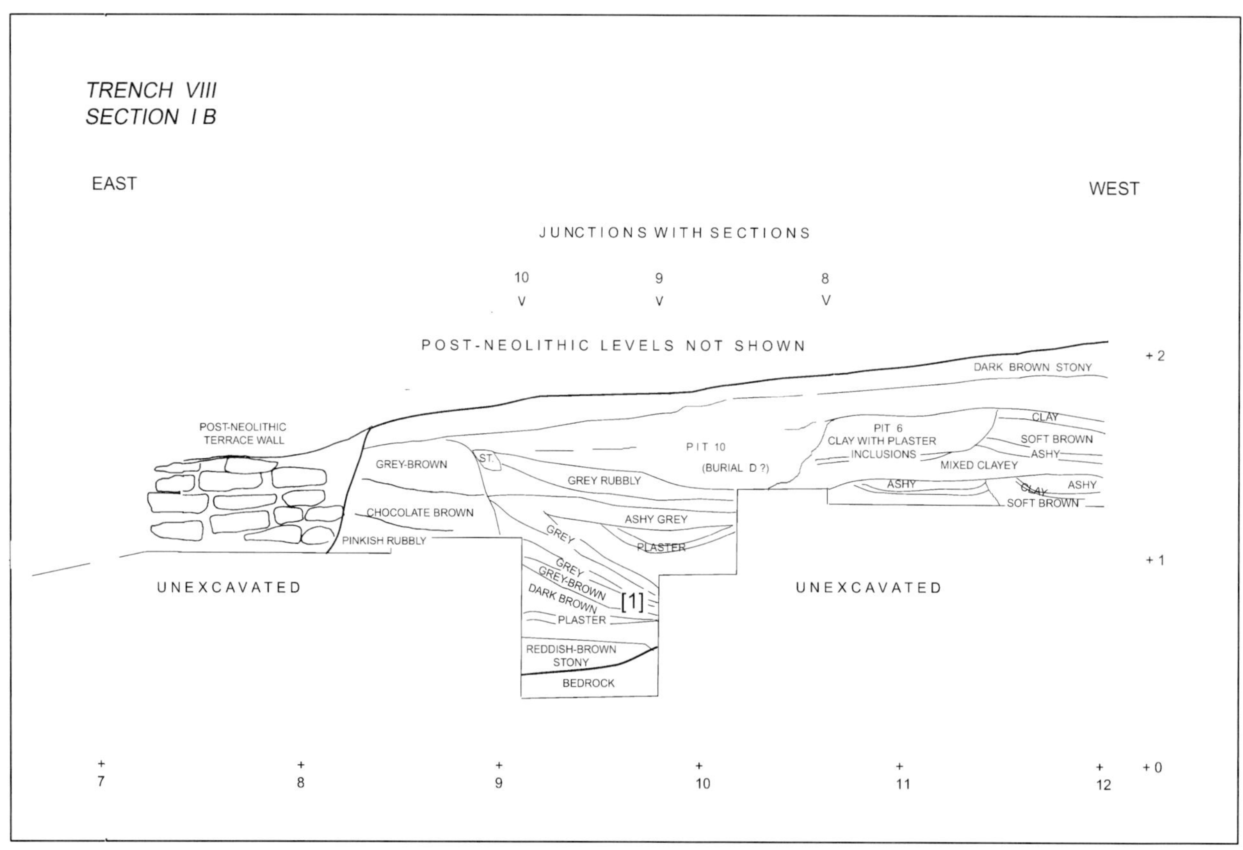

Fig. 2.13. Section 1B.

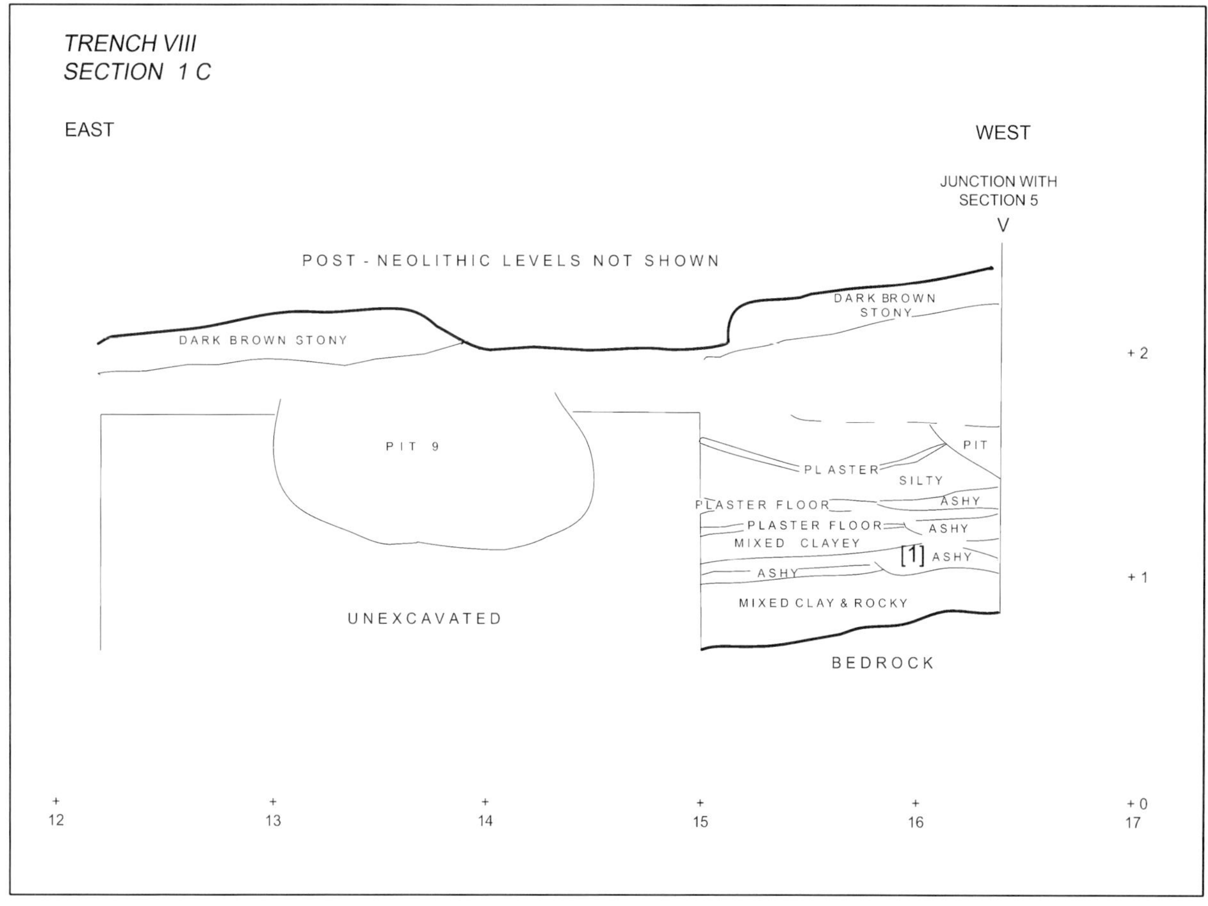

Fig. 2.14. Section 1C.

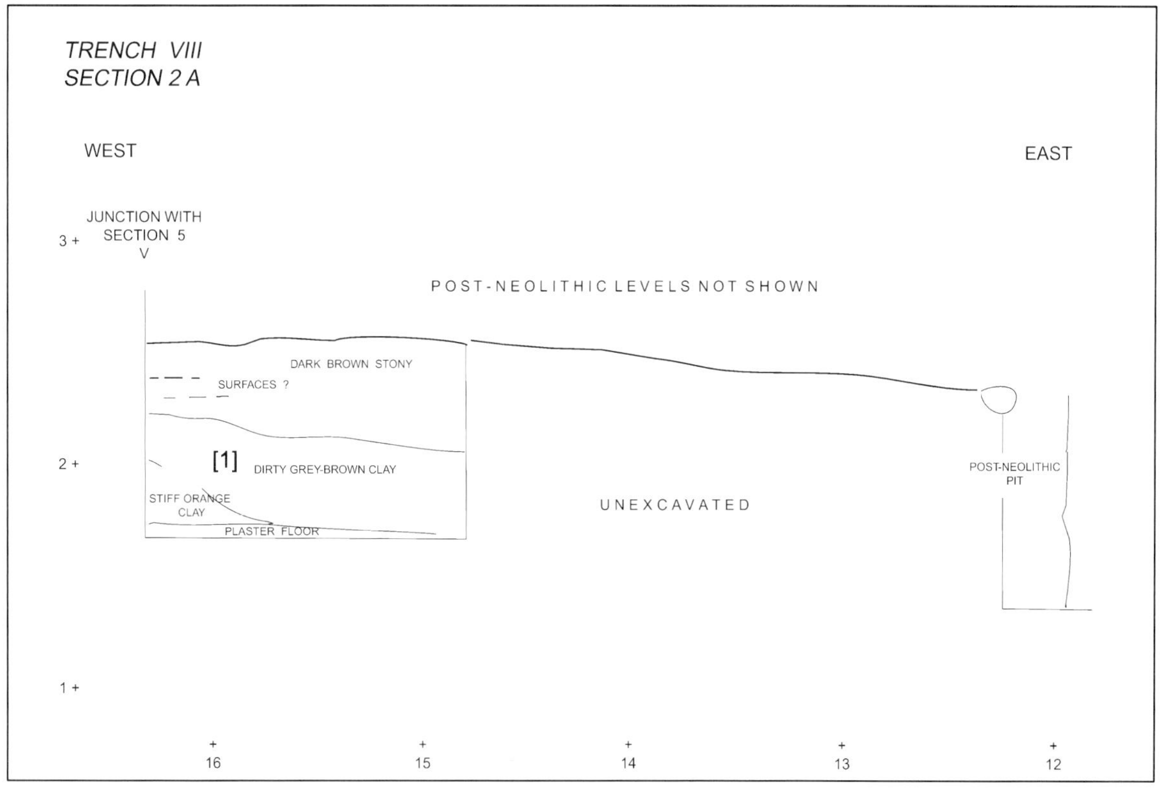

Fig. 2.15. Section 2A.

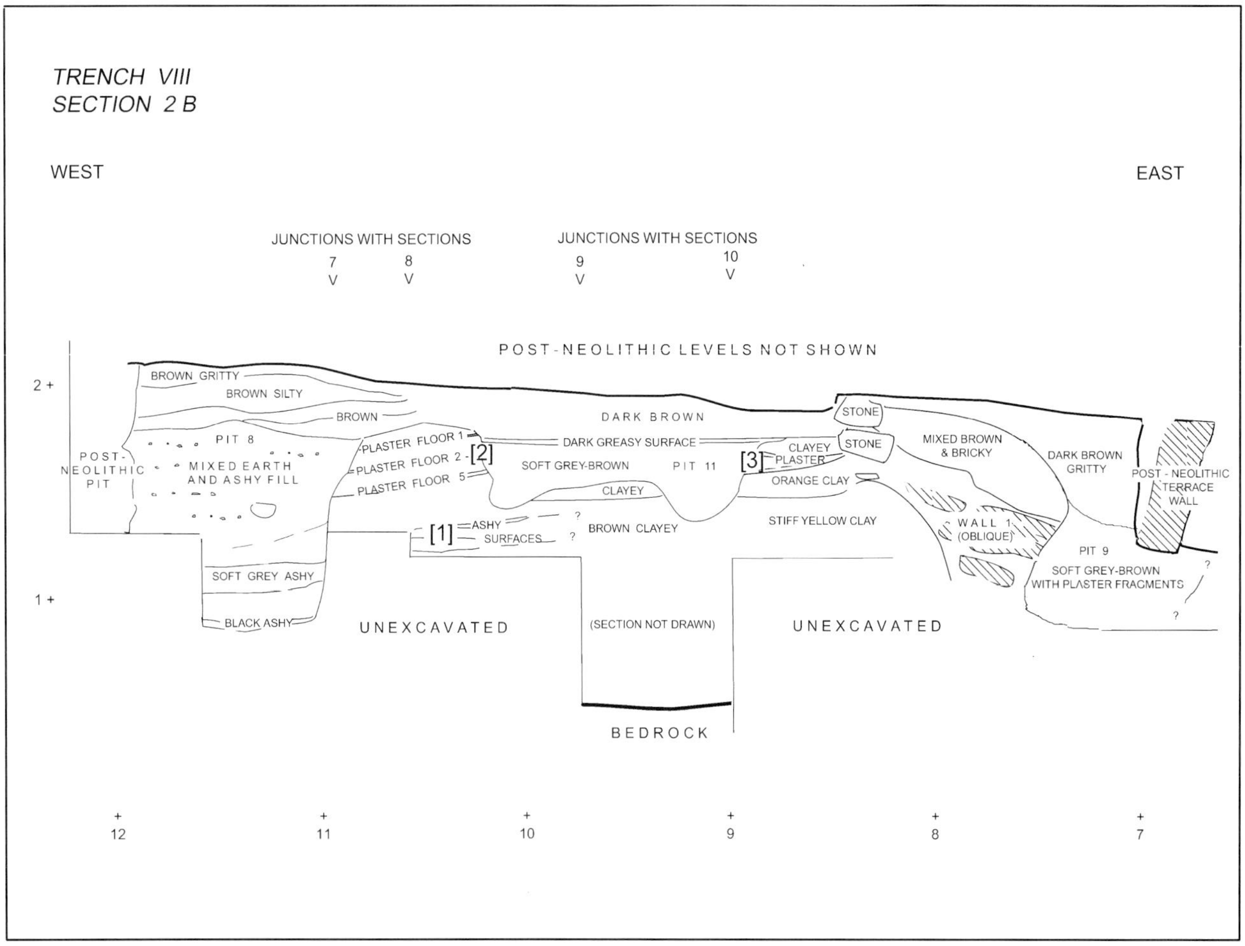

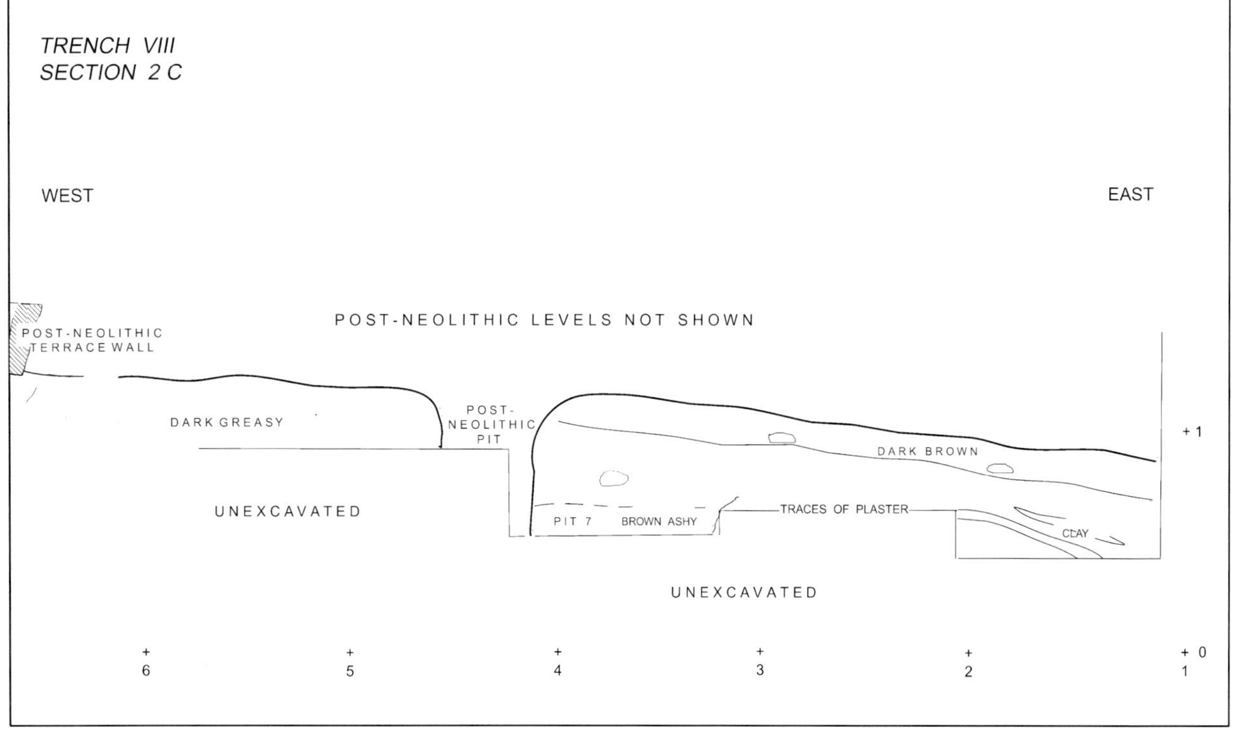

Fig. 2.16. Section 2B.

Fig. 2.17. Section 2C.

Fig. 2.18. Section 3.

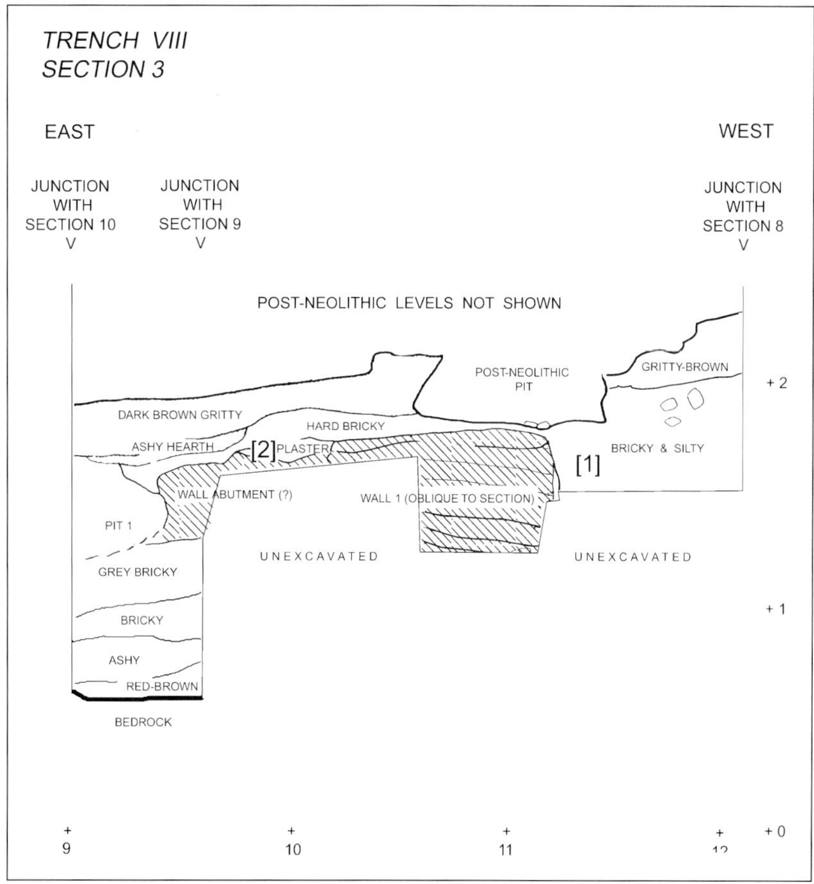

Fig. 2.19. Section 4.

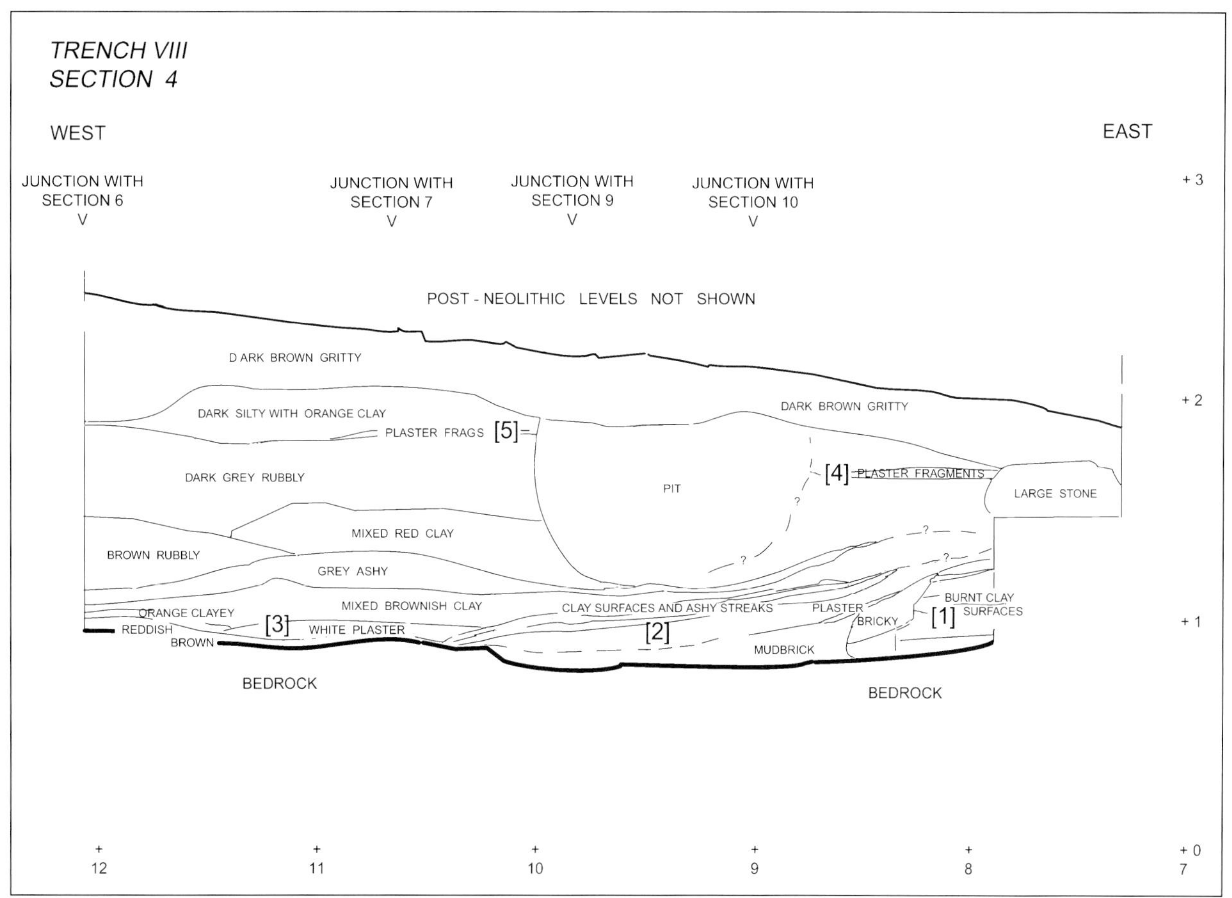

Virginia Mathias and Peter J. Parr

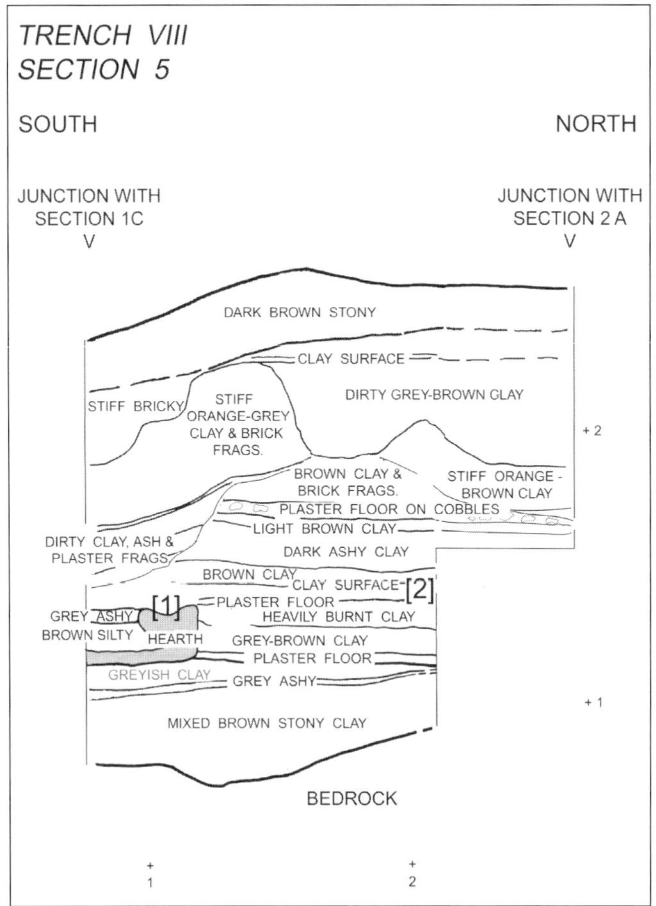

Fig. 2.20. Section 5.

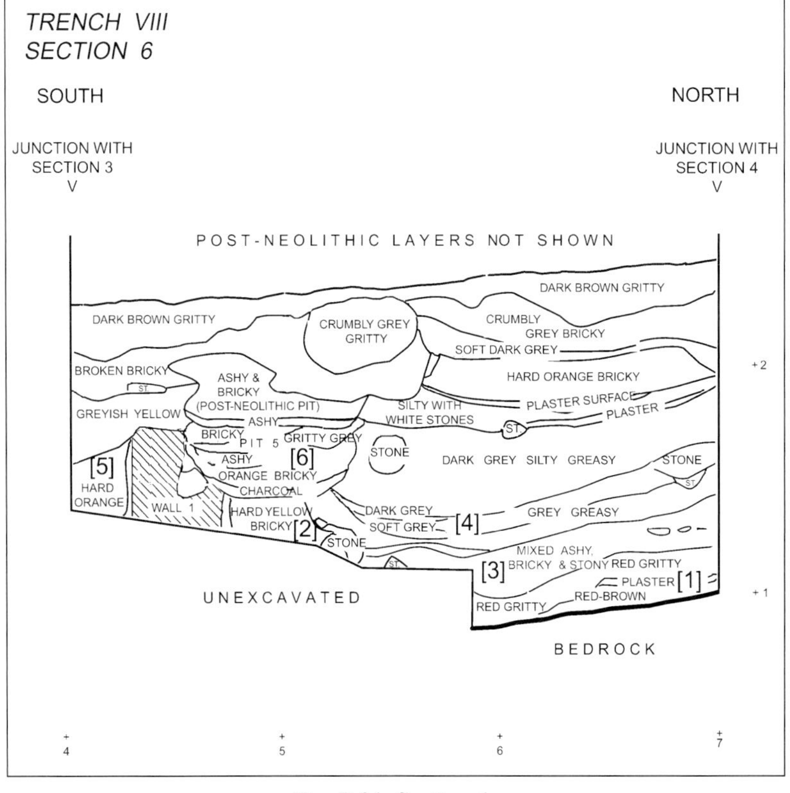

Fig. 2.21. Section 6.

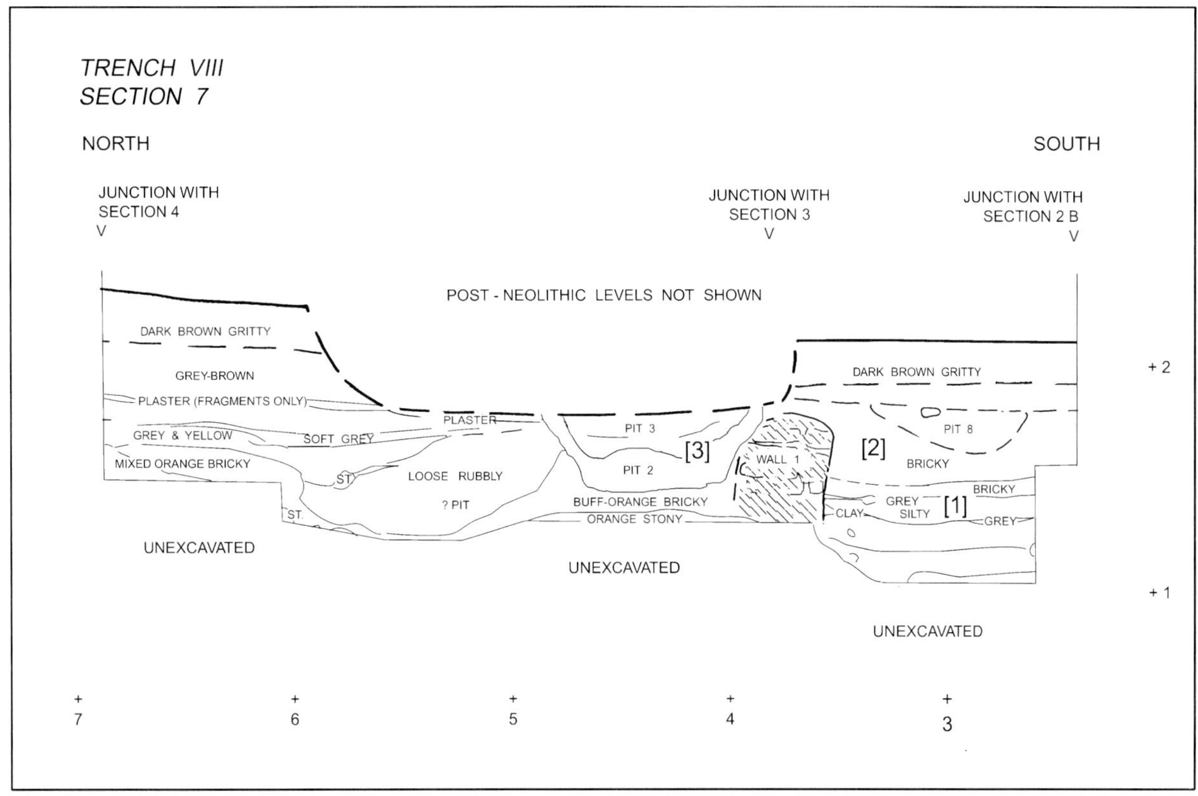

Fig. 2.22. Section 7.

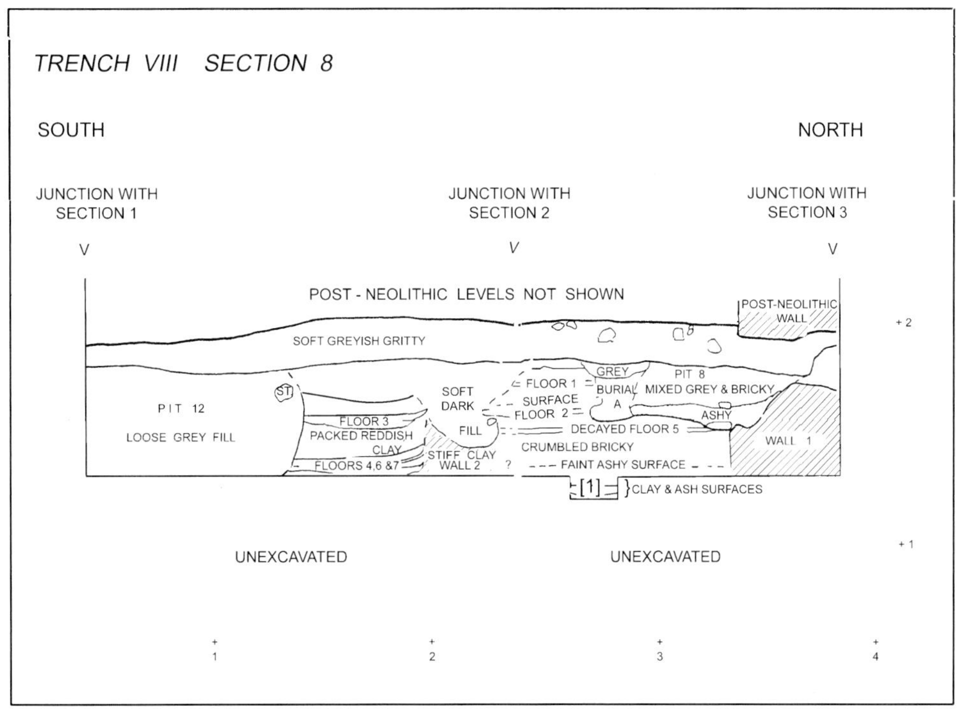

Fig. 2.23. Section 8.

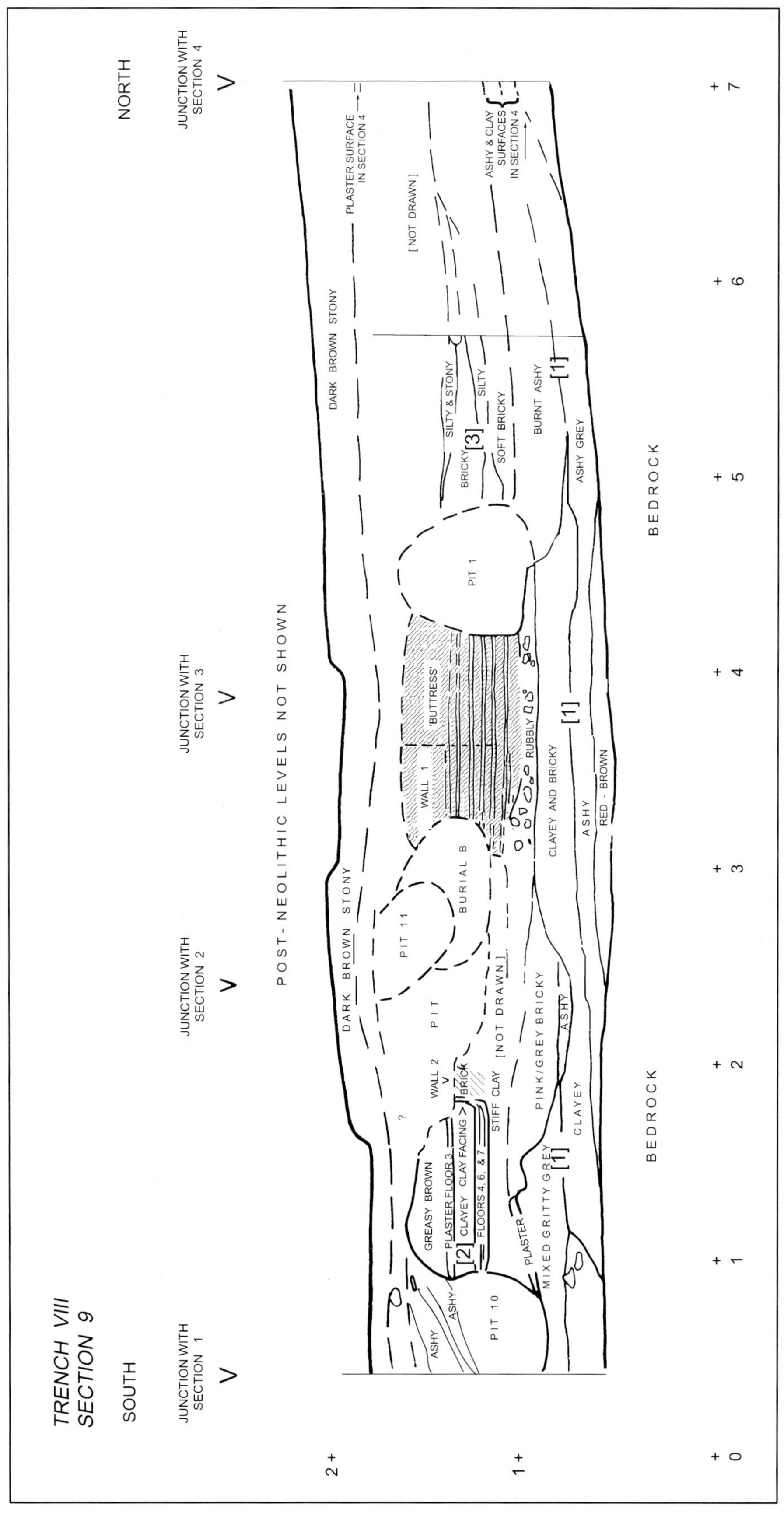

Fig. 2.24. Section 9.

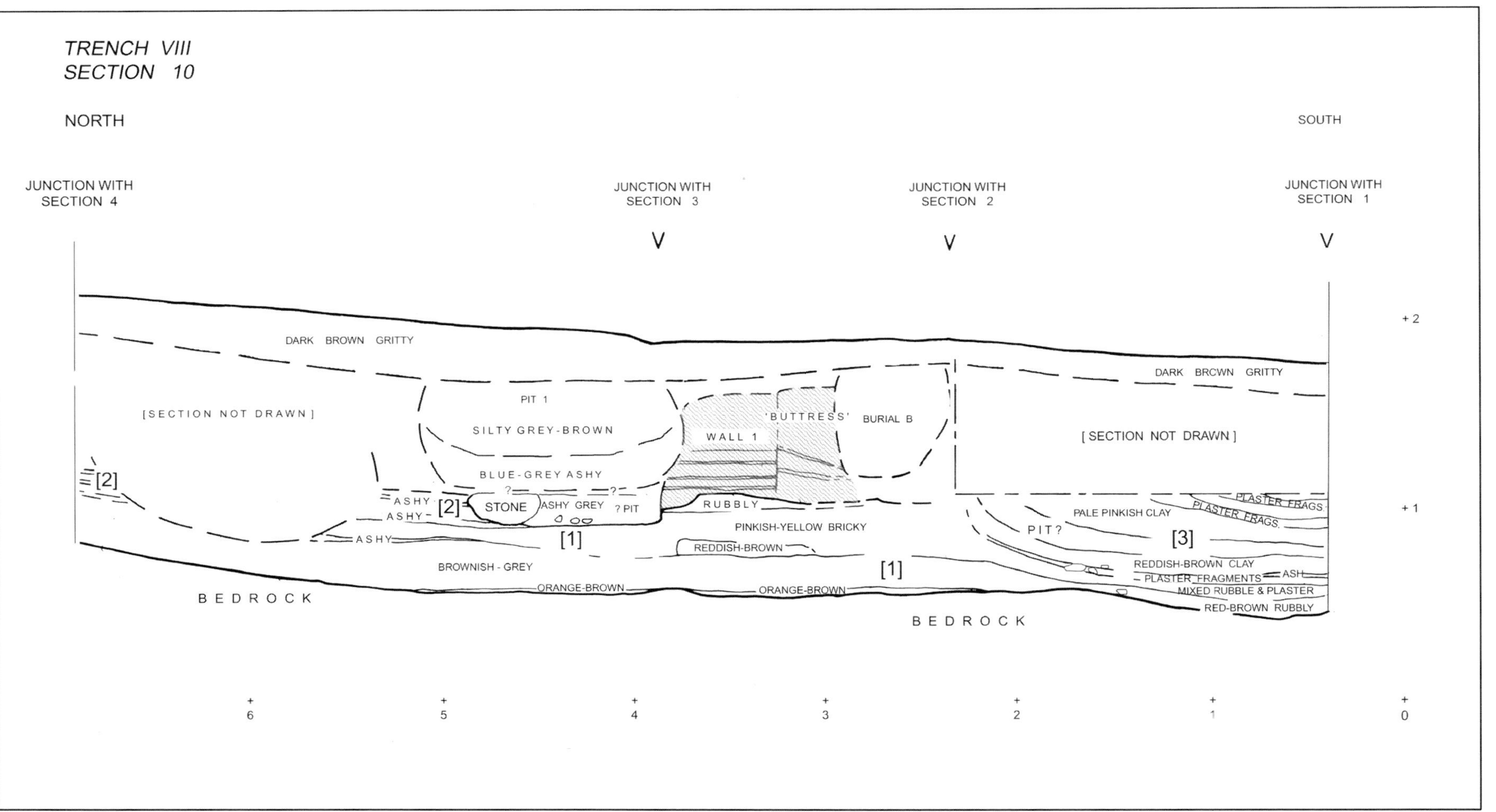

Fig. 2.25. Section 10.

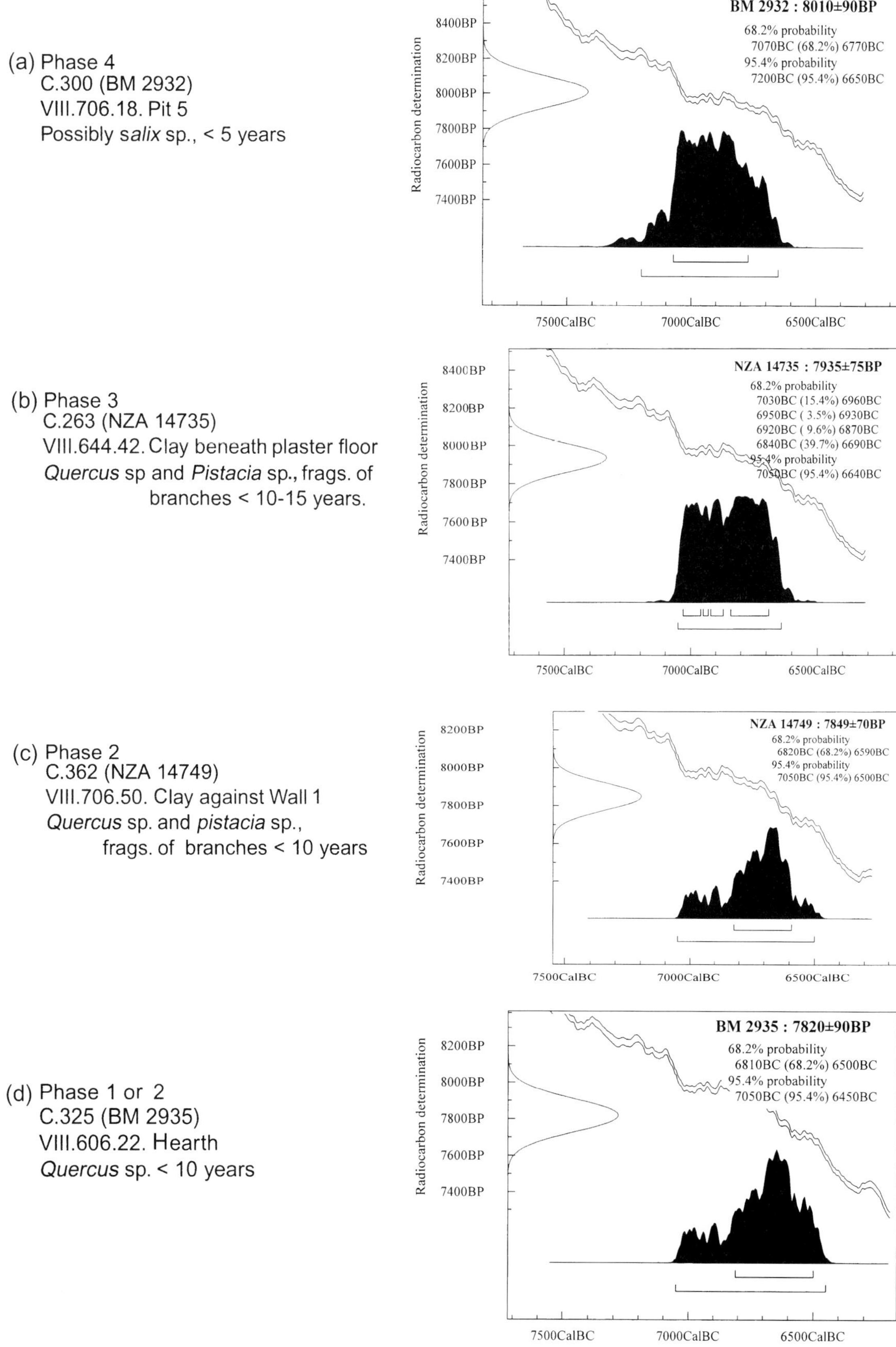

Fig. 2.26. Radiocarbon dates.

Table 2.2. Comparative radiocarbon dates.

The following table lists the majority of the published radiocarbon dates from those Neolithic sites mentioned in the text of this volume. References are normally to the original site reports, but occasionally to secondary sources; references to Radiocarbon are not normally given. With the exception of the Tell Nebi Mend data, where the calibration was carried out by the laboratories concerened, it has been calculated by the author of this report, using the OxCal v.3.1 program (Bronk Ramsey 1995; 2001). These dates are printed in italics in the table.When the calibration results in multiple ranges of values, those ranges separated by 20 years or less have been combined.

Site	Period or Level	Material (if known)	Lab. Ref.	C14 Date	*CalBC 68.2%*	*CalBC 95.4%*	Reference
ABU HUREIRA	Late Ph. 2a. (Aceramic)	—	BM 1424	8190 ± 77	*7310–7070*	*7460–7040*	Moore *et al.* 2000, 251–9, Appendix A
	Early Ph. 2b (Aceramic)	Human bone	OxA 4660	8180 + 200	*7500–6800*	*7600–6650*	
	Early Ph. 2b (Aceramic)	Wild grain	OxA 1930	8189 ± 100	*7340–7060*	*7550–6800; 7100–6500*	
	Early Ph. 2b (Aceramic)	Domestic wheat	OxA 1931	7890 ± 90	*7030–6880; 6840–6640*		
ABU THAWWAB	Yarmukian	—	GrN 13321	6350 ± 90	*5470–5220*	*5490–5060*	Kafafi 2001, 18
			GrN 15192	5540 ± 110	*4510–4260*	*4700–4050*	
'AIN GHAZAL	Late PPNB/PPNC	—	AA 5198	7960 ± 75	*7040–6770*	*7050–6650*	Rollefson *et al.* 1992, 445; Rollefson 1998
	Late PPNB/PPNC	—	GrN 17495	7915 + 95	*7030–6870; 6840–6650*	*7070–6590*	
	Late PPNB/PPNC	—	AA 5205	7895 + 95	*7030–6880; 6840–6640*	*7100–6500*	
	Late PPNB/PPNC	—	GrN 17494	7825 ± 65	*6780–6570*	*7050–6450*	
	Late PPNB/PPNC	—	AA 1165	7820 + 240	*7050–6450*	*7500–6200*	
	Late PPNB/PPNC	—	AA 5196	7670 ± 100	*6610–6430*	*6700–6260*	
'AIN ER-RAHUB	Yarmukian	—	GrN 14539	7580 ± 65	*6500–6380*	*6590–6250*	Muheisin *et al.* 1988
ASHKELON	Level 1 PPNC	Ash	OxA 7915	7995 ± 50	*7050–6820*	*7030–6700*	Garfinkel 1999b, 2
	Level 2 PPNC	Ash	OxA 7916	7935 ± 50	*7030–6880; 6940–6690*	*7040–6670*	
	Level 4 PPNC	Ash	OxA 7881	7630 ± 50	*6560–6550; 6510–6430*	*6600–6420*	
	Level 5 PPNC	Ash	OxA 7882	8000 + 110	*7060–6750; 6720–6700*	*7300–6600*	
	Level 6 PPNC	Ash	OxA 7883	7990 ± 90	*7050–6770*	*7140–6640*	
ATLIT-YAM	Late PPN	Wood charcoal	RT 707	8140 ± 120	*7350–6800*	*7500–6700*	Galili *et al.* 1993, 133–57
	Late PPN	Wood charcoal	Pta 3950	8000 ± 90	*7060–6770*	*7200–6600*	
	Late PPN	Wheat charcoal	RT 944A	7670 ± 85	*6600–6450*	*6680–6380*	
	Late PPN	Wood charcoal	RT 944C	7610 ± 90	*6590–6390*	*6640–6250*	
	Late PPN	Wheat charcoal	PITT 0622	7550 ± 80	*6480–6350; 6310–6260*	*6570–6230*	
'AIN EL-JAMMAM	Aceramic	—	–	8520 ± 190	*7850–7300*	*8200–7000*	Waheeb and Fino 1997
	PPNC?	—		8030 ± 120	*7130–6700*	*7350–6600*	
BYBLOS	Néolitique ancien (upper)	—	GrN 1544	7360 ± 120	*6370–6090*	*6440–6010*	Dunand 1973, 34; Hours *et al.* 1994, 89

Table 2.2. Comparative radiocarbon dates (continued).

Site	Period or Level	Material (if known)	Lab. Ref.	C14 Date	CalBC 68.2%	CalBC 95.4%	Reference
ÇATAL HÜYÜK	Level XII	Wood charcoal	P 1374	7757 ± 92	6660–6470	7050–6400	Radiocarbon 7 (1965), 399₇1; Radiocarbon (1969), 154–5; Hours et al. 1994, 390–91
	Level X	Wood charcoal	P 782	8092 ± 98	7290–7230; 7190–6820	7350–6650	
	Level X	Wood charcoal	P 1369	7937 ± 109	7030–6690	7150–6500	
	Level X Ash	Ash	P 1370	8036 ± 104	7130–6760	7300–6650	
	Level X	Wood charcoal	P 1371	7844 ± 102	7010–6970; 6830–6530	7050–6450	
	Level X	Wood charcoal	P 1372	7915 ± 85	7030–6880; 6840–6650	7050–6600	
	Level IX	Wood charcoal	P 779	8190 ± 99	7330–7060	7550–6800	
JERICHO	PPNB (latest date)	—	GL-28	8200 ± 200	7550–7000; 6950–6850	7600–6650	Kenyon 1981, 504
KAFAR GILADI	DFBW; pre-Yarmukian	—	MATJ-1	8905 ± 320	8450–7550	9200–7100	Kaplan 1966, 273
LABWE	Latest PPNB	Charcoal	K 1430	7990 ± 140	7070–6680	7350–6500	Kirkbride 1969, 50; Garfinkel 1999b, 6
	Latest PPNB	Charcoal	K 1428	7860 ± 140	7030–6590	7100–6400	
	Latest PPNB	Charcoal	K 1429	7850 ± 140	7030–6570; 6540–6530	7100–6400	
MATARRAH	Samarran	—	W-623	7570 ± 250	6700–6050	7100–5900	Smith 1952
MUNHATA	Niveau 2 (Yarmukian)	—	M 1792	7370 ± 400	6650–5800	7200–5400	Radiocarbon 12, 60
			Ly 4927	7330 ± 70	6600–5750	6380–6050	
RAS SHAMRA	Phase VC2 (aceramic)	—	GIF-3960	7900 ± 140	7030–6640	7150–6450	Contenson 1992, 14–16 and 191–3
	Phase VB (ceramic)	—	P.458	7686 ± 112	6640–6440	6850–6250	
SHA'AR HA-GOLAN	Level 9	Seed	OxA 9417	7285 ± 45	6220–6090	6230–6050	Garfinkel 1999b, 5; Garfinkel and Miller 2001, 29–30
	Level 7	Charcoal	OxA 7885	7270 ± 80	6220–6060	6360–5990	
	Level 6	Charcoal	OxA 7920	7245 ± 50	6210–6050	6220–6020	
	Level 4	Charcoal	OxA 7919	7495 ± 50	6430–6350; 6310–6260	6400–6240	
	Level 3	Charcoal	OxA 7918	7465 ± 50	6400–6250	6430–6230	
	Level 2	Charcoal	OxA 7917	7410 ± 50	6370–6230	6420–6000	
	Level 1	Charcoal	OxA 7884	6980 ± 100	5980–5760	6030–5670	

Table 2.2. Comparative radiocarbon dates (continued).

Site	Period or Level	Material (if known)	Lab. Ref.	C14 Date	CalBC 68.2%	CalBC 95.4%	Reference
TELL 'ALI	Level 2 PPNC	Charcoal	OxA 7886	7975 ± 70	*7050–6770*	*7070–6680*	Garfinkel 1999b, 5
	Level 1 PPNC	Charcoal	OxA 7921	7940 ± 50	*7030–6870; 6840–6690*	*7040–6680*	
TELL ASSOUAD	Level VIII	—	MC 864	8450 ± 120	*7600–7350*	*7750–7100*	Cauvin 1978; Hours *et al.* 1994, 385
	Level III	—	MC 865	8620 ± 120	*7820–7530*	*8200–7450*	
T. DAMISHLIYAH	Levels 5–7	Chaff in sherds	UtC 1094–6	7920 ± 110	*7030–6650*	*7100–6500*	Akkermans 1993, 114
	Levels 5–7	Chaff in sherds	UtC 1097–9	7670 ± 60	*6590–6450*	*6640–6430*	
	Levels 5–7	Chaff in sherds	UtC 1124	7700 ± 90	*6610–6460*	*6760–6390*	
TELL EL-KERKH	Er-Rouj 1 (aceramic)	Charcoal	N 6548	8070 ± 275	*7350–6650*	*7600–6400*	Iwasaki and Tsuneki 2003, 193–4
	Er-Rouj 2 (ceramic)	Charcoal	N 6545	8680 ± 355	*8300–7350*	*8800–6800*	
TELL NEBI MEND	Trench VIII Phase 4	Wood charcoal	BM 2932	8010 ± 90	*7070–6770*	*7200–6650*	Kromer and Becker 1993
	Trench VIII Phase 3	Wood charcoal	NZA 14735	7935 ± 75	*7030–6870; 6840–6690*	*7050–6640*	Rafter
	Trench VIII Phase 2	Humic fraction	NZA 14749	7849 ± 70	*6820–6590*	*7050–6500*	Rafter
	Trench VIII Phase 1?	Wood charcoal	BM 2935	7820 ± 90	*6810–6500*	*7050–6450*	
TELL RAMAD	Period II or III pit	—	GrN 4427	7920 ± 50	*7020–6960; 6830–6680*	*7030–6650*	Contenson 2000, 21 and Table 9
	Period II or III pit	—	GrN 4822	7900 ± 50	*6910–6880; 6830–6650*	*7030–6640*	
	Period II or III pit	—	GrN 4823	7880 ± 55	*6900–6890; 6830–6640*	*7030–6600*	
WADI SHU'EIB	Late PPNB–PPNC	—	Beta 35086/WS-9	8500 ± 160	*7740–7330*	*8000–7000*	Simmons *et al.* 2001, 28
		—	Beta 35085/WS-7	8120 ± 280	*7500–6700*	*7700–6400*	

3. Human burials

Virginia Mathias and Theya Molleson

Of the four Neolithic burials, two were primary: one, undisturbed, was of a neonate or small infant and the other, half destroyed by a later pit, was of a young woman. The other two burials – both incomplete and disarticulated, and both adult, one certainly and the other possibly male – probably comprised remains from earlier graves disturbed by the digging of pits and subsequently reinterred. Of the two primary burials, that of the infant can certainly be attributed to Phase 4, and that of the young woman most probably may be as well. The phasing of the two secondary burials is less certain. Both were found in deep pits close to bedrock, one in a very restricted sounding and the other in a narrow baulk, and in both cases the stratigraphy was unclear. However, it seems probable that they also belong to Phase 4, their upper parts having been removed by an later pit in the first case and having been missed in excavation in the second. All four burials were located within a band running north–south across the trench, which may be chance but could indicate that the graves were at the edge of, or at a certain distance away from, an area of contemporary settlement outside the limits of excavation (Fig. 3.1).

In addition to these four burials there were a number of isolated fragments of human bone, some presumably from disturbed burials but some perhaps no more than the results of domestic accidents and injury.

Burial A (VIII.709.9)

This undisturbed articulated burial of a small infant or neonate was found in a shallow oval scoop some 0.4 m × 0.6 m in size that cut into the sloping upper part of the eastern edge of a fairly large existing pit, Pit 8, and into Burial B (see below). The body was laid on its right side with the spine and skull against the southern side of the scoop, its head orientated approximately towards the south-east. It was lightly flexed with the legs drawn up and the arms in front of its face in a natural sleeping position; the hands and feet were present. Also in the scoop – which was four or five times larger than the area taken up by the skeleton – and adjacent to the burial was an arrangement of cobbles dipping slightly in the middle. This was a hearth apparently associated with the burial, since the cobbles and part of the skeleton were covered with grey ash. There were no grave goods, and overlying everything was a shallow fill of grey soil and crumbled mudbrick covering roughly the same oval area.

Burial B (VIII.709.10)

Immediately to the east of Burial A – and apparently somewhat earlier than it, since it had been cut into by the former burial – was a simple grave (709.10) dug into the silty levels and surfaces associated with Wall 1 of Phase 2 and deeply undercutting the top of the wall itself (see plan, Fig. 2.8 and Section 9, Fig. 2.24). A line of three or four spaced stones, each about 0.2 m long, set into the wall marked the northern side of the grave, but much of the rest had been destroyed by a later pit (Pit 11), which had also removed any levels contemporary with the cutting of the grave. Despite this absence of conclusive stratigraphic evidence, a date early in Phase 4 for the burial seems likely, although Phase 3 cannot be entirely ruled out.

The grave contained the articulated, though poorly preserved, remains of the lower part of a young adult female. The upper part of the body had been removed by the later pit, which had cut through the spine above the pelvis and hacked off the upper ends of the forearms. The individual lay on her right side with the lumbar vertebrae and pelvis to the south and the legs quite tightly flexed. Both feet were well preserved and lay close to the pelvis, one pointing west and the other north-west. Most of the

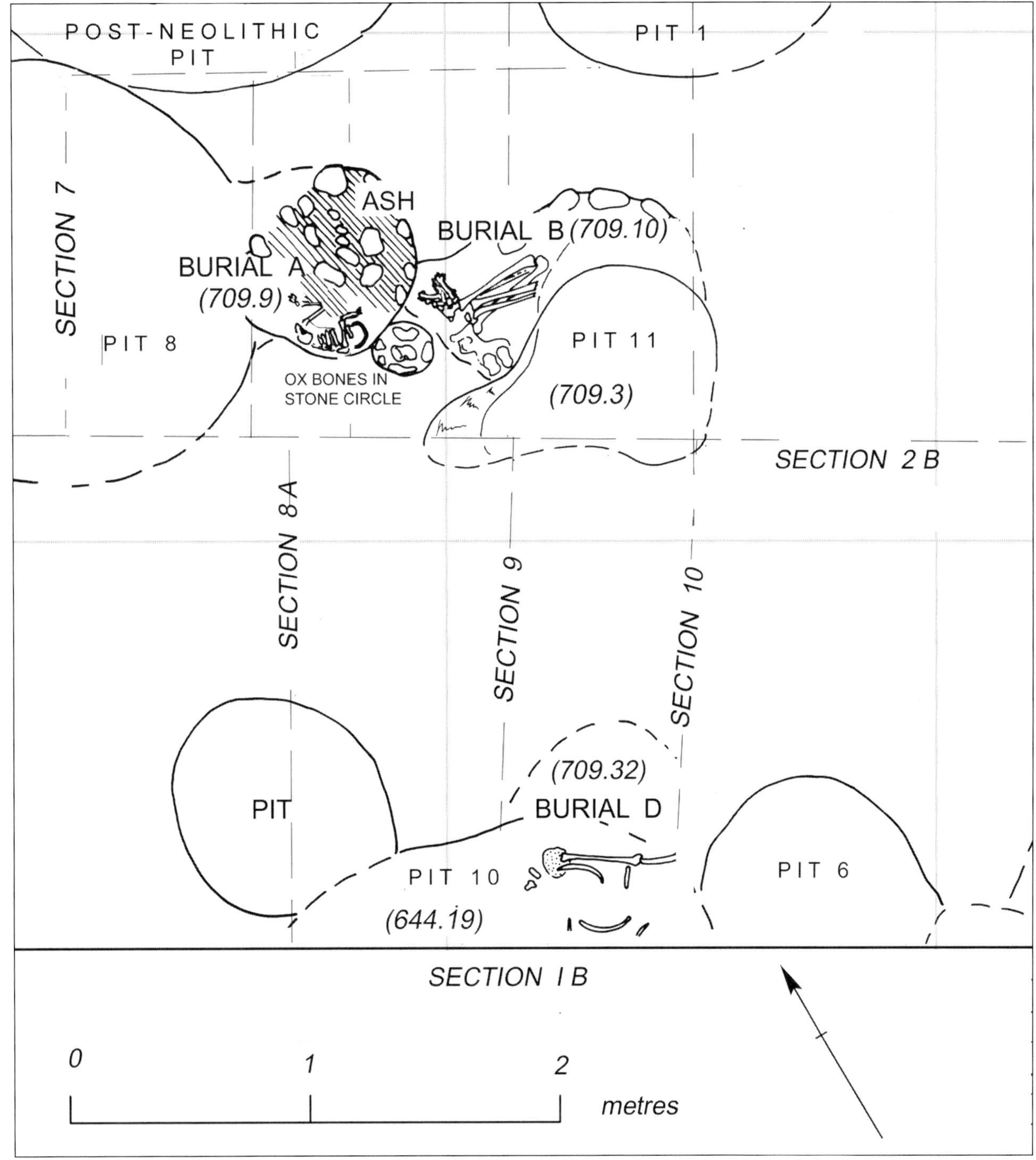

Fig. 3.1. Plan of Burials A, B and D.

left hand and some fragments of thoracic vertebrae and ribs were also recovered from the grave. A faint stain line just behind the pelvis and feet may possibly have resulted from the decay of some kind of wrapping. The fill among the bones was of the silty material containing flecks of plaster and charcoal and small stones, into which the grave was cut. There were no grave goods, but in a small contemporary pit (709.11) next to the feet was a curious arrangement of a circle of four unworked white stones – two of which could conceivably suggest crude human figures – and a large shell, with the articulated navicular and metatarsal of a wild ox set vertically on end in the middle (Fig. 3.2).

The later pit (Pit 11)) was orientated north-west–south-east, with an extension (or another roughly contemporary pit) orientated north-east–south-west (see Section 2). Part of a left forearm, presumably from Burial B, came from the fill of this upper pit.

Fig. 3.2. Burial B, articulated navicular and metatarsal of a wild ox in stone circle.

The osteological report (below) draws attention to the effects on the leg and foot bones of this individual of squatting and maintaining a kneeling posture with the toes flexed during repetitive activity such as grinding grain on a quern. There were signs also of a healed fracture in the left forearm, typically suffered when warding off a blow.

Burial C (VIII.708.3 and ?735.4)

The disarticulated and incomplete remains of a young male were found in a narrow baulk which had been left exposed for two years between excavation seasons and was consequently very weathered and difficult to interpret (Plan Phase 4, Fig. 2.10, Grid E1–2). They were discovered only after a considerable depth of the dried-out baulk had already been removed, and no plan was made. The burial appears to have been made in a pit which was slightly wider than the baulk but which did not reach the nearby Section 4, where the stratigraphy was clearer, while, unfortunately, the relevant part of the adjacent Section 10 was not drawn. The phasing is therefore uncertain, but since the pit had cut into a series of ashy levels (708.4) only 0.2–0.4 m above bedrock and attributed to Phase 1, it is at least definitely of Phase 2 or later. Most of the skeleton was

missing, but a mandible of a young adult male recovered from near bedrock in the adjacent area to the east (735.4), and probably in the same pit, is in all likelihood from the same individual. Although the evidence is inconclusive, in view of the depth of the pit and the nature of the remains it seems probable that Burial C is in fact the reburial of a collection of bones surviving from an earlier primary burial that was disturbed by the digging of this – or perhaps another – pit in Phase 4.

Burial D (709.32)

Disarticulated human remains were also found not far above bedrock at the southern end of the narrow Sounding C across the middle of the trench. This burial (or reburial) seems to have extended further into the main South Section (Section 1), and could not therefore be completely excavated. These deposits had also been exposed for some time between excavation seasons and had dried out, making the stratigraphy difficult to establish. The surrounding sections, Sections 1B (Fig. 2.13), 9 (Fig. 2.24) and 10 (Fig. 2.25), show a pit, Pit 10, cutting the adjacent plaster floors of Phase 3, and layered deposits slumping into it, and the probability must be that the burial was at the bottom of this pit, or perhaps low down in an earlier one. The pit fill was mixed and compacted, with stone rubble, clay, charcoal flecks, fragments of White Ware and lumps of plaster, the latter presumably from the floors of Phase 3 that had been cut by the pit – that is, floors 3, 4, 6 and 7 (see Phase 3 plan, Fig. 2.9). The fact that large pieces of plaster were mingled with the bones supports an attribution of the burial, in its present position, to Phase 4.

In addition to scattered teeth (all from the lower jaw), some thoracic vertebrae and fragments of ribs – all too fragile to be retrieved for analysis – the human remains of Burial D comprised only a humerus, with one end resting on a thick body sherd of White Ware (Reg. No. 5341; not illustrated, but described in Chapter 6) and the other end articulated with, probably, a radius. Nothing of the lower body was identified, although it may be assumed that other elements of the skeleton are present in that part of the grave remaining unexcavated beneath Section 1. As in the case of Burial C, it seems likely that these miscellaneous human remains are the surviving fragments of an earlier burial, disturbed and reinterred in Phase 4.

Isolated human remains

In addition to the burials and reburials, 16 isolated human bones, listed in Table 3.2, were found in Neolithic contexts, mostly from the Phase 4 pits or the Phase 5 abandonment layers, although three came from occupation layers of Phase 3 and one may be from Phase 1. Some of these solitary bones – for example, the tooth and the foot and hand bones – might well be the result of everyday occurrences and accidents, but others are presumably the result of disturbances to earlier inhumations similar to those which led to Burials C and D described above. The four from Phase 3 and (possibly) Phase 1 are not in themselves proof that burials were being made in this part of the site prior to Phase 4, when – as has been argued above – this part of the site was devoid of domestic occupation.

Summary and conclusions

The burials are clearly too few to provide a definitive picture of Neolithic funerary practices at Tell Nebi Mend, and it can only be noted that both of the primary burials, A and B, are articulated and flexed on their right sides, with their heads orientated roughly towards the east. The small hearth beside Burial A, ash from which partly covered the bones, and the cow bones set, apparently deliberately, on end within a circle of stones near Burial B, are suggestive of some sort of ritual activity associated with these burials. Burial B also provided some slight evidence that it may have been wrapped or enclosed in a bag. The absence of grave goods also needs to be noted. Similar flexed burials, laid on their sides in small oval pits and without grave goods, are found, for example, at Byblos, in the rather later Néolithique Ancien period, along with other burials in

stone-lined cists accompanied by pottery bowls, beads and ornaments (Dunand 1973, 29–33, pls XXXIV–XXXVIII). Nothing resembling this latter type of burial is known from Tell Nebi Mend, but in view of the extremely small proportion of the site excavated no conclusions should be drawn from this.

Osteological report (Theya Molleson)

The human bone from Tell Nebi Mend is stored in London at the Institute of Archaeology, University College, and in Amman at the premises of the Council for British Research in the Levant, where it was sorted from animal bone by Caroline Grigson. The two collections were examined by the present writer in March 1999 and September 2000 respectively. The data are given in Table 3.1.

Table 3.1. Osteological data.

Burial A (VIII.709.9) Neonate. Cranial, post-cranial skeleton. Dimensions (mm)

Humerus length	67.3
Mid-shaft AP × ML	5.5 × 6.0
Distal metaphysis	17.2
Radius length	52.8
Ulna length	60.1
Ilium length × breadth	32.0 × 35.2
Femur length	76.0
Mid-shaft AP × ML	6.7 × 6.8
Head diameter	18.5
Tibia length	66.1
Fibula length	64.1
Metatarsal I length	13.0

Burial B (VIII.709.10) Young adult, female. Postcranial. Dimensions (mm)

Metacarpal I length	41.8
Femur sub-trochanteric AP × ML	20.04 × 28.4
Patella length × breadth	38.4 × 37.1
Talus articulation/length	29.5/46.6
	Index 63.3
(?)VIII.709.3 Adult. Ulna, with healed parry fracture	

Burial C (VIII.708.3) Young adult, male. Dimensions (mm)

Radius length	225 (est.)
Patella length × breadth	39.7 × 43.7
R. Tibia cnemic	35.5 × 22.5
Talus articulation/length	31.0/51.4
	Index 60.3
(?VIII.735.4) Adult, male. Mandible	

Burial D (VIII.709.32) Adult, ?male. Mandible; post-cranial

Table 3.2. Isolated finds.

Layer	Description	Phase	Age	Sex	Summary of parts	Comments
606.27	Pit	4	Adult	–	Hand bone	
644.14	Chocolate brown	5		–	Postcranial	
644.20	Brown debris	?4	Juvenile	–	Postcranial	
644.20	Debris	?4		–	Hand bone	
644.21	Cobbles	4(?3)	Adult	–	Foot bone	
644.24	Greasy black surface	3	Juvenile	–	Postcranial	
644.24	Greasy black surface	3		–	Hand bone	
644.27	Pit	4	Adult	–	Postcranial	
644.27	Pit	4	Adult	–	Foot bone	
644.34	Chocolate brown	5		–	Hand bone	
644.36	Debris	?4/5	Adult	F	Mandible ramus	
646.10	Brown gritty	5		–	Foot bone	Extended articulation of the first metatarsal
648.20	Brown ashy	3		–	Tooth	
654.09	Chocolate brown	5		–	Occipital fragment	Bitumen stained (special treatment?)
680.42	Dark sandy	5		–	Hand bone	
709.15	Ashy	?1	Juvenile	–	Hand bone	

The bone of all individuals was highly fragmented, except for the skeleton of the neonate (Burial A). While all other parts of the skeleton, including parts of lower jaws, were identified, the general absence of cranial fragments of adults is notable. Age and sex determinations are based on criteria in Brothwell (1981).

Although the sample is too small to make generalisations, a dimorphism in size between the female of Burial B and the male of Burial C is displayed by the talus, which is longer in the male, and by the patella, which is relatively much wider. Interestingly, the bone did not develop a vastus notch, which in males at Çatal Hüyük is associated with the presumed habit of resting in a squatting position. Squatting facets were noted on the anterior of the tibia in the female of Burial B (709.10), however. She also had an extended articulation of the first metatarsal, a feature which is identified with the habit of kneeling with the toes curled under in order to carry out various tasks, such as grinding grain or using a pestle and mortar (Molleson 1989). (Another first metatarsal, a find from Phase 5 (646.10), showed the same feature). This woman, who was not old, had at some point in the years previous to her death fractured her left ulna, a type of injury usually sustained while warding off a blow to the head, the right arm being used to attack. The bone had healed well without misalignment, implying that the radius, the other bone of the forearm, had not been broken and had acted as a natural splint during the healing process.

Evidence for loading stress is seen in the buttressing of the superior facet of a thoracic vertebra from Burial D (709.32), which can develop in response to the carrying of heavy loads on the back (Sofaer Derevenski 2000). There is also a large olecranon fossa in the elbow of this individual. The isolated jaw of another female (644.36), older than the female of Burial B, had a broad ramus (RB' = 35.5 mm) and a pronounced forward development of the coronoid process, a form noted in the 'basket maker' from Abu Hureyra (Molleson 1994).

Neither dental caries nor abscesses were noted in the Neolithic material. The jaw (735.4) probably from the male Burial C showed evidence of anterior crowding of the teeth and an impacted third molar, and the adult female (644.36) possibly had an impacted wisdom tooth. These conditions suggest reduction of the jaws such as comes about from the introduction of a soft porridge-like diet, but could indicate a relationship between the two individuals.

4. The pottery

Virginia Mathias

Introduction

The Neolithic pottery of Tell Nebi Mend belongs to the broad tradition of dark burnished wares common in the northern Levant from very early in the production of ceramics. Calibrated radiocarbon dates suggest a time towards the beginning of the 7th millennium BC for its initial appearance, compared with indications of some centuries later for its advent in the southern Levant, where, in contrast to the north, the earliest material is usually light-coloured, lending itself to decoration with paint or coloured wash with incised bands. However, the basic shapes – simple open bowls, holemouth jars and jars with a high neck – recur widely in both north and south, and must reflect the use of the same basic technology, whether through diffusion or convergent development. Despite its early date, there are no signs of experimental beginnings or gradual introduction at Tell Nebi Mend, at least not in the earliest stratigraphic phase so far uncovered, and the pottery must therefore belong to a later stage of common use and well-established local characteristics. (For the early development of pottery technology in north-west Syria see Le Mière and Picon 1999; Nieuwenhuyse *et al.* 2010).

Although it is fairly low-fired and confined to basic shapes, the repertory from the earliest deposits at Tell Nebi Mend includes remarkably fine wares, some quite thin and many very well finished. The first three stratigraphic phases associated with remains of architecture, Phases 1–3, contain almost exclusively fine- or medium-fabric vessels, generally of fairly small size, with a preponderance of open bowls. While burnishing is a very common interior and exterior surface treatment, particularly on small bowls, cord-impression all over the outside or below a burnished or plain rim is the most typical decoration, especially on the jars and larger bowls.

Phase 4 is dominated by pits (as described in Chapter 2 above), which yielded large amounts of pottery, but as these pits were dug into the earlier phases there had inevitably been some – perhaps considerable – mixing of material. However, even allowing for this, there does appear to be a development in Phase 4, marked by the presence of coarse-fabric vessels of rougher workmanship, and these are often jars of larger size, thus altering the proportions of these shapes. These coarse fabrics apparently come into common use only in this phase, though they are still in the minority compared with the medium- and fine-fabric vessels; the very few earlier examples are probably from late in Phase 3. These changes were more or less maintained in the final Neolithic phase, Phase 5, which, however, is composed of featureless deposits derived from the earlier phases or, possibly, from an eroded higher part of the mound, and must therefore also be presumed to be largely mixed. Despite these changes, overall there is marked continuity in the pottery from Phase 1 through to Phase 5.

While the chronological scheme based on excavations in the ᶜAmuq still provides a general framework for the development of Dark Faced Burnished Ware (DFBW) in the broader region of western Syria, there are undoubtedly difficulties with it, based as it is on the poorly defined stratigraphy of the excavated sites and the limitations of the statistical analysis of the pottery (on which, see below). In any case the Tell Nebi Mend pottery belongs to a more southerly province than the ᶜAmuq, at the periphery of this area of dark burnished pottery and defined by its own variations, so that no definite correlations with the ᶜAmuq can be made. The time-scale at Tell Nebi Mend may point to period A of the ᶜAmuq sequence, but the prevalence of cord-impressed decoration may rather equate with the pattern-burnish of ᶜAmuq B. The closest association of this decoration is with the nearest coastal plain, to the west, the Beqaᶜ valley, to the south, and the Ghab, to the north. The wider regional setting and chronology of the Tell Nebi Mend pottery are discussed in more detail below.

Quantification

All the Neolithic potsherds excavated were cleaned and inspected on site. In the initial small soundings into the Neolithic levels in 1982, all rims, bases, handles and so on and all decorated sherds were kept, although only a sample of the undecorated sherds were. Thereafter, however, all sherds were saved and counted, apart from a few taken for technical analysis (Bettles 1994) which may not have been included. The numbers lost were small, and would have had very little effect on the overall statistics.

All sherds were marked with their provenance, including the Trench number (a Roman numeral), the Area within the Trench (usually three digits) and the archaeological deposit or Layer number (usually two digits, separated from the Area number by a period): so, for example, VIII.603.19. In addition, all rim sherds, bases, handles and body sherds showing any unusual feature were registered with an individual sherd number that was added to the provenance number following a solidus: thus, VIII.710.9/6. In the complete Pottery Register (below) the majority of these numbered sherds are listed and described individually; the remaining few are grouped with the unnumbered sherds and listed as 'body sherds', with only a brief note of any decorative features. Finally, after the detailed report on the pottery had been completed a further selection of sherds was made to form the illustrated Catalogue, Figs 4.6–4.60.

A total of 2351 Neolithic sherds was retrieved from Trench VIII, all of them now in the collections of the Institute of Archaeology, University College London (Table 4.1). Of these, 1875 were body sherds, 332 were rims and/or necks, 142 were bases and two were probably lids, making a total of 476 shaped (that is, not body) sherds. This, of course, does not necessarily imply 476 different vessels, since it is possible that at least some of the bases and the two lids belong to the same containers as some of the rims. The same is obviously true of the body sherds: some, perhaps many, will be from the same vessels as the rims and bases. The total number of sherds which can be used to construct a typology of the Neolithic pottery based on form is therefore really no more than the 332 rims and necks, and it is also necessary to note that only 234 of these came from stratified contexts, the rest being found in disturbed or post-Neolithic deposits within Trench VIII. In view of these observations it is clear that any conclusions reached on the basis of the statistics in the following pages must be treated as tentative. (Further comments on the statistics and the reliability of quantification will be found below in the discussion of ceramic comparisons with other sites.)

A few Neolithic sherds were also found during the excavation of the Hellenistic and Roman remains in Trench X (an area immediately south of the main mound: see plan of the site, Fig. 1.18), where they were not associated with any structural remains and are most probably the result of natural dispersal; they will be discussed in the report on that work. Other derived Neolithic sherds were occasionally encountered from later periods in other excavated areas of

the *tell*, but these are not included in the statistics or the following discussion.

In the Catalogue and the Pottery Register the stratigraphic phases to which the sherds have been assigned are also given. However, as has been pointed out above in Chapter 2, although the definition of these phases is generally, if not always, quite clear, the attribution of the pottery to them can in some cases be regarded only as uncertain. In addition, pottery from Phases 1, 2 and 3 was not plentiful, totalling only 29.2% of all stratified sherds (3.6%, 10.9% and 14.7% from Phases 1, 2, and 3 respectively). In the analysis and discussion that follows, therefore, the material from these three early phases has been treated together, since any further subdivision might well have given misleading results. As for Phases 4 and 5, although these were quite clearly defined stratigraphically and the pottery was more plentiful (33.3% and 37.5% respectively), they both – especially Phase 5 – undoubtedly contained material derived from earlier contexts, and this must be borne in mind when reading the following discussion.

The substantial amount of obviously Neolithic (*i.e.* in fabric and/or decoration) pottery recovered from disturbed, later or unstratified contexts within Trench VIII has been included as a further division, representing an additional 27% of the total pottery. Much of it came from the deposits immediately overlying Phase 5, from which it was probably derived through levelling, animal disturbance and so on. This unstratified Neolithic pottery consisted mainly of types similar to those from Phases 4 and 5, with nothing that could be seen as innovative and likely to have been later than the stratified material.

In the pottery Catalogue (Figs 4.6–4.60) virtually all rims are described and illustrated, the few that are not being listed and described in the Pottery Register, with references to illustrated analogies. The Catalogue is arranged primarily by phase (Phases 1–3 being grouped together, as explained above) and then by form, although examples of bases and a few miscellaneous forms (handles, lids, etc.) from all phases are grouped together. In the Register the arrangement is by provenance and then by sherd number (*e.g.* 654.10/3). With a very few exceptions the drawings of the pottery are at a scale of 1:2, this being judged best to enable details of the incised and impressed decoration to be shown. Photographs of a selection of sherds can be found on Plates 4.1 and 4.2.

Fabric

The initial categorisation of the pottery vessels as coarse, medium or fine was based on visual inspection and refers to the general appearance of the entire vessel and not solely to the texture of the clay matrix and the nature of the inclusions. The basic clay used seems to have been light or buff-coloured, and in the coarser wares – that is, those roughly made, poorly finished and often thick-walled and coarse-tempered – this is retained through firing. Although brick-red, buff, cream and pale grey colours do occur in the finer fabrics (perhaps the lighter ones imitating limestone bowls), the commonest colours for these are black, brown, brownish-black or very dark grey. Burnish intensifies and darkens these colours, giving the typical dark-burnished effect. However, dark colours, along with lighter brown, brick-red and buff, are also frequent with cord-impressed decoration, especially for bowls. Temper is almost entirely mineral, although grog appears in some lighter-coloured fabrics, and vegetable inclusions are occasionally visible, usually in the very coarse thick fabric. (For a fuller description of the inclusions, see Appendix 4.1 below.) In addition to this initial categorisation, 34 of the sherds were subjected to petrological and elemental analyses by Elizabeth Bettles as part of an unpublished MA dissertation at the Institute of Archaeology, University College London (Bettles 1994). As this research was carried out while the excavations were still in progress and before much of the lowest levels of Neolithic occupation had been uncovered, there is almost certainly a bias in the sample against sherds from the earlier phases. Body sherds selected on the basis of their macroscopic characteristics and already divided into coarse, medium and fine wares, as described above, were used. Bettles identified four main fabric groups and several sub-groups, differentiated primarily by the relative proportions of gabbro (more accurately, dolerite/microgabbro, a basic plutonic rock associated with basalt) and carbonate grains used as inclusions. Both grog and clay pellets – not always easy to distinguish – were also sometimes present and, very occasionally, small fragments of quartz and shell. There is nothing to suggest that any of these inclusions was not of local origin. (For the complete data of Bettles' analysis and her comments, see Appendix 4.1, below.)

It is clear that the classification of specific fabric types in Bettles' technical analyses does not correspond well to the descriptions of the pottery in this report, which (as has been said) are based on general observation. Some possible correlations can be observed: for example, Bettles's Fabric A2, with an abundance of small fragmented gabbro inclusions, is only used for fine ware vessels, and Fabric A3, with less gabbro and more carbonate and quartz, seems predominately associated with medium ware vessels. Coarse-ware vessels, on the other hand, are found made in both Fabric A1, the main feature of which is the presence of large clasts of gabbro, and Fabric D, a fine textured matrix with a high carbonate content. There may be some significance to these correlations, but it is more probable, in view of the very small sample analysed and the subjectivity of the initial characterisation, that they are coincidental.

Methods of manufacture

It is likely that forming on a mat for easy manoeuvring was the normal, if not the only, method of pottery production, probably being more common than is actually apparent from the material studied. For although there are only a few bases recorded with a recognisable mat impression underneath (Cat. no. 323 is a good complete example from the post-Neolithic Phase 7, while Cat. nos 318 and 328 are smaller sherds with similar impressions round the edge of the base), these impressions are faint and not easily seen, especially if the ubiquitous all-over cord-impressed decoration – quite different from the mat impressions – and surface burnishing (see below) extends over the bases, as it frequently does, thus obscuring or destroying the impressions.

A thin slab of clay placed on a mat is therefore the probable starting point of any of the Neolithic vessels. A simple flat base is in fact usual for both bowls and jars, the juncture with the sides being smoothed over inside where the angle is shallow, as in open bowls. Outside the angle is left or may be rounded off, although sometimes a 'heel' remains where the walls were built upon, and smoothed into, the initial disc of the base. This heel may be barely noticeable on shallow bases, tending to be of fairly fine or medium fabric and likely to be from bowls, or it can be more pronounced on deeper-angled bases, which are probably jars. There are also a few examples of carefully shaped disc bases, especially on fine bowls. Interestingly, from a Phase 4 pit containing at least one fine burnished bowl with a disc base came also a fragment of a fine stone bowl of similar shape but with a low ring base, unparalleled among the ceramics (Chapter 6, Fig. 6.4, Cat. no. 25).

The method of building up the sides of the vessel with a long coil of clay prepared in advance is well suited to a flat base pressed into a mat, which can be conveniently revolved as the coil is added in a spiral. The layers of coiled clay are fused into each other by smoothing the inner and outer surfaces across the join with the fingers. There are several instances of sherds partly broken along an S- or W-shaped line through the section where the join was imperfect, which is typical of coil-built vessels. Occasionally the tapered edge of a coil has split away completely, leaving a roughened surface. On this evidence it can be assumed that this was the usual means of constructing the Neolithic pottery. Raising the vessel sides from a lump of clay turning on even a slow wheel tends to produce horizontal striations and rilling of the surfaces, which are not in evidence here, while wheel-turning is not to be expected at such an early period.

Coil-building produces a thick wall which can be thinned out by beating with a flat tool on the outside against a rounded stone pressed against the inside – the paddle-and-anvil method. On the medium- and fine-ware vessels, which form the bulk of the repertoire, careful burnishing of the surface, often on the inside as well, would have removed the signs of thinning. The all-over cord-impressed decoration, which is also very common but on the outside only, appears to have been applied by something similar to the paddle, with the cord wound round it; the same

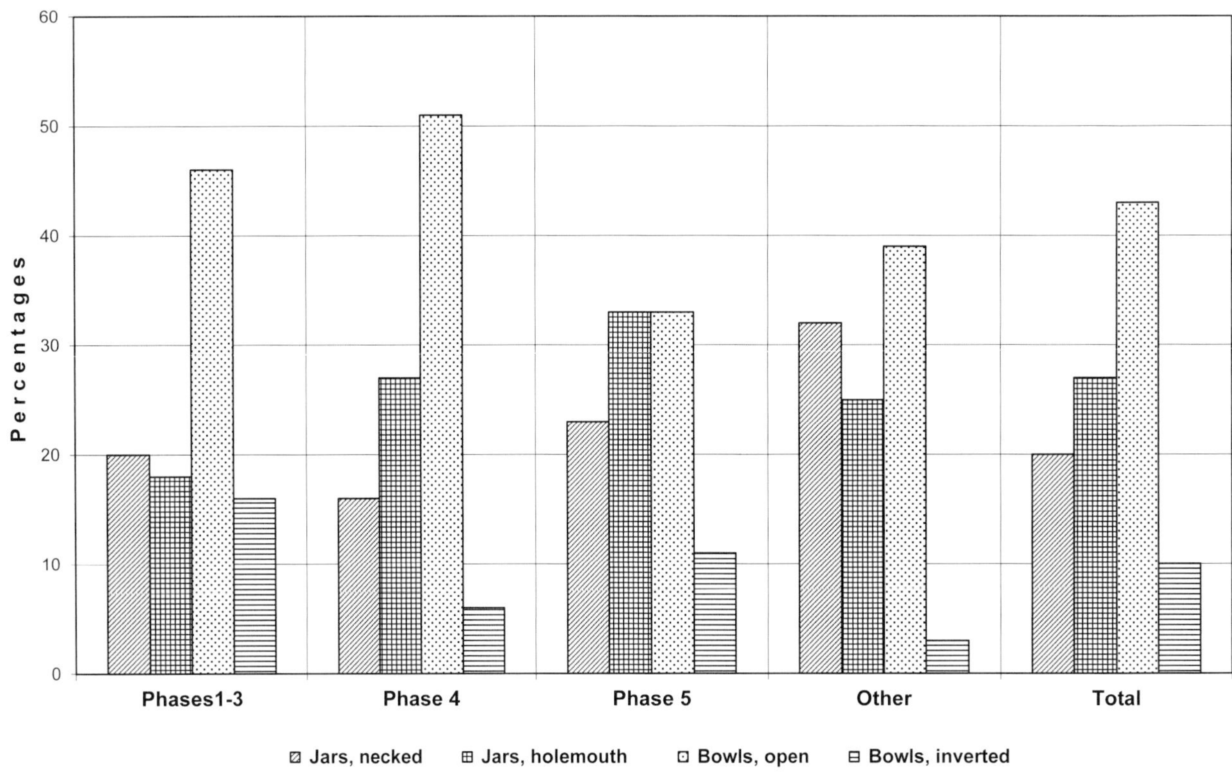

Fig. 4.1. Percentages of main vessel types.

conclusion was reached by Hole (1959, 155) in regard to the very similar cord-impressed pottery at Tabbat el-Hammam. This decoration is found predominantly on finer holemouth jars and deeper bowls, both of which would need careful thinning to produce, and also on necked jars, where the neck has been attached to the holemouth shape and sometimes shows parallel lines of smoothing and scraping to pare it down to the same thickness. Cord-impressed decoration is also used occasionally on open bowls, especially larger ones, and on the small number of bowls with slightly inverted rim. Faint-combed decoration, in which a grooved or toothed implement, or perhaps a paddle bound round with something like fine reed or grass stems, is drawn over the surface, produces a similar effect, but it is much less common and was more often used on coarser, thicker-walled vessels, and only rarely on the finest wares.

Firing temperatures were not very high, and the pottery breaks fairly easily and is permeated with fine air holes which bubble strongly when immersed in water. However, the careful burnishing of the bowls would have made them fairly watertight. The colour is generally well maintained through the thickness of the sherd, showing that the use of reducing and oxidising atmospheres in firing was well understood, and could be adjusted to produce shades of pale grey, bright brick-red, buff and cream, as well as the more common black and brown in the finer wares. Mottling does occur, even from dark grey to pale buff, but it is difficult to judge how common it was because of the lack of whole vessels. An even, dark colour was achieved on most of the finer sherds, and on the whole the surface colour is not much different from that of the core: that is, a dark 'face' is rare. The buff coarse ware is also generally consistent and only sometimes shaded with grey or pinkish mottling, which suggests that it was not baked in an open fire, the simplest method of firing. However, no remains of any kind of kiln were discovered, nor any other direct evidence of pottery production.

Forms

The basic two-fold division of the Tell Nebi Mend Neolithic pottery shapes, based on the evidence of the rim and neck sherds, is into jars, where the height is greater than the overall diameter and the rim diameter is relatively small, and bowls, which have a diameter greater than the height with a rim that is at or near the greatest overall diameter. Judging from the total sherd count bowls were slightly more common than jars (53% compared with 47%), although the figures for the stratified material suggest that in the early phases of the settlement bowls were considerably more popular (Fig. 4.1). There are very few examples of large vessels which could be for storage, and no evidence of spouted vessels. Within these categories the repertoire of shapes is fairly limited. There are necked jars – upright, slightly flared or slightly inverted, which can all be high or low, narrow or wide – or holemouth jars, those without necks, which show only minor variations. Among the bowls the most numerous type is the open bowl, which ranges

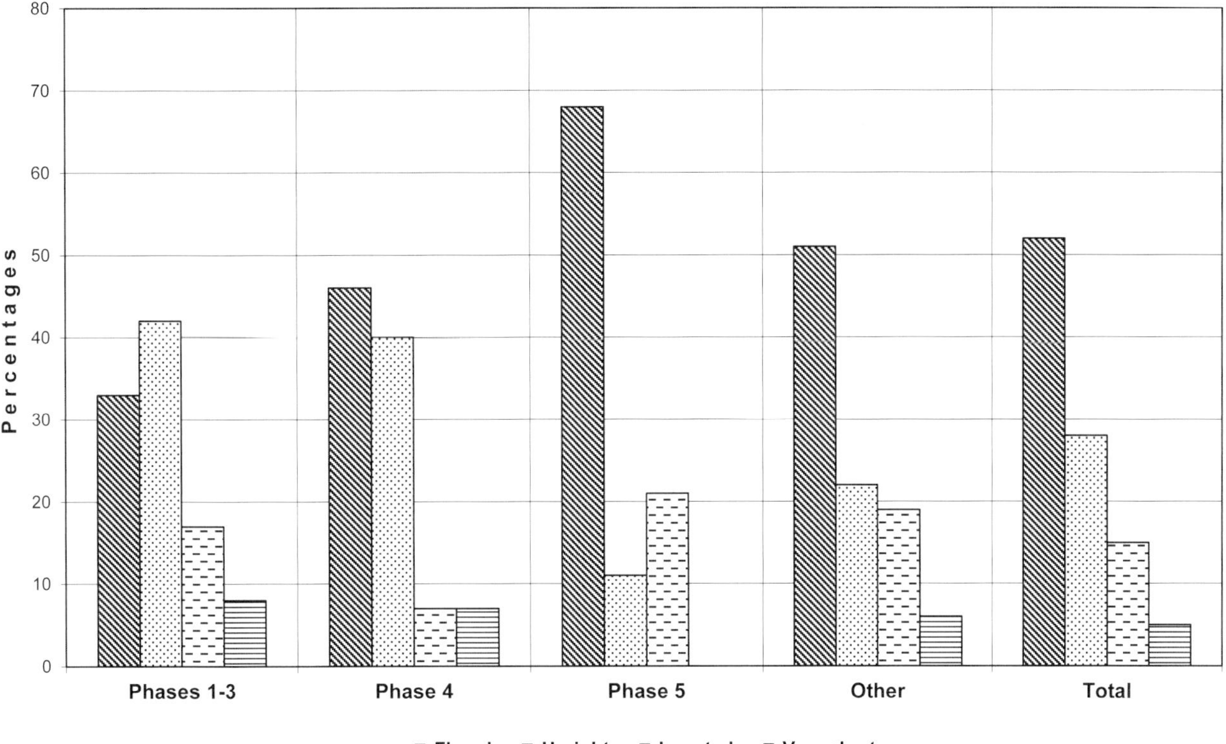

Fig. 4.2. Percentages of necked jars.

from deep through hemispherical and sub-conical (*i.e.* flat-sided) to shallow. There is also a small but distinct group with a slightly inverted rim, bordering on a holemouth but with a wider opening in proportion to the overall diameter, which itself would have been much greater than the height. Inevitably, where surviving complete profiles of vessels are rare, the overall shape, and therefore the allocation of each rim sherd to the above categories, is not always entirely certain. (Bases, generally flat, are dealt with separately, since very few whole profiles can be reconstructed from them.) Surface treatment and decoration, also dealt with later, are mentioned here wherever they relate to a particular type of vessel.

Jars: necked

There are many variations in the shapes of these in all phases, although the varieties shade into one another and are not rigidly divided. Nor is it always possible to assign an individual vessel to a particular variety, especially when only a small sherd survives; some attributions can only be subjective. The opening may be narrow or fairly wide, the junction between neck and shoulder either a sharp angle or (more often) just a slight change of direction. The neck itself can be high, medium or short (a few very short), sometimes tapered or thickened towards the rim, curved or straight. Despite this variability four categories can be distinguished (Fig. 4.2).

Flared necks (Cat. nos 2, 3, 8, 9 [Phases 1–3]; Cat. nos 52–58 [Phase 4]; Cat. nos 141–143, 147–150, 152–156 [Phase 5]; Cat. nos 214–227 [unstratified])
These occur in fine, medium and coarse fabrics and on wide- or narrow-necked vessels. High necks, with thin walls not tapering towards the rim, appear in fine fabric, burnished (Cat. no. 3, Phase 3; Cat. no. 141, Phase 5); or medium–fine fabric, smoothed only (Cat. no. 155, Phase 5; Cat. no. 223, from a post-Neolithic context). Of similar shape but shorter are Cat. nos 54 and 142 of Phase 4. There are high necks flared only at the rim, like Cat. nos 148 and 149 of Phase 5; see also Cat. nos 216 and 227 (thickened) from later contexts. All of the above are fairly narrow necks, with no indication of the shape of the body.

Wider and shorter flared necks include a single example (Cat. no. 2, Phase 2) in a very thin-walled fine fabric, black-burnished (as is common in fine bowls); examples in fine fabric, lightly burnished or smoothed, such as Cat. nos 53 (Phase 4), 153, 154 (Phase 5), 217 and another similar (from a post-Neolithic context); Cat. no. 218 with cord-impressed decoration; and Cat. no. 221 in medium fabric. Similar short necks, but narrower, are Cat. nos 52 (Phase 4) and 147 (Phase 5), and the very small jar Cat. no. 220 (post-Neolithic context), all fairly fine.

High, narrow, flared necks can also be more roughly made. Cat. no. 55 (Phase 4) is of quite coarse fabric though thin-walled, with a rare red slip. Cat. no. 143 (also Phase 4), is cord-impressed, while Cat. no. 215 (unstratified) also has cord-impressions but only on the shoulder; both are fairly fine. Similar flared necks come in thicker, medium fabric. From the earlier phases there are, for example, Cat. nos 8 and 9 (both from Phase 3), the latter wider in the neck and cord-impressed, and Cat. no. 222 (from a disturbed context). From later phases are Cat. nos 56–57 (Phase 4), 150, 152 (Phase 5) and 224 (post-Neolithic) – all high and narrow – and Cat. nos 58 (Phase 4) and 225 (post-Neolithic), which are wider. Two unusually wide necks, thickened and probably rolled, in quite fine fabric and burnished, are both late: Cat. nos 156 (Phase 5) and 214 (post-Neolithic).

Upright necks (Cat. nos 4, 5, 7, 59 [Phases 1–3]; Cat. nos 60–64 [Phase 4]; Cat. nos 144, 151 [Phase 5]; Cat. nos 228–229, 232–233, 235–236 [unstratified])
Two fairly high and narrow upright necks in fine fabric occur in Phase 3: Cat. no. 4, with combed decoration, and Cat. no. 5, with cord-impressed. A similar but shorter example is Cat. no. 233, with cord-impressed decoration (unstratified). The only other fine-fabric examples are shorter and wider necks on jars with sloping shoulders, both with a rare small horizontally pierced vertical lug: Cat. no. 60 (Phase 4), cord-impressed on the shoulder (which probably had four lugs), and Cat. no. 144 (Phase 5).

Wider, shorter necks on jars of rather coarse thick fabric appear first in Phase 4, such as Cat. no. 61, with red slip or paint round the neck, and Cat. nos 62–64, which are plain. A narrower-necked type, Cat. no. 151, is the only one in Phase 5, with another (Cat. no. 228) in a post-Neolithic context.

A higher-necked jar in medium–coarse fabric is Cat. no. 59 (probably Phase 3), and there is also a thinner-walled fine-fabric example of the same neck diameter, with fine cord-impressions on the body (Phase 4). A similar shape, but much larger, was found in a contaminated context and could be late (Cat. no. 232); despite its size the fabric was relatively fine, the surfaces being roughly burnished. Two jar necks, Cat. no. 7 and another not illustrated, of medium height and width, in medium–fine fabric and rather thick and roughly shaped, come from the early Phases 2 and 3. Four more (Cat. nos 229, 235, 236 and one not illustrated) of medium or fairly fine fabric, similar overall but better shaped, are all from unstratified or post-Neolithic contexts. All of these are undecorated and appear to have wider and less sloping shoulders (*cf.* perhaps Cat. no. 61).

Inverted necks (Cat. no. 1 [Phases 1–3]; Cat. no. 84 [Phase 4]; Cat. nos 145–146, 157–158 [Phase 5]; Cat. nos 234, 237–240 [unstratified])
An early type is the high, narrow inverted neck on fine-fabric jar, probably with sloping shoulders at only a slight angle to the base of the neck. Cat. no. 1, which is cord-impressed, is the only rim (apart from a fragment not illustrated, both from Phase 2), but it was apparently quite a common and long-lived type (see below). A smaller version

with a shorter narrow neck is represented by two in Phase 5, Cat. nos 145 (incised) and 146 (cord-impressed), and by another, Cat. no. 234, from a post-Neolithic context.

Short inverted necks, both small in fine fabric and larger in medium fabric, are present in single stratified examples all from Phase 5: Cat. nos 157 (cord-impressed) and 158 (plain). One (Cat. no. 84) in very coarse thick fabric came from Phase 4, and another four (Cat. nos 237–240), ranging from fairly fine to very coarse fabric, from post-Neolithic contexts.

Very short necks (Cat. no. 6 [Phases 1–3]; Cat. no. 51 [Phase 4]; Cat. nos 230 and 231 [unstratified])
In addition to the three main categories discussed above, there are just four jars with unusually short necks. Cat. no. 6 (*cf.* Plate 4.1) from Phase 3 is thick and probably rolled, the aperture being relatively wide and the shoulders steeply sloping and impressed with very fine cords. It is also unusual in having a small vertical lug, horizontally pierced with a small hole (one of only three known). There are indications of another lug on the broken edge, and the spacing would allow for six. The small vessel Cat. no. 51 from Phase 4 is made of buff-coloured medium fabric which is thick and poorly fired; the rim is pinched outwards and the sides are almost vertical. The shape suggests a little cup or beaker, but the red slip covering it is rather fugitive and would be unsuitable for a drinking vessel. The other two jars, Cat. nos 230 and 231, are both from very deep pits of post-Neolithic date. They are larger, and alike in having steeply sloping shoulders with the scar of a small knob or lug set well below the short rounded rim, presumably one of at least two. The smaller, Cat. no. 230, has a ledge inside which would support a lid (*cf.* two probable ceramic lid fragments in Phase 4, Cat. nos 139 and 140). Cat. no. 231, which is of typical though less common Neolithic fabric, with dense pale inclusions (probably carbonate), has a horizontal band of deep herringbone incisions on either side of the knob, cut through a rough burnish.

Overall, necked jars are not very numerous, forming only 20% of all rims and 43% of all jar rims (see Table 4.1 and Fig. 4.1). Of these, more than half are of the flared type, far outnumbering the next most popular type, that with an upright neck (see Fig. 4.2), although the statistics suggest that in Phases 1–3 and 4 the proportions are more equal. Inverted necks are much less common, and very short necks, as mentioned above, very rare. It may be noted that in all phases jars with narrow necks, usually high or medium, are consistently more frequent than those with wider necks, which are usually shorter, and this seems to hold good for both small and larger jars, as far as the size can be judged from incomplete profiles. In these jars (as for other shapes) coarse fabrics hardly occur before Phase 4, and really large jars, such as Cat. nos 158, 232 and 240, begin to come in only near the end of the Neolithic occupation.

Jars: holemouth (Cat. nos 10–20 [Phases 1–3]; Cat. nos 65–83, 85–87, 91–93 [Phase 4]; Cat. nos 159–183 [Phase 5]; Cat. nos 241–263 [unstratified])

Holemouth jars occur in roughly the same quantities as the necked jars in Phases 1–3 and seem to become more popular later; overall they account for about 54% of the total rim sherds (see Fig. 4.1). There are no complete profiles of holemouth jars, but from those relatively few rim sherds which include part of the shoulder it appears that the widest part is often fairly high up, and that the sides probably taper quite steeply to a small base. The angle of the shoulder in handmade holemouths is particularly difficult to ascertain from small rim sherds, and the variations in rim profile are probably not very significant. The most obvious differences occur between those vessels which are well made in fine fabric, thin-walled and usually decorated, and the heavier, roughly finished and usually thicker-walled version, which comes in with the introduction of coarse fabrics.

Holemouth jars in fine fabric
In the early Phases 1–3, 10 out of the 11 holemouth jars are of fine fabric and thin-walled, although relatively quite large. At least two came from the generally poorly represented Phase 1 and five or six from Phase 2. Typically they are cord-impressed on the outside and burnished on the inside; some, especially the finer examples, are burnished over the rim and in an upper band on the outside as well: examples include Cat. nos 10 (*cf.* Plate 4.1), 16, 17 (*cf.* Plate 4.1) and 14. The last of these, however, shows only burnish inside and out but may have been cord-impressed lower down. Others, usually more roughly finished, have a band around the outside left plain, the burnish inside often being rather streaky or scrappy over an uneven surface: see Cat. nos 11 (*cf.* Plate 4.1) and 20. Cat. no. 13 (*cf.* Plate 4.1) is carefully smoothed inside and on the outside of the rim but the impressions below are not of cords, but are perhaps from bunched grass or some leafy plant. Cat. no. 15, a small sherd, is thicker-walled, of medium fabric and smoothed on the outside only, but, again, it could have been decorated lower down. The shaping of the rim itself varies considerably in profile: it may be rolled and thickened (Cat. no. 10 [*cf.* Plate 4.1], where the complex folding of the coil can be seen on the break, and perhaps the much thinner Cat. no. 16); tapered (Cat. no. 14 [rounded] or Cat. no. 18 [to a point]); rounded, (Cat. nos 13 and 17); blunted (Cat. nos 19 and 20); or square-cut (Cat. nos 11 and 12 [also thickened]).

The standard fine thin-walled holemouth jar, with cord-impressed decoration outside and often burnish over the rim and inside – at least on the upper parts – continues to be well represented in Phases 4 and 5. Even the exact shaping of the rim continues with the same variations: rolled and thickened (Cat. no. 74 [Phase 4]; Cat. nos 164–167 [Phase 5]; and Cat. nos 247–251 from later or uncertain contexts); tapered, almost to a point (the very finely-made examples

Cat. nos 85–87 [Phase 4], and, similarly, Cat. nos 179 and 180 [Phase 5]); rounded (Cat. nos 65–68, 71 (undecorated) and 92–93 [Phase 4]; Cat. nos 169–170 [Phase 5]; and Cat. nos 252–253 and 255, from later contexts); and more squared-off rims, often noticeably large, thin-walled and well fired (Cat. nos 70, 72, 73 [Phase 4], Cat. nos 168, 171 and steeped-sided 182–183 [Phase 5], and Cat. nos 258–260, from later or uncertain contexts). A few others with blunted rim in profile (*i.e.* roughly cut and rounded off, as Cat. nos 19 and 20), tend to be thicker-walled, though still of fine fabric, like Cat. no. 91 in Phase 4, and often rather large, as Cat. no. 181 (Phase 5) and Cat. nos 254 and 256 (from post-Neolithic contexts).

A few horizontal ledge handles or lugs occur on holemouth jars, near or a little below the rim, as Cat. no. 66 from Phase 4, Cat. nos 171 and 183 from Phase 5 and the very similar Cat. no. 258, unstratified. No such lugs on holemouth jars have been recovered from the early Phases, but a few on body sherds (listed in the Catalogue) from Phases 2 and 3 prove that they were already in use. Presumably they would have been attached in pairs, at least. They are also to be found on inverted-rim bowls (see below).

The rise in numbers of holemouth jars from Phase 4 onwards is more than accounted for by the appearance of coarse-fabric holemouths in fairly small but persistent numbers and the increasing numbers in medium fabrics, especially in Phase 5.

Holemouth jars in fairly fine or medium fabric
Some of these are slightly rougher versions of the fine ones mentioned above, such as Cat. nos 67 and 74 in Phase 4, Cat. nos 164–165 in Phase 5 and Cat. nos 257 and 261–263 (unstratified). However, others are really versions of coarse-fabric jars in better fabric and finish, and share with them the characteristics of smoothed or at most lightly burnished surfaces, with occasionally light-combed decoration. They can be quite thick-walled, such as Cat. nos 75–77, all tapered (Phase 4), and Cat. no. 172 (Phase 5); thinner-walled, such as Cat. no. 170 (relatively fine and well smoothed, with some combed decoration) and Cat. no. 169 (barely smoothed surfaces); or large and verging on coarse ware, such as Cat. no. 173. These last three all have rounded rims and are from Phase 5.

Also from Phase 5 is a distinct group of holemouth jars in medium or medium–coarse fabric, Cat. nos 159–163 (and two more, similar, not illustrated), rather roughly made but quite well fired and thin-walled, and much less clumsy than the medium- and coarse-fabric holemouths of Phase 4, Cat. nos 77–80. However, they are also light-coloured, buff or pinkish-buff. They have a relatively small aperture and wide shallow shoulders with a quasi-carination at the widest extent, where they tended to break. The upper and lower parts of these jars may have been made separately, leaving a weakness at the junction. The surfaces are smoothed only, but combing or incising is a common decoration. The rims are sometimes rounded (Cat. no. 163) but more often roughly squared off, and one (Cat. no. 159: *cf.* Plate 4.2) has the scar of a broken-off knob (not a ledge-handle) close to the rim. A specific fabric was used for this group of holemouth jars (Group D; Bettles 1994).

Holemouth jars in coarse fabric
These first occur in Phase 4 and are relatively large and thick-walled, some with wide shallow shoulders: Cat. nos 69, 78–79 (with combed decoration) in Phase 4; Cat. no. 174 (very coarse) in Phase 5; and Cat. nos 241 and 242 (with red-brown slip) from later contexts. Others are fairly steep-sided: Cat. nos 80 (faint-combed decoration), 81 and 82 (with possibly the edge of a knob or lug), and 83 (with a slightly indented rim – *cf.* Cat. no. 84, with a short inverted neck), all from Phase 4; and Cat. nos 175–177 from Phase 5. Unstratified are Cat. nos 243–246; the last is of very coarse fabric and twice the size of any other coarse holemouth jar, and can fairly be described as a storage jar, a category probably coming into use only late in the Neolithic settlement.

Bowls: open (Cat. nos 25–9, 34–50; 96, 287, 297 [Phases 1–3]; Cat. nos 97–138; 190, 278, 301; 96 [Phase 4]; Cat. nos 269–305 [unstratified])

These are by far the most numerous shape overall: 81% of all bowls and 43% of all rims (see Table 4.1 and Fig. 4.1). The sherd count suggests they were more predominant in the earlier phases than in the later, when jars increase in proportion.

There are a very few large bowls (up to 300 mm diameter), and a small number of thick-walled bowls in coarse or medium fabric from Phase 4 onwards (see below), but the great majority of open bowls are of fine fabric and small to medium in size.

Open bowls, fine fabric
The majority fall within the range 120–200 mm (some a little larger), and are mostly well burnished inside and outside; other decoration is uncommon, at least around the preserved rim and upper parts (whole profiles are few). The colours are predominantly darkish, ranging from mushroom, grey and brick-red through grey-brown and dark brown to black. Some are very fine and thin-walled, usually black with a fine glossy burnish.

The basic open shape has a number of variations. Examples have curved sides, upright at the rim (which is generally rounded) or even marginally inverted, usually at the upper end of the size range, and are relatively shallow, such as Cat. nos 34 and perhaps 39 (Phase 2), Cat. no. 36 (Phase 3), Cat. nos 98 (and perhaps also 100), 105 and the very fine and thin 106 [all Phase 4]); possibly Cat. no. 195 (Phase 5); and Cat. nos 272 (with faint-combed decoration below a deep band of burnish) and 275 (both unstratified). Two bowls of similar overall dimension and shape (Cat. nos 108 and 109, both Phase 4) have thicker sides tapering

towards the rim, a faint carination high up and a slight flattening of the sides below; both have small disc bases.

This simple curved shape occurs also in small sizes, usually rather deeper in proportion, giving a more hemispherical profile: examples include Cat. no. 42 and the miniature version Cat. no. 41 in Phase 2; Cat. no. 27 (with faint-combed decoration) and the small Cat. no. 35, both in Phase 3; Cat. nos 102, 107 and 110 and Cat. nos 111 and 112 (which look like smaller versions of the thicker, slightly carinated and flattened Cat. nos 108 and 109 mentioned above, though they may be relatively deeper) from Phase 4. The unusual Cat. no. 269 is of the same overall shape but has incised decoration of three curved lines in swags around the rim. Other unstratified examples are Cat. nos 270, 271 and 273 and the small, thicker-walled Cat. no. 274.

Still upright at the rim, but with straighter sides and correspondingly deeper, is another sub-type of mainly medium diameter, which tends to have a tapered rim. Cat. no. 25, with faint-combed decoration below a deep burnish band, is a good example from Phase 2; Cat. no. 96 (with a large diameter) is from Phase 4. Cat. no. 104 is also typical of this variant, as is the larger Cat. no. 103 (with comb decoration), the small sherd Cat. no. 97 (rounded at the rim), Cat. no. 190 and, probably, the small, thicker-walled Cat. no. 101, all from Phase 4. (Note the same light-combed decoration below a deep burnish band on the unstratified Cat. no. 272 as on Cat. no. 25, although the bowl itself is shallower and more curved.)

Given that the exact angle cannot be certainly determined from a small sherd, slightly flared shapes with a similar tapered rim in profile look like a minor variation of this last group, with a bias towards the larger end of the range and towards thicker walls. Of these, Cat. no. 43 is from Phase 2 and Cat. no. 45 from Phase 3; there are also probably the fragments Cat. nos 113–114 (Phase 4), Cat. nos 200–202 and perhaps 195 (Phase 5) and Cat. nos 277–279 from later contexts. There is little indication of the depth of these bowls, but Cat. no. 43 could be fairly shallow.

Apparently deeper bowls, flared with very straight sides (*i.e.* conical in shape), form a related larger group. They vary greatly in diameter from well over 200 mm to a miniature variant of less than 100 mm; some taper inwards in a slight curve at the rim, others are straight and blunted. One of the latter is Cat. no. 40 (cord-impressed) from Phase 3, but both rim variations are well represented in Phase 4: Cat. nos 115 and 116 (large), and Cat. nos 118–124 in a variety of sizes; Cat. no. 122 is rather roughly made, with cord-impressed decoration. Other large examples are Cat. no. 191 and perhaps the fragment Cat. no. 192, while smaller and very fine examples are Cat. nos 193 and 194 (with cord decoration below wide burnish bands), Cat. no. 196, the tiny Cat. no. 197 (all Phase 5) and the very fine and thin Cat. nos 280–284 (combed), as well as, perhaps, the larger thicker fragments Cat. nos 285 and 286 (unstratified).

Widely flared shallow bowls are quite common from the early Phases in a range of sizes. They may be tapered and curved (*e.g.* Cat. nos 44, 48 and 49 from Phase 2) or straight (Cat. no. 47 from Phase 2 and Cat. no. 50 from Phase 3). From Phase 4 are Cat. nos 130–134 (132 being thick-walled with a knob or lug, Cat. nos 133 and 134 with comb decoration, the latter also rather thick). From Phase 5 there are Cat. nos 205 and 206 (with four oblique straight lines incised through the burnish, rather as with the small bowl Cat. no. 269, but done after firing), while Cat. nos 287–294 were unstratified. Of these last Cat. no. 287 has some irregular reddish paint or slip on the outside, Cat. no. 289 is combed or scored, Cat. no. 293 cord-impressed and Cat. no. 294 thick-walled, with a knob or lug indicated.

Also fairly shallow, but more curved and thickened, are a small number of bowls, most rather small: probably Cat. no. 37 from Phase 2, Cat. nos 127–129 (129 in less fine fabric and smoothed rather than burnished) from Phase 4, while from post-Neolithic contexts come the larger examples Cat. nos 295 and 298 (cord-impressed) and the smaller Cat. no. 299 (smoothed only).

Large-diameter fine-fabric bowls, as mentioned earlier, occur occasionally in all phases, burnished inside but usually cord-impressed outside. Examples are Cat. no. 46 (Phase 2) and Cat. no. 29 (Phase 3), which is deeper and roughly hemispherical, with a square-cut rim. Cat. no. 125 is the only example of a large-diameter bowl among the numerous fine open bowls in Phase 4, but the much smaller Cat. no. 99 might be mentioned because of its cord-impressed decoration outside, rougher finish and very perfunctory burnish inside and horizontal lug, a feature never found on the fine, thin-walled burnished bowls of similar size and shape. Cat. no. 207 has too short a rim to calculate the diameter, but it is certainly from a large bowl of this type from Phase 5, and Cat. no. 296 is a rather smaller unstratified example. Cat. no. 297, with a horizontal lug, was illegibly marked and another rim sherd from the same vessel was found in the fill of a deep late post-Neolithic pit. However, the base illustrated came from a nearby Phase 2 context and almost certainly belonged to the same bowl (given size, fabric, colour and surface treatment), and the suggested reconstruction fits well with the large bowls already mentioned.

A number of other rim sherds of fine bowls were too small to assign to any grouping, and although most are illustrated some need further mention. Cat. no. 26 (Phase 3) is a unique small bowl, probably quite shallow, with cord-impressed decoration. Cat. no. 117 (Phase 4) is also an unparalleled small bowl, thick-walled and roughly made, with faint-combing or score marks which may have been keying for white plaster, traces of which remain on the inside and outside. The two square-cut fragments of rims Cat. nos 203 and 204 (Phase 5) are both of very fine fabric and much smaller than the similar rims Cat. nos 28 and 29; there is no indication that Cat. no. 204 was the neck of a jar, as might be expected from its very small size (compare Cat. nos 41 and 197).

Open bowls, medium and coarse fabric
Compared with the large numbers of fine bowls, these are almost insignificant. There are none at all in Phases 1–3 and in Phase 4 only the small shallow bowl Cat. no. 135, the two massively thick fragments Cat. nos 136 and 137 (also of small diameter) and the more interesting item Cat. no. 138, apparently a small dish or platter; all of these are in light-coloured coarse fabric. From Phase 5 Cat. nos 208–213 include some slightly finer (Cat. no. 209) and better-finished bowls, again all fairly small and shallow, some with a little burnish (Cat. no. 209). Cat. no. 211 is similar to the platter Cat. no. 138, though much smaller. Unstratified examples of these bowls are Cat. nos 300–305.

Bowls: inverted (Cat. nos 21–24, 30–33 [Phases 1–3]; Cat. nos 88–90, 94–95 [Phase 4]; Cat. nos 184–189 [Phase 5]; Cat. nos 264–268 [unstratified])

Rims from this group of slightly inverted-rim bowls are sometimes difficult to distinguish from those of holemouth jars (*i.e.* vessels which are substantially higher than they are wide) in the absence of any complete profiles of either category. A clear example, however, is Cat. no. 23, a rim large enough to give the angle of the sides reliably, with enough of the body to fix the shape and show that the depth, even if the base was small, must have been much less than the diameter. (A rounded base, very similar in fabric and decoration to Cat. no. 23 and found close by, is probably from this vessel, and suggests a depth to the bowl of about 130 mm). In reality these slightly inverted-rim bowls probably had less in common with holemouth jars than is apparent from small rim sherds and, rather, were a variation on such hemispherical or shallower bowls as, for example, Cat. no. 29 (Phase 3), Cat. no. 99 (Phase 4) or Cat. no. 297 (probably Phase 2). Nevertheless, smaller sherds have here been generally presumed to belong to holemouth jars where there was any doubt, especially if they resembled others in that category, and only those which had both steep sides and a wide aperture have been classified as inverted-rim bowls. On this basis some salient characteristics have emerged.

These bowls are mostly of fine fabric, with a few in medium fabric; there is no version made of coarse fabric. Only in the early stages (nearly all in Phase 3) do they form a substantial proportion – about 16% – of all vessel rims, but small numbers continued to occur in Phases 4 and 5. They can be large – such as Cat. nos 23 and 24 (Phase 3) and Cat. no. 95 (Phase 4), though these are fine and very thin-walled for their size, and Cat. no. 186 (Phase 5), which is in medium fabric and thicker, especially towards the rim. Rather smaller and tapering towards the rim are Cat. no. 22 (Phase 3), Cat. no. 184 (with an unusual wide horizontal lug) and Cat. no. 187, both from Phase 5. Also medium to small in diameter, roughly shaped and with rather thick walls are Cat. no. 21

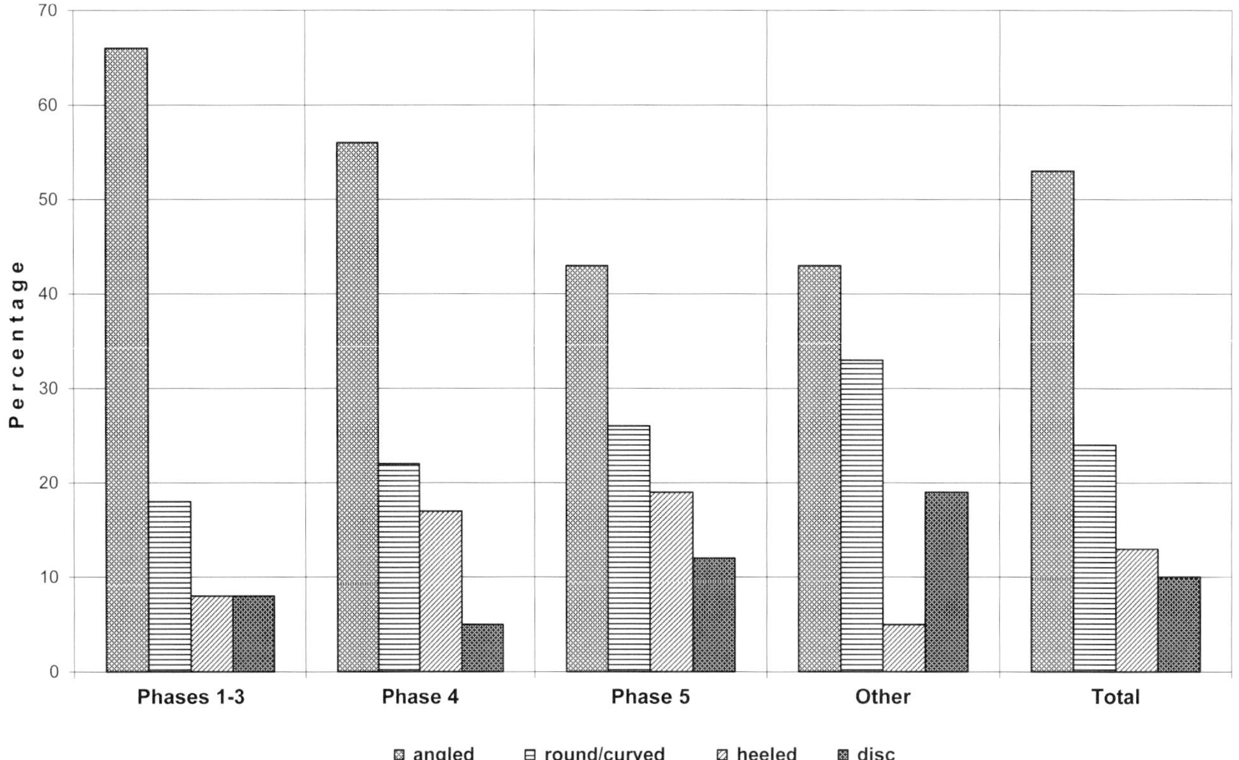

Fig. 4.3. Percentages of base types.

(Phase 3), Cat. no. 94 (Phase 4), Cat. nos 185 and 188 (Phase 5) and Cat. nos 264 and 265 (unstratified), both of these last examples with a horizontal lug. Cat. no. 266 (from a mixed post-Neolithic context, but in what appears to be Neolithic fabric) looks like a miniature version of the same type, with a broken small lug- or knob-handle or possibly a 'coffee-bean' decoration (*cf.* Cat. no. 332). Rare examples of miniature vessels are found in all shape categories, but this may be a cup or deep beaker rather than a bowl.

The above vessels are mostly cord-impressed or faint-combed outside, the latter decoration being unusually well represented, but the inside is not always burnished and often the burnishing is rather perfunctory. Cat. nos 22 and 185, both in medium fabric, are apparently undecorated, and Cat. no. 188 has streaky burnish on the inside only. However, there are several examples at the small end of the range which are fine or very fine, thin-walled and well burnished, like the more common open bowls. With these the shaping of the rims parallels all the heavier examples – thickened, tapered, rounded and so on – and again they are most numerous in the early Phases: Cat. nos 30–33 come from Phases 1–3; Cat. nos 88–90 from Phase 4; Cat. no. 189, very fine and thin, from Phase 5; and Cat. nos 267, also fine and thin, but with cord-impressions, and 268 from disturbed or later contexts.

Bowl: pedestal

Cat. no. 330 (Phase 5), without a surviving rim, is probably the sole example of a pedestal bowl. It is of coarse ware and apparently rather large; the hidden under surface is rougher than the outside and inside surfaces.

Bases (Cat. nos 23, 108, 138, 297, 306–330)

These are virtually all flat, either curved into the sides (some nearly round) or meeting at an angle or with a 'heel', or a more definite disc (Fig. 4.3). Where the sherd is large enough to judge it appears that very many bases are slightly concave underneath, a feature that would give some additional strength to the base against shock. There is one fragment of what is probably a pedestal base (Cat. no. 330) on a large coarse-ware bowl: see above, 'Bowls'.

Angled bases

The most common base has the side-wall set on at an angle with a definite edge (see Cat. nos 310–315 and bowl Cat. no. 138), the profile being thickest at this point and the angle being smoothed out on the inside. This is true of fine, medium and coarse wares, though the angle tends to be less sharp the coarser the fabric and the less well-finished the vessel. (If the angle between side and base is shallow it probably comes from an open bowl.) A base with a shallow angle in a fine fabric (*e.g.* Cat. nos 312, 314) is the most numerous variety. The outside surfaces have overall burnish or cord-impression, rarely faint-combing, which often continues underneath the base (where burnish may, however, wear off, especially at the edge). The inside surfaces are usually burnished or well smoothed, a further indication of an open bowl. Shallow-angled bases in medium fabric are much less common: out of a total of ten, six are from Phase 4, three from Phase 5 and only one is definitely early, from Phase 1. All of these are cord-impressed outside except one (Phase 4), and only smoothed or lightly burnished inside. Coarse, thick bases of this type are even rarer (a total of three, one each from Phases 4 and 5 and one unstratified).

A more steeply angled base is assumed to belong to a jar (or deeper bowl: see above). It is also a common type in fine vessels, especially in the earlier periods (Cat. nos 310, 311). There are 15 in all: eight in Phases 1–3, five in Phase 4 and only two in Phase 5, representing a sharp decline in percentages. Deeper bases (*e.g.* Cat. no. 313) are less numerous but proportionally the largest grouping in medium-fabric vessels; there are 13 in all: six in Phases 1–2, one each in Phases 4 and 5 and five from post-Neolithic contexts. In coarse-fabric heavy vessels (*e.g.* Cat. no. 315) there are seven: two in Phase 4 and five in Phase 5, three of which were so steep-angled as to be almost certainly jars. In fine vessels the inside is still usually well burnished and the outside is again burnished or sometimes cord-impressed, though underneath is more likely to be left plain. Medium vessels, however, though normally cord-impressed outside, may be left plain or even rough on the outside and underneath, while the inside is only smoothed or sometimes also left rough. On the coarse vessels finger-smoothing of the inside and outside surfaces is the norm, with some rough burnish, faint-combing or cord-impressions on the outside of the body only; alternatively all surfaces may be left rough.

Angled bases predominate throughout, but occur most frequently in the three earlier phases (where they represent two-thirds of all bases), except in the coarse ware, which is, as usual, not very common and confined to the later pits and abandonment phases.

Curved or rounded bases

A substantial minority (27, plus seven unstratified) is formed by the category of base where the juncture of the flat base and the side wall is a fairly continuous curve (see Cat. nos 23, 105 and 306–309), the surfaces more or less parallel – that is, without a thickening at the join (see Cat. nos 308 and 309 [Phases 4 and 5] and bowl Cat. no. 297, where the base of the reconstructed profile is from Phase 2). Smaller bases in fine fabric tend to have a very small flat area underneath, so that the base simply seems round, as with Cat. nos 306 (Phase 3) and 307 and bowl Cat. no. 105 (both Phase 4), but even here the slight concavity at the centre is noticeable. The 16 fine, thin examples – six from Phases 1–3, six from Phase 4, one from Phase 5 and

three unstratified – are either burnished on both surfaces or cord-impressed outside (one has faint-combing only and one is lightly incised or scored) and lightly burnished or smoothed inside, and are often left rough underneath. There are only seven medium-fabric examples (*e.g.* Cat. no. 309): one from Phase 4, four from Phase 5 and two from later contexts. Apart from faint cord-impressions on Cat. no. 309 and one other, they are only smoothed or roughly burnished, one from Phase 5 having a thin chalky coating inside. Coarse-fabric curved bases are relatively common (*e.g.* Cat. no. 308), there being 12 in all, including one apparently from late in Phase 3, three from Phase 4, five from Phase 5 and three unstratified. Only one or two of these had cord or comb decoration, while two had a rare brown slip on the outside and one had possible red paint inside. Burnish or smoothing was minimal, with some examples being left rough inside.

There is quite good evidence that the small rounded base was used on fine bowls, such as the near-complete profile Cat. no. 105 and the base similar to Cat. no. 307 but larger, which almost certainly belongs to the inverted-rim bowl Cat. no. 23. The wider bases curved at the edge were also employed on larger open bowls such as Cat. no. 297. In the absence of any whole profiles the curvature makes it hard to judge whether these could, alternatively, be the bases of jars; the rather perfunctory treatment of the inside surfaces, even on finer fabrics, would, for instance, be compatible with the common holemouth jars.

Although some fine curved bases come from the early Phases there are more in the Phase 4 pits, and the medium- and coarse-fabric versions do not occur earlier than this. However, such bases are difficult to identify from small sherds, and they could be both more numerous and more widely distributed than indicated.

Heeled bases (Cat. nos 316–323)

These are much less common than either the curved or angled bases. The base here, which is more roughly joined to the sides of the vessel, is found mainly in medium and coarse ware. Usually the heel is fairly pronounced, but in some examples the indentation is slight (*e.g.* Cat. nos 316 and 320), while in others it is low down and vestigial (Cat. nos 317, 318). Of the heeled bases, only four are of fine fabric: one in Phase 2 (Cat. no. 317, shallow and probably a bowl, cord-impressed on the outside and slightly burnished inside), two in Phase 4 (both also cord-impressed) and the fourth (undecorated) from Phase 5. There are six in medium fabric: one from Phase 3, two in each of Phases 4 and 5 and one from a disturbed context. Of these six, two are cord-impressed, one has faint-combing and three are only smoothed on the outside (one of these, Cat. no. 323, has a complete mat impression underneath). None are more than smoothed on the inside and, though varying from fairly shallow (Cat. no. 322) to deep (Cat. no. 323), they may all be the bases of jars. Unusually, coarse fabric occurs most frequently in this category of base, with a total of nine: one apparently early, from Phases 1–3, three from

Phase 4 and five from Phase 5. Two of the least coarse have cord-impressions or faint-combing outside, and on the other examples either there is minimal smoothing only or the surface is left rough. Those instances in which enough of the side-wall is present from which to judge seem to be probably the bases of jars, and Cat. nos 318 and 321, for example, are almost certainly so.

Disc bases (Cat. nos 324–329)
There are even fewer true disc bases – only 14 – but they are distributed somewhat more evenly between the phases. Four, including two of the three from Phases 1–3, are of very fine fabric, very thin-walled and well made; one, Cat. no. 324, has the remains of a thick white plaster layer inside; and the other two are burnished inside and outside. Cat. no. 328, probably from Phase 4, has a pronounced high disc base with a clear mat-impression (see below); it is of fine fabric but with no signs of burnish. Cat. no. 327 (Phase 4 or 5), though worn on both surfaces, shows its original high gloss in the groove above the disc and must have been a delicate and impressive bowl. Bowl Cat. no. 108, from a Phase 4 pit, was also burnished, but was heavier and much less carefully made, the base being an irregular oval, and Bowl Cat. no. 109 probably also had a disc base. Other bases, such as Cat. nos 325, 326 and 329 (all Phase 5), are of coarse fabric, roughly finished and similar to the heeled bases above. Three more medium-fabric examples, without surface decoration (but one mat-impressed underneath), were from unstratified contexts.

Taken together, disc and heeled bases represent a significant proportion of bases, though with rather wide variations, that originate early and continue throughout the sequence. However, in all probability most vessels were begun as a disc of clay on which the walls were built up and, in the earlier phases, where only fine and medium vessels were produced, the original disc would be habitually smoothed into the walls, particularly where the cord-impressed decoration or burnish on the walls was continued unbroken over the base. Perhaps only on very thin-walled examples was it necessary to leave the disc as a thicker base for support. Many of the later heeled bases in coarser fabric, on the other hand, give the appearance of simply being more roughly constructed, so that the disc could still be seen.

It is on such undecorated medium- and coarse-fabric bases that the few clear mat impressions, already mentioned, were identified (Cat. nos 318, 323 and 328 [though this is of somewhat finer fabric]). These are all late (Phases 4 or 5), but this may be no more than coincidence, since not only are mat impressions difficult to see on small sherds but many impressions may have been obliterated by surface decoration.

Lids (Cat. nos 139–140)

Only two sherds, both from Phase 4, could be identified with any confidence as lids. They are too flat in shape for a bowl and have a rather irregular rim with a noticeably flattened horizontal edge underneath. Cat. no. 139 is of medium–coarse fabric and cord-impressed outside; Cat. no. 140 is of very coarse fabric and undecorated. Their diameters were particularly difficult to estimate, but are likely to be at least 170 mm and 200 mm respectively, sufficient to cover smaller holemouth jars or bowls. A suitably sized bowl inverted would do just as well, which may explain the scarcity of true lids, and other materials such as matting or cloth could also have been used, if tied down (see below under lugs). Jars with necks would have been even easier to cover or seal. There is only one jar with an internal ledge around the neck (Cat. no. 230) that would take a solid lid, and this was found in a much later context.

Handles (note: since these are all attached to either bowls or jars they are not listed separately in Table 4.1)

Ledge handles or lugs
These are rather rare, especially if we assume they occurred in pairs, but nevertheless are a persistent feature throughout the phases. There are a total of 17, varying from very short (projecting only 10 mm from the pot wall) to quite long (up to 30 mm), and from wide (70 mm) to quite narrow (25 mm). They taper towards the outer edge, which may be chipped and worn. Of the 10 still attached to rim sherds, four are on holemouth jars (Cat. nos 66, 171, 183 and 258 – the latter two are classified as holemouths rather than bowls, though the aperture is rather wide and the rims are too short to be certain of the angle); three or possibly four are on rather small slightly inverted-rim bowls (Cat. nos 184, 264, 265 and perhaps the small bowl Cat. no. 266: see below, *Appliqué*); and four more are on open bowls (the small hemispherical bowl Cat. no. 99, the large shallow bowl Cat. no. 297, the small shallow thick-walled bowl Cat. no. 294 and a very similar shallow bowl, Cat. no. 132, which has possible signs of a ledge or knob). Apart from the last, which was burnished, and Cat. no. 265, which was decorated with faint-combing, all of the ledge handles – 15 of the 17 – had cord-impressed decoration, often all over the ledge itself. The fabric of all the vessels was fine or medium–fine, and no signs of ledge handles were found on any coarse-fabric sherds. They were not found on any necked jars, and the numerous fine, thin-walled, burnished open bowls did not have them either.

The ledges on holemouth jars are short and near the rim, and could hardly have been used to lift the vessel, but rather to tilt it, or possibly to tie on a lid (perhaps of matting or leather). The same applies to the two inverted-rim bowls, Cat. nos 264–265, although that on Cat. no. 184, being set lower down and projecting more, would, if one of a pair, be suitable for lifting the vessel, as also would the handles on the open bowls Cat. nos 99 and 297. Of the seven on body sherds, three are short, three are long and one has broken, unusually, on the join, leaving only a scar. The ledge handles are normally well smoothed and luted to the vessel wall, reinforcing it, so that, with one exception, the surrounding wall breaks rather than the ledge breaking off at the join, although the break may be through the vessel wall and across the ledge.

Although no rim sherds with a ledge handle were found from clear early contexts, the large bowl Cat. no. 297, with a handle set low, is probably from Phase 2 (on the evidence of the matching base), and there are also two on body sherds of Phase 2, indicating that they were present in the early phases. From Phase 4 there were five: one short and wide on a holemouth jar, one longer and narrower on an open bowl, two more long and narrow on body sherds and one with only the scar remaining. In Phase 5 there are two short ledges on holemouth jars and one long ledge on an inverted-rim bowl. The six from unstratified contexts are all short.

Vertical lugs, horizontally pierced
Of these rare examples, Cat. nos 6, 60 and 144 come from Phase 3, 4 and 5 respectively. All are on the junction of the upright neck and sloping shoulder on fine-fabric jars: Cat. no. 6 on a small cord-impressed jar with a short rolled rim which has signs on the break of possibly another lug, giving at least four if all round the neck and six if evenly spaced. The other two examples are both on slightly larger jars: Cat. no. 60 shows clear signs of the next lug out of a probable four, with burnish in between and fine cord-impressions below, while Cat. no. 144 is too small a sherd to give any signs of further lugs and has only sketchy burnish. In all three cases the lugs are small, 25–30 mm deep and about 10 mm wide, pinched out to a ridge 20 mm high or more overall. The holes are between 2.5 and 4 mm in diameter and thus suitable only for the threading through of a fine cord or thong – that is, for suspension or to tie down a cover or lid.

The only other example of a pierced vertical lug, Cat. no. 331 from Phase 5, is also on the neck and shoulder of a jar of medium–small size (rim missing) and of very coarse fabric. It is represented by little more than scars, having broken more or less on the join with the body, probably owing to poorer preparation and perhaps a lower firing temperature for coarse ware. It appears to have been at least 30 mm wide and 20 mm high at the lower end, possibly slightly smaller at the upper end, and the circular hole between was 17 mm or more in diameter. This lug is much bigger than the three above and more like a loop formed around a stick or finger: that is, it is large enough to be used for lifting and carrying.

Knob handles
These are also rare. There is only one complete, Cat. no. 333 (from a deep post-Neolithic pit), on a coarse-fabric body sherd with the join clearly visible. It projects about 15 mm and is slightly oval, nearly 30 mm × 35 mm at the root and rounded at the top; the sherd is evidently from a vessel with a fairly large diameter. All other examples have little more than the scar, indicating that a good join was not achieved in firing (compare the ledge-handles, where this type of break hardly ever happens). Cat. no. 159, a medium–coarse holemouth jar of Phase 5, has a vertically flattened oblong 15 mm × 20 mm in size very close to the rim (compare sherd Cat. no. 333; but there the knob could be simply decoration: see below, *Appliqué*).

Two more are on the steeply sloping shoulder of jars with a short upright neck: one *c.*20 mm × 20 mm (? broken across) on jar Cat. no. 230, which also has an inside ledge, perhaps for a solid lid; the other, on jar Cat. no. 231 (*cf.* Plate 4.2), is a vertically flattened oval 15 mm × 25 mm in size broken off at a length of 10 mm and placed in the middle of a horizontal band of herringbone incisions. Both of these jars are from later pit fills, but Cat. no. 231 is of a typical Neolithic fabric despite its unusual features. There are faint indications of part of a scar on the broken edge of the sherd on one or two holemouth jars – Cat. nos 72 (Phase 4) and 243, both further from the rim – and on one body sherd. No clear example of a knob is earlier than the abandonment Phase 5.

Surface treatment and decoration

More than 80% of the total sherds have some form of surface treatment or decoration, and in the earlier phases the proportion is even higher. Surface burnishing and all-over cord-impressions are by far the most common treatment, but the relative popularity of the two is not easy to gauge accurately. This is because many vessels, especially the jars, originally had both, with a cord-impressed outer surface to the body and a band of burnish around the rim (for example, Cat. nos 16–19), and many small sherds, either from the body or from the rim, do not necessarily provide evidence for this combination. It is for this reason that the two accompanying charts, Figs 4.4 and 4.5 – the former based on the count of all sherds and the latter on that of rim sherds only – display considerable discrepancies, with, in particular, the relative proportions of burnishing and cord-impressions being reversed in all phases. However, both charts are consistent in showing a decline in the combined percentage of burnished and impressed sherds over the course of the occupation of the settlement, probably because of the introduction in Phase 4 of a new coarse fabric used for heavier roughly made vessels which are only rarely lightly burnished or cord-impressed.

Faint-combing is a variation of cord-impression used to produce a similar effect, but it occurs much less often. In addition, a few sherds are only smoothed – that is, wet-wiped or self-slipped – although all surfaces must originally have been similarly prepared before decoration. Almost all the fabric of the decorated sherds is fine (some very fine), or occasionally medium (under 6%), although a few decorated coarse-fabric sherds (3%) occur in Phase 3.

 Virginia Mathias

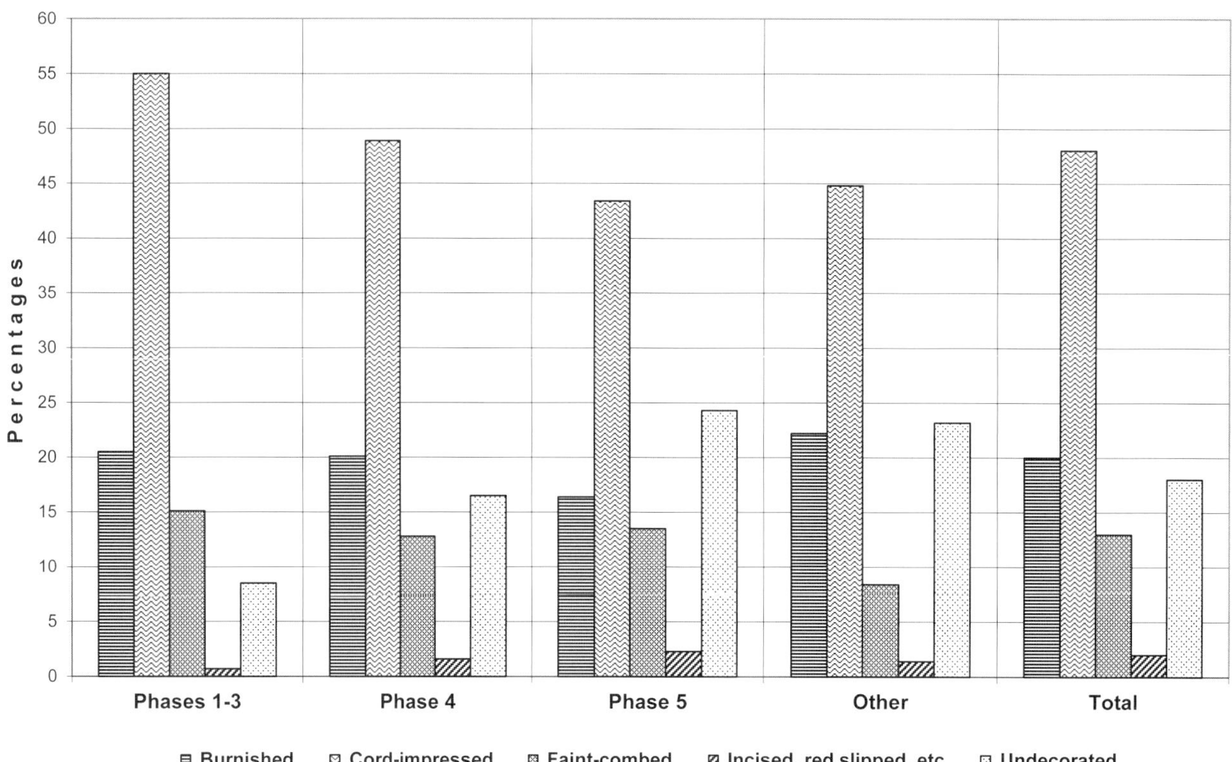

Fig. 4.4. Percentages of surface treatment: all sherds.

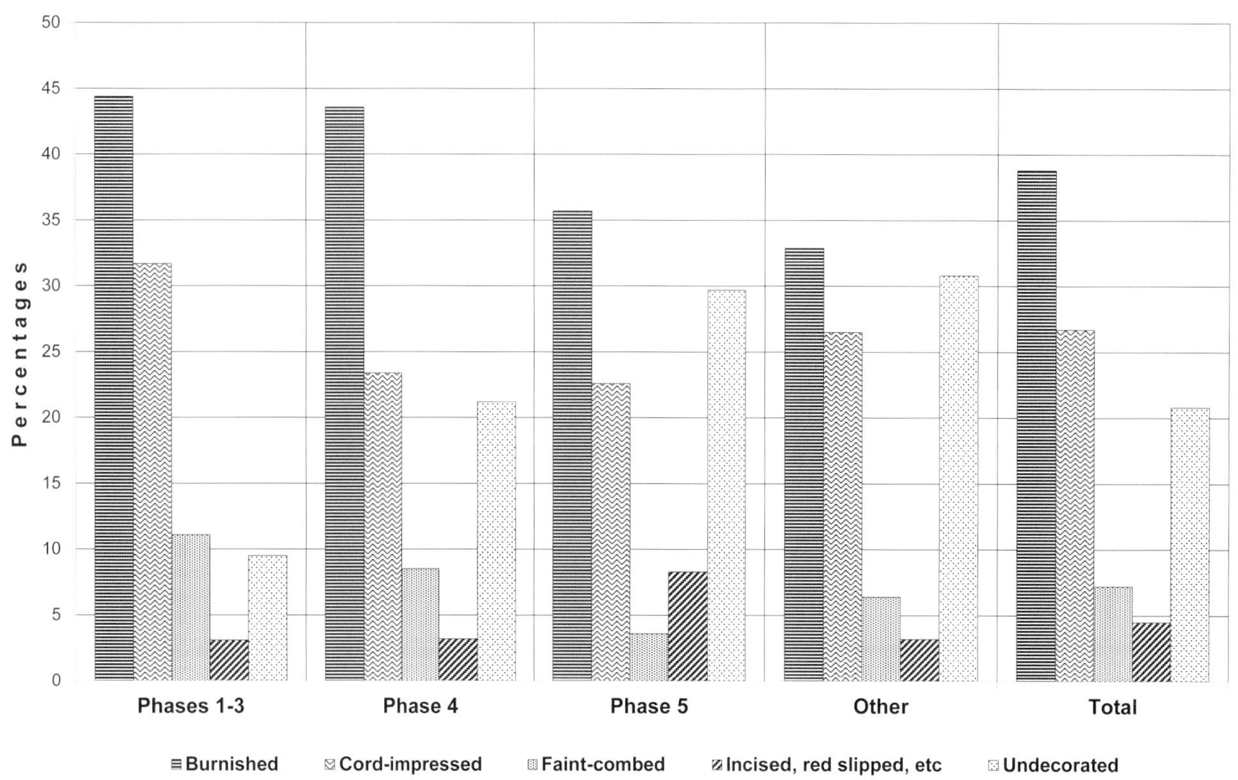

Fig. 4.5. Percentages of surface treatment: rims only.

Burnish (note: represented by solid dark shading in the illustrations, even if actually light-coloured)

Burnish is most common on the inside of open and wide-mouthed vessels, but it is also found on the inside and outside of jar rims. Judged by the care often taken with it, it can surely be considered as decoration as well as a waterproofing device.

Often the burnish is finely finished, varying from a high gloss (*e.g.* Cat. no. 130 [*cf.* Plate 4.1]) through to a smooth matt effect (*e.g.* Cat. no. 42 [*cf.* Plate 4.1]), with the individual strokes undetectable by eye or touch; compare this with many published descriptions of DFBW at other sites, where the strokes are usually said to be visible. However, the burnish may also be rather roughly done, streaky or irregular (*e.g.* Cat. nos 99 and 108 [*cf.* Plate 4.2]), especially on thicker-walled fine or medium ware, or sometimes even on coarse ware. The burnish has a considerable darkening effect: black (on black or dark grey fabric) and blackish-brown are the most common colours, but lighter brown (*e.g.* Cat. no. 108 [*cf.* Plate 4.2]), grey, buff (*e.g.* Cat. Nos 10 and 13 [*cf.* Plate 4.1]) and occasionally brick-red (*e.g.* Cat. no. 111 [*cf.* Plate 4.2]) occur. Some mottling of buff with grey or black may mean that buff was the original colour of the clay before firing. However, as noted above ('Methods of manufacture'), the fabric is usually much the same colour throughout its thickness and does not appear to have been deliberately given a dark surface in firing: that is, it is not so much 'Dark Faced Burnished Ware' as 'dark burnished ware'.

Burnish on the inside of vessels is quite common, whether these are burnished or cord-impressed outside, and this is usually well finished on bowls. Alternatively, the inside may be smoothed with strokes of some tool (or with the fingertips) or with a few burnish streaks only, this tending to be the case with holemouth jars and on medium- or coarse-fabric vessels generally.

Burnish is also quite common over the rims of vessels decorated externally with cord-impressions or combing, and there may also be a band of burnish around the outside of the rim, sometimes quite deep (*e.g.* Cat. nos 10 [*cf.* Plate 4.1], 25 [*cf.* Plate 4.1], 60, 164, 187, 194, 272, 300); which, as mentioned above, is the reason for the much higher percentage of burnish on rim sherds alone, as compared with body sherds. Rarely, incised pattern decoration (see below) is made through the burnish (*e.g.* Cat. nos 206, 231 [*cf.* Plate 4.2] and 269 [*cf.* Plate 4.2]).

Cord-impressions

Cord-impressed decoration all over the vessel, frequently set off by a well-burnished band around the rim, is the defining characteristic of the Tell Nebi Mend Neolithic pottery and is especially dominant in the early phases of occupation if the total sherd count is considered, although this, as already mentioned, may be deceptive. Nearly 45%

of the unstratified material is also cord-impressed. It is found almost always on fine or fairly fine ware, and only rarely on coarse. It apparently covers the whole of the outside surface, including ledge-handles, up to the rim, and often even under the base, especially on finer vessels (*e.g.* Cat. nos 313 and 314). However, if the inside is burnished, as with open bowls and some holemouth jars, or even if just smoothed or left quite rough, then the rim and a band below the rim outside may be burnished too, or this band left plain, *e.g.* Cat. nos 11 (*cf.* Plate 4.1), 13 (*cf.* Plate 2.1), 99, 122, 134, 215). The cords were impressed on a smooth surface but not on burnish, though there is occasional overlap (*e.g.* Cat. no. 180).

The impressions seem mostly to have been applied with a wide flat instrument, and it seems likely that the paddle used to thin out the vessel wall was bound round with spaced cord and used for this purpose; the edge or overlap of segments of the pattern is sometimes clearly visible on larger sherds. The impression was evidently made on a wet surface, probably a self-slip, while the fabric was still soft, and the result is clear and sharp. The cords vary from very fine indeed (0.5 mm), more like a strong thread, to occasionally quite thick, but are commonly around 1.5 mm and are neatly twisted. The lack of fuzziness or impressions of stray fibres suggests that these cords were made of long vegetable fibres or stalks rather than of spun animal hair (see remarks on the textile impression, Chapter 6). The holemouth jar Cat. no. 13 (*cf.* Plate 4.1) has decoration of the same impressed type which does not appear to have been made with cords; rather, a simple bunch of grass or other vegetation may have been used. While mats were certainly used to hold the clay base on which vessels were built up, the impressions from these were arranged differently and are rather unclear. The cords used for decoration may have been made for the purpose or originated from a different use.

Faint-combing

This is also found on the outside only and all over, giving a similar effect to cord-impression, and in some cases it may have been applied in the same way but with smooth fibres such as reed or grass stems wound around the paddle (*e.g.* Cat. nos 23 [*cf.* Plate 4.1] and 170). However, in other cases it was evidently done by dragging a 'comb' across the surface; the number of teeth – usually around six – can sometimes be clearly seen (*e.g.* Cat. nos 54, 79, 80, 160, 163 and 302). Experiments by Khalaily and Kamaisky (2002, fig. 6) using denticulated flint blades to make impressed decoration on Wadi Rabah Late Neolithic pottery showed that dragging such blades over the clay surface also produces a similar effect. Combing on finer vessels is rare (*e.g.* Cat. nos 23 [*cf.* Plate 4.1], 25 [*cf.* Plate 4.1], 265 and 272), but was the preferred decoration for coarse ware. Overall, however, it was much less common than cord-impression.

With the possible exception of the holemouth jar Cat. no. 163, patterned combed decoration is confined to a few body sherds. Cat. no. 340 (*cf.* Plate 4.2) shows a diamond or lattice pattern on fine or medium fabric, while Cat. no. 341 (*cf.* Plate 4.2) has a more complex pattern on the shoulder of a jar of unusual coarse grey fabric.

Some sherds have very faintly scored parallel lines, which may be the result of wiping, smoothing or scoring rather than intended as deliberate decoration (*e.g.* Cat. nos 4, 21, 24 77, 117, 133, 226, 284 and 289).

Incisions

The fine-fabric open bowl Cat. no. 269 (*cf.* Plate 4.2), which is rather small and deep, has incised decoration in the form of a swag of three incised lines descending from the rim to halfway down (and probably up to the rim again), and is roughly burnished over the incisions and inside (the two rim sherds shown are both from disturbed contexts, but a body sherd from the same bowl, with decoration, is from a Phase 4 pit). A larger shallow bowl Cat. no. 206 (Phase 5), with thicker walls, has a similar row of four lines running obliquely from the rim, but incised through the streaky burnish after firing.

There is just one example of an incised herringbone band, which occurs on either side of a knob on the shoulder of a jar (Cat. no. 231: *cf.* Plate 4.2), with streaky burnish above and below; it may represent the stitching on a leather vessel, as might the band of jab-marks described below. A small jar, Cat. no. 145, with a narrow inverted neck, has some deep oblique and irregular lines resembling cord or other impressions; and the incised lines (some quite light) on the shoulder of the holemouth jar Cat. no. 159 (*cf.* Plate 4.2) look like a rough imitation of combing (*cf.* jar Cat. no. 163). There are occasional body sherds similarly incised or deep-combed (*e.g.* Cat. no. 339 from Phase 5). The body sherd Cat. no. 338, also from Phase 5, with a basket-pattern of deeply incised parallel lines in opposed blocks, is unique. All these incised sherds are from Phases 4, 5 or disturbed contexts, and perhaps represent a late development.

Jab-marks

There are four examples of a row of close vertical jabs on the shoulder of a jar; in the two cases where the sherds are large enough to show this (Cat. nos 334 and 336), they are just below the junction with the neck. On Cat. no. 335 the indentations were made very neatly with a fingernail on a slightly raised or applied band, and there are extremely fine cord-impressions on one side of (or below) the band and burnish on the other; the inside of the vessel is also burnished. The fact that this small body sherd is from a fine, thin-walled vessel from early in Phase 2 gives an indication that some rare forms of decoration may have originated early in the settlement rather than in the later phases. Cat. no. 334 (*cf.* Plate 4.2) is also quite fine and

has a more irregular row of small jabs through burnish, while on Cat. no. 336 a corresponding line of larger jabs is made with the end of a reed or similar instrument on a large coarse-fabric jar. Both 334 and 336 are from post-Neolithic contexts, but another smaller sherd with fairly deep narrow jabs close together on the broken edge (not illustrated) is from a Phase 4 pit. These bands, both of jab-marks and herringbone incisions (see above), may well copy the stitching or drawstring line on a leather vessel.

The small fine body sherd Cat. no. 337 has all-over fingernail impressions outside and burnish inside; this is a unique example at Tell Nebi Mend of a type of decoration much more common on sites further north. Unfortunately this sherd was found in a post-Neolithic level.

Red slip or wash

This occurs very occasionally on poorly finished smoothed light-coloured pottery, either on the typical buff coarse fabric or on a finer, thinner version which is still poorly finished. In a few cases the slip has traces of burnish on top. Of three jars from Phase 4, a matt and rather fugitive slip is found on both the inside and outside (as far as preserved) of the small thick-walled jar Cat. no. 51, and on the outside only of the thin-walled flared-neck jar Cat. no. 55, where it is worn off round the rim. The thicker-walled upright-necked jar Cat. no. 61 has red slip both inside and outside, but only on the neck, with traces of burnish on top, no doubt to fix the slip. Cat. no. 242 (from a later context but most probably Neolithic) is a coarse-fabric holemouth jar with brownish-red slip outside and patchily inside. The very coarse-fabric bowl Cat. no. 304 (also from a later context) has a brick-red slip on the outside; the inside surface has worn away. Two fine shallow burnished bowls Cat. nos 126 (Phase 4) and 287 (from a later context again) apparently have a partial brownish slip or possibly paint on the pale surface under the burnish, but not in any recognisable pattern and in both cases it is possibly accidental.

Appliqué

The coarse buff body sherd Cat. no. 332 (*cf.* Plate 4.2), from Phase 5, evidently from quite a large vessel, has a roughly applied small 'coffee-bean', recalling the simple 'face-pots' from northern Iraq, as at Matarrah, an early Samarran site with a basal date 6700–6050 cal BC (Smith 1952, fig. 6 and pl. IX). Umm Dabaghiyah also has a tradition of relief designs of animals, human figures and faces applied to primitive local pottery, including apparent 'coffee-bean' eyes (Kirkbride 1972, pl. VII–XI). 'Coffee-bean' eyes are, of course, very common over a far wider area on clay figurines in the later Pottery Neolithic period. The unstratified small inverted-rim bowl Cat. no. 266 may have a similar broken 'coffee-bean' a little below the rim, although this could instead be the edge of a small lug. Cat. no. 333 is also a roughly applied knob on a coarse-fabric vessel, and may be functional, but could possibly be a nose on a 'face-pot'. At the Late Neolithic site of Shir, much closer to Tell Nebi Mend, dating to *c.*6500–6400 cal BC, a few coarse-ware sherds with plastic decoration also suggest these contacts; they include a body sherd with two 'coffee-bean' eyes and another with a human figure (Bartl and Nieuwenhuyse 2008).

Plaster coating

This is very rare, five examples in all having been found from Phases 1, 3 and 4. It comprises a thick (3–5 mm) lining on the inside of both fine- and medium-ware vessels (the traces of plaster on the outside of some vessels are perhaps most likely to have been left accidentally during application). On one fine body sherd the plaster has a smoothed and reddish-tinted surface. Often the plaster has worn or split off; the small deep bowl Cat. no. 117 had traces on the inside and outside, which could have been a thinner layer or wash, or accidental.

The plaster coating or lining of pottery vessels is common in the north-west of Syria, as at Tell 'Ain el-Kerkh, Ras Shamra, Tell Sukas, and in the ᶜAmuq. It does also occur further south, at Shir (where it is common), Hama (more rarely), Byblos and, in Jordan, at Wadi Shu'aib. It could have had a specific function, or hark back to the waterproofing of baskets in the pre-pottery era; it may also be related to the 'White Ware' vessels made of plaster (see Chapter 6).

Background and antecedents

As already observed, the Neolithic pottery of Tell Nebi Mend is well developed right from Phase 1. It does not belong to the initial stages of ceramic production, though it is always possible that earlier phases could still be buried under the later *tell*. The four calibrated radiocarbon determinations from around the first part of the 7th millennium BC are early compared with the date of the first appearance of pottery in the southern Levant, but there has long been evidence that pottery technology had a still earlier history further east and north, with simple coarse-fabric vessels going back into the 8th millennium BC (Le Mière and Picon 1999; the Tell Nebi Mend pottery corresponds to the third stage in this scheme). At Çatal Hüyük in Anatolia the lowest levels reached (XIII–IX) had small amounts of pottery and several calibrated dates going back to the end of the 8th millennium BC (Mellaart 1967; Hours *et al.* 1994, 390–1). On the western Iranian plateau recent surveys have found a number of Pottery Neolithic sites, some with pre-ceramic levels beneath. There were indications that pottery appeared equally early in this region, as, for example, at Zaghe (Negahban 1979), though current Iranian research indicate that the ceramic Neolithic is rather later.

Small quantities of primitive sherds, friable and often tempered with vegetable matter, have been reported from some sites in western Syria, which may have a bearing on the development and adoption of pottery. For instance, at Tell Ramad period II, which is largely aceramic and dated to the later 8th millennium cal BC, they precede the DFBW of Ramad III; at Late Neolithic Shir, near Hama, three sherds of 'soft ware' from the earlier period (among DFBW) were heavily vegetable-tempered and not definitely identifiable as pottery; at Tell el-Kerkh light-coloured sand-tempered 'Kerkh ware' of period 2a from a deep sounding was earlier than the DFBW of 2b; at Ras Shamra a small quantity of friable vegetable-tempered soft ware was found in the lower levels of period VB, which mainly had DFBW in its lower levels, overlying the aceramic period VC; and there was crumbly coarse ware late in Abu Hureyra period 2B, otherwise aceramic (see below in this section). At ᶜAin Ghazal in Jordan there were occasional sun-dried and even fired sherds from a long aceramic sequence (see individual reviews of these sites for references). Clay was used for many other purposes in aceramic times as well as during the Early Pottery Neolithic (EPN) and later: for example, in bins, lining storage pits, plastering walls and platforms and also for making small objects: figurines, beads and so on.

A number of sites in northern central Syria, especially a group in the Balikh valley, were previously reported to have produced coarse vegetable-tempered pottery in simple shapes and roughly finished, which was then believed to be at the beginning of a ceramic sequence for the region and of an early date. More recent excavations, notably at Sabi Abyad, show that this coarse ware was preceded by finer mineral-tempered and better-made pottery in more complex shapes, with some painted decoration in stripes. There is also a long aceramic sequence here on an adjacent mound, where radiocarbon dates indicate that the initial pottery phase is around 7000–6800 cal BC. These results from Sabi Abyad, and other current excavations at sites in the wider region of the upper Mesopotamian steppe, have prompted an interesting debate over the earliest appearance of pottery and the reasons for its adoption and development. It may well be relevant that pottery is scarce in this initial phase at Sabi Abyad and other sites in the region (Nieuwenhuyse 2009), while at Tell Nebi Mend it appeared in regular use in the lowest levels.

Further west on the Euphrates, the site of Abu Hureyra is mainly aceramic until late in period 2B, and pottery is still scarce in period 2C. The 2B settlement was estimated to cover approximately the late 8th–late 7th millennium BC (Moore *et al.* 2000, 251–9). This pottery was coarse, straw-tempered and crumbly, and mostly burnished to some degree; there were some traces of paint and also cordon decoration.

Subsequent ceramic development in north-eastern Syria is related more to the Hassuna culture to the east and to Umm Dabaghiyah, El-Kowm and Bouqras, further south. The pottery of the Euphrates is largely different from that of north-west Syria, where, however, mineral-tempered DFBW appeared at a comparable time and was similarly followed by coarser vegetable-tempered vessels. The rest of this review is therefore limited to western Syria and the

Levant, where the best parallels for the Tell Nebi Mend Neolithic pottery are to be found.

Regional comparisons

The northern Levant

There is still plenty of uncertainty in the framework of the EPN in the northern Levant, especially in the placing of material from older excavations and where dating is sparse. The chronological setting for the Tell Nebi Mend Neolithic, on present evidence, seems to be (moving from north to south) ᶜAmuq A, Qoueiq A, Tell el-Kerkh 2b, Ras Shamra VB, Sukas N lower levels, Qalᶜat el-Mudiq V, Hama M, Shir I–III, basal Tabbat el-Hammam, Tell Hmeira Neolithic, Labwe PN and, perhaps, Tell Ramad III. Byblos Néolithique Ancien is probably later. In the southern Levant the general use of pottery comes later, after an aceramic period referred to as PPNC which continues to develop well into the mid-7th millennium BC, especially along the western edge of the Jordanian plateau. The following Ceramic Neolithic of the Yarmuk tradition has antecedents here (ᶜAin Ghazal) as well as in the Yarmuk and Galilee areas. In the Jordan valley separate traditions of light-coloured pottery grew up, represented chiefly by the PNA and PNB at Jericho, which is at least partly contemporary with the Yarmukian to the east. Though the late Pre-Pottery Neolithic B (PPNB) and Pre-Pottery Neolithic C (PPNC) are missing at Jericho, these periods are represented on the coastal plain at Atlit Yam and Ashkelon (for references see below under each site).

By the time of the advent of the DFBW of the ᶜAmuq A horizon in the northern Levant, around 7000 cal BC, refinements in pottery techniques had taken place. Better understanding of the properties of clays, better choice and preparation of the clay, use of fine grit in preference to unsorted and vegetable temper, coil-building with more skillful drawing up and smoothing followed by careful beating out with paddle and anvil, and improved firing techniques had permitted the development of finer wares (Courtois 1992, 212–3) – smaller, thinner-walled vessels, no longer simply utilitarian containers, but attractive and practical, lending themselves to surface decoration or burnish as well as being easier to produce in quantity than fine stone vessels. Their uses were no doubt primarily as the link between the storage bin or water-skin and consumption, in transporting and preparing food and drink.

The shapes in this secondary period remained simple, and were similar for both finer and coarser vessels: open bowls, often curved in profile, commonly burnished and fairly small (100–200 mm in diameter), and therefore likely to have been drinking vessels; similar bowls with straighter sides (*i.e.* a more conical profile), and also some wider and shallower shapes, more like plates; other bowls, often larger and deeper, slightly inverted at the rim, probably to prevent the spilling of liquids – all these are well represented at Tell Nebi Mend. Holemouth jars can be achieved by extending the inverted rim of a bowl into a deeper vessel by the coil-building technique and narrowing the aperture, and a neck can then be added to facilitate both pouring and the plugging or covering of the opening. Knobs, ledges and lugs, already in use in the earliest forms, were retained for lifting and sometimes pierced for the tying of a cord. Some of the older shapes, such as oval and oblong vessels, perhaps derived from fixed bins or wood, leather and basketry containers, tended to disappear except for a few specialised categories; however, the basic shapes recur not only in the dark burnished wares but over a wide area from northern Syria to both the coast and inland in the central Levant, and eventually far to the south, while each region was developing its own characteristics.

The classic DFBW of the ᶜAmuq period A is from Judaidah (Braidwood and Braidwood 1960, 49), where it was reckoned at between 79% and 84% of the selected sample of sherds. Since comparisons between Tell Nebi Mend and the ᶜAmuq sites will figure largely in the following paragraphs, it is appropriate here to note that the basis of the statistical analysis of the ᶜAmuq pottery is not the same as that of the Tell Nebi Mend material. As has already been mentioned, at Tell Nebi Mend every sherd was counted. At the ᶜAmuq sites, on the other hand, according to the Braidwoods (1960, 30–1) 'the count is based on the field sortings, which are "by eye" proportionate reductions of the total sherds of any findspot to 10% of the original bulk'. It was only this estimated 10% which was then accurately counted, to give the statistics used in 'expressing the proportionate strengths of the wares which characterise' each phase. Furthermore, in order to avoid giving 'an impression of numerical accuracy which is not justified', these percentage proportions are only cited 'in terms of a range of 5%'; hence the figures quoted above for the DFBW of period A. Unfortunately, not every publication details the field sampling procedures as carefully and honestly as does the ᶜAmuq report, and when making the kind of inter-site statistical comparisons such as appear in the following paragraphs it is rarely possible to judge to what extent the data are strictly comparable. It can only be assumed that they indicate, at best, what the Braidwoods term an 'approximation to accuracy', making further mathematical manipulation impossible, and demanding only a cautious acceptance of any conclusions.

At Tell Nebi Mend, where all forms of decoration decline gradually through the phases of the settlement, burnish is found on some 39% reckoned on rim sherds alone, or 20% of all sherds, stratified and unstratified. The common cord-impressed decoration, usually on similar fabric to the burnished pottery, is often accompanied by a burnished band on the rim and burnish inside, especially on bowls; impressions are not made on top of burnish, as they cover the surface closely anyway. Together the dark-burnished and the cord-impressed decoration account for about 66% of the rims at Tell Nebi Mend, and almost the same proportion, 68%, of the total sherds. The same applies to the rarer faint-combed decoration (7% of all rims and

13% of all sherds), though this can also be found on coarser fabrics, which is rarely the case with cord-impression. The element of impressed or incised decoration at Judaidah, in bands or all over the outside (occurring on bowls only), is on burnished surfaces and counts as DFBW in the statistics; at 11% (Braidwood and Braidwood 1960, 51) it is much rarer than the cord-impressed and combed decoration at Tell Nebi Mend, where the percentages are 34% (rims) and 61% (all sherds), occurring mainly on jars and slightly inverted-rim bowls, and on a few, usually large, open bowls. (For details of the Tell Nebi Mend pottery surface treatment see Figs 4.4 and 4.5.) As much as two-thirds of the ᶜAmuq DFBW at Judaidah was found to have an oxidised layer or zone between a dark core and the black outer surface – hence 'dark-faced' (Braidwood and Braidwood 1960, 49). At Tell Nebi Mend the material is better described as dark-burnished: that is, the burnish merely intensifies the generally even colour through the fabric. Occasionally lighter reddish, grey or buff sherds have been given a darker surface by reduction, or an otherwise dark-fired sherd has thin light surfaces, almost certainly deliberate. Darker cores through incomplete oxidisation are rare, even in the buff coarse ware, though mottling does occur even in the finer fabrics. The Tell Nebi Mend burnish, though sometimes streaky (*i.e.* there are gaps between the strokes, as in the ᶜAmuq A ware: see illustrations), is generally finer and more even, especially in the earlier periods; the finest wares (some extraordinarily thin) are very well finished, often to a glossy polish (see above, 'Surface treatment and decoration'). These differing features are sometimes mentioned under descriptions of pottery called DFBW at other sites, and will be noted below.

The Judaidah DFBW is dominated by rather straight-sided bowls (95% of all rims: Braidwood and Braidwood 1960, 50), whereas at Tell Nebi Mend all bowls – straight-sided or rounded, open or slightly inverted at the rim, deep or shallow – decline from 62% to 43% during the period of settlement and account for only 52% of all registered rims. The small percentage of collared jars in DFBW at Judaidah has only a few parallels with Tell Nebi Mend necked jars, whose typical narrow upright or slightly inverted necks do not feature in the Judaidah assemblage; nor are holemouth jars mentioned. The latter do occur, thickened and rounded at the rim, at Dhahab (the other ᶜAmuq A site on typological grounds), as do simple hemispherical bowls; but there are other types here which are unknown at Tell Nebi Mend: shallow carinated bowls and larger deeper bowls heavily thickened and flattened at the rim and often also pinched out on the inner side (Braidwood and Braidwood 1960, 52, fig. 27). Ledge-handles are quite common on the ᶜAmuq sites (23% at Judaidah: Braidwood and Braidwood 1960, 51), but are rare at Tell Nebi Mend, numbering only 11, or less than 5%, of the total stratified rim-sherds. Red wash, mostly inside and in a band around bowl rims, is reported from Dhahab in ᶜAmuq A and Judaidah A and B, while at Tell Nebi Mend it is found only on a very few sherds in rather coarse buff fabric, including three necked jars,

a holemouth jar and a large bowl (see above, 'Surface treatment and decoration'), all late in the sequence or unstratified. The bases illustrated and described at Judaidah, simple flat or disc in DFBW, and disc or curved in coarse ware, are strikingly similar to Tell Nebi Mend bases, but the coarse-ware bowls and collared jars illustrated from Judaidah are not very close.

The pottery from the Qoueiq River Survey ascribed to period Qoueiq A ('Middle Neolithic', equating to ᶜAmuq A: Mellaart 1981) has, again, only some shapes similar to those at Tell Nebi Mend, and almost none among the decorated sherds (incised, impressed, etc.), whether burnished, colour-washed or coarse. The similarities are to be found, rather, with the monochrome burnished ware mainly from the site of Bahouerte: for example, the fairly high and narrow-necked jars Cat. nos 81 and 83 (Mellaart 1981, fig. 77) are quite like some Tell Nebi Mend shapes (*e.g.* Cat. nos 4, 5; 59, 61; 145, 146, 148–150; 227–229, 233, 234), although they belong to a group of over-fired 'clinky' ware usually tempered with white grits. From the site of ᶜAin et-Tell, the jar Cat. no. 112 with high narrow and slightly inverted neck (Mellaart 1981, fig. 80) is similar to a Tell Nebi Mend form (Cat. no. 1), though it is also in 'clinky' ware, and holemouths Cat. nos 105–107 from ᶜAin et-Tell look like the finer (and earlier) Tell Nebi Mend version of this shape. Qoueiq has very fine and well-fired burnished pottery, apparently earlier than in the neighbouring ᶜAmuq in period A, but the colours are lighter, buff to red, with black burnish appearing only in the following period B.

The large Neolithic complex of Tell el-Kerkh in the Rouj basin is shedding more light on the beginnings of pottery. Above late PPNB-type material (er-Rouj period 1) in the small mound Tell el-Kerkh 2 a sounding found the earliest pottery, Kerkh ware (er-Rouj 2a: Iwasaki *et al.* 1995; Iwasaki and Tsuneki 2003), already mentioned above. A few sherds of this ware, which is fine, sand-tempered and lightly burnished, were also found in excavation of the north-west area of the main Neolithic mound, Tell ᶜAin el-Kerkh, along with a few more of a thick, light-coloured coarse ware, heavily chaff-tempered; but the more common pottery was already Dark Faced Burnished Ware (Tsuneki *et al.* 1998, 12–14). In the succeeding period (er-Rouj Period 2b, equating to ᶜAmuq A) DFBW becomes predominant (up to 95%), with the remainder coarse ware, and Kerkh ware disappears (Iwasaki and Tsuneki 2003, table 32). A satisfactory sequence of radiocarbon dating is not yet available: one (rather imprecise) date for late aceramic er-Rouj 1 of 7350–6650 cal BC seems about right (Iwasaki and Tsuneki 2003, Appendix 1).

The repertoire of er-Rouj 2b has, in addition to typical early DFBW, some variations such as: (1) red-washed, which may be earlier than that of the ᶜAmuq at Dhahab (continuing into ᶜAmuq B) or the few pieces at Tell Nebi Mend (Phase 4 and later); (2) heavily white-grit-tempered, not seen at Tell Nebi Mend, though a small sub-group of usually cord-impressed sherds have copious amounts of pale greyish carbonate inclusions; (3) DFBW with some chaff temper (not seen at Tell Nebi Mend except rarely in very coarse ware, late in the sequence); and (4) a thick-walled variant, similar to occasional larger vessels at Tell Nebi Mend, such as a jar with upright neck of fairly fine fabric but roughly finished, darkish red and burnished inside and out (Cat. no. 232), or the large holemouth jar Cat. no. 246, both unstratified. The er-Rouj coarse ware, though present in small amounts from the earliest levels with ceramics, is rather more common in the later part of the 2b period and roughly equates to the Tell Nebi Mend coarse ware, which comes in only at Phase 4. At both sites the proportion of coarse ware to finer burnished or decorated pottery remains quite low.

Er-Rouj 2b shapes (Iwasaki and Tsuneki 2003, figs 54–58 and plates 11, 12; Tsuneki *et al.* 1998, fig. 11) are predominantly hemispherical and deeper bowls, and some necked jars, very similar to Tell Nebi Mend. The jars shown are all in DFBW (Tsuneki *et al.* 1988, fig. 11: 24 and 25; Iwasaki and Tsuneki 2003, figs 55:17–19; 57:4–10; 58:12–26), with variations including wide and narrow necks, low and high, upright and flared; and a few (not very close) resemblances can be found with Tell Nebi Mend examples. However, the thin-walled er-Rouj jars with high and fairly wide necks (Iwaskaki and Tsuneki 2003, figs 57:7–10; 58:24–26) are not seen at Tell Nebi Mend, nor are the very short-necked jars (Iwasaki and Tsuneki 2003, figs 57: 4; 58; 13); and all the thicker-walled jars with high, narrow or low, wide necks, which form the bulk of necked jars at Tell Nebi Mend, do not feature in the er-Rouj repertory. The jar with a long, slightly inverted neck at Tell Nebi Mend (Cat. no. 1, and many neck–shoulder sherds) is not represented either, and, most notably, no holemouth jars are mentioned.

Burnished bowls with curved or hemispherical sides are numerous in er-Rouj, and this simple shape differs little from those very common at Tell Nebi Mend; but the flatter-sided bowl, deep or shallow, that is also typical of Tell Nebi Mend is apparently rare (Iwasaki and Tsuneki 2003, fig. 57:18–20) and shallow bowls are unknown. Some bowls with slightly inverted rim or sides (*e.g.* Tsuneki *et al.* 1998, fig. 11:8–12) are quite comparable to the class of cord-impressed bowls of similar profile at Tell Nebi Mend, some with ledge handles or knobs. Open bowls, often larger and heavier, seem to be well represented (Iwasaki and Tsuneki 2003, figs 54:18; 55:15, 16; 56:17–23) and compare with a probably smaller percentage of large bowls at Tell Nebi Mend (Cat. nos 46, 125, 207, 297), all cord-impressed. Interestingly enough, the er-Rouj bowls are also often decorated all over, probably in imitation of the basketry or woven reed containers which preceded pottery. However, those bowls with a heavily thickened and flattened rim, often furnished with ledge-handles (*e.g.* Tsuneki *et al.* 1998, fig.11: 3–7), described as typical of er-Rouj 2b and widespread at other sites, are absent at Tell Nebi Mend.

The er-Rouj decoration (34% of DFBW: Tsuneki *et al.* 1998, 12) of nail-impressions, finger-pinching, pointed impressions and so on, overall and often in rows, is quite different from the cord-impressed and faint-combed decoration at Tell Nebi Mend (61% of all sherds), but the effect is similar. The er-Rouj decoration occurs almost entirely on bowls, while at Tell Nebi Mend it is on jars, especially holemouths, or on slightly-inverted rim bowls, and only on a few open bowls. The few bases shown (*e.g.* Tsuneki *et al.* 1998, fig. 11:18–20) are mostly flat, with the wall set on at a fairly well-defined angle; this type accounts for over half (55%) at Tell Nebi Mend.

There are therefore strong general resemblances between the Tell Nebi Mend Neolithic and the er-Rouj 2b pottery repertoire, although the details diverge in many ways, as should be expected from broadly related assemblages separated by a considerable distance.

Ras Shamra on the north Syrian coast has a similar sequence, from preceramic (Niveau VC) through Neolithic with Dark Faced Burnished Wares (VB and VA) to the advent of painted pottery (IVC) and Halaf-related wares (IVB) (Contenson 1977; 1992). The latest of three radiocarbon dates from the aceramic levels is 7060–6640 cal BC. The earliest pottery period (VB) can be equated with ᶜAmuq A, and has a single radiocarbon date which puts its end at around 6640–6440 cal BC. This period contains a very high proportion of DFBW, at 94%, plus an additional 2.7% of unburnished ware in the same fabric. The remainder is 'soft ware' (3.2%), friable and vegetable-tempered, mostly in the lowest levels of VB and therefore probably earlier than this date (Courtois 1992, 212–3), though the fabric and shapes – thick-walled basins – sound similar to the er-Rouj coarse ware (also very sparse, but continuing throughout the Neolithic). The DFBW shapes at Ras Shamra are mostly open bowls, some slightly inverted at the rim (*cf.* Tell Nebi Mend), rounded in outline (*bols, bassins*), and either tapered or thickened at the rim with incised decoration below (*i.e.* the common type at er-Rouj, missing at Tell Nebi Mend). There are also a few jars with a low wide neck, slightly flared, but there are no holemouth jars. Decoration is rare, at under 3%: fingernail impressions (*lunules*) are the most common, but rows of short lines and other forms of decoration are also present (decoration continues into period VA). Along with the customary knobs and ledge-handles there are also horizontally pierced knobs near the rim, though not the narrow vertically flattened type found on just three jar necks at Tell Nebi Mend (Cat. nos 6, 60, and 144). The DFBW pottery of Ras Shamra VB is well fired and described as already well developed; this, and the radiocarbon dating, correspond well with Tell Nebi Mend.

At Tell Sukas, further south along the coast, a small deep sounding was made to bedrock through some 2.5–3.0 m and 11 major levels of Neolithic deposits (Riis and Thrane 1974). No dating is available, but pottery was found from directly above bedrock (stratum N11). White Ware (lime plaster) was common (over 50% of all sherds) and though elsewhere this occurs only early in the Pottery Neolithic and in the preceding aceramic, here it continued in use throughout the Pottery Neolithic period. In N11 there was the familiar predominance of bowls (75%), the rest being collared jars. The bulk of the pottery was DFBW from the beginning: hemispherical bowls, some with the local peculiarity of a groove below the rim on the outside (Riis and Thrane 1974, figs 38–41, pl. I), the rims otherwise thickened or tapered; a few had ledge- or knob-handles, such as a deep bowl with a large horizontal lug in level N10 (Riis and Thrane 1974, fig. 75). Jars had both high and low necks, upright or slightly flared, as at Tell Nebi Mend; holemouths, however, were absent. Another local feature was that bases were usually round, flat bases being very rare: Riis and Thrane (1974, fig. 85) show one disc foot from level N9. Apart from burnish surface decoration was also rare: one sherd from N11 is illustrated with pattern burnish (Riis and Thrane 1974, fig. 56), which became common in the next period (ᶜAmuq B, er-Rouj 2c), and one with lentoid impressions (Riis and Thrane 1974, fig. 55). Though lacking the confirmation of absolute dates, the depth of the Pottery Neolithic deposits and the pottery itself suggest that the lower levels at Tell Sukas belong with ᶜAmuq A and the Tell Nebi Mend Neolithic.

Inland at Qalᶜat el-Mudiq the lowest level reported in soundings, Niveau V, was identified as Neolithic although, like the succeeding levels, it was redeposited in separate episodes of slump from the flanks of the *tell* (Collon *et al.* 1975), with the possible inversion of the stratigraphy and consequent contamination. A further sounding (Otte 1976) clarified the evidence of the Neolithic. The upper deposit Va contained some thick-walled coarse ware (also occurring in Niveau 4 with Ubaid-type painted pottery, but there probably intrusive). Apart from this Va contained dark pottery, black or brown and some red, which was fine-tempered and burnished on the outside. The relatively small quantities reported from the 1974 soundings comprised globular vessels; jars with upright necks (Collon *et al.* 1975, *e.g.* pl. III: 21), some quite high and some very short; rather straight-sided open bowls (Collon *et al.* 1975, pl. III: 22) similar to common shapes at Tell Nebi Mend; and a few horizontal ledge-handles and fingernail impressions, all on deep bowls with thickened and flattened rim (Collon *et al.* 1975, pl.III: 23), which is a common type at Tell el-Kerkh and occurs on several other DFBW sites, though not at Tell Nebi Mend.

The lower Neolithic deposit at al-Mudiq, Vb, considered free of contamination though also redeposited, had similar dark fine fabrics, burnished outside, colours (out of 181 DFBW sherds from the 1974 sounding 97 were black, 59 dark brown, 11 red and 14 cream – much as at Tell Nebi Mend) and shapes, such as bowls with slightly inverted rim and fingernail decoration (Otte 1976, pl. VII: 55), hemispherical bowls (Otte 1976 pl. VII: 51); jars with high upright necks (Otte 1976, pl. VII: 54) and very low short necks (Otte 1976, pl. VII: 52, 53) – present but uncommon at Tell Nebi Mend (*e.g.* Cat. nos 6, 230–231); and horizontal ledge-handles (Otte 1976, pl. VII: 55), all in DFBW. A total of 123 of the sherds from the earlier soundings (around

two-thirds) apparently are of small globular jars with round bases, very different proportions from most of the comparable Neolithic assemblages, where bowls usually predominate. Both levels Va and Vb contained White Ware.

At Qminas, not far from Idlib, midway between Aleppo and Hama, Neolithic deposits were found in a small sounding (Masuda and Shu'ath 1983). No pottery was discovered in the lower levels, but the upper levels, with at least two phases of stone-built architecture, had mostly DFBW, some incised, along with mineral-tempered orange coarse ware and straw-tempered soft ware, increasing in amounts towards the top. Shapes were hemispherical bowls and collared jars, bases were flat or roundish, heeled (Masuda and Shu'ath 1983, pl. 5:12, orange coarse ware) and disc (Masuda and Shu'ath 1983, pl. 4:10 and pl. 17:4, DFBW, incised), comparable to vessels at Tell Nebi Mend. Some finer vessels, such as a jar with a high upright neck (Masuda and Shu'ath 1983, pl. 3:2 lower fig. and pl. 16:4, burnished, red-washed), had notably thin walls (*cf.* Tell Nebi Mend types [Cat. nos 4, 5, 59, 148, 149], though these are often smaller). Coarse pottery jars had flared necks, as at Tell Nebi Mend. The heavy thickened and flattened rims on deep bowls (absent at Tell Nebi Mend) were also found at Qminas, as occasionally were small knobs applied near the rim (which are found at Tell Nebi Mend mostly in the later Phases), but ledge handles were apparently not. There was no radiocarbon dating, but the ceramic Neolithic levels were equated with ᶜAmuq A and B. The Qminas pottery may correspond to the later material from Tell Nebi Mend.

At Hama, on the Orontes and at no great distance from Tell Nebi Mend, the Neolithic Period M (layers 16–36) was characterised by DFBW and, in view of the depth of deposit (5.5 m), the lower part probably goes back as early as the Tell Nebi Mend Neolithic (Thuesen and Riis 1988). Halfway through the deposit (layer 26) plain unburnished wares appear; these are lighter in colour with a reddish wash (*cf.* the few red-slipped coarse fabric vessels at Tell Nebi Mend; necked jars Cat. nos 51, 55, 61; holemouth jar 242, bowl 304), mostly coarse, with heavy vegetable or mineral temper, and poorly fired, with a thick dark core. Open bowls were the only shape in these unburnished wares, and accounted for about 50% of the pottery.

The burnished wares were mineral-tempered and well fired, though with variations in the surface colour: as with the ᶜAmuq A sherds, light oxidised layers enclosed a dark core, and the surfaces were darker. Dark brown-grey was the most common colour, followed by black, although a few were light grey or orange, with the same dark core but without the darkened surfaces. Burnish strokes were distinguishable and left narrow, concave, horizontal or oblique traces. The shapes were mainly open bowls – upright or slightly inward-leaning, rounded, parallel-sided, straight-ish or curved in profile, but rarely flared and shallow. The few jars were holemouth or slightly inward-leaning with sloping shoulders; a single short upright neck is published (Thuesen and Riis 1988, 215, Cat. no. 10, from layer 17) and others may be indicated by neck/shoulder sherds. A few knobs and ledge-handles occurred, and bases could be flat or round. All these shapes are standard at Tell Nebi Mend, except the bowls with upright parallel sides, which do not occur at all. Decoration, on burnished ware only, was either incised or the usual fingernail impressions in horizontal bands, similar to the faint-combed decoration at Tell Nebi Mend, which occasionally was done in bands instead of overall (*e.g.* Cat. nos 163 and 315).

The recently excavated site of Shir,12 km north-west of Hama, is situated on a natural terrace above a tributary of the Orontes and covers about 4 ha. (For a recent summary, see Prehistoric Research: Excavation Shir. www.dainst. org/en/projects/shir 2013. [accessed February 2014].) A sounding revealed 6 m of Neolithic deposits. Immediately over bedrock and sterile clay was a burnt layer 0.2 m thick which already contained pottery, and from which carbonised grain provided a radiocarbon date of around 7000 cal BC. Above this, three successive occupation levels (I–III) contained hearths and fragmentary architecture, including plaster floors, and pottery, predominantly DFBW. There followed 1.0–1.5 m of earth, clay and ash containing much animal bone but no buildings, perhaps representing an open space for domestic activities. This was succeeded by three more levels (IV–VI) with rectilinear buildings having pisé or mudbrick walls and lime plaster floors, with a number of burials. The latest phase, VI, was dated to around 6500–6400 cal BC. This part of the site was abandoned before the end of the 7th millennium BC, though excavation in a different part of the site revealed deposits which may be a little later.

The parallels at Shir, approximately 80 km upstream, are considerable. The dating is similar, though Shir goes on until much later; both have buildings with lime plaster floors and pisé/mudbrick walls; both have fine DBFW pottery superseded by coarse, poorly finished wares, while the cord-impressed and combed decoration so typical of Tell Nebi Mend is also found at Shir and the hiatus in occupation at Shir between levels III and IV sounds remarkably like the final Phase 5 at Tell Nebi Mend; The differences, however, are interesting too. While the calibration ranges for the dates of the two sites make it impossible to relate them precisely, the earliest pottery at Shir is thought to be rather sparse, DFBW includes a considerable minority of oxidised sherds and, in the earlier period levels I–III, only an additional category of Light-faced Burnished Wares, and the coarse ware occurs here in a definite if minor proportion; none of these observations hold for Tell Nebi Mend Phases 1, 2 and 3. More important, it is only in Shir levels IV–VI that there are appreciable amounts of cord-impressed decoration, as part of a much-reduced occurrence of DFBW at around 10% (of a much greater quantity of pottery than earlier); the remaining 90% coarse unburnished ware is darker in colour than that at Tell Nebi Mend (where it is usually buff, and dark cores are rare). Cord-impression was the second most common surface decoration at Tell Nebi Mend (nearly as common

as overall burnish, included under plain DFBW at Shir) and most frequent in the earlier Phases 1–3. Though holemouth jars and inverted-rim and various other shapes of bowl occur at both sites, some with similar horizontal 'ear-shaped' lugs, Shir has a wider range of shapes, such as the burnished globular vessel with rather short and wide upright neck, which has not been identified at Tell Nebi Mend. The remains from the later period at Shir, including silos, large storage vessels and several burials, and the small finds – particularly stamp seals – surely point to a more developed era than the Tell Nebi Mend sequence. The beginnings may be earlier than at Tell Nebi Mend (Nieuwenhuyse 2009; Nieuwenhuyse *et al.* 2012).

The central Levant

In the central Levant there existed links which included the distribution of cord-impressed decoration, the definitive characteristic of the Tell Nebi Mend Neolithic pottery. To the west the natural route of the Homs–Tripoli gap through the Lebanese mountains leads across to the coastal plain, where a little to the north, at Tabbat el-Hammam, a sounding in a step-trench (TT1) found a 0.5 m thick layer above bedrock containing dark burnished pottery and unburnished cord-marked ware (Braidwood and Braidwood 1940). Of the 215 sherds selected by eye in the field, in approximate proportion to types, 85 were DFBW, 55 were cord-marked, 10 were coarse ware (apparently from one or two jars let into a floor from the next level I-2, above a thin sterile layer), 28 were indeterminate fragments, some probably early, and the rest were Early Bronze Age (EBA) or later.

Despite the stratigraphic problems a reappraisal by Hole (1959) presented a coherent assemblage of DFBW and cord-marked ware, which had the same vessel shapes and clay as the burnished pottery, though heavier inclusions were noted. The cord-impressions were all over the outside from rim to base and even underneath, and were thought to have been applied by a flat paddle wound round with closely spaced cord to give a textured effect (Hole 1959, 157). In the illustrations this decoration appears exactly the same as at Tell Nebi Mend, and was combined with burnish on the inside of bowls and even holemouth jars, continuing over the rim. The burnish, however, is described as consisting of irregular strokes, not the fine, even effect often achieved at Tell Nebi Mend. Colours of the fabric varied from red-orange-buff to brown and black and was duller where unburnished. The temper was mineral only, mostly white (limestone or flint) but also red and grey.

Braidwood indicates a predominance of hemispherical bowls (Braidwood and Braidwood 1940, 198) that are curved in profile, and Hole's fig. 3:1–3 demonstrates that this included cord-marked as well as burnished examples. Flatter-sided or more conical bowls evidently also occurred (Hole 1959, fig. 2:27, 29), at least in DFBW, with incised decoration (*cf.* Tell Nebi Mend Cat. nos 120, 124, 282); there were also some with a low carination (Hole 1959, fig. 2:7, 8), a type unknown at Tell Nebi Mend.

Hole notes that very deep bowls or holemouths are the most common shapes (Hole 1959, 154), and these correspond more or less to the Tell Nebi Mend categories of bowls with slightly inverted sides, usually tapered or roughly rounded at the rim (Cat. nos 21–24, 90, 95, etc.), and holemouth jars (Cat. nos 10–20, 65–83, 85–87, 91–93, 159–183 and 241–263). However, his illustrations show only a few resembling the former Tell Nebi Mend category – perhaps his fig. 2:9 and 30 (incised decoration), and fig. 3:4 (cord-marked) with a shallow but very long ledge-handle. This type of deep bowl with slightly incurving rim is represented at Tabbat el-Hammam also by the thickened and flattened rim, usually pinched inwards, that is evidently quite common on fairly large to very large vessels (Hole 1959, fig. 2:1, 2, 9(?), 11–14, these last better described as bevelled inwards; Braidwood and Braidwood 1940, fig.13:9, 10). Some of these have the standard cord-marked decoration (Hole 1959, fig. 3:7 and 8) and around half of them are furnished with a ledge-handle. This type of deep bowl with distinctive rim is similar (apart from the cord decoration) to those common at Tell el-Kherkh and occurring at most of the northern sites, while unknown at Tell Nebi Mend; the only tentative exceptions are perhaps Cat. no. 30 (small, fine), and Cat. no. 186, with cord-impressions.

True holemouths (*i.e.* more inverted to a narrower aperture) are also present at Tabbat el-Hammam, with a simple rounded rim (Hole 1959, fig. 2:10, 15), cord-impressions (fig. 3:5, 6) and ledge-handles, either near the rim (fig. 3:6) – compare Tell Nebi Mend (Cat. nos 171, 183 and 258) – or lower down (Hole 1959, fig. 3:5).

A straighter, slightly inverted shape (Hole 1959, fig. 3:9), of unknown diameter and, unusually, not burnished inside, may be neither of the above but rather an example of a jar with long inverted narrow neck set on a sloping shoulder, quite common at Tell Nebi Mend, where it is also usually cord-impressed (*e.g.* Cat. no. 1). However, the coarse-fabric, thicker-walled version at Tell Nebi Mend (Cat. nos 83, 84; and perhaps 238–240) has no illustrated parallels at Tabbat el-Hammam.

Of the collared jars (*i.e.* those with neck) at Tabbat el-Hammam, the short-necked type (Hole 1959, fig. 2:16; Braidwood and Braidwood 1940, fig. 13:6) is different from the few at Tell Nebi Mend (Cat. nos 6; 51; 230, 231). The medium-height examples of uncertain diameter are perhaps closer (Hole 1959, fig. 2:18 ; *cf.* Tell Nebi Mend Cat. nos 59, 60, 144; Hole 1959, fig. 3:10; *cf.* Tell Nebi Mend 61, 63, 64, 151–2, 143 and 156). The thinner-walled burnished and narrow-necked example (Hole 1959, fig. 2:19; Braidwood and Braidwood 1940, fig. 13:7) roughly resembles a unique fine black-burnished jar rim at Tell Nebi Mend (Cat. no. 2, and perhaps Cat. nos 154 and 155). The only higher upright neck (Hole 1959, fig. 2:17; Braidwood and Braidwood 1940, fig. 13:8) is much wider than the correspondingly high but narrow-necked jars of Tell Nebi Mend. The larger jars with wide flared neck and steeply sloping shoulders (Hole 1959, fig. 4; Braidwood and

Braidwood 1940, fig. 13:1–4) belong to the coarse wares mentioned above, presumed later, and are unlike the Tell Nebi Mend coarse-fabric jars.

The two bases shown, which are burnished (Hole 1959, fig. 2:20) and cord-marked (fig. 3:11), have simple shallow angles very common at Tell Nebi Mend. Ledge-handles occur on holemouth jars and deep bowls, as at Tell Nebi Mend, varying from narrow to deep, short to long, angular to rounded, and outward-tapering to squarer-cut. At Tabbat el-Hammam they are apparently fairly common and are found not only on cord-marked vessels but also on burnished bowls, which is not the case at Tell Nebi Mend, where they are rather rare. Oval or rounded knobs (Hole 1959, fig. 2:3, 4) are, likewise, rarer, but the flatter shape, vertically pierced (Hole 1959, fig. 2:23), has no parallel at Tell Nebi Mend, nor has the proper lug handle, squat and horizontally pierced (Hole 1959, fig. 2:24).

About a third of the DFBW at Tabbat el-Hammam also had incised or combed patterns round the rim of bowls or shoulder of jars. The herringbone bands on bowls (Hole 1959, fig. 2:27–29; Braidwood and Braidwood 1940, pl. XXII 2, 2nd row right) are similar to that on a burnished low-necked jar of Neolithic fabric at Tell Nebi Mend (Cat. no. 231), and the swags on a bowl (Hole 1959, fig. 2:31) and the zigzags on the shoulder of a jar (fig. 2:33) have possible parallels on both brownish/buff burnished bowls at Tell Nebi Mend (Cat. nos 206, 269).

Further south, at Byblos, the earliest period, Néolithique Ancien, is ascribed to a later development of the Pottery Neolithic, with comparisons with ʿAmuq B and equivalent deposits in the north Levant, as well as with the Yarmukian pottery culture of the south; one calibrated radiocarbon date suggests a date in the latter part of the 7th millennium BC (Dunand 1973, 34; Hours *et al.* 1994, 89, 389). However, among the body of excavated and published material from Byblos Néolithique Ancien deposits a few sherds of typical cord-impressed pottery can also be noted (Dunand 1973, pl. XLIX, middle row, 1st left), including a bowl with a ledge-handle and vertical cord-impressions (same row, 3rd left). This is not one of the common Néolithique Ancien forms of decoration, which, however, often have a similar textured effect, and these sherds may have arrived at Byblos by trade or exchange, although the rather later date could mean that they are residual from an earlier settlement somewhere else on this large site.

As for shapes, the Byblos Néolithique Ancien has not only a much larger repertoire but one which includes many whole profiles, so often lacking in the smaller samples from deeper soundings elsewhere (Dunand 1973, 42–61, figs 16–28). Among this greater wealth of shapes can be found most of those already identified at earlier sites further north: the usual simple hemispherical or shallower bowls (*coupes*) in the range of 120–150 mm diameter, mostly upright at the rim and with curving profile (though a few inverted above a low carination); the round or slightly flattened bases; the deeper, heavier basins (*jattes*), about as wide as they are high (Dunand 1973, figs 17, 20, 21, 23, 24), with upright or slightly inverted sides and sometimes with various lugs or ledges near the rim (an indication perhaps of the full profile of some of the slightly inverted-rim bowls at Tell Nebi Mend, such as Cat. no. 23); some holemouth jars (Dunand 1973, figs 17, 18, 25); the jars with inverted neck and bulbous body (Dunand 1973, figs 17, 27), or with short upright neck, either fairly narrow, wide (Dunand 1973, figs 17, 18) or everted (Dunand 1973, figs 18, 25, 26); and jars with very high cylindrical necks (Dunand 1973, figs 18, 25) typical of the ^cAmuq B horizon and of Tell el-Kerkh (er-Rouj 2c). Some of these shapes common to the earlier period seem at Byblos to be heavier and more roughly made, and while burnish is still common it is not universal. Probably these basic shapes continued in use and are likely to be found even in rather later contexts, especially on larger sites where the repertoire is wide.

There are examples at Byblos of white lime-plaster lining to the insides of bowls (*e.g.* Dunand 1973, pl. LVI), which is rare at Tell Nebi Mend but very common at sites further north. White Ware occurs only as occasional fragments.

Inland, to the east of the mountains, the northern and central Beqa^c valley is more easily accessible to western Syria than the narrow littoral of the Lebanese coast. At the headwaters of the Orontes, some 50 km south-west of Tell Nebi Mend, the site of Labwe was found to have early Neolithic pottery during detailed surveys of the region (Copeland and Wescombe 1966, figs XXXVI and XXXVII, pls 7 and 11). Some sparse surface material from Tell Labwe North included DFBW sherds with cord-impressed decoration. At the edges of the extensive low mound of Tell Labwe South both EBA and EPN were exposed by terracing and bulldozing for a road. At the southern end and in the central area of the latter tell, substantial plaster floors and walls were visible, possibly of pre-ceramic periods. To the north-west, recent terracing had exposed further plaster floors and walls, with flints of Byblos Néolithique Ancien type and cord-impressed DFBW on the surface.

The northern end of Labwe South was also an EPN site, and this was the location of two soundings (Kirkbride 1969). The excavations produced in one area (A) two substantial stone-walled buildings with plaster floors; the lower one apparently contained only White Ware, but the upper also had pottery in small amounts: fine, hard DFBW coloured red, black and brown, burnished on both sides or with combed or cord-impressed patterning. One whole profile is of a hemispherical bowl slightly inverted towards the rim and with a high angular ledge-handle, a slightly flattened base and combed decoration (Kirkbride 1969, fig. 1 lower) which could easily have come from Tell Nebi Mend (*e.g.* Cat. nos 183, 258 and 265, all of similar size with ledge-handles or knobs and cord or combed decoration, or the smaller versions Cat. nos 99, 183, and 264). There were similar bowls with cord-impressions, and also globular vessels, perhaps holemouths, but necked jars are not recorded. The DFBW is said to be similar to that

from Tabbat-el-Hammam. There was no coarse pottery (*cf.* the earlier Phases at Tell Nebi Mend), but White Ware was abundant.

In the other excavated area (B), of about 4 m of Neolithic deposits the upper part was cut into by large pits, destroying any architecture except fragments of plaster floors, as at Tell Nebi Mend. The lower part apparently consisted of courtyard deposits, also badly cut by pits. The upper pits contained White Ware and pottery, the lower pits White Ware only, and in small soundings of the lowest metre of deposits neither were found. The latest PPNB levels produced three calibrated radiocarbon dates of around the early part of the 7th millennium BC (Kirkbride 1969, 50; Garfinkel 1999b, 6).

The survey illustrations include a curved bowl with slightly inverted rim and cord-impressed decoration (Copeland and Wescombe 1966, fig. XXXVII (a) and pl. 7a, 1) which is absolutely typical of this category at Tell Nebi Mend (*e.g.* Cat. no. 23). Also shown are shallower and deeper bowls, both curved and straighter-sided, and a holemouth jar, all with standard all-over or more widely spaced cord decoration. Colours are dark red, reddish-buff, black, dark grey and buff, and diameters range from 160 mm to 200 mm – that is, comparable to the same types at Tell Nebi Mend. Overall the amount of pottery obtained from Labwe is small, but all indications are that it is very close to that of Tell Nebi Mend.

At Ard Tlaïli, mainly a later Neolithic and Chalcolithic site between the headwaters of the Orontes and the Litani, occasional sherds of Labwe type are found, such as cord-impressed (Kirkbride 1969, pl. V, top left and 2nd row centre), presumably residual sherds (as at Byblos), indicating that occupation of Labwe/Tell Nebi Mend type continued further south. But other (unexcavated) early Neolithic sites in the central Beqa^c had no cord-impressed pottery, such as Tell Neb^ca Faour, where DFBW (some incised, brushed or comb-marked: Copeland 1969, 87–90) and coarser pottery were found, or nearby Tell Shamshine, which had DFBW and coarse pottery (Copeland and Wescombe 1966, fig. XLVII). These were equated with Byblos Néolithique Ancien, and may therefore be later than Labwe, as perhaps is Tell Hashbai, with DFBW and red slipped pottery, some incised (Copeland and Wescombe 1966, fig. XXXV); *cf.* the few late examples of both at Tell Nebi Mend.

The style of cord-impressed decoration found in the Beqa^c and on the central coastal plains is so distinctive, and so close to that of Tell Nebi Mend, that there can be no doubt as to a common chronological horizon and close contacts within these areas.

In the Damascene region further to the south-east, Tell Ramad is interesting for the southernmost occurrence of dark burnished ware as its predominant type, in pits or silos and on an earth floor of Period III. It was accompanied by White Ware (which had been more plentiful in the previous substantially aceramic period II) of PPNB type, accompanied by a very few sherds of primitive vegetable-tempered friable pottery (Contenson and Van Lière 1964, 1966; Contenson 1971; 2000). Three radiocarbon dates in Period II (there are none from Period III) range, when calibrated, over the first half of the 7th millennium BC (Contenson 2000, 21, tableau 9), which the excavator equated with the PPNC of the southern Levant.

In Period III 87% of the pottery was DFBW-related (including coarse ware of the same fabric type). It was mineral-tempered and usually dark-coloured – brown, black, grey and more rarely buff. Common shapes were hemispherical bowls, some with slightly inverted rim, or shallower bowls of small to medium size (around 150 mm in diameter) with flattened or rounded rims, some with knobs or ledges below the rim, and commonly with ring-bases, also some flat; and jars with low cylindrical or slightly everted necks, some with horizontally pierced vertical lugs and one shown with a large loop lug or handle (Contenson 2000, fig. 107:2; *cf.* Tell Nebi Mend Cat. no. 331). The surfaces were burnished entirely or around the rim and base only, with the zone between either left undecorated or with incised (including vertical lines, zigzags, fingernail-impressed), combed or scratched all-over decoration that was applied before firing (*e.g.* Contenson 2000, fig. 105:9); however, the proportion of decorated vessels was under 10% (Contenson 2000, 235, tableau 69). There were also larger vessels (*bassins*) with the outside surface smoothed only and a layer of white plaster on the inside (*cf.* this common practice in the northern Levant, and the few examples at Tell Nebi Mend). This pottery was equated with ᶜAmuq A and Ras Shamra VB, and also Byblos Néolithique Ancien, though from the description the pottery is less developed and may be earlier than the latter. It was said to be closely related to that of Tabbat el-Hammam and the Beqaᶜ sites, and the decoration could well be a local equivalent of the Labwe/Tell Nebi Mend type. Light-coloured red-slipped sherds were found on the surface and equated with Byblos Néolithique Moyen; compare the few from the later Phases at Tell Nebi Mend.

The southern Levant

Further south still, in the southern half of the Levant, the tradition of dark or dark-faced burnished pottery all but disappears. This is partly due to the persistence of aceramic traditions well into the first half of 7th millennium BC, followed by the later development of pottery of different fabric from that of the north, usually light-coloured and often painted or red-slipped. As in the north, there are difficulties with the chronology and radiocarbon dates are few, as are stratified sites (but see Garfinkel 1999b). Roughly speaking, the widespread and stable pattern of the PPNB breaks down around 7000 BC, and is replaced by, or develops into, a further aceramic culture centred mainly on large sites on the western side of the Jordanian plateau and associated wadis, with well-developed architecture and a rather impoverished flint industry, for which the term PPNC has been coined. This in turn is replaced towards the

middle of the 7th millennium BC by the Yarmukian pottery culture, which extends to the upper Jordan valley and lasts into the 6th millennium. A rather different pottery culture develops in the Jordan valley and to the west, defined by the Jericho assemblage of Jericho IX/PNA and PNB. The Yarmukian pottery has resemblances to the Jericho material, and both have some affinities in shapes and decoration to the Néolithique Ancien and Moyen of Byblos.

At Tell Batashi on the coast (Kaplan 1958a) DFBW was reported from the lower levels, 4b; it may not be directly related to the DFBW of the northern Levant, but the presence of any pottery produced in a reducing atmosphere so far south is noteworthy, especially as it is at or near the beginning of the pottery sequence for this region. The lower levels also contained painted pottery, considered by the excavator to be in the initial stages of this craft. The painted pottery was more developed in the upper levels, 4a, where the burnishing of unpainted vessels continued. This Neolithic pottery was equated with that of Jericho IX, but it is not clear from the brief English summary whether 4b might be even earlier. The shapes of the undecorated pottery (Kaplan 1958a, figs 7 and 8, Hebrew section) are crude and thick-walled, and there is not much resemblance to northern types. The following Stratum 3, above, was mainly Chalcolithic but also contained some Yarmukian pottery, which may therefore be later than Jericho IX, at least in this area. Similarly, at Lod, a thin Neolithic deposit was found containing Jericho IX painted pottery together with pottery burnished inside and out; most was light-coloured, but some was blackish (Kaplan 1977, 291*).

Kefar Giladi, in Upper Galilee, has two Neolithic phases, the upper containing a substantial stone wall and the lower ashy occupation debris resting on bedrock. There are no differences in pottery or flints between the two. The pottery, some of which was cord-impressed, is referred to as DFBW and was thought to be the earliest pottery in the area (a small number of Yarmukian sherds were intrusive). The only radiocarbon date of 8450–7550 cal BC, from the lower phase, must be considered unacceptably early (Kaplan 1958b; 1966). It should be noted that this site is not very far distant from Tell Ramad in the Damascene area, and connections with the Beqaᶜ valley cannot be ruled out.

At Jericho there are no radiocarbon dates for the Pottery Neolithic, neither PNA nor PNB, which follow the PPNB after a period of abandonment. (The latest date for the PPNB – apart from one that is clearly aberrant – has a range of 7550–6850 cal BC.) Among the large amount of Neolithic pottery published parallels can be seen for many of the simple shapes found at Tell Nebi Mend: various open bowls, curved or hemispherical in profile, with tapered, rounded or squared-off rims (Kenyon and Holland 1982, fig. 1); straighter-sided, shallow/flared bowls (fig. 3); flat platters (fig. 4); deep upright-sided bowls or basins (figs 5, 7); inverted-rim bowls bordering on holemouth jars, some with projecting knobs (fig. 6); slightly inverted-neck jars (figs 8, 10); high narrow-neck jars; low wider-neck jars with thicker walls (fig. 10); true holemouth jars with variously shaped rims, some also with knobs (fig. 12); and a variety of handles including pierced lugs and ledges, especially on slightly inverted-rim bowls (figs 13, 14). However, the general impression is that Jericho PNA has a much greater proportion of larger and probably coarser-fabric vessels, and that there are features which are common here but unknown at Tell Nebi Mend, such as proper lug or loop handles on jars (though *cf.* Tell Nebi Mend Cat. no. 331), jars with high wide necks, very straight-sided or conical bowls, wide flat bases and so on. The fabrics of the PNA vessels are mostly light-coloured; reddish slip is quite common, though burnish rather less so. There is some simple painted decoration, rarely incised, but no dark burnish or overall patterning as in the central Levant and Byblos Néolithique Ancien.

In Jericho PNB (Kenyon and Holland 1982, figs 21–30, various) mat red slip is even more common than in PNA, and occurs with reserve bands of herringbone incisions typical of Yarmukian decoration. Many of the simple Tell Nebi Mend shapes are still found, a further indication that these parallels may be due to similar technology and/or functions rather than to any direct link, as the PNB repertoire is certainly some centuries later: Garfinkel (1999a, 1–7 and 106) equates this period with the Chalcolithic Wadi Rabah culture.

ᶜAin Ghazal, on the Jordanian plateau just north of Amman, has a stratified sequence from PPNB, its late phase extending to the turn of the 8th–7th millennium BC through PPNC, with buildings imposed directly on PPNB structures and dates ranging from 7050 to 6130 cal BC. This is followed by a Yarmukian period, when some PPNC walls were reused or incorporated into the new buildings, and there is strong evidence for continuity in the lithic material. These buildings were associated with crude undecorated pottery similar in fabric and technology to Yarmukian pottery (Rollefson 1993, 92), presumably representing an earlier stage, and these undecorated sherds continued to occur among those with more typical Yarmukian decoration. The excavators consider that pottery technology evolved at the site, in view of the occasional sun-dried and fired sherds which occurred throughout the long aceramic sequence. The earliest specifically Yarmukian pottery was red-painted or slipped, and the classic bands of incisions, with or without fields of red paint or slip between, were apparently a later development (Rollefson *et al.* 1993, 117). Pottery shapes include the usual straight and curved open bowls, possible holemouth jars and slightly inverted-rim bowls; and the classical Yarmukian decoration of red slip and herringbone bands is present (Rollefson *et al.* 1993, figs 9–10).

Wadi Shuʾaib, in a fertile wadi descending from the Jordanian plateau, is another large site of the mid–late PPNB and PPNC, with both Yarmukian and Jericho PNA pottery (possibly contemporary) in apparently undisturbed upper layers. The pottery illustrated (Simmons *et al.* 1989, figs 3 and 4; 2001, figs 12–13) includes straight-sided and curved open bowls, possible holemouth jars, jars with

high and narrow or short and wide necks, and both flat and heeled bases. Out of several dates for the aceramic periods one, from late PPNB, fell around the mid-8th millennium BC (other late PPNB dates seem either too old or too recent), and one from PPNC levels in the late 8th millennium BC (another is older still and unsatisfactory). There are no dates reported for the Pottery Neolithic levels (Simons *et al.* 2001, 28, table 10).

Overall, dates for the Yarmukian period are still rather sparse (Garfinkel 1999b, 10). ᶜAin er-Rahub, near Irbid in northern Jordan, has one of the earliest, 6500–6380 cal BC (Muheisen *et al.* 1988). As well as a variety of bowls and necked jars, this site has true holemouth jars (Kafafi 1989, Cat. nos 36, 40), and one jar-neck designated DFBW (Kafafi 1989, Cat. no. 33), a relatively thin sherd with a high gloss on a dark slip (see also Kafafi 1993). Otherwise the vessels appear to be rather thick-walled and heavier than the earlier dark-burnished or DFBW of the ᶜAmuq A chronological horizon. Munhata, in the north Jordan Valley, has PPNB deposits (Niveau 3) in which were found a few brown burnished sherds, assumed to be intrusive; one had a thick white layer inside well known from DFBW sites in the northern Levant and also occurring at Tell Ramad and sporadically at Tell Nebi Mend. Following a hiatus in occupation equated by the excavator with Byblos Néolithique Ancien, there were deposits with Yarmukian pottery (Niveau 2) that gave two dates of 6650–5800 and 6600–5750 cal BC, equated with Néolithique Moyen.

Other sites have Yarmukian deposits only, such as Shaʾar Hagolan on the Yarmuk river (Stekelis 1972; Garfinkel and Miller 2001) and Abu Thawwab on the Jordanian plateau (Kafafi 1988; Kafafi 2001), the latter with two dates ranging around 5470–4260 cal BC.

Descriptions of Yarmukian pottery are sometimes brief for the smaller sites or where there have been only small-scale excavations. However, more material is now available from the recent excavations at Shaʾar Hagolan (Garfinkel and Miller 2001), Munhata (Garfinkel 1992) and Abu Thawwab (Obeidat 1995; Kafafi 2001). The following comparisons with the Tell Nebi Mend Neolithic pottery rely largely on the analysis of the Yarmukian assemblages by Garfinkel (1999a), with reference to the illustrations therein.

In size, the Tell Nebi Mend vessels mostly come within the range of the small Yarmukian types, the former's largest (usually coarse) vessels being only medium-sized in Yarmukian terms. In fact, medium and large vessels account for the great majority of the Yarmukian pottery, as at Munhata (Garfinkel 1999a, fig. 7). Among the smaller types, examples occur of open bowls with curved or straight profiles, slightly inverted-rim bowls or possible holemouth jars (fig. 8), shallow bowls (fig. 15) and jars with various kinds of high, low, flared or upright necks, often with small loop handles (fig. 24). However, most of these smaller vessels seem rather thicker-walled that the common types at Tell Nebi Mend. The typical Yarmukian large jars with high wide neck, loop handles from neck to shoulder and incised-band decoration (fig. 26) bear little resemblance even to the later coarse-ware jars from Tell Nebi Mend, although loop handles are apparently coming in by the end of the Tell Nebi Mend sequence (Cat. no. 331). Chalices or footed bowls are common in the Yarmukian assemblages but absent at Tell Nebi Mend, though the basic shape occurs in White Ware there and elsewhere. The fabric of Yarmukian pottery is usually light-coloured, rather coarse and mineral-tempered, sometimes with vegetable matter added. The distinctive incised, slipped or painted decoration is also quite different from any at Tell Nebi Mend. Small quantities of White Ware are usually found on Yarmukian sites, surviving from its long tradition in the PPNB.

It appears, therefore, that the dark burnished pottery of the north and central Levant begins considerably before both the Yarmukian and the tradition represented by Jericho IX/PNA (which was probably not substantially earlier and overlapped in space as well as time). In both the Yarmukian and the Jericho Pottery Neolithic pottery seems to have developed initially with coarse utilitarian vessels, rather than with the fine, small pottery vessels which predominated in the northern half of the Levant, perhaps in imitation of the fine stone bowls which originated in the aceramic period. Prior to this, while in the south the aceramic tradition continued to develop as the PPNC, there are a few indications that the earlier northern technology may have filtered a little way down the coast to, for example, Tell Batashi and inland to sites such as Munhata and ᶜAin er-Rahub, and may have been one factor in the acceptance of pottery into common use in the south.

Summary and conclusions

The evidence for the origins of pottery is still sparse. There are still gaps in the chronology as well, and a satisfactory sequence of dates for the transition from aceramic to ceramic deposits has not yet been established everywhere. However, the indications from calibrated dates so far are that, before 7000 BC in the region of northern Syria, and perhaps even earlier on the Anatolian plateau, the first pottery was beginning to be used in a few areas. The significant sites of Ras Shamra on the coast and Tell el-Kerkh inland, with well-established aceramic settlements, are among those reporting this development, which will probably prove to be the foundation on which the succeeding appearance of 'Dark Faced Burnished Ware' was based, spreading out over the whole of the northern Levant. Other centres of early development of pottery technology may yet be uncovered in areas favourable to settlement, such as the Damascus basin (Tell Ramad) and northern Jordan valley, and even on the coast, where Byblos is perhaps the best candidate.

The Neolithic settlement at Tell Nebi Mend is part of this wider province of dark burnished pottery covering the northern half of the Levant, but more specifically it belongs to a smaller region extending down to the coast (Tabbat el-Hammam and probably Byblos), up the Beqaᶜ valley (Labwe) and with connections down the Orontes valley at least as far as Shir. The close connection between sites in this restricted area is shown above all by the identical decoration of their pottery with all-over cord-impression, and must surely represent a tribal grouping or similar relationship.

Pottery catalogue: prefatory notes

The Catalogue of drawn pottery is arranged initially by phase (Phases 1–3 being grouped together, for reasons already explained) and then by form, the only exception being that examples of bases and a few miscellaneous pieces (handles, decorated sherds, etc.) are grouped together at the end irrespective of phase. In those cases where there is some doubt as to the precise phase of a vessel it is included in the most likely section of the Catalogue, but a question mark or a possible alternative phase is inserted in the appropriate column. If the vessel, although clearly Neolithic by virtue of its attributes, comes from a known post-Neolithic phase, that phase is given in square brackets (*e.g.* [7]), or if from an as yet undefined phase simply as [Post-Neo.]. Disturbed contexts are termed 'Mixed' or 'Disturbed' in the Phase column.

All the pottery drawings here are printed, unusually, at the scale of 1:2, since this enables the full variety of the typical cord-impressed and combed decoration to be shown most clearly. Unfortunately it is not possible to show the variations in the colour and quality of the other characteristic surface treatment, surface burnishing, with similar accuracy in a line drawing. In their ᶜAmuq report the Braidwoods attempted to solve this problem by marking the limits of the burnishing with small arrows alongside the drawn profiles of the sherds (Braidwood and Braidwood 1960, 37), but this is only effective when the burnishing is fairly regular and well defined. At Tell Nebi Mend much of it is not, but is patchy and variable in both quality and colour. It was decided, therefore, to show as precisely as possible the actual extent of the burnished surfaces by black shading, even though this prevents significant differences in colour and luminousness – which range from glossy black through dull brown to matt red – being shown. For these important details reference must be made to the verbal descriptions and to the colour photographs of selected sherds on Plates A and B.

Virginia Mathias

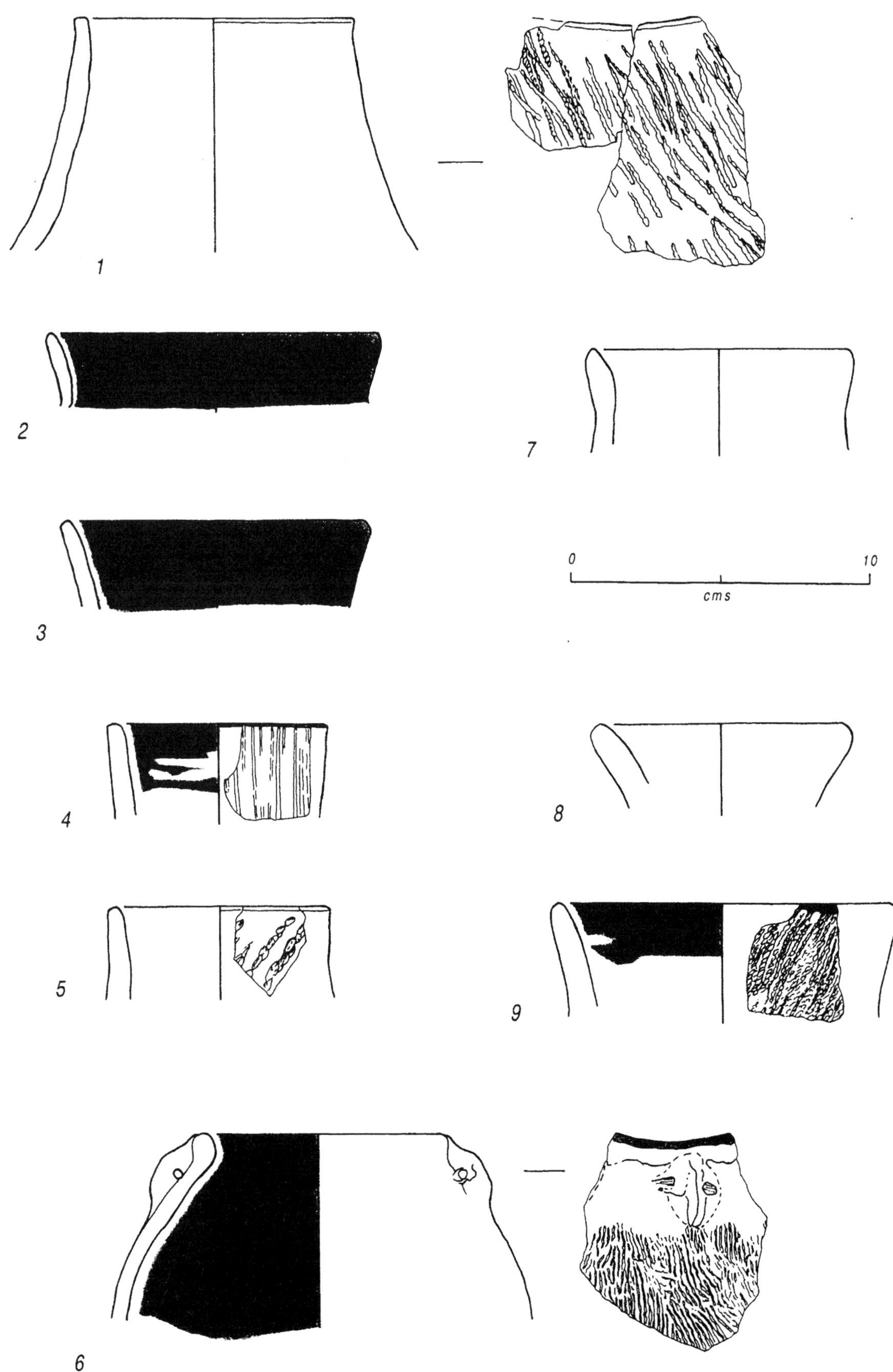

Figure 4.6
Phases 1–3

Jars, necked

Cat. no.	Provenance and sherd no.	Phase	Description
1	706.22/1	2	Jar with neck, inverted, narrow, high; flat rim. Fine fabric; fine dark grey grits; dull brick-red mottled darker surfaces lower down. Cord-impressions outside, inside surface uneven. (*cf.* Plate 4.1)
2	710.11/1	2	Jar with neck, flared, short. Fine fabric; fine dark and light grits; black. Fine burnish outside and inside.
3	648.13/1	3	Jar with neck, flared, wide, short. Very fine fabric; very fine grits; brick-red, dark grey-brown surfaces below rim. Horizontal burnish outside and inside.
4	644.30/2	3	Jar with neck, upright, narrow. Very fine fabric, poorly fired and crumbly; fine light-coloured grits; bricky-brown, dark grey surfaces. Faint-combed or scored outside, streaky horizontal burnish inside on upper 20 mm.
5	606.8/1	3	Jar with neck, upright, narrow. Fine fabric; fine dark grey grits; dark grey outside, brick-red inside. Cord-impressed outside, smoothed inside.
6	644.32/1	3	Jar with neck, very short, rolled. Lug(s), vertical, horizontally pierced. Very fine fabric, quite hard; fine dark grits; brownish black. Fine cord-impressions below lug(s), burnished on rim, and inside on uneven surface. (*cf.* Plate 4.1)
7	706.26/1	2	Jar with neck, upright, narrow. Fine fabric, roughly shaped; dark grey grits; buff, mottled grey. Smoothed over very uneven surfaces.
8	644.24/35	3	Jar with neck, flared. Medium fabric; dark and light grits; brownish grey. Surfaces smoothed only.
9	648.18/1	3	Jar with neck, flared. Medium–fine fabric; small grey grits; buff, grey mottling. Cord-impressed outside, burnished on rim and 20 mm inside.

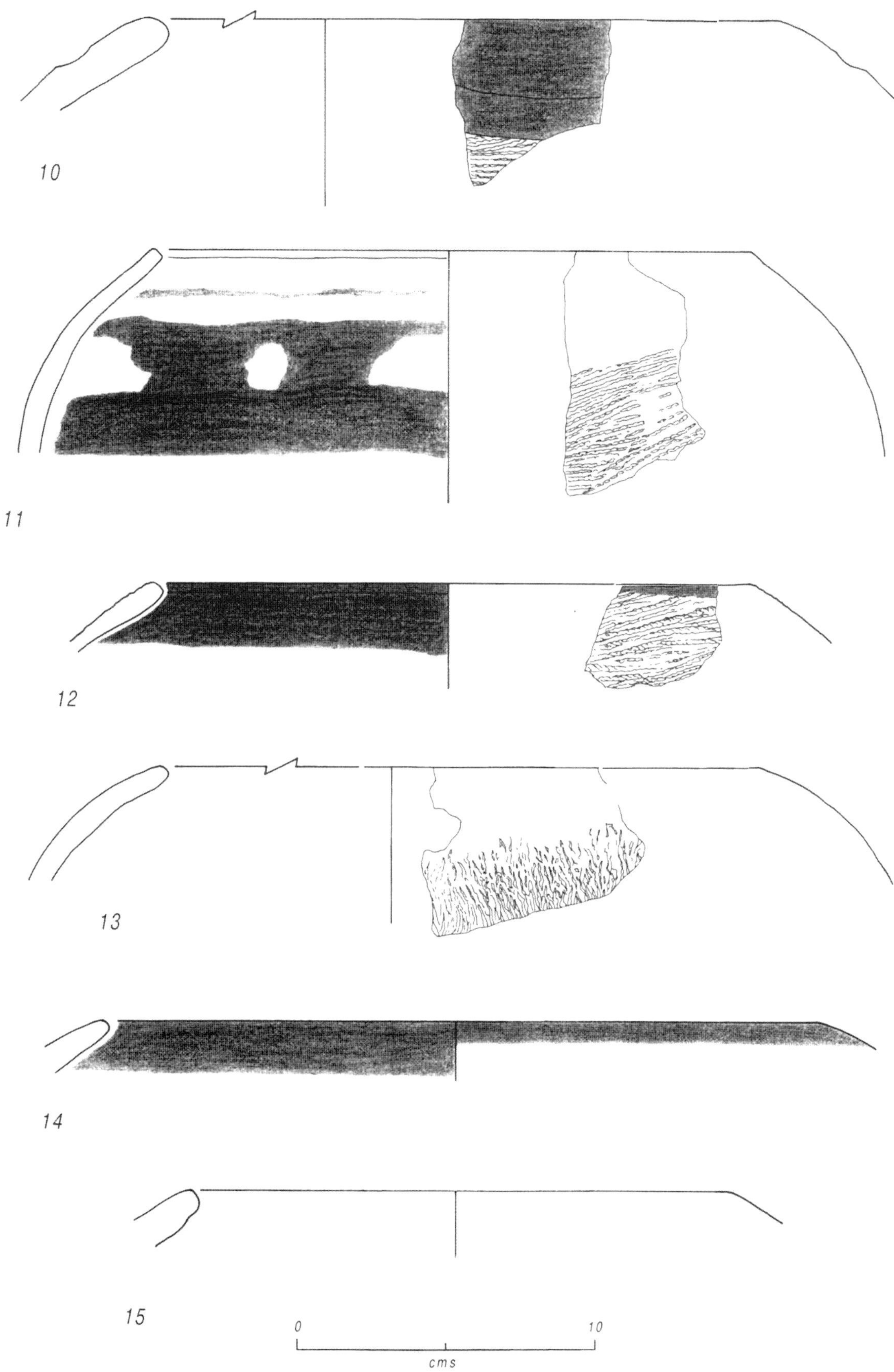

10
11
12
13
14
15
0
10
cms

Figure 4.7
Phases 1–3 (continued)

<u>*Jars, holemouth*</u>

Cat. no.	Provenance and sherd no.	Phase	Description
10	647.15/2	1	Jar, holemouth, shallow, large. Rim rolled outwards and smoothed in, leaving a slight horizontal groove. Fine fabric; fine pale-grey grits; dark grey with pale orange surfaces. Cord-impressed outside below groove, burnish in groove, up to and over rim, traces inside. (*cf.* Plate 4.1)
11	706.22/3	2	Jar, holemouth, shallow. Fine fabric; dark grey grits; dark bricky brown, blackish inside and upper parts outside; cord-impressed outside, below 40 mm band left plain with traces of burnish, patchy burnish inside on uneven surfaces. (*cf.* Plate 4.1)
12	706.22/2	2	Jar, holemouth, shallow. Fine fabric; dense pale-grey angular grits; grey/brown mottled. Cord-impressed outside, burnished over rim and inside.
13	644.30/1	3	Jar, holemouth, shallow. Fine fabric; fine dark grits; pale cream-grey. Irregular impressions outside (not cord – bunched grass or similar) below 25 mm smoothed band, also smoothed inside. (*cf.* Plate 4.1)
14	644.24/19	3	Jar, holemouth, shallow. Fairly fine fabric; small light-grey grits; brick-red, buff surfaces. Burnish outside and inside.
15	735.12/1	3	Jar, holemouth, shallow. Medium fabric; grey grits, grog; pale pink, grey-buff core. Smoothed outside, fairly rough inside.

Virginia Mathias

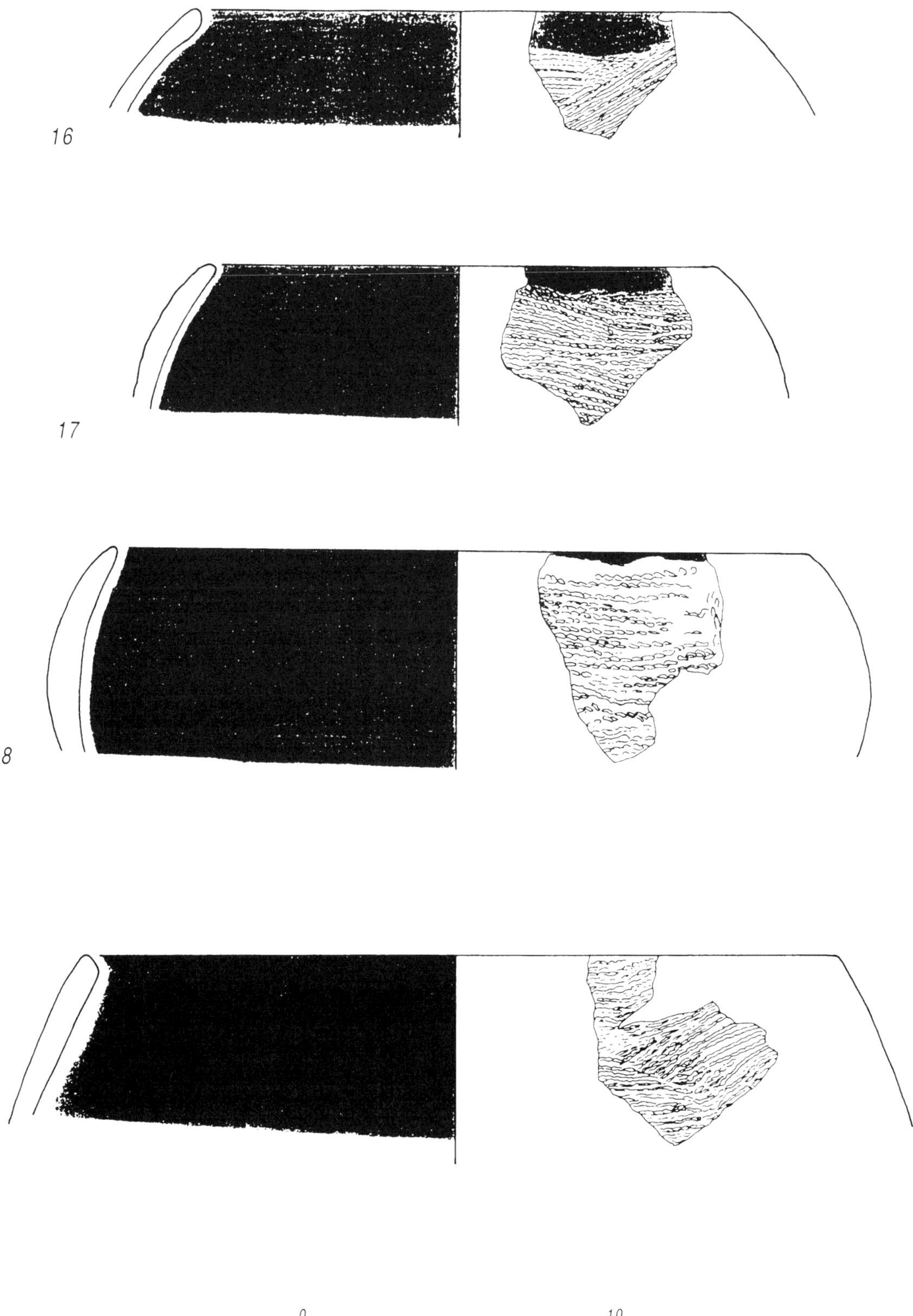

Figure 4.8
Phases 1–3 (continued)

Jars, holemouth

Cat. no.	Provenance and sherd no.	Phase	Description
16	706.12/1	2	Jar, holemouth, steep. Fine fabric; fine pale-grey angular grits; brick-red, brown-mottled surfaces, grey core. Cord-impressed outside below 14 mm band of light horizontal burnish outside, continuing over rim and inside.
17	706.30/2	2	Jar, holemouth, steep. Fine fabric; fine whitish grits; dark grey. Cord-impressed outside, slightly overlapping 10 mm band of light horizontal burnish, continuing inside. (*cf.* Plate 4.1)
18	607.42/4	2	Jar, holemouth, steep. Fine fabric; fine shiny grits; black. Cord-impressed outside, fine burnish on rim and inside. (*cf.* Plate 4.1)
19	706.6/2	2 (?3)	Jar, holemouth, steep. Fine fabric; fine dark grits, some whitish; pale buff mottled dark grey inside. Cord-impressed outside, fine burnish on rim and inside. (*cf.* Plate 4.1)

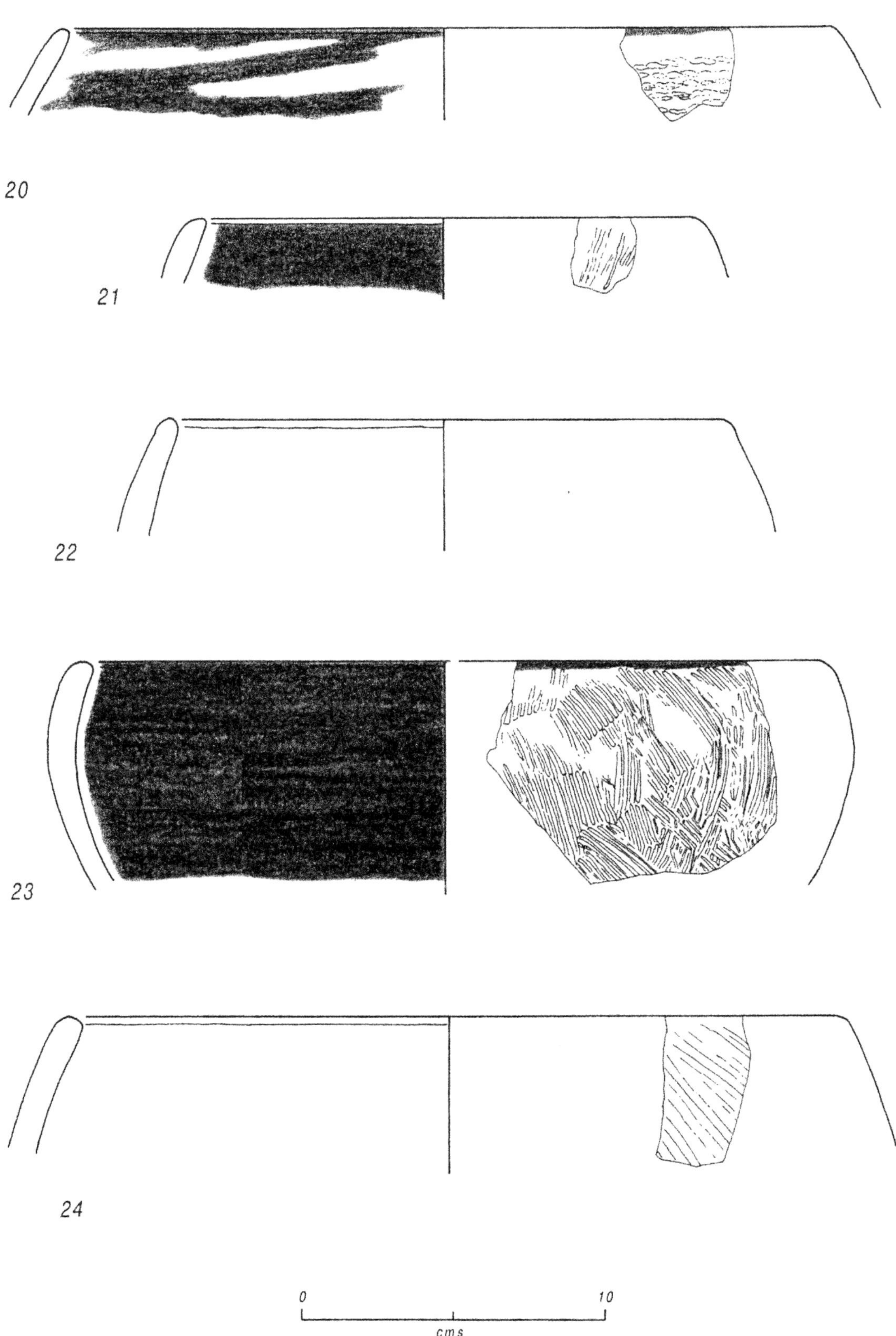

20
21
22
23
24
0
10
cms

Figure 4.9
Phases 1–3 (continued)

<u>*Bowls*</u>

Cat. no.	*Provenance and sherd no.*	*Phase*	*Description*
20	706.44/1	1	Jar, holemouth, steep. Fine fabric; fine light-grey grits; black. Very faint cord-impressions outside, burnish on rim, and sketchy inside.
21	606.5/10	3	Bowl, slightly inverted rim. Fine fabric; very fine light and dark grits; light brick-red, grey core and mottling outside; faint and very sketchy combing outside, light burnish inside below rim.
22	644.24/17	3	Bowl, slightly inverted rim. Medium–fine fabric; small light-coloured grits; dull greyish pink. Smoothed outside, rough horizontal scraping inside.
23	606.25/1	3	Bowl, slightly inverted rim, base rounded. Fine fabric; small dark grey and whitish grits; dull dark brown outside and rim, blackish inside and core. Faint impressed or combed in short strokes outside, burnished rim and inside. Sherds of rounded base, matching size, fabric, temper, unusual combed decoration. (*cf.* Plate 4.1)
24	705.68/4	3(?2)	Bowl, slightly inverted rim. Fine fabric; fine whitish grits; dull brown, blackish inside and core. Very faint-combed outside, smoothed or very light burnish inside.

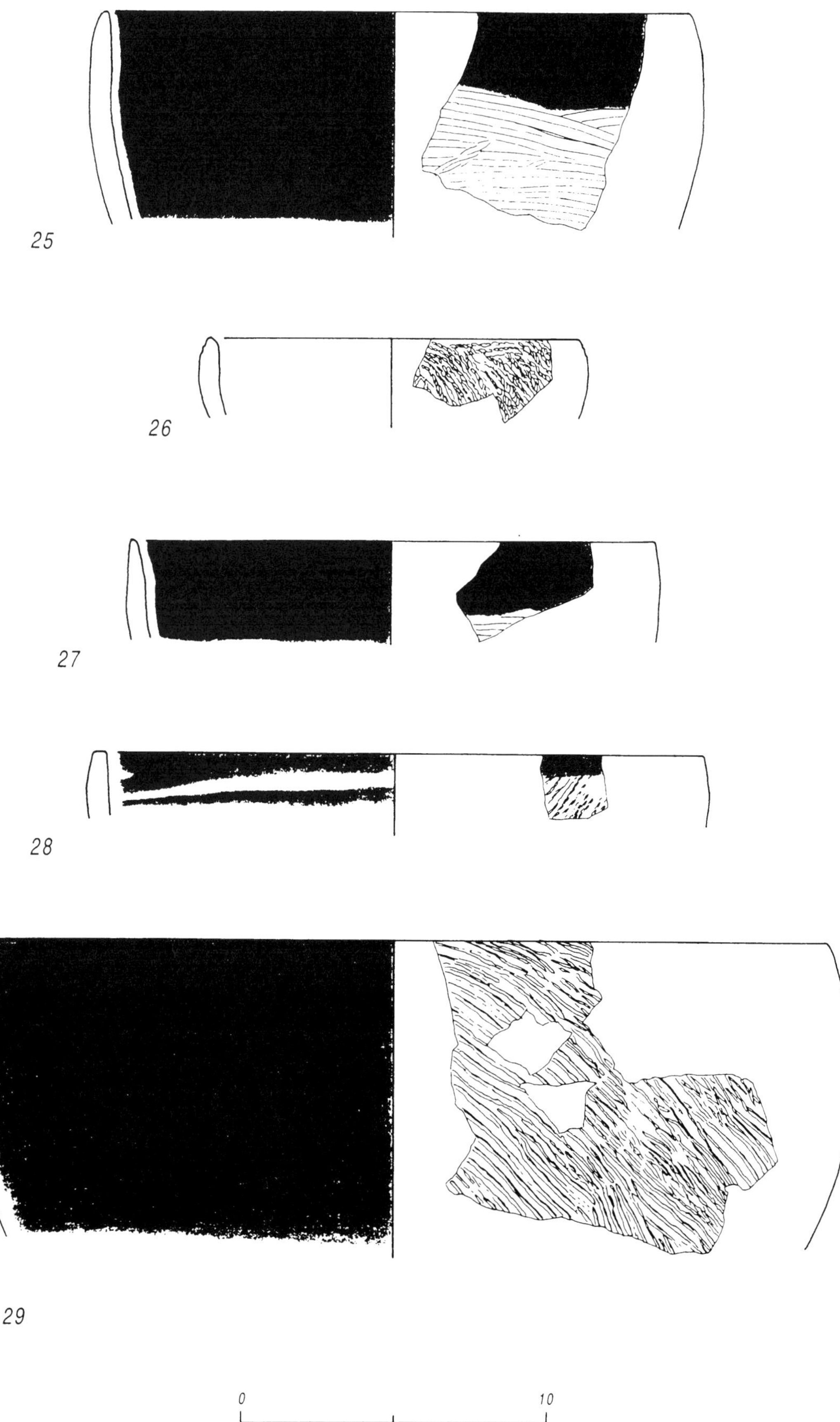

25

26

27

28

29

Figure 4.10
Phases 1–3 (continued)

<u>*Bowls*</u>

Cat. no.	Provenance and sherd no.	Phase	Description
25	706.6/1	2(?3)	Bowl, upright rim. Fine fabric; fine dark grits; black. Faint-combed outside below 30 mm band of glossy burnish, continuing inside. (*cf.* Plate 4.1)
26	606.8/23	3	Bowl, upright rim. Fine fabric; fine grits; dull bricky-brown, mottled grey outside; cord-impressed outside, slight burnish on rim, smoothed inside.
27	644.24/2	3	Bowl, upright rim. Very fine fabric; very fine grits; black. Faint-combed outside below 24 mm band of glossy horizontal burnish, continuing inside.
28	709.17/1	3	Bowl, upright rim, flattened. Fine fabric; very fine black grits; pinkish buff. Fine cord-impressions outside below 6 mm band of burnish, continuing over rim, and streaky inside.
29	606.25/6	3	Bowl, upright rim, flattened. Fine fabric; fine light-coloured and shiny grits; dull brick-red, greyish-red surfaces. Deep but blurred cord-impressions outside, light burnish on rim and inside. (*cf.* Plate 4.1)

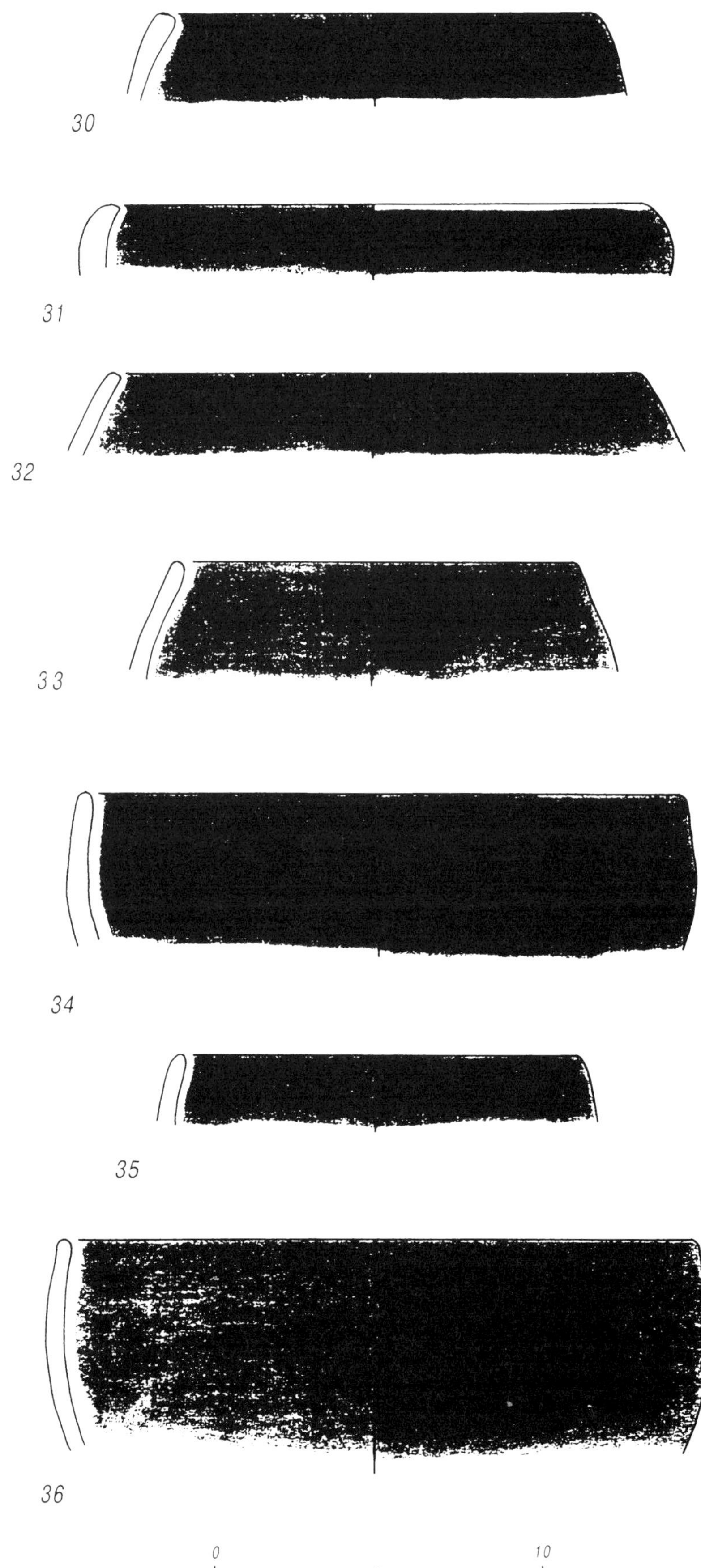

Figure 4.11

Phases 1–3 (continued)

Bowls

Cat. no.	Provenance and sherd no.	Phase	Description
30	606.20/1	1(?2)	Bowl, slightly inverted rim. Fine fabric; fine grits, mostly dark; dark buff, greyish outside surface. Fine horizontal burnish outside, rim and inside.
31	606.25/5	3	Bowl, slightly inverted rim. Very fine fabric; fine grits; greyish brown, dull brick-red core; matt burnish outside (streaky on rim) and inside.
32	648.13/2	3	Bowl, slightly inverted rim. Very fine; fine white and dark grits; dark brownish grey. Burnish outside and inside.
33	709.14/1	3	Bowl, slightly inverted rim (small). Fine fabric; fine light and dark grits; brick-red, grey-brown surfaces. Horizontal burnish (streaky) outside and inside.
34	706.42/1	2	Bowl, upright rim. Fine fabric; fine light and dark grits; black, mottled cream at rim. Fine burnish outside and inside, rim worn.
35	606.25/8	3	Bowl, slightly inverted rim. Fine fabric; fine brown grits; brown, dark-grey core. Burnish outside and (uneven) inside.
36	709.4/1	3	Bowl, upright rim. Fine fabric; small dark-grey and whitish grits; brick-red, grey-brown surface: Horizontal burnish (streaky) outside and inside.

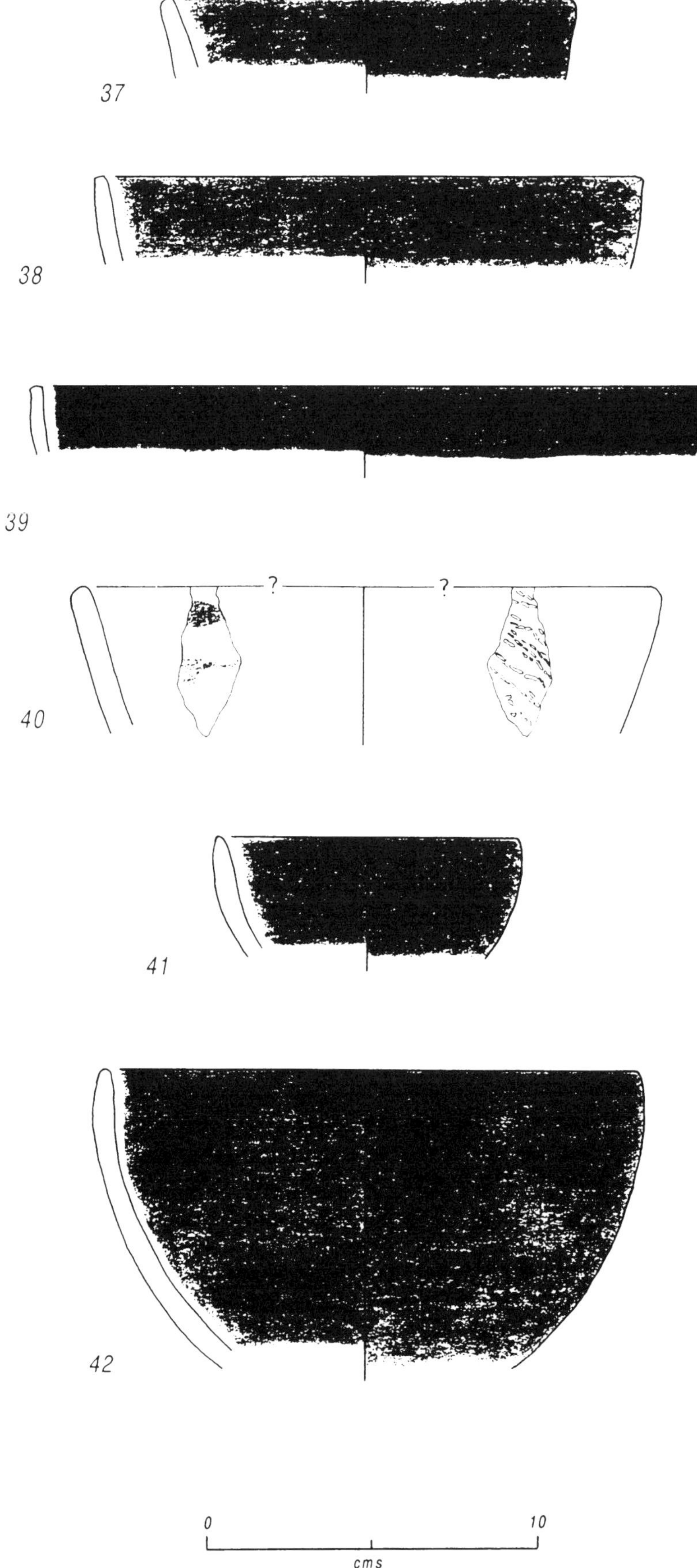

37
38
39
40
?   ?
41
42
0
10
cms

Figure 4.12

Phases 1–3 (continued)

Bowls, open

Cat. no.	Provenance and sherd no.	Phase	Description
37	706.42/2	2	Bowl, upright rim. Fairly fine fabric; small to fine light-coloured grits; mushroom. Light burnish outside and inside.
38	706.26/2	2	Bowl, upright rim. Fine fabric; fine grey grits; greyish cream. Burnish outside and inside.
39	647.15/1	1(?2)	Bowl, upright rim. Very fine fabric; very fine grits; black; glossy burnish outside and inside.
40	705.67/1	3(?2)	Bowl, flared, conical. Fine fabric; fine light and dark grey grits; reddish grey, brick-red core. Faint cord-impressions outside, very sketchy burnish inside.
41	706.30/1	2(?3)	Bowl, hemispherical. Fine fabric; fine light grits; mottled dark grey and light brick-red, with grey-buff surfaces. Fine matt burnish outside and inside.
42	706.22/5	2	Bowl, hemispherical. Fine fabric; fine grey and light grits; dark brick-red upper parts outside and core, dark brown-black below and inside. Vertical/oblique burnish outside, horizontal inside. (*cf.* Plate 4.1)

 Virginia Mathias

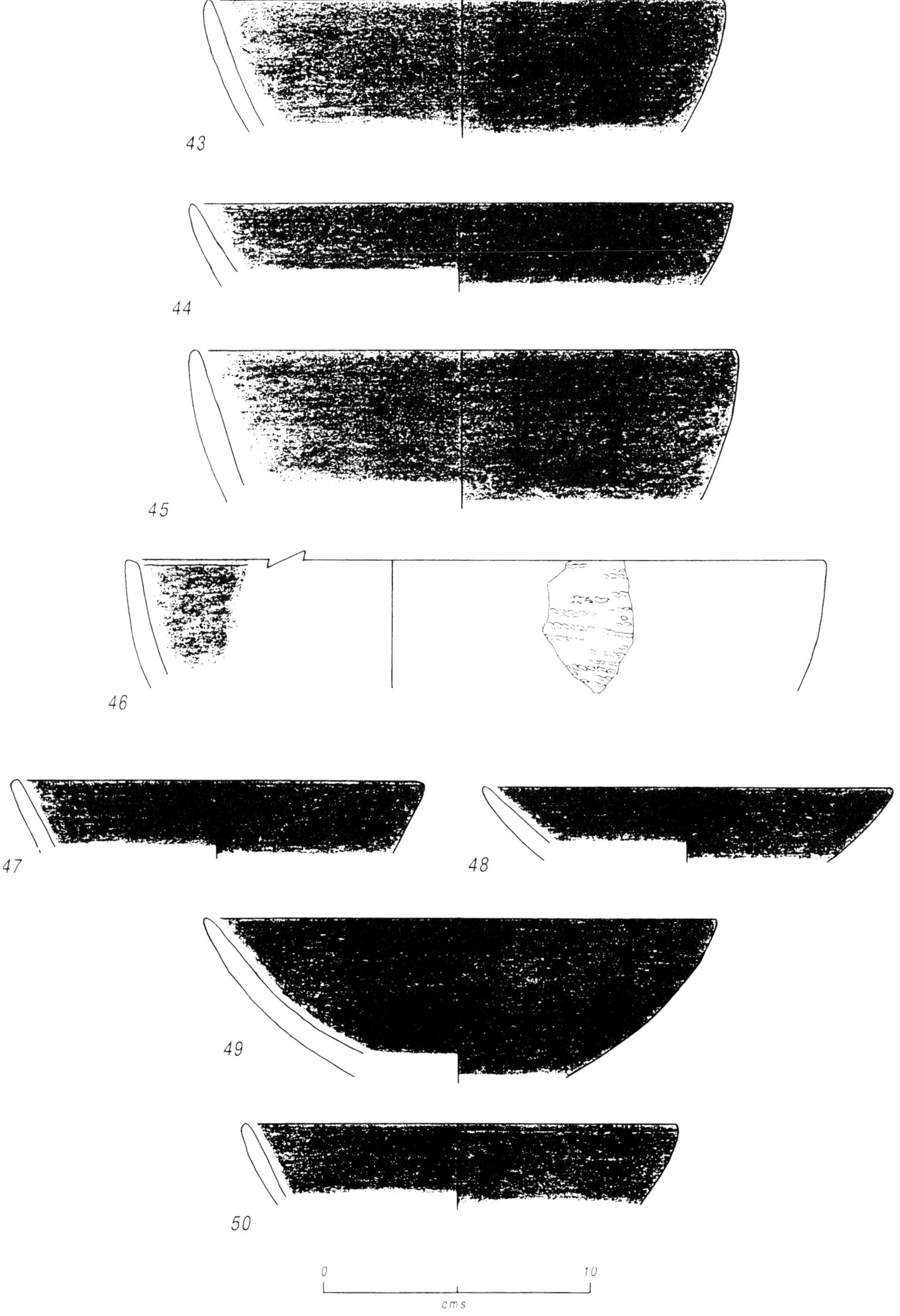

Figure 4.13
Phases 1–3 (continued)

Bowls, open

Cat. no.	Provenance and sherd no.	Phase	Description
43	706.22/11	2	Bowl, flared, shallow. Fine fabric; fine whitish grits; brownish black, brown core. Fine burnish outside and inside.
44	607.42/2	2	Bowl, flared, shallow. Very fine fabric; very fine whitish grits; black; glossy burnish outside and inside.
45	606.25/7	3	Bowl, flared, flat-sided. Medium–fine fabric; small angular whitish grits; brownish black, grey-brown inside. Horizontal burnish outside and inside.
46	706.43/1	2	Bowl, flared, shallow (large). Fine fabric; fine light and dark grits; dull brown mottled blackish. Faint cord-impressions outside, light horizontal burnish inside.
47	607.42/3	2	Bowl, flared, shallow. Fine fabric; very fine grits; brown, black core and mottling. Fine matt burnish outside and inside.
48	706.22/4	2	Bowl, flared, shallow. Fine fabric, small light grits, black. Glossy burnish inside and outside.
49	607.42/1	2	Bowl, flared, shallow. Fine fabric; fine light and dark grits; dark red, mottled black. Fine burnish outside and inside.
50	648.21/1	3	Bowl, flared, shallow. Very fine fabric; very fine grits; mushroom, mottled black. Light burnish outside and inside.

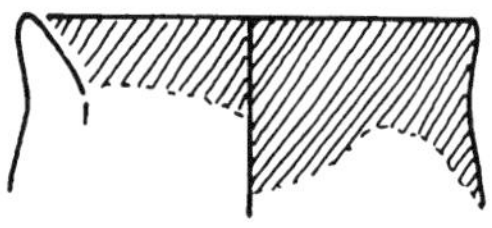

Virginia Mathias

51

52

53

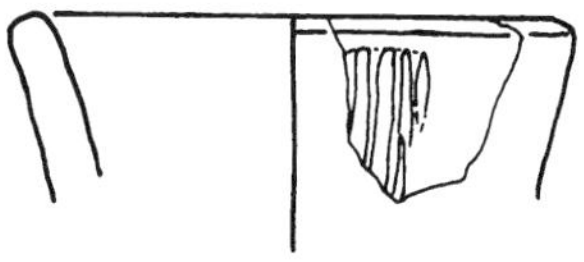

54

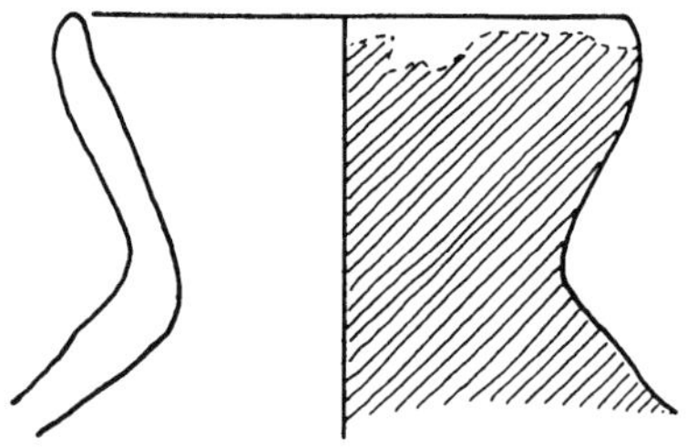

55

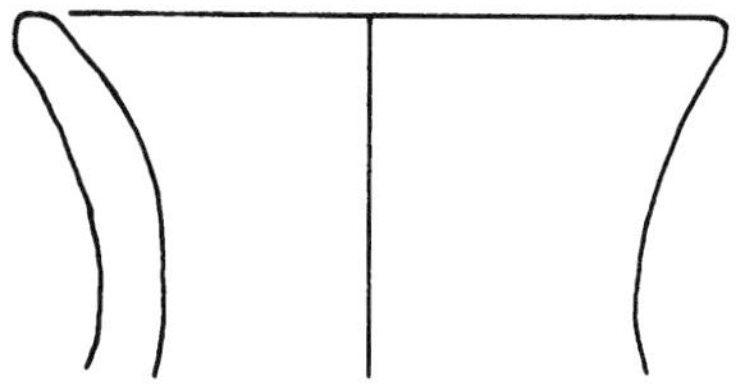

56

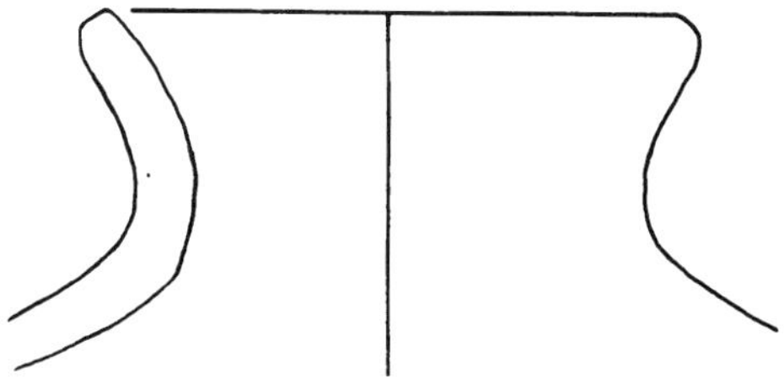

57

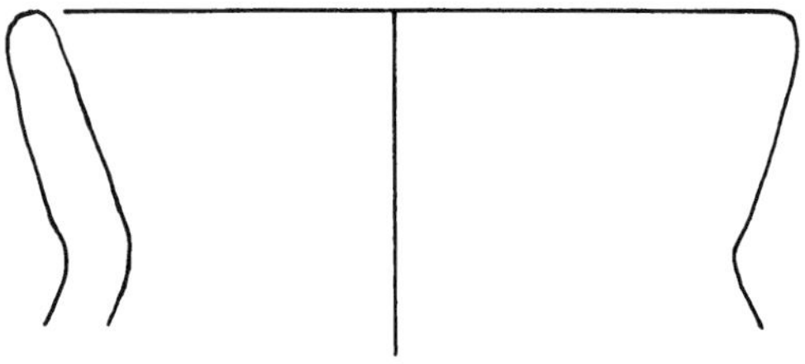

58

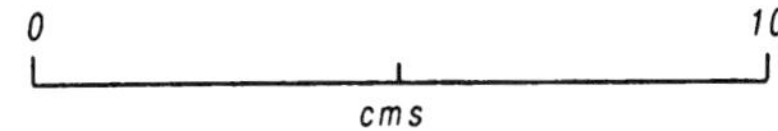

Figure 4.14
Phase 4

Jars, flared neck

Cat. no.	Provenance and sherd no.	Phase	Description
51	706.10/1	4	Jar with neck, narrow, very short (small). Medium–fine fabric, soft; small whitish and grey grits; buff. Pinkish-red matt slip outside and inside.
52	654.10/1	4	Jar with neck, flared, narrow. Fine fabric; small light-grey grits; buff. Smoothed only outside and inside.
53	708.2/5	4	Jar with neck, flared. Fine fabric; fine light and shiny grits; blackish-brown. Light horizontal burnish outside and inside.
54	708.3/1	?4	Jar with neck, flared, narrow. Fine fabric; fine light grits; blackish-brown. Faint-combing (4 teeth at least, spaced) outside, inside rough.
55	706.18/2	4	Jar with neck, flared, narrow, high. Medium–coarse fabric, thin-walled and uneven; medium-size light-grey grits and fine vegetable temper; buff. Matt pinkish-red fugitive slip outside, worn rim, inside rough.
56	606.27/2	4	Jar with neck, flared, narrow, high. Coarse fabric; medium-size dark-grey grits; buff, blackened outside on neck. Finger-smoothed, slight sheen in band 25–30 mm from rim outside, 20 mm inside (perhaps from handling rather than burnish).
57	655.7/1	4	Jar with neck, flared, narrow, high. Coarse fabric; small dark-grey and reddish grits, some vegetable temper; light buff. Smoothed outside and lightly inside.
58	735.9/1	4	Jar with neck, flared, high. Very coarse fabric; large and small dark-grey grits, some light; grey-buff, blackened rim. Slight burnish or sheen outside, on rim and 10–15 mm inside (over blackening – may be from handling).

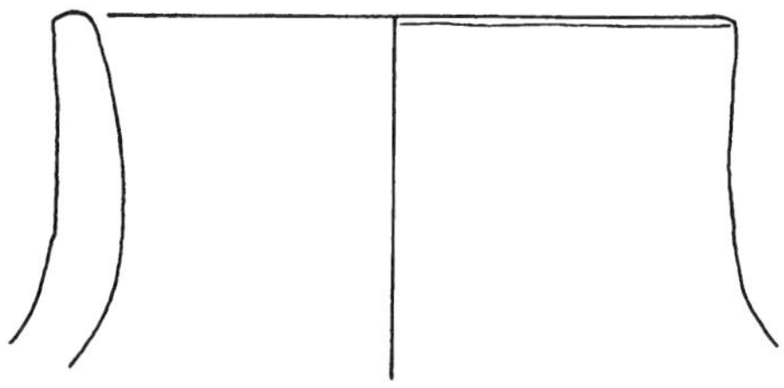

59

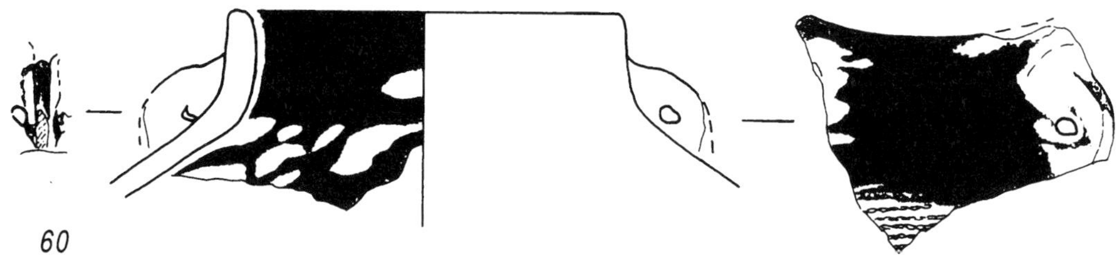

60

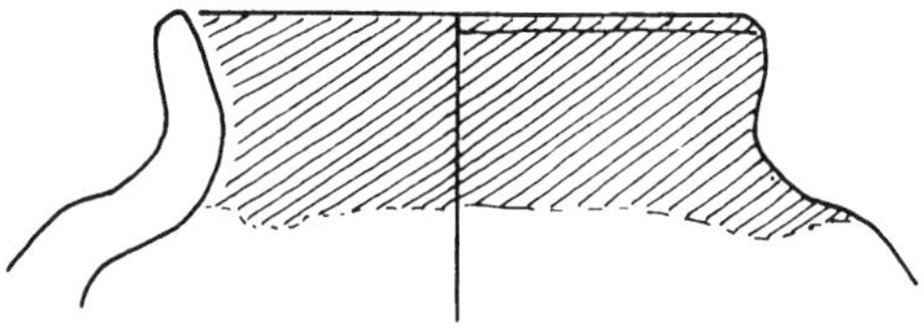

61

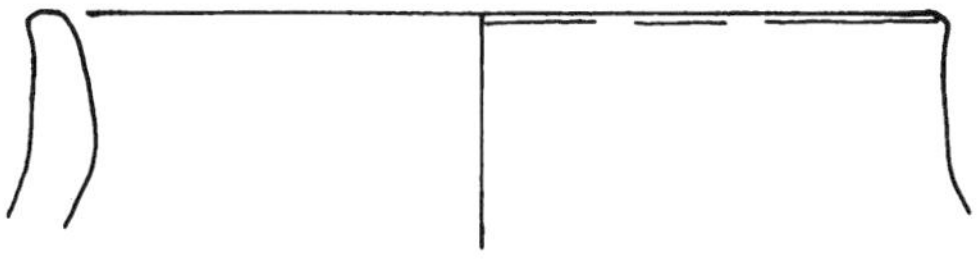

62

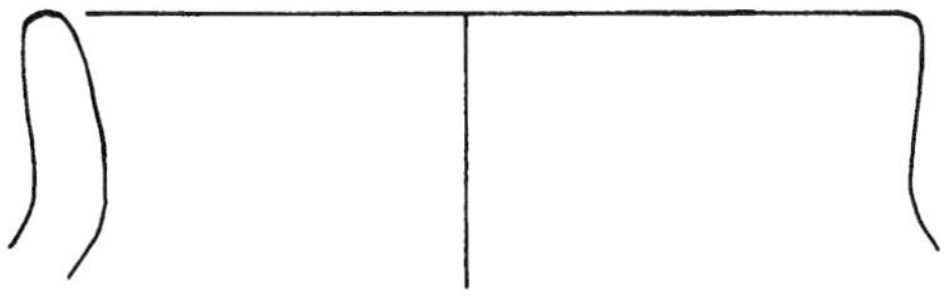

63

64

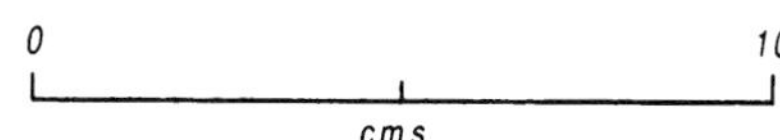

Figure 4.15
Phase 4 (continued)

Jars, upright neck

Cat. no.	Provenance and sherd no.	Phase	Description
59	655.3/1	3	Jar with neck, upright, narrow, high. Medium–coarse fabric; small dark-grey grits, some red grog, possibly some fine vegetable temper; buff, with grey discoloration. Smoothed outside and inside.
60	606.27/1	4	Jar with neck, upright. Vertical horizontally pierced lug handles. Very fine fabric; fine light and dark grits; grey, buff surfaces, mottled. Cord-impressed on shoulder outside, burnish on neck between lugs, also inside rim, and sketchy below on less even surface.
61	706.10/3	4	Jar with neck, upright. Coarse fabric, very variable thickness of wall; small grey and white grits. Red slip on rim and neck outside and inside, burnish over slip in streaky lines on rim and outside only (not shown in drawing).
62	644.16/1	4(?3)	Jar with neck, upright. Medium–fine fabric; fine grey and light grits; dark grey, buff surfaces. Smoothed outside and inside.
63	602.27/1	4	Jar with neck, upright. Medium–coarse fabric; medium and small grey grits, probably some vegetable temper; buff, light brick-red surfaces. Outside and inside surfaces rough or worn.
64	735.7/1	4	Jar with neck, upright. Medium–coarse fabric; much small grey grit, probably some vegetable temper; buff. Smoothed outside and inside.

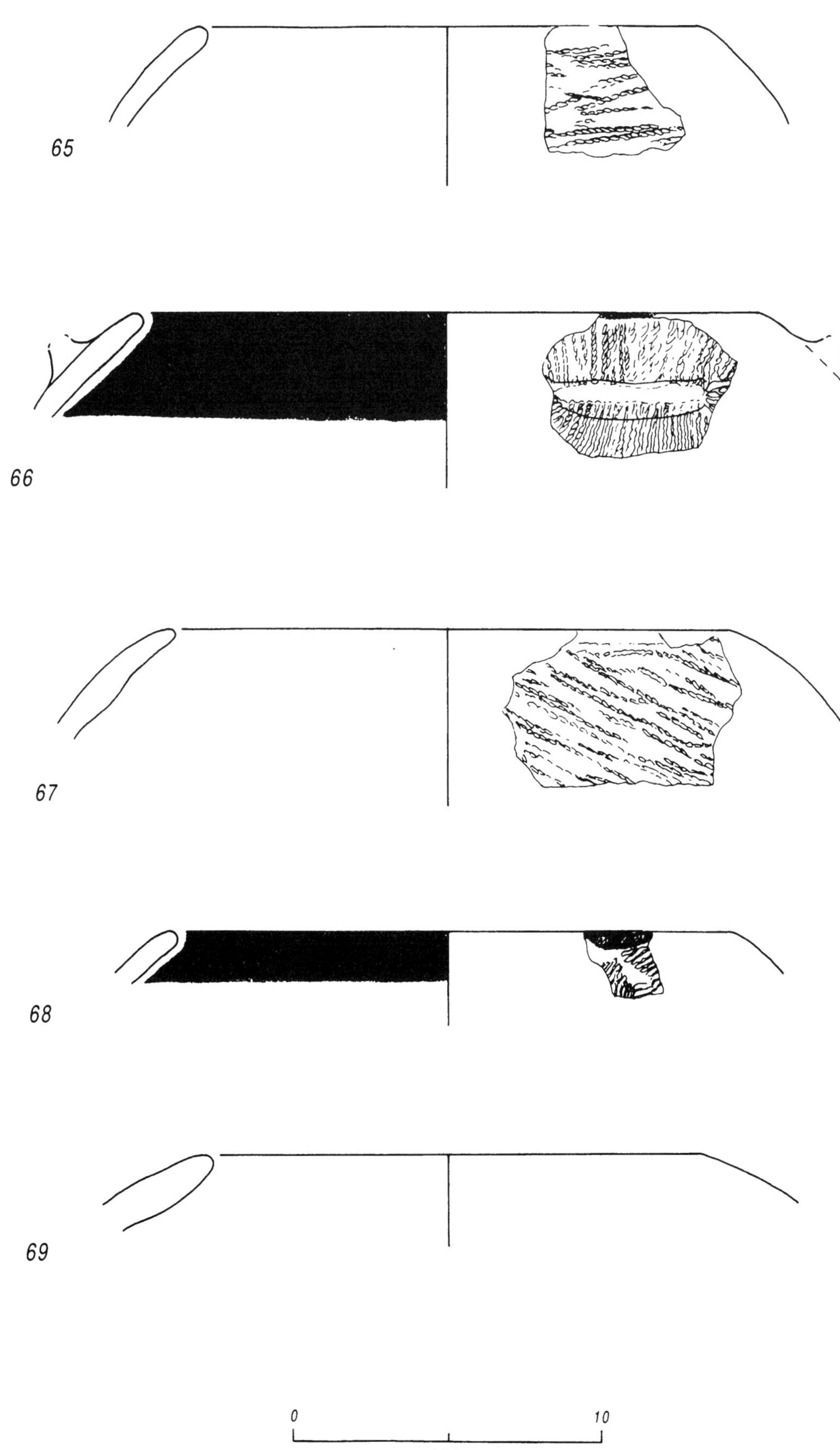

65
66
67
68
69
0
10
cms

Figure 4.16
Phase 4 (continued)

Jars, holemouth

Cat. no.	*Provenance and sherd no.*	*Phase*	*Description*
65	706.40/2	?4	Jar, holemouth, shallow. Fine fabric; fine dark and light grits; dull brick-red, grey surfaces. Cord-impressed outside, smoothed or light sketchy burnish inside.
66	706.41/5	?4	Jar, holemouth, shallow. Horizontal lug/ledge handle. Fine fabric; fine light and dark grits; brown-black. Cord-impressed outside and on horizontal ledge/lug; matt burnish on rim and inside.
67	644.27/25 +30	4	Jar, holemouth, shallow. Medium–fine fabric, small light and dark grits, possibly some vegetable temper; mid-grey, blackened or discoloured inside; cord-impressed outside, smoothed inside. (May be same vessel as no. 168.)
68	709.30/1	?4	Jar, holemouth, shallow. Fine fabric; fine grey grits; bright brick-red. Very shallow cord-impressions outside, horizontal burnish inside, over rim and 5 mm band outside.
69	735.15/1	?4	Jar, holemouth, shallow. Medium–coarse fabric; small grey and red grits or grog; pale grey-buff. Smoothed outside, rather rough inside, possibly traces of orange slip.

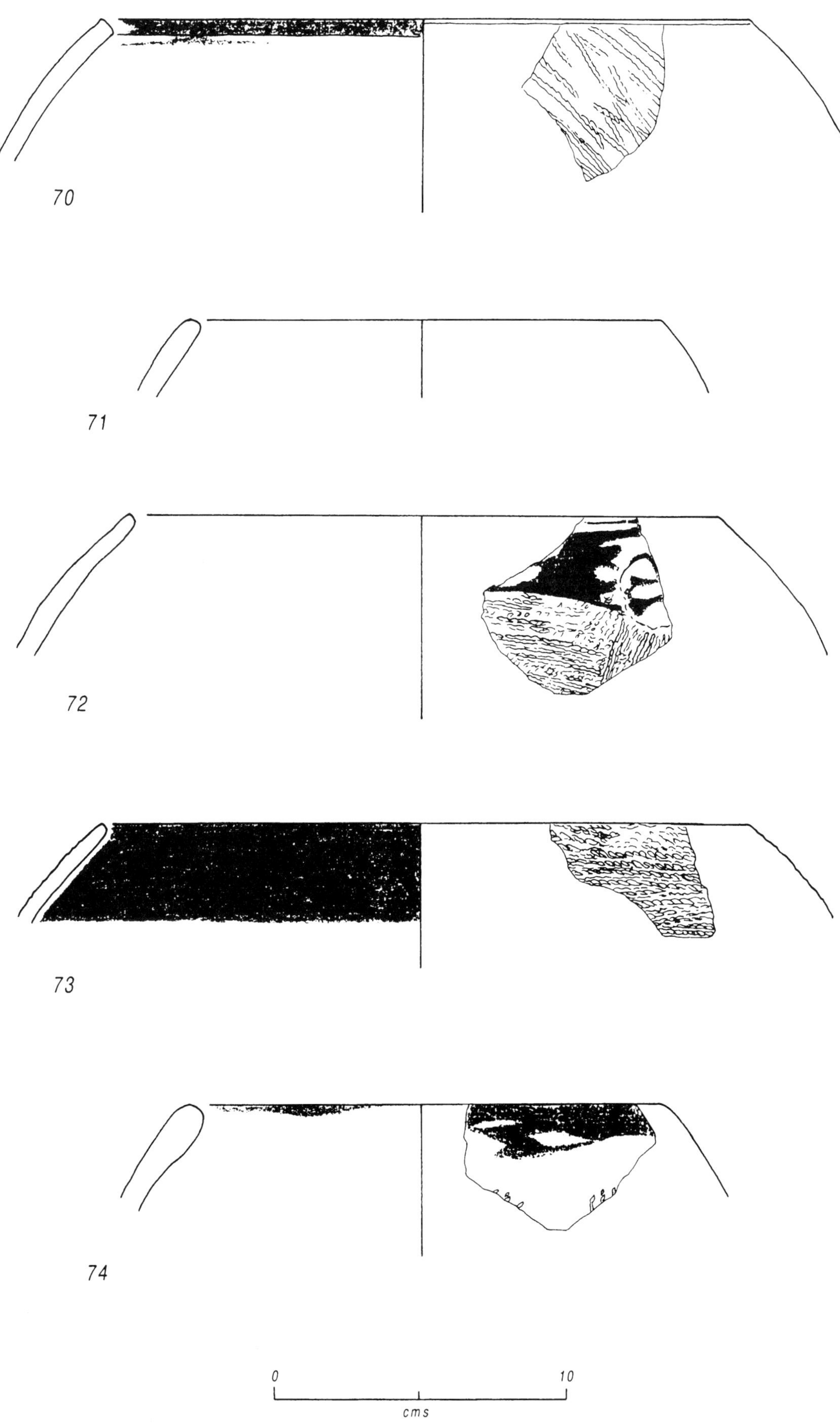

70
71
72
73
74
0
10
cms

Figure 4.17
Phase 4 (continued)

Jars, holemouth

Cat. no.	Provenance and sherd no.	Phase	Description
70	708.3/3	?4	Jar, holemouth, shallow. Fine fabric; fine dark and light grits; dull brick-red, black core and mottling. Spaced cord-impressions outside, faint horizontal burnish inside rim, smoothing or light matt burnish inside.
71	735.14/1	4	Jar, holemouth, steep. Fine but soft fabric; fine dark grits; cream/buff. Well smoothed or light matt burnish outside and inside.
72	705.63/11	?4	Jar, holemouth, shallow. Fine fabric; fine dark grey grits. Cord-impressed outside below 30 mm band of streaky burnish, also on rim and very sketchy inside. Possible knob/lug scar (thickening on broken edge).
73	710.9/6	4	Jar, holemouth, shallow. Very fine fabric; fine light and dark grits; blackish brown, dull brick-red core. Deeply cord-impressed outside, uneven horizontal burnish on rim and inside. (*cf.* Plate 4.1)
74	644.21/15	?4	Jar, holemouth, steep, rolled rim. Fairly fine fabric; fine dark grey grits; buff mottled dark grey. Sketchy horizontal burnish on rim and on band outside, with spaced cord-impressions below; inside very sketchily smoothed.

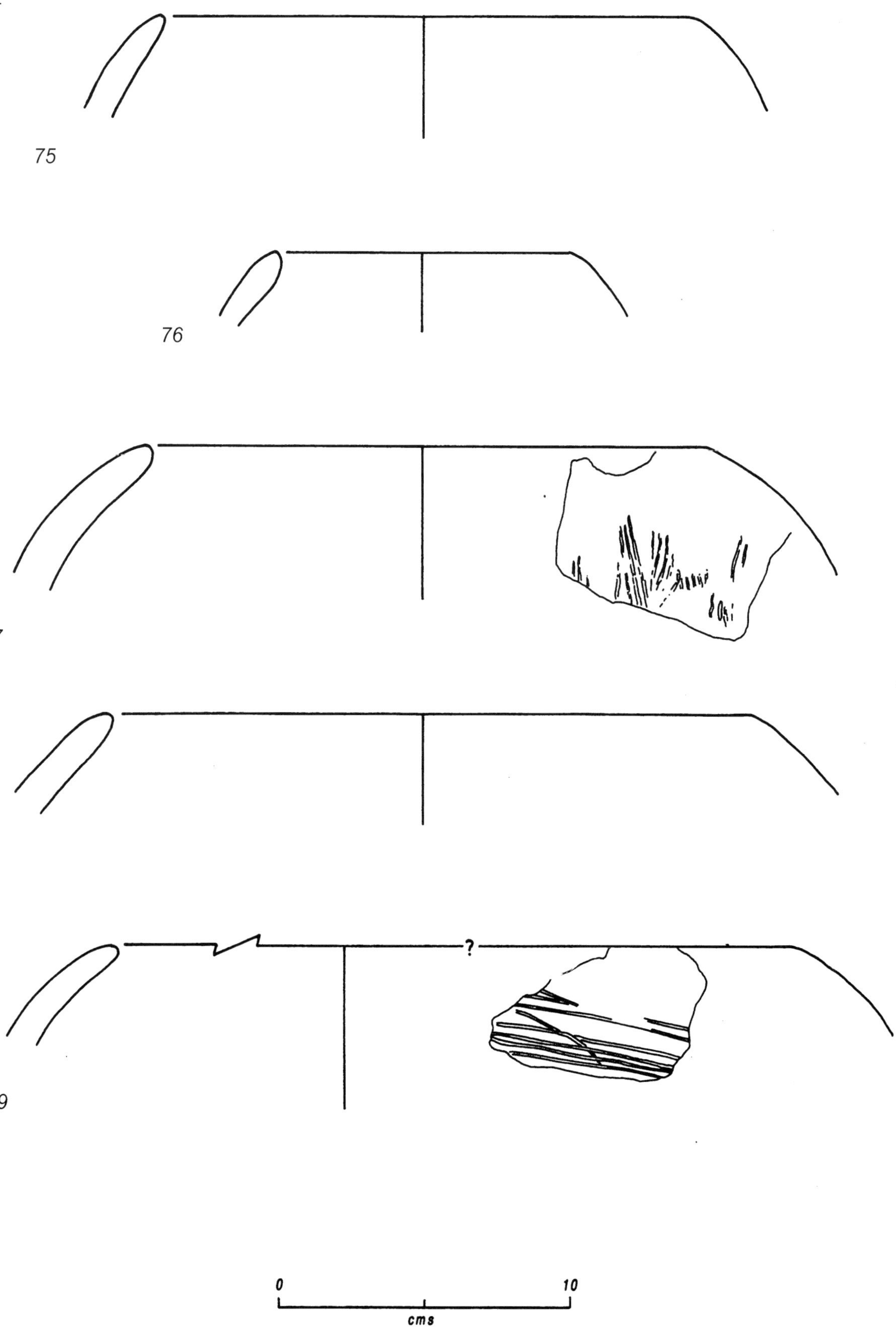

75

76

77

78

79

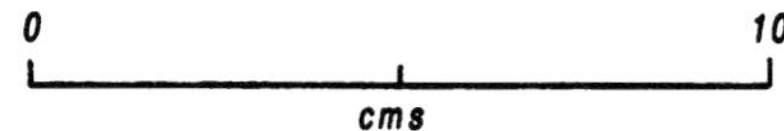

0 10
cms

Figure 4.18
Phase 4 (continued)

Jars, holemouth

Cat. no.	Provenance and sherd no.	Phase	Description
75	709.29/3	?4	Jar, holemouth, steep. Fairly fine fabric; fine dark and light grits; dark brick-red, dark grey core. Smoothed or very sketchy burnish outside and inside.
76	606.2/5	?4	Jar, holemouth, steep. Fairly fine fabric; fine dark grits; dark brick-red, dark grey surfaces. Well smoothed or light matt burnish outside and inside.
77	606.7/2	4	Jar, holemouth, shallow. Medium fabric; small dark grits; greyish-buff; well smoothed or light matt burnish outside and inside; Traces of very faint combing outside, and possibly of reddish paint or slip.
78	606.27/4	4	Jar, holemouth, shallow. Coarse fabric; medium-size dark grey angular grits, possible vegetable temper; light buff, dull greyish-red surfaces. Smoothed outside only, inside rather rough.
79	735.8/1	4	Jar, holemouth, shallow. Coarse fabric; large to fine grey grits, possibly some red grog and fine vegetable temper; greyish buff, light-grey core. Faint-combed outside, smoothed outside and inside.

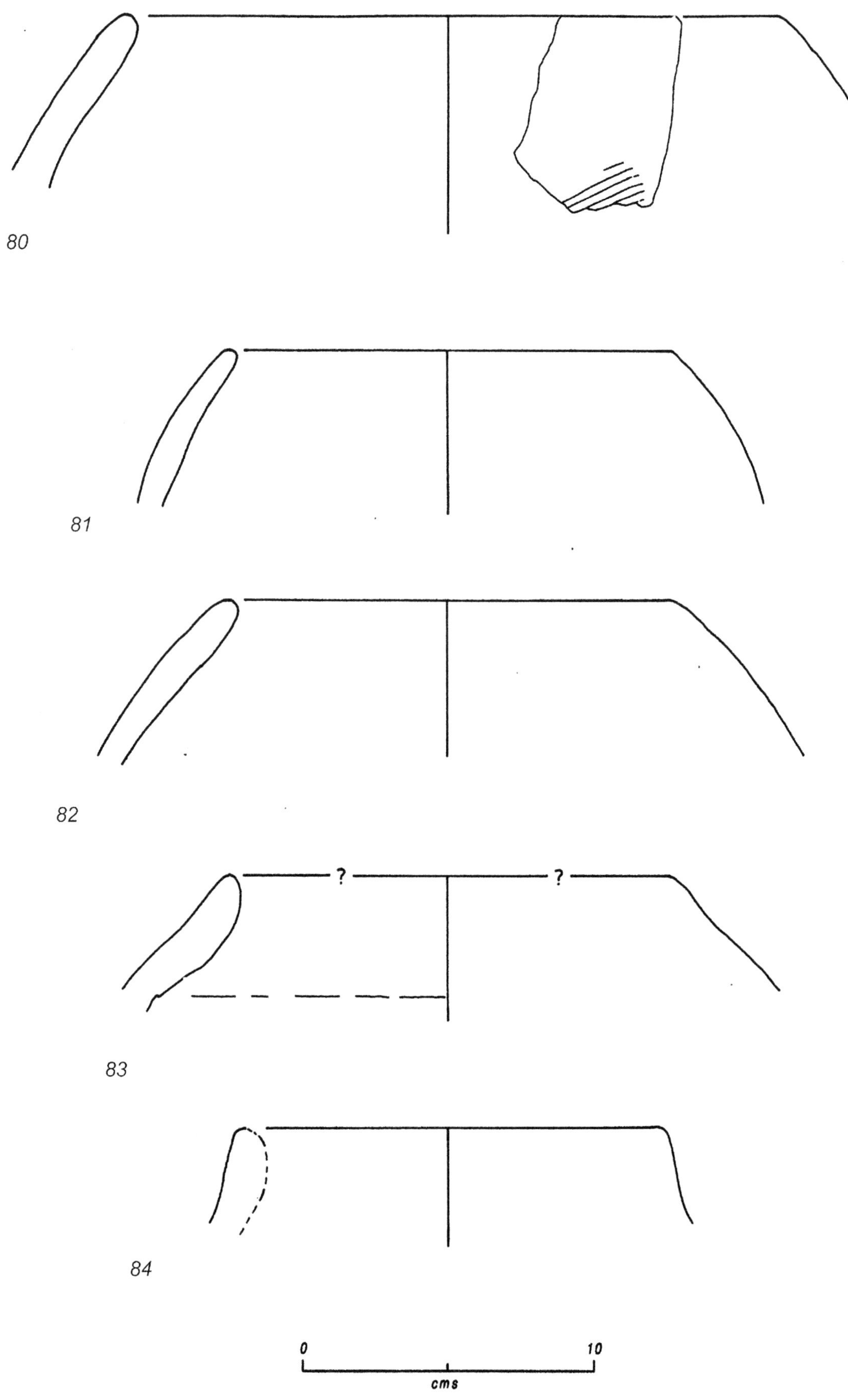
80
81
82
83
?   ?
84
0
10
cms

Figure 4.19
Phase 4 (Continued)

Jars, holemouth or slightly inverted-neck

Cat. no.	Provenance and sherd no.	Phase	Description
80	644.40/1	4	Jar, holemouth, steep. Coarse fabric; small white grits, and probably vegetable temper; buff. Faint-combed (not impressed) starting 50 mm below rim outside, smoothed above and inside.
81	606.27/3	4	Jar, holemouth, steep. Coarse fabric; medium to small whitish and grey grits, some fine vegetable temper; pale brick-red mottled buff, buff core. Smoothed outside and inside but poor finish with crackled surfaces.
82	606.27/6	4	Jar, holemouth, steep. Coarse fabric; large dark-grey grits, fine vegetable temper; greyish buff, discoloured. Smoothed outside and inside; indication of knob or lug on broken edge (thickness of wall is variable).
83	606.27/5	4	Jar, holemouth, steep. Coarse fabric; medium to small dark-grey angular grits; buff. Smoothed outside and inside. (Rim folded inwards and roughly flattened, with join still visible.)
84	706.10/2	4	Jar with neck, inverted, narrow, low. Coarse fabric; large to small dark-grey grits, a few light; pale brick-red, buff core. Smoothed outside, inside surface missing.

Virginia Mathias

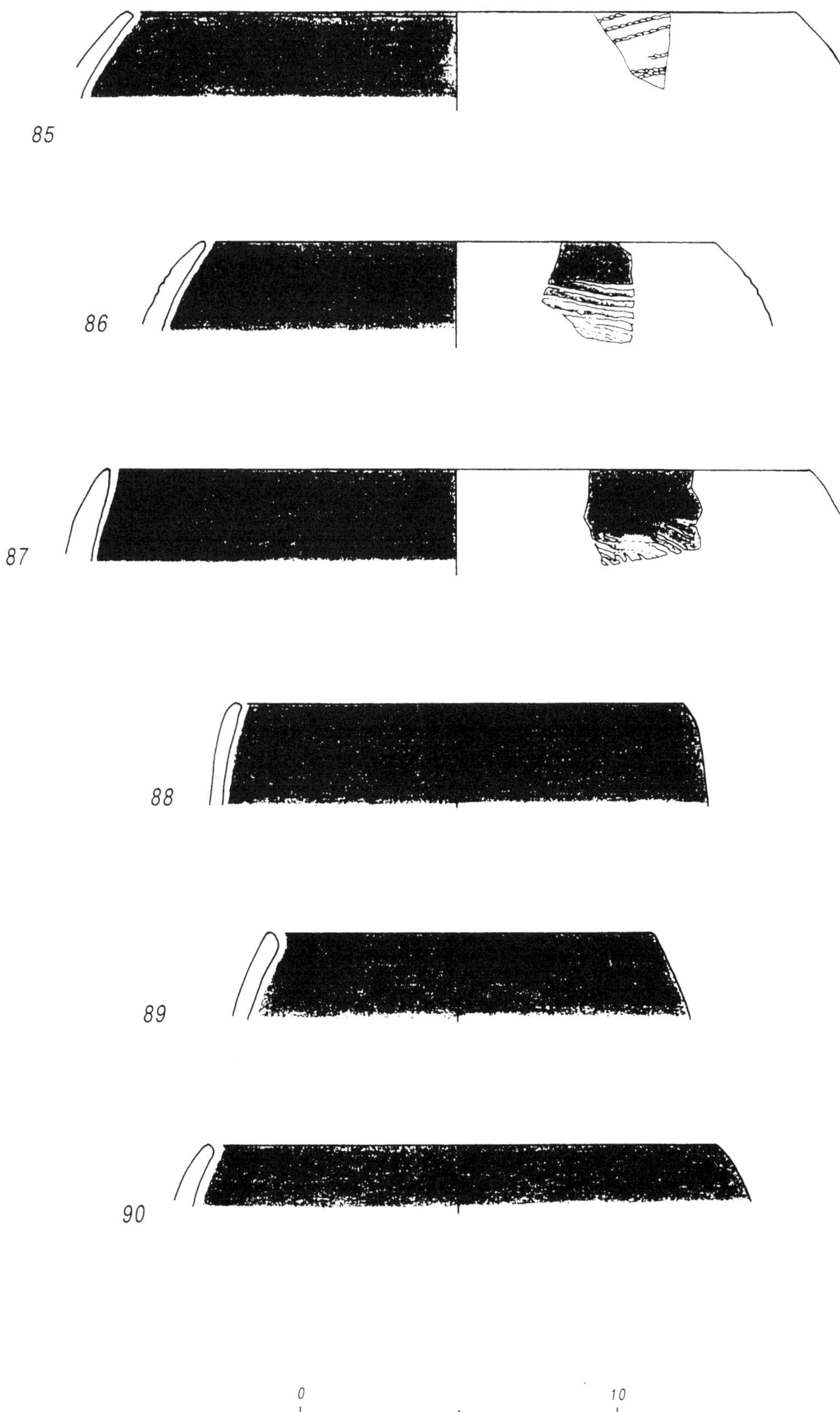

Figure 4.20
Phase 4 (continued)

Jars, holemouth or bowls, slightly inverted

Cat. no.	Provenance and sherd no.	Phase	Description
85	708.3/2	?4	Jar, holemouth, steep. Very fine fabric; very fine dark and light grits. Spaced cord-impressions outside, horizontal burnish on rim and inside.
86	710.6/1	4	Jar, holemouth, steep. Very fine fabric; very fine dark and light grits; blackish brown, mottling. Cord-impressions outside blurred by 20 mm band of burnish above; rough burnish inside.
87	710.7/1	4	Jar, holemouth, steep. Fine fabric; fine light and dark grits; brown surfaces mottled darker/greyish. Cord-impressions outside blurred by 25 mm band of matt burnish above, continues inside.
88	706.41/1	?4	Bowl, slightly inverted rim. Very fine fabric; fine grey grits; black. Glossy burnish outside and inside.
89	709.8/2	?4	Bowl, slightly inverted rim (small). Fine fabric; fine light and dark grits; greyish brown, brick-red core. Horizontal burnish outside, rather streaky inside.
90	644.15/1	?4	Bowl, slightly inverted rim. Fine fabric; fine dark grits; buff, thin pale-grey core and mottling outside. Horizontal burnish outside and inside.

Virginia Mathias

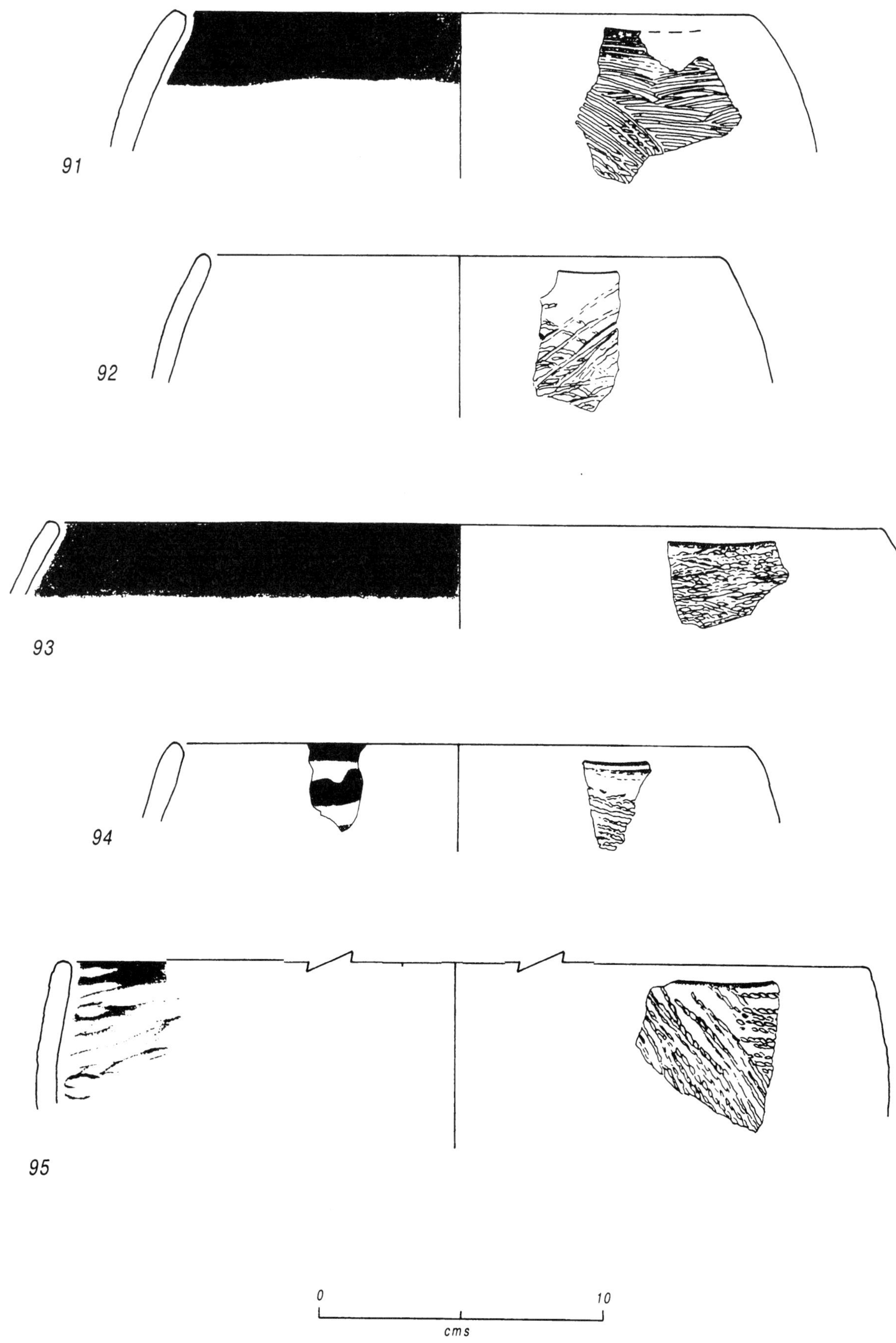

Figure 4.21
Phase 4 (continued)

Jars, holemouth or bowls, slightly inverted

Cat. no.	Provenance and sherd no.	Phase	Description
91	709.29/2	?4	Jar, holemouth, steep. Fine fabric; fine grey and light grits; dull brick-red, grey outside surface. Cord-impressions blurred under 11 mm burnished band outside, matt burnish 25 mm inside, and well smoothed below.
92	708.2/6	4	Jar, holemouth, steep. Fine fabric; fine light and dark grits; bricky brown, dark-grey rim, core and inside. Cord-impressed outside, well smoothed or light matt burnish on rim and inside.
93	646.2/1	4	Jar, holemouth, steep (large). Fine fabric; fine light and dark grits; black surfaces, dark brick-red core. Faint cord-impressions outside, horizontal burnish over rim and inside.
94	710.6/2	4	Bowl, slightly inverted rim. Fine fabric; fine light and dark grits; dull brick-red, darker/greyish surfaces. Blurred cord-impressions outside, streaky horizontal burnish on rim and on uneven surface inside.
95	706.31/1	4	Bowl, slightly inverted rim (large). Fairly fine fabric; small greyish grits; blackish, black-brown outside surface. Cord-impressed outside, sketchy burnish over rim and inside.

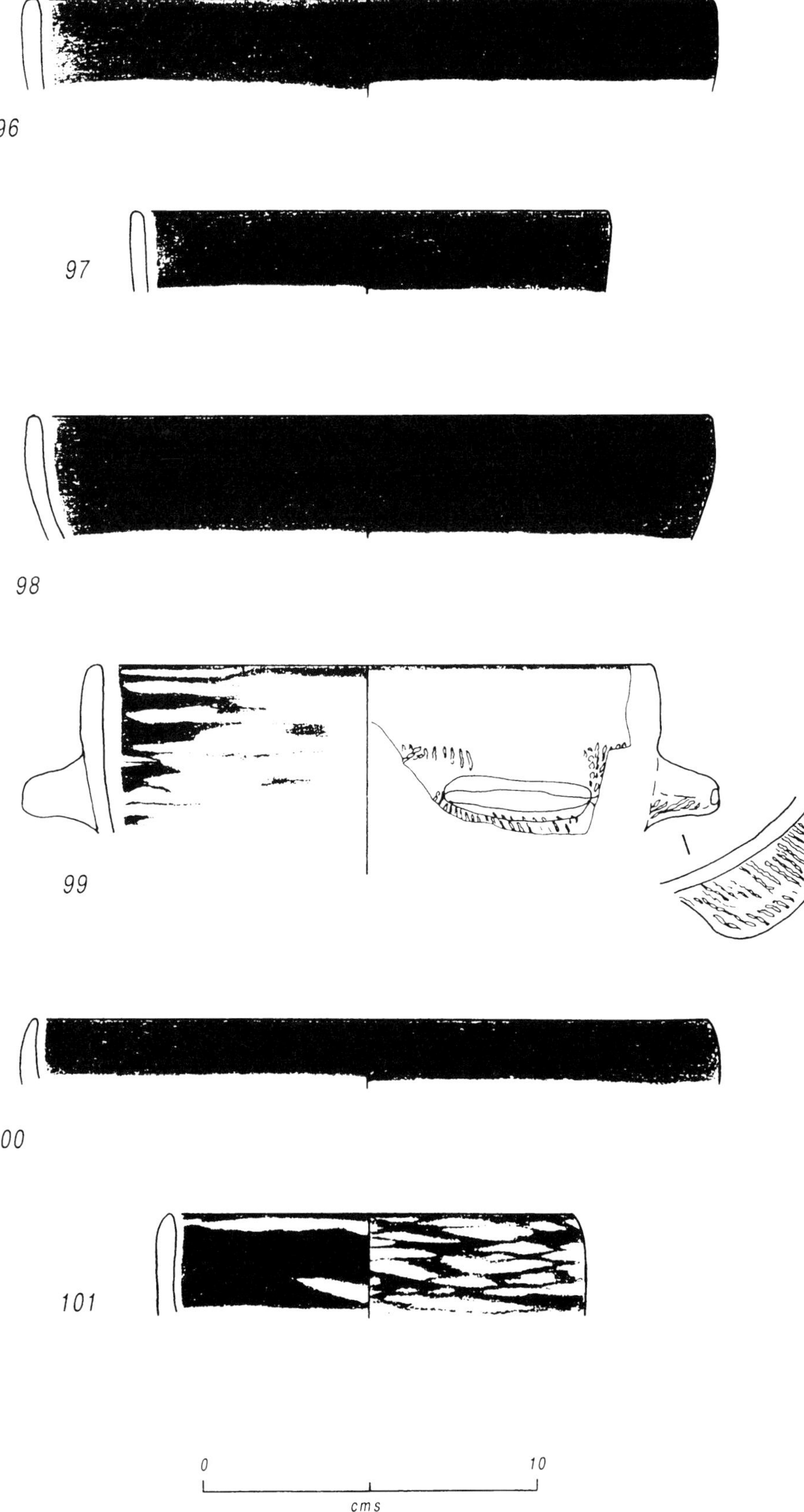

96

97

98

99

100

101

Figure 4.22
Phase 4 (continued)

<u>*Bowls, open*</u>

Cat. no.	*Provenance and sherd no.*	*Phase*	*Description*
96	705.84/1	?4	Bowl, upright rim. Fine fabric; fine grey grits, some whitish; pinkish-buff, some dark-grey mottling. Fine horizontal burnish outside (may be upper 25 mm from rim only) and inside.
97	644.27/15	4	Bowl, upright rim. Fine fabric; fine grits; bricky-orange. Fine burnish outside and outside.
98	708.2/3	4	Bowl, hemispherical. Very fine fabric; fine grits; dark grey, black surfaces. Very fine glossy burnish outside and inside. (*cf.* Plate 4.1)
99	710.6/5	4	Bowl, hemispherical. Horizontal lug/ledge handle. Fine fabric; fine grey and whitish grits; dull brick-red, some greyish mottling. Cord-impressed outside and on underside of handle, upper 20 mm left rough/scraped, burnished on rim and very streakily inside over well-smoothed surface.
100	709.29/1	?4	Bowl, upright rim. Very fine fabric; fine light-grey grits; brick-red, dark-grey inside surface. Horizontal burnish outside and inside.
101	709.8/1	?4	Bowl, upright rim (small). Fine fabric; fine dark grits; dull brick-red, brown surfaces. Horizontal burnish outside (streaky) and inside.

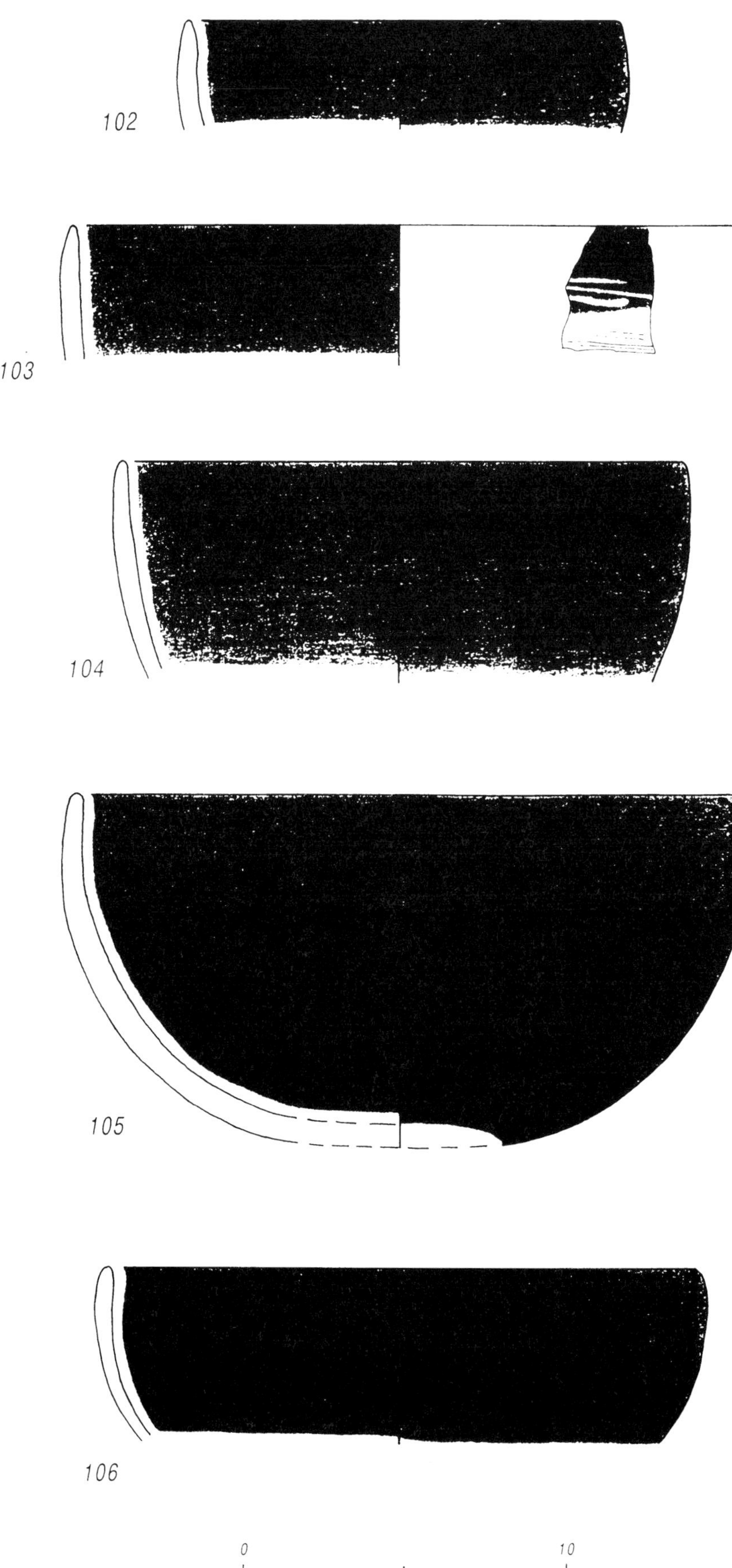

102
103
104
105
106
0
10
cms

Figure 4.23
Phase 4 (continued)

<u>*Bowls, open*</u>

Cat. no.	Provenance and sherd no.	Phase	Description
102	708.3/4	?4	Bowl, hemispherical (small). Fine fabric; fine light grits; dark brown, blackish-brown surfaces. Fine burnish outside and inside.
103	708.2/4	4	Bowl, upright rim. Fine fabric; fine light grits; dark brown/black. Very faint combing outside, below 26 mm band of glossy burnish, continuing inside.
104	708.2/1	4	Bowl, hemispherical. Fine fabric; fine grits; black mottled brown. Horizontal/oblique glossy burnish outside and inside. (*cf.* Plate 4.1)

<u>*Bowls, hemispherical*</u>

Cat. no.	Provenance and sherd no.	Phase	Description
105	710.9/3	4	Bowl, hemispherical. Base, round? Fine fabric; fine light and dark grits; bricky-brown, darker surfaces, black/brown at the base. Horizontal burnish outside and inside, rather streaky towards rim.
106	710.6/4	4	Bowl, hemispherical. Very fine fabric; fine light-grey grits; blackish brown, lighter brown outside surface. Fine burnish outside and inside.

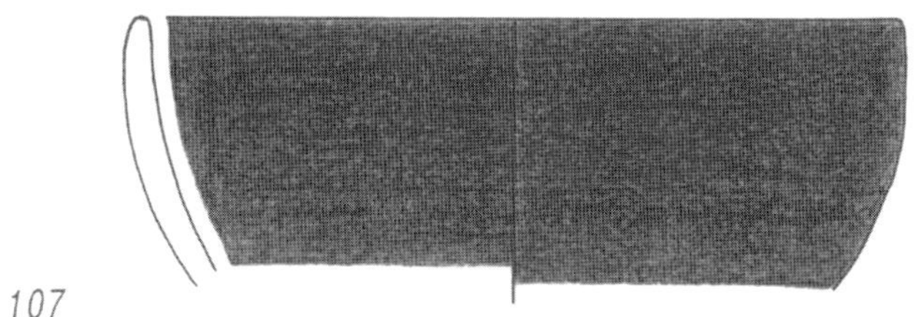

107

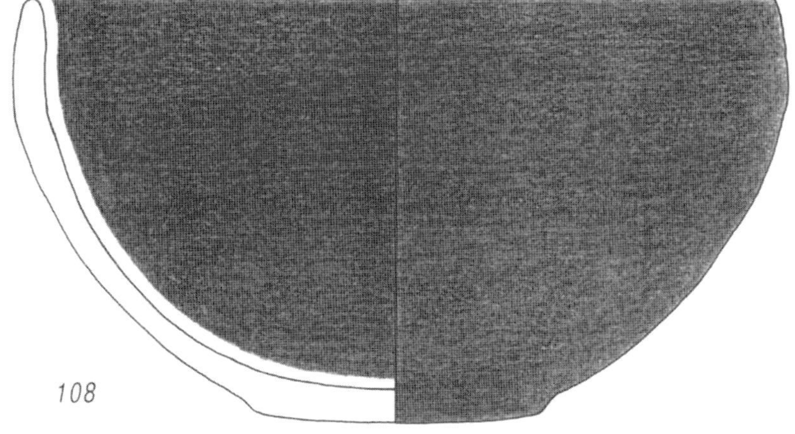

108

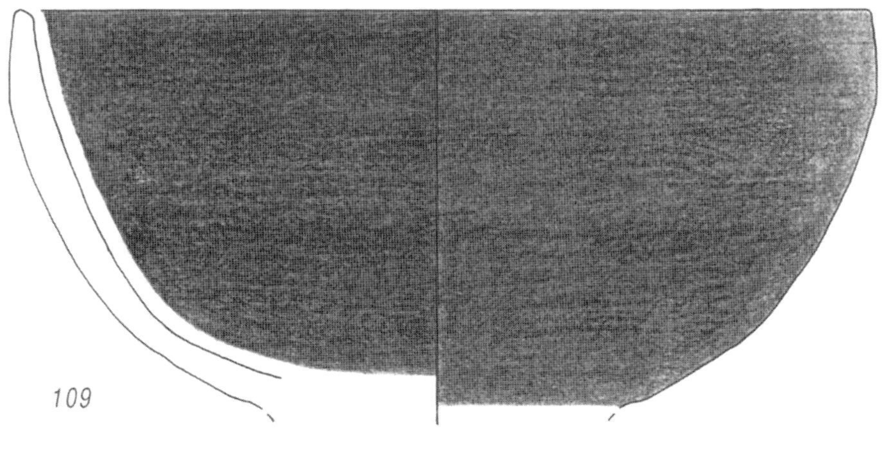

109

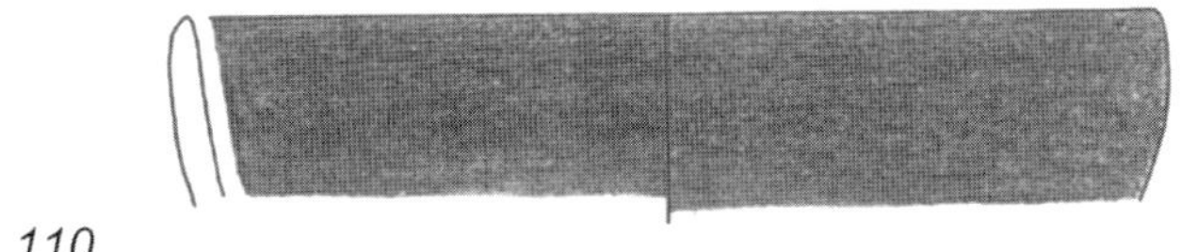

110

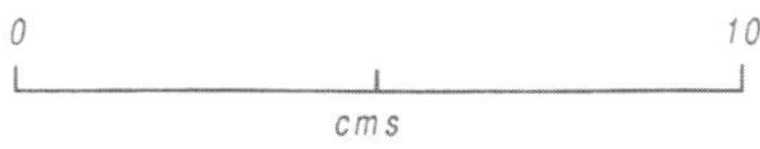

Figure 4.24
Phase 4 (continued)

Bowls, hemispherical

Cat. no.	Provenance and sherd no.	Phase	Description
107	644.41/4	4(?3)	Bowl, hemispherical. Fine fabric; small dark-grey grits; deep brick-red, dark-brown outside surface mottled black. Fine burnish outside and inside.
108	710.9/1	4	Bowl, hemispherical. Base, disc. Fine fabric; fine dark-grey grits, some light buff, a few larger; orange/brown, a little greyish mottling, heavily but unevenly blackened surface inside base. Streaky matt poorly applied burnish outside (except under centre of base where surface is rough or worn) and inside. (*cf.* Plate 4.2)
109	710.9/2	4	Bowl, hemispherical. (Base, disc, similar to no. 108?) Fine fabric; fine dark and light grits, some larger; dull mushroom-brown, blackish/mottled outside, heavily blackened surface inside base. Uneven/streaky matt burnish outside and inside.
110	708.3/7	?4	Bowl, flared. Very fine fabric; very fine light and dark grits; mid-brown, blackish inside below rim. Very fine glossy burnish outside and inside.

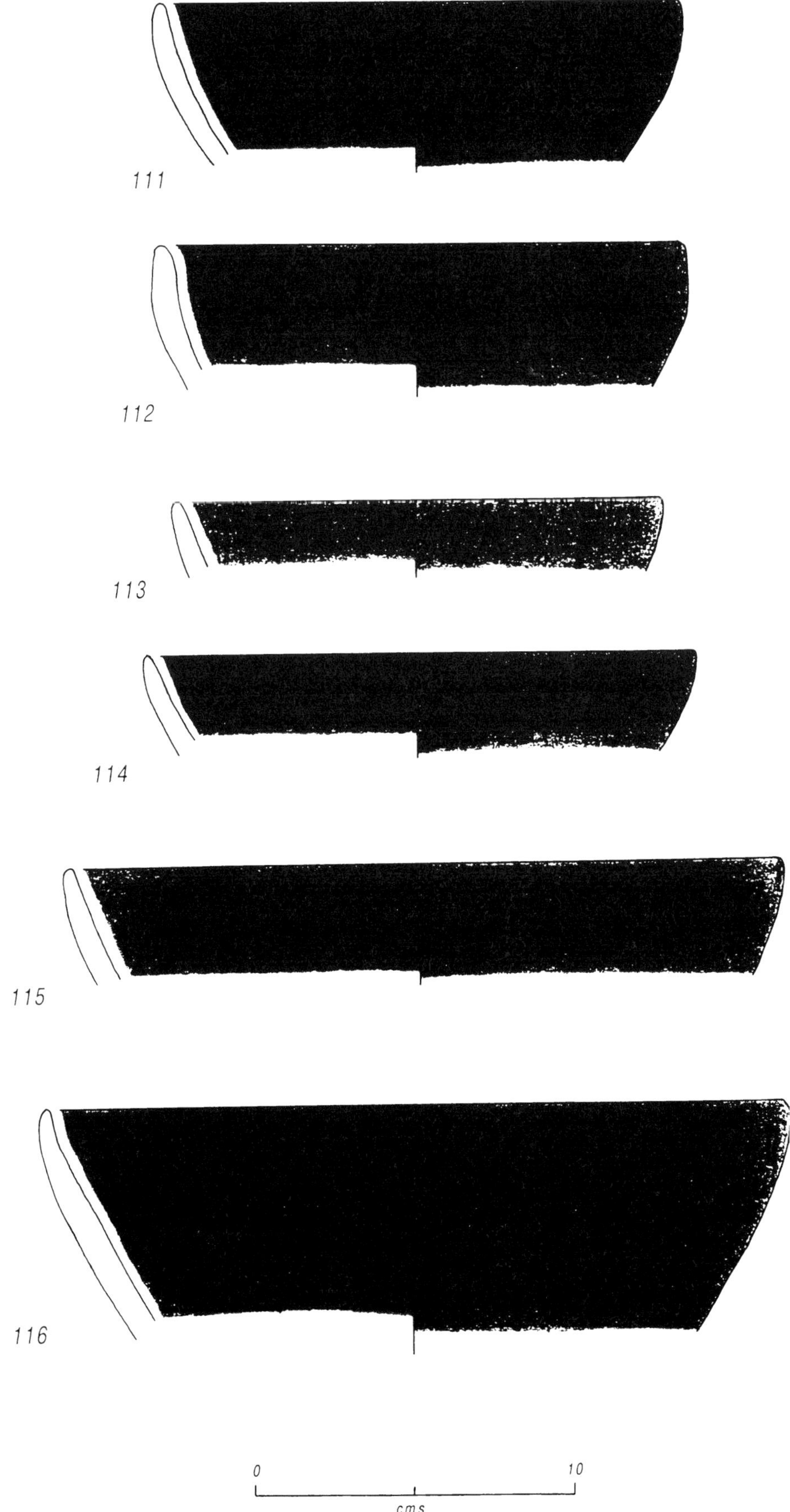

111
112
113
114
115
116
0
10
cms

Figure 4.25
Phase 4 (continued)

Bowls, rounded or conical

Cat. no.	Provenance and sherd no.	Phase	Description
111	606.2/1	?4	Bowl, flared. Fine fabric; fine grey and light grits; brick-red, some faint greyish mottling. Light matt burnish outside and inside on well smoothed surfaces. (*cf.* Plate 4.2)
112	710.9/5	4	Bowl, flared. Fine fabric but thick-walled; fine light and dark grits; blackish mottling outside, and inside below rim. Overall but streaky horizontal burnish outside and inside.
113	706.29/1	4(?3)	Bowl, flared. Fine fabric; fine light and dark grits. Black; glossy burnish outside and inside.
114	706.41/3	?4	Bowl, flared, shallow. Fine fabric; fine light and dark grits; black. Glossy burnish outside and inside.
115	708.3/5	?4	Bowl, flared. Fine fabric; fine light and dark grits; black, dark brown surfaces. Glossy burnish outside and inside.
116	706.10/4	4	Bowl, flared, conical. Fine fabric but thick-walled; fine light and dark grits; brick-red mottled grey/black. Fine burnish outside and inside.

Virginia Mathias

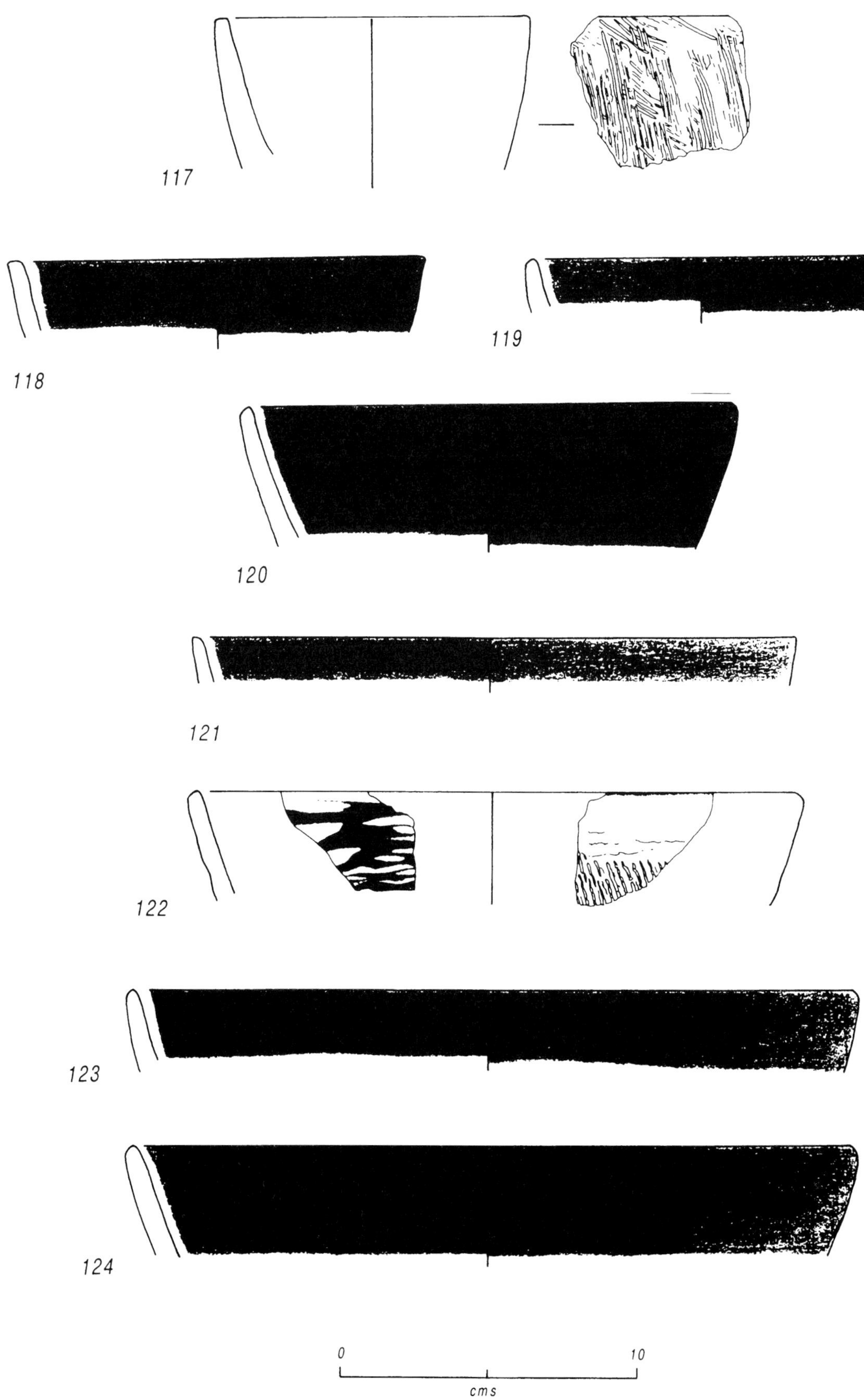

Figure 4.26
Phase 4 (continued)

Bowls, straight-sided/conical

Cat. no.	Provenance and sherd no.	Phase	Description
117	708.2/7	4	Bowl, flared, deep, small. Fine fabric but thick-walled; small dark-grey grits; light brick-red. Very faint combing outside, smoothed or faint-burnished inside on very uneven surface, with traces of white plaster inside and out. (*cf.* Plate 4.2)
118	706.40/1	?4	Bowl, flared. Very fine fabric; fine light and black grits; black. Very fine glossy burnish outside and inside.
119	708.3/6	?4	Bowl, flared (small). Very fine fabric; very fine light and dark grits; black; very fine glossy burnish outside and inside.
120	710.9/4	4	Bowl, flared, conical. Very fine fabric; fine light and dark grits; black. Very fine glossy burnish outside and inside.
121	705.69/8	?4	Bowl, flared. Very fine fabric; very fine light and dark grits; black. Very fine glossy burnish outside and inside.
122	710.6/6	4	Bowl, flared. Fine fabric; fine light grits; dull brown, blackish surfaces. Cord-impressed below 20 mm rough-scraped band outside, streaky horizontal burnish on rim and inside.
123	646.2/2	4	Bowl, flared. Fine fabric; small light grits; dark grey. Horizontal burnish outside and inside, scratched oblique lines inside through burnish, probably accidental.
124	705.63/4	?4	Bowl, flared. Fine fabric; fine black and light grits; dark brownish grey. Matt horizontal burnish outside and inside.

 Virginia Mathias

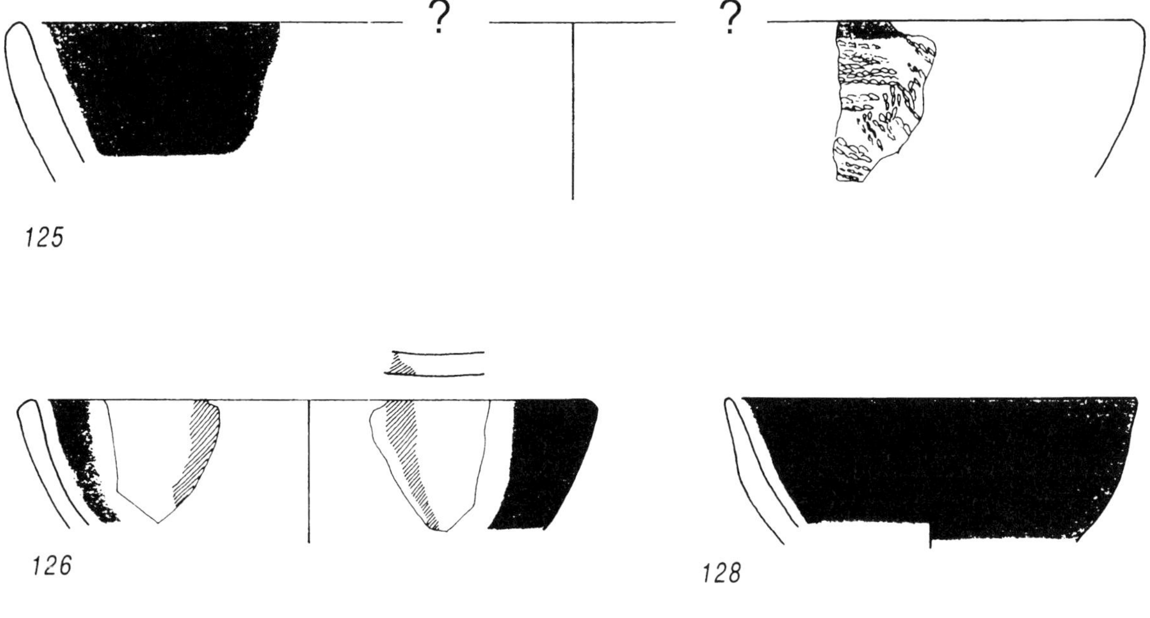

125

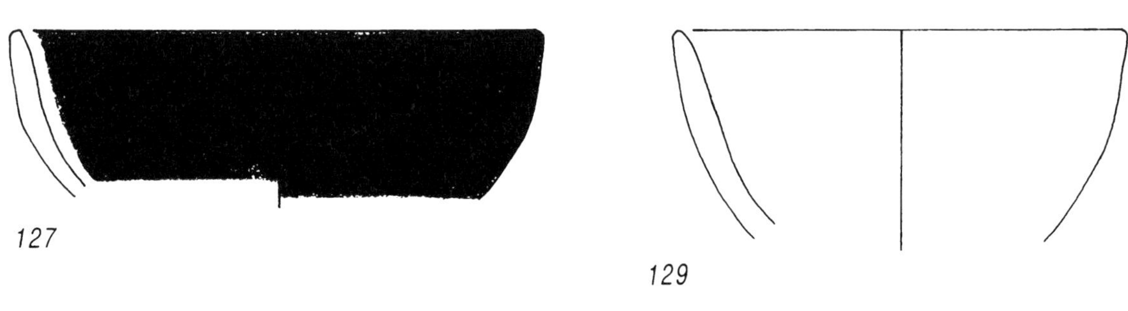

126

128

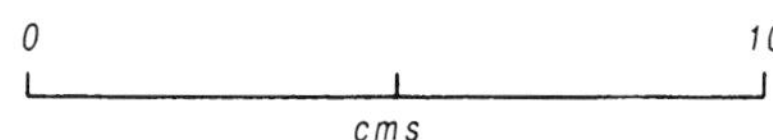

127

129

0   10
cms

Figure 4.27
Phase 4 (continued)

Bowls, shallow, rounded profile

Cat. no.	Provenance and sherd No.	Phase	Description
125	648.3/1	3	Bowl, shallow (large). Fine fabric; brick-red; fine light grits. Faint cord-impressions outside, burnish over rim and inside.
126	706.41/4	4(?3)	Bowl, curved, shallow. Fine fabric; fine dark grits; pale buff, thin light-grey core and surface mottling. Light burnish outside and inside, possible brownish paint or staining.
127	644.41.3	4(?3)	Bowl, curved, shallow. Fine fabric; fine grey and light grits; brick-red, grey-brown surfaces (possibly a slip). Matt burnish outside and inside.
128	710.6/3	4	Bowl, curved, shallow (small). Fine fabric; fine light grits; dark brownish grey. Glossy burnish outside and inside.
129	706.7/1	4	Bowl, curved, shallow (small). Fairly fine fabric; small whitish grits (causing some surface pitting); light brick-red, light greyish inside. Surfaces smoothed, traces of faint burnish, inside uneven.

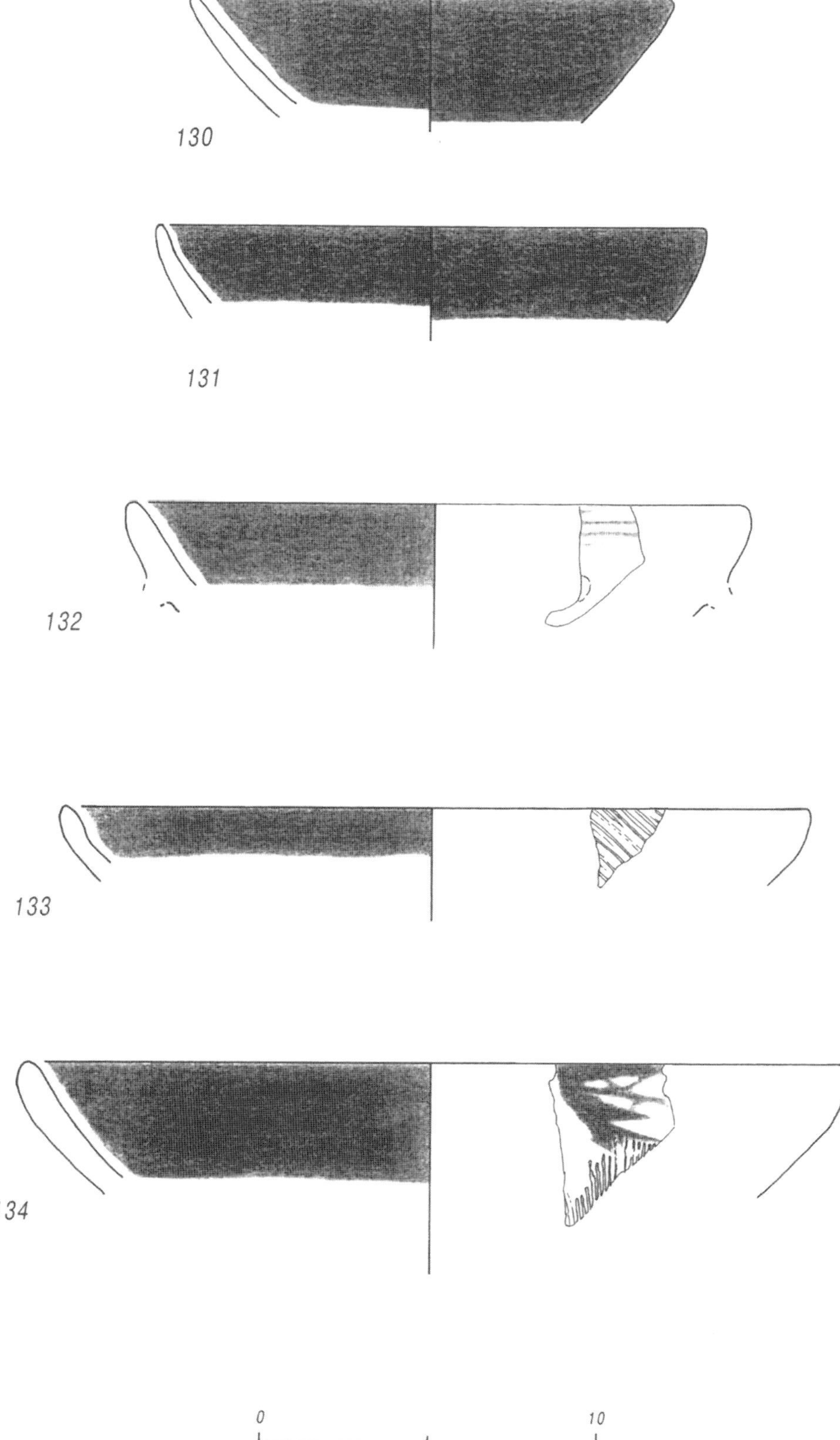

130

131

132

133

134

0   10

cms

Figure 4.28
Phase 4 (continued)

Bowls, shallow, flared

Cat. no.	Provenance and sherd No.	Phase	Description
130	706.41/2	?4	Bowl, flared, shallow (small). Very fine fabric; very fine light and dark grits; blackish brown. Fine glossy burnish outside and inside.
131	708.2/2	4	Bowl, flared, shallow. Fine fabric; fine light and dark grits; black. Fine glossy burnish outside and inside.
132	644.27/34	4	Bowl, flared, shallow. Lug or knob handle? Fine fabric but thick-walled; fine light and dark grits; blackish grey, lighter core. Horizontal burnish in a 10 mm band outside (very streaky), over rim and inside.
133	710.9/7	4	Bowl, flared, shallow. Fine fabric; fine light grits; brown mottled black, especially inside. Faint-combing outside, horizontal burnish on rim and inside.
134	646.2/3	4	Bowl, flared, shallow. Fine fabric; fine light and grey grits; brown, black mottled on rim (similar to a wick mark). Smudged combing outside, 25 mm band of streaky burnish above, and over rim, inside even but matt.

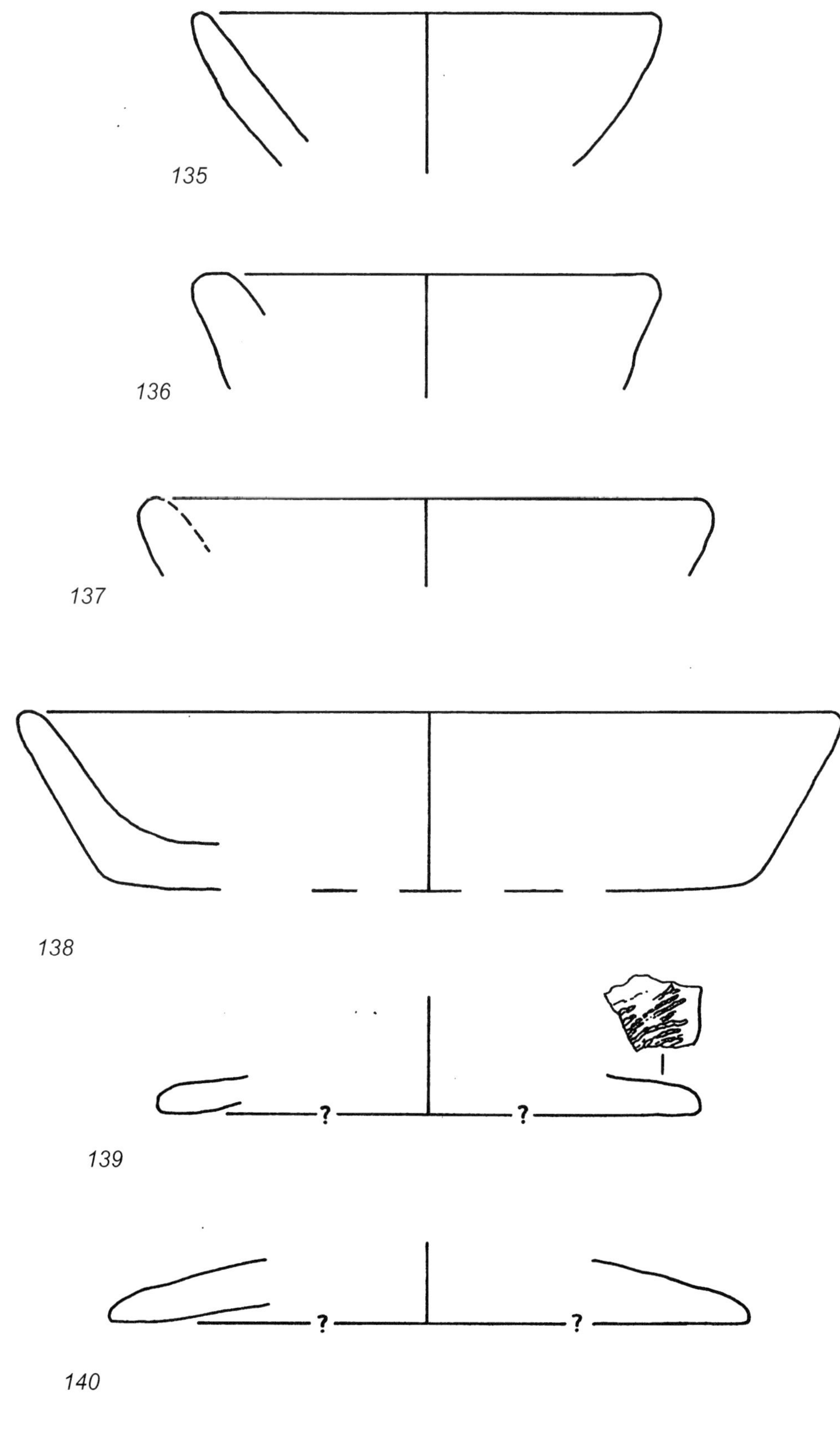

135

136

137

138

139

140

Figure 4.29
Phase 4 (continued)

Bowls, coarse fabric; lids

Cat. no.	Provenance and sherd No.	Phase	Description
135	606.27/7	4	Bowl, flared, shallow. Coarse fabric; medium-size dark-grey grits; pale buff-pink, light-grey core. Smoothed surfaces. Blackened inside.
136	706.7/2	4	Bowl, flared, shallow (small). Very coarse fabric, very thick-walled; medium-size dark-grey and light grits, some vegetable temper; buff-pink, grey core. Smoothed surfaces, slightly blackened on rim.
137	706.11/1	4	Bowl, flared. Coarse fabric, thick-walled; medium-size dark-grey grits, some vegetable temper; light brick-red, buff-and-grey core. Smoothed outside and on rim, inside surface missing.
138	606.7/3	4	Platter, flared, shallow. Coarse fabric; large dark-grey grits; buff. Well smoothed outside and inside, rougher underneath. (*cf.* Plate 4.2)

Lids

Cat. no.	Provenance and sherd No.	Phase	Description
139	735.7/2	4	Lid? Medium–coarse fabric; small grey and white grits, grog, fine vegetable temper; buff, mottled grey inside; cord-impressed outside, lightly smoothed inside; flattened underneath outside edge.
140	706.11/2	4	Lid? Flattened edge. Very coarse fabric; large dark-grey and small white grits; buff-pink, grey core; fairly rough surfaces; flattened underneath outside edge.

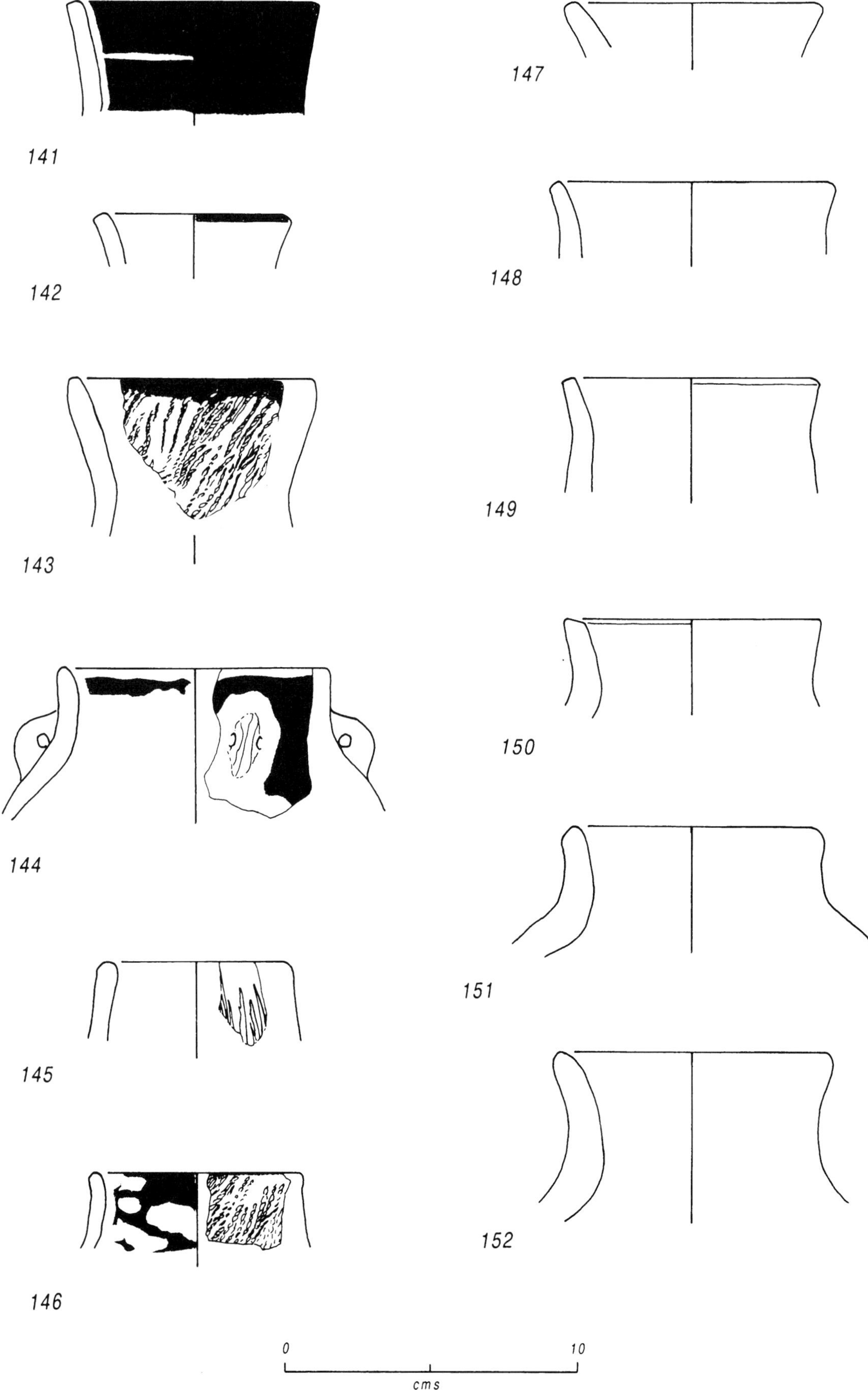

Figure 4.30
Phase 5

Jars, necked, narrow

Cat. no.	Provenance and sherd no.	Phase	Description
141	708.1/3	5	Jar with neck, flared, narrow, high. Very fine fabric; very fine dark and light-grey grits; brownish-buff, faint greyish mottling. Rather streaky burnish, vertical outside, horizontal inside, on very even surfaces.
142	735.2/1	5	Jar with neck, flared, narrow (small). Fine fabric; small pale-grey grits; buff. Burnish on rim, very slight outside and inside.
143	706.1/1	5	Jar with neck, flared, narrow, high. Fairly fine fabric; small white grits, dark-red grog; brownish-black surfaces, reddish-brown core. Cord-impressed outside, slight burnish over rim, inside smoothed over uneven surface.
144	708.1/1	5	Jar with neck, upright. Vertical lug handle, horizontally pierced. Fine fabric; fine dark-grey grits; buff surfaces, thick dark-grey core. Sketchy burnish outside (but not around lug), over rim.
145	680.42/1	5	Jar with neck, slightly inverted, narrow. Fine fabric; fine dark grits; dull dark-red outside surface, black core and inside. Irregular incised vertical lines outside (some deep), rough inside.
146	708.1/4	5	Jar with neck, slightly inverted, narrow. Fine fabric; fine pale-grey grits; pale brick-red, mottled buff. Cord-impressed outside, streaky burnish on rim and inside on uneven surface.
147	654.7/2	5	Jar with neck, flared, narrow. Fairly fine fabric; small pale-grey grits; brick-red, thick black core. Smoothed outside and inside.
148	735.3/5	5	Jar with neck, upright. Fairly fine fabric; small dark-grey grits. Very sketchy burnish outside, smoothed inside.
149	654.7/1	5	Jar with neck, upright, narrow, high. Medium fabric, roughly made; small dark-grey grits; light brick-red, buff core. Smoothed outside and inside
150	735.2/2	5	Jar with neck, upright, narrow. Coarse fabric; small dark-grey grits; buff. Rough-scraped outside and inside.
151	650.14/1	5	Jar with neck, upright, narrow. Coarse fabric; medium-size dark-grey grits; buff, possible brownish slip. Smoothed outside and inside.
152	606.62/1	5	Jar with neck, flared, narrow. Coarse fabric; large dark-grey grits; buff. Smoothed outside and inside.

Virginia Mathias

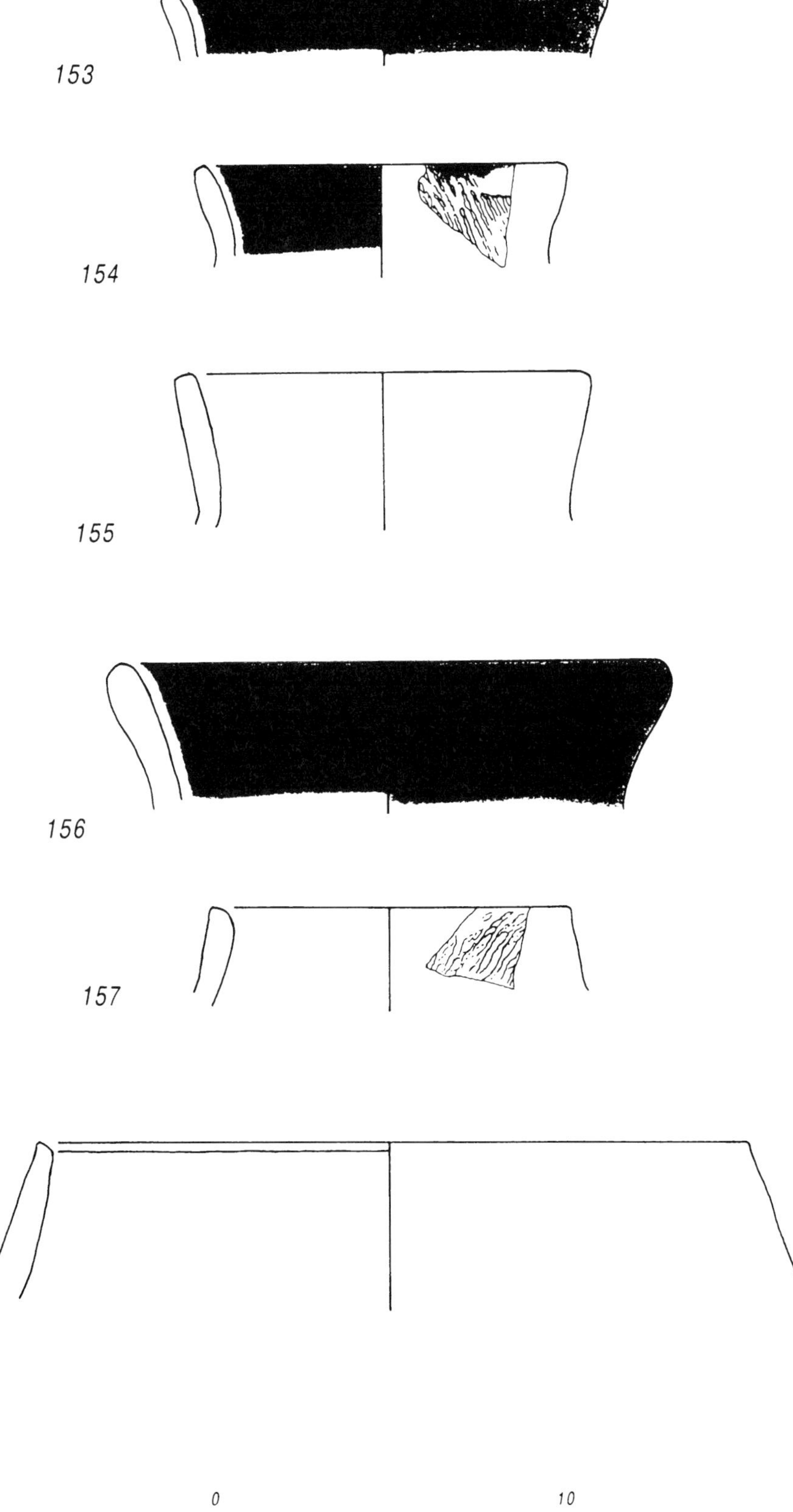

Figure 4.31
Phase 5 (continued)

Jars, necked, wide

Cat. no.	Provenance and sherd no.	Phase	Description
153	648.1/2	5	Jar with neck, flared. Fairly fine fabric; small whitish grits; brick-red, thin blue-grey core. Rough burnish outside and inside on a yellowish surface, possibly a slip.
154	602.19/1	5	Jar with neck, flared. Fine fabric; fine dark grits; dull brick-red. Cord-impressed outside, light burnish on rim and inside.
155	644.34/20	5	Jar with neck, flared, high. Fairly fine fabric, hard-fired; small grey and light grits, some pitting the surface; brick-red, thin dark-grey core; surface. Lightly smoothed outside and inside.
156	648.1/1	5	Jar with neck, flared, thickened. Fairly fine fabric; dense small pale-grey grits; light brick-red, thick grey core. Rough burnish outside and inside on pale buff surface or slip.
157	710.3/1	5	Jar with neck, slightly inverted, narrow. Fine fabric; fine light and dark grits; dark brick-red. Cord-impressed outside, well smoothed inside.
158	644.34/9	5	Jar with neck, slightly inverted, wide. Medium fabric; dense small dark-grey grits; buff. Lightly smoothed outside and upper 25 mm inside, rough below.

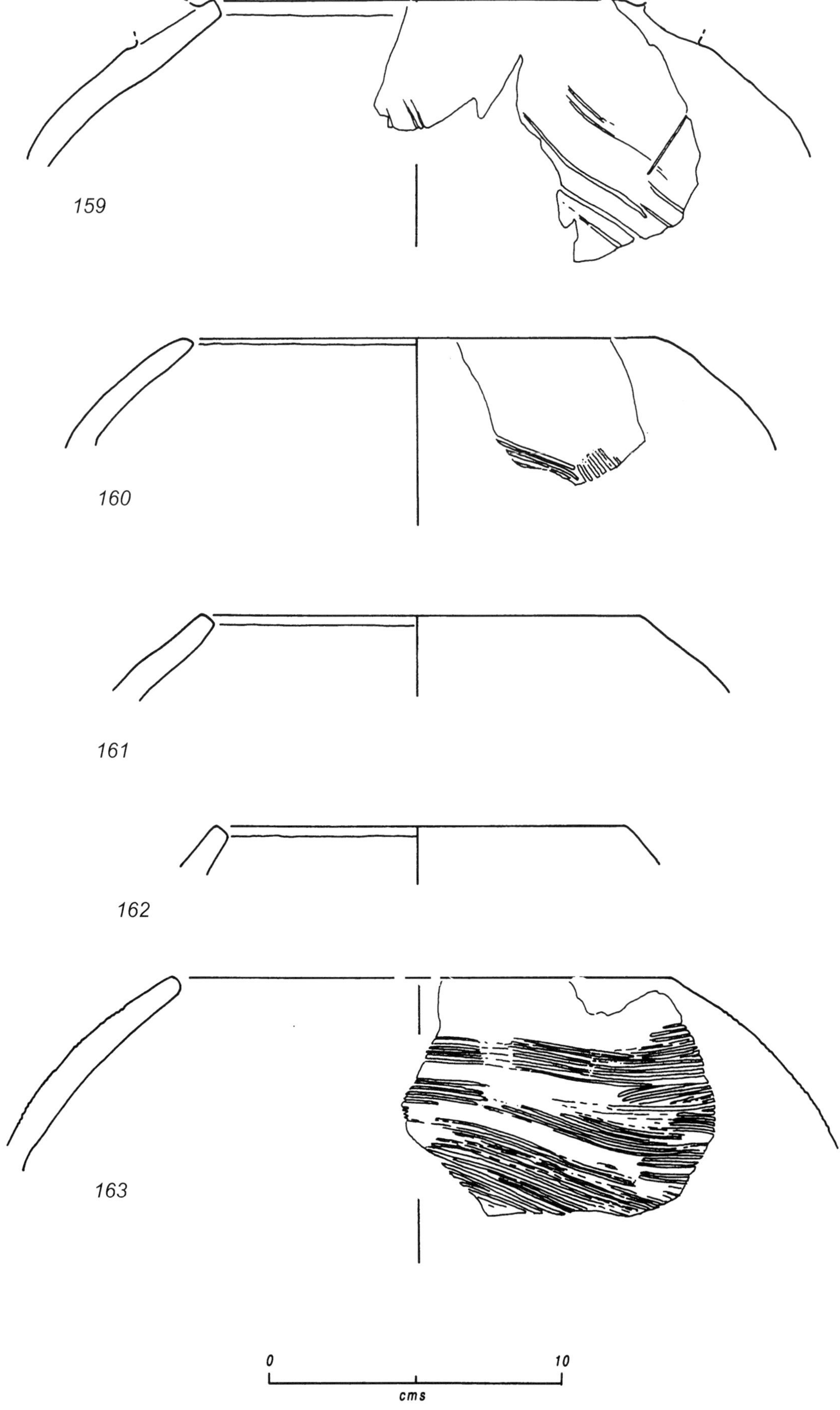

159

160

161

162

163

Figure 4.32
Phase 5 (continued)

Jars, holemouth, shallow angle; medium to coarse fabric

Cat. no.	Provenance and sherd no.	Phase	Description
159	735.1/1	5	Jar, holemouth, shallow. Knob handle? Medium–fine fabric, hard-fired but roughly made and uneven; small dark and light grits, red grog; pale brick-red, buff core and mottling. Surfaces finger-smoothed (especially inside), incised parallel lines outside on shoulder (some very light), below rectangular knob (broken on join: scar only close to rim. (*cf.* Plate 4.2)
160	654.7/3	5	Jar, holemouth, shallow. Medium fabric, thin-walled (uneven); fine dark and light grits; pale brick-red, pale buff core. Finger-smoothed outside with faint-combing or impressed lines on shoulder starting 40 mm down from rim, rather rough inside.
161	735.3/2	5	Jar, holemouth, shallow. Medium–coarse fabric, roughly made and uneven; small light and grey grits, fine vegetable temper; pinkish-buff, grey core and mottling. Finger-smoothed on uneven surfaces.
162	735.3/3	5	Jar, holemouth, shallow. Medium fabric; small grey grits; pale buff, slight grey core. Finger-smoothed outside, uneven surface inside.
163	708.1/2	5	Jar, holemouth, shallow. Medium fabric; small dark grey and whitish grits; light brick-red; partial red-brown wash or discoloration outside. Combed decoration (6-tooth?) in horizontal and swirling bands starting 25 mm below rim; vertical finger-smoothing inside, on uneven surfaces.

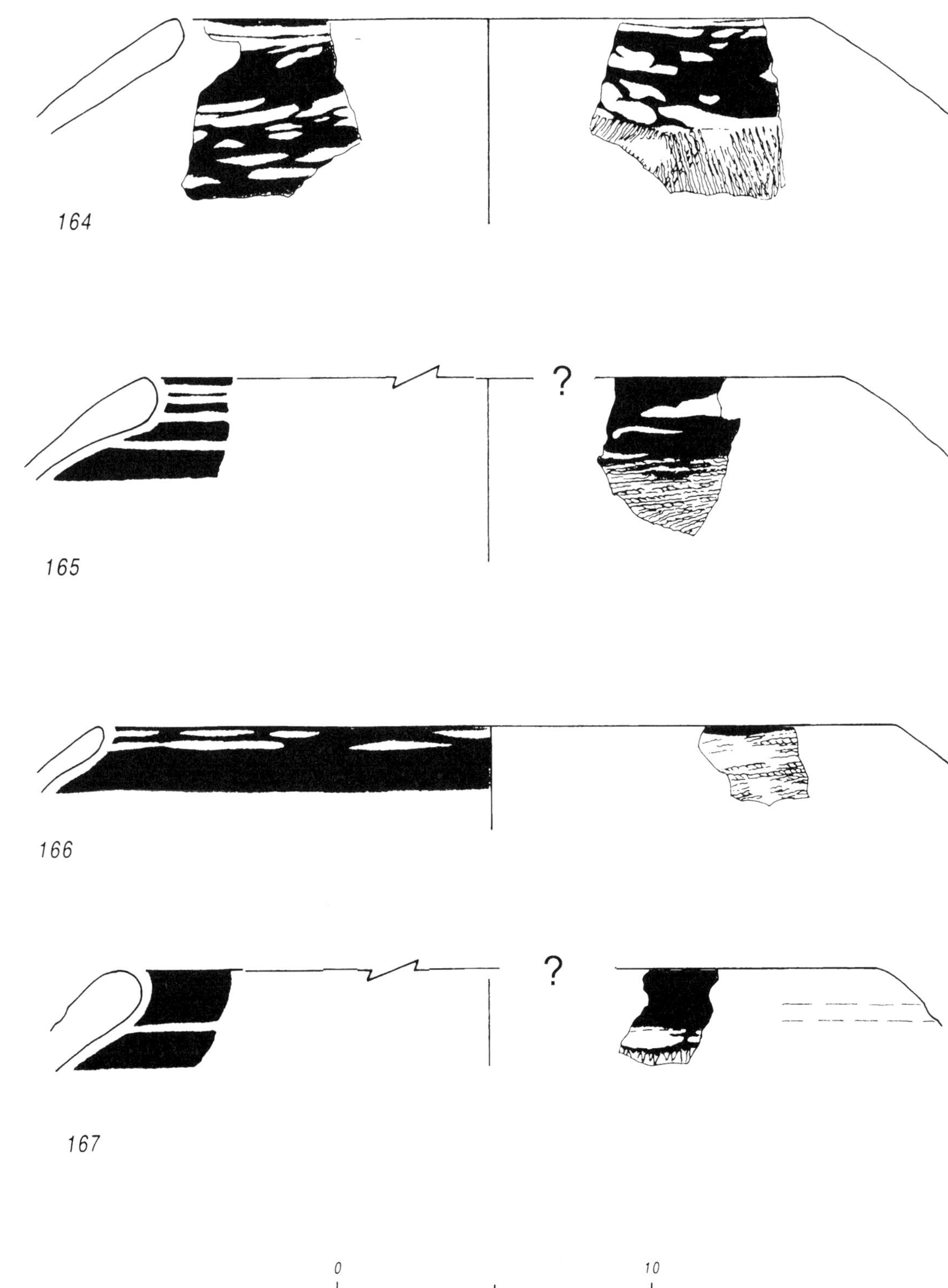

164

165

166

167

Figure 4.33
Phase 5 (continued)

Jars, holemouth, shallow angle, rolled rim; fine fabric

Cat. no.	Provenance and sherd no.	Phase	Description
164	606.62/3	5	Jar, holemouth, shallow, rolled rim. Medium–fine fabric; dense small pale-grey grits; light orange, grey mottling. Streaky burnish inside and in band above cord-impressions outside.
165	654.9/1	5	Jar, holemouth, shallow, rolled rim. Fairly fine fabric; dense small pale-grey grits; dull brick-red, grey-brown core. Cord-impressed outside slightly overlapping 30 mm band of streaky burnish, also inside, on roughly finished surfaces.
166	706.1/3	5	Jar, holemouth, shallow, rolled rim. Fine fabric; fine light and dark grits; dull brick-red, dark grey towards inside surface. Faint cord-impressions outside, matt horizontal burnish over rim (streaky) and inside.
167	735.2/3	5	Jar, holemouth, shallow, rolled rim. Fine fabric, thick-walled, with multiple or rolled-over coils visible on break; small light and dark grits; black, light orange-buff surface on rim and inside and parts of core (may be heavy mottling). Cord-impressions outside below slight groove and 27 mm band of horizontal burnish, burnish inside.

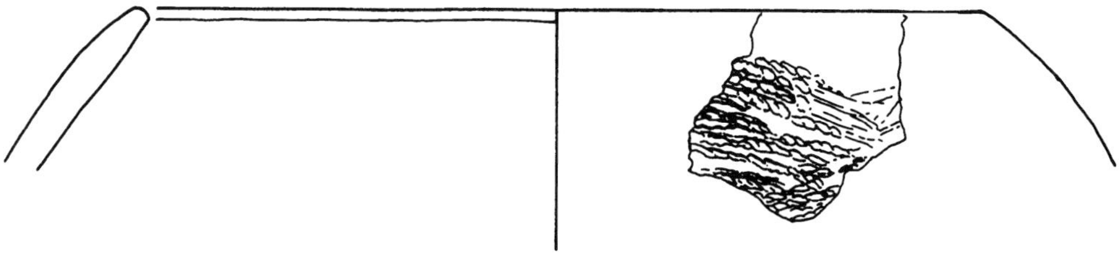

168

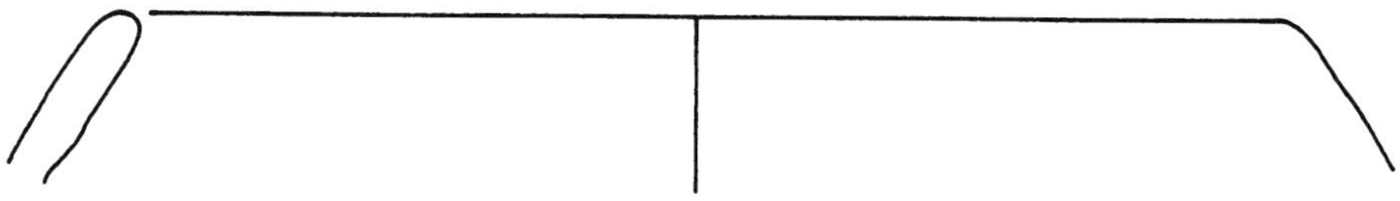

169

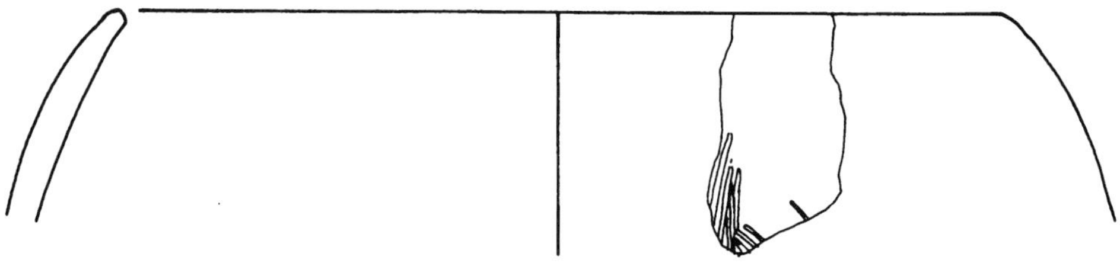

170

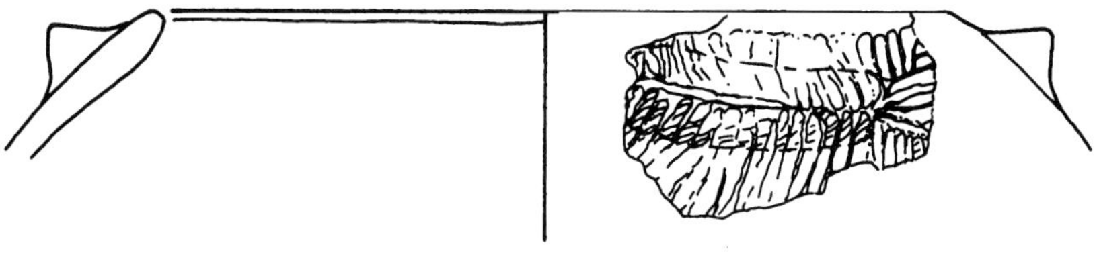

171

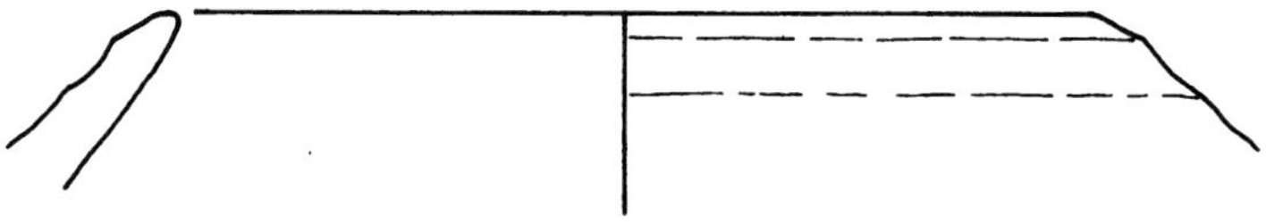

172

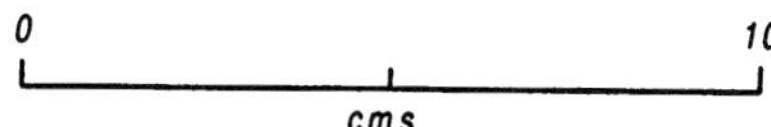

Figure 4.34
Phase 5 (continued)

Jars, holemouth, steeper angle; medium fabric

Cat. no.	Provenance and sherd no.	Phase	Description
168	646.10/2	5	Jar, holemouth, steep. Fine fabric; fine white and dark grits; black, rim and outside surface cream-grey (possibly a slip). Cord-impressed (thick cord) outside below *c.*15 mm band left rather rough, horizontal smoothing inside.
169	735.6/2	?5	Jar, holemouth, steep. Medium fabric, light and porous; small whitish and dark grits, vegetable temper; dull greyish buff, thick dark-grey core. Slightly smoothed outside and inside.
170	735.3/9	5	Jar, holemouth, steep. Medium–fine fabric; medium-size dark-grey angular grits, some vegetable temper, possibly chaff. Well smoothed or very light burnish outside, with very faint combing starting 27 mm below rim, lightly finger-smoothed inside.
171	709.1/1	5	Jar, holemouth, shallow. Long narrow ledge/lug. Fine fabric; small dark and light grits; dull dark brownish-grey. Cord-impressed outside, including over ledge handle, horizontal and oblique smoothing inside.
172	644.14/20	5	Jar, holemouth, shallow. Medium–fine fabric, hard-fired; medium-size dark grey grits, a few white, and red grog; pale brick-red, buff core. Well smoothed or light burnished on rilled outside surface, inside slightly finger-smoothed on uneven surface.

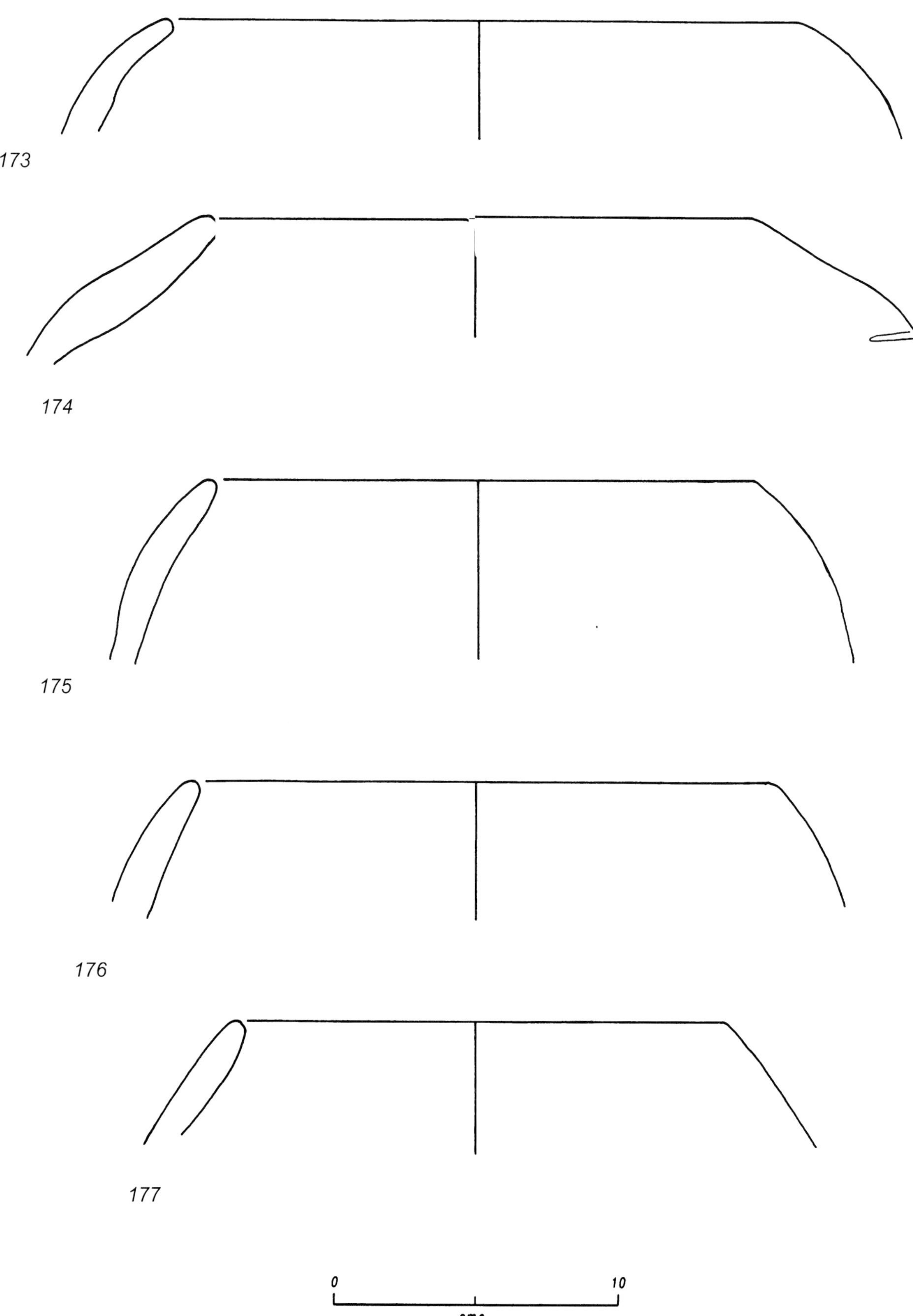

173
174
175
176
177
0
10
cms

Figure 4.35
Phase 5 (continued)

Jars, holemouth; coarse fabric

Cat. no.	Provenance and sherd no.	Phase	Description
173	735.6/3	?5	Jar, holemouth, shallow. Medium fabric; medium-size dark grey grits, some vegetable temper, (may be chaff); buff. Well smoothed or very light matt burnish outside, light finger-smoothing inside.
174	606.61/1	5	Jar, holemouth, shallow. Very coarse fabric; medium-size dark grey and white grits, red grog. Lightly smoothed or wiped outside and inside (uneven surface). Shallow incised or indented mark on shoulder (could be accidental).
175	735.3/8	5	Jar, holemouth, steep. Coarse fabric; small grey, white and brown grits, some vegetable temper; pinkish buff, slightly blackened outside surface. Finger-smoothed outside and inside.
176	650.14/2	5	Jar, holemouth, steep. Coarse fabric; medium-size dark-grey grits, a few white, some vegetable temper; buff. Well smoothed inside and outside.
177	706.47/6	5	Jar, holemouth, steep. Coarse; medium-size blackish grits; buff, thick black core. Well smoothed or light matt burnish outside and inside.

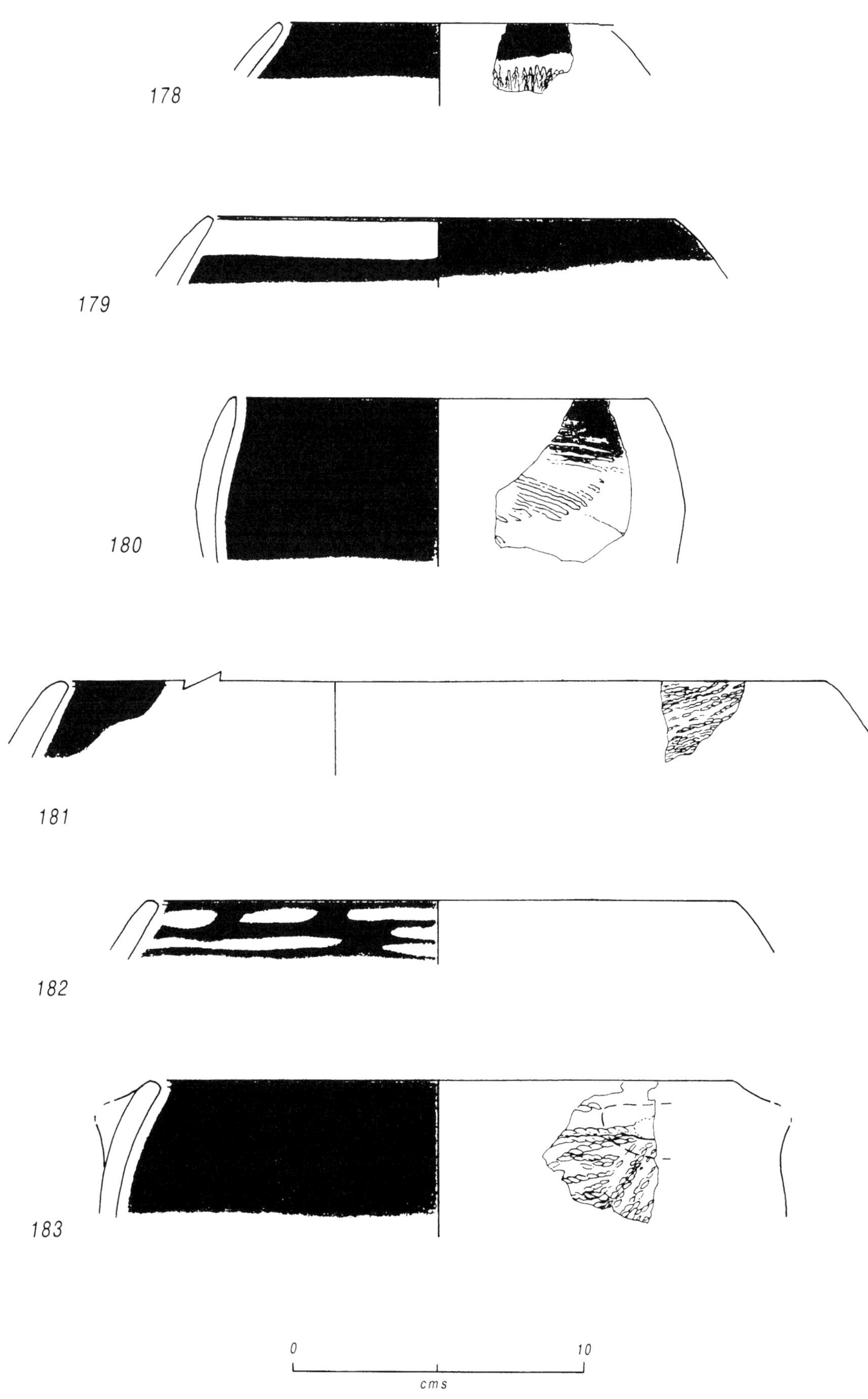

178
179
180
181
182
183
0
10
cms

Figure 4.36
Phase 5 (continued)

Jars, holemouth, steeply sloping; fine fabric

Cat. no.	Provenance and sherd no.	Phase	Description
178	644.34/12	5	Jar, holemouth, steep (small). Fine fabric; fine light and dark grits; greyish-buff surfaces, thick dark-grey core. Fine cord-impressions below 12 mm band of matt burnish, also burnish inside.
179	710.5/1	5	Jar, holemouth, steep. Fine fabric; fine light and shiny grits; dull brick-red, dark grey inside surface and mottling outside. Matt burnish outside and (sketchy) inside.
180	710.5/2	5	Jar, holemouth, steep (small). Fine fabric; small to fine dark and light grits; dull brick-red outside, dark grey inside and rim. Cord-impressed outside below and overlapping 20 mm matt burnish band, also inside.
181	602.19/2	5	Jar, holemouth, steep (large). Fine fabric; fine dark-grey grits; bricky brown. Shallow cord-impressions outside, horizontal burnish on rim and inside.

Bowls, slightly inverted rim; fine fabric

Cat. no.	Provenance and sherd no.	Phase	Description
182	706.1/2	5	Jar, holemouth, steep. Fine fabric; small dark-grey grits; buff. Smoothed outside, very sketchy burnish inside.
183	735.1/2	5	Jar, holemouth, steep. Lug or knob handle. Fine fabric; fine grey grits; dark grey outside, black inside and core. Well smoothed outside under cord-impressions (thick cord), light matt burnish inside.

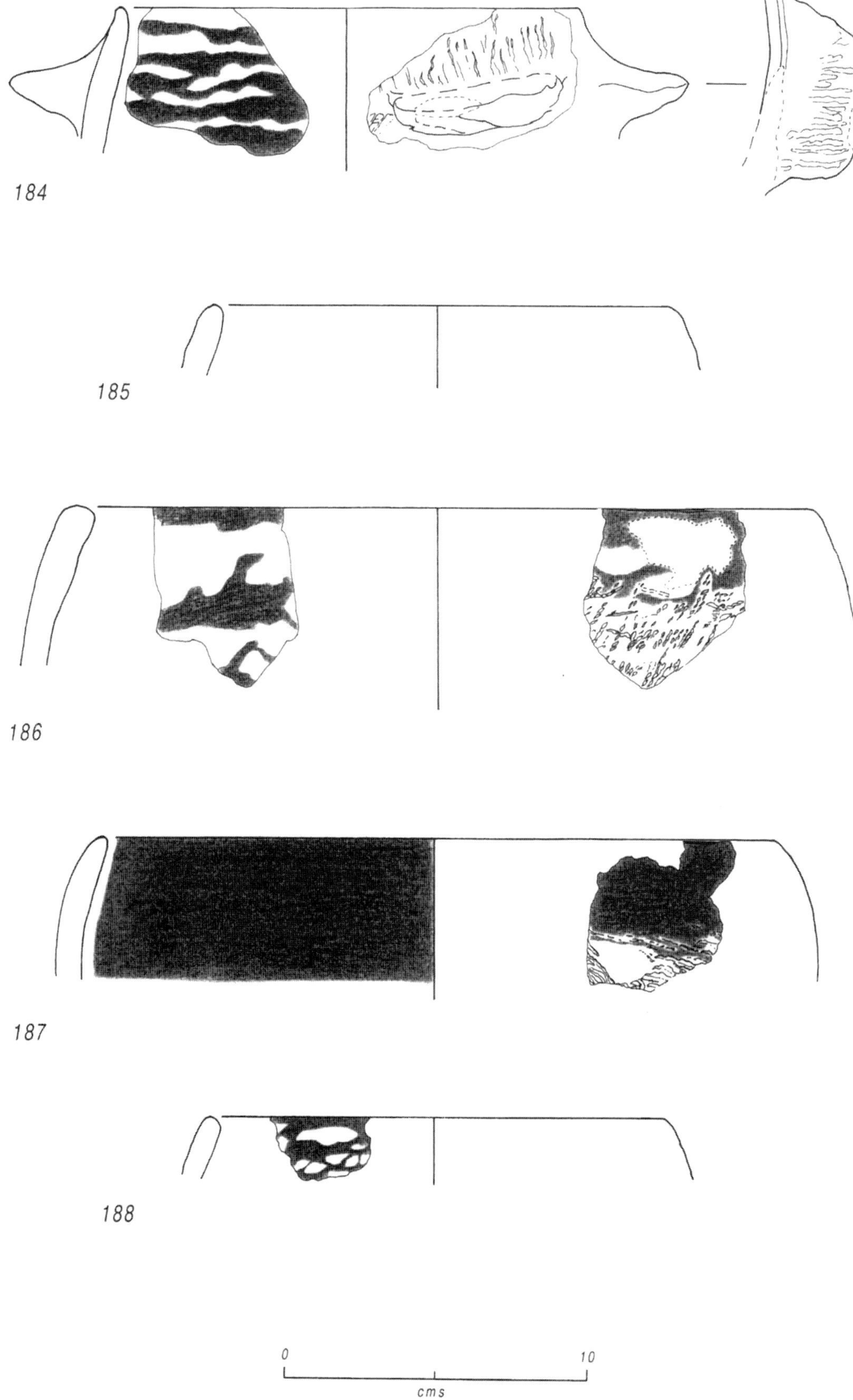

184

185

186

187

188

Figure 4.37
Phase 5 (continued)

Bowls, slightly inverted rim; fine and medium fabric

Cat. no.	Provenance and sherd no.	Phase	Description
184	606.62/2	5	Bowl, slightly inverted rim. Deep horizontal lug/ledge handle. Fine fabric, roughly finished; small dark and shiny grits; dull brick-red, brown core and surfaces. Worn and indistinct cord-impressions outside on uneven surface of body and upper side only of broad ledge handle, under-side rough and very uneven, streaky burnish on inside surface.
185	735.3/4	5	Bowl, slightly inverted rim. Medium fabric; small dark and light grits; dull pinkish-buff, blackened/greyish outside surface. Smoothed outside, barely inside.
186	646.10/3	5	Bowl, slightly inverted rim (large). Medium fabric; small dark and light grits, fine vegetable temper; light brick-red, thick dark-grey core and darkened or mottled surfaces. Cord-impressed outside, apparently overlapping 30 mm band of sketchy matt burnish (part of surface missing), also sketchy burnish inside on uneven surface.
187	706.1/4	5	Bowl, slightly inverted rim. Fairly fine fabric; fine dark grits and red grog; pinkish buff, greyish mottled surfaces. Cord-impressed outside, slightly overlapping 37 mm band of light matt horizontal burnish, continuing inside.
188	644.18/8	5	Bowl, slightly inverted rim. Fine fabric; small dark-grey grits; brownish buff. Smoothed outside, streaky burnish on rim and inside.

Virginia Mathias

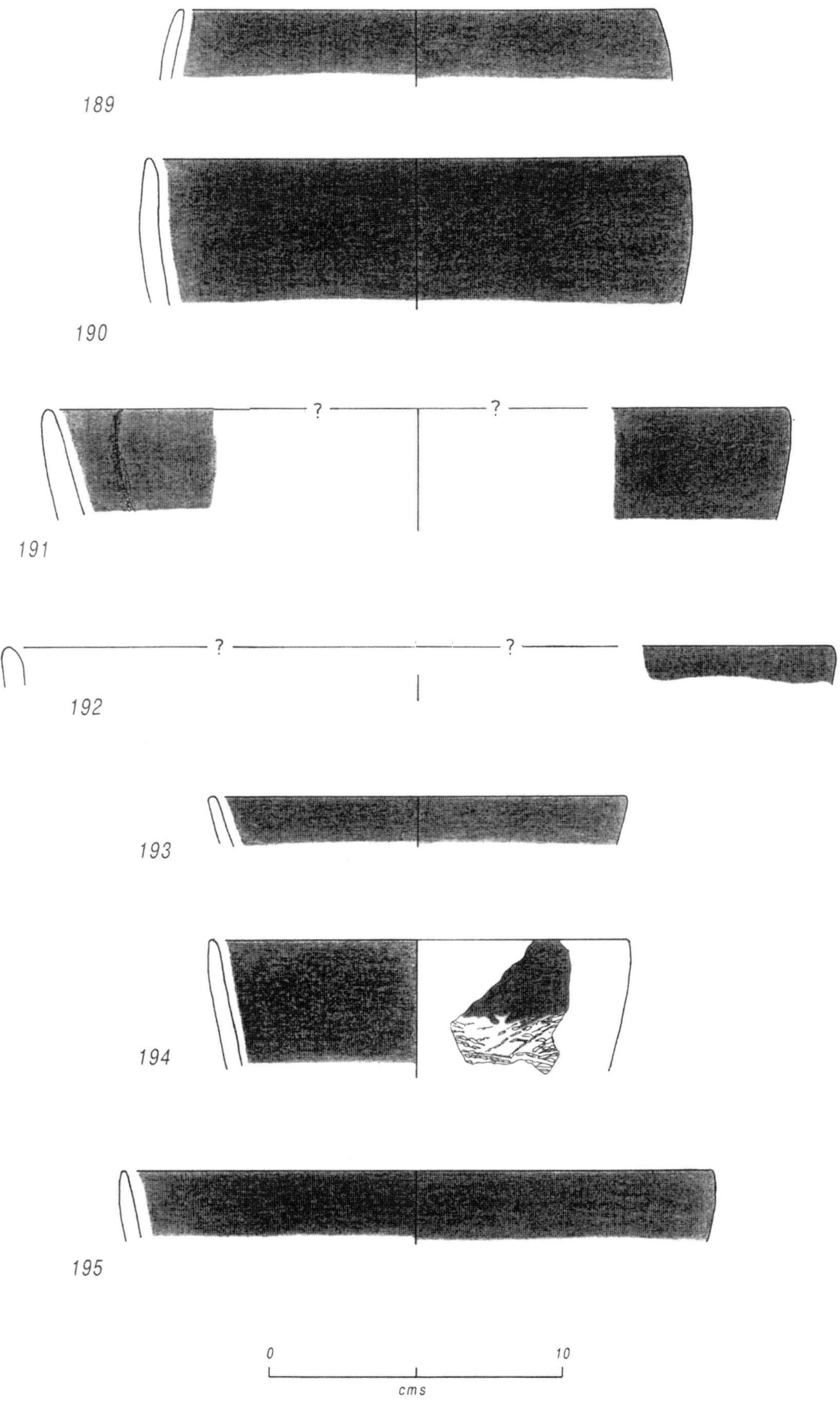

Figure 4.38
Phase 5 (continued)

Bowls, open, deep; fine fabric

Cat. no.	Provenance and sherd no.	Phase	Description
189	706.4/1	5	Bowl, slightly inverted rim. Very fine fabric; fine pale grey grits; black. Fine glossy burnish outside and inside.
190	647.6/1	5	Bowl, upright rim. Fairly fine fabric; small grey and light grits, red grog; brick-red mottled brown, thin grey core. Rather rough burnish, horizontal outside and over rim, oblique inside.
191	706.3/1	5	Bowl, flared (large). Fine fabric but thick-walled; fine whitish grits; black. Horizontal burnish outside and inside.
192	654.9/2	5	Bowl (large). Fine fabric but thick-walled; fine light and dark grits; black, some brown mottling. Burnish outside, worn rim and inside with traces of burnish.
193	706.3/3	5	Bowl, flared. Very fine fabric; fine light grits; black. Fine glossy burnish outside and inside.
194	646.10/1	5	Bowl, flared, conical. Fine fabric; fine light grey grits; black. Cord-impressed outside below 27 mm band of fine glossy burnish, also inside.
195	644.34/33	5	Bowl, flared. Very fine fabric; very fine dark and light grits; black. Fine glossy burnish outside and inside.

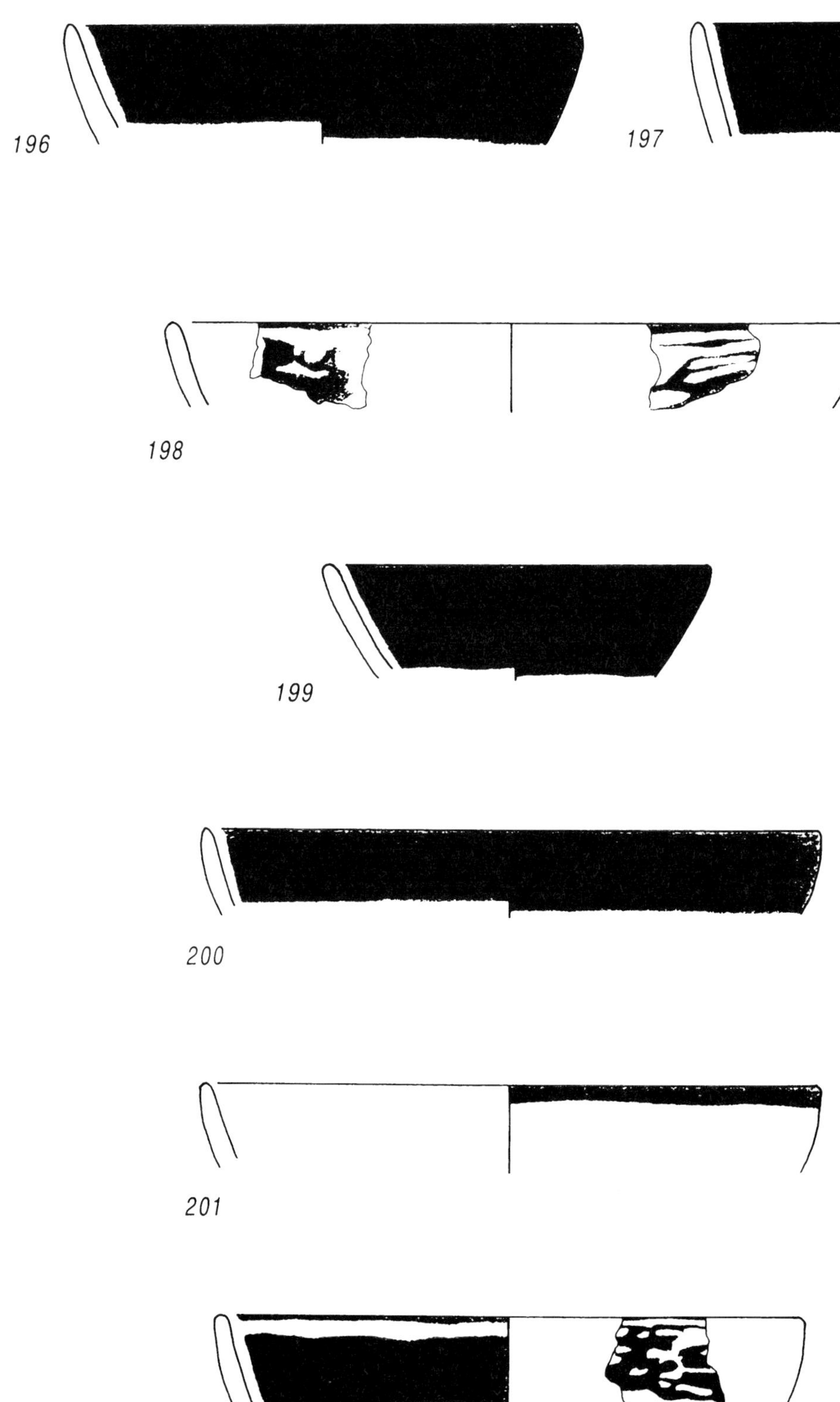

196
197
198
199
200
201
202
0
10
c m s

Figure 4.39
Phase 5 (continued)

Bowls, open, deep; fine fabric (continued)

Cat. no.	Provenance and sherd no.	Phase	Description
196	648.1/3	5	Bowl, flared, conical. Very fine fabric but thick-walled; very fine grits; black. Fine matt burnish outside and inside.
197	708.1/5	5	Bowl, flared, conical (small). Very fine fabric; fine grey/shiny grits; black. Fine glossy burnish outside and inside.
198	650.14/12	5	Bowl, flared, shallow. Fine fabric; small dark-grey grits; cream-buff, possible cream slip. Streaky matt burnish outside, faint inside.
199	644.34/37	5	Bowl, flared, shallow (small). Very fine fabric; fine dark and light grits; brown, heavily mottled black towards the rim. Very fine glossy burnish outside and inside.
200	710.4/1	5	Bowl, curved, shallow. Very fine fabric; fine dark and light grits; brownish-black, black core. Fine glossy burnish outside and inside.
201	709.2/2	5	Bowl, curved, shallow. Very fine fabric; fine dark and light grits; dark pinkish-grey. Light burnish around rim and 10 mm band outside, smoothed below and inside.
202	644.14/8	5	Bowl, curved, shallow. Fine fabric, variable thickness of wall; fine dark and light grits; reddish brown. Streaky matt burnish on uneven surface outside in a band 20–25 mm around rim, and inside.

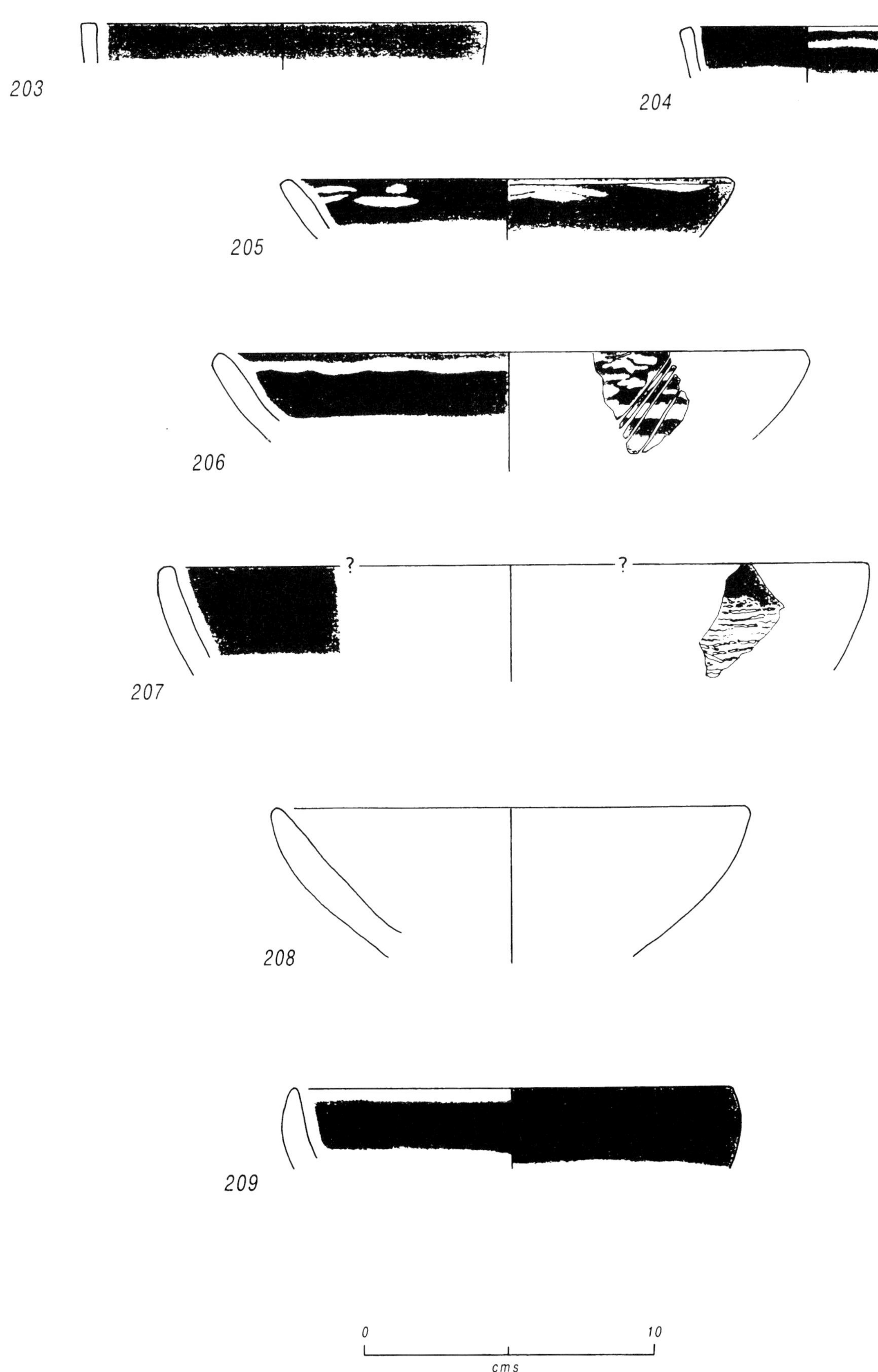

203
204
205
206
207
?
?
208
209
0
10
cms

Figure 4.40
Phase 5 (continued)

Bowls, hemispherical, shallow; fine fabric

Cat. no.	Provenance and sherd No	Phase	Description
203	706.47/8	5	Bowl, upright rim, flat. Very fine fabric; very fine grits; buff. Burnish outside, rim and inside.
204	735.2/4	5	Bowl, flared (small). Very fine fabric; very fine grits; light brick-red, light grey surfaces. Burnish outside, rim (streaky) and inside.
205	709.2/1	5	Bowl, flared, shallow. Fine fabric; fine light and dark grits; dull brick-red, dark-grey surfaces. Streaky matt burnish outside and inside.
206	644.18/12	5	Bowl, shallow, curved. Medium–fine fabric; medium-size grey and reddish grits; brick-red, faint grey core, surfaces greyish/blackened, especially inside. Streaky burnish outside and inside, 4 incised lines (parallel, oblique) through burnish after firing.
207	650.14/4	5	Bowl, curved, shallow (large). Fine fabric; fine dark and light grits; pinkish red. Cord-impressed outside, slightly overlapping a 16 mm band of matt burnish, continuing inside.
208	606.63/1	5	Bowl, flared, shallow; probably a 'heeled' base. Coarse fabric; medium-size dark-grey angular grits, a little red grog; buff, pale-grey core. Finger-smoothed outside and inside.
209	606.62/4	5	Bowl, curved, shallow. Medium fabric; small dark-grey grits; greyish buff. Light burnish outside, fainter inside.

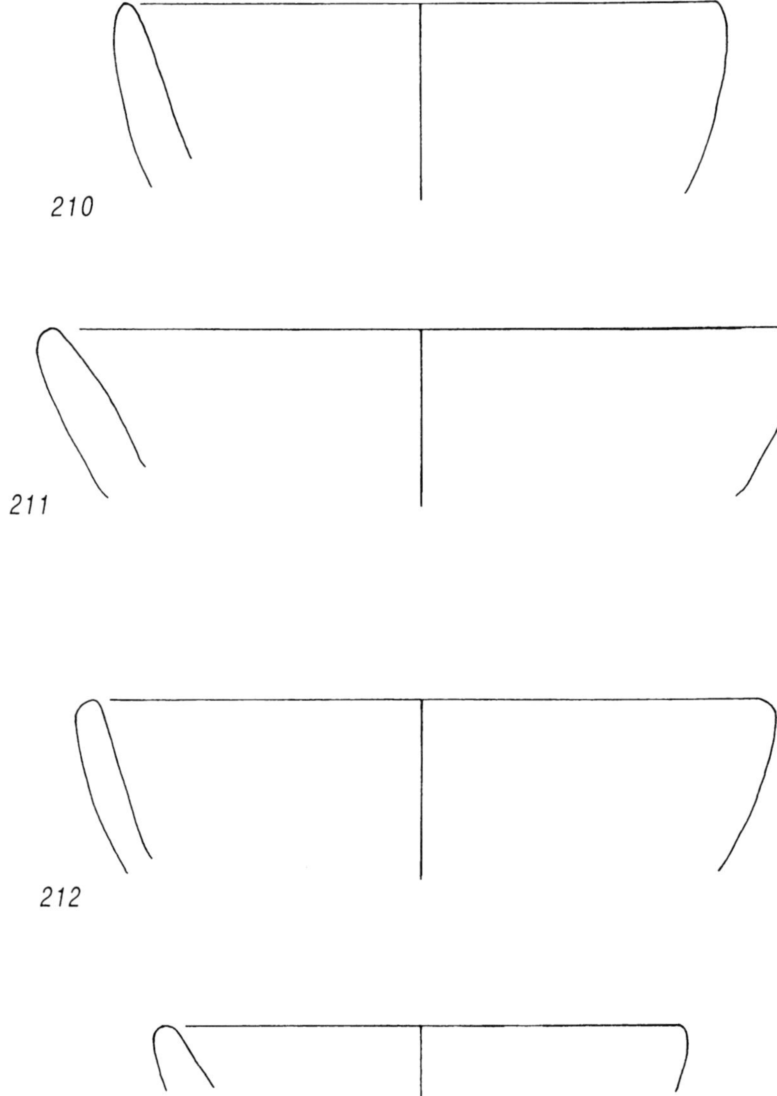

210
211
212
213

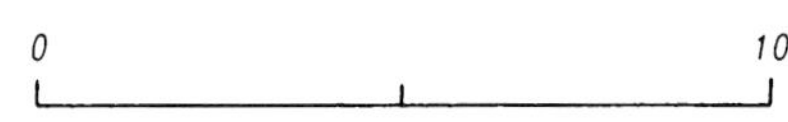

0
10
c m s

Figure 4.41
Phase 5 (continued)

Bowls, open; coarse fabric

Cat. no.	Provenance and sherd no.	Phase	Description
210	606.62/5	5	Bowl, curved, shallow. Coarse fabric; medium-size dark-grey angular grits, some fine vegetable temper; buff. Smoothed (possibly light matt burnish) outside and inside.
211	650.14/3	5	Bowl, flared, shallow. Very coarse fabric; large dark-grey angular grits, a little red grog and fine vegetable temper; buff. Lightly smoothed or wiped on uneven surfaces outside and inside rim, rough below.
212	654.7/5	5	Bowl, curved, shallow. Medium–coarse fabric; medium-size dark-grey angular and light-grey rounded grits, some fine vegetable temper; buff, some pinkish mottling. Slight burnish inside, even less outside.
213	706.4/2	5	Bowl, flared, shallow. Coarse fabric; medium-size dark-grey angular grits, some fine vegetable temper; pale pinkish-buff, dark-grey core. Smoothed outside, slight burnish over rim and inside.

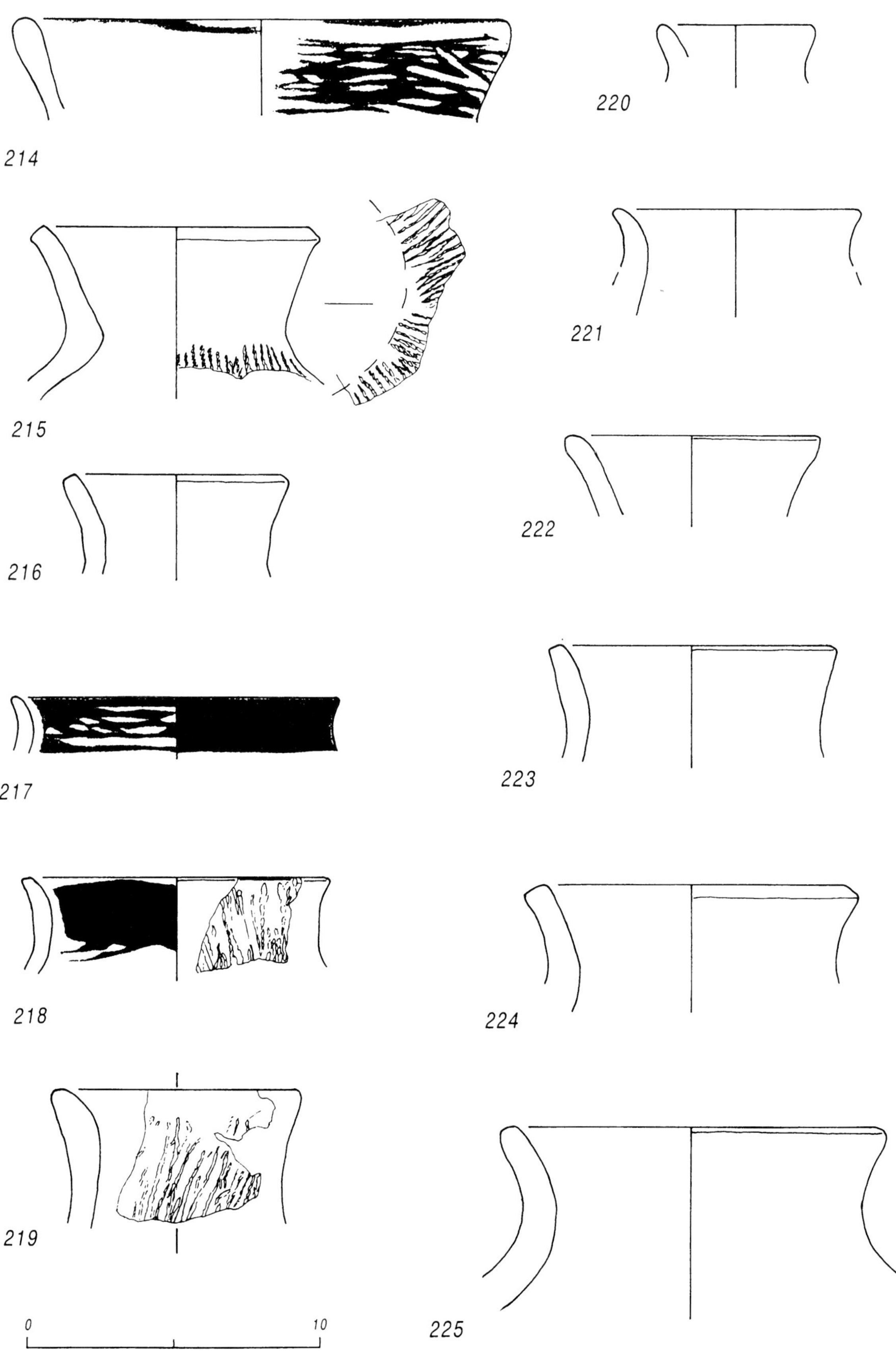
214
220
215
221
216
222
217
223
218
224
219
225
0
10
cms

Figure 4.42
Neolithic pottery from disturbed or later contexts

Jars, necked, flared

Cat. no.	Provenance and sherd no.	Phase	Description
214	653.8/4	[6 fill]	Jar with neck, flared. Fairly fine fabric; dense small pale-grey grits; light brick-red, greyish red inside. Streaky burnish outside and on rim, on uneven surface, inside rough.
215	735.4/3	Mixed	Jar with neck, flared, narrow, high. Fine fabric; fine white and grey grits; brick-red, dark reddish-grey surfaces. Fine cord-impressions outside on shoulder, lightly smoothed on neck and rim, inside uneven.
216	750.1/1	[8]	Jar with neck, flared, narrow. Fairly fine fabric; small dark-grey and light grits; buff, greyish core and mottling. Lightly smoothed outside, rough inside.
217	644.2/68	[6 fill]	Jar with neck, upright, short. Fine fabric; small dark-grey and whitish grits; dark brick-red, greyish-brown surfaces. Horizontal burnish outside and inside (rather streaky).
218	680.62/1	[10]	Jar with neck, upright. Fairly fine fabric; small pale-grey angular grits; light brick-red, slight grey core, greyish-brown slip. Cord-impressed outside, matt burnish inside neck.
219	708.+/1	Surface	Jar with neck, upright, narrow. Fairly fine fabric; fine light and shiny grits; dull brick-red, dark-grey core and inside surface mottling. Light blurred cord-impressions outside, light smoothing over rim and inside.
220	905.2/3	[9–12].	Jar with neck, flared (small). Medium–fine fabric; fine grits, a little fine vegetable temper; buff, blackened throughout; very uneven surfaces.
221	905.8/5	[14]	Jar with neck, flared, short. Medium–fine fabric; fine dark grits, possibly grog; greyish buff, pale bricky-buff slip outside and inside, blackened. Smoothed surfaces.
222	644.35/10	Mixed	Jar with neck, flared, narrow. Medium fabric; fine grey grits and red grog; light brick-red, thin grey core. Darker more reddish slip; lightly smoothed on uneven surfaces.
223	650.10/1	[Post-Neo.]	Jar with neck, flared, narrow. Medium fabric, variable thickness of wall; small grey and light grits, light-red grog; buff-pink, faint grey core, darker slip. Lightly smoothed outside and inside.
224	614.1/1	[?7/8]	Jar with neck, flared, narrow. Coarse fabric; small grey grits; pale brick-red. Smoothed outside, rough inside.
225	735.11/6	[6 fill]	Jar with neck, flared. Very coarse fabric; large dark-grey angular grits; buff. Smoothed outside, rough inside.

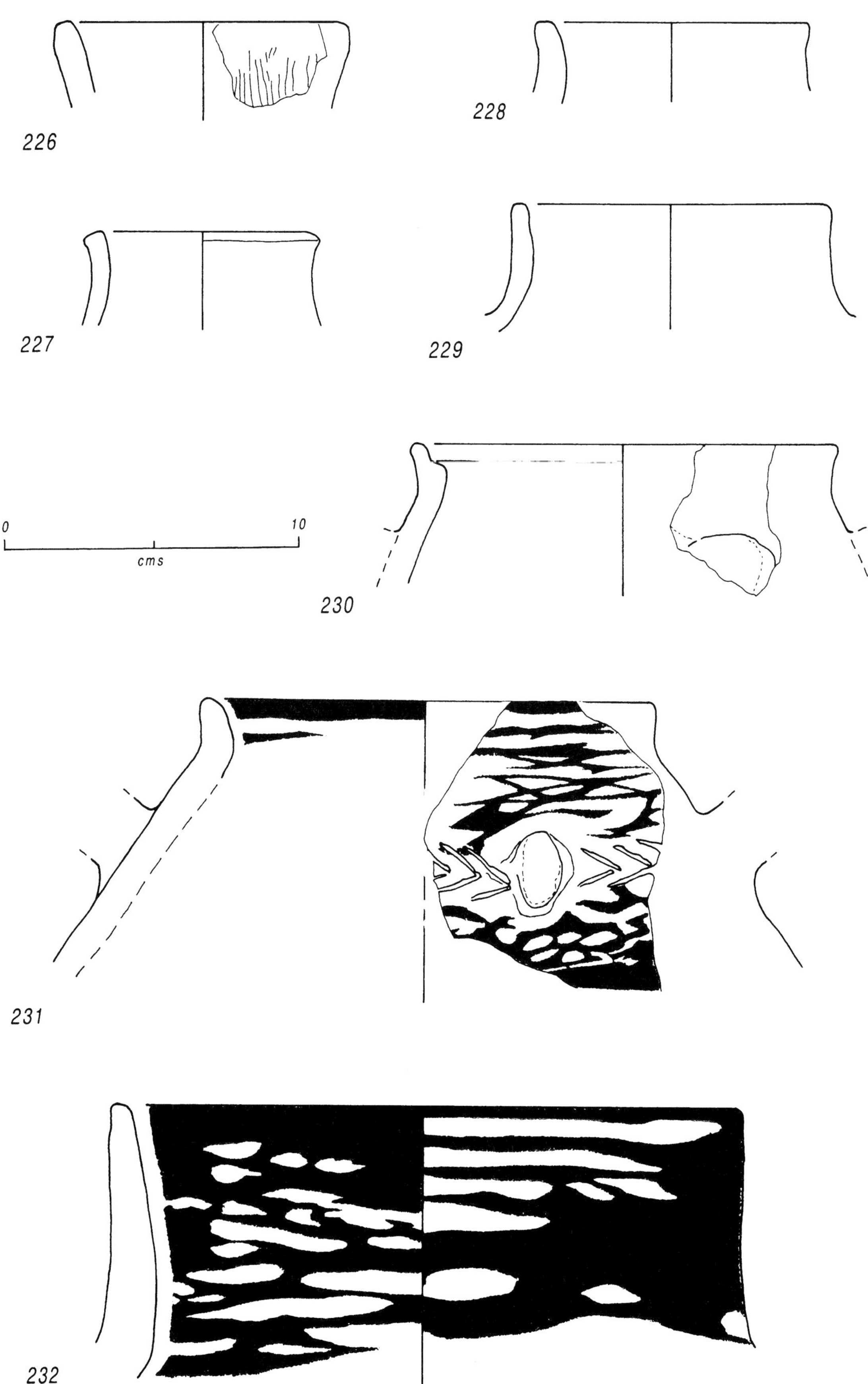

226

228

227

229

230

231

232

Figure 4.43
Neolithic pottery from disturbed or later contexts (continued)

Jars, necked, slightly flared or upright

Cat. no.	Provenance and sherd no.	Phase	Description
226	610.41/2	[15 fill]	Jar with neck, flared. Medium–fine fabric, but thick-walled; small dark grits; dull brick-red; faint-combed outside, smoothed inside.
227	606.60/1	Mixed	Jar with neck, upright, narrow. Medium–fine fabric, thin-walled; small dark-grey and light grits; pale buff-grey. Very roughly finger-smoothed outside and inside.
228	608.1/1	[7]	Jar with neck, upright, narrow. Medium–coarse; fine grey and light grits, some reddish, and fine vegetable temper; pale orange-buff, mottled grey; rough outside, lightly smoothed inside.
229	644.12/5	[7]	Jar with neck, upright. Medium fabric, thin-walled; fine grey grits and red grog; pinkish buff, darker slip. Slightly smoothed outside, and inside on uneven surface.
230	652.2/10	[Post-Neo.]	Jar with neck, upright, very short; inside ledge (for lid?) Ledge/knob handle. Medium–coarse fabric; small grey and white grits, some vegetable temper; dull orange-buff surface outside and on rim, grey core and inside. Smoothed outside and inside. Scar of broken knob or handle on shoulder.
231	680.11/29	[14a]	Jar with neck, upright, very short. Vertically flattened knob handle. Medium fabric; very dense medium-size buff-grey grits; brick-red, greyish-buff surfaces. Streaky horizontal burnish outside and inside neck on uneven surface (lower surface inside worn away), deeply incised herringbone-pattern band (through burnish) on shoulder, either side of vertically flattened knob or handle (broken off). (*cf.* Plate 4.2)
232	644.36/3	[Post-Neo.]	Jar with neck, upright, high (large). Fairly fine fabric, thick-walled large jar; bright brick-red, thick black core. Streaky horizontal burnish outside and inside on rather uneven surfaces.

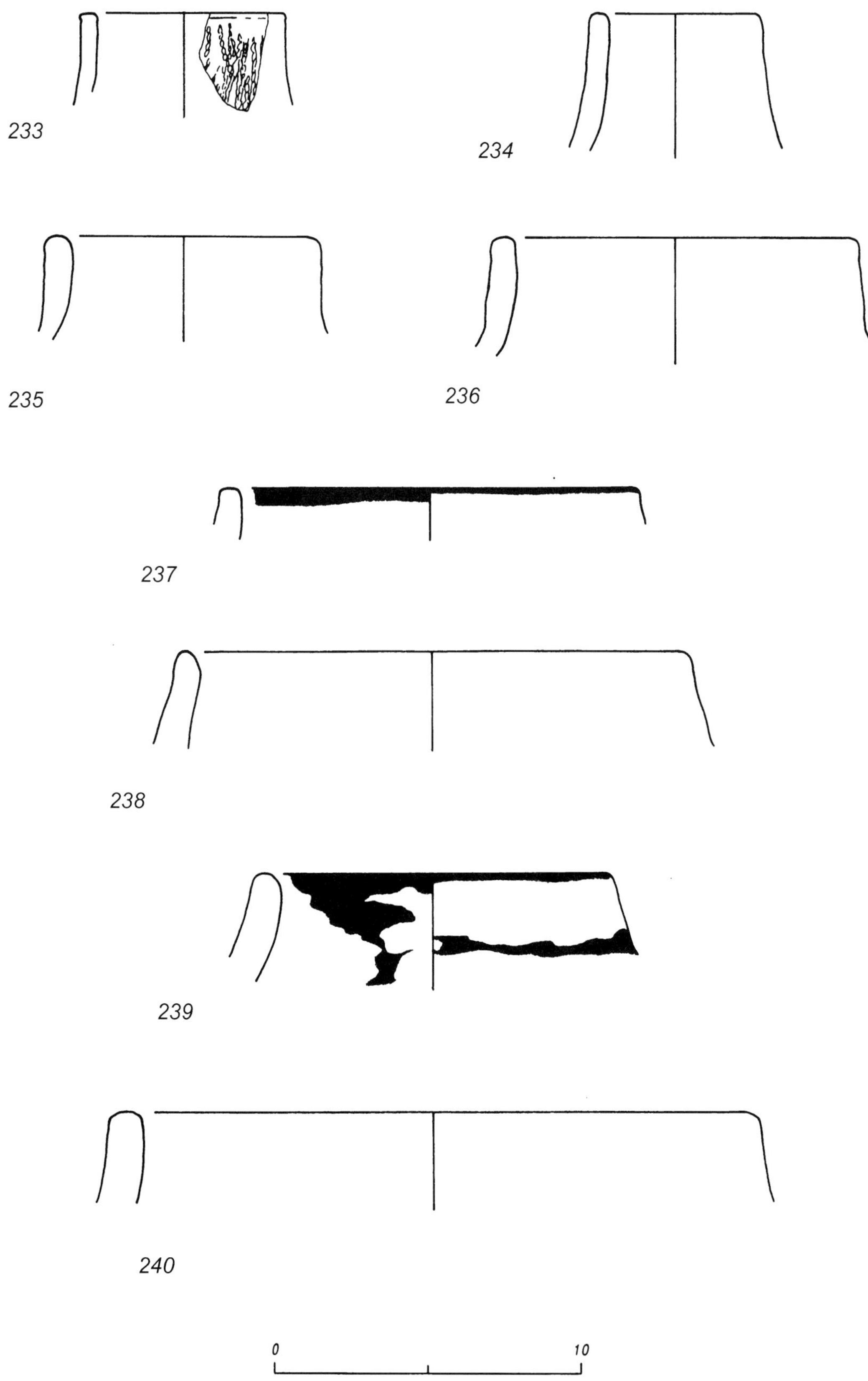

233

234

235

236

237

238

239

240

Figure 4.44
Neolithic pottery from disturbed or later contexts (continued)

Jars, necked, upright or slightly inverted

Cat. no.	Provenance and sherd no.	Phase	Description
233	++/02	Unstrat-ified	Jar with neck, upright, narrow (small). Fine fabric; fine dark grits; greyish buff, surfaces mottled grey. Cord-impressed outside, flat rim and inside lightly smoothed.
234	705.81/2	[Post-Neo.]	Jar with neck, slightly inverted, narrow (small). Fine fabric; fine dark grits; cream-buff, thick pale-grey core and mottling. Well smoothed outside and over rim, slightly inside.
235	++/03	Unstrat-ified	Jar with neck, upright, narrow. Medium–fine fabric; medium to small grey grits, red grog, a little fine vegetable temper; light brick-red, mottled buff, light grey core. Very slightly smoothed or wiped outside and inside.
236	604.26/2	[15]	Jar with neck, upright. Fairly fine fabric; small dark-grey angular grits, some fine vegetable temper; cream-buff, thin grey core. Smoothed outside and inside on uneven surfaces.
237	644.2/63	[6 fill]	Jar with neck, slightly inverted. Fairly fine fabric, thick-walled; fine dark and light grits; light brick-red, thick grey core. Streaky burnish over rim.
238	614.1/2	[?7/8]	Jar with neck, slightly inverted. Medium–coarse fabric; small dark-grey angular grits; buff. Well smoothed outside, slightly inside rim, rough below.
239	652.17/9	[Post-Neo.]	Jar with neck, slightly inverted, narrow. Medium–coarse fabric; small dark-grey and light grits, red grog; buff. Burnished over rim, and sketchily outside and inside.
240	642.11/1	[?9/14]	Jar with neck, slightly inverted. Very coarse fabric; large dark-grey angular grits; buff. Lightly smoothed outside and on rim, rough inside.

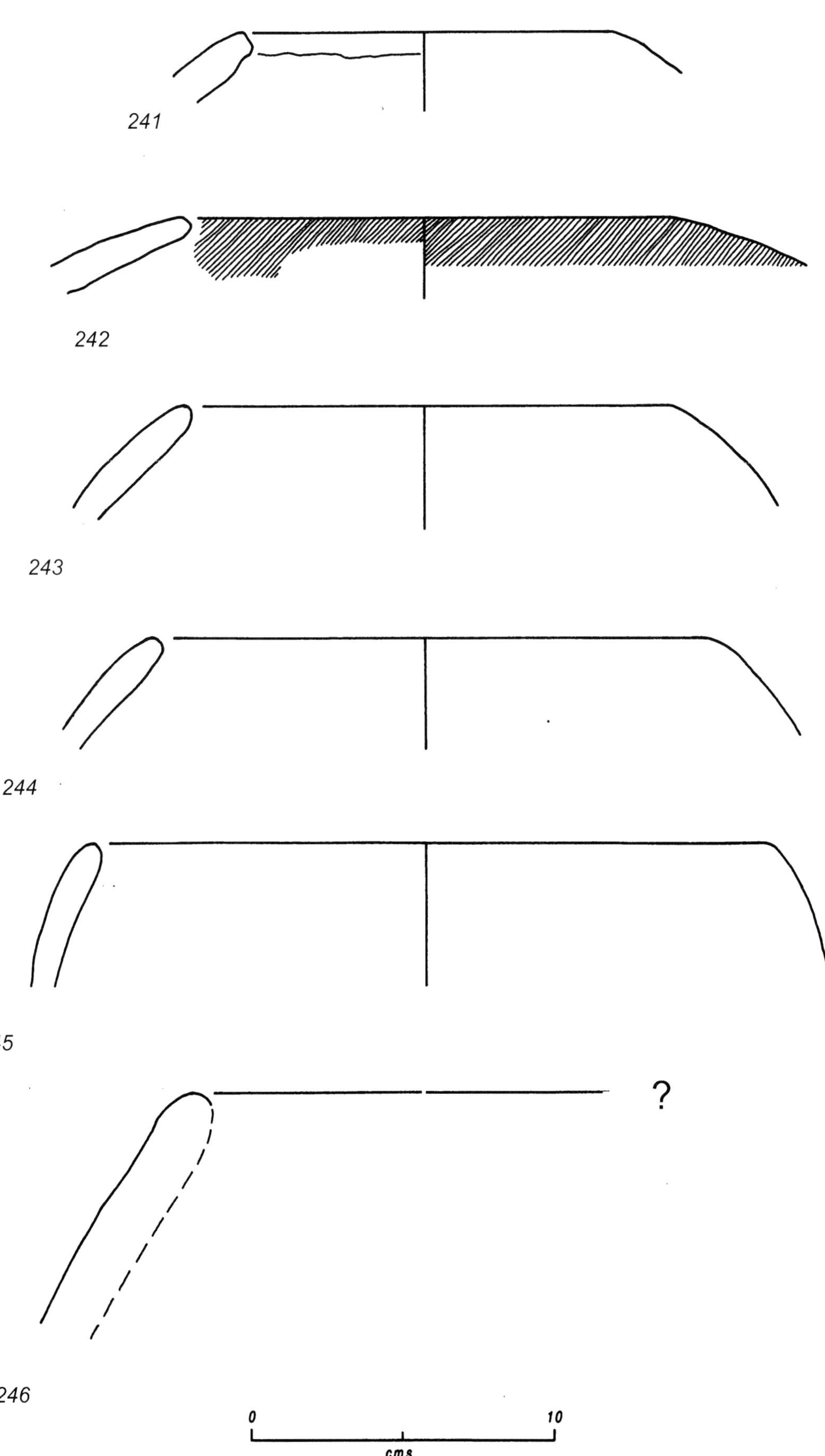
241
242
243
244
245
246
?
0
10
cms

Figure 4.45
Neolithic pottery from disturbed or later contexts (continued)

Jars, holemouth; coarse fabric

Cat. no.	Provenance and sherd no.	Phase	Description
241	735.11/5	[6 fill]	Jar, holemouth, shallow. Medium–coarse fabric, thick; small grey and whitish grits, red grog; buff, thin light-grey core. Smoothed outside and lightly inside.
242	699.+/1	[?8]	Jar, holemouth, shallow. Coarse fabric, walls of variable thickness; medium-size dark-grey grits, light grits or grog, some fine vegetable temper; buff, light-grey core. Brownish-red slip outside, over rim and irregularly inside; smoothed outside and inside on uneven surfaces.
243	680.59/13	[?9]	Jar, holemouth, shallow. Lug/knob handle. Very coarse fabric; very large dark-grey angular grits, fine vegetable temper, red grog; pale orange-buff, greyish core and blackening inside. Lightly smoothed outside and inside. Signs of lug or knob on broken edge, 33 mm down from rim.
244	709.21/1	[Post-Neo.]	Jar, holemouth, shallow. Probable knob handle. Coarse fabric; small light grits, fine vegetable temper; dull light brick-red, thick dark-grey core, greyish or blackened outside. Smoothed outside and inside.
245	707.9/1	[7]	Jar, holemouth, steep. Coarse fabric; medium-size dark-grey and light grits; buff, mottled light brick-red. Well smoothed outside, less inside.
246	614.1/4	[?7/8]	Jar, holemouth, steep. Very coarse fabric; very large dark-grey grits, a few white, fine vegetable temper, a little red grog; light brick-red, brownish core. Slightly smoothed outside, inside surface entirely lost. Diameter and angle of profile approximate.

Virginia Mathias

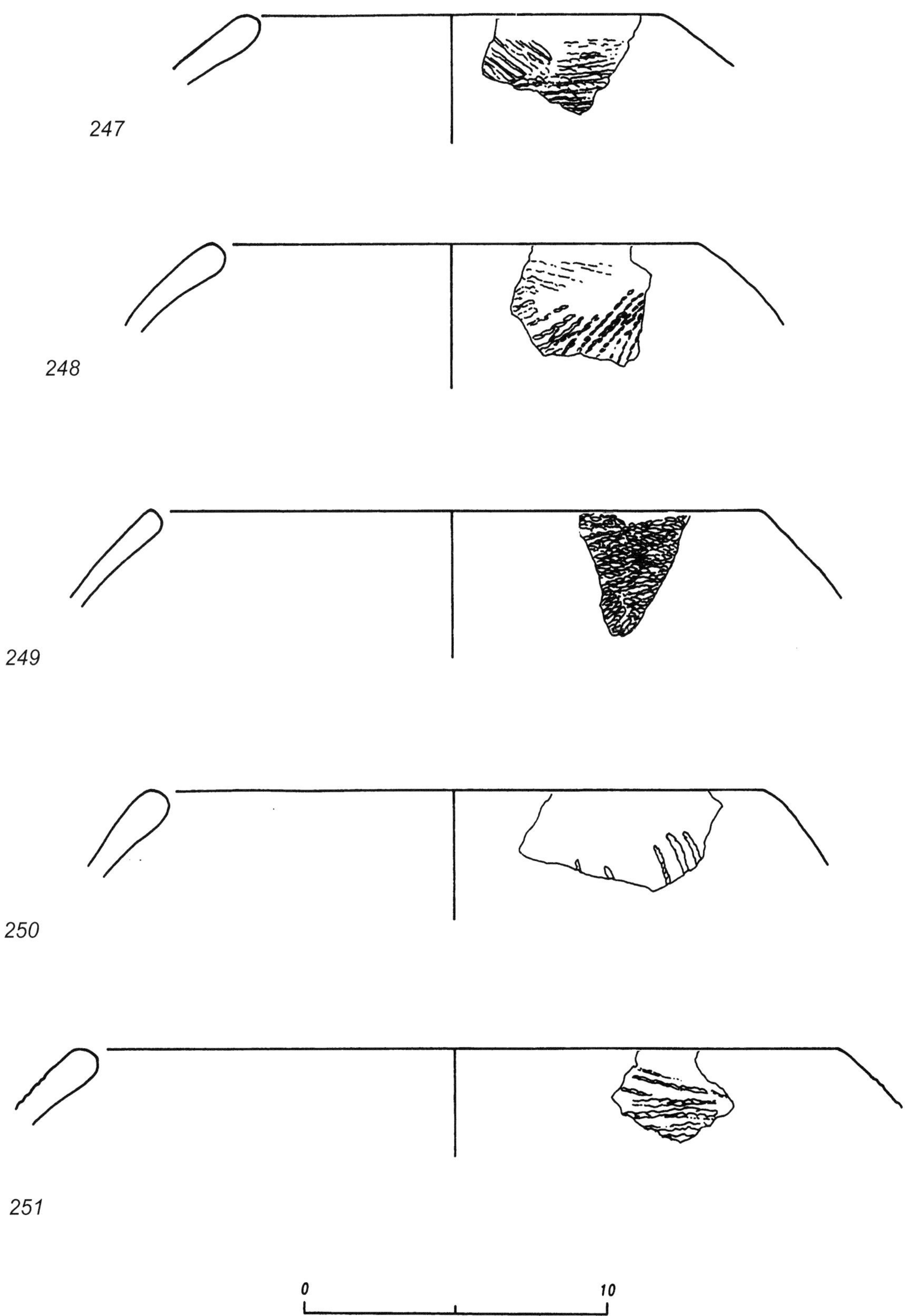

Figure 4.46
Neolithic pottery from disturbed or later contexts (continued)

Jars, holemouth, shallow to medium angle, rolled rim; fine fabric

Cat. no.	Provenance and sherd no.	Phase	Description
247	680.38/2	[10]	Jar, holemouth, shallow, rolled rim. Fairly fine fabric; dense small pale grits; dull reddish grey, mottled black. Faint cord-impressions outside, faint streaky burnish or smoothing on rim and inside.
248	644.13/2	[6]	Jar, holemouth, shallow, rolled rim. Fine fabric; dense small pale-grey grits, a little red grog; buff, dark-grey core and mottling, especially inside. Faint cord-impressions outside, smoothed on rim and inside.
249	705.81/1	[Post-Neo.]	Jar, holemouth, shallow, rolled rim. Fine fabric; fine dark-grey and brown grits (or grog); greyish buff. Cord-impressed outside, light burnish over rim, inside surface uneven.
250	644.20/4+5	[Post-Neo.]	Jar, holemouth, shallow, rolled rim. Fairly fine fabric; small dark-grey grits; dull blackish brown. Widely spaced cord-impressions outside, below 15 mm band of horizontal smoothing/faint streaky burnish, continuing over rim and inside.
251	640.22/4	[Post-Neo.]	Jar, holemouth, shallow, rolled rim. Fairly fine fabric; small pale-grey grits; light brick-red, thick dark-grey core. Blurred cord-impressions outside below 10 mm band of finger-smoothing or light matt burnish over rim and inside.

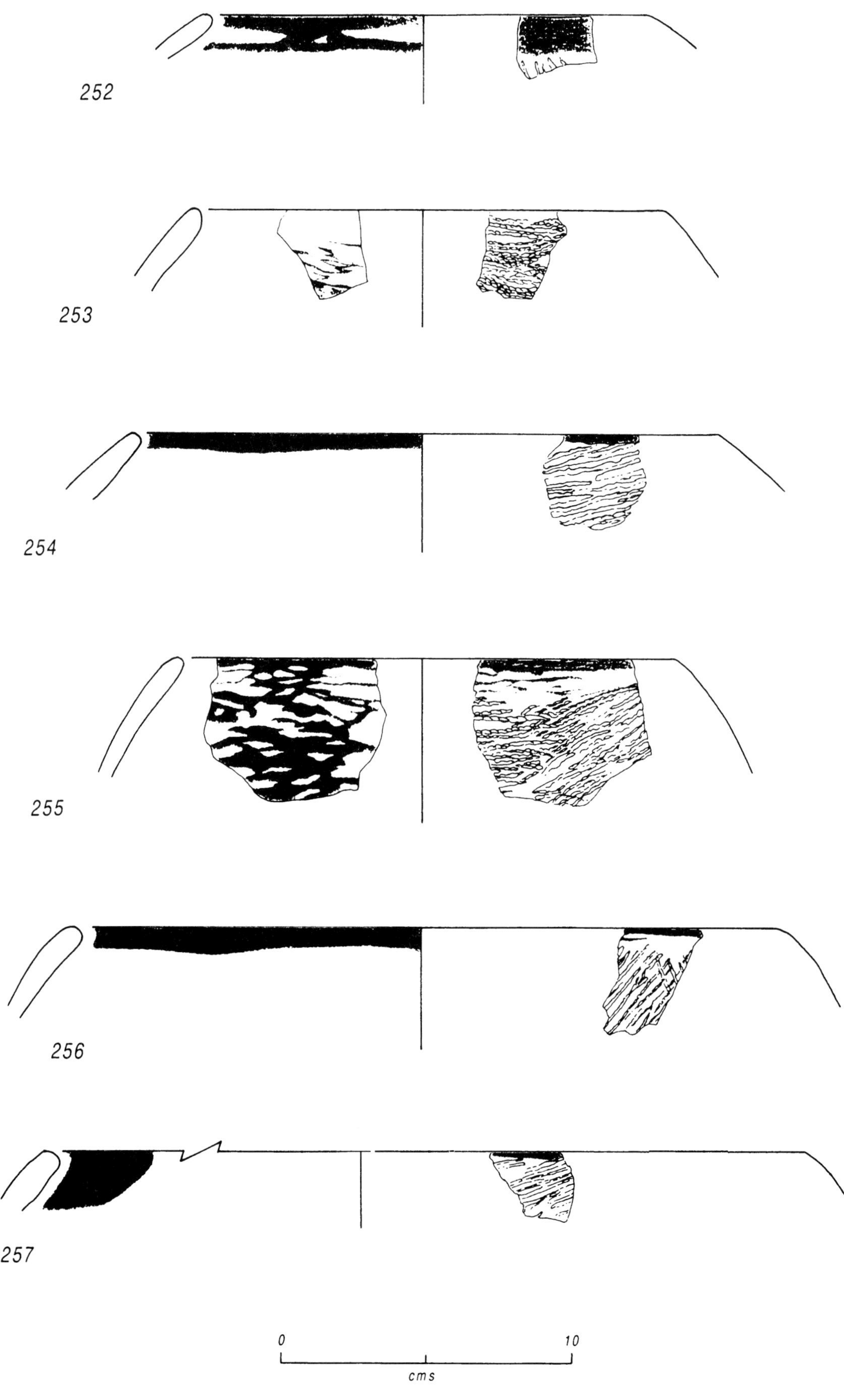

252
253
254
255
256
257
0
10
cms

Figure 4.47
Neolithic pottery from disturbed or later contexts (continued)

Jars, holemouth, shallow to medium angle, plain rim; fine fabric

Cat. no.	Provenance and sherd no.	Phase	Description
252	605.1/22	[9]	Jar, holemouth, shallow. Very fine fabric; very fine light and dark grits; grey-brown, mottling. Faint cord-impressions outside, below 13 mm band of fine horizontal burnish, continuing over rim and (streaky) inside.
253	735.4/1	Mixed	Jar, holemouth, steep. Fine fabric; dense small pale-grey grits; light brick-red. Shallow cord-impressions outside, very sketchy burnish over rim and inside.
254	735.10/1	[7]	Jar, holemouth, shallow. Fairly fine fabric; small dark-grey shiny grits; dull bricky-grey. Blurred cord-impressions outside, light matt burnish over rim, inside well smoothed.
255	644.46/1	Mixed	Jar, holemouth, steep. Fine fabric; small grey and light grits; dull brick-red outside, greyish brown inside. Cord-impressed outside, below 10 mm band of streaky horizontal burnish, continuing over rim and inside. (*cf.* Plate 4.2)
256	Trench I I.194.6/1	[Post-Neo.]	Jar, holemouth, steep. Fine fabric; small dark-grey grits; pale buff, slight grey mottling. Cord-impressions outside, below light horizontal burnish over rim, smoothed inside.
257	642.22/6	[8]	Jar, holemouth, steep (large). Medium–fine fabric; medium-size pale-grey grits; pale orange-buff. Faint-combed outside on uneven surface, burnished on rim and inside. Thickening on broken edge suggesting end of horizontal lug or knob, 10 mm from rim.

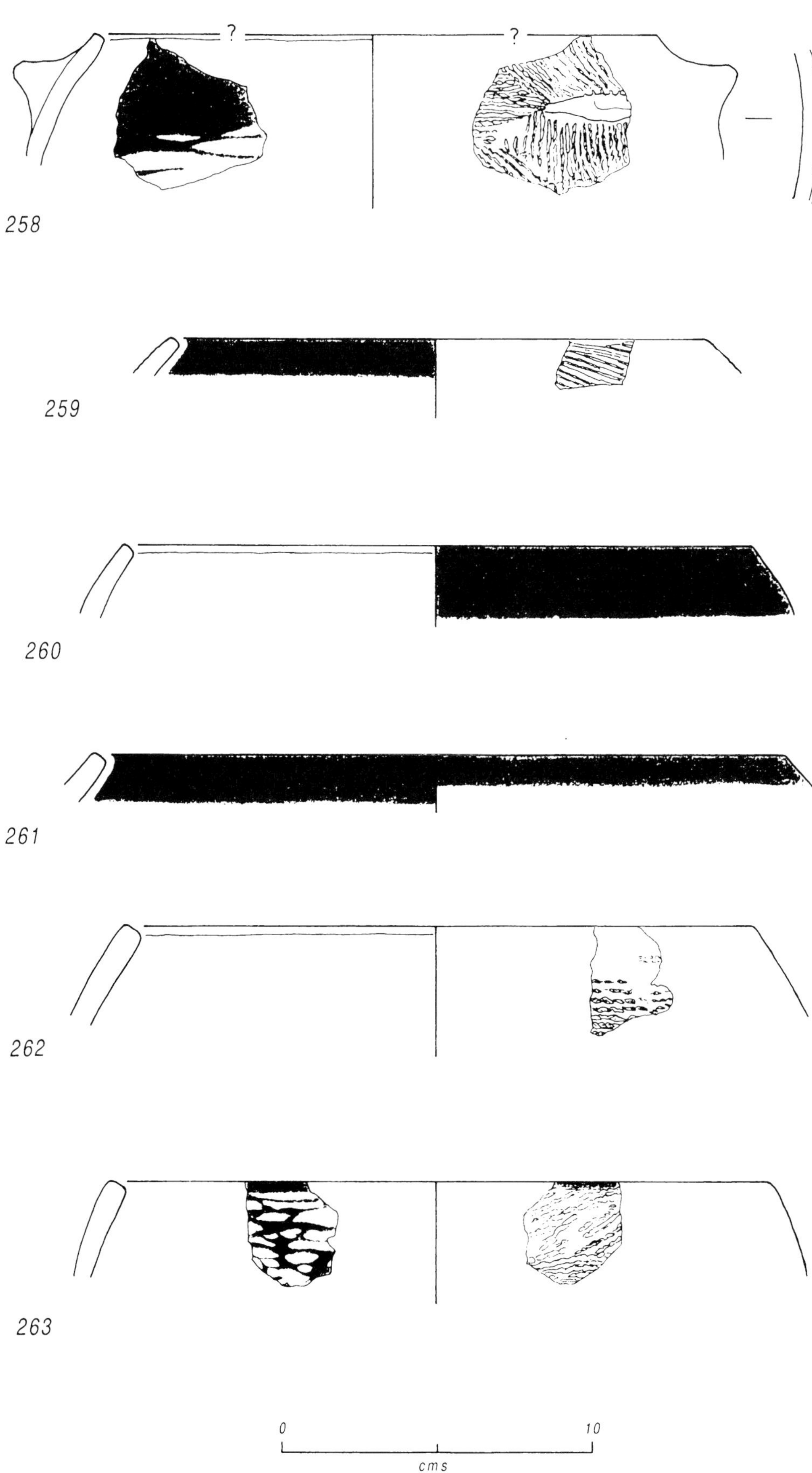

258

259

260

261

262

263

Figure 4.48
Neolithic pottery from disturbed or later contexts (continued)

Jars, holemouth, medium-steep angle

Cat. no.	Provenance and sherd no.	Phase	Description
258	701.20/3	[?16 fill]	Jar, holemouth, steep. Lug/horizontal ledge handle. Very fine fabric; very fine light and dark grits; light brick-red, reddish grey towards surfaces. Cord-impressed outside and upper and lower surfaces of handle, horizontal matt burnish inside.
259	644.47/2	Mixed	Jar, holemouth, steep. Fine fabric; fine grey and light grits; light brick-red, greyish brown inside. Light-combed outside, light burnish on flat rim and (matt) inside.
260	606.59/1	[7]	Jar, holemouth, steep. Fine fabric; small grey grits; buff/light red mottled, thin grey core near to inside surface. Light matt burnish outside, signs of cord-impressions below, inside finger-smoothed.
261	705.61/4	[7]	Jar, holemouth, steep Medium fabric; small dark-grey grits; buff, light-grey surfaces. Light burnish outside, over rim and inside.
262	735.4/2	Mixed	Medium fabric; small dark-grey grits, a few medium-large white (chalk?); pale pinkish grey, medium-grey surfaces. Thick cord-impressions outside, below and partly under 28 mm band well-smoothed or faint matt burnish, continuing over rim, and very sketchy inside on uneven surface.
263	680.31/1	[12]	Fairly fine fabric; small pale-grey grits; light dull brick-red, mottled black on rim and inside. Faint cord-impressions outside, streaky burnish over rim and inside.

Virginia Mathias

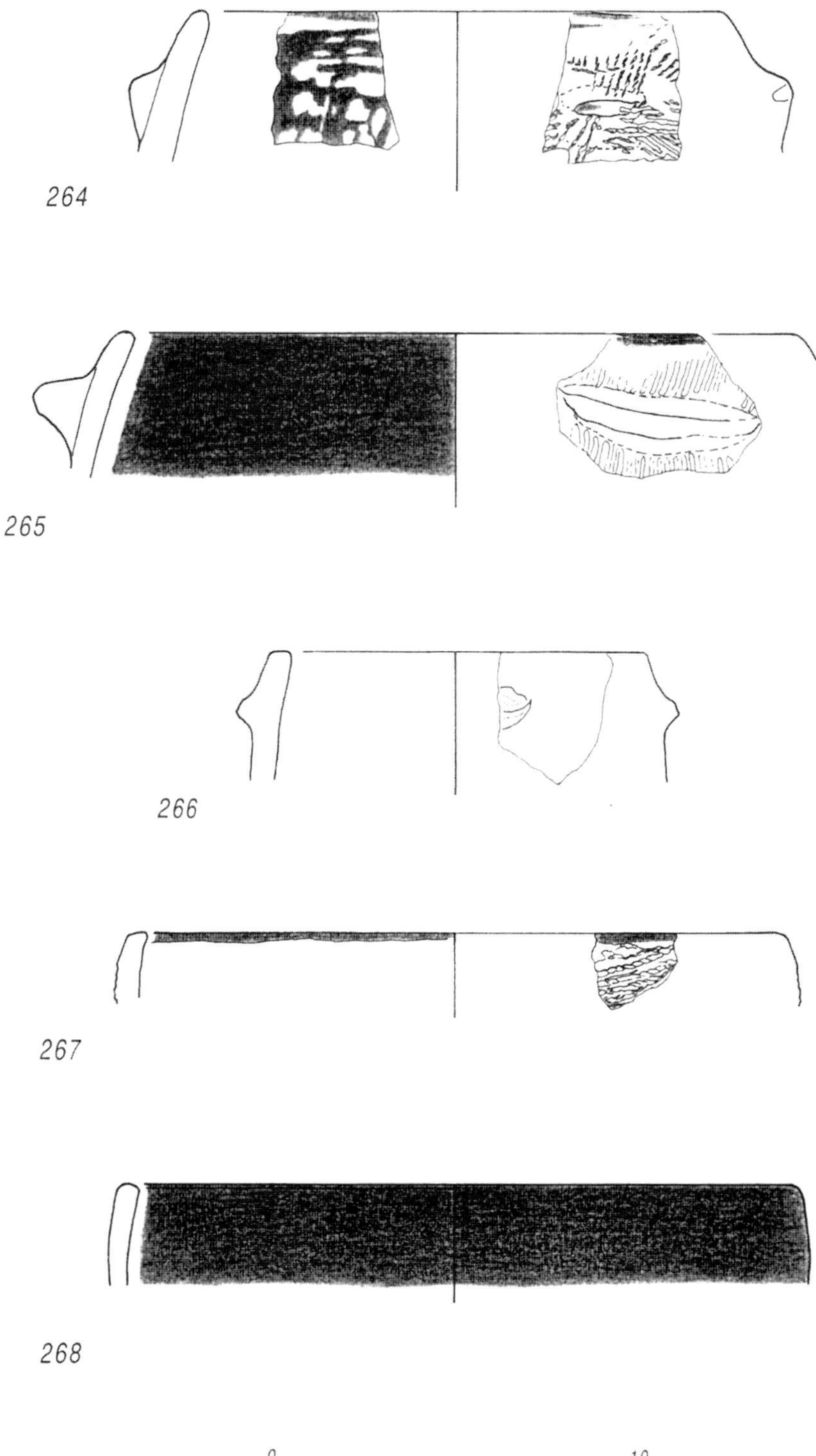

Figure 4.49
Neolithic pottery from disturbed or later contexts (continued)

Bowls, slightly inverted rim

Cat. no.	*Provenance and sherd no.*	*Phase*	*Description*
264	735.4/7	Mixed	Bowl, slightly inverted rim. Horizontal ledge/lug handle. Fairly fine fabric; small dark-grey and whitish grits; bright brick-red, buff-brown surfaces, probably a slip. Deep cord-impressions outside, below 6–12 mm band smoothed only, streaky burnish on rim and inside; very shallow horizontal oval lug or knob, partly cord-impressed.
265	++6	Unstrat- ified	Bowl, slightly inverted rim. Narrow horizontal ledge handle, slightly askew. Fine fabric; fine white and dark grits; black, mottled dull brick-red outside. Very faint combing outside, light matt burnish over rim and inside.
266	614.3/1	[9]	Bowl, slightly inverted rim, flattened (small) appliqué knob/ lug handle or 'coffee-bean' decoration. Fine fabric; fine dark and light grits; buff mottled dark-grey towards surfaces, brick-red core. Surfaces smoothed near rim, rough below.
267	606.13/1	Mixed	Bowl, upright rim. Fine fabric; fine dark shiny grits, some medium-size dull red, may be grog. Black. Cord-impressed outside, burnish over rim, and very sketchy inside on rough surface.
268	610.27/9	[16]	Bowl, upright rim. Very fine fabric; very fine dark and light grits; mid-brown, slight greyish mottling outside; fine horizontal burnish outside, rim and inside.

Virginia Mathias

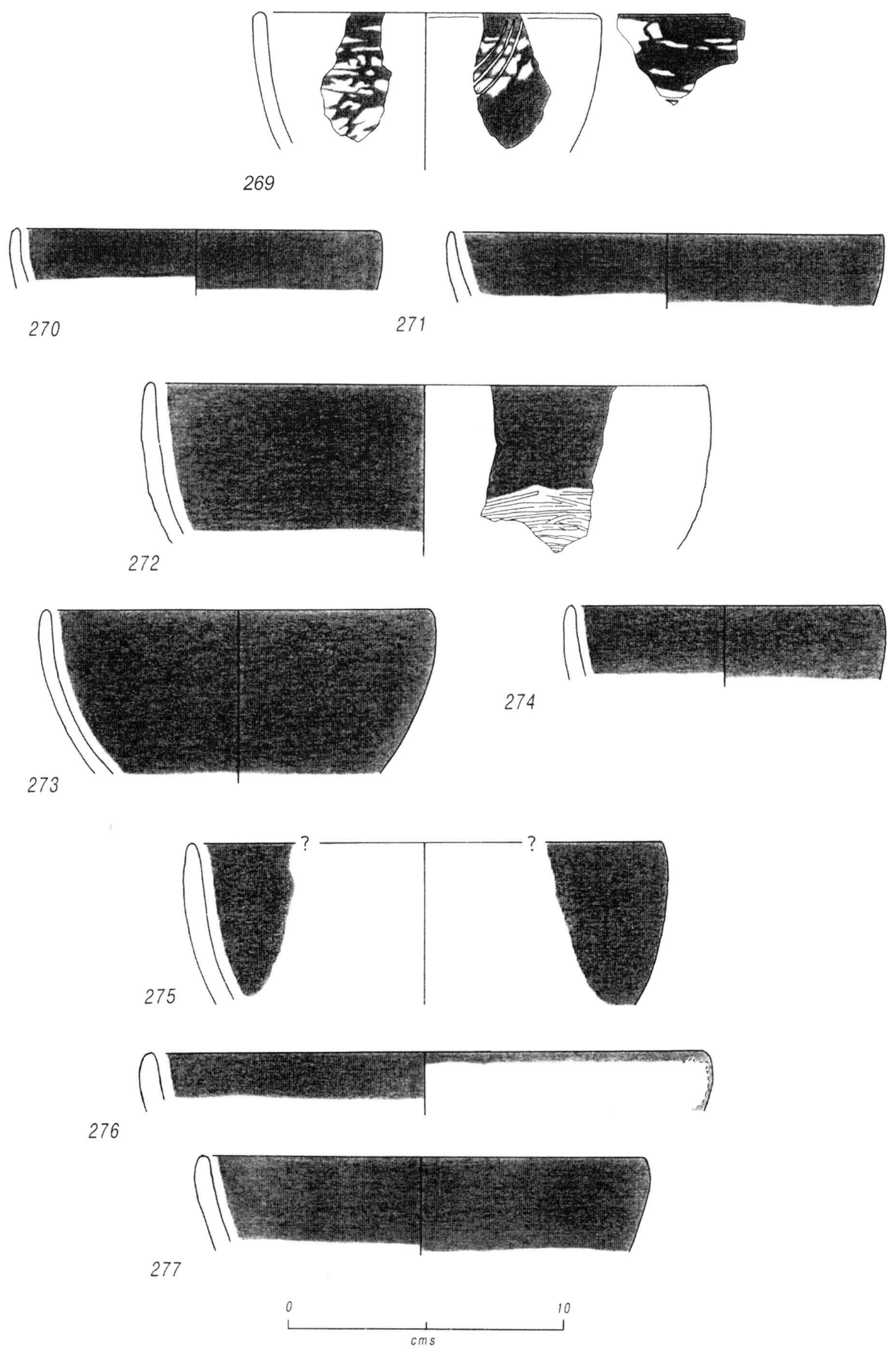

269

270

271

272

273

274

275

276

277

Figure 4.50
Neolithic pottery from disturbed or later contexts (continued)

Bowls, open, hemispherical and flared; fine fabric

Cat. no.	Provenance and sherd no.	Phase	Description
269	648.2/1	Mixed	Bowl. Fine fabric; small grey grits; brick-red, greyish mottling at surfaces. Three incised lines depending from rim in semicircular swag pattern (extending about a quarter-way around rim, i.e. would fit four times around circumference). Burnished over incisions outside (sketchy in places), and streaky inside. (*cf.* Plate 4.2)
270	644.47/1	Mixed	Bowl, hemispherical. Fine fabric; fine dark shiny grits; brownish black. Fine burnish outside and inside.
271	735.4/5	Mixed	Bowl, hemispherical. Fine fabric; small light-grey grits; black. Fine glossy burnish outside and inside.
272	730.2/1	Mixed	Bowl, hemispherical. Fine fabric; fine whitish grits; black. Light combing outside below 40 mm band of fine glossy burnish, also inside but worn.
273	705.65/1+2	Mixed	Bowl, hemispherical. Very fine fabric; very fine white and fine dark grits; dull dark brick-red, black towards surfaces. Fine burnish outside and inside.
274	707.11/1	[7]	Bowl, hemispherical. Fine fabric; very fine greyish grits; light grey. Fine burnish outside and inside.
275	702.46/120	[14a]	Bowl, hemispherical. Fine fabric; fine dark-grey grits; pale grey. Fine glossy burnish outside and inside. (*cf.* Plate 4.2)
276	606.13/3	Mixed	Bowl, flared. Fine fabric; fine dark-red and light grits; brick-red, dark-red surfaces. Matt burnish outside and inside.
277	730.32/4	[8 fill]	Bowl, flared. Very fine fabric; very fine grits, mostly dark grey; light brown, dark grey inside. Matt burnish outside, slightly streaky inside.

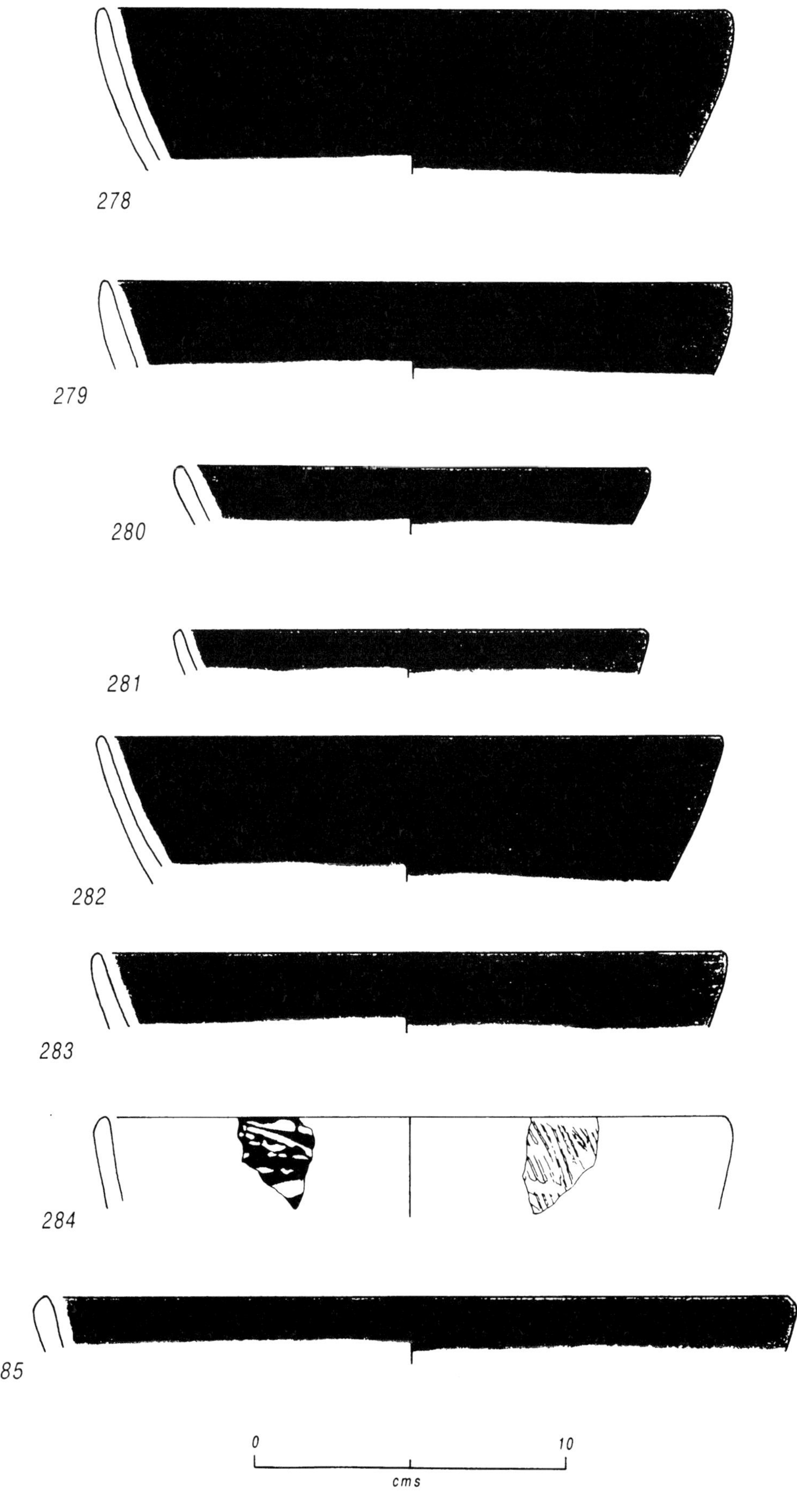

278

279

280

281

282

283

284

285

Figure 4.51
Neolithic pottery from disturbed or later contexts (continued)

Bowls, open, flared; fine fabric

Cat. no.	Provenance and sherd no.	Phase	Description
278	735.4/13	Mixed	Bowl, flared. Fine fabric; fine grey grits; brownish black, browner core. Fine glossy burnish outside and inside.
279	614.3/5	[9]	Bowl, flared. Fine fabric; fine greyish grits; black. Glossy but slightly streaky horizontal burnish outside and inside.
280	705.65/3	Mixed	Bowl, flared. Fine fabric; small light-grey grits; black. Fine burnish outside and inside.
281	705.61/10	[7]	Bowl, flared. Very fine fabric; very fine light and dark grits; black. Fine glossy burnish outside and inside.
282	702.46/28	[14a]	Bowl, flared. Very fine fabric; fine light and dark grits; black. Fine glossy burnish outside and inside.
283	705.61/7	[7]	Bowl, flared. Very fine fabric; very fine light and dark grits; black. Very fine burnish outside and inside.
284	(Trench I) I.176.4/3	[Post-Neo.]	Bowl, flared. Fine fabric; fine light and dark grits; dark brick-red (outside) mottled black (inside). Very faint combing outside, streaky burnish inside.
285	702.22/5	[16]	Bowl, flared. Fine fabric; fine grey grits; black. Fine burnish outside and inside, crackled.

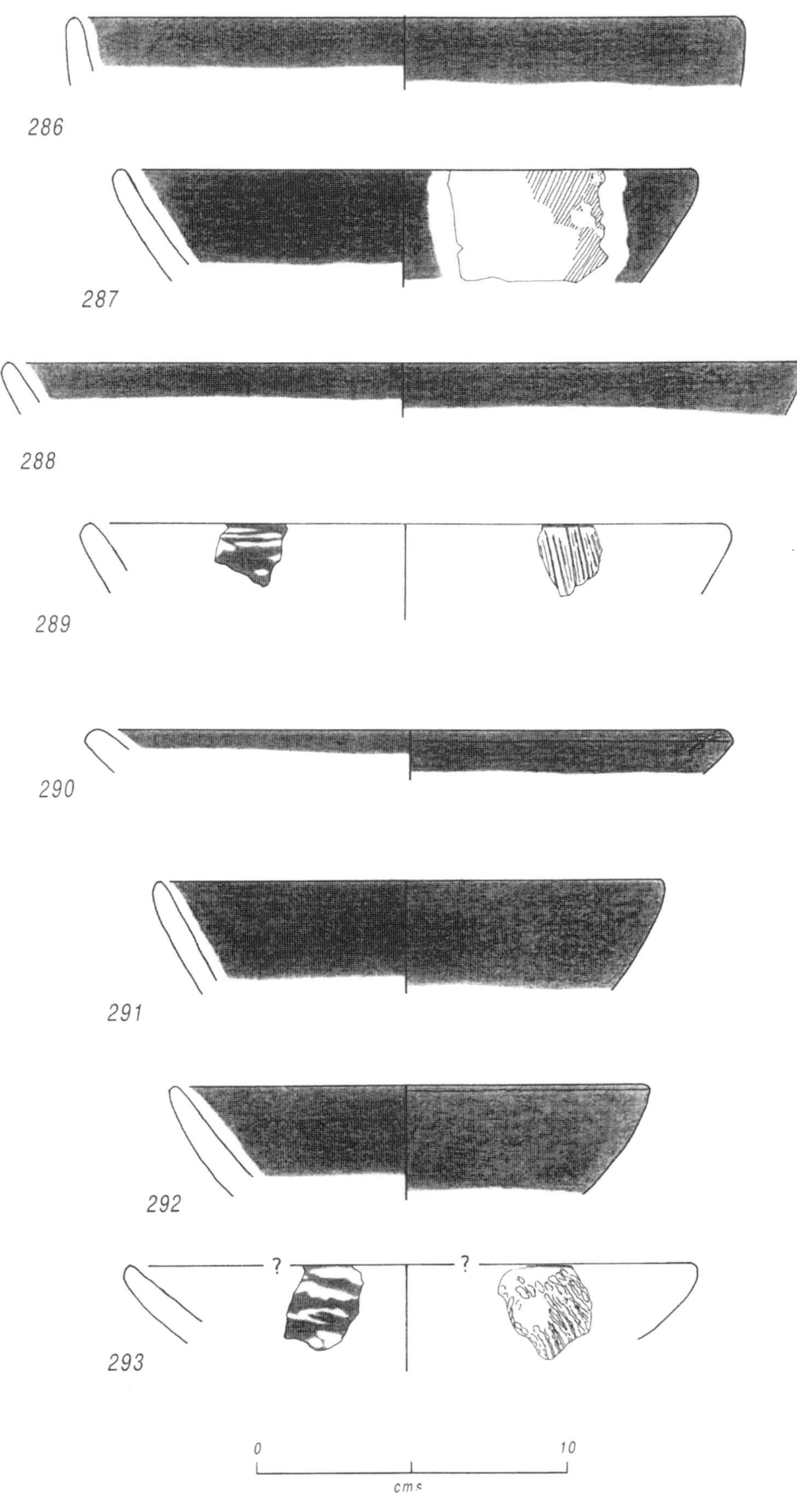

286
287
288
289
290
291
292
293
?   ?
0   10
c m s

Figure 4.52
Neolithic pottery from disturbed or later contexts (continued)

Bowls, open, shallow; fine fabric

Cat. no	Provenance and sherd no.	Phase	Description
286	656.6/6	[Post-Neo.]	Bowl, upright rim. Fine fabric; fine grey and white grits, some red grog; brick-red. Horizontal burnish outside and inside. (Perhaps Neolithic.)
287	706.32/5	Mixed	Bowl, flared, shallow. Very fine fabric; very fine dark and light grits; dark grey, mottled buff outside. Brownish-red paint (or partial slip) outside, no obvious pattern, fine burnish outside and inside.
288	644.3/12	[6 fill]	Bowl, flared, shallow. Fine fabric; fine light and dark grits; black. Burnished outside and inside.
289	608.1/2	[7]	Bowl, flared, shallow. Fine fabric; fine grey and light grits; brick-red, darker/greyish inside; very faint combing outside, streaky horizontal burnish inside.
290	646.9/1	[7]	Bowl, flared, shallow. Fine fabric; fine grey grits, a few light; brick-red. Light matt burnish outside and inside.
291	707.3/6	[8]	Bowl, flared, shallow. Fine fabric; fine dark and light grits; very dark grey. Matt burnish outside and inside.
292	644.17/1	[6]	Bowl, flared, shallow. Fine fabric; small light and dark grits; brownish black, a little buff mottling outside. Glossy horizontal burnish outside and inside, apparently over horizontal scoring.
293	610.21/14	[16 fill]	Bowl, curved, shallow. Fine fabric; fine light and dark grits; black outside, brownish inside, thin brick-red core; faint cord-impressions outside, streaky burnish inside.

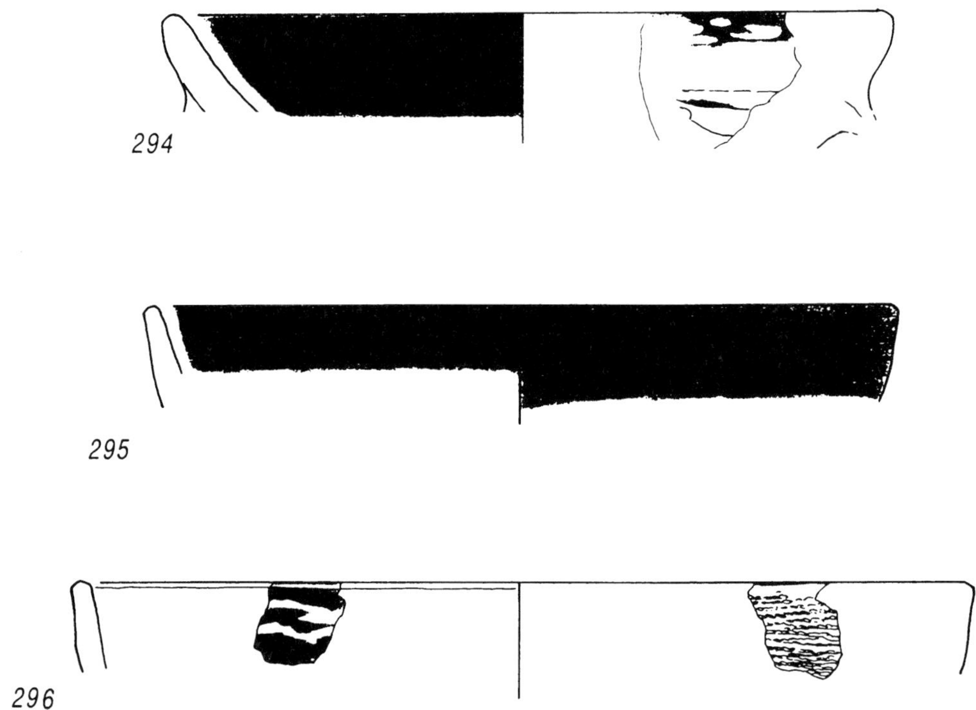

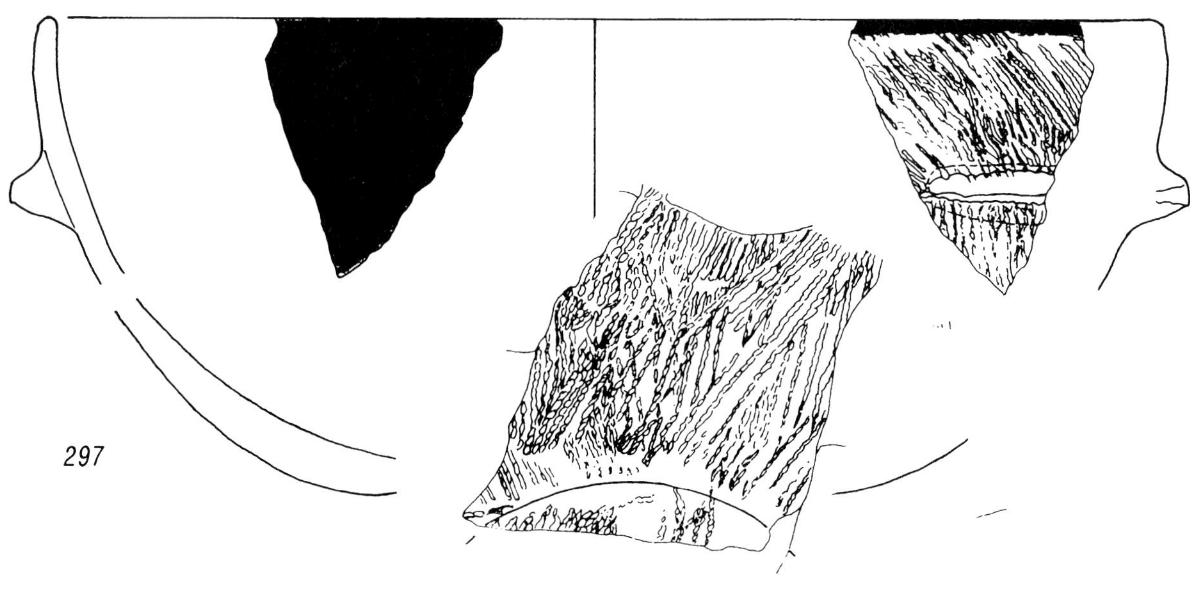

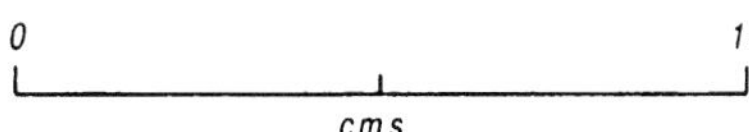
0
10
cms

Figure 4.53
Neolithic pottery from disturbed or later contexts (continued)

Bowls, open, shallow, rounded

Cat. no.	Provenance and sherd no.	Phase	Description
294	644.35/5	Mixed	Bowl, curved, shallow. Lug/ledge handle. Fairly fine fabric, thick-walled; fine grey grits; dull brick-red, blackish inside, like a slip. Smoothed outside, streaky burnish on outside rim, matt burnish inside.
295	680.15/2	[10]	Bowl, hemispherical? Fine fabric; small light and dark grits; black. Burnished outside and inside.
296	702.23/1	[16]	Bowl, hemispherical? Very fine fabric; very fine grey and light grits; buff, buff-brown inside. Cord-impressed outside, streaky burnish on rim and inside.
297	++/1	Unstratified	Bowl, curved, shallow, large. Horizontal ledge/knob handle. Fine fabric; fine grey grits; dark greyish-red outside with some blackish mottling, black core and inside. Cord-impressed outside, and upper and lower sides of lug, light matt burnish over rim and inside; horizontal ledge handle.

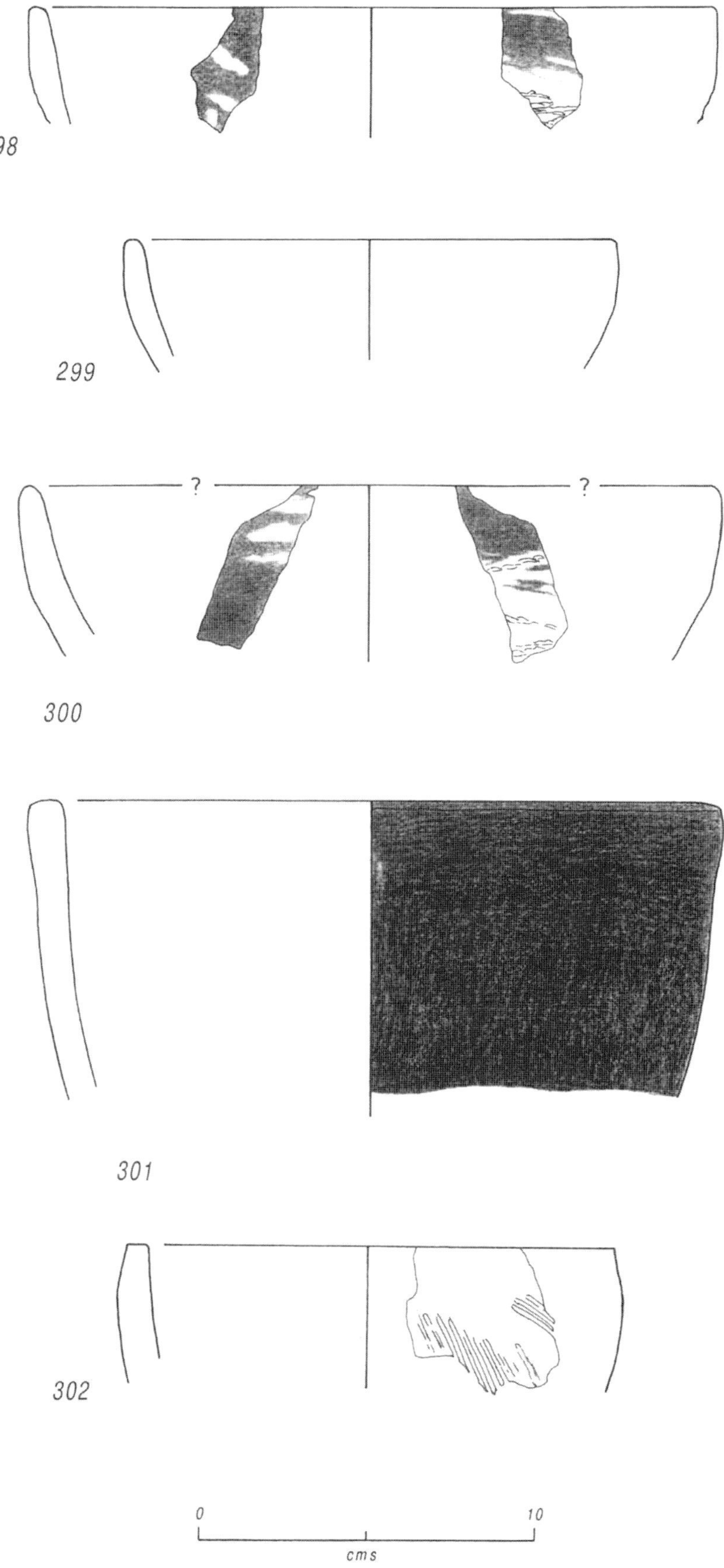

298
299
300
302
301
0
10
cms

Figure 4.54
Neolithic pottery from disturbed or later contexts (continued)

Bowls, open; medium and coarse fabric

Cat. no.	Provenance and sherd no.	Phase	Description
298	654.5/1	[6]	Bowl, curved, shallow. Fine fabric; fine light grits; dark greyish-brown. Cord-impressed outside, below 18 mm band of streaky burnish, continuing inside.
299	750.1/2	[8]	Bowl, curved, shallow. Fairly fine; fine grey grits; greyish buff; slightly brownish or self-slip; well smoothed outside and inside.
300	690.27/1	Mixed	Bowl, upright rim, curved. Fairly fine fabric but thick-walled; small dark-grey grits; buff. A few very faint cord-impressions outside, below a 22 mm band of burnish (streaks overlapping), burnish inside, upper part streaky.
301	735.4/14	Mixed	Bowl, upright rim, deep. Fairly fine fabric, roughly finished; dense small dark-grey grits; light brown, blackish mottling outside. Rough burnish outside on uneven surface (horizontal near rim, vertical on body), over rim and very sketchy inside.
302	735.11/4	[6 fill]	Bowl, upright rim (flat), deep. Medium–coarse fabric; small grey grits, shell; pale orange-buff. Faint-combed outside to within 14 mm of rim, finger-smoothed above, rim and inside.

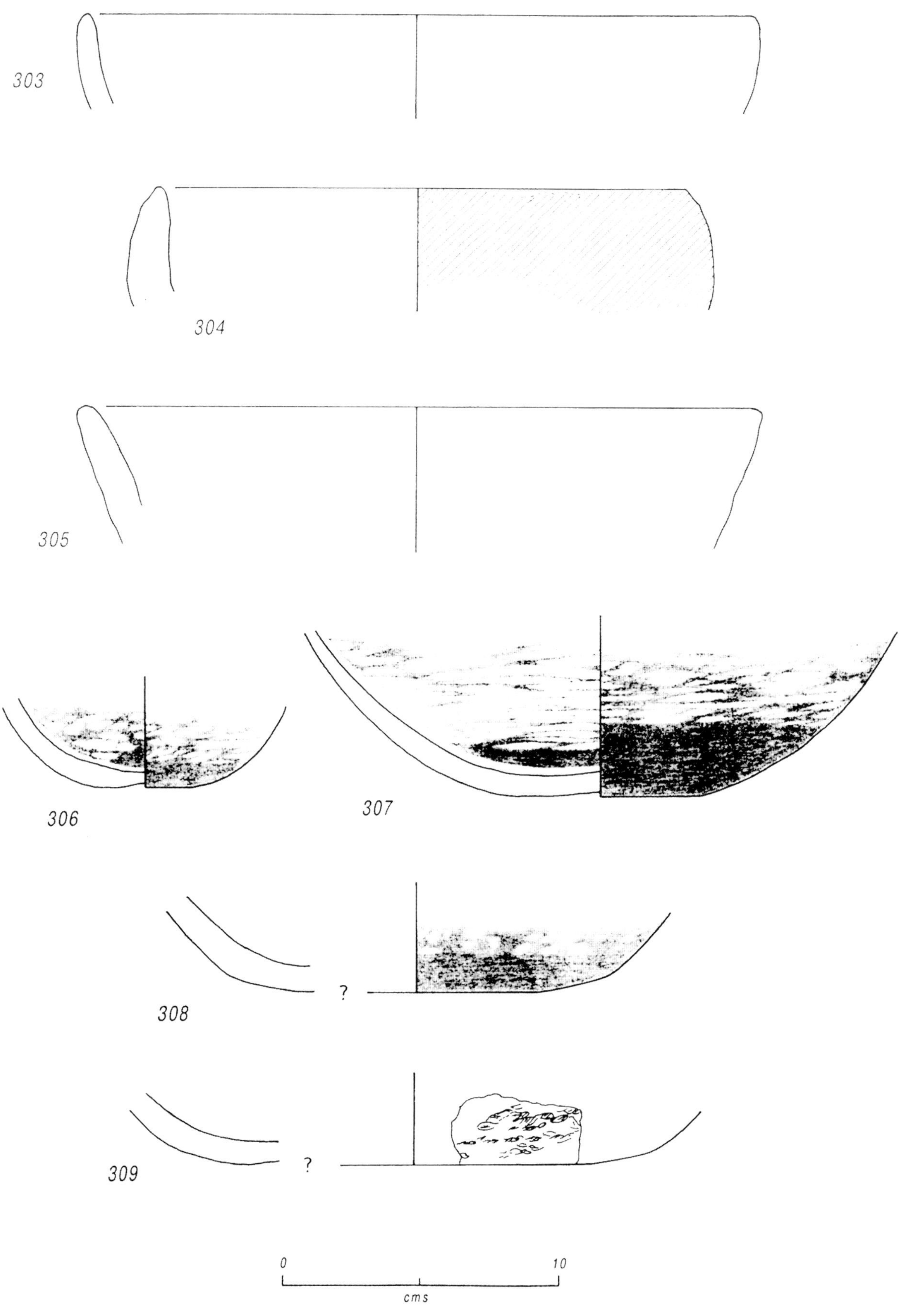

Figure 4.55
Neolithic pottery from disturbed or later contexts (continued)

Bowls, open; medium and coarse fabric continued

Cat. no.	Provenance and sherd no.	Phase	Description
303	644.2/11	[6 fill]	Bowl, upright rim, curved. Coarse fabric but thin-walled; small dark grits, some fine vegetable temper; pale buff. Smoothed outside and inside.
304	614.1/3	[?7/8]	Bowl, upright rim, curved, shallow. Very coarse fabric, thick-walled; medium-size dark-grey grits, fine vegetable temper; buff, pink surfaces. Light brick-red slip outside, inside worn.
305	606.60/2	Mixed	Bowl, flared (conical or platter?). Very coarse fabric; medium-size dark-grey grits, fine vegetable temper; buff. Lightly smoothed on uneven surfaces outside and inside.

Bases, all phases

Bases, round, with rounded-off angle

Cat. no.	Provenance and sherd no.	Phase	Description
306	648.13/3	3	Small round base with slightly concave centre, worn at the edge; fine fabric; small light and dark grits; black surfaces, greyish-red core. Slight streaky burnish outside, under base and inside.
307	710.9/8	4	Base, round (small base of quite large vessel). Fine fabric; fine light and dark grits; black, mottled buff on upper outside surfaces. Matt streaky burnish outside and inside, rough under base.
308	706.7/3	4	Base, flat, rounded edge. Coarse fabric; medium-size grits, a few large; buff, light grey under base. Light streaky burnish outside and under base, lightly smoothed inside.
309	602.19/4	5	Wide base, rounded at the edge and flattened or slightly concave in the middle; Medium–fine fabric; medium-size dark-grey and shiny grits, a few large white; dull buff, mottled greyish outside not under base, blackened over whole inside surface. Faint thick, widely spaced cord-impressions outside and under centre of concave base worn or rough ring 25 mm wide at edge of base, slight smoothing inside.

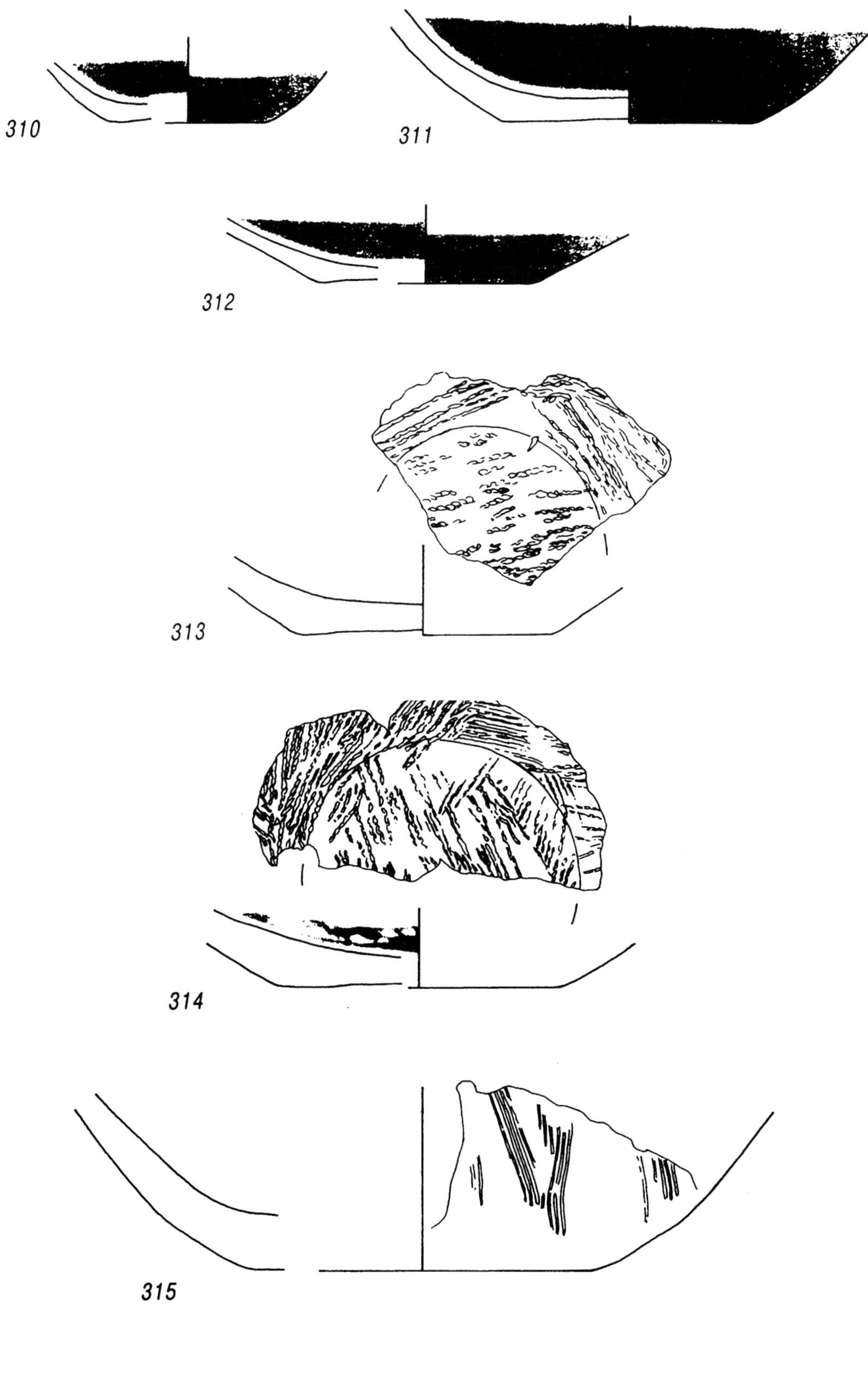

310
311
312
313
314
315
cms

Figure 4.56
Bases, all phases (continued)

Bases, angled

Cat. no.	Provenance and sherd no.	Phase	Description
310	706.12/2	2	Base, flat, steeper angle (probably a jar). Fairly fine fabric, thin-walled; small (few medium) light- and dark-grey grits; black. Glossy burnish outside, under base and inside.
311	706.33/1	1	Base, flat, steeper angle (probably a jar). Very fine fabric, fairly thick-walled; fine light and dark grits; black. Glossy burnish on all surfaces.
312	709.15/1	?1	Base, flat, shallow angle (probably a bowl). Extremely fine fabric; very fine light and dark grits; mushroom-colour outside, dark grey inside. Glossy burnish outside, under base and inside.
313	646.2/5	4	Base, flat, steeper angle (probably a jar). Medium fabric; dense small dark-grey grits; brick-red, blackened inside and lightly outside on walls only. Light cord-impressions outside and under base, worn at edge, inside lightly smoothed.
314	706.26/4	2	Base, flat, shallow angle (probably a bowl). Fairly fine fabric, but thick-walled; small dark-grey and lighter grits; buff outside, thick grey core and blackening inside. Cord-impressed outside and under base; streaky burnish inside.
315	644.14/22	5	Base, flat, steeper angle (probably a jar). Medium–coarse fabric, thick-walled; small dark and light grits; buff, light-red surfaces. Possible reddish slip outside; faint-combing over faint burnish outside, inside slightly smoothed.

Virginia Mathias

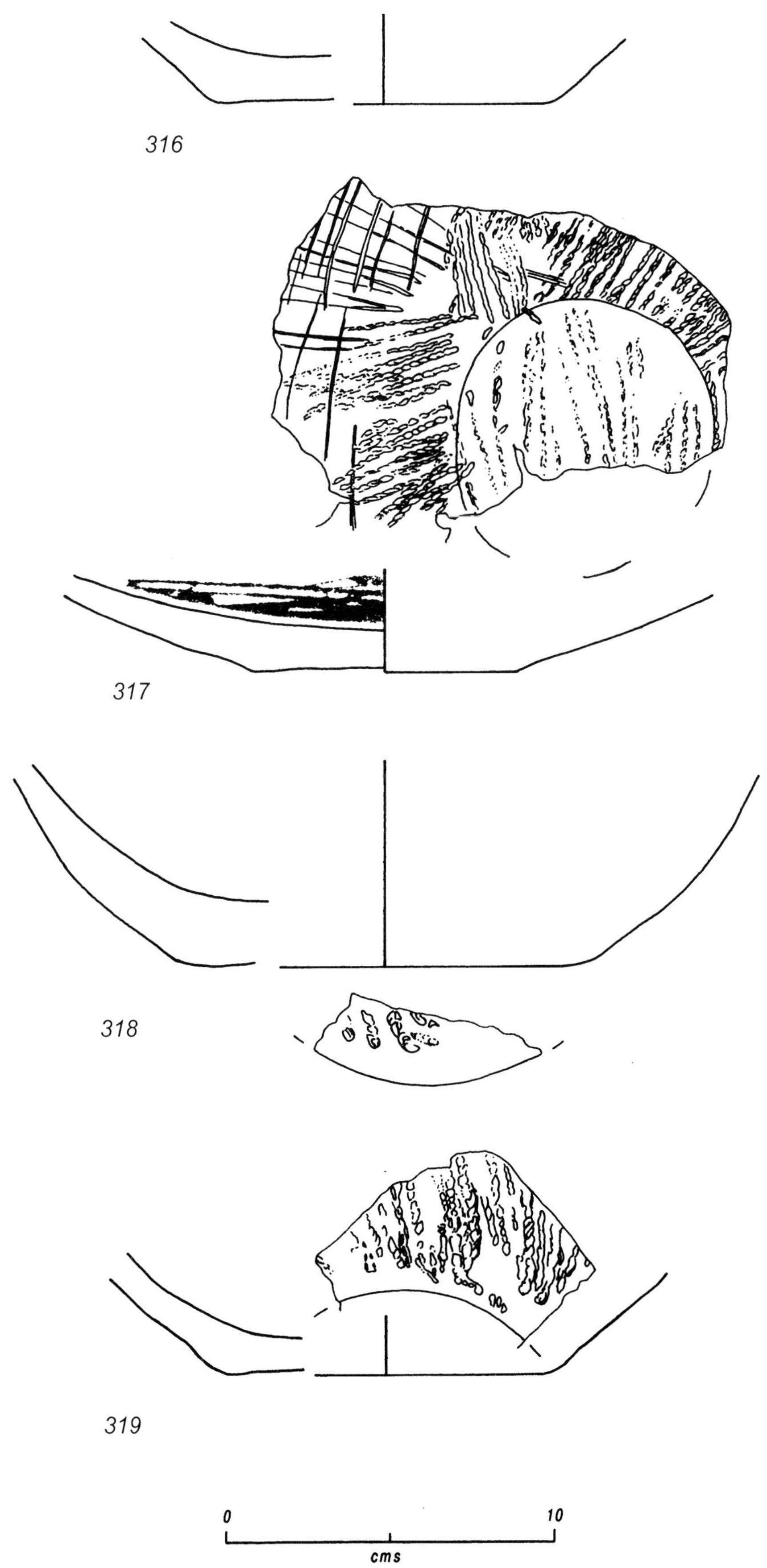

316

317

318

319

Figure 4.57
Bases, all phases (continued)

Bases, angled, with slight 'heel'

Cat. no.	Provenance and sherd no.	Phase	Description
316	735.3/11	5	Coarse fabric; small light and dark grits; bricky-buff, blackened outside; smoothed/faint burnished outside, inside barely smoothed.
317	706.42/4	2	Shallow-angled small base, very slightly concave; fine fabric; small dark-grey and white grits; light greyish-red, black core and mottling, especially inside; cord-impressed and scored lines outside and under base blurred over faint matt burnish, matt streaky burnish inside.
318	650.14/10	5	Base with clear mat impression, slightly concave; very coarse fabric; vegetable temper, pale grits, grog; light brick-red outside, light-grey core, buff-grey under base and inside; slightly smoothed on uneven surfaces.
319	735.13/1	5	Base, 'heeled' (probably a jar). Medium–coarse fabric; small dark-grey and light grits, a little fine vegetable temper; dull greyish buff, dark-grey surfaces outside and inside, inside also partly light orange (mostly upper part, may be original surface). Roughly applied cord-impressions outside, worn ring at edge of base, smoothed underneath, inside surface rough or worn.

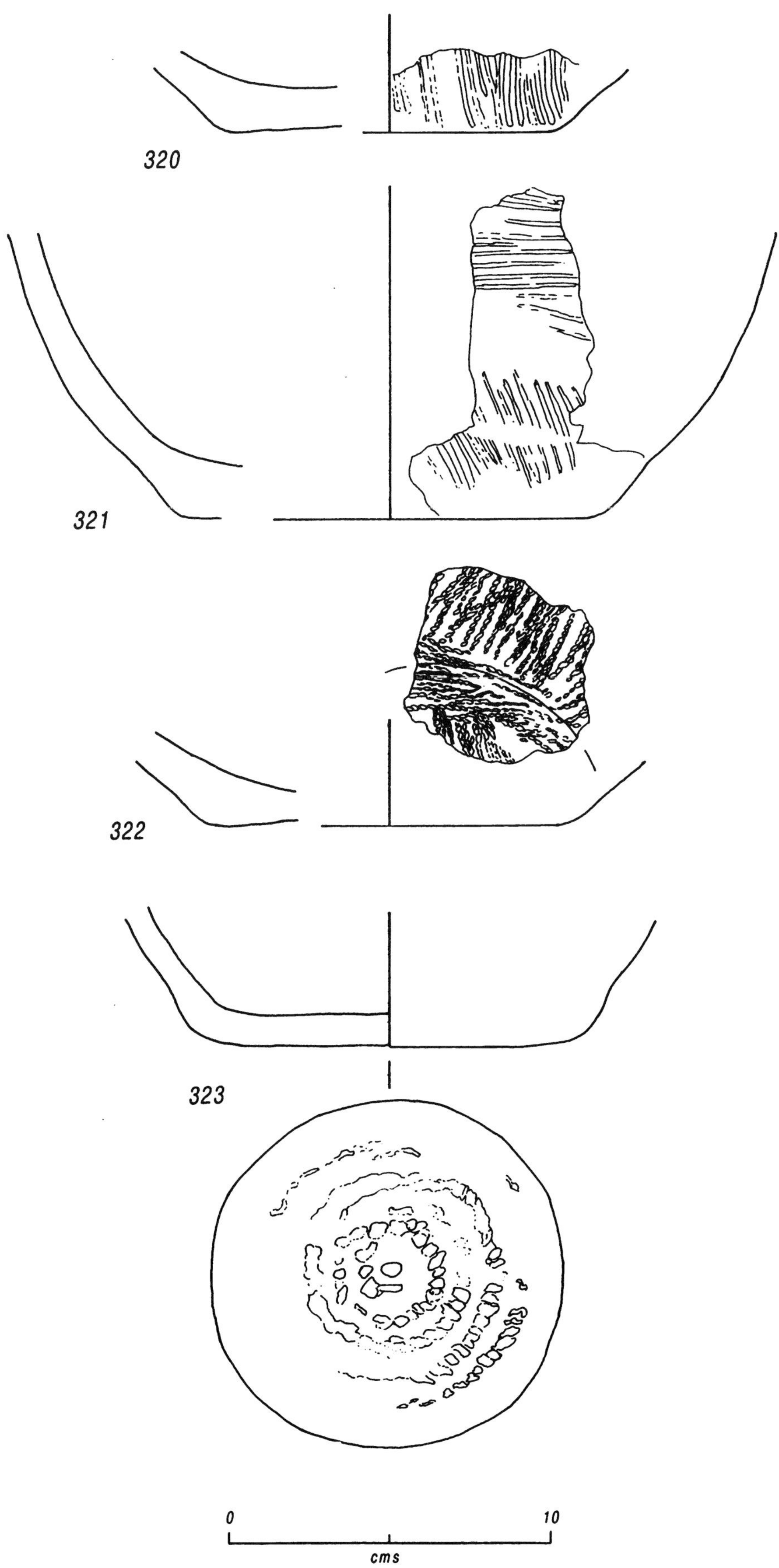

320
321
322
323
0
10
cms

Figure 4.58
Bases, all phases (continued)

Bases, 'heeled'

Cat. no.	*Provenance and sherd no.*	*Phase*	*Description*
320	654.10/4	4	Base, 'heeled' (probably a jar). Very coarse fabric; small pale-grey angular grits, coarse vegetable temper, a little red grog; light pinkish-buff, reddish on heel, pale grey inside, darker grey core and under centre of base outside. Faint-combed outside, smoothed under base and inside.
321	654.10/3	4	Base, 'heeled', deep (jar). Very coarse fabric; small pale-grey angular grits, coarse vegetable temper, a little red grog; light pinkish-buff, cream-buff on outside higher up, reddish on heel, pale grey inside, darker grey core and under centre of base outside. Faint-combed outside, smoothed under base and inside.
322	735.11/7	[6 fill]	Base, 'heeled', (probably a jar). Medium fabric; small dark-grey angular grits, some pale; dull buff, some dark-grey mottling. Cord-impressed outside and under base, rough inside.
323	644.31/2	[7]	Base, 'heeled', deep (jar), complete mat impression. Medium fabric; small dark-grey angular grits, some pale and larger, some vegetable temper, a little red grog; dull buff, partial thin dark-grey core, a little blackish mottling outside (may be post-depositional). Smoothed outside on uneven surface, mat impression under base, inside rough or worn with prominent grits.

Virginia Mathias

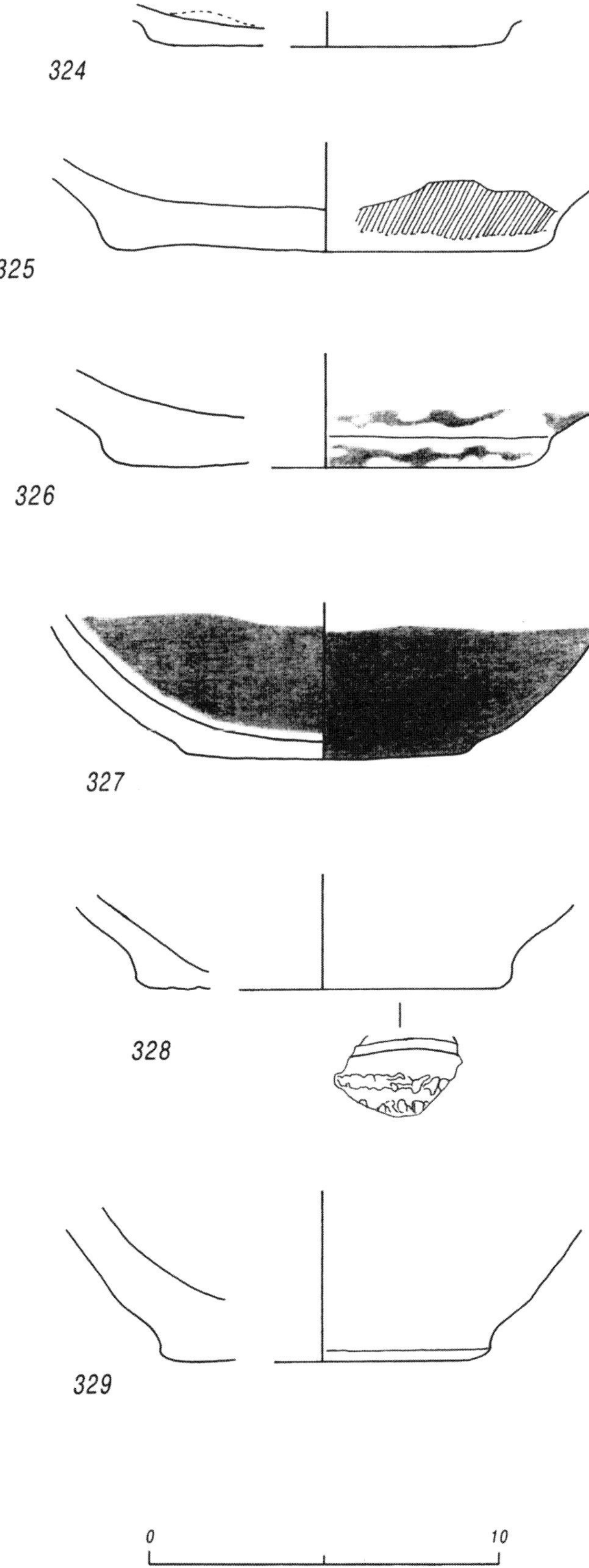

324

325

326

327

328

329

0   10

cms

Figure 4.59
Bases, all phases (continued)

Disc bases

Cat. no.	Provenance and sherd no.	Phase	Description
324	709.14/2	3	Base, disc. Very fine fabric; fine dark grits; dull darkish brick-red. Smooth surfaces. Remains of thick lime plaster coating (>3 mm) inside, possible traces under base and outside.
325	650.14/5	5	Base, disc. Medium–coarse fabric; medium and small light-grey angular grits, some dark-grey, some vegetable temper; blackish-grey core and underneath base only, walls and inside base bricky-buff, thin reddish surface outside (walls). Smoothed outside, probably on bright-red slip, base uneven, inside very worn.
326	680.42/2	5	Base, disc. Coarse fabric; medium to small dark-grey grits, some pale; brick-red, blackened outside surface, and thicker under base. Scrappy burnish outside and under base on very uneven surfaces, inside very worn and rough.
327	710.5/4	5	Base, disc. Very fine fabric; fine pale-grey and whitish grits, a few dark. Fine matt burnish inside, very fine glossy burnish outside, worn at edge and centre of convex base, and partially on outside wall.
328	735.4/8	Mixed	Base, disc, with mat impression. Fine fabric; fine dark-grey angular grits, some light, some red grog. Smoothed outside, possibly on darker slip, rough inside.
329	650.14/7	Mixed	Base, disc. Coarse fabric, thick base; small dark- and light-grey grits, vegetable temper, some red grog; buff-grey core, dark-grey inside, pale buff mottled orange outside. Burnished on uneven surface outside, possibly on darker slip, inside barely smoothed.

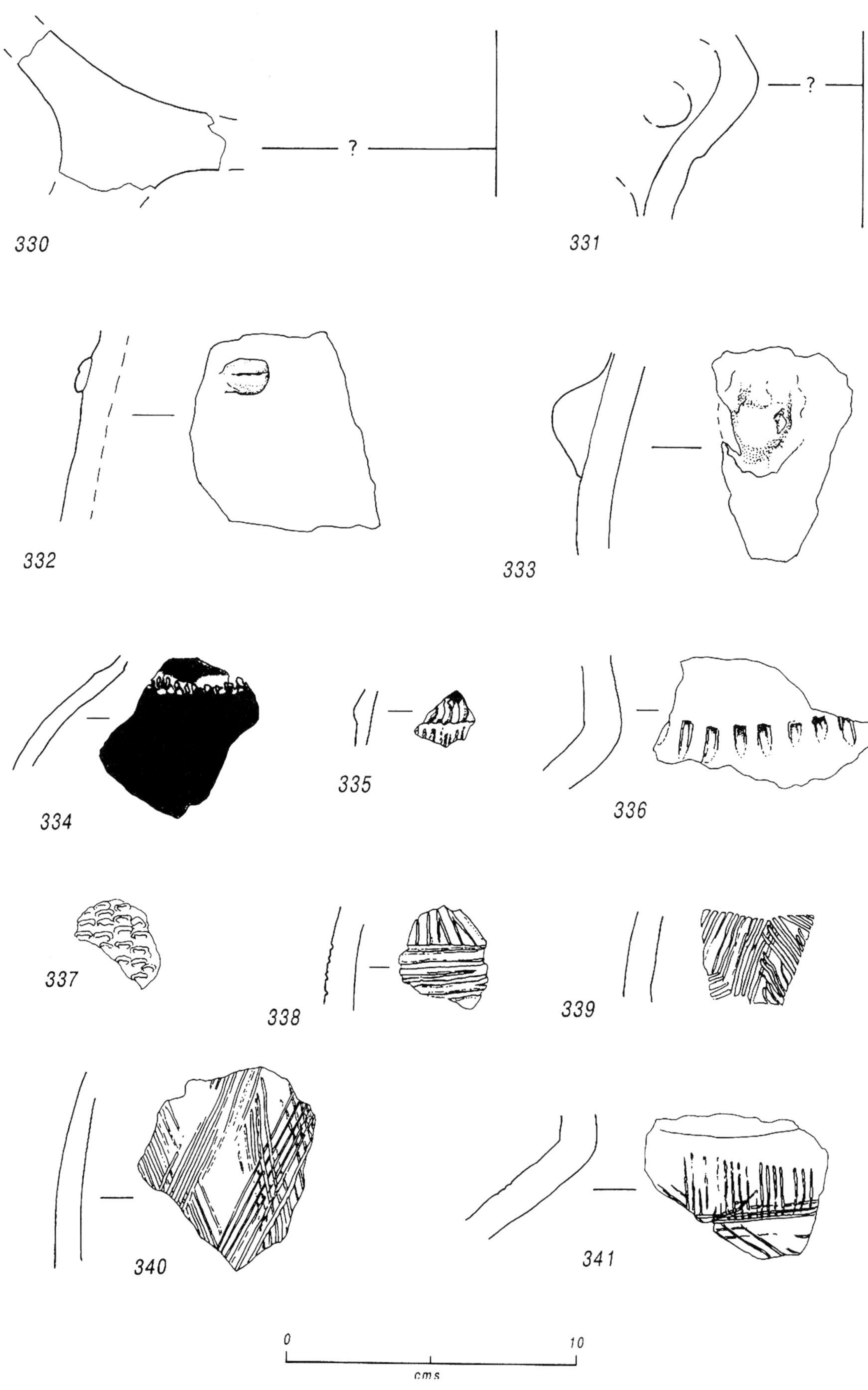

330

331

332

333

334

335

336

337

338

339

340

341

0   10

cms

Figure 4.60
Miscellaneous shapes and decoration (all phases)

Cat. no.	Provenance and sherd no.	Phase	Description
330	606.62/7	5	Pedestal bowl (?). Very coarse fabric; medium-size dark-grey grits; buff. Smoothed on all surfaces, best finish is on probable inside of bowl.
331	606.63/2	5	Lug handle, large, circular, on jar neck. Very coarse fabric; medium-size dark-grey grits; buff. Smoothed surfaces, broken off close to neck and shoulder of a fairly small jar with flaring neck; probably circular or oval in section.
332	650.14/8	5	Appliqué 'coffee-bean'. Very coarse fabric; medium-size dark-grey grits; buff; smoothed outside, worn inside. May represent an eye on a crude face-pot. (*cf.* Plate 4.2)
333	680.11/26	[14a]	Appliqué knob. Very coarse fabric; medium-size dark-grey grits; buff; smoothed outside, worn inside. Appliqué knob, probably on shoulder of jar. Perhaps a nose on a crude face-pot.
334	680.11/31	[14a]	Incised decoration, row of jabs (body sherd). Fairly fine fabric, thin-walled; medium-size pale grits, and small dark; reddish brown outside, partial black core, mottled inside. Fairly fine burnish outside, around neck inside, scrappy below; one irregular row of small jabs (through burnish), on shoulder just below neck of jar. (*cf.* Plate 4.2)
335	706.22/10	2	Fingernail impressions on band, and cord-impressions. Fine fabric, thin-walled; small white grits; pinkish mushroom. Raised or appliqué band with deep fingernail impressions. Faint very fine cord-impressions below band, burnished above, and inside.
336	602.35/5	[13]	Body sherd. Coarse fabric; medium to small dark-grey grits; buff. Lightly smoothed outside, rough inside. One irregular row of deep jabs, on shoulder of jar just below neck.
337	642.27/4	[8]	Incised decoration, row of jabs (body sherd). Fairly fine fabric, thin-walled; medium-size pale grits, and small dark; reddish brown outside, partial black core, mottled inside. Fairly fine burnish outside, around neck inside, scrappy below; one irregular row of small jabs (through burnish), on shoulder just below neck of jar.
338	602.19/5	5	Body sherd. Medium fabric; medium to small dark-red and pale grits; dark brick-red, dark-grey core. Smoothed inside. Deeply incised parallel lines in opposed blocks, probable basket-pattern.
339	644.14/1	5	Body sherd. Medium–fine fabric; small grey and red grits; buff. Scraped inside. Deeply combed or incised outside in possible basket pattern.
340	735.4/17	Mixed	Body sherd with faint-combed decoration of parallel lines in diamond pattern. Fairly fine fabric; small light grits; orange-brown. Lightly smoothed inside.
341	735.4/19	Mixed	Body sherd (shoulder of jar) with deep pattern-combed decoration. Coarse, unusual fabric, thick; large pale grits; pale grey. Smoothed outside and lightly inside.

                                    Virginia Mathias

Table 4.1. Number of sherds.

	STRATIFIED Phases			NEOLITHIC Total Stratified	OTHER	TOTALS
	1 – 3	*4*	*5*			
JAR RIMS						
Necked						
flared	4	7	13	24	16	40
upright	5	6	2	13	7	20
inverted	2	1	4	7	6	13
very short	1	1	0	2	2	4
Total necked	12	15	19	46	31	77
Holemouth	11	25	27	63	26	89
Total jar rims	23	40	46	109	57	166
BOWL RIMS						
inverted	10	5	9	24	3	27
						13
open	28	46	27	101	38	9
Total bowl rims	38	51	36	125	41	166
Total jar + bowl rims				234	98	332
BASES						
round/curved	7	9	11	27	7	34
angled	25	23	18	66	9	75
heeled	3	7	8	18	1	19
disc	3	2	5	10	4	14
Total bases	38	41	42	121	21	142
LIDS	0	0	2	2	0	2
TOTAL RIMS/BASES/LIDS	99	132	126	357	119	476
BODY SHERDS	440	481	569	1490	385	1875
TOTAL SHERDS	539	613	695	1847	504	2351

Table 4.2. Types of surface treatment.

	STRATIFIED				OTHER	TOTALS
	Phases 1–3	*Phase 4*	*Phase 5*	*Total Stratified*		
RIMS						
Burnished	28	41	30	99	31	130
Cord-impressed	20	22	19	61	25	86
Faint-combed	7	8	3	18	6	24
Incised, red slipped, etc.	2	3	7	12	3	15
Undecorated	6	20	25	51	29	80
	63	94	84	241	94	335
BASES						
Burnished	12	10	7	29	6	35
Cord-impressed	18	22	13	53	6	59
Faint-combed	4	3	4	11	1	12
Incised, red slipped, etc.	0	2	3	5	0	5
Undecorated	4	4	15	23	8	31
	38	41	42	121	21	142
BODY SHERDS						
Burnished	71	73	77	221	74	295
Cord-impressed	260	258	270	788	191	979
Faint-combed	71	68	87	226	35	261
Incised, red slipped, etc.	2	5	6	13	4	17
Undecorated	36	78	129	243	79	322
	440	482	569	1491	383	1874
ALL SHERDS						
Burnished	111	124	114	349	111	460
Cord-impressed	298	302	302	902	222	1126
Faint-combed	82	79	94	255	42	297
Incised, red slipped, etc.	4	10	16	30	7	37
Undecorated	46	102	169	317	116	433
	541	617	695	1853	498	2351

POTTERY REGISTER

	Area	Layer	Sherd	Vessel	Description	Phase	Cat. No
TRENCH I							
176	176	4	3	Bowl, flared.	Fine fabric; fine light and dark grits; dark brick-red (outside) mottled black (inside). Very faint combing outside, streaky burnish inside.	[MB]	284
192	192	66	4	Jar, holemouth, shallow, rolled rim.	Fairly fine fabric; dense small pale-grey grits; light brick-red, buff surface over rim and inside. Cord-impressed outside below band of light burnish, continuing over rim and inside.	[EB or MB]	*cf. 248*
194	194	6	1	Jar, holemouth, steep.	Fine fabric; small dark-grey grits; pale buff, slight grey mottling. Cord-impressions outside, below light horizontal burnish over rim, smoothed inside.	[EB or MB]	256
TRENCH VIII							
600	600	22	22	Base, flat, steeper angle.	Medium fabric and thickness; medium-size pale grits; pale grey. Undecorated? Worn outside and inside.	[15 fill]	*cf. 310, 311, 313, 315*
602	602	15	–	9 body sherds.	5 cord-impressed (2 roughly burnished inside); 4 undecorated coarse fabric (2 burnish traces outside).	5	–
	602	16	1	Base, flat, shallow angle probably a bowl).	Fine fabric, thin-walled. Cord-impressed outside, smoothed inside.	?4	*cf. 312, 314*
	602	16	–	12 body sherds.	11 cord-impressed (2 burnished inside; 1 with chalky coating, esp. inside); 1 undecorated coarse fabric.	4	–
	602	19	2	Jar, holemouth, steep (large).	Fine fabric; fine dark-grey grits; bricky brown. Shallow cord-impressions outside, horizontal burnish on rim and inside.	5	181
	602	19	3	Base, disc.	Very fine fabric, thin-walled; dense fine dark and light grits; black surfaces, dull brick-red core. Cord-impressed outside, burnished under base, fine burnish inside.	5	*cf. 108, 109*
	602	19	4	Base, flat, wide.	Medium-fine fabric; medium-size dark-grey and shiny grits, a few large white; dull buff, mottled greyish outside (not under base), blackened over whole inside surface. Faint thick, and widely spaced cord-impressions outside and under centre of concave base (worn or rough ring 25 mm wide at edge of base); slight smoothing inside.	5	309
	602	19	5	Body sherd.	Medium fabric; medium to small dark-red and pale grits; dark brick-red, dark-grey core. Smoothed inside. Deeply incised parallel lines in opposed blocks, probable basket-pattern.	5	338

	602	19	–	31 body sherds.	3 burnished (2 outside and inside, 1 inside only); 25 cord-impressed (3 burnished inside); 3 undecorated coarse fabric.	5	–
	602	20	–	2 body sherds.	1 cord-impressed; 1 undecorated coarse fabric.	4	–
	602	23	1	Jar with neck.	Fine fabric, thin-walled; fine dark shiny grits, a few light; dull brick-red. Very fine cord-impressions on shallow shoulder and body, neck smoothed/scraped with regular vertical strokes.	4	Plate 4.2 (Not catalogued)
	602	24	–	1 body sherd.	Fine red ware, burnished outside and inside.	4	–
	602	27	1	Jar with neck, upright.	Medium-coarse fabric; medium and small grey grits, probably some vegetable temper; buff, light brick-red surfaces. Outside and inside surfaces rough or worn.	4	63
	602	27	–	16 body sherds.	2 burnished outside and inside; 11 cord-impressed (5 burnished inside, most streaky); 3 undecorated coarse fabric.	4	–
	602	30	1	Base, flat, shallow angle (probably a bowl).	Fine fabric, thin-walled; fine dark grits; brownish, black outside surface. Fine cord-impressions outside, burnished base, rough inside.	4	cf. 312, 314
	602	30	–	2 body sherds.	1 cord-impressed; 1 undecorated coarse fabric.	4	–
	602	34	–	7 body sherds.	1 burnished outside; 1 cord-impressed; 5 undecorated coarse fabric.	4	–
	602	35	5	Body sherd.	Coarse fabric; medium to small dark-grey grits; buff. Lightly smoothed outside, rough inside. One irregular row of deep jabs, on shoulder of jar just below neck.	[13]	336
	602	36	15	Body sherd.	Undecorated, coarse fabric.	5	–
	602	36	17	Body sherd.	Undecorated, coarse fabric.	5	–
604	604	9	5	Lug, ledge handle.	Fine fabric; small-fine light and dark grits; buff-orange, slightly blackened or mottled. Cord-impressed outside, well-smoothed inside.	[post 16]	–
	604	26	2	Jar with neck, upright.	Fairly fine fabric; small dark-grey angular grits, some fine vegetable temper; cream-buff, thin grey core. Smoothed outside and inside on uneven surfaces.	[15]	236
	604	34	1	Base, flat, steeper angle (probably a jar).	Medium fabric and thickness; medium-fine light and dark grits; blackish outside and core, inside dark brick-red. Burnish (crackled) outside, smoothed or light burnish inside.	[post 16]	cf. 310 311, 313, 315
	604	35	4	Base, flat, rounded edge.	Medium fabric; small-fine grey grits; buff. Rough burnish outside, lightly smoothed inside.	[post 16]	cf. 306–309, 297
	605	1	22	Jar, holemouth, shallow.	Very fine fabric; very fine light and dark grits; grey-brown, mottling. Faint cord-impressions outside, below 13 mm band of fine horizontal burnish, continuing over rim and (streaky) inside.	[9]	252

606	606	2	5	Jar, holemouth, steep.	Fairly fine fabric; fine dark grits; dark brick-red, dark grey surfaces. Well smoothed or light matt burnish outside and inside.	?4	76
	606	2	1	Bowl, flared.	Fine fabric; fine grey and light grits; brick-red, some faint greyish mottling. Light matt burnish outside and inside on well smoothed surfaces.	?4	111
	606	2	–	11 body sherds.	Medium-coarse fabric. 1 burnished inside and outside; 1 burnished outside only; 3 cord-impressed; 4 faint-combed; 2 undecorated.	4	–
	606	4	–	3 body sherds.	1 burnished outside and inside; 2 cord-impressed.	3	–
	606	5	10	Bowl, slightly inverted rim.	Fine fabric; very fine light and dark grits; light brick-red, grey core and mottling outside; faint and very sketchy combing outside, light burnish inside below rim.	3	21
	606	5	45	Jar with neck, inverted	Fine fabric; fine light-coloured grits; dull blackish. Cord-impressions outside, burnish inside on uneven surface.	3	cf. 1
	606	5	–	45 body sherds.	Medium-fine fabric. 4 burnished outside and inside; 20 cord-impressed; 15 faint-combed; 6 undecorated.	3	–
	606	7	2	Jar, holemouth, shallow.	Medium fabric; small dark grits; greyish-buff; well smoothed or light matt burnish outside and inside; Traces of very faint combing outside, and possibly of reddish paint or slip.	4	77
	606	7	3	Platter, flared, shallow.	Coarse fabric; large dark-grey grits; buff. Well smoothed outside and inside, rougher underneath.	4	138
	606	7	–	8 body sherds.	1 roughly burnished; 5 cord-impressed (1 very faint); 1 faint-combed or incised; 1 undecorated. Coarse fabric.	4	–
	606	8	1	Jar with neck, upright, narrow.	Fine fabric; fine dark grey grits; dark grey outside, brick-red inside. Cord-impressed outside, smoothed inside.	3	5
	606	8	23	Bowl, upright rim.	Fine fabric; fine grits; dull bricky-brown, mottled grey outside; Cord-impressed outside, slight burnish on rim, smoothed inside.	3	26
	606	8	–	23 body sherds.	4 burnished outside and inside; 12 cord-impressed; 7 faint-combed.	3	–
	606	9	–	5 body sherds.	2 cord-impressed; 2 faint-combed (or grass-wiped?); 1 burnished inside.	3	–
	606	9	1	Body sherd with lime plaster lining.	Fairly fine fabric; small-fine dark-grey grits; dull brick-red. Cord-impressed outside. Thick (3 mm) white plaster lining, surface stained (?) pale reddish-buff.	3	–
	606	13	1	Bowl, upright rim.	Fine fabric; fine dark shiny grits, some medium-size dull red, may be grog. black. Cord-impressed outside, burnish over rim, and very sketchy inside on rough surface.	Mixed	267
	606	13	3	Bowl, flared.	Fine fabric; fine dark-red and light grits; brick-red, dark-red surfaces. Matt burnish outside and inside.	Mixed	276

606	13	–	8 body sherds.	3 burnished outside and inside; 2 cord-impressed outside, burnished inside; 2 faint-combed, basket pattern(?); 1 undecorated. Coarse fabric.	3	–
606	15	–	5 body sherds.	2 cord-impressed (1 burnished inside); 3 burnished outside and inside.	3	–
606	17	–	5 body sherds.	2 burnished outside and inside; 3 cord-impressed.	?4	–
606	19	–	4 body sherds.	1 burnished outside and inside; 2 cord-impressed (1 burnished inside, 1 smoothed); 1 scraped/combed (fine fabric, brick-red, neck/shoulder).	2	–
606	20	1	Bowl, slightly inverted rim.	Fine fabric; fine grits, mostly dark; dark buff, greyish outside surface. Fine horizontal burnish outside, rim and inside.	1 (?2)	30
606	20	–	4 body sherds.	2 burnished outside and inside; 1 cord-impressed, burnished inside; 1 faint-combed or scraped.	1	–
606	21	–	3 body sherds.	2 cord-impressed and burnished inside; 1 undecorated coarse fabric.	1	–
606	25	1	Bowl, slightly inverted rim, base rounded.	Fine fabric; small dark grey and whitish grits; dull dark brown outside and rim, blackish inside and core. Faint impressed or combed in short strokes outside, burnished rim and inside. Sherds of rounded base, matching size, fabric, temper, unusual combed decoration.	3	23
606	25	5	Bowl, slightly inverted rim.	Very fine fabric; fine grits; greyish brown, dull brick-red core; matt burnish outside (streaky on rim) and inside.	3	31
606	25	6	Bowl, upright rim, flattened.	Fine fabric; fine light-coloured and shiny grits; dull brick-red, greyish-red surfaces. Deep but blurred cord impressions outside, light burnish on rim and inside.	3	29
606	25	7	Bowl, flared, flat-sided.	Medium-fine fabric; small angular whitish grits; brownish black, grey-brown inside. Horizontal burnish outside and inside.	3	45
606	25	8	Bowl, slightly inverted rim.	Fine fabric; fine brown grits; brown, dark-grey core. Burnish outside and (uneven) inside.	3	35
606	27	1	Jar with neck, upright. Vertical horizontally pierced lug handles.	Very fine fabric; fine light and dark grits; grey, buff surfaces, mottled. Cord-impressed on shoulder outside, burnish on neck between lugs, also inside rim, and sketchy below on less even surface.	4	60
606	27	2	Jar with neck, flared, narrow, high.	Coarse fabric; medium-size dark-grey grits; buff, blackened outside on neck. Finger-smoothed, slight sheen in band 25–30 mm from rim outside, 20 mm inside (perhaps from handling rather than burnish).	4	56
606	27	3	Jar, holemouth, steep.	Coarse fabric; medium to small whitish and grey grits, some fine vegetable temper; pale brick-red mottled buff, buff core. Smoothed outside and inside but poor finish with crackled surfaces.	4	81
606	27	4	Jar, holemouth, shallow.	Coarse fabric; medium-size dark grey angular grits, possible vegetable temper; light buff, dull greyish-red surfaces. Smoothed outside only, inside rather rough.	4	78

606	27	5	Jar, holemouth, steep.	Coarse fabric; medium to small dark-grey angular grits; buff. Smoothed outside and inside. (Rim folded inwards and roughly flattened, with join still visible.)	4	83
606	27	6	Jar, holemouth, steep.	Coarse fabric; large dark-grey grits, fine vegetable temper; greyish buff, discoloured. Smoothed outside and inside; indication of knob or lug on broken edge (thickness of wall is variable).	4	82
606	27	7	Bowl, flared, shallow.	Coarse fabric; medium-size dark-grey grits; pale buff-pink, light-grey core. Smoothed surfaces. Blackened inside.	4	135
606	27	8	Base, disc (jar?).	Coarse fabric, fairly thin; medium-fine dark-greyish grits, some vegetable temper; buff. Light burnish outside, red slip inside.	4	*cf. 324–9*
606	27	9	Base, flat, shallow angle (probably a bowl).	Medium fabric and thickness; dense small-fine light-greyish grits, some darker; dull bricky grey. Cord-impressed outside, smoothed inside.	4	*cf. 312, 314*
606	27	10	Base, angled, shallow, with slight heel (bowl?).	Medium fabric; dense small-fine dark grits, some light. Cord-impressed outside (including under base), smoothed inside.	4	*cf. 317*
606	27	11	Base, flat, deep angle (jar).	Coarse fabric; small-fine dark and light grits; buff discoloured grey, light brick-red inside surface. Cord-impressed on brown slip outside, smoothed inside.	4	*cf. 310, 311, 313, 315*
606	27	12	Lug, ledge (on body sherd).	Complete, long deep tapering ledge; fine fabric; fine light and dark grits; dull brick-red. Cord-impressed outside, matt burnish inside.	4	–
606	27	–	27 body sherds.	3 burnished outside and inside; 8 cord-impressed, smoothed inside; 3 faint-combed/scored/scraped outside, smoothed/light-burnished inside; 13 undecorated (2 medium fabric, thin; 11 coarse fabric, mostly thick).	4	–
606	59	1	Jar, holemouth, steep.	Fine fabric; small grey grits; buff/light red mottled, thin grey core near to inside surface. Light matt burnish outside, signs of cord-impressions below, inside finger-smoothed.	[7]	260
606	59	2	Base, flat, steeper angle (probably a jar).	Medium fabric and thickness; small grey grits; dull brown, greyish core, black inside, mottled outside. Cord-impressed outside, smoothed inside.	[7]	*cf. 310, 311, 313, 315*
606	59	3	Base, flat, shallow angle (of a bowl?).	Coarse fabric, thick-walled; medium-fine grey and light grits, red grog, a little fine vegetable temper; buff-greyish, mottled outside (worn), pale orange inside.	[7]	*cf. 312, 314*
606	59	–	2 body sherds.	1 burnished outside and inside; 1 cord-impressed, roughly burnished inside.	5	–
606	60	1	Jar with neck, upright, narrow.	Medium-fine fabric, thin-walled; small dark-grey and light grits; pale buff-grey. Very roughly finger-smoothed outside and inside.	Mixed	227
606	60	2	Bowl, flared (conical or platter?).	Very coarse fabric; medium-size dark-grey grits, fine vegetable temper; buff. Lightly smoothed on uneven surfaces outside and inside.	Mixed	305
606	61	1	Jar, holemouth, shallow.	Very coarse fabric; medium-size dark grey and white grits, red grog. Lightly smoothed or wiped outside and inside (uneven surface). Shallow incised or indented mark on shoulder (could be accidental).	5	174

606	61	2	Base, flat, medium angle.	Medium fabric, thick at base; medium-fine dark-grey grits, some large, pale; light pinkish-grey, faint grey core; cord-impressed outside, well-smoothed or matt burnish inside.	5	cf. 310, 311, 313, 315
606	61	3	Base, flat, rounded edge (without sides).	Coarse fabric, thick; very large-fine dark-grey angular grits, shell?; buff. Light burnish outside, possible red paint on smoothed surface inside.	5	cf. 306–309, 297
606	61	–	5 body sherds.	1 roughly burnished outside; 3 cord-impressed (1 roughly burnished inside); 1 undecorated coarse fabric.	5	–
606	62	1	Jar with neck, flared, narrow.	Coarse fabric; large dark-grey grits; buff. Smoothed outside and inside.	5	152
606	62	2	Bowl, slightly inverted rim. Deep horizontal lug/ledge handle.	Fine fabric, roughly finished; small dark and shiny grits; dull brick-red, brown core and surfaces. Worn and indistinct cord-impressions outside on uneven surface of body and upper side only of broad ledge-handle, under-side rough and very uneven, streaky burnish on inside surface.	5	184
606	62	3	Jar, holemouth, shallow, rolled rim.	Medium-fine fabric; dense small pale-grey grits; light orange, grey mottling. Streaky burnish inside and in band above cord-impressions outside.	5	164
606	62	4	Bowl, curved, shallow.	Medium fabric; small dark-grey grits; greyish buff. Light burnish outside, fainter inside.	5	209
606	62	5	Bowl, curved, shallow.	Coarse fabric; medium-size dark-grey angular grits, some fine vegetable temper; buff. Smoothed (possibly light matt burnish) outside and inside.	5	210
606	62	6	Base, angled, steeper, with slight 'heel' (jar?).	Very coarse fabric, thick-walled; dense medium-fine dark-grey angular grits, some fine vegetable temper; buff, light bricky-orange surfaces. Smoothed outside and inside.	5	cf. 316, 318–323
606	62	7	Pedestal bowl (?)	Very coarse fabric; medium-size dark-grey grits; buff. Smoothed on all surfaces, best finish is on probable inside of bowl.	5	330
606	62	13	Base, flat, shallow angle (probably a bowl).	Fine fabric, thin-walled; fine light and grey grits, red grog?; blackish-brown surfaces, bricky-brown core. Burnish outside and inside.	5	cf. 312, 314
606	62	–	5 body sherds.	5 cord-impressed (2 burnished/smoothed inside).	5	–
606	63	1	Bowl, flared, shallow; probably a 'heeled' base.	Coarse fabric; medium-size dark-grey angular grits, a little red grog; buff, pale-grey core. Finger-smoothed outside and inside.	5	208
606	63	2	Lug handle, large, circular, on jar neck.	Very coarse fabric; medium-size dark-grey grits; buff. Smoothed surfaces, broken off close to neck and shoulder of a fairly small jar with flaring neck; probably circular or oval in section.	5	331
606	63	–	2 body sherds.	2 cord-impressed.	5	–
606	64	–	5 body sherds.	4 cord-impressed outside, smoothed inside; 1 undecorated coarse fabric.	5	–
606	66	–	3 body sherds.	1 burnished outside and inside; 1 cord-impressed with burnished band outside, and burnished inside; 1 undecorated medium-coarse fabric.	3	–

607	607	42	1	Bowl, flared, shallow.	Fine fabric; fine light and dark grits; dark red, mottled black. Fine burnish outside and inside.	2	49
	607	42	2	Bowl, flared, shallow.	Very fine fabric; very fine whitish grits; black; glossy burnish outside and inside.	2	44
	607	42	3	Bowl, flared, shallow.	Fine fabric; very fine grits; brown, black core and mottling. Fine matt burnish outside and inside.	2	47
	607	42	4	Jar, holemouth, steep.	Fine fabric; fine shiny grits; black. Cord-impressed outside, fine burnish on rim and inside.	2	18
	607	42	5	Base, flat, steeper angle (probably a jar).	Very fine fabric, very thin-walled; very fine grits; buff-grey, blackened inside. Fine diagonal burnish outside, and inside (cross-scoring).	2	*cf. 310, 311, 313, 315*
	607	42	6	Base, flat, steeper angle (jar?).	Medium fabric and thickness; small-fine light grits; dull brick-red, darker or blackened surfaces. Faintly cord-impressed outside, smoothed inside.	2	*cf. 310, 311, 313, 315*
	607	42	–	8 body sherds.	2 burnished outside and inside; 12 cord-impressed (7 burnished, 3 smoothed/wiped, 2 rough inside); 3 faint-combed/scraped outside (1 burnished inside); 1 undecorated medium fabric, thick.	2	–
608	608	1	1	Jar with neck, upright, narrow.	Medium-coarse; fine grey and light grits, some reddish, and fine vegetable temper; pale orange-buff, mottled grey; rough outside, lightly smoothed inside.	[7]	228
	608	1	2	Bowl, flared, shallow.	Fine fabric; fine grey and light grits; brick-red, darker/greyish inside; very faint combing outside, streaky horizontal burnish inside.	[7]	289
	608	1	3	Base, disc.	Medium fabric; small-fine whitish and dark grits; dull light brick-red; undecorated? (small sherd); mat impression underneath, indented.	[7]	*cf. 325, 326–328*
	608	1	–	7 body sherds.	2 rough-burnished outside (1 fine fabric, rough-burnished inside; 1 coarse fabric); 5 cord-impressed (1 burnished inside).	[7]	–
	608	2	–	5 body sherds.	1 burnished outside and inside (very fine fabric); 1 rough-burnished outside and inside (medium fabric); 2 cord-impressed (1 light-burnished inside); 1 undecorated coarse fabric.	[7]	–
	608	3	1	Jar, holemouth, shallow.	Coarse fabric; medium-size dark-grey grits, light grits/grog, some veg; buff; smoothed outside and inside.	[7]	*cf. 242*
	608	3	–	4 body sherds.	2 cord-impressed; 2 undecorated coarse fabric.	[7]	–
610	610	21	14	Bowl, curved, shallow.	Fine fabric; fine light and dark grits; black outside, brownish inside, thin brick-red core; faint cord-impressions outside, streaky burnish inside.	[16 fill]	293
	610	27	9	Bowl, upright rim.	Very fine fabric; very fine dark and light grits; mid-brown, slight greyish mottling outside; fine horizontal burnish outside, rim and inside.	[16]	268
	610	41	2	Jar with neck, flared.	Medium-fine fabric, but thick-walled; small dark grits; dull brick-red; faint-combed outside, smoothed inside.	[15 fill]	226

614	614	1	1	Jar with neck, flared, narrow.	Coarse fabric; small grey grits; pale brick-red. Smoothed outside, rough inside.	[?7 ?8]	224
	614	1	2	Jar with neck, slightly inverted.	Medium-coarse fabric; small dark-grey angular grits; buff. Well smoothed outside, slightly inside rim, rough below.	[?7 ?8]	238
	614	1	3	Bowl, upright rim, curved, shallow.	Very coarse fabric, thick-walled; medium-size dark-grey grits, fine vegetable temper; buff, pink surfaces. Light brick-red slip outside, inside worn.	[?7 ?8]	304
	614	1	4	Jar, holemouth, steep.	Very coarse fabric; very large dark-grey grits, a few white, fine vegetable temper, a little red grog; light brick-red, brownish core. Slightly smoothed outside, inside surface entirely lost. Diameter and angle of profile approximate.	[?7 ?8]	246
	614	1	–	1 body sherd.	Cord-impressed (rough inside).	[Post-Neo.]	–
	614	3	1	Bowl, slightly inverted rim, flattened (small) appliqué knob/lug handle or 'coffee-bean' decoration.	Fine fabric; fine dark and light grits; buff mottled dark-grey towards surfaces, brick-red core. Surfaces smoothed near rim, rough below.	[9]	266
	614	3	5	Bowl, flared.	Fine fabric; fine greyish grits; black. Glossy but slightly streaky horizontal burnish outside and inside.	[9]	279
	614	3	6	Base, flat, rounded edge.	Coarse fabric; large-fine dark-grey grits; orange-buff, buff core. Smoothed outside, slightly smoothed inside.	[9]	*cf. 306–309, 297*
	614	3	–	3 body sherds.	1 burnished outside and inside; 1 cord-impressed (rough-burnished/smoothed inside); 1 faint-combed.	[9]	–
640	640	22	4	Jar, holemouth, shallow, rolled rim.	Fairly fine fabric; small pale-grey grits; light brick-red, thick dark-grey core. Blurred cord impressions outside below 10 mm band of finger-smoothing or light matt burnish over rim and inside.	[Post-Neo.]	251
642	642	10	–	3 body sherds.	2 burnished/well smoothed outside and inside; 1 cord-impressed outside, smoothed inside.	[14a]	–
	642	11	1	Body sherd.	Very coarse fabric; large dark-grey angular grits; buff. Lightly smoothed outside and on rim, rough inside.	[?9-14]	240
	642	11	–	1 body sherd.	1 undecorated coarse fabric.	[? 14a]	–
	642	22	6	Jar, holemouth, steep (large).	Medium-fine fabric; medium-size pale-grey grits; pale orange-buff. Faint-combed outside on uneven surface, burnished on rim and inside. Thickening on broken edge suggesting end of horizontal lug or knob, 10 mm from rim.	[8]	257
	642	22	–	2 body sherds.	1 cord-impressed; 1 faint-combed.	[8]	–
	642	26	–	3 body sherds.	2 burnished outside and inside; 1 cord-impressed (light burnish inside).	[8]	–

	642	27	4	Body sherd.	Fine fabric, fine dark grits, also some small white; outside dark reddish-grey, inside black. Fine burnish inside. All-over deep scale-shaped jabs, probably fingernail impressions.	[8]	337
	642	27	–	2 body sherds.	1 burnished outside and inside; 1 cord-impressed.	[8]	–
644	644	1	–	16 body sherds.	1 burnished outside and inside; 8 cord-impressed (2 light burnish/smoothed inside); 2 rough burnished outside only (coarse fabric); 5 undecorated (medium-coarse fabric, thick).	[7]	–
	644	2	11	Bowl, upright rim, curved.	Coarse fabric but thin-walled; small dark grits, some fine vegetable temper; pale buff. Smoothed outside and inside.	[6 fill]	303
	644	2	63	Jar with neck, slightly inverted.	Fairly fine fabric, thick-walled; fine dark and light grits; light brick-red, thick grey core. Streaky burnish over rim.	[6 fill]	237
	644	2	68	Jar with neck, upright, short.	Fine fabric; small dark-grey and whitish grits; dark brick-red, greyish-brown surfaces. Horizontal burnish outside and inside (rather streaky).	[6 fill]	217
	644	2		43 body sherds.	2 burnished outside and inside; 32 cord-impressed, (5 burnished inside); 9 undecorated medium and coarse.	[6 fill]	–
	644	3	12	Bowl, flared, shallow.	Fine fabric; fine light and dark grits; black. Burnished outside and inside.	[6 fill]	288
	644	3		17 body sherds.	3 burnished outside and inside; 5 cord-impressed, (2 burnished/smoothed inside); 2 faint-combed outside; 1 rough burnished outside only (coarse fabric); 6 undecorated coarse fabric.	[6 fill]	–
	644	6	–	1 body sherd.	Undecorated, coarse fabric.	[7]	–
	644	7	–	2 body sherds.	Cord-impressed.	[7 + 8]	–
	644	12	5	Jar with neck, upright.	Medium fabric, thin-walled; fine grey grits and red grog; pinkish buff, darker slip. Slightly smoothed outside, and inside on uneven surface.	[7]	229
	644	12	15	Jar with neck, upright, narrow.	Medium fabric, thin-walled; fine grey grits, red grog; buff, mottled/blackened, darker slip. Slightly smoothed outside and inside.	[7]	*cf. 229*
	644	12	–	8 body sherds.	2 burnished outside and inside; 5 cord-impressed; 1 rough burnished (medium-coarse fabric.	[7]	–
	644	13	2	Jar, holemouth, shallow, rolled rim.	Fine fabric; dense small pale-grey grits, a little red grog; buff, dark-grey core and mottling, especially inside. Faint cord-impressions outside, smoothed on rim and inside.	[6]	248
	644	14	1	Body sherd.	Medium-fine fabric; small grey and red grits; buff. Scraped inside. Deeply combed or incised outside in possible basket pattern.	5	339
	644	14	8	Bowl, curved, shallow.	Fine fabric, variable thickness of wall; fine dark and light grits; reddish brown. Streaky matt burnish on uneven surface outside in a band 20-25 mm around rim, and inside.	5	202

644	14	14	Base, flat, steeper angle (probably a jar).	Coarse fabric; small grits; buff-grey; rough inside and outside.	5	cf. 310, 311, 313, 315
644	14	20	Jar, holemouth, shallow.	Medium-fine fabric, hard-fired; medium-size dark grey grits, a few white, and red grog; pale brick-red, buff core. Well smoothed or light burnished on rilled outside surface, inside slightly finger-smoothed on uneven surface.	5	172
644	14	21	Jar, holemouth, shallow.	Medium fabric; small dark grey and whitish grits; buff, grey mottling. Lightly smoothed outside and inside.	5	cf. 163
644	14	22	Base, flat, steeper angle (probably a jar).	Medium-coarse fabric, thick-walled; small dark and light grits; buff, light-red surfaces. Possible reddish slip outside; faint combing over faint burnish outside, inside slightly smoothed.	5	315
644	14	–	29 body sherds.	2 burnished outside and inside; 3 burnished outside only (1 coarse fabric); 18 cord-impressed (some burnished inside); 3 faint-combed outside; 6 undecorated coarse fabric.	5	–
644	15	1	Bowl, slightly inverted rim.	Fine fabric; fine dark grits; buff, thin pale-grey core and mottling outside. Horizontal burnish outside and inside.	?4	90
644	15	2	Base, flat, steeper angle (probably a jar).	Fine fabric, thin-walled; black. Fine burnish outside except beneath base, and inside.	?4	cf. 310, 311, 313, 315
644	15	–	6 body sherds.	2 burnished outside and inside; 1 burnished outside only (fine fabric); 3 cord-impressed (1 also burnished outside only – band?).	4 (? 5)	–
644	16	1	Jar with neck, upright.	Medium-fine fabric; fine grey and light grits; dark grey, buff surfaces. Smoothed outside and inside.	4 (?3)	62
644	16	2	Base, flat, shallow angle (probably a bowl).	Fine fabric, thin-walled; very fine grits; brick-red, grey outside surface. Cord-impressed outside, rough inside.	4 (?3)	cf. 312, 314
644	16	–	23 body sherds.	1 burnished outside and inside; 9 cord-impressed (some also roughly burnished inside); 2 roughly burnished inside only (medium-fine fabric); 1 roughly burnished (?) outside (coarse fabric).	4 (? 3)	–
644	17	1	Bowl, flared, shallow.	Fine fabric; small light and dark grits; brownish black, a little buff mottling outside. Glossy horizontal burnish outside and inside, apparently over horizontal scoring.	[6]	292
644	17	–	1 body sherd.	Faint-combed outside (medium-coarse fabric).	[6]	–
644	18	8	Bowl, slightly inverted rim.	Fine fabric; small dark-grey grits; brownish buff. Smoothed outside. streaky burnish on rim and inside.	5	188
644	18	11	Base, flat, shallow angle (probably a bowl).	Medium fabric and thickness; small grits; pale buff. Cord-impressed, burnished on angle, lightly smoothed inside.	5	cf. 312, 314

644	18	12	Bowl, shallow, curved.	Medium-fine fabric; medium-size grey and reddish grits; brick-red, faint grey core, surfaces greyish/blackened, especially inside. Streaky burnish outside and inside, 4 incised lines (parallel, oblique) through burnish after firing.	5	206
644	18	–	16 body sherds.	10 cord-impressed; 1 faint-combed outside; 6 undecorated coarse fabric.	5	–
644	20	2	Base, flat, rounded edge.	Fine fabric, thin-walled; fine grits; black. Burnished outside and inside.	[Post-Neo.]	*cf.* 306–309, 297
644	20	10	Base, flat, rounded edge.	Coarse fabric; small dark-grey grits; buff-grey (blackened). Traces of cord impressions, smoothed outside, inside rough.	[Post-Neo.]	*cf.* 306–309, 297
644	20	4 + 5	Jar, holemouth, shallow, rolled rim.	Fairly fine fabric; small dark-grey grits; dull blackish brown. Widely spaced cord impressions outside, below 15 mm band of horizontal smoothing/faint streaky burnish, continuing over rim and inside.	[Post-Neo.]	250
644	21	12	Base, angled, steeper, with slight 'heel' (jar?).	Fine fabric; fine grits; dull brown, blackened outside and heavily on inside surface. Cord-impressed outside, rough burnish under base and inside.	?4	*cf.* 316, 318–323
644	21	15	Jar, holemouth, steep, rolled rim.	Fairly fine fabric; fine dark grey grits; buff mottled dark grey. Sketchy horizontal burnish on rim and on band outside, with spaced cord impressions below; inside very sketchily smoothed.	?4	74
644	21	–	23 body sherds.	3 burnished outside and inside; 12 cord-impressed (1 also roughly burnished outside); 3 faint-combed outside; 5 undecorated medium or fine fabric.	4 (? 3)	–
644	23	–	2 body sherds.	Cord-impressed.	3	
644	24	1	Base? flat, rounded edge.	Coarse fabric; small grey grits, vegetable temper? orange-buff outside, grey core and inside. Smoothed or very rough burnish outside, smoothed or wiped inside.	3	*cf.* 306–309, 297
644	24	2	Bowl, upright rim.	Very fine fabric; very fine grits; black. Faint-combed outside below 24 mm band of glossy horizontal burnish, continuing inside.	3	27
644	24	7	Base, angled, shallow, with slight heel (bowl?).	Medium fabric; small grits; buff, pale orange inside. Smoothed outside and inside.	3	*cf.* 317
644	24	17	Bowl, slightly inverted rim.	Medium-fine fabric; small light-coloured grits; dull greyish pink. Smoothed outside, rough horizontal scraping inside.	3	22
644	24	19	Jar, holemouth, shallow.	Fairly fine fabric; small light-grey grits; brick-red, buff surfaces. Burnish outside and inside.	3	14
644	24	35	Jar with neck, flared.	Medium fabric; dark and light grits; brownish grey. Surfaces smoothed only.	3	8
644	26	–	1 body sherd.	Cord-impressed.	4	–
644	27	2	Base, flat, steeper angle (probably a jar).	Fine fabric, thin-walled; fine pale grits; mushroom grey, darkened outside surface. Cord-impressed outside, including base, light burnish inside.	4	*cf.* 310 311, 313, 315
644	27	15	Bowl, upright rim.	Fine fabric; fine grits; bricky-orange. Fine burnish outside and outside.	4	97
644	27	34	Bowl, flared, shallow. Lug or knob handle?	Fine fabric but thick-walled; fine light and dark grits; blackish grey, lighter core. Horizontal burnish in a 10 mm band outside (very streaky), over rim and inside.	4	132

644	27	25	Jar, holemouth, shallow.	Medium-fine fabric, small light and dark grits, possibly some vegetable temper; mid-grey, blackened or discoloured inside; cord-impressed outside, smoothed inside. (May be same vessel as Cat. no. 168.)	4	67
644	27	–	24 body sherds.	2 burnished outside only (medium fabric); 17 cord-impressed (a few also roughly burnished inside); 4 faint-combed; 1 undecorated medium-fine fabric.	4	–
644	29	–	5 body sherds.	2 burnished outside and inside; 1 cord-impressed; 1 faint-combed; 1 undecorated medium-fine fabric.	5	–
644	30	1	Jar, holemouth, shallow.	Fine fabric; fine dark grits; pale cream-grey. Irregular impressions outside (not cord – bunched grass or similar) below 25 mm smoothed band, also smoothed inside.	3	13
644	30	2	Jar with neck, upright, narrow.	Very fine fabric, poorly fired and crumbly; fine light-coloured grits; bricky-brown, dark grey surfaces. Faint-combed or scored outside, streaky horizontal burnish inside on upper 20 mm.	3	4
644	30	3	Jar with neck, upright.	Medium-fine fabric; dark grey grits; pinkish buff. Smoothed surfaces.	3	cf. 7
644	30		Body sherds.	1 burnished inside only (medium fabric); 1 cord-impressed.	3	–
644	31	2	Base, 'heeled', deep (jar), complete mat impression.	Medium fabric; small dark-grey angular grits, some pale and larger, some vegetable temper, a little red grog; dull buff, partial thin dark-grey core, a little blackish mottling outside (may be post-depositional). Smoothed outside on uneven surface, mat impression under base, inside rough or worn with prominent grits.	[7]	323
644	32	1	Jar with neck, very short, rolled. Lug(s), vertical, horizontally pierced.	Very fine fabric, quite hard; fine dark grits; brownish black. Fine cord-impressions below lug(s), burnished on rim, and inside on uneven surface.	3	6
644	33	–	4 body sherds.	2 burnished outside and inside; 1 faint-combed; 1 undecorated medium-fine fabric.	[7]	–
644	34	5	Base, flat, rounded edge.	Coarse fabric; small grits; buff, greyish inside surface. Smoothed outside, inside rough.	5	cf. 306–309, 297
644	34	9	Jar with neck, slightly inverted, wide.	Medium fabric; dense small dark-grey grits; buff. Lightly smoothed outside and upper 25 mm inside, rough below.	5	158
644	34	12	Jar, holemouth, steep (small).	Fine fabric; fine light and dark grits; greyish-buff surfaces, thick dark-grey core. Fine cord impressions below 12 mm band of matt burnish, also burnish inside.	5	178
644	34	20	Jar with neck, flared, high.	Fairly fine fabric, hard-fired; small grey and light grits, some pitting the surface; brick-red, thin dark-grey core; surface. Lightly smoothed outside and inside.	5	155
644	34	33	Bowl, flared.	Very fine fabric; very fine dark and light grits; black. Fine glossy burnish outside and inside.	5	195

644	34	37	Bowl, flared, shallow (small).	Very fine fabric; fine dark and light grits; brown, heavily mottled black towards the rim. Very fine glossy burnish outside and inside.	5	199
644	34	–	33 body sherds.	8 burnished outside (some also inside); 9 cord-impressed; 8 faint-combed; 8 undecorated medium-fine fabric.	5	–
644	35	2	Base, flat, rounded edge.	Medium fabric; small dark-grey and light gits; orange-brown, mottled grey. Rough burnish outside, smoothed or light burnish inside.	Mixed	*cf. 306–309, 297*
644	35	5	Bowl, curved, shallow. Lug/ledge handle.	Fairly fine fabric, thick-walled; fine grey grits; dull brick-red, blackish inside, like a slip. Smoothed outside, streaky burnish on outside rim, matt burnish inside.	Mixed	294
644	35	10	Jar with neck, flared, narrow.	Medium fabric; fine grey grits and red grog; light brick-red, thin grey core. Darker more reddish slip; lightly smoothed on uneven surfaces.	Mixed	222
644	35	–	Body sherds.	3 burnished outside (2 also inside); 1 cord-impressed; 2 undecorated fine and medium fabric.	[Post-Neo.]	–
644	36	3	Jar with neck, upright, high (large).	Fairly fine fabric, thick-walled large jar; bright brick-red, thick black core. Streaky horizontal burnish outside and inside on rather uneven surfaces.	[Post-Neo.]	232
644	36	5	Body sherd.	Medium fabric; medium-small light grits; black and brick-red mottled. Pattter-combed decoration on light burnish.	[Post-Neo.]	*cf. 340*
644	36	–	6 body sherds.	3 burnished outside and inside; 1 faint-combed (criss-cross); 2 undecorated coarse fabric.	[Post-Neo.]	–
644	38	–	1 body sherd.	Burnished outside and inside.	[Post-Neo.]	–
644	40	1	Jar, holemouth, steep.	Coarse fabric; small white grits, and probably vegetable temper; buff. Faint combed (not impressed) starting 50 mm below rim outside, smoothed above and inside.	4	80
644	41	3	Bowl, curved, shallow.	Fine fabric; fine grey and light grits; brick-red, grey-brown surfaces (possibly a slip). Matt burnish outside and inside.	4 (?3)	127
644	41	4	Bowl, hemispherical.	Fine fabric; small dark-grey grits; deep brick-red, dark-brown outside surface mottled black. Fine burnish outside and inside.	4 (?3)	107
644	41	–	5 body sherds.	3 burnished outside and inside; 2 cord-impressed (1 burnished inside).	3	–
644	42	2	Base, flat, steeper angle (probably a jar).	Very fine fabric, thin-walled; dark brick-red, darker surfaces. Fine burnish outside (vertical) including under base and inside (horizontal).	3	*cf. 310, 311, 313, 315*
644	42	–	2 body sherds.	1 burnished outside and inside; 1 cord-impressed (smoothed inside).	3	–
644	46	1	Jar, holemouth, steep.	Fine fabric; small grey and light grits; dull brick-red outside, greyish brown inside. Cord-impressed outside, below 10 mm band of streaky horizontal burnish, continuing over rim and inside.	Mixed	255
644	47	1	Bowl, hemispherical.	Fine fabric; fine dark shiny grits; brownish black. Fine burnish outside and inside.	Mixed	270

	644	47	2	Jar, holemouth, steep.	Fine fabric; fine grey and light grits; light brick-red, greyish brown inside. Light-combed outside, light burnish on flat rim and (matt) inside.	Mixed	259
646	646	2	1	Jar, holemouth, steep (large).	Fine fabric; fine light and dark grits; black surfaces, dark brick-red core. Faint cord impressions outside, horizontal burnish over rim and inside.	4	93
	646	2	2	Bowl, flared.	Fine fabric; small light grits; dark grey. Horizontal burnish outside and inside, scratched oblique lines inside through burnish, probably accidental.	4	123
	646	2	3	Bowl, flared, shallow.	Fine fabric; fine light and grey grits; brown, black mottled on rim (similar to a wick mark). Smudged combing outside, 25 mm band of streaky burnish above, and over rim, inside even but matt.	4	134
	646	2	4	Base, flat, steeper angle (probably a jar).	Fine fabric, thick-walled; small-fine light brown and dark grits; black, brownish-grey outside surface. Fine burnish outside and inside, worn under base.	4	*cf. 310, 311, 313, 315*
	646	2	5	Base, flat, steeper angle (probably a jar).	Medium fabric; dense small dark-grey grits; brick-red, blackened inside and lightly outside on walls only. Light cord-impressions outside and under base, worn at edge, inside lightly smoothed.	4	313
	646	2	–	19 body sherds.	3 burnished outside and inside (1 thick-walled); 6 cord-impressed (4 burnished or smoothed inside); 8 faint-combed (4 burnished inside, 1 also partly outside); 2 undecorated (1 medium, 1 coarse).	4	–
	646	3	–	1 body sherd.	1 burnished outside and inside.	4	–
	646	9	1	Bowl, flared, shallow.	Fine fabric; fine grey grits, a few light; brick-red. Light matt burnish outside and inside.	[7]	290
	646	10	1	Bowl, flared, conical.	Fine fabric; fine light grey grits; black. Cord-impressed outside below 27 mm band of fine glossy burnish, also inside.	5	194
	646	10	2	Jar, holemouth, steep.	Fine fabric; fine white and dark grits; black, rim and outside surface cream-grey (possibly a slip). Cord-impressed (thick cord) outside below *c.*15 mm band left rather rough, horizontal smoothing inside.	5	168
	646	10	3	Bowl, slightly inverted rim (large).	Medium fabric; small dark and light grits, fine vegetable temper; light brick-red, thick dark-grey core and darkened or mottled surfaces. Cord-impressed outside, apparently overlapping 30 mm band of sketchy matt burnish (part of surface missing), also sketchy burnish inside on uneven surface.	5	186
	646	10	–	28 body sherds.	6 burnished outside (3 roughly) and smoothed/light-burnished inside; 16 cord-impressed (10 burnished or smoothed inside); 5 faint-combed, rough inside; 1 undecorated coarse fabric.	5	–
	646	12	–	6 body sherds.	2 burnished outside (1 inside); 3 cord-impressed (1 burnished inside); 1 sherd undecorated fine fabric.	2 (? 3)	–

647	647	6	1	Bowl, upright rim.	Fairly fine fabric; small grey and light grits, red grog; brick-red mottled brown, thin grey core. Rather rough burnish, horizontal outside and over rim, oblique inside.	4	190
	647	6	–	3 body sherds.	3 cord-impressed (1 burnished inside; 1 medium-coarse fabric).	4	–
	647	15	–	5 body sherds.	1 rough-burnished outside, well burnished inside cord-impressed; 1 light-burnished inside; 1 smoothed/scraped; 1 rough; 1 undecorated fine fabric, rough-burnished inside.	1	–
	647	15	1	Bowl, upright rim.	Very fine fabric; very fine grits; black; glossy burnish outside and inside.	1 (?2)	39
	647	15	2	Jar, holemouth, shallow, rolled rim (large).	Fine fabric; fine pale-grey grits; dark grey with pale orange surfaces. Cord-impressed outside below groove, burnish in groove, up to and over rim, traces inside.	1	10
648	648	1	1	Jar with neck, flared, thickened.	Fairly fine fabric; dense small pale-grey grits; light brick-red, thick grey core. Rough burnish outside and inside on pale buff surface or slip.	5	156
	648	1	3	Bowl, flared, conical.	Very fine fabric but thick-walled; very fine grits; black. Fine matt burnish outside and inside.	5	196
	648	1	21	Jar with neck, flared.	Fairly fine fabric; small whitish grits; brick-red, thin blue-grey core. Rough burnish outside and inside on a yellowish surface, possibly a slip.	5	153
	648	1	–	19 body sherds.	1 burnished outside and inside; 17 cord-impressed (4 burnished inside, 6 smoothed; 2 neck/shoulder of jar); 1 undecorated medium fabric.	5	–
	648	2	1	Bowl.	Fine fabric; small grey grits; brick-red, greyish mottling at surfaces. Three incised lines depending from rim in semicircular swag pattern (extending about a quarter-way around rim, *i.e.* would fit four times around circumference). Burnished over incisions outside (sketchy in places), and streaky inside.	Mixed	269
	648	3	1	Bowl, shallow (large).	Fine fabric; brick-red; fine light grits. Faint cord impressions outside, burnish over rim and inside.	3	125
	648	3	–	7 body sherds.	1 burnished outside and inside; 2 cord-impressed (1 rough-burnished inside, 1 smoothed); 2 faint-combed (1 plaster-lined; 1 deeper combed, smoothed inside); 2 undecorated coarse fabric.	3	–
	648	4		2 body sherds.	1 cord-impressed; 1 undecorated outside (fine fabric, traces of burnish inside).	3	–
	648	13	1	Jar with neck, flared, wide, short.	Very fine fabric; very fine grits; brick-red, dark grey-brown surfaces below rim. Horizontal burnish outside and inside.	3	3
	648	13	2	Bowl, slightly inverted rim.	Very fine; fine white and dark grits; dark brownish grey. Burnish outside and inside.	3	32

	648	13	3	Base, round.	Small round base with slightly concave centre, worn at the edge; fine fabric; small light and dark grits; black surfaces, greyish-red core. Slight streaky burnish outside, under base and inside.	3	306
	648	13	–	5 body sherds.	3 burnished outside and inside; 1 cord-impressed (burnished inside); 1 faint-combed (rough inside).	3	–
	648	18	1	Jar with neck, flared.	Medium-fine fabric; small grey grits; buff, grey mottling. Cord-impressed outside, burnished on rim and 20 mm inside.	3	9
	648	18	–	1 body sherd.	Faint-combed/scraped outside.	3	–
	648	21	1	Bowl, flared, shallow.	Very fine fabric; very fine grits; mushroom, mottled black. Light burnish outside and inside.	3	50
650	650	10	1	Jar with neck, flared, narrow.	Medium fabric, variable thickness of wall; small grey and light grits, light-red grog; buff-pink, faint grey core, darker slip. Lightly smoothed outside and inside.	[Post-Neo.]	223
	650	14	1	Jar with neck, upright, narrow.	Coarse fabric; medium-size dark-grey grits; buff, possible brownish slip. Smoothed outside and inside.	5	151
	650	14	2	Jar, holemouth, steep.	Coarse fabric; medium-size dark-grey grits, a few white, some vegetable temper; buff. Well smoothed inside and outside	5	176
	650	14	3	Bowl, flared, shallow.	Very coarse fabric; large dark-grey angular grits, a little red grog and fine vegetable temper; buff. Lightly smoothed or wiped on uneven surfaces outside and inside rim, rough below.	5	211
	650	14	4	Bowl, curved, shallow (large).	Fine fabric; fine dark and light grits; pinkish red. Cord-impressed outside, slightly overlapping a 16 mm band of matt burnish, continuing inside.	5	207
	650	14	5	Base, disc.	Medium-coarse fabric; medium and small light-grey angular grits, some dark-grey, some vegetable temper; blackish-grey core and underneath base only, walls and inside base bricky-buff, thin reddish surface outside (walls). Smoothed outside, probably on bright-red slip, base uneven, inside very worn.	5	325
	650	14	7	Base, disc.	Coarse fabric, thick base; small dark- and light-grey grits, vegetable temper, some red grog; buff-grey core, dark-grey inside, pale buff mottled orange outside. Burnished on uneven surface outside, possibly on darker slip, inside barely smoothed.	5	329
	650	14	8	Appliqué 'coffee-bean'.	Very coarse fabric; medium-size dark-grey grits; buff; smoothed outside, worn inside. May represent an eye on a crude face-pot.	5	332
	650	14	9	Base (?), flat.	Medium fabric; small-fine grey grits; buff, mottled orange inside, blackened outside surface. Faint-combed, pattern? (criss-cross or diamond), inside worn.	5	*cf. 306–309, 297*

	650	14	10	Base, angled, deep, with slight 'heel' (probably a jar).	Very coarse fabric; vegetable temper, pale grits, grog; light brick-red outside, light-grey core, buff-grey under base and inside. Slightly smoothed on uneven surfaces; base with clear mat impression, slightly concave.	5	318
	650	14	11	Base? flat, rounded edge.	Coarse fabric; medium-small grey grits; buff; dark-brow. Slip and burnish outside, lightly smoothed inside; broken on coil.	5	cf. 306–309, 297
	650	14	12	Bowl, flared, shallow.	Fine fabric; small dark-grey grits; cream-buff, possible cream slip. Streaky matt burnish outside, faint inside.	5	198
	650	14	13	Base, angled, steeper, with slight 'heel' (jar?).	Medium fabric; small light and dark grits; blackish, mottled dark-grey outside surface. Faint-combed or scored outside, slightly smoothed inside.	5	cf. 316, 318–323
	650	14	–	25 body sherds.	2 burnished outside (1 also inside); 9 cord-impressed (2 burnished inside); 6 faint-combed (5 coarse, 1 medium fabric); 1 rough-burnished outside, coarse fabric; 7 undecorated coarse fabric.	5	–
	650	16	–	2 body sherds.	1 cord-impressed, blackened slightly inside; 1 undecorated coarse fabric.	?	–
	650	17	–	10 body sherds.	10 cord-impressed, medium and coarse fabric.	?	–
652	652	2	10	Jar with neck, upright, very short; inside ledge (for lid?) Ledge/knob handle.	Medium-coarse fabric; small grey and white grits, some vegetable temper; dull orange-buff surface outside and on rim, grey core and inside. Smoothed outside and inside. Scar of broken knob or handle on shoulder.	[Post-Neo.]	230
	652	17	9	Jar with neck, slightly inverted, narrow.	Medium-coarse fabric; small dark-grey and light grits, red grog; buff. Burnished over rim, and sketchily outside and inside.	[Post-Neo.]	239
653	653	8	4	Jar with neck, flared.	Fairly fine fabric; dense small pale-grey grits; light brick-red, greyish red inside. Streaky burnish outside and on rim, on uneven surface, inside rough.	[6 fill]	214
	653	8	–	7 body sherds.	3 burnished outside (1 traces only), medium and coarse fabric; 2 cord-impressed, lightly burnished inside; 2 undecorated medium and coarse fabric.	[6 fill]	–
654	654	2	1	Base, disc.	Medium fabric; dense fine dark shiny grits; greyish buff, blackened inside surface; lightly smoothed outside (uneven) and inside.	[6]	cf. 108, 109
	654	2	2	Base, flat, steeper angle (probably a jar).	Medium fabric and thickness; dense small-fine dark grits; buff, greyish surfaces. Possible rough cord-impressions outside, smoothed inside.	[6]	cf. 310, 311, 313, 315
	654	2	–	2 body sherds.	1 burnished outside only (streaky) cord-impressed; 1 undecorated, medium fabric.	[6]	–
	654	5	1	Bowl, curved, shallow.	Fine fabric; fine light grits; dark greyish-brown. Cord-impressed outside, below 18 mm band of streaky burnish, continuing inside.	[6]	298
	654	7	1	Jar with neck, upright, narrow, high.	Medium fabric, roughly made; small dark-grey grits; light brick-red, buff core. Smoothed outside and inside	5	149

654	7	2	Jar with neck, flared, narrow.	Fairly fine fabric; small pale-grey grits; brick-red, thick black core. Smoothed outside and inside.	5	147
654	7	3	Jar, holemouth, shallow.	Medium fabric, thin-walled (uneven); fine dark and light grits; pale brick-red, pale buff core. Finger-smoothed outside with faint combing or impressed lines on shoulder starting 40 mm down from rim, rather rough inside.	5	160
654	7	5	Bowl, curved, shallow.	Medium-coarse fabric; medium-size dark-grey angular and light-grey rounded grits, some fine vegetable temper; buff, some pinkish mottling. Slight burnish inside, even less outside.	5	212
654	7	6	Base, flat, steeper angle (probably a jar).	Fine fabric, thin-walled; fine light grits; black. Very fine burnish outside, fine burnish inside.	5	cf. 310, 311, 313, 315
654	7	7	Base, flat, shallow angle (probably a bowl).	Medium fabric and thickness; small angular dark grits; dark grey outside and core, buff-grey inside surface. Cord-impressed outside and under base, smoothed inside.	5	cf. 312, 314
654?	7	10	Body sherd.	Medium fabric; small dark-grey grits; buff-grey, blackened. Pattern-combed decoration, curved lines.	5	cf. 269?
654	7	–	9 body sherds.	1 burnished outside only; 7 cord-impressed (4 burnished/smoothed inside, fine-medium fabric; 3 fairly coarse); 1 undecorated coarse fabric.	5	–
654	9	1	Jar, holemouth, shallow, rolled rim.	Fairly fine fabric; dense small pale-grey grits; dull brick-red, grey-brown core. Cord-impressed outside slightly overlapping 30 mm band of streaky burnish, also inside, on roughly finished surfaces.	5	165
654	9	2	Bowl (large).	Fine fabric but thick-walled; fine light and dark grits; black, some brown mottling. Burnish outside, worn rim and inside with traces of burnish.	5	192
654	9	3	Base, flat, steeper angle (probably a jar).	Fine fabric, thin-walled; dense pale grits; buff. Cord-impressed outside, smoothed inside.	5	cf. 310, 311, 313, 315
654	9	4	Base, flat, shallow angle (probably a bowl).	Coarse fabric, thick-walled; medium-small dark shiny angular grits, some light, also some vegetable temper; grey-buff. Cord-impressed or faint-combed (smoothed over) outside, smoothed inside.	5	cf. 312, 314
654	9	–	23 body sherds.	1 burnished outside (smoothed inside); 5 cord-impressed (1 burnished/smoothed inside); 1 faint-combed, burnished inside (fine fabric); 1 burnished (worn, on black mottling; coarse fabric); 5 undecorated coarse fabric (1 neck of jar).	5(? 4)	–
654	10	1	Jar with neck, flared, narrow.	Fine fabric; small light-grey grits; buff. Smoothed only outside and inside.	4	52
654	10	2	Base, angled, steeper, with slight 'heel' (jar?).	Medium-coarse fabric, very thick base; medium-fine angular dark-grey grits; buff, grey core. Smoothed outside, rough or worn inside.	4	cf. 316, 318–323
654	10	3	Base, 'heeled', deep (jar).	Very coarse fabric; small pale-grey angular grits, coarse vegetable temper, a little red grog; light pinkish-buff, cream-buff on outside higher up, reddish on heel, pale grey inside, darker grey core and under centre of base outside. Faint-combed outside, smoothed under base and inside.	4	321

	654	10	4	Base, 'heeled' (probably a jar).	Very coarse fabric; small pale-grey angular grits, coarse vegetable temper, a little red grog; light pinkish-buff, reddish on heel, pale grey inside, darker grey core and under centre of base outside. Faint-combed outside, smoothed under base and inside.	4	320
	654	10	–	14 body sherds.	4 burnished outside only (very worn/rough; 1 medium, 3 coarse fabric); 7 cord-impressed (1 sooty inside); 1 brown slip, over a few score-marks (coarse fabric); 2 undecorated (medium/coarse fabric).	4	–
655	655	1	–	2 body sherds.	1 burnished outside (worn) and inside; 1 cord-impressed	4	–
	655	2	–	9 body sherds.	1 burnished outside and inside; 6 cord-impressed (1 burnished inside); 1 faint-combed with burnish band outside, burnished inside (fine fabric); 1 undecorated fairly fine fabric (neck/shoulder of jar).	4	–
	655	3	1	Jar with neck, upright, narrow, high.	Medium-coarse fabric; small dark-grey grits, some red grog, possibly some fine vegetable temper; buff, with grey discoloration. Smoothed outside and inside.	3	59
	655	4	–	1 body sherd.	1 cord-impressed.	?3	–
	655	5	–	5 body sherds.	2 faint-combed (coarse fabric); 3 undecorated medium-coarse fabric.	? (2/1?)	–
	655	6	–	1 body sherd.	1 undecorated coarse fabric.	4?	–
	655	7	1	Jar with neck, flared, narrow, high.	Coarse fabric; small dark-grey and reddish grits, some vegetable temper; light buff. Smoothed outside and lightly inside.	4	57
	655	7	–	11 body sherds.	1 burnished (smoothed inside); 4 cord-impressed (1 smoothed inside; fine-fairly coarse fabric; 6 undecorated coarse fabric.	4	–
656	656	6	6	Bowl, upright rim.	Fine fabric; fine grey and white grits, some red grog; brick-red. Horizontal burnish outside and inside.	[Post-Neo.]	286
680	680	11	26	Appliqué knob.	Very coarse fabric; medium-size dark-grey grits; buff; smoothed outside, worn inside. Appliqué knob, probably on shoulder of jar. Perhaps a nose on a crude face-pot.	[14a]	333
	680	11	29	Jar with neck, upright, very short. Vertically flattened knob handle.	Medium fabric; very dense medium-size buff-grey grits; brick-red, greyish-buff surfaces. Streaky horizontal burnish outside and inside neck on uneven surface (lower surface inside worn away), deeply incised herringbone-pattern band (through burnish) on shoulder, either side of vertically flattened knob or handle (broken off).	[14a]	231
	680	11	31	Incised decoration, row of jabs (body sherd).	Fairly fine fabric, thin-walled; medium-size pale grits, and small dark; reddish brown outside, partial black core, mottled inside. Fairly fine burnish outside, around neck inside, scrappy below; one irregular row of small jabs (through burnish), on shoulder just below neck of jar.	[14a]	334 (Plate 4.2)

	680	11	–	15 body sherds.	1 burnished outside and inside; 11 cord-impressed (3 burnished inside; 1 sooty inside); 3 undecorated coarse fabric, rough inside (1 with appliqué knob scar; 1 sooty inside).	[14a]	–
	680	14	–	3 body sherds.	2 burnished outside and inside (1 traces only); 1 cord-impressed.	[12]	–
	680	31	1	Jar, holemouth, steep.	Fairly fine fabric; small pale-grey grits; light dull brick-red, mottled black on rim and inside. Faint cord-impressions outside, streaky burnish over rim and inside.	[12]	263
	680	31		2 body sherds.	1 burnished outside (well smoothed inside); 1 cord-impressed.	[12]	–
	680	38	1	Jar with neck, upright.	Medium fabric; small to medium-size pale-grey grits; buff, light-grey core. Wiped or rough outside, lightly smoothed inside.	[10]	*cf. 217*
	680	38	2	Jar, holemouth, shallow, rolled rim.	Fairly fine fabric; dense small pale grits; dull reddish grey, mottled black. Faint cord-impressions outside, faint streaky burnish or smoothing on rim and inside.	[10]	247
	680	42	1	Jar with neck, slightly inverted, narrow.	Fine fabric; fine dark grits; dull dark-red outside surface, black core and inside. Irregular incised vertical lines outside (some deep), rough inside.	5	145
	680	42	2	Base, disc.	Coarse fabric; medium to small dark-grey grits, some pale; brick-red, blackened outside surface, and thicker under base. Scrappy burnish outside and under base on very uneven surfaces, inside very worn and rough.	5	326
	680	42	–	24 body sherds.	3 burnished (2 also inside); 3 cord-impressed (2 coarse fabric); 2 faint-combed (1 burnished inside, fine fabric); 16 undecorated (15 coarse fabric, 1 with possible dark slip outside; 1 fine fabric).	5	–
	680	56	12	Base, disc.	Medium fabric; fine light and dark grits; pale orange. Smoothed or slight burnish outside, slightly smoothed/rough inside.	[? 8]	*cf. 108, 109*
	680	59	13	Jar, holemouth, shallow. Lug/knob handle.	Very coarse fabric; very large dark-grey angular grits, fine vegetable temper, red grog; pale orange-buff, greyish core and blackening inside. Lightly smoothed outside and inside. Signs of lug or knob on broken edge, 33 mm down from rim.	[? 9]	243
	680	62	1	Jar with neck, upright.	Fairly fine fabric; small pale-grey angular grits; light brick-red, slight grey core, greyish-brown slip. Cord-impressed outside, matt burnish inside neck.	[10]	218
690	690	26	–	2 body sherds.	1 cord-impressed; 1 rough-burnished outside (coarse fabric).	[Post-Neo.]	–
	690	27	1	Bowl, upright rim, curved.	Fairly fine fabric but thick-walled; small dark-grey grits; buff. A few very faint cord-impressions outside, below a 22 mm band of burnish (streaks overlapping), burnish inside, upper part streaky.	Mixed	300
	690	27	–	3 body sherds.	1 cord-impressed (light-burnished/smoothed inside); 2 rough-burnished outside and inside.	[Post-Neo.]	–

699	699	+	1	Jar, holemouth, shallow.	Coarse fabric, walls of variable thickness; medium-size dark-grey grits, light grits or grog, some fine vegetable temper; buff, light-grey core. Brownish-red slip outside, over rim and irregularly inside; smoothed outside and inside on uneven surfaces.	[?8]	242
701	701	20	3	Jar, holemouth, steep. Lug/ horizontal ledge handle.	Very fine fabric; very fine light and dark grits; light brick-red, reddish grey towards surfaces. Cord-impressed outside and upper and lower surfaces of handle, horizontal matt burnish inside.	[? 16 fill]	258
702	702	22	5	Bowl, flared.	Fine fabric; fine grey grits; black. Fine burnish outside and inside, crackled.	[16]	285
	702	23	1	Bowl, hemispherical?	Very fine fabric; very fine grey and light grits; buff, buff-brown inside. Cord-impressed outside, streaky burnish on rim and inside.	[16]	296
	702	27	2	Bowl, hemispherical.	Fine fabric; fine dark grits; black and buff mottled. Fine burnish outside and inside	[Post-16]	*cf. 270*
	702	46	28	Bowl, flared.	Very fine fabric; fine light and dark grits; black. Fine glossy burnish outside and inside.	[14a]	282
	702	46	120	Bowl, hemispherical.	Fine fabric; fine dark-grey grits; pale grey. Fine glossy burnish outside and inside.	[14a]	275
	702	46	–	14 body sherds.	2 burnished outside (traces only); 5 cord-impressed (4 burnished/smoothed inside); 1 faint-combed; 6 undecorated coarse fabric.	[14a]	–
705	705	59	12	Bowl, hemispherical.	Fine fabric; fine dark grits; greyish buff. Fine glossy burnish outside and inside; very small sherd.	[8]	*cf. 270*
	705	61	4	Jar, holemouth, steep.	Medium fabric; small dark-grey grits; buff, light-grey surfaces. Light burnish outside, over rim and inside.	[7]	261
	705	61	7	Bowl, flared.	Very fine fabric; very fine light and dark grits; black. Very fine burnish outside and inside.	[7]	283
	705	61	9	Base, flat, shallow angle (probably a bowl).	Fine fabric, thin-walled; black. Cord-impressed outside, fine burnish inside.	[7]	*cf. 312, 314*
	705	61	10	Bowl, flared.	Very fine fabric; very fine light and dark grits; black. Fine glossy burnish outside and inside.	[7]	281
	705	61	–	4 body sherds.	1 burnished outside and inside; 3 cord-impressed (1 burnished inside).	[7]	–
	705	63	4	Bowl, flared.	Fine fabric; fine black and light grits; dark brownish grey. Matt horizontal burnish outside and inside.	?4	124

705	63	11	Jar, holemouth, shallow.	Fine fabric; fine dark grey grits. Cord-impressed outside below 30 mm band of streaky burnish, also on rim and very sketchy inside. Possible knob/lug scar (thickening on broken edge).	?4	72
705	63	–	3 body sherds.	1 burnished outside only; 6 cord-impressed (3 burnished inside); 2 faint-combed (fine fabric).	4 (? 3)	–
705	65	3	Bowl, flared.	Fine fabric; small light-grey grits; black. Fine burnish outside and inside.	Mixed	280
705	65	1 + 2	Bowl, hemispherical.	Very fine fabric; very fine white and fine dark grits; dull dark brick-red, black towards surfaces. Fine burnish outside and inside.	Mixed	273
705	65	–	2 body sherds.	2 cord-impressed (1 very faint, sooty inside).	[Post-Neo.]	–
705	66	–	2 body sherds.	2 cord-impressed, burnished inside.	4	–
705	67	1	Bowl, flared, conical.	Fine fabric; fine light and dark grey grits; reddish grey, brick-red core. Faint cord impressions outside, very sketchy burnish inside.	3 (? 2)	40
705	67	2	Base, flat, shallow angle (probably a bowl).	Fine fabric, thin-walled; dull brick-red, blackened outside. Faint-combed outside, light burnish inside.	3 (? 2)	312, 314
705	67	–	2 body sherds.	2 faint-combed, streaky burnish inside.	3 (? 2)	–
705	68	4	Bowl, slightly inverted rim.	Fine fabric; fine whitish grits; dull brown, blackish inside and core. Very faint combed outside, smoothed or very light burnish inside.	3 (? 2)	24
705	68	13	Base, angled, steeper, with slight 'heel' (jar?).	Medium-coarse fabric, thick-walled; small grits; buff, black inside surface. Smoothed unevenly outside, rough or lightly smoothed inside.	3 (? 2)	cf. 316, 318–323
705	69	5	Base, flat, shallow angle (probably a bowl).	Fine fabric, thin-walled; black. Fine cord-impressions outside, fine burnished base and inside.	?3 ?4	cf. 312, 314
705	69	8	Bowl, flared.	Very fine fabric; very fine light and dark grits; black. Very fine glossy burnish outside and inside.	?3 ?4	121
705	69	9	Base, flat, shallow angle (probably a bowl).	Medium fabric and thickness; dull brick-red. Cord-impressed outside, rough or worn inside.	?3 ?4	cf. 312, 314
705	69	–	8 body sherds.	8 cord-impressed (4 burnished inside; 2 blackened inside).	4 (? 2)	–
705	70	–	1 body sherd.	Undecorated coarse fabric.	4	–
705	81	1	Jar, holemouth, shallow, rolled rim.	Fine fabric; fine dark-grey and brown grits (or grog); greyish buff. Cord-impressed outside, light burnish over rim, inside surface uneven.	[Post-Neo.]	249
705	81	2	Jar with neck, slightly inverted, narrow (small).	Fine fabric; fine dark grits; cream-buff, thick pale-grey core and mottling. Well smoothed outside and over rim, slightly inside.	[Post-Neo.]	234
705	81	3	Base, flat, steeper angle (probably a jar).	Medium fabric and thickness; small-fine dark-grey grits, a few light (larger); dull light brick-red. Cord-impressed outside, smoothed inside.	[Post-Neo.]	cf. 310, 311, 313, 315
705	81	–	5 body sherds.	1 burnished outside and inside; 3 cord-impressed (1 burnished inside, and partly outside); 1 faint-combed, burnished inside (fine fabric).	[Post-Neo.]	–

	705	83	–	5 body sherds.	1 burnished outside and inside; 2 cord-impressed; 2 faint-combed (1 burnished inside, and partly outside).	4	–
	705	84	1	Bowl, upright rim.	Fine fabric; fine grey grits, some whitish; pinkish-buff, some dark-grey mottling. Fine horizontal burnish outside (may be upper 25 mm from rim only) and inside.	? 4	–
	705	84	2	Base, flat, steeper angle (probably a jar).	Fine fabric, thin-walled; fine dark and light grits; thin bricky-brown surface, black core and inside surface. Cord-impressed outside, rough burnish inside.	?4	*cf. 310, 311, 313, 315*
	705	84	–	4 body sherds.	4 cord-impressed (2 light-burnished/smoothed inside; 2 rough).	3 (? 4)	–
706	706	1	1	Jar with neck, flared, narrow, high.	Fairly fine fabric; small white grits, dark-red grog; brownish-black surfaces, reddish-brown core. Cord-impressed outside, slight burnish over rim, inside smoothed over uneven surface.	5	143
	706	1	2	Jar, holemouth, steep.	Fine fabric; small dark-grey grits; buff. Smoothed outside, very sketchy burnish inside.	5	182
	706	1	3	Jar, holemouth, shallow, rolled rim.	Fine fabric; fine light and dark grits; dull brick-red, dark grey towards inside surface. Faint cord-impressions outside, matt horizontal burnish over rim (streaky) and inside.	5	166
	706	1	4	Bowl, slightly inverted rim.	Fairly fine fabric; fine dark grits and red grog; pinkish buff, greyish mottled surfaces. Cord-impressed outside, slightly overlapping 37 mm band of light matt horizontal burnish, continuing inside.	5	187
	706	1	–	5 body sherds.	1 burnished outside and inside; 3 cord-impressed (1 burnished inside, 1 rough-burnished); 1 faint-combed (light burnish inside).	5	–
	706	2	–	1 body sherd.	Cord-impressed (fine).	5	–
	706	3	1	Bowl, flared (large).	Fine fabric but thick-walled; fine whitish grits; black. Horizontal burnish outside and inside.	5	191
	706	3	3	Bowl, flared.	Very fine fabric; fine light grits; black. Fine glossy burnish outside and inside.	5	193
	706	3	4	Jar, holemouth, shallow.	Medium fabric; small dark grey grits; pinkish buff, some blackening or mottling. Smoothed outside and inside.	5	*cf. 163*
	706	3	5	Base, flat, shallow angle (probably a bowl).	Fine fabric, thin-walled; small-fine dark grits; blackish-brown outside, black inside. Burnish outside and inside; worn at edge and centre.	5	*cf. 312, 314*
	706	3	–	27 body sherds.	3 burnished outside and inside; 16 cord-impressed (8 burnished inside; 2 scraped/smoothed); 1 faint-combed (rough inside); 1 burnish traces outside, smoothed inside; 3 smoothed outside (parallel strokes), burnished inside; 3 undecorated (medium-fine fabric).	5	–
	706	4	1	Bowl, slightly inverted rim.	Very fine fabric; fine pale grey grits; black. Fine glossy burnish outside and inside.	5	189

706	4	2	Bowl, flared, shallow.	Coarse fabric; medium-size dark-grey angular grits, some fine vegetable temper; pale pinkish-buff, dark-grey core. Smoothed outside, slight burnish over rim and inside.	5	213
706	4	3	Base, flat, shallow angle (probably a bowl).	Fine fabric, thin-walled; fine dark and light grits; dull bricky-brown, grey inside surface. Cord-impressed/base plain, smoothed/very light burnish inside.	5	cf. 312, 314
706	4	–	22 body sherds.	3 rough-burnished outside only (coarse fabric); 12 cord-impressed (4 burnished inside, 1 scraped/smoothed); 2 faint-combed (burnished, 1 roughly, inside); 5 undecorated (1 fine fabric, rough burnished inside; 4 coarse fabric).	5	–
706	5	–	2 body sherds.	2 cord-impressed (1 roughly burnished inside).		–
706	6	1	Bowl, upright rim.	Fine fabric; fine dark grits; black. Faint-combed outside below 30 mm band of glossy burnish, continuing inside.	2 (?3)	25
706	6	2	Jar, holemouth, steep.	Fine fabric; fine dark grits, some whitish; pale buff mottled dark grey inside. Cord-impressed outside, fine burnish on rim and inside.	2 (?3)	19
706	6	3	Base, flat, shallow angle (probably a bowl).	Fine fabric; medium-fine light- and dark-grey grits; black, mottled dark grey. Cord-impressed outside, burnish inside.	2 (?3)	cf. 314
706	6	–	25 body sherds.	3 rough-burnished outside (2 inside); 18 cord-impressed (3 well burnished inside, 6 lightly burnished); 2 faint-combed, burnished inside; 2 undecorated, fine fabric (1 rough-burnished inside; 1 thick, flat – part of base?).	2	–
706	7	1	Bowl, curved, shallow (small).	Fairly fine fabric; small whitish grits (causing some surface pitting); light brick-red, light greyish inside. Surfaces smoothed, traces of faint burnish, inside uneven.	4	129
706	7	2	Bowl, flared, shallow (small).	Very coarse fabric, very thick-walled; medium-size dark-grey and light grits, some vegetable temper; buff-pink, grey core. Smoothed surfaces, slightly blackened on rim.	4	136
706	7	3	Base, flat, rounded edge.	Coarse fabric; medium-size grits, a few large; buff, light grey under base. Light streaky burnish outside and under base, lightly smoothed inside.	4	308
706	7	4	Incised decoration, diamond pattern (body sherd).	Fine buff fabric. Lightly burnished on dark slip outside, with diamond-pattern decoration of two spaced lines incised post-firing; inside surface rough.	4	cf. 340
706	7	5	Base, flat, rounded edge.	Coarse fabric; large-fine dark angular grits; buff. Brown slip and light burnish outside, inside rough.	4	cf. 306–309, 297
706	7	9	Base, flat, rounded edge.	Coarse fabric; small-fine grey and whitish grits, vegetable temper; pale brick-red and cream, slightly blackened inside. Rough burnish outside, inside rough/worn .	4	cf. 306–309, 297
706	7	–	8 body sherds.	2 burnished outside (1 inside, possible reddish slip); 6 cord-impressed (2 burnished inside).	4	–
706	8	–	2 body sherds.	1 cord-impressed (roughly burnished inside), very fine and thin; 1 faint-combed, very fine lines (burnished inside).		–

706	9	1	Lug, ledge (on body sherd).	Scar, broken across; fine fabric, thin; dark brick-red, dark surfaces. Cord-impressed outside, streaky burnish inside.	4	–
706	10	1	Jar with neck, narrow, very short (small).	Medium-fine fabric, soft; small whitish and grey grits: buff. Pinkish-red matt slip outside and inside.	4	51
706	10	2	Jar with neck, inverted, narrow, low.	Coarse fabric; large to small dark-grey grits, a few light; pale brick-red, buff core. Smoothed outside, inside surface missing.	4	84
706	10	3	Jar with neck, upright.	Coarse fabric, very variable thickness of wall; small grey and white grits. Red slip on rim and neck outside and inside, burnish over slip in streaky lines on rim and outside only (not shown in drawing).	4	61
706	10	4	Bowl, flared, conical.	Fine fabric but thick-walled; fine light and dark grits; brick-red mottled grey/black. Fine burnish outside and inside.	4	116
706	10	–	14 body sherds.	4 burnished outside only (very worn/rough; 1 medium, 3 coarse fabric); 7 cord-impressed (1 sooty inside); 1 brown slip, over a few score-marks (coarse fabric); 2 undecorated (medium/coarse fabric).	4	–
706	11	1	Bowl, flared.	Coarse fabric, thick-walled; medium-size dark-grey grits, some vegetable temper; light brick-red, buff-and-grey core. Smoothed outside and on rim, inside surface missing.	4	137
706	11	2	Lid (?), flattened edge.	Very coarse fabric; large dark-grey and small white grits; buff-pink, grey core; fairly rough surfaces; flattened underneath outside edge.	4	140
706	11	–	2 body sherds.	1 burnished outside only, coarse fabric; 1 undecorated (inside surface worn away), very coarse fabric, thick.	4	–
706	12	1	Jar, holemouth, steep.	Fine fabric; fine pale-grey angular grits; brick-red, brown-mottled surfaces, grey core. Cord-impressed outside below 14 mm band of light horizontal burnish outside, continuing over rim and inside.	2	16
706	12	2	Base, flat, steeper angle (probably a jar).	Fairly fine fabric, thin-walled; small (few medium) light- and dark-grey grits; black. Glossy burnish outside, under base and inside.	2	310
706	12	3	Base, flat, steeper angle (probably a jar).	Medium fabric and thickness; fine grits; dull dark bricky-brown, mottled black outside, heavily blackened inside, sooty. Faint cord-impressions outside.	2	*cf. 310, 311, 313, 315*
706	12	–	5 body sherds.	1 burnished outside and inside; 4 cord-impressed (1 smoothed inside; 3 rough (same vessel?).	2	–
706	14	1	Base, flat, shallow angle (probably a bowl).	Fine fabric, thin-walled; fine dark and light grits; bricky-brown, grey/mottled inside. Cord-impressed outside and under base, light burnish inside.	2	*cf. 312, 314*
706	14	–	4 body sherds.	4 cord-impressed.	2	–
706	15	1	Lug, ledge (on body sherd).	Long shallow ledge, chipped; medium fabric; small light grits; dull bricky-brown, dark-red surfaces. Cord-impressed outside, rather streaky burnish inside.	2	–

706	15	–	5 body sherds.	2 burnished outside and inside; 2 cord-impressed (1 sooty inside, same vessel as base 706.12/3); 1 faint-combed.	2	–
706	16	–	9 body sherds.	5 burnished outside and inside; 4 cord-impressed.	2	–
706	17	–	2 body sherds.	1 cord-impressed; 1 undecorated (wiped or scraped), fine fabric, thick (heavily blackened inside).	2	–
706	18	2	Jar with neck, flared, narrow, high.	Medium-coarse fabric, thin-walled and uneven; medium-size light-grey grits and fine vegetable temper; buff. Matt pinkish-red fugitive slip outside, worn rim, inside rough.	4	55
706	18	–	1 body sherd.	Faint cord-impressed.	4	–
706	19	1	Base, angled, shallow, with slight heel (bowl?).	Fine fabric; small-fine dark-grey and whitish grits, and red grog (?); pale bricky-buff, mottled light grey, especially outside. Cord-impressed outside, burnished under base, light burnish inside.	Mixed	*cf. 317*
706	20	1	Base, disc.	Fairly fine fabric; small-fine dark-grey grits, few whitish; brick-red. Faint burnish outside and inside on dark-grey surface, not under base.	2 (?3)	*cf. 324–329*
706	20	–	4 body sherds.	2 burnished outside and inside; 1 cord-impressed (lightly burnished inside); 1 faint-combed, remains of chalky coating outside and inside.	2	–
706	22	1	Jar with neck, inverted, narrow, high; flat rim.	Fine fabric; fine dark grey grits; dull brick-red mottled darker surfaces lower down. Cord-impressions outside, inside surface uneven.	2	1
706	22	2	Jar, holemouth, shallow.	Fine fabric; dense pale-grey angular grits; grey/brown mottled. Cord-impressed outside, burnished over rim and inside.	2	12
706	22	3	Jar, holemouth, shallow.	Fine fabric; dark grey grits; dark bricky brown, blackish inside and upper parts outside. Cord-impressed outside, below 40 mm band left plain with traces of burnish; patchy burnish inside on uneven surfaces.	2	11
706	22	4	Bowl, flared, shallow.	Fine fabric, small light grits, black. Glossy burnish outside and inside.	2	48
706	22	5	Bowl, hemispherical.	Fine fabric; fine grey and light grits; dark brick-red upper parts outside and core, dark brown-black below and inside. Vertical/oblique burnish outside, horizontal inside.	2	42
706	22	7	Base, flat, shallow angle (probably a bowl).	Fine fabric, thin-walled; fine light grits; black, mottled dark grey. Fine cord-impressions outside, fine burnish under base and inside.	2	*cf. 312, 314*
706	22	8	Base, flat, shallow angle (probably a bowl).	Fine fabric, thin-walled; small-fine light and brownish-grey grits; black, mottled brown-grey inside. Faint-combed outside and under base, smoothed inside.	2	*cf. 312, 314*
706	22	9	Base, flat, shallow angle (probably a bowl).	Fine fabric, thin-walled; small-fine whitish and dark-grey grits. Cord-impressed outside, smoothed base, light burnish inside.	2	*cf. 312, 314*
706	22	10	Fingernail impressions on band, + cord-impressions.	Fine fabric, thin-walled; small white grits; pinkish mushroom. Raised or appliqué band with deep fingernail impressions. Faint very fine cord impressions below band, burnished above, and inside.	2	335

706	22	11	Bowl, flared, shallow.	Fine fabric; fine whitish grits; brownish black, brown core. Fine burnish outside and inside.	2	43
706	22	–	21 body sherds.	6 burnished outside and inside; 15 cord-impressed (7 burnished inside; 8 rough, 1 sooty inside; 1 faint-combed (burnished inside and partly outside).	2	–
706	24	–	5 body sherds.	2 burnished outside and inside; 3 cord-impressed.	2	–
706	26	1	Jar with neck, upright, narrow.	Fine fabric, roughly shaped; dark grey grits; buff, mottled grey. Smoothed over very uneven surfaces.	2	7
706	26	2	Bowl, upright rim.	Fine fabric; fine grey grits; greyish cream. Burnish outside and inside.	2	38
706	26	3	Bowl, flared, shallow.	Fine fabric; small-fine greyish-brown grits; black. Fine burnish outside and inside (horizontal, diagonal and vertical).	2	cf. 43
706	26	4	Base, flat, shallow angle (probably a bowl).	Fairly fine fabric, but thick-walled; small dark-grey and lighter grits; buff outside, thick grey core and blackening inside. Cord-impressed outside and under base; streaky burnish inside.	2	314
706	26	5	Base, flat, rounded edge.	Fine fabric, thin-walled; small-fine light and greyish grits; brick-red mottled blackish. Cord-impressed outside except underneath; smoothed inside.	2	cf. 306–309, 297
706	26	6	Base, flat, steeper angle.	Fine fabric, thin-walled; fine dark grits; bricky-brown core, black surfaces. Burnish outside (base very worn) and inside.	2	cf. 310–311, 313, 315
706	26	–	15 body sherds.	3 burnished outside and inside; 5 cord-impressed; 1 with burnish band; 3 faint-combed; 1 burnished inside; 1 with chalky coating inside; 1 with traces of coating outside.	2	–
706	27	1	Base, flat, steeper angle (probably a jar).	Medium fabric and thickness; small-fine dark-grey grits, some shiny, light; bricky-brown, blackened/mottled outside. Cord-impressed outside and under base, encrusted inside but probably smoothed.	2	cf. 310–311, 313, 315
706	29	1	Bowl, flared.	Fine fabric; fine light and dark grits. Black; glossy burnish outside and inside.	4 (?3)	113
706	29	2	Base, flat, shallow angle (probably a bowl).	Medium fabric and thickness; small-fine whitish grits; brick-red, blackened outside, brownish core. Smoothed or wiped outside, smoothed inside.	4 (?3)	cf. 312, 314
706	29		4 body sherds.	1 burnished outside and inside, fine, thin (3 mm) 3 cord-impressed.	4	–
706	30	1	Bowl, hemispherical (small).	Fine fabric; fine light grits; mottled dark grey and light brick-red, with grey-buff surfaces. Fine matt burnish outside and inside.	2 (?3)	41
706	30	2	Jar, holemouth, steep.	Fine fabric; fine whitish grits; dark grey. Cord-impressed outside, slightly overlapping 10 mm band of light horizontal burnish, continuing inside.	2	17
706	30	3	Base, flat, steeper angle (probably a jar).	Very fine fabric, very thin-walled; fine light and dark grits; black, brown-black core. Fine burnish (diagonal) outside and inside (horizontal).	2	cf. 310–311 313, 315
706	30	4	Base, flat, rounded edge.	Fine fabric, thin-walled; fine dark and light grits; bricky-buff, some grey mottling outside. Cord-impressed (faint) outside, but not under base, smoothed inside.	2	cf. 306–309, 297

706	30	5	Base, flat, rounded edge.	Fine fabric, thin-walled; small-fine light and dark grits; dull bricky-brown, slightly blackened outside, heavily inside (sooty). Cord-impressed (faint) outside and under base.	2	cf. 306–309, 297
706	30	–	1 body sherd.	Cord-impressed.	2	–
706	31	1	Bowl, slightly inverted rim (large).	Fairly fine fabric; small greyish grits; blackish, black-brown outside surface. Cord-impressed outside, sketchy burnish over rim and inside.	4	95
706	32	5	Bowl, flared, shallow.	Very fine fabric; very fine dark and light grits; dark grey, mottled buff outside. Brownish-red paint (or partial slip) outside, no obvious pattern, fine burnish outside and inside.	Mixed	287
706	32	–	2 body sherds.	1 cord-impressed; 1 faint-combed.	2	–
706	33	1	Base, flat, steeper angle (probably a jar).	Very fine fabric, fairly thick-walled; fine light and dark grits; black; glossy burnish on all surfaces.	1	311
706	33	2	Base, flat, steeper angle (probably a jar).	Fine fabric, thin-walled; small-fine brownish grits; brownish-black. Fine burnish outside and inside; very fine and thin.	1	cf. 310–311, 313, 315
706	33	3	Base, flat, shallow angle (probably a bowl).	Medium fabric and thickness; small-fine dark-grey and light grits. Cord-impressed outside and under base, thick chalky lining (3-5 mm) inside, and traces underneath.	1	cf. 314
706	33	–	8 body sherds.	2 burnished outside and inside; 5 cord-impressed (4 burnished inside, 1 sooty; 1 rough); 1 faint-combed.	2 (? + 3-4)	–
706	40	1	Bowl, flared.	Very fine fabric; fine light and black grits; black. Very fine glossy burnish outside and inside.	?4	118
706	40	2	Jar, holemouth, shallow.	Fine fabric; fine dark and light grits; dull brick-red, grey surfaces. Cord-impressed outside, smoothed or light sketchy burnish inside.	?4	65
706	40	3	Base, flat, shallow angle (probably a bowl).	Fine fabric, thin-walled; small-fine dark and light grits; greyish-buff outside, heavily blackened inside. Cord-impressed outside, light burnish inside and under base.	?4	cf. 312, 314
706	40	4	Base, flat, shallow angle (probably a bowl).	Fine fabric, thin-walled; small-fine pale-grey and dark grits; bricky-brown outside, black core-inside. Cord-impressed outside and under base, smoothed inside.	?4	cf. 312, 314
706	40	–	6 body sherds.	6 cord-impressed (2 burnished inside, 1 smoothed, 1 rough).	2 (? + 3- 4)	–
706	41	1	Bowl, slightly inverted rim.	Very fine fabric; fine grey grits; black. Glossy burnish outside and inside.	?4	88
706	41	2	Bowl, flared, shallow (small).	Very fine fabric; very fine light and dark grits; blackish brown. Fine glossy burnish outside and inside.	?4	130
706	41	3	Bowl, flared, shallow.	Fine fabric; fine light and dark grits; black. Glossy burnish outside and inside.	?4	114
706	41	4	Bowl, curved, shallow.	Fine fabric; fine dark grits; pale buff, thin light-grey core and surface mottling. Light burnish outside and inside, possible brownish paint or staining.	?4	126

706	41	5	Jar, holemouth, shallow. Horizontal lug/ledge handle.	Fine fabric; fine light and dark grits; brown-black. Cord-impressed outside and on horizontal ledge/lug; matt burnish on rim and inside.	?4	66
706	41	6	Base, flat, shallow angle (probably a bowl).	Fine fabric, thin-walled; small-fine grey grits; black. Faint-combed outside and under base; fine burnish inside.	?4	cf. 312, 314
706	41	7	Base, flat, rounded edge.	Fine fabric, thin-walled; small-fine brown-grey and shiny grits; dark brown, blackened inside, mottled outside. Cord-impressed (faint) outside, faint/worn burnish inside.	?4	cf. 306–309, 297
706	41	8	Base, flat, shallow angle (probably a bowl).	Medium fabric and thickness; dense small-fine light grey grits; dull brick-red outside, black core and inside. Cord-impressed outside, smoothed inside.	?4	cf. 312, 314
706	41	9	Base, flat, shallow angle (probably a bowl).	Medium fabric and thickness; small-fine dark-grey angular grits, a few whitish; greyish-buff, greyish surfaces. Cord-impressed outside, smoothed inside.	?4	cf. 312, 314
706	41	–	18 body sherds.	17 cord-impressed (2 burnished inside; 4 blackened outside/inside; 1 with thin uneven chalky coating inside; 1 faint-combed.	2 (? + 3- 4)	–
706	42	1	Bowl, upright rim.	Fine fabric; fine light and dark grits; black, mottled cream at rim. Fine burnish outside and inside, rim worn.	2	34
706	42	2	Bowl, upright rim (small).	Fairly fine fabric; small to fine light-coloured grits; mushroom. Light burnish outside and inside.	2	37
706	42	4	Base, angled, shallow, with slight 'heel' (probably a bowl).	Fine fabric; small dark-grey and white grits; light greyish-red, black core and mottling, especially inside. Cord-impressed and scored lines outside and under base (blurred) over faint matt burnish, matt streaky burnish inside.	2	317
706	42	5	Base, flat, shallow angle (probably a bowl).	Fine fabric, thin-walled; dense pale grits, possibly some vegetable temper, dull brick-red, greyish surfaces. Cord-impressed outside, burnish under base, and traces on (rough) inside.	2	cf. 312, 314
706	42	–	13 body sherds.	1 burnished outside and inside; 11 cord-impressed (2 light-burnished inside, 6 rough; 1 undecorated, rough outside, smoothed inside [fine fabric]).	2	–
706	43	1	Bowl, flared, shallow (large).	Fine fabric; fine light and dark grits; dull brown mottled blackish. Faint cord impressions outside, light horizontal burnish inside.	2	46
706	43	–	3 body sherds.	2 cord-impressed (1 burnished inside, 1 rough, blackened outside); 1 undecorated, very roughly finished outside and inside (medium fabric).	2	–
706	44	1	Jar, holemouth, steep.	Fine fabric; fine light-grey grits; black. Very faint cord-impressions outside, burnish on rim, and sketchy inside.	1	20
706	44	–	4 body sherds.	4 cord-impressed (1 smoothed, 1 scraped, 2 rough inside).	1	–
706	47	6	Jar, holemouth, steep.	Coarse; medium-size blackish grits; buff, thick black core. Well smoothed or light matt burnish outside and inside.	5	177
706	47	7	Bowl, upright or slightly inverted.	Fine fabric, very thin (3 mm); small-fine light greyish grits; black. Fine burnish outside and inside.	5	cf. 189

	706	47	8	Bowl, upright rim, flat.	Very fine fabric; very fine grits; buff. Burnish outside, rim and inside.	5	203
	706	47	11	Body sherd with incised row of jabs.	Coarse fabric; medium-size grey grits, some fine vegetable temper; pale buff-orange. Lightly smoothed on uneven surface outside, very uneven inside. Row of deep jabs (broken near edge).	5	*cf. 336*
	706	47	–	34 body sherds.	3 burnished outside (1 inside); 10 cord-impressed; 6 burnished inside (2 blackened); 4 rough; 1 faint-combed; 10 undecorated (coarse fabric).	5 (? + 4)	–
	706	50	–	3 body sherds.	1 burnished outside and inside; 2 cord-impressed, inside rough.	2	–
707	707	3	6	Bowl, flared, shallow.	Fine fabric; fine dark and light grits; very dark grey. Matt burnish outside and inside.	[8]	291
	707	9	1	Jar, holemouth, steep.	Coarse fabric; medium-size dark-grey and light grits; buff, mottled light brick-red. Well smoothed outside, less inside.	[7]	245
	707	11	1	Bowl, hemispherical.	Fine fabric; very fine greyish grits; light grey. Fine burnish outside and inside.	[7]	274
	707	11	2	Base, flat, shallow angle (probably a bowl).	Fine fabric, thin-walled; dense pale grits; pale orange-buff. Cord-impressed outside and under base, burnish inside.	[7]	*cf. 312, 314*
708	708	1	1	Jar with neck, upright. Vertical lug handle, horizontally pierced.	Fine fabric; fine dark-grey grits; buff surfaces, thick dark-grey core. Sketchy burnish outside (but not around lug), over rim.	5	144
	708	1	2	Jar, holemouth, shallow.	Medium fabric; small dark grey and whitish grits; light brick-red; partial red-brown wash or discoloration outside. Combed decoration (6-tooth?) in horizontal and swirling bands starting 25 mm below rim; vertical finger-smoothing inside, on uneven surfaces.	5	163
	708	1	3	Jar with neck, flared, narrow, high.	Very fine fabric; very fine dark and light-grey grits; brownish-buff, faint greyish mottling. Rather streaky burnish, vertical outside, horizontal inside, on very even surfaces.	5	141
	708	1	4	Jar with neck, slightly inverted, narrow.	Fine fabric; fine pale-grey grits; pale brick-red, mottled buff. Cord-impressed outside, streaky burnish on rim and inside on uneven surface.	5	146
	708	1	5	Bowl, flared, conical (small).	Very fine fabric; fine grey/shiny grits; black. Fine glossy burnish outside and inside.	5	197
	708	1	6	Base, flat, steeper angle (probably a jar).	Coarse fabric; small-fine dark-grey grits, a few light; cream, faint grey core, blackened inside. Faint-combed outside (except beneath base), smoothed inside.	5	*cf. 310, 311, 313, 315*
	708	1	–	7 body sherds.	2 cord-impressed (1 blackened inside); 4 faint-combed, some criss-cross (deliberate pattern?); 1 undecorated.	5	–
	708	2	1	Bowl, hemispherical.	Fine fabric; fine grits; black mottled brown. Horizontal/oblique glossy burnish outside and inside.	4	104

708	2	2	Bowl, flared, shallow.	Fine fabric; fine light and dark grits; black. Fine glossy burnish outside and inside.	4	131
708	2	3	Bowl, hemispherical.	Very fine fabric; fine grits; dark grey, black surfaces. Very fine glossy burnish outside and inside.	4	98
708	2	4	Bowl, upright rim.	Fine fabric; fine light grits; dark brown/black. Very faint combing outside, below 26 mm band of glossy burnish, continuing inside.	4	103
708	2	5	Jar with neck, flared.	Fine fabric; fine light and shiny grits; blackish-brown. Light horizontal burnish outside and inside.	4	53
708	2	6	Jar, holemouth, steep.	Fine fabric; fine light and dark grits; bricky brown, dark-grey rim, core and inside. Cord-impressed outside, well smoothed or light matt burnish on rim and inside.	4	92
708	2	7	Bowl, flared, deep, small.	Fine fabric but thick-walled; small dark-grey grits; light brick-red. Very faint combing outside, smoothed or faint-burnished inside on very uneven surface, with traces of white plaster inside and out.	4	117
708	2	–	4 body sherds.	3 burnished outside and inside; 1 cord-impressed, partial thick chalky coating on top (inside rough).	4	–
708	3	1	Jar with neck, flared, narrow.	Fine fabric; fine light grits; blackish-brown. Faint-combing (4 teeth at least, spaced) outside, inside rough.	?4	54
708	3	2	Jar, holemouth, steep.	Very fine fabric; very fine dark and light grits. Spaced cord impressions outside, horizontal burnish on rim and inside.	?4	85
708	3	3	Jar, holemouth, shallow.	Fine fabric; fine dark and light grits; dull brick-red, black core and mottling. Spaced cord impressions outside, faint horizontal burnish inside rim, smoothing or light matt burnish inside.	?4	70
708	3	4	Bowl, hemispherical (small).	Fine fabric; fine light grits; dark brown, blackish-brown surfaces. Fine burnish outside and inside.	?4	102
708	3	5	Bowl, flared.	Fine fabric; fine light and dark grits; black, dark brown surfaces. Glossy burnish outside and inside.	?4	115
708	3	6	Bowl, flared (small).	Very fine fabric; very fine light and dark grits; black; very fine glossy burnish outside and inside.	?4	119
708	3	7	Bowl, flared.	Very fine fabric; very fine light and dark grits; mid-brown, blackish inside below rim. Very fine glossy burnish outside and inside.	?4	110
708	3	8	Base, flat, rounded edge.	Fine fabric, thin-walled; fine dark and light grits; mushroom-buff, mottled/blackened inside. Cord-impressed outside (except beneath base), very light burnish inside.	?4	*cf. 306–309, 297*
708	3	9	Base, flat, steeper angle (probably a jar).	Fine fabric, thin-walled; small-fine grey grits, a few medium, white; brown-bricky. Light burnish outside, rough burnish inside.	?4	*cf. 310–311, 313, 315*

	708	3	–	32 body sherds.	1 burnished outside and inside; 25 cord-impressed (11 burnished/smoothed inside, 14 rough, 1 with thick chalky layer); 5 faint-combed or scraped outside (4 burnished inside); 1 undecorated (fine fabric).	4	–
	708	4	1	Bowl, upright (hemispherical?).	Fine fabric; fine light and dark grits; brownish-black. Burnished outside and inside.	?1	cf. 42
	708	4	–	25 body sherds.	2 burnished outside and inside; 12 cord-impressed, 1 with burnish band outside; 4 burnished inside; 7 rough.	1	–
	708	5	–	12 body sherds.	1 burnished outside and inside; 10 cord-impressed (5 lightly burnished inside, 5 rough); 1 faint-combed, blackened outside (rough inside).	1	–
	708	+	1	Jar with neck, upright, narrow.	Fairly fine fabric; fine light and shiny grits; dull brick-red, dark-grey core and inside surface mottling. Light blurred cord-impressions outside, light smoothing over rim and inside.	Surface	219
709	709	1	1	Jar, holemouth, shallow. Long narrow ledge/lug.	Fine fabric; small dark and light grits; dull dark brownish-grey. Cord-impressed outside, including over ledge-handle, horizontal and oblique smoothing inside.	5	171
	709	1	2	Bowl, flared.	Very fine fabric; fine dark and light grits; brown, blackish mottling. Burnish outside, streaky inside.	5	cf. 196
	709	1	3	Base, flat, rounded edge.	Medium fabric; small-fine dark, reddish and light grits (grog?); buff, brick-red outside surfaces, pale-grey core. Smoothed outside, thin chalky coating inside.	5	306–309, 297
	709	1	3	Base, flat, deep angle (jar).	Coarse fabric; small-fine dark and light grits, shell; buff, blackened under base. Smoothed outside, probably inside.	5	cf. 310, 311, 313, 315
	709	1	–	15 body sherds.	3 burnished outside and inside; 2 light/smoothed only; 10 cord-impressed (4 burnished inside, 3 smoothed, 3 rough).		–
	709	2	1	Bowl, flared, shallow.	Fine fabric; fine light and dark grits; dull brick-red, dark-grey surfaces. Streaky matt burnish outside and inside.	5	205
	709	2	2	Bowl, curved, shallow.	Very fine fabric; fine dark and light grits; dark pinkish-grey. Light burnish around rim and 10 mm band outside, smoothed below and inside.	5	201
	709	2	3	Base, rounded.	Base, rounded; medium fabric. Smoothed outside, thin chalky coating inside.	5	306–309, 323, 297
	709	2	–	5 body sherds.	1 burnished outside and inside; 4 cord-impressed (1 burnished inside, 2 smoothed, 1 rough).	5	–
	709	3	–	2 body sherds.	1 lightly burnished/smoothed outside and inside (medium fabric); 1 cord-impressed, burnished inside.	4	–
	709	4	1	Bowl, upright rim.	Fine fabric; small dark-grey and whitish grits; brick-red, grey-brown surface: Horizontal burnish (streaky) outside and inside.	3	36
	709	4	2	Base, flat, shallow angle.	Fine fabric, thin-walled: Rough burnish outside and inside.	3	cf. 312, 314
	709	4	–	1 body sherd.	Undecorated, coarse fabric.	3	–

709	5	–	2 body sherds.	1 smoothed outside and lightly burnished inside (fine fabric); 1 cord-impressed, burnished inside.	3	–
709	8	1	Bowl, upright rim (small).	Fine fabric; fine dark grits; dull brick-red, brown surfaces. Horizontal burnish outside (streaky) and inside.	?4	101
709	8	2	Bowl, slightly inverted rim (small).	Fine fabric; fine light and dark grits; greyish brown, brick-red core. Horizontal burnish outside, rather streaky inside.	?4	89
709	8	–	3 body sherds.	2 burnished outside and inside; 1 faint-combed, rough-burnished inside.	4 (? 2 + 3)	–
709	11	–	2 body sherds.	1 cord-impressed, dec. burnish line on neck-shoulder of fine jar, rough burnish inside; 1 faint-combed, burnish/smoothing strokes inside.	4 (? + 3)	–
709	14	1	Bowl, slightly inverted rim (small).	Fine fabric; fine light and dark grits; brick-red, grey-brown surfaces. Horizontal burnish (streaky) outside and inside.	3	33
709	14	2	Base, disc.	Very fine fabric; fine dark grits; dull darkish brick-red. Smooth surfaces. Remains of thick lime plaster coating (>3 mm) inside, possible traces under base and outside.	3	324
709	14	–	1 body sherd.	1 cord-impressed, smoothed inside.	3 (? + 2)	–
709	15	1	Base, flat, shallow angle (probably a bowl).	Extremely fine fabric; very fine light and dark grits; mushroom-colour outside, dark grey inside. Glossy burnish outside, under base and inside.	?1	312
709	15	2	Base, flat, steeper angle (probably a jar).	Medium fabric and thickness; fine light-grey grits; dull greyish-brown. Cord-impressed outside and under base, smoothed inside.	?1	310–311, 313, 315
709	15	–	2 body sherds.	1 smoothed outside and lightly burnished inside (fine fabric); 1 cord-impressed, burnished inside.	1	–
709	16	–	5 body sherds.	3 cord-impressed, light burnish inside; 2 faint-combed, light burnish inside.	3	–
709	17	1	Bowl, upright rim, flattened.	Fine fabric; very fine black grits; pinkish buff. Fine cord-impressions outside below 6 mm band of burnish, continuing over rim, and streaky inside.	3	28
709	17	–	1 body sherd.	1 cord-impressed, light-burnished inside.	3	–
709	21	1	Jar, holemouth, shallow. Probable knob handle.	Coarse fabric; small light grits, fine vegetable temper; dull light brick-red, thick dark-grey core, greyish or blackened outside. Smoothed outside and inside.	[Post-Neo.]	244
709	21	–	12 body sherds.	2 burnished (1 rough; 1 light-burnished outside and inside); 3 cord-impressed (2 smoothed inside); 6 faint-combed, coarse fabric; 1 very fine fabric, well burnished inside, lightly outside?	5 (? + Post-Neo.)	–
709	22	–	4 body sherds.	1 cord-impressed (burnished inside); 2 faint-combed (smoothed/burnish strokes inside, probably same vessel); 1 thin.	2	–
709	28	–	2 body sherds.	2 cord-impressed (burnished inside).	40269	–
709	29	1	Bowl, upright rim.	Very fine fabric; fine light-grey grits; brick-red, dark-grey inside surface. Horizontal burnish outside and inside.	?4	100

	709	29	2	Jar, holemouth, steep.	Fine fabric; fine grey and light grits; dull brick-red, grey outside surface. Cord impressions blurred under 11 mm burnished band outside, matt burnish 25 mm inside, and well smoothed below.	?4	91
	709	29	3	Jar, holemouth, steep.	Fairly fine fabric; fine dark and light grits; dark brick-red, dark grey core. Smoothed or very sketchy burnish outside and inside.	?4	75
	709	29	–	12 body sherds.	2 burnished outside and inside; 10 cord-impressed (5 burnished inside; 1 scraped; 2 blackened, 1 jar-neck/shoulder).	40269	–
	709	30	1	Jar, holemouth, shallow.	Fine fabric; fine grey grits; bright brick-red. Very shallow cord-impressions outside, horizontal burnish inside, over rim and 5 mm band outside.	?4	68
	709	30	–	3 body sherds.	1 burnished outside and inside; 2 cord-impressed (lightly smoothed or rough inside).	40269	–
	709	31	1	Base, flat, steeper angle (probably a jar).	Medium fabric and thickness; small-fine dark-grey and light grits; dull greyish-buff, blackened inside. Cord-impressed outside and under base; smoothed inside.	1	cf. 310–311, 313, 315
	709	31	–	2 body sherds.	2 cord-impressed (burnished/smoothed inside; mottled/blackened, esp. inside).	1	–
710	710	1	–	2 body sherds.	2 undecorated (medium-fine fabric, thick).	[7]	–
	710	2	–	5 body sherds.	4 cord-impressed (1 light-burnished, 3 lightly smoothed inside); 1 faint-combed (rough inside); 1 undecorated (fine fabric), neck of jar.	5	–
	710	3	1	Jar with neck, slightly inverted, narrow.	Fine fabric; fine light and dark grits; dark brick-red. Cord-impressed outside, well smoothed inside.	5	157
	710	3	2	Bowl, slightly inverted.	Fine fabric; fine light and dark grits; black. Glossy burnish outside, partly worn, inside chipped off.	5	cf. 189
	710	3	3	Base, flat, shallow angle (probably a bowl).	Medium fabric and thickness; medium-fine light and pale-grey grits, possibly some red grog; dark grey black where burnished. Cord-impressed outside, light burnish inside.	5	cf. 312, 314
	710	3	–	5 body sherds.	1 burnished outside and inside (lightly); 3 cord-impressed (2 light-burnished inside).	5	–
	710	4	1	Bowl, curved, shallow.	Very fine fabric; fine dark and light grits; brownish-black, black core. Fine glossy burnish outside and inside.	5	200
	710	4	2	Base, flat, shallow angle (probably a bowl).	Fine fabric, thin-walled; small-fine whitish grits; black. Cord-impressed outside and under base, burnished inside.	5	cf. 312, 314
	710	4	3	Base (? rounded-edge only).	Fine fabric; fine light and dark grits; dark brown. Incised/scored outside (c.5 mm apart), burnished inside.	5	cf. 306, 307?
	710	4	1	Bowl, curved, shallow.	Very fine fabric; fine dark and light grits; brownish-black, black core. Fine glossy burnish outside and inside.	5	200

710	4	–	9 body sherds.	1 burnished outside and inside (lightly); 7 cord-impressed (1 burnished inside, 3 smoothed, 2 scraped or rough); 1 faint-combed (scraped inside).	5	–
710	5	1	Jar, holemouth, steep.	Fine fabric; fine light and shiny grits; dull brick-red, dark grey inside surface and mottling outside. Matt burnish outside and (sketchy) inside.	5	179
710	5	2	Jar, holemouth, steep (small).	Fine fabric; small to fine dark and light grits; dull brick-red outside, dark grey inside and rim. Cord-impressed outside below and overlapping 20 mm matt burnish band, also inside.	5	180
710	5	3	Base, flat, rounded edge.	Fine fabric, thin-walled; very fine dark and light grits; dark grey, black where burnished. Glossy burnish outside (except under base – worn off?) and inside.	5	*cf. 306–309, 297*
710	5	4	Base, disc.	Very fine fabric; fine pale-grey and whitish grits, a few dark. Fine matt burnish inside, very fine glossy burnish outside, worn at edge and centre of convex base, and partially on outside wall.	5	327
710	6	1	Jar, holemouth, steep.	Very fine fabric; very fine dark and light grits; blackish brown, mottling. Cord impressions outside blurred by 20 mm band of burnish above; rough burnish inside.	4	86
710	6	2	Bowl, slightly inverted rim.	Fine fabric; fine light and dark grits; dull brick-red, darker/greyish surfaces. Blurred cord-impressions outside, streaky horizontal burnish on rim and on uneven surface inside.	4	94
710	6	3	Bowl, curved, shallow (small).	Fine fabric; fine light grits; dark brownish grey. Glossy burnish outside and inside.	4	128
710	6	4	Bowl, hemispherical.	Very fine fabric; fine light-grey grits; blackish brown, lighter brown outside surface. Fine burnish outside and inside.	4	106
710	6	5	Bowl, hemispherical, with horizontal lug/ledge handle.	Fine fabric; fine grey and whitish grits; dull brick-red, some greyish mottling. Cord-impressed outside and on underside of handle, upper 20 mm left rough/scraped, burnished on rim and very streakily inside over well-smoothed surface.	4	99
710	6	6	Bowl, flared.	Fine fabric; fine light grits; dull brown, blackish surfaces. Cord-impressed below 20 mm rough-scraped band outside, streaky horizontal burnish on rim and inside.	4	122
710	6	7	Base, flat, steeper angle (probably a jar).	Fine fabric, thin-walled; fine dark shiny and light grits; bricky-brown, blackish outside surface. Light burnish outside (base worn), burnish inside.	4	310–311, 313, 315
710	6	–	19 body sherds.	5 burnished outside (4 inside, 1 rough); 9 cord-impressed (5 burnished inside (1 jar-neck/shoulder; 1 scraped); 4 faint-combed (1 burnished inside), 1 on shoulder only, with high flaring neck.	4	–
710	7	1	Jar, holemouth, steep.	Fine fabric; fine light and dark grits; brown surfaces mottled darker/greyish. Cord impressions outside blurred by 25 mm band of matt burnish above, continues inside.	4	87

710	7	2	Base, flat, shallow angle (probably a bowl).	Medium fabric and thickness; small-fine dark-grey grits, few light, red (grog?); pale greyish-buff, pink core. Cord-impressed outside, light burnish inside.	4	*cf. 312, 314*
710	7	–	4 body sherds.	2 burnished outside and inside; 1 cord-impressed (light-burnished inside); 1 faint-combed? (very faint; possible lime or clay coating inside).	4	–
710	9	1	Bowl, hemispherical. Base, disc.	Fine fabric; fine dark-grey grits, some light buff, a few larger; orange/brown, a little greyish mottling, heavily but unevenly blackened surface inside base. Streaky matt poorly applied burnish outside (except under centre of base where surface is rough or worn) and inside.	4	108
710	9	2	Bowl, hemispherical. Base, disc?	Bowl, hemispherical. Fine fabric; fine dark and light grits, some larger; dull mushroom-brown, blackish/mottled outside, heavily blackened surface inside base. Uneven/streaky matt burnish outside and inside.	4	109
710	9	3	Bowl, hemispherical. Base, round?	Fine fabric; fine light and dark grits; bricky-brown, darker surfaces, black/brown at the base. Horizontal burnish outside and inside, rather streaky towards rim.	4	105
710	9	4	Bowl, flared, conical.	Very fine fabric; fine light and dark grits; black. Very fine glossy burnish outside and inside.	4	120
710	9	5	Bowl, flared.	Fine fabric but thick-walled; fine light and dark grits; blackish mottling outside, and inside below rim. Overall but streaky horizontal burnish outside and inside.	4	112
710	9	6	Jar, holemouth, shallow.	Very fine fabric; fine light and dark grits; blackish brown, dull brick-red core. Deeply cord-impressed outside, uneven horizontal burnish on rim and inside.	4	73
710	9	7	Bowl, flared, shallow.	Fine fabric; fine light grits; brown mottled black, especially inside. Faint combing outside, horizontal burnish on rim and inside.	4	133
710	9	8	Base, round (small base of quite large vessel).	Fine fabric; fine light and dark grits; black, mottled buff on upper outside surfaces. Matt streaky burnish outside and inside, rough under base.	4	307
710–9	9	9	Base, flat, rounded edge (probable base).	Medium fabric; small- fine light and dark grits; dull bricky-brown. Cord-impressed (few, spaced) over smoothed surface outside; brown slip and rough burnish inside.	4	*cf. 306–9, 297*
710	9	10	Base, flat, rounded edge.	Fine fabric, thin-walled; fine-very fine brown and light grits; dull bricky-brown with greyer surfaces. Light burnished outside and inside; rough beneath base.	4	*cf. 306–309, 297*
710	9	14	Base, flat, shallow angle (probably a bowl).	Fine fabric, thin-walled; fine dark and light grits; dull bricky-orange. Cord-impressed under base; sides abraded, and possible traces of plaster; lightly smoothed inside.	4	*cf. 312, 314*
710	9	–	36 body sherds.	7 burnished outside and inside; 17 cord-impressed (11 burnished inside, 8 roughly); 6 smoothed or rough; 7 faint-combed (rough inside); 1 neck/shoulder of jar.	4	–
710	10	1	Base, flat, steeper angle (probably a jar).	Fine fabric; small-fine dark-grey and light grits; grey, mushroom inside, brick-red core in thickness of base. Faint-combed outside, light burnish under base, smoothed inside.	2	310–311, 313, 315

	710	10	–	1 body sherd.	Cord-impressed (burnished inside).	2	–
	710	11	1	Jar with neck, flared, short.	Fine fabric; fine dark and light grits; black. Fine burnish inside and outside.	2	2
	710	11	2	Base, disc.	Very fine fabric, very thin-walled; very fine light and dark grits; black, brownish-grey core. Burnished outside, worn under base, light burnish inside.	2	cf. 324–329
	710	11	–	3 body sherds.	3 burnished outside and inside (1 neck-shoulder of jar).	2	–
730	730	2	1	Bowl, hemispherical.	Fine fabric; fine whitish grits; black. Light combing outside below 40 mm band of fine glossy burnish, also inside but worn.	Mixed	272
	730	32	4	Bowl, flared.	Very fine fabric; very fine grits, mostly dark grey; light brown, dark grey inside. Matt burnish outside, slightly streaky inside.	[8 fill]	277
735	735	1	1	Jar, holemouth, shallow. Knob handle?	Medium-fine fabric, hard-fired but roughly made and uneven; small dark and light grits, red grog; pale brick-red, buff core and mottling. Surfaces finger-smoothed (especially inside), incised parallel lines outside on shoulder (some very light), below rectangular knob (scar only – broken on join) close to rim.	5	159
	735	1	2	Jar, holemouth, steep. Lug or knob handle.	Fine fabric; fine grey grits; dark grey outside, black inside and core. Well smoothed outside under cord impressions (thick cord), light matt burnish inside.	5	183
	735	1	4	Base, flat, rounded edge (base without sides).	Coarse fabric; small, fine grey grits, some medium, pale; buff/cream, grey core, blackened inside. Cord-impressed (thick) outside, inside rough.	5	cf. 306–309, 297
	735	1	5	Body sherd.	Medium fabric, thick, hard-fired, but very roughly finished, especially inside; small-fine dark and light grits; dull orange-buff, slight grey mottling. Combed diamond pattern, roughly done.	5	cf. 340
	735	1	–	16 body sherds.	3 burnished outside (1 inside; 1 coarse fabric, rough burnish outside, inside worn); 5 cord-impressed (1 burnished inside, 4 rough); 3 faint-combed (1 burnished inside, 2 rough); 5 undecorated, smoothed outside and inside (1 fine fabric; 4 coarse).		–
	735	2	1	Jar with neck, flared, narrow (small).	Fine fabric; small pale-grey grits; buff. Burnish on rim, very slight outside and inside.	5	142
	735	2	2	Jar with neck, upright, narrow.	Coarse fabric; small dark-grey grits; buff. Rough-scraped outside and inside.	5	150
	735	2	3	Jar, holemouth, shallow, rolled rim.	Fine fabric, thick-walled, with multiple or rolled-over coils visible on break; small light and dark grits; black, light orange-buff surface on rim and inside and parts of core (may be heavy mottling). Cord impressions outside below slight groove and 27 mm band of horizontal burnish, burnish inside.	5	167
	735	2	4	Bowl, flared (small).	Very fine fabric; very fine grits; light brick-red, light grey surfaces. Burnish outside, rim (streaky) and inside.	5	204

735	2	5	Base, angled, shallow, with slight heel (bowl?).	Medium fabric; medium-fine dark-grey and light grits; buff, cream surface outside, blackened under base. Smoothed outside and inside.	5	*cf. 317*
735	2	–	18 body sherds.	4 burnished outside and inside; 5 cord-impressed (1 burnished inside, 4 rough); 4 faint-combed (smoothed inside); 5 undecorated (1 fine fabric; 4 coarse, 1 blackened inside).	5	–
735	3	2	Jar, holemouth, shallow.	Medium-coarse fabric, roughly made and uneven; small light and grey grits, fine vegetable temper; pinkish-buff, grey core and mottling. Finger-smoothed on uneven surfaces.	5	161
735	3	3	Jar, holemouth, shallow.	Medium fabric; small grey grits; pale buff, slight grey core. Finger-smoothed outside, uneven surface inside.	5	162
735	3	4	Bowl, slightly inverted rim.	Medium fabric; small dark and light grits; dull pinkish-buff, blackened/greyish outside surface. Smoothed outside, barely inside.	5	185
735	3	5	Jar with neck, upright.	Fairly fine fabric; small dark-grey grits. Very sketchy burnish outside, smoothed inside.	5	148
735	3	6	Bowl, slightly inverted rim.	Fine light and dark grits. Fine glossy burnish outside and inside.	5	*cf. 189*
735	3	7	Bowl, flared.	Fine fabric; fine pale grey grits; brownish brick-red. Fine glossy burnish outside and inside.	5	*cf. 196*
735	3	8	Jar, holemouth, steep.	Coarse fabric; small grey, white and brown grits, some vegetable temper; pinkish buff, slightly blackened outside surface. Finger-smoothed outside and inside.	5	175
735	3	9	Jar, holemouth, steep.	Medium-fine fabric; medium-size dark-grey angular grits, some vegetable temper, possibly chaff. Well smoothed or very light burnish outside, with very faint combing starting 27 mm below rim, lightly finger-smoothed inside.	5	170
735	3	10	Base, angled, steeper, with slight 'heel' (jar?).	Medium-coarse fabric; medium-fine light and dark grits; brick-red, buff under base, mottled/blackened. Smoothed outside, rough inside.	5	*cf. 316, 318–323*
735	3	11	Base, angled, with slight 'heel'.	Coarse fabric; small light and dark grits; bricky-buff, blackened outside. Smoothed/faint burnished outside, inside barely smoothed.	5	316
735	3	12	Base, flat, rounded edge (base without sides).	Medium fabric; small, fine light and dark grits; cream-buff outside, heavily blackened from core to inside; worn outside. Smoothed or light burnish inside.	5	*cf. 306–309, 297*
735	3	13	Base, flat, rounded edge.	Medium fabric; medium-fine light and greyish grits; cream-buff outside, heavily blackened from core to inside. Smoothed outside and inside.	5	*cf. 306–309, 297*
735	3	–	89 body sherds.	5 burnished outside and inside; 28 cord-impressed (7 burnished inside, 5 smoothed, 16 rough); 31 faint-combed, some very slight (6 burnished inside); 25 undecorated (med. or coarse fabric, some slightly burnished, 1 jar-neck/shoulder).	5(? 4)	–
735	4	1	Jar, holemouth, steep.	Fine fabric; dense small pale-grey grits; light brick-red. Shallow cord impressions outside, very sketchy burnish over rim and inside.	Mixed	253

735	4	2	Jar, holemouth, steep.	Medium fabric; small dark-grey grits, a few medium-large white (chalk?); pale pinkish grey, medium-grey surfaces. Thick cord impressions outside, below and partly under 28 mm band well-smoothed or faint matt burnish, continuing over rim, and very sketchy inside on uneven surface.	Mixed	262
735	4	3	Jar with neck, flared, narrow, high.	Fine fabric; fine white and grey grits; brick-red, dark reddish-grey surfaces. Fine cord impressions outside on shoulder, lightly smoothed on neck and rim, inside uneven.	Mixed	215
735	4	5	Bowl, hemispherical.	Fine fabric; small light-grey grits; black. Fine glossy burnish outside and inside.	Mixed	271
735	4	6	Bowl, flared, shallow.	Fine fabric; small light grits; dark brick-red, blackish inside surface. Fine burnish outside and inside.	Mixed	*cf. 291*
735	4	7	Bowl, slightly inverted rim. Horizontal ledge/lug handle.	Fairly fine fabric; small dark-grey and whitish grits; bright brick-red, buff-brown surfaces, probably a slip. Deep cord impressions outside, below 6–12 mm band smoothed only, streaky burnish on rim and inside; very shallow horizontal oval lug or knob, partly cord-impressed.	Mixed	264
735	4	8	Base, disc, with mat impression.	Fine fabric; fine dark-grey angular grits, some light, some red grog. Smoothed outside, possibly on darker slip, rough inside.	Mixed	328
735	4	9	Base, flat, shallow angle (probably a bowl).	Fine fabric, thin-walled; fine grits; black. Faint-combed outside, fine burnish inside.	Mixed	*cf. 312, 314*
735	4	10	Base, flat, rounded edge.	Coarse fabric; small-fine light-grey and dark-grey grits; pale buff, greyish outside. Smoothed outside, lightly smoothed inside.	Mixed	*cf. 306–309, 297*
735	4	14	Bowl, upright rim, deep.	Fairly fine fabric, roughly finished; dense small dark-grey grits; light brown, blackish mottling outside. Rough burnish outside on uneven surface (horizontal near rim, vertical on body), over rim and very sketchy inside.	Mixed	301
735	4	16	Base (? round or rounded edge).	Fine fabric, thin-walled; small light-grey and dark grits; black. Burnished outside and inside.	Mixed	*cf. 306–309, 297*
735	4	17	Body sherd.	Fairly fine fabric; small light grits; orange-brown. Lightly smoothed inside. Faint combed decoration of parallel lines in diamond pattern.	Mixed	340
735	4	19	Body sherd (shoulder of jar).	Coarse, unusual fabric, thick; large pale grits; pale grey. Smoothed outside and lightly inside. Deep pattern-combed decoration.	Mixed	341
735	4	–	65 body sherds.	7 burnished outside and inside; 31 cord-impressed (13 burnished or smoothed inside; fine-coarse fabric); 9 faint-combed (2 light-burnished inside); 12 undecorated (fine-coarse fabric, some slightly burnished outside); (6 sherds late EB).	Mixed Neo. + Post.-Neo	–
735	5	–	9 body sherds.	2 cord-impressed (rough inside); 5 faint-combed (1 smoothed inside; 4 rough); 2 undecorated, wiped or scored outside (medium fabric).	? 4	–
735	6	1	Jar with neck, flared.	Coarse fabric but thin, pinkish-red slip or paint outside.	? 5	*cf. 55*

735	6	2	Jar, holemouth, steep.	Medium fabric, light and porous; small whitish and dark grits, vegetable temper; dull greyish buff, thick dark-grey core. Slightly smoothed outside and inside.	? 5	169
735	6	3	Jar, holemouth, shallow.	Medium fabric; medium-size dark grey grits, some vegetable temper (may be chaff); buff. Well smoothed or very light matt burnish outside, light finger-smoothing inside.	? 5	173
735	7	1	Jar with neck, upright.	Medium-coarse fabric; much small grey grit, probably some vegetable temper; buff. Smoothed outside and inside.	4	64
735	7	2	Lid?	Medium-coarse fabric; small grey and white grits, grog, fine vegetable temper; buff, mottled grey inside; cord-impressed outside, lightly smoothed inside; flattened underneath outside edge.	4	139
735	7	–	14 body sherds.	2 burnished outside (1 burnished inside, 1 rough); 7 cord-impressed (1 burnished inside, 2 lightly smoothed, 1 rough); 2 faint-combed; 3 undecorated, smoothed outside (medium fabric).	4	–
735	8	1	Jar, holemouth, shallow.	Coarse fabric; large to fine grey grits, possibly some red grog and fine vegetable temper; greyish buff, light-grey core. Faint-combed outside, smoothed outside and inside.	4	79
735	8	–	5 body sherds.	2 cord-impressed (blackened inside and core, 1 a few strokes on very uneven surface); 3 undecorated (medium fabric; 1 blackened inside).	4	–
735	9	1	Jar with neck, flared, high.	Very coarse fabric; large and small dark-grey grits, some light; grey-buff, blackened rim. Slight burnish or sheen outside, on rim and 10–15 mm inside (over blackening – may be from handling).	4	58
735	9	–	7 body sherds.	4 cord-impressed (1 light-burnished inside, 3 rough); 1 faint-combed (smoothed inside, blackened); 2 undecorated, smoothed outside (1 rough-burnished); medium-coarse fabric.	4	–
735	10	1	Jar, holemouth, shallow.	Fairly fine fabric; small dark-grey shiny grits; dull bricky-grey. Blurred cord impressions outside, light matt burnish over rim, inside well smoothed.	[7]	254
735	10	–	2 body sherds.	2 cord-impressed (1 light-burnished inside); 1 faint-combed on light burnish (rough inside).	[7]	–
735	11	4	Bowl, upright rim (flat), deep.	Medium-coarse fabric; small grey grits, shell; pale orange-buff. Faint combed outside to within 14 mm of rim, finger-smoothed above, rim and inside.	[6 fill]	302
735	11	5	Jar, holemouth, shallow.	Medium-coarse fabric, thick; small grey and whitish grits, red grog; buff, thin light-grey core. Smoothed outside and lightly inside.	[6 fill]	241
735	11	6	Jar with neck, flared.	Very coarse fabric; large dark-grey angular grits; buff. Smoothed outside, rough inside.	[6 fill]	225
735	11	7	Base, 'heeled' (probably a jar).	Medium fabric; small dark-grey angular grits, some pale; dull buff, some dark-grey mottling. Cord-impressed outside and under base, rough inside.	[6 fill]	322

735	11	–	6 body sherds.	5 cord-impressed (1 blackened outside, coarse, coil-break; 1 light-burnished inside); 1 faint-combed (1 smoothed inside, blackened).	[6 fill]	–
735	12	1	Jar, holemouth, shallow.	Medium fabric; grey grits, grog; pale pink, grey-buff core. Smoothed outside, fairly rough inside.	3	15
735	13	1	Base, 'heeled', probably a jar).	Medium-coarse fabric; small dark-grey and light grits, a little fine vegetable temper; dull greyish buff, dark-grey surfaces outside and inside, inside also partly light orange (mostly upper part, may be original surface). Roughly applied cord-impressions outside, worn ring at edge of base, smoothed underneath, inside surface rough or worn.	5	319
735	13	2	Base, flat, steeper angle (probably a jar).	Coarse fabric, thick; dense small-fine brownish grits; buff outside, dark core, blackish-brown inside. Probably smoothed outside, rough inside.	? 5	310–311, 313, 315
735	13	3	Body sherd with incised decoration (?).	Coarse fabric, thick; dense dark-grey grits; orange-buff. Incised irregular zigzag lines, post-firing (intentional?).	? 5	*cf. 340, 341?*
735	13	–	6 body sherds.	2 burnished outside (lightly; 1 neck/shoulder of jar); 2 cord-impressed, 1 blackened (rough inside); 2 faint-combed; 2 undecorated.	? 5	–
735	14	1	Jar, holemouth, steep.	Fine but soft fabric; fine dark grits; cream/buff. Well smoothed or light matt burnish outside and inside.	4	71
735	14	12	Jar, holemouth, steep.	Fairly fine fabric; small whitish and dark-grey grits; dark dull brick-red, blackened inside. Outside rough or scraped (perhaps flattened coil lost before firing), streaky horizontal burnish inside.	4	*cf. 256*
735	14	13	Bowl, flared.	Fine fabric; fine grey grits; brownish black, browner core. Fine glossy burnish outside and inside.	4	278
735	14	15	Base, flat, steeper angle (probably a jar).	Coarse fabric; small-fine dark-grey and whitish grits; buff, slightly blackened outside. Cord-impressed outside, smoothed inside.	4	*cf. 310, 311, 313, 315*
735	15	1	Jar, holemouth, shallow.	Medium-coarse fabric; small grey and red grits or grog; pale grey-buff. Smoothed outside, rather rough inside, possibly traces of orange slip.	?4	69
735	15	–	10 body sherds.	7 cord-impressed (4 burnished inside, 3 rough); 1 faint-combed; 2 undecorated.	4	–
750	1	1	Jar with neck, flared, narrow.	Fairly fine fabric; small dark-grey and light grits; buff, greyish core and mottling. Lightly smoothed outside, rough inside.	[8]	216
750	1	2	Bowl, curved, shallow.	Fairly fine; fine grey grits; greyish buff; slightly brownish or self-slip; well smoothed outside and inside.	[8]	299
905	2	3	Jar with neck, flared (small).	Medium-fine fabric; fine grits, a little fine vegetable temper; buff, blackened throughout; very uneven surfaces.	[9-12]	220
905	8	5	Jar with neck, flared, short.	Medium-fine fabric; fine dark grits, possibly grog; greyish buff, pale bricky-buff slip outside and inside, blackened. Smoothed surfaces.	[? 14 /15]	221

905

UNSTRATIFIED

++	++	1	Bowl, curved, shallow, large. Horizontal ledge/knob handle.	Fine fabric; fine grey grits; dark greyish-red outside with some blackish mottling, black core and inside. Cord-impressed outside, and upper and lower sides of lug, light matt burnish over rim and inside; horizontal ledge-handle.	–	297
++	++	2	Jar with neck, upright, narrow (small).	Fine fabric; fine dark grits; greyish buff, surfaces mottled grey. Cord-impressed outside, flat rim and inside lightly smoothed.	–	233
++	++	3	Jar with neck, upright, narrow.	Medium-fine fabric; medium to small grey grits, red grog, a little fine vegetable temper; light brick-red, mottled buff, light grey core. Very slightly smoothed or wiped outside and inside.	–	235
++	++	4	Jar with neck, slightly inverted.	Medium fabric; buff; small grey grits. Smoothed or streaky burnish outside and inside.	–	*cf. 237*
++	++	6	Bowl, slightly inverted rim. Narrow horizontal ledge handle, slightly askew.	Fine fabric; fine white and dark grits; black, mottled dull brick-red outside. Very faint combing outside, light matt burnish over rim and inside.	–	265

Virginia Mathias

Table 4.3. Petrographic analysis of inclusions.

ID.No	Sherd No.	Phase	G	O	C	CH	Q	F	SH	G/CP	Ware	Fabric Group
1	VIII.602.15/1	4+5	o	o	++vp	+	+			++	C	D
2	VIII.602.15/2	4+5	+	+	+		+	+		+	M	A3
3	VIII.602.27/1	4+5	++vp	+	+		+	+		+	C	A1
4	VIII.602.27/2	4+5?	++vp	+	+		+	+	o	+	C	A1
5	VIII.606.7/1	4	++fs	+	+	+	+	+	o	+	F	A2
6	VIII.606.7/4	4	+	+	+	+	+	+	o	+	M	B
7	VIII.606/8/8	3	++vp	+		+	+	+		+	F	A2
8	VIII.644.12/7		++vp	+		+	+	+		o	C	A1
9	VIII.644.14/36	5	+	+	+	+	+		+		C	B
10	VIII.644.14/37	5	++vp	+	+		+	+		+	M	A1
11	VIII.644.18/4	5	o	+	+		+		o	+	M	D
12	VIII.644.21/2	4(3?)	++fs	+	+		+	+		+	F	A2
13	VIII.644.21/8	4(3?)	+		++		+				M	A3
14	VIII.644.21/24	4(3?)		+	+		+		o	++	M	D
15	VIII.644.21/25	4(3?)	+	+	+	+	+	+	o	+	M	A3
16	VIII.644.27/37	4	+	+	+		+	+	o	+	M	A3
17	VIII.644.30/8	3	+		+		+	+		+	C	B
18	VIII.644.33/1			+	++vp		+	+		++	M	D
19	VIII.644.34/3	5	++fs	+	+		+	+	o	+	F	A2
20	VIII.644.34/4	5	++vp	+	+		+	+	o	+	F	A1
21	VIII.644.34/14	5	+	+	+		+	+			M	A3
22	VIII.650.14/2	5	o	+	+	+	+	+			M	D
23	VIII.654/9	5	o	+	++fs	+	+	+	+		C	D
24	VIII.705.61/1				++vp		o				F	C1
25	VIII.705.61/3				++vp		o				M	C1
26	VIII.705.61/5		++vp	+			+	+		+	C	A1
27	VIII.705.61/8				++vp		+	+			F	C1
28	VIII.705.63/5	?4	++fs	+	+		+	+		+	F	A2
29	VIII.705.66/2	4(?3)	++fs	+	+	+	+	+	o		F	A2
30	VIII.705.67/3	3(?2)	+	+	+		+		o	+	F	A3
31	VIII.705.68/7	3(?2)	++vs	+	+	+	+	+		+	F	A2
32	VIII.705.68/8	3(?2)	++fs	+	+		+	+			F	A1
33	VIII.705.68/9	3(?2)			++vp		++vp		o		M	C2
34	VIII.705.69/4	3?4?	+	+	++vp		+				M	A3

Key: G = Gabbro; O = Olivine; C = Carbonate; CH = Chert; Q = Quartz; F = Felspar; SH = Shell; G/CP = Grog/Clay Pellet;
vp = very poorly sorted grains;
C = Coarse; M = Medium; F = Fine

Table 4.4. Elemental analysis of clay matrices.

	Si	Al	Na	K	Ca	Mg	Fe	S	Ti	Cl
26	53.3 (1.3)	17,8 (0.4)	1	3.7	9.1 (0.8)	3.2	9.1 (0.4)	1.2	1.3	0.3
6	38.6 (0.6)	10.9 (0.1)	0.5	3.2	33.1 (1)	5.3	6.8 (0.2)	0.5	0.9	0.2
30	45.6 (1)	19.1 (0.6)	0.8	3.2	16 (1)	1.7	11.3 (0.3)	0.2	1.9	0.2
22	26.1 (0,8)	9.9 (0.6)	0.8	2.6	48.8 (4)	1.6	5.9 (1.1)	2.8	0.9	0.6
12	53.1 (1.3)	20.8 (1.1)	1.4	1.7	4.7 (0.5)	1,8	13.6 (0.4)	0.3	2.4	0.1
24	40.2 (1.4)	15.2 (0.4)	1.5	2.9	24.2 (3)	2.8	10.4 (2.4)	0.4	1.7	0.1
17	53.2 (2.4)	23.9 (1.1)	0.8	4.6	4.5 (0.5)	1.1	9.4 (0.7)	0.8	2.5	0.1
9	35.5 (1.7)	7.3*(0.7)	0,6	3.4	42.8 (3.5)	3.6	5 (0.2)	0.9	0.6	0.3
11	31.6 (0.8)	7.3 (0.5)	0.4	3.4	44.9 (3.9)	4.3	5.5 (0.7)	0.9	0.6	0.2
14	28.7 (1.9)	7.4 (0.6)	0.4	2.7	46.2 (2.3)	7.2	4.9 (0.3)	1.8	0.8	0.2

Note: the data given are the means of 4–6 tests on each sample, and show the normalised wt% of the oxides present in the clay matrices. The figures in brackets show the range of variability, and are only provided for some elements as the data are given to within one decimal point. For further details of the sherds involved, see Table 4.3.

Appendix 4.1

Summary of a petrological and elemental analysis of a sample of the Neolithic pottery

E. A. Bettles[1]

Petrology and texture

After a detailed examination of the TNM thin sections through a polarising microscope, it was possible to create a table of the petrographic inclusions identified and a general indication of their frequency (Table 4.3). However, the data cannot be considered as definitive because pottery is not a homogenous material: some of the rarer inclusions may be more abundant than is here apparent, and some may have been absent from the particular sherd but might have occurred in other parts of the same vessel. On the basis of this study the sherds were divided into the following fabric groups. A sample sherd from each group was drawn and its fabric texture sketched (Fig. 4.61).

Group A1

The main feature of this group is the presence of large clasts of dolerite/micro-gabbro, frequently up to 2 mm or more in diameter. Within the gabbro are crystals of plagioclase feldspar (showing repeated twinning under crossed polars), olivine crystals (euhedral in shape and reddened by oxidation and high iron content) and clinopyroxene (blue/green or pink in colour under crossed polars, owing to the presence of titanium). There are a few carbonate grains and grog fragments, the occasional piece of chert and a very little freshwater shell. The clay matrix is quite coarse-grained.

Group A2

The main feature of this group is also the abundance of gabbro inclusions, but here they are in a smaller, very fragmented form. For a visual display of the difference between the A1 and the A2 fabric see Fig. 4.61. Otherwise the inclusions and the clay matrix are very similar to those of A1.

Group A3

This fabric group contains some gabbro clasts, though not in the quantity seen in A1 and A2. It has a higher concentration of carbonate and quartz grains (a feature also of the C groups). Small pieces of grog are normally present, but, as with the other A sub-groups, they are not plentiful. The clay matrix is fairly coarse.

Group B

The most notable feature of this group is the texture of the matrix, which is several orders of magnitude finer than in the A groups. Otherwise it comprises the same inclusion types as the A groups, though the grain sorting is particularly poor and the percentage of inclusions in the matrix seems lower than in the A groups (Fig. 4.61). Gabbro clasts are present, but are not as frequent as in groups A1 and A2. There appears to be more carbonate grains and pieces of grog than in the A groups.

Group C1

The preponderant inclusion-type here is carbonate, where the sorting of the grains is very poor. Some quartz grains and grog fragments are evident but there are no gabbro clasts, no chert and no pieces of shell. There is possibly one small piece of chalcedony in Sample 27. The clay matrix is similar in texture to that of the A groups.

Group C2

This group comprises only one sherd, Sample 33. Like group C1 it has a very high carbonate content, but there is a noticeably larger number of quartz grains in the matrix, of sub-rounded rather than angular shape. Both carbonate and quartz grains are poorly sorted. A few grog pieces and freshwater shell fragments are present. There are no gabbro clasts, and the matrix is coarsely grained.

Group D

The essential feature of this group is, as with group B, the fine texture of the clay matrix. Otherwise it is very similar to the C groups, with a high carbonate content. Like group B, the grain sorting is poor and the percentage of the inclusions in the matrix appears comparatively low (Fig. 4.61). The proportion of grog seems higher than in the C groups and traces of shell can sometimes be seen. There are rare instances of small pieces of gabbro and olivine.

The inclusions

Gabbro (or more accurately dolerite/micro-gabbro) is a basic plutonic rock which has cooled and solidified at some depth in the earth (Pough 1953, 18). Although its presence in the geology of this part of Syria is not acknowledged on maps or books on its geology (see Ponikarov 1966 for the most comprehensive geological study of the area), it is probably included under the term 'basalts', of which there are large outcrops north of the Homs lake and which is plentiful at Tell Nebi Mend itself both in the form of natural boulders and as heavy-duty implements. Some of the larger clasts in the thin sections have rounded to sub-rounded edges, suggesting some transportation and deposition,

Virginia Mathias

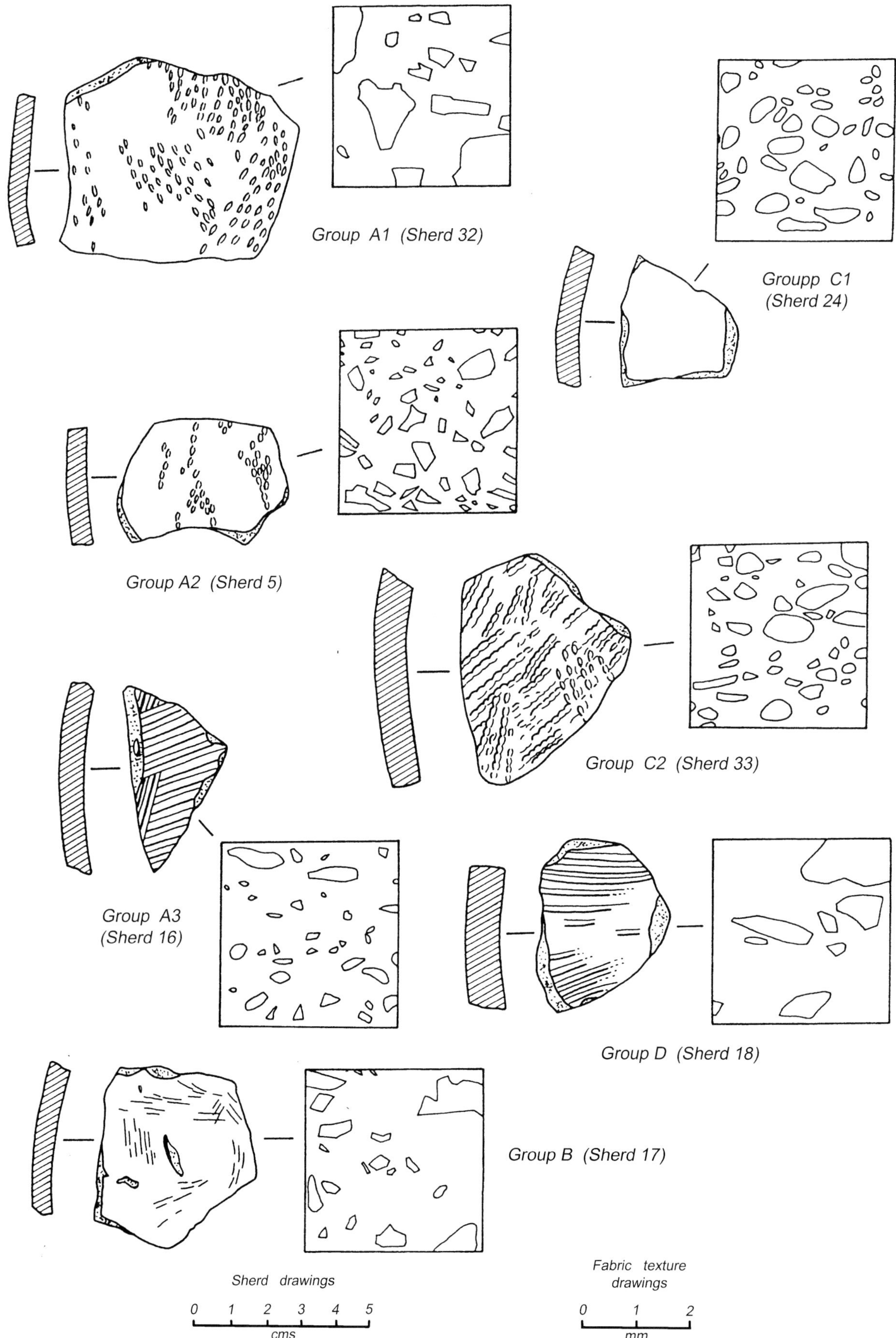

Fig. 4.61. Texture of fabric groups (after Bettles 1994).

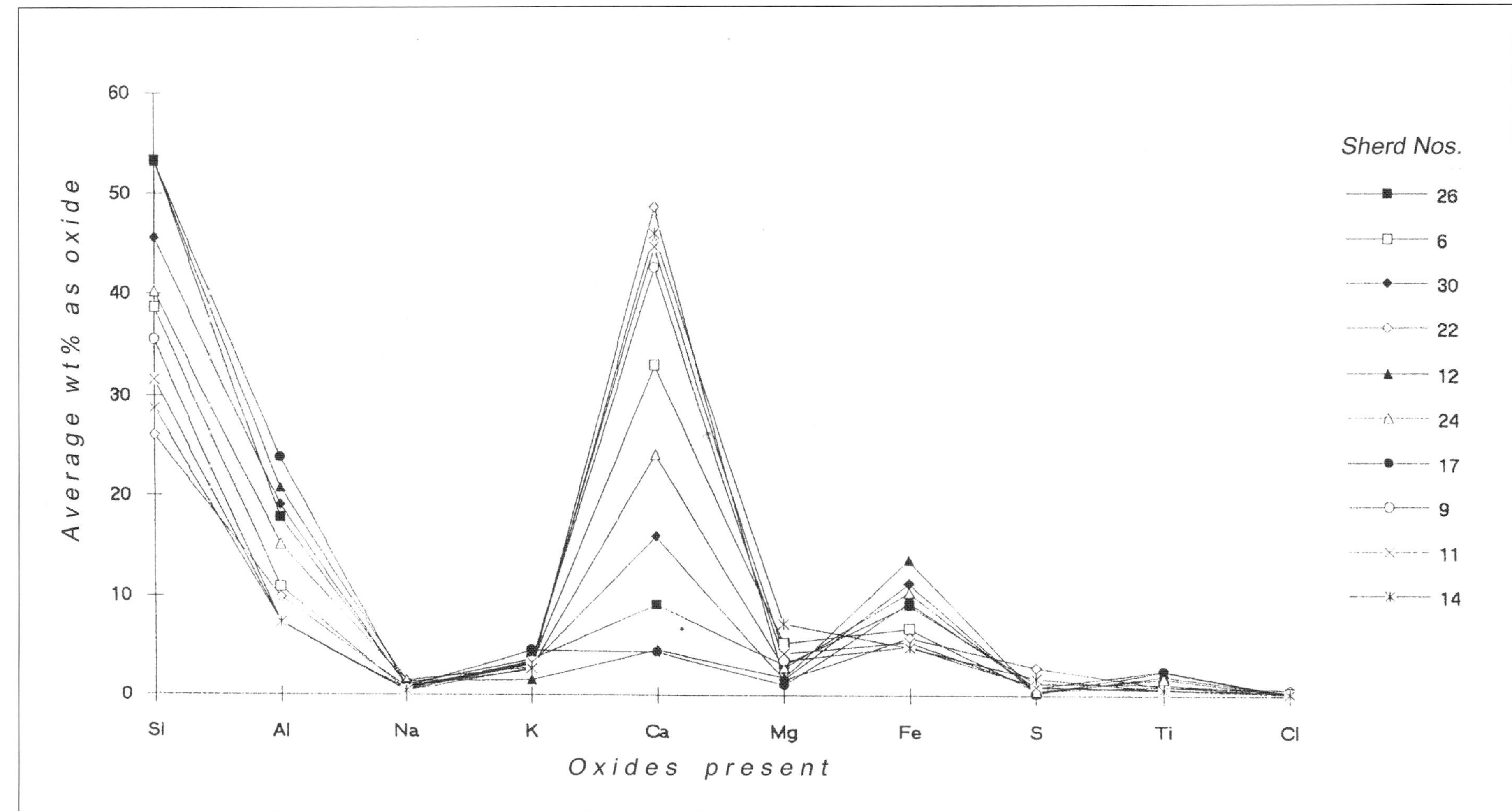

Fig. 4.62. S.E.M. clay matrix analysis (after Bettles 1994).

but for the vast majority of clasts, both the larger and the broken crystals, the shape is angular.

The carbonate grains, a characteristic of limestone, are both single and polycrystalline in section, though examples of the latter, with its polygonal internal structure, are the more frequent. Lamellae twinning under crossed polars, a feature of marble, is not apparent. The identification of particular carbonate grains can be difficult, and those with rhomb-shaped grains may possibly be dolomite.

As regards the grog, the fragments are normally of a fabric different in colour and alignment from that in which they are embedded. In one instance a piece of grog with fabric identifiable as group C type appears within a group A1 sherd. Most of the fragments are not of great size, generally about 0.5 mm in diameter, unlike some of the clay pellets, which can be well over 2 mm.

Occasionally a few fragments of chert can be discerned in the thin sections. This is a microscopically grained quartz found commonly in sedimentary rocks, and is stable and resistant to weathering. Consequently the grains are very angular in shape, with a polycrystalline surface and are fairly easy to identify.

Shell occurs mainly in small amounts in the Tell Nebi Mend thin sections and can be identified as freshwater bivalve/mollusc species, shaped in long thin curves or in thicker chunks. There is one example of a whole gastropod within the body of a sherd. Like bivalves, gastropods are common components of limestone, and they can live in freshwater, marine or brackish water.

Elemental composition

The mean results of the S.E.M. tests on ten of the sherds are displayed in Table 4.4 and in graph form in Fig. 4.62. It is apparent, especially from the latter, that there are two distinct categories of fabric. The sherds denoted by solid symbols have a comparatively high content of Si, Al, Fe and Ti, but low Ca. Open symbols are comparatively low in Si, Al, Fe and Ti, but are high in Ca. The former (*i.e.* nos 17, 12, 30 and 26) are attributed to groups B, A2, A3 and A1 respectively. The latter (*i.e.* nos 24, 6, 22, 9, 11 and 14 are attributed to groups C1 , B, D, B, D and D respectively (see Table 4.3). This bears direct relation to the petrologically defined fabric groups, where the fundamental division is based on the presence of gabbro or the high carbonate content. Gabbro clasts include Si, Al, Fe and Ti within their elemental composition, whereas carbonate is Ca-based.

Only the group B sherds are caught between both elemental categories. This also reflects the definition of the petrologically based fabric group, in that this fabric has a medium quantity of gabbro clasts and the carbonate grains are more plentiful than in the A groups. It can also be noted that there is a tendency for the B and D group sherds to be located on the extremities of the percentage range for each element. Too much emphasis cannot be put on this since the number of sherds tested is so small, but it may be some reflection of the different, fine-textured clay used in these groups. Additionally, it is noticeable how divergent is the percentage of calcia content, and therefore the covarying Si, among the sherds tested. As noted above, this is not because of the variable use of shell as temper, as little shell is in fact evident in the thin sections studied, but rather because of the abundant carbonate constituent. It seems, therefore, that the petrographic inclusions in the paste have a strong direct bearing on the elemental composition of the clay matrix.

Finally, none of the results of the S.E.M. tests are distinctly different from what might be expected to arise from the local geology, and conseqently there is no evidence that any of the sherds are not of local manufacture.

Note

1   Bettles 1994, 19–29.

5. The flint and obsidian artefacts

Lorraine Copeland†

Introduction

The lithic finds from Tell Nebi Mend to be discussed here consist of 1444 flint and obsidian artefacts (306 tools and 1138 debitage) excavated between 1982 and 1995 (Mathias and Parr 1989; Parr 1991). Of these, 354 artefacts (120 tools and 334 debitage) from the 1988 season were studied by Y. Nishiaki as part of his doctoral thesis at the Institute of Archaeology on the 'material procurement, core reduction and manufacturing processes' at Neolithic sites in Syria (Nishiaki 1992; 2000). Nishiaki paid careful attention to the technical aspects of the artefacts and the relationships of these to the various kinds of stone raw materials used to make tools and weapons. His totals are shown in our Tables 5.1 and 5.2, a summary of his conclusions will appear in the Appendix to this chapter and his results will be constantly referred to in this report. The remaining 1140 artefacts (referred to below as 'the present sample') were studied by the author. Not studied here are a number of Neolithic artefacts retrieved from post-Neolithic pits that had disturbed the Neolithic levels. All the material is stored at the Institute of Archaeology, University College London.

Although analysis of the Neolithic stratigraphy enables four broad successive phases of occupation/utilisation and one phase of abandonment to be identified, the fragmentary nature of the remains and the presence of many disturbances of both Neolithic and post-Neolithic date – as explained in Chapter 2 – make the attribution of individual artefacts to a specific phase not always reliable. In the circumstances, therefore, it has been considered advisable not to treat the flint and obsidian material from each of the five phases separately, and in the following analyses the numbers of artefacts have been amalgamated (Tables 5.1–5.4) and no attempt has been made to trace any chronological development in the material.

Raw material

The different qualities of such raw material as was apparently available to the Tell Nebi Mend flint knappers were assessed, bearing in mind that one of Nishiaki's most interesting findings was that flint blanks of different grades were used to make different tool types. For example, only the finest-grain flint was used for the arrowheads and sickle elements, while coarser-grain flint was used for burins or other heavy-duty tools. He eventually divided the artefacts into two groups, fine-grain and coarse-grain (with an intermediate group which was eventually dropped); flint colour often differed in each group. In the larger sample studied by the author, although very fine and very coarse material was easily distinguished, it proved difficult to assign large numbers of artefacts to one or the other group, especially as similar colours occurred in each group. In addition, often the original colour had clearly been altered by thermal action and so had to be classed as 'grey' or 'black'. Roughly half the artefacts are considered as coarse-grain and half as fine-grain (Table 5.3); most of the fine-grain flint is beige or varying shades of brown, but smaller percentages of grey and black, and a translucent type, are also present. The coarse-grain flint is mainly grey, beige or light brown, and there is a dense, reddish material only slightly resembling flint. Both classes include one-colour and multi-colour (mottled) specimens, including piebald (included with 'whitish'; see Table 5.3).

Primary raw material flint sources in the regions surrounding Tell Nebi Mend are apparently scarce, as has been discussed by Unger-Hamilton (1988) in connection with her study of sickles from the nearby site of Arjoune, and also by Dorrell (2003). According to the latter, the nearest known available sources are the 'short stretches of conglomerated flint gravel, presumably the relics of old shingle bars', forming small vertical cliffs east of the present course of the Orontes. However, 'some 10–15 km to the east … a series of deep seasonal wadis drain the western flanks of the Anti-Lebanon, and these wadis are at present cutting down through extensive beds of rounded cobbles, mostly flint but including other hard stone' (Dorrell 2003, 8). However, imported flint (as well as obsidian) was apparently used at Tell Nebi Mend as well as local materials since the flint-type of many artefacts does not match the types present in the gravels.

Physical condition

The present physical condition of the artefacts was found to be mainly fresh and unpatinated, with sharp edges, but a considerable number (particularly the blades) have been broken deliberately by several methods. Many pieces, including 'debris', have been damaged by heating, as can be seen by pot-lid fractures, calcination, blackened colour and fragmentation. The artefacts have not been studied by microscopy to detect use/wear.

Obsidian items are in fresh condition in colours ranging from pale grey to dense black. The sources of the obsidian have not been determined.

Technical features

Each artefact was individually examined and its technical attributes – for example, the types of butt, from which reduction techniques can be deduced – recorded (Table 5.4). The formal technical classification of the artefacts (as between flakes, blades, cores, etc.) is seen in Table 5.2.

Analysis of the retouched flint tools

The retouched tools (Table 5.1) are classified in a type-list that differs slightly from that of Nishiaki, but only as concerns the criteria for the sub-types. The obsidian artefacts are listed separately to reflect the very different nature of their manufacture and origin. It should be noted that not all the Neolithic sites mentioned in the following discussion are referenced in the bibliography; those missing are listed in Hours *et al.* 1994.

Axes (Fig. 5.3: nos 1–3)

Four axes occur in our sample and one in Nishiaki's material. All are consistent in their dimensions and basic morphology, but differ in the detail. Of the three illustrated, nos 1 and 3 have been flaked and then polished at the tip (working end) and partially down the length on both faces. They were evidently heavily used and have post-polish damage. (Nishiaki's specimen has in fact been damaged and then reshaped as a chisel.) They are made in beige chert, no. 1 having a biconvex profile and no. 3 a plano-convex profile. In contrast, no. 2 is made of coarse grey chert without polish and may be a rough-out (a large

hinge-fracture has spoiled one face, which is incompletely decorticated); this piece has vertical sides and represents a type familiar at other Neolithic sites (*e.g.* in the Néolithique Ancien of Byblos – *hache* à *pans verticaux*: Cauvin 1968, fig. 27, 1 and 2). Nos 1 and 3 correspond closely to Byblos Néolithique Ancien types (*e.g.* Cauvin's *hache plat* à *taillant droit*: Cauvin 1968, fig. 24, 1). No. 1 has traces of a black, sticky substance on both faces, which may represent bitumen used as an adhesive to attach the axe to a haft. The fourth (unillustrated) axe is a reworked specimen with traces of the original polish on one side.

As will be discussed further later, these flaked then tip-polished flint axes represent types well known in the central–coastal and southern Levant from PPNB and early Pottery Neolithic sites. They contrast with northern styles where axes were fully polished and mainly made in non-flint materials (limestone, basalt, greenstone). Curiously, the site of Labwe (which, to judge by the dates and the presence of a special cord-impressed pottery, was contemporary with Tell Nebi Mend) had non-flint axes, as did Shir and Tabbat al-Hammam. However, these were usually polished only at the tip (Kirkbride 1969; Bartl *et al.* 2006a; 2006b; Hole 1959).

Most scholars assume that Neolithic axes were hafted (see illustration in, for example, Cauvin 1968, fig. 60), and that they were hafted with the tip in line with the haft, as are modern wood-cutting axes. This is in contrast to adzes, where the tip was attached transversally, as in *herminettes* or mattocks (Unger-Hamilton 1988, 165). The function of the axes – for wood-cutting or soil cultivation, for example – has been much discussed; according to Unger-Hamilton (1988, 165), wear traces on axes from Jericho and Mureybet suggest that these were used on wood.

Pebble tool (Fig. 5.6: no. 6)

A smooth and nearly flat limestone river pebble with oval outline has been retouched at each end to produce concave areas. It has slight scratches and percussion marks on one face. It may have been used as a net-sinker or the like: compare the nearby site of Arjoune, where heavy-duty limestone tools were numerous (Copeland 2003). Similar objects occur at Ras Shamra VA and VB, where they are called *galets* à *encoches* (Contenson 1992, figs 128 and 131). (For a similar tool from Tell Nebi Mend and other heavy stone implements, see Chapter 6 and Fig. 6.4.)

One artefact may be a chopper although made on a chert flake; the distal edge was coarsely retouched to form a wavy edge.

Arrowheads (Fig. 5.1: nos 1–10)

None of the 26 projectile point specimens are intact, although no. 7 is nearly so. All but one are made on fine-grain blanks, usually in brown flint in dark to light tones. Typical Byblos and ᶜAmuq Points are present, the former characterised by a narrow tang separated from the main body by notched shoulders, as in nos 1 and 4, and the latter characterised by a smoothly tapering tang, as in no. 6. These occur mainly in the form of tang fragments which may combine attributes of both point types, as in no. 7. Some specimens are extensively pressure-flaked, either on one face (nos 2 and 10) or on both (nos 3 and 7), with the facets running obliquely across the width of the blade. Tip fragments also occur, and show the typical distal inverse pressure-flaking (nos 9 and 10). It is not clear whether the 'burin blows' seen on nos 1 and 7 are breaks due to impact fracture or to the refashioning of damaged pieces as burins (*cf.* Azoury and Bergman 1980).

In our sample the arrowheads, both as a group and individually, are closely comparable to those from the early pottery Neolithic of Byblos, as can be seen from Cauvin's publication of 1968, especially his figs 5–8. The points also closely resemble those from neighbouring Labwe, where most are invasively pressure-flaked (Mortensen n.d., fig. 1). In northern Levant terms, the styles belong to the Early Pottery Neolithic (EPN) phase and, in a larger context, to the 'Big Arrowhead Industries' of the PPNB/EPN of the 8th–7th millennia (Aurenche and Kozlowski 1999); this accords well with the radiocarbon dates from Tell Nebi Mend, of which more later.

Byblos and ᶜAmuq Points were first so named at Byblos (Cauvin 1968). Numbers of each form varied from site to site, but at Halula the ᶜAmuq types increased upwards, to dominate in the EPN ('pre-Halaf') level (Molist Montana 1996). Large specimens (sometimes called javelins or *poignards*) are found at some sites (Tabbat-al-Hammam; Janoudiyeh) and may correspond to our no. 7 from Tell Nebi Mend; but the even larger, completely pressure-flaked types, such as at Byblos (Cauvin 1968, fig. 17, pls 4 and 5), are not seen in the present sample from Tell Nebi Mend.

Sickle-blade elements (Fig. 5.2: nos 1–15)

These are the most numerous tool-type in the present sample. Blades with lustre are assumed to represent elements fixed sequentially in a haft forming a sickle and used to harvest organic material. On one Tell Nebi Mend specimen (no. 8) there was a possible trace of bitumen.

The lustred pieces were mainly made on fine-grain brown flint blades of varying widths, rarely as wide as no. 2 or as narrow as no. 6 and rarely on intact blanks, as No. 12. The most numerous element type (72 of 106, Nishiaki's pieces included) was a simple blade segment of moderate size with butt and tip snapped off, having one denticulated edge on which occurred the sickle-sheen or lustre, normally on both faces (no. 1). The next most common type had one snapped end and one end truncated by retouch (nos 3, 6 and 10). Only one piece, no. 2, had backing retouch (a style very common at other Neolithic sites, *e.g.* in the Jezirah: Copeland 1996), and only one had both ends truncated (as no. 4).

The denticulations nearly always occurred on one edge only; they were either retouched from the dorsal onto the ventral face (no. 12) or *vice versa* (nos 1, 10 and 14). Some specimens had teeth on both edges (no. 5). A few had teeth retouched on both faces of the edge, suggesting reuse, but on these the opposed teeth were ragged and thus could represent damage during use (no. 9). In fact, the teeth themselves varied from small and finely defined to large and distinct; the latter may represent heavy utilisation. No non-denticulated glossed pieces occurred.

Another common feature on the elements was the position of the lustre. This invariably occurred vertically down the length of the denticulated edge and often reached the central ridge of the blank on smaller pieces. On other specimens only the points of the teeth showed lustre (nos 6 and 12). Occasionally less lustre showed on one of the faces, or less was present at one end than at the other (nos 4 and 6). The vertical position of the lustre differentiates the Tell Nebi Mend sickle elements from those from Jezirah sites, where the lustre occurs obliquely to the blade's axis (*e.g.* at Assouad: Cauvin 1973).

Although truncations were occasionally used to segment the blades in the lowest deposits, only three out of 27 pieces were so treated in later findspots, so that a stylistic development through time cannot be proved.

The function of the denticulations on the Early Neolithic sickle elements has been discussed by, among others, Cauvin, who argues (1968, 73) that cutting edges with large teeth were more efficient at cutting reeds than cereals. The Nebi Mend inhabitants probably made use of the reeds that would have been available in the riverine and lakeside vicinities of the site not only to make arrowshafts but also for use in house building. However, the more finely toothed specimens may have been used for harvesting other plants.

Compared with the sickle-blade elements at contemporary sites in other regions, the Tell Nebi Mend sample is notable for the absence on sickle elements of both invasive pressure-flaking and backing retouch such as is common in, for example, the Damascus Basin sites. However, sickles at sites nearer to Tell Nebi Mend in the central corridor (the Beqaᶜ and the Rouj basin) do resemble it in this respect.

Shape-defined sickle-blade elements

This class is defined, following Unger-Hamilton, as consisting of blade fragments that are without lustre but closely resemble lustred sickle-blade elements. Thirteen pieces are blade segments made in the same styles as the lustred pieces but showing no glossed areas. It is assumed that these were used to cut cereals or other organic matter, although not for long enough to cause lustre (Unger-Hamilton 1988). All were denticulated but none were truncated.

Burins (Fig. 5.4: nos 1–9)

The 13 burins from Tell Nebi Mend studied by the author are made on a variety of blanks, from thick flakes to slender blades, as well as on damaged tools and fragments. They can be divided into three types: (1) dihedral right angled, as in no. 1; (2) axial, as in no. 2; and (3) simple – that is, on a break surface (as in nos 5 and 6) or on lateral preparation, the latter consisting of either retouch (no. 7) or a notch (no. 9). The first two types are usually struck transversally to the axis of the blank. Nos 1 and 5 are made on older tools – an arrowhead in the case of no. 1, a sickle-blade element in the case of no. 5. Nos 3 and 4 are composite tools, no. 3 being a 'triple' tool (notch/end-scraper/burin) while no. 5 is a denticulate/burin. Truncation and polyhedric burin types are absent.

In the assemblages studied by Nishiaki (2000) a relatively large number of burins was recognised (13.44% of the retouched tools), but the present sample produced only 7.7%. The burin ensemble is matched at Byblos in the early Neolithic phase, where the same types form 9% of the Byblos retouched tool count (Cauvin 1968, fig. 31).

End-scrapers (Fig. 5.5)

With the exception of the unique circular flake-scraper no. 1 (Fig. 5.5), the few scrapers present are roughly made and are usually combined with other tools. For example, that on no. 2 (Fig. 5.5) is combined with a notch. In particular, end-of-blade scrapers are virtually absent (two specimens). The circular scraper is made on a thick cortex flake and its butt and bulb have been removed by invasive retouch; the retouch is quite abrupt and slightly undercut. The other flake-scrapers include a side-scraper, no. 6 (Fig. 5.5), and *raclette* types (no. 2), as well as pieces that may grade into notches (no. 6).

A curious scarcity of end-scrapers also occurs at Byblos in the earliest phase, where they formed just 1% of the retouched tools, in contrast to their more numerous presence at many earlier and 'Transitional' sites, such as Tell el-Kerkh (Tsuneki *et al.* 2006), Labwe (where 'cushion-shaped' scrapers occurred), and Ramad. At Tabbat al-Hammam (Hole 1959) circular, fan-shaped and blade-scrapers were common, just as they were at earlier PPNB sites (Abu Hureyra, Halula, Mureybet IV). Should we assume that the inhabitants of Tell Nebi Mend were not processing hides or wood with end-scrapers, or at least not in the areas so far excavated? In this connection, at Halula Molist Montana (1996) has remarked on the alternance of scraper and burin percentages in the different excavated areas of the site.

Backed pieces (Fig. 5.5)

On three of these the lateral retouch is abrupt, perhaps intended to constitute a back, as on no. 5.

Notches and denticulates (Fig. 5.5)

There are 13 pieces with broad notches (*e.g.* no. 9) or with roughly denticulated edges. They are made on various blank types and include combinations with other forms such as No. 7, which has a distal *bec*.

Borers (Fig. 5.5)

The three borers are made on small blades and seem designed for piercing. More robust types such as drill bits are absent.

Splintered piece

The only specimen (not illustrated) had crushed retouch at both ends of a small flake.

Variously retouched pieces (Fig. 5.5)

Twenty-one pieces have a variety of types and amounts of retouch on their lateral edges. No. 11 is a blade fragment with bilateral pressure flaking; its original shape and function are unknown. Other specimens may have ragged and crushed edges (*e.g.* no. 10) or have alternating retouch which looks suspiciously like damage due to trampling. These are omitted from the tool count.

Analysis of the retouched obsidian tools

Corner-thinned blades (Fig. 5.5: nos 12–16)

First recognised by Nishiaki at Kashkashok, these are segments of small obsidian blades with 'burin-blows' that have thinned one, two, three or all four corners of the blade segment. Twelve specimens (henceforth referred to as CTBs) were present at Tell Nebi Mend: three with a single thinned corner, two with double (no. 13), four with triple (nos 12 and 14) and two with quadruple (nos 15 and 16) thinned corners. The 'quadruple' would correspond to positions V (for Ventral) 1/V4 in Nishiaki's scheme (2000). The longest measures 44 mm and the shortest around 12 mm. Some pieces have vertical 'burin blows' that have entirely removed one edge, while others have crushed butts or a small concave notch at one end.

It is quite surprising that this obsidian tool-type occurs as far south as Tell Nebi Mend. Hitherto, its known presence has been confined to sites in north Syria and the Jezirah dating from the late PPNB to the late Pottery Neolithic, although in the latter phase (Sabi Abyad I) they are rare (Copeland 1996). The type has recently been recognised at, for example, Halula (Molist Montana 1996), Sabi Abyad II (Copeland 2000) and numerous sites in the Balikh Valley. It would be interesting if the collections from other excavated Central Corridor sites such as Labwe, Hama M, or coastal Sukas could be re-examined to see if CTBs were present there also but up until now not noticed.

Laterally retouched pieces

Nine small obsidian blades or segments have nibbling or semi-abrupt lateral (in one case, bilateral) retouch. This may have been made deliberately or it may be the result of 'utilisation'.

Analysis of the flint debitage: cores, by-products and unretouched waste

Cores (Fig. 5.6: nos 1–5)

(Cores reused as axes are excluded from the 'core' list.)

The 11 cores are so extensively worked down that one can only speculate as to their original form and as to the knapping techniques used to produce the blanks; they represent the final stage of the reduction process with average dimensions as seen in Fig. 6.5. This may explain why a typical PPNB/EPN core-type, the naviform blade-core, was absent in the sample.

The blanks were mainly rounded river pebbles. Two were patinated older pieces, which may also have been retrieved from terrace gravels. In the present assemblage eight cores are exhausted discoidal bases, where the last removals were small flakes (nos 1 and 5). Three are small prismatic specimens (no. 2), one being made on an older (patinated) artefact (no. 4). Nishiaki, who studied the Tell Nebi Mend cores in his sample in depth, also found them to be scarce and worked down. Besides the discoid core bases he also noted a change-of-orientation type but no prismatic specimens. As with our sample, the cores were small, the largest measuring 60 × 50 mm and the smallest 25 × 25 mm (Nishiaki 2000).

The presence of flakes, blades and by-products clearly show that a variety of core-reduction methods were used to produce them. For example, the long, narrow blades of fine-grain flint used for arrowheads and sickle-blade elements must have come from blade-cores (only traces of which are now present) of both single platform (unipolar) and opposed platform (bipolar) type, although it is also possible that the smaller blades of fine flint were produced from conical (prismatic) core types with flat bases, such as were used in the Near East since the late Palaeolithic. The cresting method of core preparation was used, as was the removal of overhang to revive core-platforms. Although no hammerstones were present in this sample, hard hammer percussion was evidently used to produce many of the flakes with large butts (no. 1) and soft hammers must have been employed to strike off the blades with punctiform butts. To carry out the pressure flaking some kind of punch must have been used.

A similar poverty of cores has been noted by authors as occurring at other EPN sites. At Halula cores formed only 1.67% of the PPNB assemblages, and the knappers often merely used Euphrates river terrace pebbles of suitable shape. It was suggested that these were not the blanks for producing the blades of fine-grain flint, which may have been imported ready-made (Molist Montana 1996); however, unlike the Tell Nebi Mend sample, naviform cores were present at Halula. Cauvin illustrates some bladelet cores that might correspond to our prismatic types, although more reduced (Cauvin 1968, fig. 33). Cores at Rouj basin sites were varied and include bipolar types with transverse back preparation as well as prismatic and naviform cores

(Iwasaki and Tsuneki 2003). The cores from Balikh sites (*e.g.* Damishliyya) are, according to Nishiaki (Appendix 5.1), comparable to those from Tell Nebi Mend – that is, similarly scarce and without naviform types. He, too, points out that the differences between flake- and blade-production technologies that are often evidenced at early Neolithic sites are so marked as to suggest that they represent different industries or importation of the blades from elsewhere (Nishiaki 2000).

By-products

There are 25 by-products: five burin spalls, 13 core edge revival flakes (Fig. 5.5, no. 9) and seven tool refreshment flakes (Fig. 5.6, no. 7). The distinction between the last two categories is not always clear. All are small and have the retouch along one edge rather than two, as would be the case with normal crested flakes. Nishiaki reported two crested flakes in his sample and concluded that crest removal was done only after the core had been much reduced (Nishiaki 2000).

The presence of this group shows that knapping procedures such as tool repair and core revival took place at the site.

Products (unretouched non-cortex flint flakes)

It is difficult to determine whether the Tell Nebi Mend industry was flake- or blade-dominated. Most of the 86 unretouched non-cortex flint flakes are small and broken, sometimes owing to heating, as shown by, for example, pot-lid fractures. Both they and the small preparation-flakes (102 pieces less than 30 mm in diameter) have varied, but predominantly plain or punctiform, butt forms (Table 5.4). A few larger pieces are present but these usually retain some cortex (*cf.* Fig. 5.4, no. 9).

There are 19 unretouched cortex flakes and 68 un-retouched part-cortex flakes which form 25.9% of the unretouched flake debitage. This is a relatively modest number. Perhaps initial core-peeling procedures took place elsewhere in the village, or off-site altogether. No pieces are large and most were fashioned of coarse-grain flint. Only five cortex flakes were used to make tools (Fig. 5.5, no. 1).

Only 69 of the unretouched blades were intact, the rest (139) consisting of segments, tips and butts. Segments predominate and, just as at other Neolithic sites in the Near East, a variety of methods was used to detach the central segment of the blade: notching, snapping, percussion and so on (Azoury and Bergman 1980). As Table 5.4 shows, most breaks must have been made by soft hammer, punch or pressure techniques. Punctiform butts form almost 45% of the recognisable butts. Only one example of a characteristic feature seen on PPNB blades, the proximal ventral scar, was present and only one wide-ended 'Upsilon blade' was noted (Calley 1988).

There are 130 unretouched fragments that appear to be artefacts but may be parts of either flakes or blades.

Debris

This group of consists of 99 small, ill-defined pieces including burned fragments and chunks.

Natural stones

There are 30 natural, mainly intact, pebbles with smooth faces and dark patinas, which may have formed part of the gravelly topsoil. A relatively larger number (122) was noted by Nishiaki in his material. This group is not included when artefact percentages are computed.

Analysis of the obsidian debitage

Only one very small and amorphous core was present. There were also two by-products (spalls) and 20 unretouched products (two being flakes, the rest blades).

Summary and conclusions

As a whole, the flint assemblage clearly refers to that of the 8th–6th millennia PPNB/EPN culture of the central Fertile Crescent, the latter part of which is distinguished from the first by the presence of ceramics and is sometimes known as ᶜAmuq A (as at Judaidah). The lithics of both ceramic and aceramic phases have more recently been combined as the 'Big Arrowhead Industries (BAI)' by Aurenche and Kozlowski (1999). The calibrated radiocarbon dates from Tell Nebi Mend (see Chapter 2 and Fig. 2.26), spanning the period between the very late 8th and the middle of the 7th millennium with 95.4% probability, would place the assemblages in the second phase of the long span of the BAI, herein referred to as the EPN.

From the range of tool types one can conclude that the inhabitants belonged to a hunting and farming community (see the flora and fauna reports, Chapters 7 and 8) that had settled beside the river, or possibly a lake, in the upper Orontes Valley. It is not known if PPNB deposits exist, as yet unfound, below the EPN, as they do at Labwe.

The above-mentioned dates indicate that the settlement was in existence during the long period of transition when certain (but not all) of the northern/central Levant villages were undergoing cultural adaptations such as the adoption of ceramics. We find that PPNB folk were sometimes the last to occupy a site, while at others the founding inhabitants were pottery-using groups (*e.g.* Byblos), of which Tell Nebi Mend and Judaidah may or may not be examples. At yet other sites in both northern and central areas the stratigraphy shows continuity from aceramic to ceramic traditions, as at Bouqras, Assouad, Damishliyya, Halula, Ramad, and Labwe. Here the PPNB was directly overlain by levels containing broadly similar lithics, but with the addition of pottery and/or 'White Ware'.

As to the main tool types, as noted above, tanged arrowheads of Byblos and ᶜAmuq Points type are regarded as the defining features of the stone repertoire and have given rise to the term 'BAI'. The projectile points suggest that the hunting of wild fauna continued (see Chapter 7). Although Naviform core techniques (as used in the PPNB to fashion points) are absent at Tell Nebi Mend, perhaps at least partly because of the absence of suitable raw material, the point styles were clearly related to those of the PPNB cultures, especially those in northern Fertile Crescent sites. Tanged Byblos and ᶜAmuq type points were used until the end of the EPN/ᶜAmuq A phase. Only a few fragmentary specimens occur in sites of the Late Neolithic/ᶜAmuq B, such as at Tell Nebi Mend's neighbour, Arjoune (Copeland 2003).

Farming and/or harvesting activities are evidenced by the numerous sickle-blade elements at Tell Nebi Mend. They include types that seem to be regionally and temporally diagnostic – that is, limited to EPN sites in the central Levant: the sickle blades are unlike the PPNB forms, where long, usually unretouched blades were used, as at Sa'aideh in the Beqaᶜ (Hours 1969). They also differ, as the vertical position of the lustre indicates, from those in Jezirah sites both in the PPNB and the EPN, such as Halula (Molist Montana 1996), Assouad (Cauvin 1973) and Sabi Abyad II (Copeland and Verhoeven 1997). At the last two sites the lustre occurs obliquely across the blank, indicating that the elements were mounted in curved rather than straight hafts, and most often the elements were attached with a bitumen adhesive. The straight position of the lustre at Tell Nebi Mend is the same as that at Byblos and neighbouring Labwe. Curiously, at Tell el-Kerkh both lustre positions occur (reflecting its location between the Jezirah and the Central Corridor?).

The distinctive denticulated cutting edges of the sickle elements is another characteristic of EPN sites in the central Levant (Byblos, Labwe, Ramad) and to a certain extent in the southern Levant (Sha'ar ha-Golan). As mentioned earlier, the denticulations may have had to do with use on hard material such as reeds. Truncations on sickle elements appear far more rarely at EPN sites in the southern Levant (*e.g.* Byblos, Ramad III, Sha'ar ha-Golan), while unretouched truncations are more common at northern sites (Judaidah, Ras Shamra VB). Together with Labwe, Tell Nebi Mend seems to 'have a foot in both camps' as regards this feature.

One could say the same for the two main tool-types at Tell Nebi Mend: the arrowheads refer stylistically to northern/central Syria, and the sickles – at least in the way they were hafted – to the central Levant/Tripoli Gap area.

A few flint axes are present in the assemblages, and may indicate (if used for felling trees) that forested areas existed close to the river and the village; these must have included gallery forests of poplar and plain trees such as still occur today in the Orontes bottom land and in the gorges between Homs and Hama (Dorrell 2003). The numerous burins present, if used for woodworking, tend to reinforce this supposition. As mentioned earlier, burins were present at contemporary EPN sites such as Byblos and Qalᶜat el-Mudiq in the Ghab, while end-scrapers were mysteriously scarce; this was not the case in northern Syrian sites, such as Neolithic 2 at Abu Hureyra (Moore 1981). Compared with the often rich scraper component in other EPN sites in the region (*e.g.* at Tabbat al-Hammam), the poor scraper sample at Tell Nebi Mend may indicate that the inhabitants were not processing hides or wood, or at least not in the parts of the site so far excavated.

Most surprising is the finding of the obsidian CTBs at Tell Nebi Mend. So far as we know, this is the southernmost instance of the presence of this enigmatic tool-type. It is clearly a northern form, occurring prolifically in Jeirah sites of the Pre-Halaf/Halaf transition period such as Assouad, Damishliyya, Kashkashok II (Nishiaki 1990; Molist Montana 1996, fig. 7,18), Halula (Molist Montana 1996) and Sabi Abyad II (Copeland 2000) and continuing, albeit less frequently, into the Late Neolithic, as at Sabi Abyad I (Copeland 1996). The Nebi Mend inhabitants, therefore, had some kind of contact with settlements to the north, but whether this was direct or whether, as with other obsidian artefacts, the obsidian was traded 'down the line' from its far-away sources in Anatolia has not been established. A specimen from Tell Nebi Mend could usefully be analysed to see which Anatolian zone was involved. Certain CTBs have attributes such as the crushing of the butt and/or tip that were not seen by this writer in Balikh sites. The function of CTBs is unknown, although it has been suggested that they represented small burins or a way of thinning blades in order to insert them into hafts (Nishiaki 1990). These artefacts were not listed among the various boundary- or territory-defining characteristics of the Neolithic by Aurenche and Kozlowski (2005).

As to the debitage, in his dissertation on the north Syrian Neolithic lithics, Nishiaki (2000) focused on the technical aspects of stone tool use as seen in the northern Levant. He noted that the change from blade-orientated to flake-orientated technical methods came about towards the latter part of the EPN span, seemingly concurrent with the increased use of pottery. He suggested that a combination of factors may have led to the change: an increase in dependence on produced food in contrast to that hunted; an increase in other hunting methods (traps, nets, bolas, wood weapons); less time spent on flint knapping and more on agriculture; and the break-down of imported flint distribution networks. Explanations such as these could well explain the rather poor assemblage of debitage flakes and broken blades at Tell Nebi Mend.

To sum up, taking the whole of the Levant in consideration, the Tell Nebi Mend stone tool repertoires show an interesting mix of both northern Levant (*e.g.* CTBs) and certain southern/central Levant stylistic traits (*e.g.* flaked flint axes), which is perhaps not surprising given the 'crossroads' position of the *tell* in the Homs–Tripoli Gap arena. For the moment we lack evidence at the site itself either of the villagers' antecedents (the PPNB?) or of their final fate (there is at least a thousand-year gap between them and the Late Neolithic occupiers of adjacent Arjoune; see Chapter 4; Parr 2003).

Tell Nebi Mend in its region

Until about 40 years ago Neolithic settlements in the Gap region were scarce (Hama M, Tabbat al-Hammam) or absent; the area between the coast and Homs on both sides of the Syrian–Lebanese border seemed to form a frontier zone between the northern and southern Levant. However, surveys carried out since then and recent excavations produced both aceramic and ceramic sites (Tell Nebi Mend itself, Labwe, Hmaira, Shir). Ongoing work in the Homs–Tripoli Gap area (including the Bouqeia basin) has resulted in the finding of possibly PPNB and numerous EPN and Late Neolithic sites (Haidar-Boustani *et al.* 2007). The EPN appears to be related to ᶜAmuq A and Byblos. Other Orontes valley sites further north have been re-evaluated (Hama M, Qalᶜat el-Mudiq). An entirely unknown complex of PPNB and EPN sites has been found and excavated in the Rouj basin (*e.g.* Tell el-Kerkh, Tell ᶜAin el-Kerkh, Riz). It appears, then, that the Tell Nebi Mend settlement was far from isolated and that it, with its neighbours – albeit with their own characteristics – formed a part of the widely dispersed Big Arrowhead Industries of Aurenche and Kozlowski (2005).

The fact that there is a ceramic feature (cord-impressed pottery) distinctive to this area suggests that a 'mini-province' of perhaps related populations lived here during the early Pottery Neolithic period (for pottery comparisons see Chapter 4). This consisted of Tell Nebi Mend's nearest neighbours, some of whom occupied Tell Labwe, located at the northern end or 'vestibule' of the Beqaᶜ valley. It is a large but low *tell* beside a powerful spring, one of the sources of the Orontes. It was discovered (a road cutting revealed pits, plastered floors and ash layers) by the present writer and P. Wescombe in 1964, and was subsequently excavated by D. Kirkbride (1969). It is characterised by the frequent use of white lime plaster to make floors, containers and furniture in the second level. Pottery appeared in Level III. The Labwe flint industry was compared to those of Ramad and Byblos by Mortensen (n.d.) and, as we have seen, there are close comparisons between the lithics of Labwe and Tell Nebi Mend.

Similarities can be seen between Tell Nebi Mend and the huge *tell* at Hama, which also has a historic overburden and is also located in the Orontes flood plain. The discovery of the Neolithic occupation in layer M at Hama was largely fortuitous, owing to the presence of the cistern G11X. This allowed access to the prehistoric levels, attributed at the time of discovery to *c.*6000 BC uncalibrated (Thuesen and Riis 1988). The Neolithic sample from Hama M includes flint and obsidian blades and an ᶜAmuq Point, while the sherds consist of DFBW and impressed/incised types reminiscent of ᶜAmuq A and Byblos; one sherd appears to represent the distinctive cord-impressed decoration method mentioned above and one pot was lined with white plaster. We could assume that the Neolithic at Hama M and Tell Nebi Mend were broadly contemporary.

The site of Shir was located by a German/Syrian team on the Nahr Sarut, a left-bank Orontes tributary 12 km north-west of Hama (Bartl *et al.* 2006a). Described as a large, exclusively ceramic Neolithic settlement, it was found thanks to a bulldozer section and was subsequently excavated, revealing 6 m of both EPN/ᶜAmuq A and Late Neolithic/ᶜAmuq B layers that were radiocarbon dated to between about 7000 cal BC and 6400 cal BC. Present were small structures with lime plastered floors and walls, ash layers, pits and burials (some with missing skulls) (Bartl *et al.* 2006b). The flint material included many sickle-blade elements, scrapers and rare Byblos and ᶜAmuq Points. There were stone axes, and the ceramics included DFBW (one sherd described as 'cord-impressed'), coarse ware and white lime plaster wares, the whole compared to those of Kerkh, Byblos and Judaidah.

Further down the Orontes Valley in the Ghab basin is the ᶜAmuq A/B site at Qalᶜat el-Mudiq (Apamea) (Balty and Zakzouk 1970). Yet further north of the Gap area but still in the Orontes drainage, the Japanese excavations in the Rouj basin have revealed a number of large PPNB and EPN sites along the easternmost 'arm' of the Levantine corridor.

As noted above, the Tell Nebi Mend settlement was linked to the west and the Mediterranean coast through the Homs–Tripoli Gap. The recent surveys of a Spanish/Lebanese/Syrian team took place west of Homs and included the Boqueia basin margins. Several large multi-period sites were found dating to the Natufian, Neolithic and Early Bronze periods. Two sites reported by the survey team are Tell el-Marj on the eastern Boqueia margin, and Tell Ezou near Lake Qattina, both of which had late PPNB and EPN material (Haidar-Boustani *et al.* 2007 and references therein); certain types were likened to those of the later site of Arjoune (Parr 2003).

The apparently contemporary coastal site known as Tabbat al-Hammam (Hole 1959) contained, beside the cord-impressed pottery already mentioned, typical ᶜAmuq A materials such as tanged points and javelins, flaked flint axes, DFBW and impressed/incised pottery of Byblos type. At the time Hole noted that the assemblage seemed to refer more to Byblos and Palestine than to the ᶜAmuq. Another site is Hmaira, in the ᶜAkkar Plain north of Tripoli, found by the German/Syrian team (Müller-Neuhof 1998). It is an EPN site with BAI stone tools and DFBW and cord-impressed ceramics. Tabbat al-Hammam and Hmaira form part of the north–south chain of EPN/ᶜAmuq A settlements that occur along the coasts of Lebanon and Syria. Curiously, only two of them seem to have been preceded by a PPNB phase (Tel aux Scies and Ras Shamra VC).

Tell Nebi Mend may also have had cultural connections to the east. From the Homs basin there is an easy passage alongside the Palmyrides to inland Syria: from Palmyra via the desert highways to Mesopotamia; or to the Euphrates and the Balikh via El-Kowm. Both EPN and PPNB communities flourished in these regions (*cf. e.g.* Akkermans 1990: Fujii *et al.* 1987). The frequent use of white plaster (although in this case gypsum rather than lime plaster) at, for example, El-Kowm 1 and 2, as well as similar lithics and ceramics, links these settlements with both the Syrian and the Mesopotamian Euphrates sites.

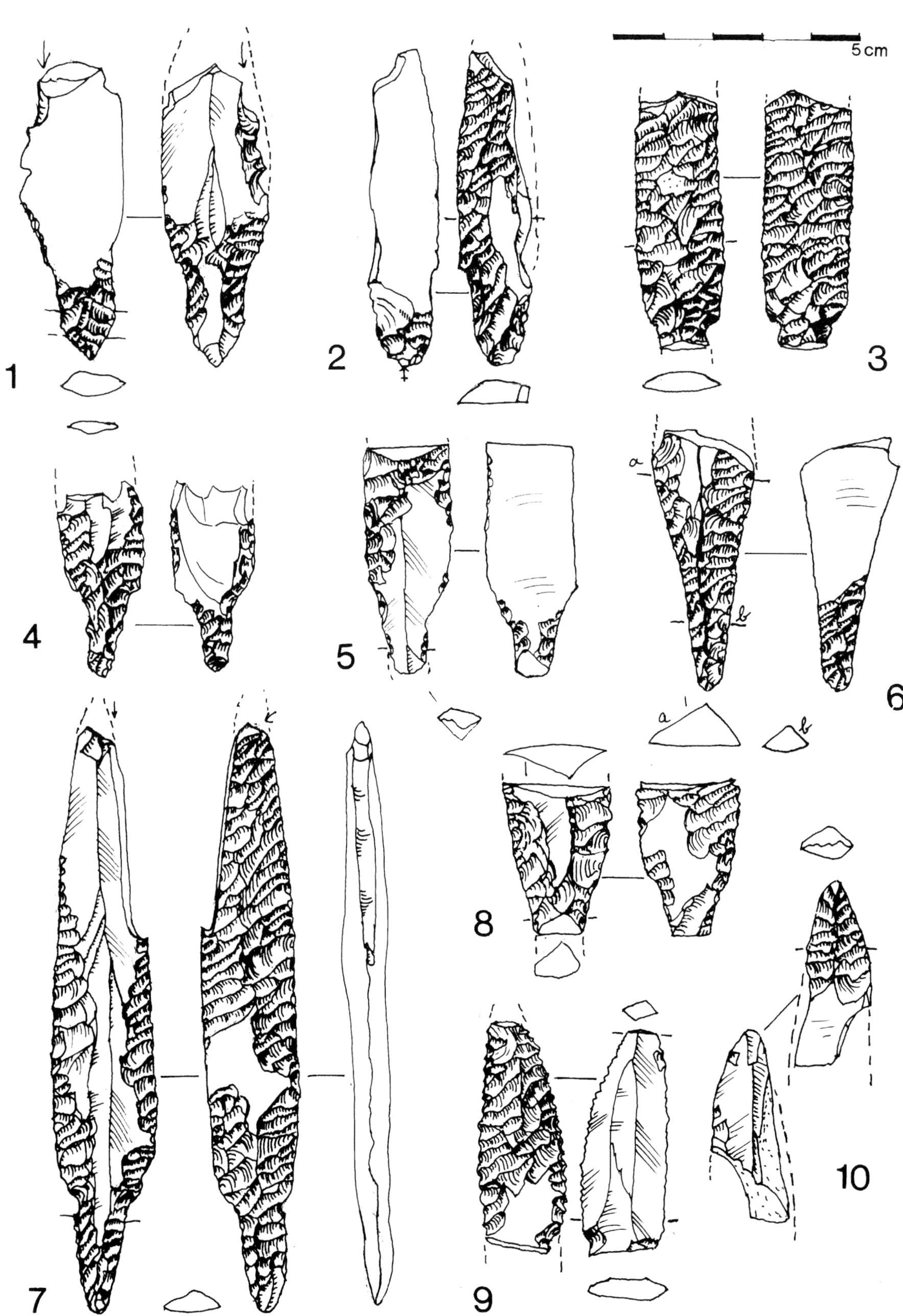

Figure 5.1

Projectile points

1	706.22	Tang of Byblos Point. Brown.
2	706.22	Broken Amuq Point. Light brown.
3	706.43	Mid-section of thin, bifacially-pressure-flaked point. Whitish.
4	606.11	Tang of Byblos Point. Dark brown.
5	707.1	Tang of Byblos Point. Light brown.
6	Unstratified	Tang of Amuq Point. Light brown.
7	706.24	Amuq point with broken tip in form of burin blow. Light brown.
8	706.17	Tang fragment of possible Amuq Point on a crested blade. Dark brown.
9	709.4	Distal portion of point with inverse pressure-flaking. Beige.
10	709.1	Tip fragment of Byblos Point with typical inverse tip retouch. Dark brown.

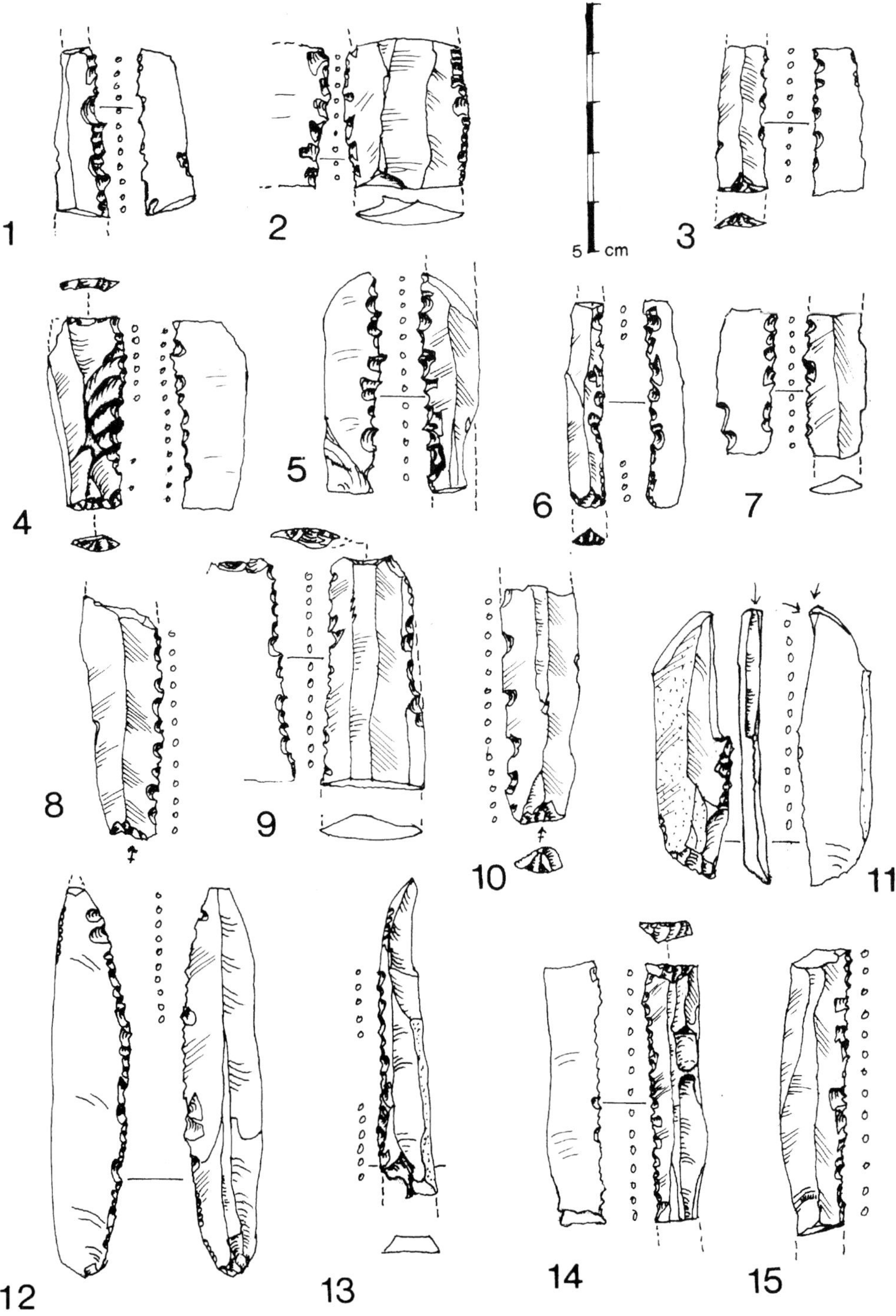

Figure 5.2

Sickle-blade elements (vertical lines of circles indicate gloss on both sides of edge in the positions shown, except in the case of No. 1, which has inverse gloss only).

1	735.1	Blade segment with ragged teeth, two snaps, inverse gloss. Brown.
2	605.59	Wide blade segment, teeth one edge, abrupt retouch on other, slight gloss. Dark brown.
3	735.6	Blade segment truncated by retouch one end, small teeth on the inverse. Light brown.
4	706.22	Segment, both ends truncated, more glossed on ventral than dorsal edge. Brown mottled.
5	708.1	Well-defined teeth on blade segment obliquely snapped one end. Black.
6	644.43	Narrow blade segment, truncated one end, slight gloss, teeth mainly on inverse. Brown.
7	709.4	Blade segment, teeth mainly on inverse edge, slight damage other edge. Grey-brown.
8	706.42	Truncated blade butt, fine regular teeth, trace of bitumen. Grey-brown.
9	654.7	Wide segment, one truncated end, fine teeth on inverse opposed to ragged retouch. Light brown, coarse grain.
10	706.22	Truncated blade with widely spaced teeth. Beige.
11	646.3	Cortex-sided blade butt with distal end retouched into a dihedral burin, rest of edge heavily glossed. Beige.
12	602.27	Intact blade with very fine teeth on the inverse, slight gloss one side. Dark brown.
13	708.5	Tip of twisted blade, cortex back, slight gloss on one edge. Grey.
14	706.42	Truncated segment with fine teeth. Brown.
15	735.7	Tip of snapped, finely toothed blade. Beige.

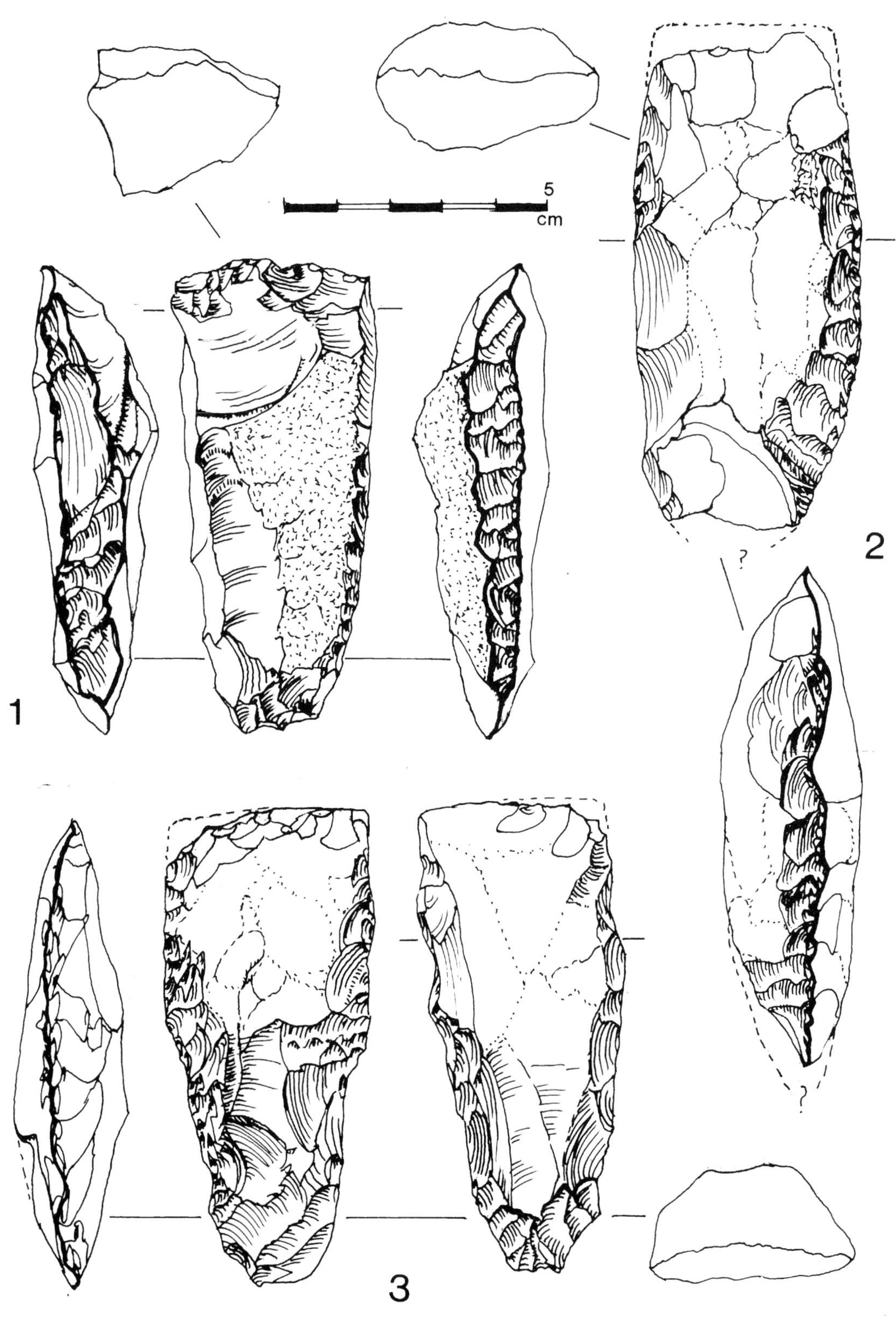

Figure 5.3

Axes (white areas and dotted lines indicate polished areas, unshaded facets indicate post-polish damage).

1   647.1   Partially polished axe with straight bit and biconvex profile; the base is missing. Traces of a black, sticky substance occur on both faces. Beige chert.

2   798.4   Unpolished axe with straight bit and vertical sides, possibly incompletely fashioned. Coarse grained greyish chert.

3   602.19   Partially polished axe with plano-convex profile and straight bit. Beige chert.

Lorraine Copeland

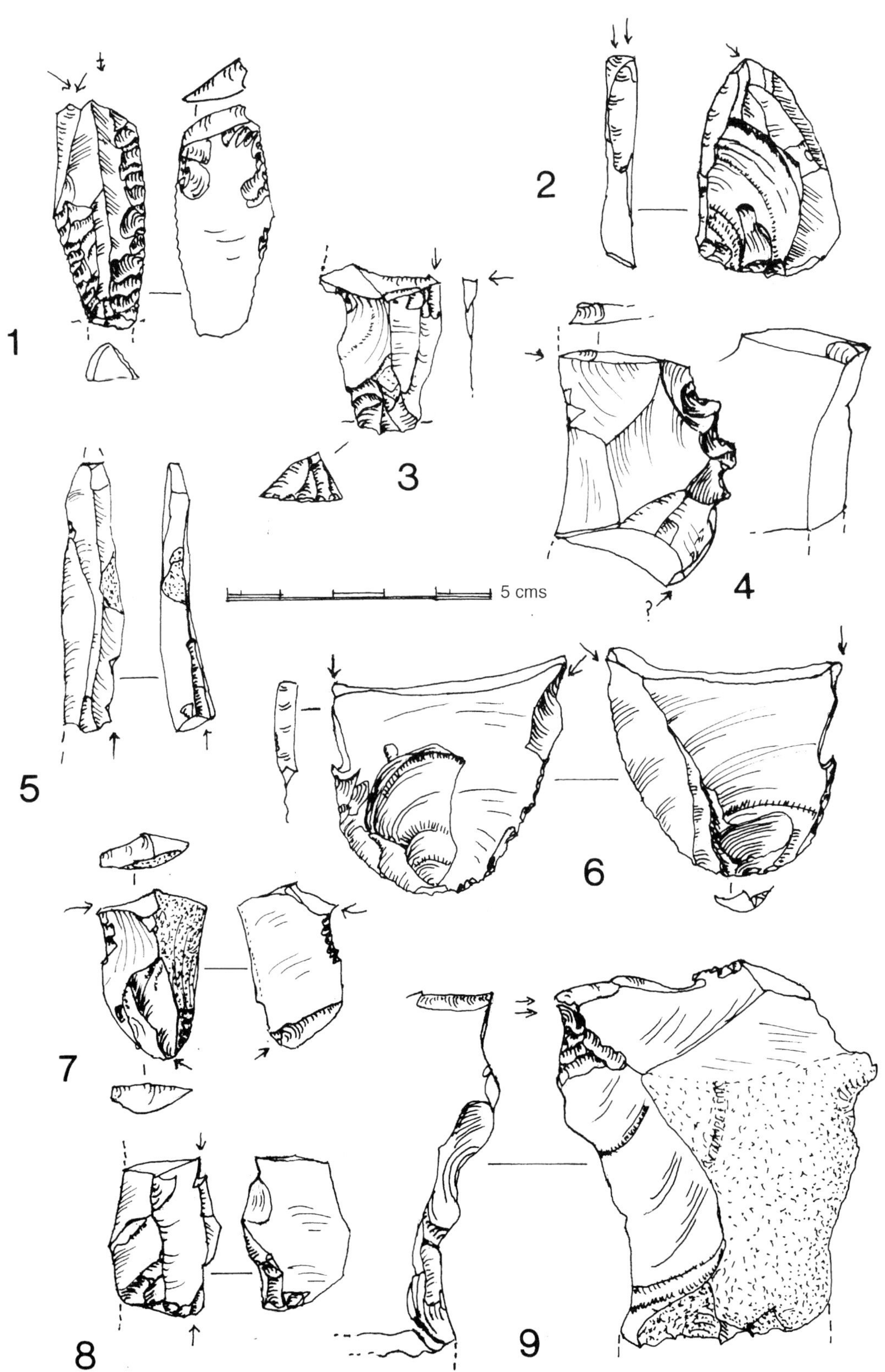

Figure 5.4

Burins.

1	735.3	Right angle dihedral burin on the mid-section of a pressure-flaked arrowhead. Blackish.
2	706.11	Axial dihedral burin on a flake. Whitish.
3	706.3	Right angle dihedral burin on a thick fragment with pronounced notch and opposed end-scraper. Beige chert.
4	735.3	Burin on a break-surface; the blank is a thick fragment with large denticulations. Dark brown.
5	643.3	Dihedral burin on a small blade with traces of gloss. Beige, coarse-grained.
6	735.8	Double dihedral burin, the burin blows struck at right angles to a distal break. Black.
7	646.2	Double burin, transverse on lateral preparation both ends. Beige.
8	709.1	Double burin on break-surfaces, on same edge. Translucent brown.
9	709.1	Right angle burin on lateral notch, made on a large cortex flake. Coarse brown.

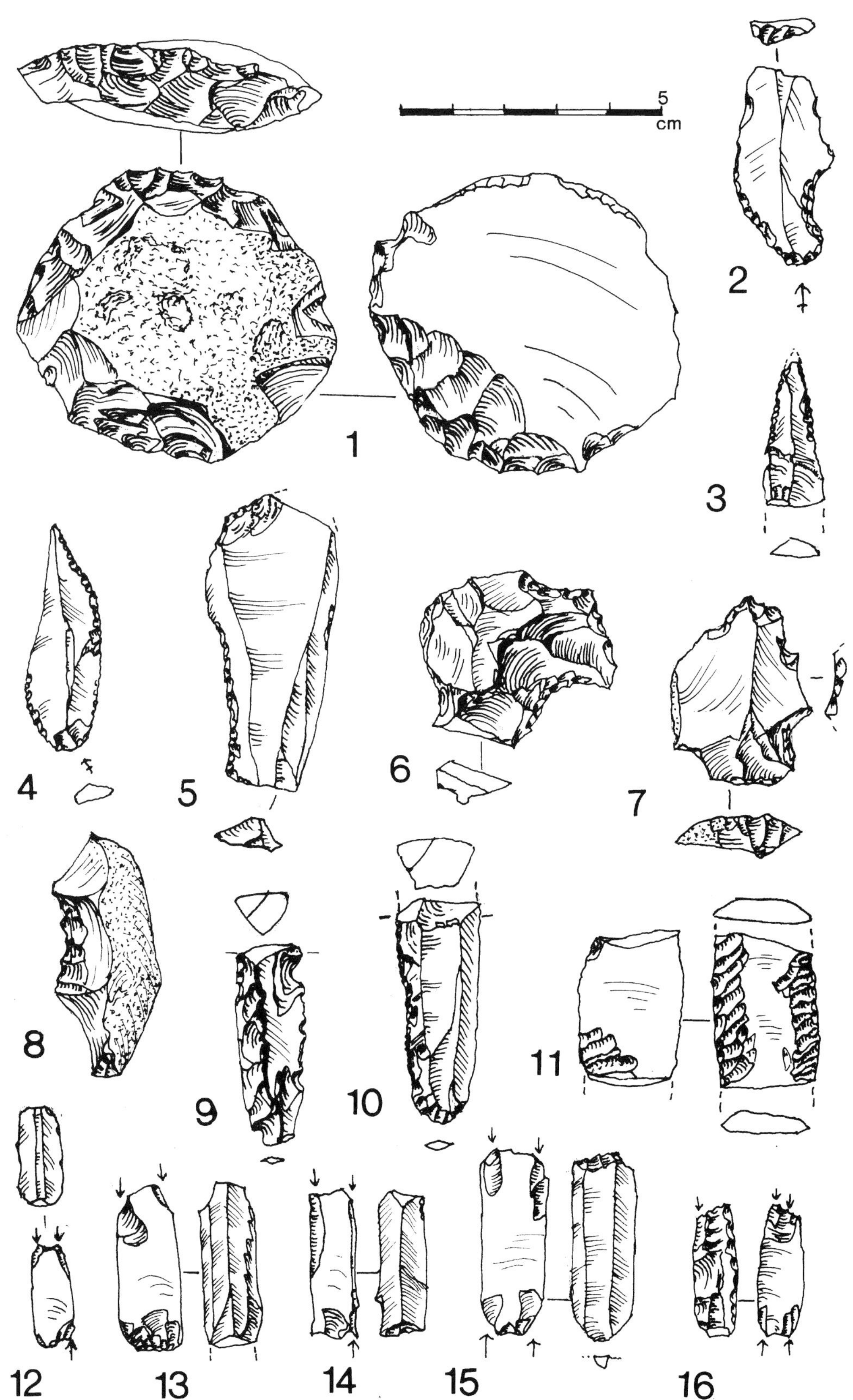

Figure 5.5

Various flint and obsidian tools.

1	709.29	Circular scraper on a thick cortex flake with butt and bulb removed and a little undercut (*cf.* fan-scraper). Coarse beige chert.
2	648.5	Raclette type side-scraper with concave notch. Dark brown.
3	709.3	Borer on a small blade. Beige.
4	709.3	Borer on a small pointed flake. Dark brown.
5	646.10	Backed blade, truncated, with traces of distal end-scraper retouch. Brown.
6	709.14	Concave side-scraper on a core-refreshment flake. Coarse beige.
7	647.1	Denticulate with bec on a part-cortex flake. Translucent.
8	706.18	Notch on a cortex-backed flake. Coarse beige chert.
9	735.10	Notch on a core-edge blade. Chestnut.
10	706.34	Thick blade butt with ragged. Piebald flint abrupt lateral retouch.
11	606.16	Blade segment made trapezoidal by bilateral pressure-flaking. Whitish.
12	606.17	Obsidian: small triple corner-thinned blade (CTB). Pale grey.
13	735.4	CTB, double on same end with retouched base.
14	606.16	CTB, triple with truncated base.
15	735.14	CTB, quadruple on a blade with distal truncation.
16	706.42	CTB, quadruple with fine lateral retouch and truncated base.

Lorraine Copeland

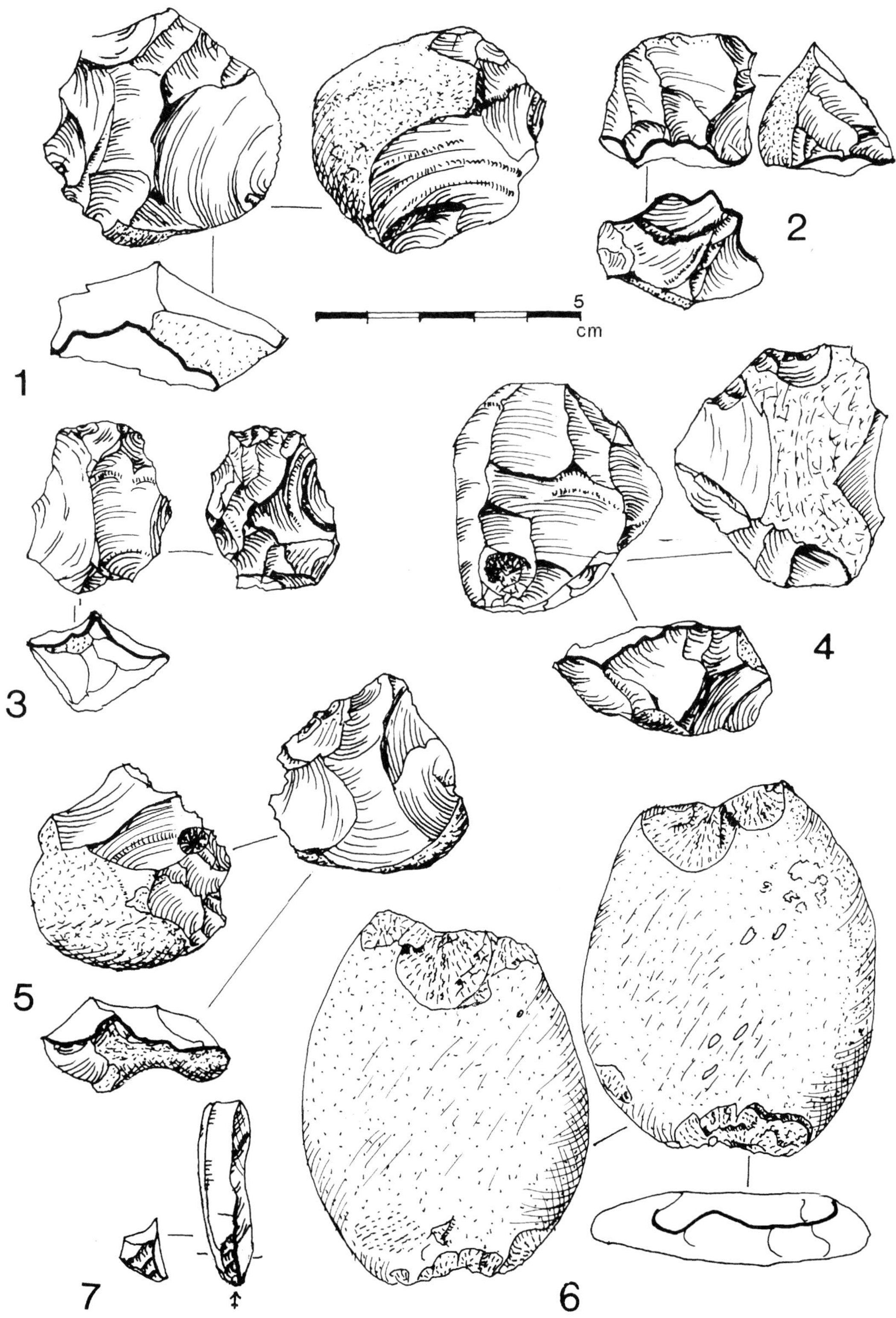

Figure 5.6

Cores.

1	706.22	Exhausted discoid core on a pebble. Translucent
2	706.22	Prismatic core for blades, refreshed base. Light brown, coarse.
3	709.21	Exhausted discoid core, fully flaked base. Black.
4	735.3	Unipolar semi-prismatic core on older artefact. Brown.
5	706.22	Exhausted discoid core on pebble. Beige.
6	706.26	Smoothed thin river pebble of limestone, perhaps a 'net-sinker', with opposed distal/proximal notches and traces of percussion and scratching.
7	735.10	Refreshment flake possibly for end-scraper revival. Dark brown.

Appendix 5.1

Summary of the study by Y. Nishiaki of the 1988 season's lithics from Tell Nebi Mend

Although he examined and classified the artefacts into retouched pieces (tools) and unretouched pieces (debitage) in the conventional way, Nishiaki (2000, 132–58) carried out a particularly detailed analysis of the technologies used by the flintknappers when fashioning the artefacts. The emphasis on the technological aspect derived from the wider context of his research into 'material procurement, core reduction and the manufacturing processes at Neolithic sites in Syria'; the other sites he studied included Douara Cave II, Damishliyya, Kashkashok, Abu Hureyra and Assouad (Nishiaki 2000, 2). He felt that the technical aspect of artefact production had too often been neglected by authors in favour of typological studies of particular tool forms.

At Tell Nebi Mend raw material flint sources were scarce (see above). The types of flint seen in the collection showed considerable variability in colour, texture and grain size, from fine-grain (yellow-brown, dark brown or black, reddish-grey or grey) through medium-grain (brownish, grey, pale brown) to coarse-grain (translucent, coarse matt in brownish-grey to pale brown) and included also 'miscellaneous' pieces (thermally affected). These types occurred to the tune of 10–19% each. It appeared that a strongly patterned technological variability was observable between the flint types and subject classes at Tell Nebi Mend, just as was the case at Tell Damishliyya (Nishiaki 2000, 125–6). For example, fine-grain flint was utilised for most of the blades and blade tools, while coarse and medium flint was used for tools made of flakes, cortical flakes and cores. Thus two distinct technological/behavioural patterns are represented, which Nishiaki studied separately.

Understanding the reduction sequence of the fine-grain flints was difficult owing to the absence of cores. It seemed probable that the fine-grain pieces were imported in the form of ready-made blanks or cores. Examination of the butts, facet patterns and so on on the artefacts suggested that soft-hammer or even punch flaking was used on bipolar cores after expert core preparation.

The coarse-grain flints, on the other hand, may have been procured from a local source of pebbles (Unger-Hamilton 1988, 117–8) and knapped on site. The cores resemble Levallois types; they were extensively worked down and knapped on the flat surface of the pebble in a variety of directions to produce a series of cortical and non-cortical flakes (oval, rectangular, expanding or triangular in almost equal proportions) as well as a few short, broad flakes (Nishiaki 2000, 147). Some were apparently heat-treated, perhaps intentionally.

The material studied by Nishiaki resembles very closely that found during the other excavation seasons at Tell Nebi Mend. His totals have been included in the technological and typological classifications listed in Tables 5.1 and 5.2

of the present report. The retouched tools (120 specimens and seven retouch spalls) consisted of the following types:

Points: Eight pieces were fragments of Byblos Points or ͨAmuq Points, some with invasive pressure flaking and retouched tang, others with less retouch; they were made on fine-grain flint blades, one with traces of bitumen (Nishiaki 2000, 147). One had a burin-like break at the tip that may represent impact fracture (Bergman and Newcomer 1983).

Sickle elements: The 42 pieces showed visible sickle gloss (lustre). They were made on high-quality flint blade sections knapped from core types that are not present in the collection. Various techniques were used to break the blades in order to remove butt and tip. Several elements had denticulated edges and distal and/or proximal retouch on the break surfaces. The longitudinal position of the lustre on the lateral edges suggested the use of a straight haft (Nishiaki 2000, 155).

Burins: Angle burins on breaks, transverse, dihedral or oblique/transversal burin types made up the 16 specimens, three being multi-faceted. They were made on either fine- or coarse-grain flint and on either flakes or blades.

Backed blades, borers and denticulations: These were present in low numbers (eight) and were made of either flakes or blades.

Scraper, notch, rod: One specimen of each occurred, the scraper on a thick flake, the notch in Clactonian style, the rod with abrupt bilateral retouch.

Retouched blades and flakes: These consisted of 43 pieces with irregular or nibbled retouch along one or both edges in the case of the blades, or on part of the edge in the case of the flakes. Those made on fine-grain flint might have been used as sickle elements, as their shapes and measurements were closely comparable to those of lustred specimens.

The retouched tools listed above were mostly made on very dark brown, dark brown or yellow fine-grain flint (43%: Nishiaki 2000, 157). Tools on blades were made by truncating, 'burinating' or laterally retouching the blade blank. Pressure flaking was used on the points. The Tell Nebi Mend artefacts show that a mixture of at least two operational sequences, each characterised by its own technical and behavioural features and raw material type, was in use (Nishiaki 2000, 158). Nishiaki refers the industry to the Byblos Néolithique Ancien in general, especially to those 6th-millennium sites occurring during or just after the transition from Pre-Pottery to Pottery Neolithic in the Near East.

An exhaustive set of illustrations, tables and graphs concerning both technological and typological features at Tell Nebi Mend fully supports Nishiaki's interpretations (Nishiaki 2000, figs 6.1–6.24 and tables 6.1–6.10). He concludes by proposing that profound changes were taking place in Neolithic people's lifeways at the time of the transition that were reflected in settlement systems and patterns in raw material availability and in the subsistence economy; some of these could explain the variability in lithic use seen in the industries of this period.

Table 5.1. Classification of retouched tools.

	Copeland 2007	Nishiaki 2000	Total
Flint tools			
Axe	4	1	5
Pebble tool	2		2
Arrowhead:			
Byblos Point	3	1	4
Amuq Point	4	1	5
tang/tip	9	6	15
body frag.	2		2
Sickle-blade element:			
unilateral	47	25	72
bilateral	8	6	14
truncated	8	11	19
bitruncated	1		1
Shape-defined element:			
abrupt	9		9
nibbled	5	1	6
Burin	13	16	29
Scraper: end-of-blade	2		2
flake	6	1	7
Backed piece	3	2	5
Denticulate, notch	14	4	18
Borer	3	2	5
Splintered piece	1		1
Retouched piece	21	43	64
Total flint tools	165	120	285
Obsidian tools			
Corner-thinned blade			
single	3		3
double	3		3
triple	2		2
quadruple	4		4
Lateral retouch	9		9
Total obsidian tools	21		21
Total tools	186	120	306

Table 5.2. Technological classification of Neolithic artefacts.

	Copeland 2007	Nishiaki 2000	Total
Flint: debitage types			
Cores:			
Discoid	9	9	18
Prismatic	3	2	5
Other (axes, pebble tools, etc.)	10	2	12
By-products:			
Spall	5	7	12
Core revival	13	6	19
Tool repair	7		7
Products:			
Flakes	86	98	184
Cortex-flakes	19	26	45
Part-cortex	68	61	129
Preparation flakes	102		102
Blades	69	24	93
Blade segment/tip	93		93
Blade butts	46		46
Fragments	130	86	216
Debris	99		99
Total flint debitage	759	321	1080
Obsidian debitage types			
Core	1		1
By-products	6		6
Flakes	3		3
Blade segment/tip	20		20
Blade butts	8		8
Fragments	7		7
Total obsidian debitage	45	13	58
Total debitage	804	334	1138

Table 5.3. Colour distribution of raw flint material.

	Total	%
Raw material colour		
Pale or piebald	27	4.40
Beige	139	22.86
Light brown	111	18.25
Brown	75	12.33
Dark Brown	57	9.37
Black	68	11.18
Grey	108	17.76
Rosy	9	1.48
Translucent	14	2.30
Totals	608	99.93

Table 5.4. Types of butt.

	Total	%
Recognisable butt-type		
Cortex	29	9.89
Plain	98	33.44
Faceted	19	6.48
Linear or punctiform	131	44.7
Removed	16	5.46
Totals	293	99.97
Absent or unrecognisable type	231	
Total butts	524	

6. Miscellaneous objects, White Ware and a textile impression

Virginia Mathias

The small number of Neolithic objects from Tell Nebi Mend is presumably a reflection of the limited extent of excavation of the Neolithic levels. All 55 are catalogued and described here, and all are illustrated, with the exception of one bone point, one possible hammerstone, and some body fragments of stone vessels and White Ware. It should be noted that those objects with field registration numbers beginning with the numeral 0, together with one stone bowl, Cat. no. 25 (which was not so registered) remain in Syria, and so have not been available for re-examination prior to this publication. Objects with registration numbers beginning with the numeral 5 are now at the Institute of Archaeology, University College London, and have been re-examined.

In view of this scarcity, the presence or absence of any category of object in a particular phase cannot have real significance. The fact that the earlier Phases 1–3 are particularly lacking in objects (14) compared with Phases 4 and 5 (41) is in all probability to be explained by the nature of the later deposits – pits in Phase 4 and mixed or redeposited Neolithic material in Phase 5. A few ceramic objects – for example, the figurine Cat. no. 1 and the spindle-whorl Cat. no. 6 – although of uncertain provenance can safely be ascribed to the Neolithic occupation on account of their fabric or decoration. Any other objects which are probably Neolithic but which were intrusive in later levels will be dealt with in the forthcoming report on the post-Neolithic levels of Trench VIII.

Clay objects

Figurines (Fig. 6.1: nos 1 and 2; Plate 6.1: nos 1 and 2)

There are two apparent figurines, both incomplete, and both human. No. 1 is the base of a standing figurine, broken across low down but originally at least 100 mm high. The base is well flattened to stand firm on a flat surface and has a slightly splayed foot which is worn and chipped. The sides taper slightly upwards and are lightly smoothed. The modelling is fairly rough and the surfaces uneven with a very patchy shine representing either a sketchy and worn burnish or a sheen or polish from handling. The fabric is the same as the buff coarse pottery, with unsorted dark-grey angular grit temper and some red inclusions which may be grog. It is well-fired and light orange-buff with a pale grey core. It came from Neolithic levels but the context was not certain – possibly the accumulation of bricky material at the base of the Phase 2 wall. If so, it is an example of coarse fabric being used for another purpose long before it was in general use for the production of pottery, this fabric being practically unknown until Phase 4: see Cauvin's comments on the use of (baked) clay for ornamental or religious purposes (figurines) far earlier than for practical ones such as pottery (Cauvin 1978, 101–4).

Of course, there is the possibility that this is not the base of a figurine but is, for example, part of an implement for some use such as burnishing a plaster floor. However, a suitable flat smooth stone (see below, *e.g.* nos 31–35, 38) would easily serve this purpose without the effort of preparation and firing needed to make a ceramic substitute, while the shape of this fragment fits well with the tradition of standing or pillar figurines in the Neolithic of the Levant. (See, for example, a *'figurine en forme de pion'* at Tell Ramad in the Damascene area: Contenson 2000, pl. XX, 2a; this may be from the earlier aceramic period Ramad II.)

The other figurine (Fig. 6.1: no. 2 and Plate 6.1: no. 2) is from lower fill of a Phase 4 pit dug deep into levels of the preceding phases. It is made of fine pinkish-buff clay and the few visible white and dark grits may be natural inclusions. Blobs of similar clay found in associated

 Virginia Mathias

fills – probably from mud-plaster or the manufacture of mudbricks – were softer and dissolved readily in water, but this figurine was probably sun-dried although not fired, since, though fragile and broken during excavation, it was easily mended and showed no tendency to crumble. Initially it seemed like a simple clay lump, but has various signs of deliberate shaping. There are indications that the underside was pressed into a mat to hold it steady for modelling, a technique certainly used and probably common in the manufacture of the Neolithic pottery. The upper end has lost a substantial chip, but is tapering and shows no sign of a head. The object seems to represent a seated human figure leaning well back with knees bent. The thighs and knees, which are divided by a groove, are wide and flattened, with the lower legs barely indicated. The body tapers towards the neck, and the arms and shoulders are not shown. The surfaces, especially on the front, are well smoothed and curved. The emphasis on curved thighs and the lack of shoulders indicate a female, and from the slender torso a young one. As with no. 1, the modelling is fairly casual and at first glance might seem to have been accidental, but the features taken together place it in the very widespread genre of small seated female figurines of roughly tetrahedral shape, as from Ramad in the Damascus basin (Contenson 2000, pl. XX, 1a–b, 2c), Çayönü in southern Turkey (Broman Morales 1990, pls 22 and 23), and Jarmo on the flanks of the Zagros mountains (Broman Morales 1983, figs 156: 1–7, 9; 157: 3, 4; 160: 8).

The lack of animal figurines is unexpected, since elsewhere they tend to occur more frequently than human ones. However, this may be due solely to the limited extent of Neolithic excavation.

Other clay objects (Fig. 6.1: nos 3–5)

The two fired clay objects nos 3 and 4 both come from the lower fill of a deep Phase 4 pit. They are similar in fabric to the group of light-coloured plain holemouth jars which apparently occur only in Phase 5 (pottery illustrations Fig. 4.27, nos 159–163), but are not so hard-fired. Both are flattened and tapering; no. 3 is slightly twisted and no. 4 is curved in profile. They are similar, and could even be parts of the same piece. Their function is obscure, but the shape suggests a handle of, for example, some kind of rough spatula or spoon.

The clay object no. 5 comes from Phase 3 levels which may have been disturbed by a pit of Phase 4 at the very edge of the excavations. It has been fired, but is very roughly shaped out of a lump or flat disc of clay which has been pressed round something smooth and cylindrical, such as a stick. The outside is uneven and cracked from being stretched. On the inside of the groove are two or more deep impressions, probably made accidentally with fingernails while shaping the clay, and across the end of the groove is an impression of something like a reed or grass-stem. The piece is broken across the groove, where it is at its thickest, so must have been at least twice as

long. It could have functioned as a seal over a lid or covering, perhaps fastened down with a stick attached to pierced lugs by means of reed ties; or the groove might have been made on the rim of a vessel, though it shows no obvious curvature. If it was indeed used to seal a vessel, it may have been intended merely to keep stored food from the depredations of rodents and insects, even perhaps from pilfering by children or other members of the settlement. Stamp seals and sealings were common in the later Neolithic, as, for example, at Tell ᶜAin el-Kerkh in periods 2c and 2d (Tsuneki *et al.* 1997, 31–4, fig. 24: 1–6; 1998, 23–6, fig. 17: 3–23), and were already known in period 2b (Tsuneki *et al.* 1998, fig. 17: 1–2), equivalent to the Tell Nebi Mend Neolithic.

Reworked sherds (Fig. 6.1: nos 6–8)

The three reworked sherds nos 6–8 are all of fine fabric (although no. 8 is exceptionally thick) and cord-impressed on the outside. No. 6 is a broken spindle-whorl on a thin sherd, very carefully shaped into an exact circle with the hole accurately centred. The edges have been bevelled, more extensively on the under(concave)-side of the sherd. This object came from Phase 5, but the sherd is definitively Neolithic and the shaping is unlikely to be later. A very similar example of a spindle-whorl was found at Tabbat el-Hammam (Hole 1959, fig. 2: 25), also made on a cord-impressed sherd and also biconically drilled and bevelled at the edges. Similar examples on rounded and biconically perforated potsherds are reported from Ras Shamra VB Neolithic (Contenson 1992, vol. I, 136 and vol. II, fig. 163: 9–11), and also in Byblos Néolithique Ancien on fine sherds with all-over surface decoration (Dunand 1973, pl. CVII).

The other two sherds are complete but only roughly shaped, especially no. 7 (which also came from a later level, but is definitely Neolithic), which is quite small and of a thin fine fabric streakily burnished on the inside surface. Such sherds may seem unshaped and are likely to be overlooked in excavation. However, they do occur in most periods and are notably frequent in the Halaf and Ubaid-related deposits at neighbouring Arjoune (Parr 2003, *e.g.* fig. 62: 1–8), where there are also pierced sherds (Parr 2003, fig. 61: 1–6), some only very roughly shaped. The Neolithic sherds from Tell Nebi Mend could therefore have been intended for further shaping and for piercing, but were discarded (*cf.* Parr 2003, fig. 61: 3), although they might equally well have had some other use, such as counters in a game. No. 8 is rather more shaped but looks worn, and is so heavy that it may have been put to a different use, (*e.g.* a loom-weight or a weight for a fishing net); or it could have been abraded underfoot while lying on the paving of an outside passage or alleyway.

Such roughly circular potsherds are only rarely mentioned or illustrated in excavation reports, as at Byblos (Dunand 1973, pl. CVII) and Ras Shamra (Contenson 1992, later Neolithic and Chalcolithic periods only), but in fact they are probably quite common. They may occur naturally from breakage and were probably occasionally reused, with or without reshaping, in a variety of ways.

Bone objects (Fig 6.2: nos 9–22)

These 15 objects mostly fall into two categories. Nos 10–13 and 15 are flat shapes of various sizes; the fragment no. 9 and the flat pierced object no. 16 may also be included in this group. Nos 19–22 (plus one not illustrated) are points, while the remaining three, nos 14, 17 and 18, are all different. (Nos 11–16 were not available for study by the author of this report, and descriptions have been taken from the field register.)

No. 9 is part of a much larger object, perhaps oval in shape. The front surface has been roughly polished, while the back is the natural interior of the bone. The only surviving worked edge has been finely tapered and polished, the polish extending slightly into the rough underside. The front surface has been deliberately scored, with straight lines in two groups of three or four which come together at one end, and two slightly curved lines. These groups of lines also cross each other. The lines vary from deep and 0.5 mm wide through to fine shallow scratches. They form no definite pattern but give a decorative effect, and suggest that the original object was ornamental rather than functional, especially as it was thin and fragile.

Nos 10, 11 and 12 are all made on flat, thin bone, smooth on one surface and rougher on the other; no. 12 is polished on the smooth surface, which is slightly convex. They are similar in size and shape – a slightly tapering oblong – though no. 12, which is complete apart from a chipped corner, is broader, the wider end being straight. No. 11 has lost the broader end, but on no. 10 it is shaped into what seems to be a tang which has broken off; the tapered blade, which is partly blackish, is apparently stained or charred.

No. 13 is less regularly shaped than the above three and is half as long again, barely tapered and convex on the smooth side, like no. 12, but also curved in profile. The side edges are polished, perhaps through use. No. 15 is similar to no. 13 but twice as long, and is still more roughly shaped, with one end curved and the other transversely tapered. It is slightly thicker in proportion and slightly curved in profile, and the convex surface is polished. Both pieces are complete apart from chips. At Tell Qminas similar bone objects are referred to as razors, presumably because of their shape (Masuda and Shu'ath 1983, pl. 7: 21 [similar in size to Tell Nebi Mend no.15], nos 22 and 23 [both broken, but no. 23 is 260 mm long at least]).

All five flat narrow bone objects nos 10–13 and 15 probably had some function such as a spatula. No. 10, and possibly all the smaller pieces, may have been attached to a handle.

No. 16 (unstratified, but from a Neolithic area) is a very thin flat object tapering to a broad point at one end and pierced at the other – a pendant or needle? The only other pierced object is no. 17, where a small hole similar to that in no. 16 has been drilled in the protruding end of a

sheep or goat ulna and the shaft of the bone has broken off in the middle of the joint. The flat area between the hole and the joint has been scored on both faces with diagonal lines crossing each other, but the lines give no impression of patterning or decoration (in contrast to no. 9).

No. 14, which is probably round in section, is well shaped and suggests some sort of fastening or toggle, perhaps for clothing. It resembles the fairly ubiquitous bone pins which are of similar shape but pointed at one end only. If attached in the middle to the front of a garment near an opening it could be secured with a simple loop.

No. 18 is a delicate small implement formed on a narrow split bone, cut at one end, where it is shaped into an asymmetric curve, perhaps partly by use in smoothing or polishing; this end and the split edges are more highly polished than the rest. The other end is broken. A bone object from period A Judaidah, in the ᶜAmuq (Braidwood and Braidwood 1960, fig. 38: 5), looks similar.

Of the five points, no. 19 is the only one formed on a solid flat bone such as a rib, which is convex on one surface and fairly flat on the other. It tapers in a smooth curve towards the point, the tip of which is lost, and is evenly polished overall; the other end is broken off. The other four points are formed from rounded bones split longitudinally, but no. 20 is similar to no. 19 in shape, size and fine polish, both ends also being broken. No. 21 is broader, and only the fine tip is lost, showing how the point was sharpened in a slightly concave taper (rather like a pencil). The other end is the joint of the bone (a sheep or goat metatarsal), and all surfaces (except the rough inner) are well polished. A similar slightly larger example (not illustrated, but listed under no. 21) has been broken diagonally at the joint end and the polish does not extend so far. No. 22 has a similar point (unbroken) formed on the natural edge of a more robust bone that is lightly polished and more roughly finished than the others; it may be broken at the other end and looks unused. Bone points or awls, often formed on short, relatively dense bones such as sheep or goat metatarsals, are quite common, as at Judaidah, ᶜAmuq A (Braidwood and Braidwood 1960, fig. 38: 1, similar to our no. 21).

Stone objects (Figs 6.3, 6.4 and 6.5: nos 23–40)

Not all of the stone objects were fully described at the time of their discovery and the following descriptions of those that were not rely mainly on the field drawings. In addition, not all of the material from which the objects were made was always precisely identified, thus making a detailed petrological analysis impossible.

Stone bowls

There are six pieces of small stone bowls (130 mm to approximately 250 mm in diameter) comprising two with partial rims, one partial ring-base and three body fragments (not illustrated). There is also one rim fragment of a larger shallow dish.

The smallest is no. 23, a hemispherical bowl of fine limestone or marl that is very finely ground and polished on both inside and outside surfaces. The walls, which are thin for a stone vessel (6.5 mm), are of even thickness and evenly tapered towards a thin rim that is pointed in section. It would have made an excellent drinking vessel. No. 24 is a larger bowl of similar shape, but the surfaces, though even, are not polished and have a slightly rough feel. It is correspondingly thicker – 11 mm near the base – and tapers gradually towards a thin rounded rim. The three other small body fragments (not illustrated) fall within the range of 150–200 mm diameter and vary in thickness from as much as 13 mm down to 8 mm; they are all finely smoothed or polished on both surfaces.

There is no indication of the shape of the base for any of the above: although that of no. 24 appears to be rounded they might also have been slightly flattened, so as to stand firmly. However, the only fragment of a base found (no. 25, without rim) is a low ring, carefully and evenly shaped and polished on all surfaces except the bottom of the ring. From this fragment there is no indication of the overall shape of the vessel, but if it belonged to a bowl similar to nos 23 and 24 it would have a diameter of about 250 mm; it could also have been shallower and smaller. It is thicker, at least at the base, than the other pieces (but in proportion to its larger size), and it also tapers towards the rim. However, the surviving upper edge has been bevelled, presumably for some other use after the vessel had been broken.

All of the above are of carefully selected light-coloured stone of cream, pale buff, mushroom or grey. Despite some differences, dictated in part by the varying material, there are obvious comparisons with the large numbers of ceramic open bowls, especially with regard to the frequency of fine burnish; although the pottery bowls are predominantly black or dark brown, a few do occur in pale grey and buff. No ring-bases are known on ceramic bowls, but the disc bases look similar and strengthen the vessel in the same way.

These bowls clearly belong to a long and accomplished tradition dating from aceramic times, the pottery no doubt imitating an older stone-working tradition rather than the other way around. The stone bowls, like their ceramic counterparts, would serve well as drinking or eating vessels. Ras Shamra has three comparable fine stone bowls in period VB, with diameters of 120–140 mm (Contenson 1992, vol. I, 98; vol. II, fig. 128: 5, 6, 10).

The small fragment of a large shallow dish no. 26 is made of black basalt that is relatively coarse-grained but dense enough to have been ground to a very fine surface, especially on the inside, where it is smooth to the touch. It is also remarkably thin-walled for its size, which is estimated to be well over 300 mm in diameter. It could theoretically be oval, and therefore smaller, but there is no evidence of such a shape or indeed anything similar among the larger pottery vessels. Like the smaller bowls, it shows a high level of workmanship.

Miscellaneous small stone objects

There is one stone 'astragalus', no. 27 – a natural water-worn pebble where differential wear on a softer layer between two hard layers has resulted in a shape like an astragalus bone. A small number of such stones have been found in deposits of other periods on the site (as well as actual astragalus bones that have been further shaped and polished), and are thought to have been collected as gaming pieces. No. 27 is missing the upper hard layer, but could still have been used in this way. Its base is broad and perfectly flat with a reddish patina and a matt polish which extends a few millimetres over the edges. It could also possibly have been used as a burnishing tool.

No. 28 is another natural pebble, but it has been polished all over to a very high gloss. One flat side has a less glossy area about the size of a thumb-print. It is an unusual brownish-black colour, and its attractive appearance suggests an ornament such as a pendant, though there are no signs of attachment or suspension. It, too, might have been used as a burnishing tool, to produce a fine polish on pottery or stone bowls.

No. 29 is a unique object: a slender curved rod with a knob at one end, the other end unfortunately being broken. Despite its small size it has been carefully shaped, with four facets visible on the central part, then polished all over, including the bulbous end. The stone is light grey, but dark grey on the surface, possibly as a result of the polishing process. If the broken end had a similar knob, it may have been a stud or plug for ear, nose or lip. If it had been longer, it might conceivably have been a fastening for clothing (see the bone pin or toggle no. 14), though this seems less likely. A possibly similar object was found at the base of excavations at Judaidah, ᶜAmuq Phase A, where it was described as a 'nail-like object of soapstone'; in shape this object was slightly curved with a blunt point (the other end broken), and it showed rough facets in section (Braidwood and Braidwood 1960, 62, fig. 35: 6).

No. 30, a stone plaque or pendant, is roughly square or shield-shaped and broken across one corner. This thin flat piece has been cut along the top and left side (as drawn) so as to leave straight, right angled edges. The lower edge has been bevelled on the front surface only and the bevelling on the right side has been ground smooth with a matt polish, like the rest of the front; on the left some striations are still visible, and there are possible pecking marks made to rough-shape the edge. The squared sides and back, though very even, are not finished to the same polish as the front and the lower edge. The back is slightly concave and the front correspondingly convex. This piece was apparently not completely finished, perhaps because the need to clamp it firmly while working caused it to snap.

Stone implements (Fig. 6.4: nos 31–36; Fig. 6.5: nos 37–40)

Thirteen implements of limestone or basalt were found; 12 are catalogued here, while the remainder, a smoothed river pebble with signs of use (not unlike Cat. no. 36), is treated by Copeland in Chapter 5. Nos 32, 33, 36, 38 and 39 are not now available for examination, and descriptions have been taken from the field register or brief notes on the field drawings. Eight pieces, nos 31–35, 37, 38 and an unillustrated pebble-tool, are rubbing and/or hammerstones. No. 36 seems to be a rough-out for a tool, which was chipped but not ground to produce, for example, an axe, adze or similar. Nos 39 and 40 are fragments of basalt querns.

No. 31 is a small basalt cobble with one facet on the longer side which is worn flat by rubbing; reddish flecks or stains are probably inherent in the stone. The other surfaces, especially the ends, look rather battered, as if from hammering. A smooth limestone pebble (not illustrated) of similar size and shape but flatter is slightly battered at the ends and round the narrower sides (more than the flat sides), probably from hammering. Both of these items are dense and heavy for their size, and suitable for hammerstones.

No. 32 is another small rubbing stone. The wear traces are described as slight, with possible indications of circular scoring on the flat side. The small oval flattish implement no. 33, broken across one end, was described as 'granite' on the field drawing, but is more likely to be basalt. Although not available for examination, it appears to have a polish on the flat surface and narrow sides, and the curved end looks battered. It may have been used for polishing or burnishing and also as a hammerstone.

No. 32a is another basalt pebble similar in general shape to nos 31 and 32, but both ends have been deliberately worked to rough points, and it is perhaps more likely to have been a sling-stone than a hammerstone, at least originally.

The larger flat stone no. 34, of hard grey schist or fluvial sandstone (outcrops of which occur nearby along the Orontes), has been considerably battered (and chips split off) at both ends, and to a lesser extent on the long sides. The flat surface illustrated has a slight natural hollow which has been used for abrasion, leaving striations in two or more directions. There is a brownish stain over most of this surface and the long edges, but not in the striated area nor most of the battered ends, and on the reverse only around a large chip which was probably naturally detached before use. The stain has the appearance of grime from handling, which has been worked into the surface of the stone by heavy use.

No. 35 is another natural stone, and the chip missing from one end obviously predates any use. It is of a much softer stone than the foregoing, and the flat side not shown is battered all over, perhaps underfoot, as it came from a Phase 3 context of plaster floors. One (or both) of the long edges has been used in a rubbing or burnishing process, and in view of the nature of the stone this use is most likely to have been on the surface of the contemporary plaster floors.

No. 36 is described only as white stone (perhaps limestone). Judging from field drawings and photographs it has been roughly chipped into shape with the intention of grinding into a tool such as an axe or adze, or possibly even a hoe.

No. 37 is described as of reef-stone, perhaps fossilised coral, and has other visible fossils in its matrix. It is roughly spherical but has some flat facets, three with dark red coloration which appears to be the original surface of the stone before use. All other surfaces are heavily battered, suggesting long use as a hammerstone. Its hardness, weight and shape would be ideal for this purpose.

No. 38 is unbroken, and has apparently been shaped for use by grinding. It is oblong with both upper and lower surfaces flattened and the long sides sloping, giving a squat trapezoid in cross section. The ends are similarly sloping, and also rounded. There is no note of the type of stone, but any hard material in this shape would be suitable for a rubbing stone to grind grain on a basalt quern.

No. 39 is a fragment of a quern, no doubt of basalt (although a description of the material is not available): an end or corner of an oval or oblong with two broken edges. The upper or working surface is only very slightly concave, but could have had a deeper hollow in the centre. The unbroken edges are rounded, and the under-surface is also curved, giving a thick dish-shape in section. All surviving edges have evidently been shaped or ground, at least roughly.

No. 40 is another fragment of a basalt quern, this time with a rather more concave working surface. The under-side is probably natural, and all other edges are broken. The working surface has been worn to a polish – possibly a silica gloss from grinding seeds or grain – in patches between natural pitting.

Various other pieces of basalt were fragments of natural cobbles that had been brought to the site from nearby areas where basalt is plentiful. No large pieces were found, and none whole.

Locally available stone – that is, different kinds of limestone, basalt and natural pebbles from the river and alluvial soil deposits – were used for a variety of tools and small objects, for which there is only a small and not necessarily representative sample. Raw materials were probably being worked somewhere in the settlement, and some of the stone found, such as the broken basalt cobbles, were no doubt by-products or rejected pieces from manufacture. The angular dark grits and chips of basalt or gabbro used as temper in coarse-fabric pottery from Phase 4 onwards were presumably another by-product.

'White Ware' (Fig. 6.6: nos 41–43)

'White Ware' vessels stem from an older tradition in the preceding aceramic period, when plaster was already in common use for floors and associated installations such as bins and raised hearths. The plaster used can be either gypsum or lime, and the term 'White Ware' has been used for both, although the technology is different. Gypsum requires a much lower temperature, less than 190°C, to become workable and the material hardens quickly; lime needs at least 800°C and is at first brittle and takes a long time to harden, especially through to the core of a thick-walled vessel. However, tempering with vegetable matter speeds up the process. Application of a surface layer of fine plaster would have to be done after the base layer had hardened, but burnishing or oiling produces a fine smooth surface (Contenson and Courtois 1979, especially 178–9; Maréchal 1982). White Ware vessels would have been impermeable to liquids and could also be repaired by re-heating – they were therefore in some ways superior to early ceramics.

Only a few pieces of White Ware, produced from the same lime plaster as the floors, were excavated at Tell Nebi Mend: the three rims illustrated (nos 41–43) and six body fragments. One or two other pieces of rather irregular shape which apparently had two smoothed surfaces were probably from fixed domestic installations or even from edges of plaster floors at the point where they curved upwards against walls. (Pieces of floor plaster were found scattered throughout the Neolithic deposits, usually very small fragments one surface of which was smooth and completely flat, while the other was broken up; they could not be mistaken for White Ware.)

There appear to have been two categories of White Ware fabric, coarse and fine. The coarse version, as used in the deep bowl no. 42, like pottery often has coarse inclusions of grits or stones and also dark flecks, probably burnt organic matter. The plaster used in this bowl was greyish, crumbly and necessarily quite thick (*c.*21 mm). Interesting evidence of the method of manufacture was found when a piece of the inside surface (not a fine plaster layer) split off, revealing a perfect impression of cloth on its interior surface (see below). This cloth had been laid over a fairly thin inner core, and wet plaster then applied thickly over it, hence the clear impression on the back of the outer layer but not on the core. Further comments on this textile impression are made below.

One body piece much thicker than no. 42 was of finer plaster and had a fine layer on each surface (Reg. no. 5338; not illustrated). Another very thick body fragment (Reg. no. 5341; not illustrated) was identified as White Ware and not floor plaster by its well-smoothed inside and outside surfaces, both considerably curved. It must have been part of a massive vessel.

Vessels made entirely from finer plaster were also built up in layers. The deep jar no. 41 has lost much of the surface layer on its heavy outer flange, so the wiping or scraping of the core to key in the outer layer can be seen. There are no signs of cloth, which may not have been necessary to hold the finer plaster. Finally the surface was burnished, which would have helped adhesion of the outer layer as well as improving the appearance of the vessel.

The fine plaster also has some inclusions, but these are much finer-grained. It is stronger than the crumbly

coarse fabric and could be used to make large vessels with remarkably thin walls, such as the large flaring bowl no. 43, which had a raised foot or pedestal base, unfortunately broken off. There are blackish marks on the outside surface from the rim to about halfway down and a pale brownish area inside the rim, either of which could be the remains of paint. Paint is not unknown on White Ware and, of course, on plaster floors since the aceramic period. However, this could well be staining in use or post-deposition.

There is other evidence, especially in the northern Levant, that White Ware continued to be made long after pottery came into common use. In the deep sounding at Sukas it was found in abundance (more than half of all sherds) throughout the Neolithic; both fine white and coarser greyish plaster were reported, as were fine surface layers on a coarse core, sometimes with inclusions of grit and burnt straw, and one piece with paint on its inside surface, though traces of bitumen may have been unconnected with manufacture. The only shapes were open: conical or hemispherical bowls and shallow dishes with flat or ring bases and some ledge handles near the rim; the wall thickness varied widely between 3 mm and 26 mm. The authors of the report equate only the earliest period, N11, with ᶜAmuq A and Ras Shamra VB (comparable to the Neolithic at Tell Nebi Mend), and all the later Neolithic periods with ᶜAmuq B, Ras Shamra VA, Nebi Fa'our (in the Beqaᶜ valley) and Byblos Néolithique Ancien, or even Néolithique Moyen, but White Ware still occurs in the top Neolithic deposits at Sukas (Riis and Thrane 1974, 26–8 etc.). At Ras Shamra it was apparently found only in the later ceramic Neolithic period VA (heavy bowls with disc or high foot, carefully smoothed surfaces, occasionally painted), with a few sherds intrusive into the preceding period VB (Contenson 1992, vol. I, 150; vol. II, fig. 164). Some few White Ware vessel fragments were found at Tell ᶜAin el-Kerkh in the er-Rouj valley of north-west Syria, including some with red paint from Period 2b (equivalent to the Tell Nebi Mend Neolithic) and the succeeding Period 2c; they were thought to resemble the large pedestal bowl shapes which were characteristic of plaster-coated pottery in the latter period (Tsuneki *et al.* 1998, 16–7).

From the small sounding at Labwe in the Beqaᶜ valley, where the pottery is very close to that from Tell Nebi Mend, a White Ware bowl with a pedestal base is illustrated which is quite similar to Cat. no. 43 (Kirkbride 1969). Tell Ramad (Damascene) has some White Ware, sometimes painted, consisting of heavy bowls with a flat base or a high foot or pedestal base (Contenson 2000, fig. 108), and apparently both gypsum and lime plaster were used (Contenson and Courtois 1979, 178). At Byblos during the Néolithique Ancien White Ware is found in small amounts, the only shapes being low-footed or ring-based heavy bowls (Dunand 1973, 40–2, fig. 148; pl. XLIV).

It is noticeable that at Tell Nebi Mend the shapes of the White Ware vessels are completely different from the contemporary pottery (except perhaps for the simple shape of the deep bowl no. 42). There are no ceramic types resembling the double-flanged rim of no. 41, nor the footed bowl no. 43 (with the possible exception of a wide pedestal: see Pottery Catalogue no. 330, fig. 4.60).

White Ware could also be used for large items at a time when making pottery vessels of substantial size had scarcely been attempted at Tell Nebi Mend. Despite the relative fragility of White Ware, and the quite complicated techniques necessary for successful manufacture, the production of fine plaster vessels was skilful enough to produce a graceful, thin-walled shape such as no. 43, which had a rim diameter of around 400 mm. Some of the fine-plaster body fragments show that small vessels were also made, including some very thin and fine. In general, however, White Ware seems to have been used for different purposes from pottery, which may explain why both classes of vessel continued to be used together for a considerable time.

Textile impression (Fig. 6.6: 42 and Pl. 6.1: 42)

Woven textile had been used to build up the layers of coarse lime plaster of the heavy White Ware vessel no. 42, and a clear, sharp impression, discovered when a small piece split away, was left on the underside of the surface layer. The cloth was a plain or tabby weave (over and under alternate threads), quite loose but even, with about 10 × 10 threads per centimetre. The threads are flat and untwisted, and are therefore probably single vegetal fibres or fine stems of grass or reed which did not require spinning, but the cloth appears well made and technically skilled (see, *e.g.*, Hodges 1981, especially 128, 140).

At Hama in the Neolithic Period M no White Ware was identified, though floor and wall plaster was common, some of it coloured. However, a 30 mm × 35 mm fragment of wall plaster with a textile impression on one side was reported. This showed a finer weave than the Tell Nebi Mend piece,

at 17 × 10–12 threads per centimetre, although neither the fibre nor the direction of spin could be identified. The other surface was described as convex, pigmented and polished (which sounds rather like a White Ware body sherd, built up in a similar way to Tell Nebi Mend no. 42). This was a fine-quality plaster without inclusions (Thuesen and Riis 1988, 19 and Appendix A, 188; photo plate II, 3). Upon testing it was found to be pure lime plaster (Thuesen and Gwozdz 1982).

Actual woven textiles, and in far greater quantities, were found at Çatal Hüyük in Anatolia from below the internal platforms in houses of Level VI. The textiles were wrapped round partly defleshed skeletons in secondary burials, and had been carbonised either by fire in the overlying level or by decay. A variety of fabrics, in both coarse and fine yarn, was present, and one piece wrapped around a skull had been soaked in red ochre. The initial report identified all the yarn, apart from the strings used to tie the bundles, as being animal fibre (Helbaek 1963). Although the textiles were very fragile and powdery, it was possible to subject them to further study (Burnham 1965 and Ryder 1965). They consisted of plain tabby weave (Burnham 1965, plate XXXI (b)) and some open or net patterns of quite complicated design and technical skill; all the yarn was twisted – that is, it had been spun. While one study identified the yarn as wool, and pointed out that no flax seeds had been found among large amounts of cereal grains (Burnham 1965, 170), another study using a series of tests conclusively identified flax, but stated that carbonisation must have occurred through decay rather than fire, which would have destroyed flax fibres (Ryder 1965, 176), and suggested that both animal and vegetable fibres were being used. In any case, the extensive evidence from this site has established that textile production was already well developed at this time, and the chance preservation of impressions at both Hama and Tell Nebi Mend give an indication that this skill was known and practised over a wide area.

Fig. 6.1. Ceramic.

	Reg. No	*Provenance*	*Phase*	
1	5311	(706.20?)	Unstratified (?2)	Flat base of (standing) human figurine? Neolithic coarse fabric; medium-fine dark grey, bluish and pale grits, some red grog; buff, pale-grey core; lightly smoothed on uneven surfaces, suggestions of burnish or handling sheen.
2	5312	710.9	4	Possible seated human figurine, base may have been pressed into mat, top or head missing, unbaked clay; fine fabric; some fine white grits, may be accidental inclusions; orange-buff; surfaces smoothed.
3	5313	710.9	4	Clay object, flat, part of spatula (?) broken at both ends, slightly twisted on long axis; fine fabric, low-fired and soft; small brownish grits or grog; light brick-red; smoothed surfaces.
4	5314	710.9	4	Clay object, flat, part of spatula (?) broken at both ends; very similar to 5313.
5	0729	706.40	? 4	Clay object, roughly shaped and deeply grooved on one side, broken across one end, tapering at the other, with impression of fibres (reed or grass?) across end of groove, indentations inside and along edge of groove, probably from fingernail; low-fired and soft; brick-red; few small grey and light grits; outside surface very uneven.
6	5316	735.4	5 + Post-Neo.	Spindle-whorl fragment (nearly half) on Neolithic sherd, edges bevelled, central hole drilled biconically with grooved edge visible on upper surface; fine fabric; small dark-grey grits, a few light; brick-red, mottled grey; cord-impressed outside, smoothed inside.
7	5310	606.60/3	[7]	Disc on Neolithic sherd, very roughly shaped; fine fabric; fine light and dark grits; dull brick-red outside, black inside and core; cord-impressed outside, streaky burnish on uneven inside surface.
8	5315	710.9	4	Disc on very thick Neolithic sherd, edges roughly shaped, complete but broken across; medium–fine fabric; small dark, shiny and light grits; dull brick-red, blackish or blackened surfaces; cord-impressed outside, smoothed inside, all surfaces worn.

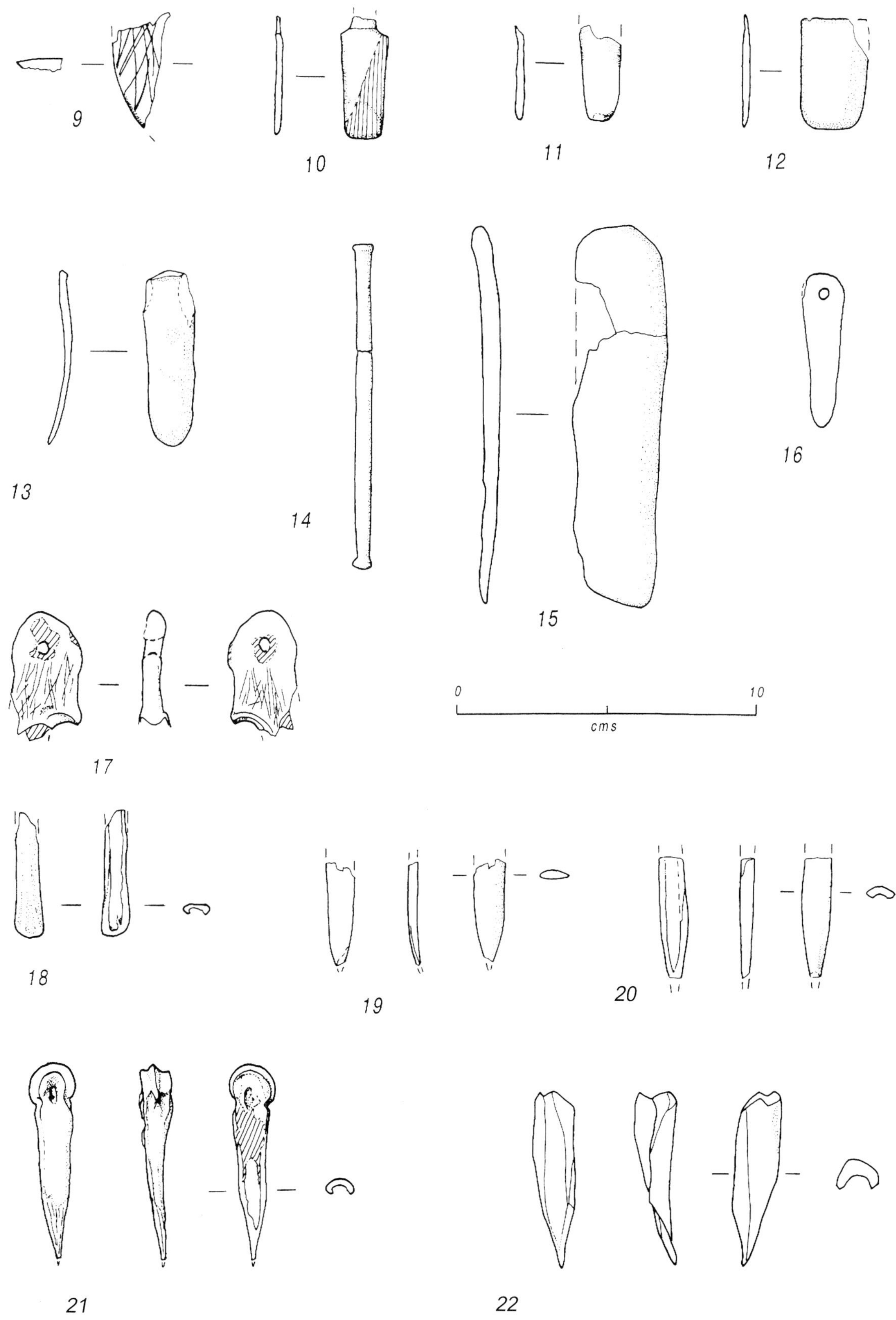

Fig. 6.2. Bone.

	Reg. No	*Provenance*	*Phase*	
9	5206	602.19	5	Bone object, flat, one edge shaped in a curve, other two broken off; outer surface polished and incised or scored in long criss-cross lines in no apparent pattern, underside is rough natural interior of bone.
10	0720	735.14	?4	Bone object, flat, slightly tapering, broader end indented like a tang (broken off); one surface smooth, slightly concave, partly blackish, other flat, rougher.
11	0735	606.15	3	Bone object, flat, one end broken, other end slightly tapering; smoothed on one surface, other rougher.
12	0725	606.15	3	Bone object, flat, complete apart from one broken corner, ends cracked, and some surface damage; one end straight, one rounded; one surface convex and may be polished, other flat and rough.
13	0722	648.4	3	Bone object, thin, curved in profile, complete (apart from two broken corners), one end straight, one rounded; one surface convex and smoothed, other flat and rough, edges polished.
14	0706	606.2	?4	Bone pin or toggle, complete but broken in two, and carved into slightly protruding and flattened head at both ends. (Drawing from sketch/measurements in register.)
15	0721	706.42	2	Bone object, flat (broken in two, piece missing at one edge on break), roughly rounded at thicker end, transversely tapered at the other; one surface slightly convex and polished, other flatter and rough.
16	0718	735.+	Unstratified	Bone object pierced one end, 1 mm thick [no description].
17	5350	606.17	4	Bone object, sheep/goat ulna, pierced end (edges crumbled), broken on shaft; random scoring and light polish between hole and joint.
18	5351	735.7	4	Bone object smoothing tool, on split bone with rounded end; polish on end and split surfaces.
19	5317	644.14	5	Bone point, slightly curved outwards towards point (tip and other end broken), carefully shaped and tapered on flat solid bone, one surface convex and one flat; fine polish on all surfaces.
20	5319	735.3	5	Bone point on split hollow bone (tip of point, other end and part of edge broken), carefully shaped and tapered; fine polish on convex surface and shaped edges; greyish coloration.
21	5352	706.18	4	Bone point on split sheep/goat metatarsal, complete; sharply tapered, partly concave and faceted point (tip broken); polished over all protruding surfaces.
---	5320	735.3	5	Bone point on split hollow bone, joint end broken; partly concave and faceted point (tip broken) polished. (Not illustrated.)
22	5321	735.3	5	Bone point on split hollow bone (robust), split again transversely to make a concave point on natural edge; light polish on outer surface only, may be unfinished.

 Virginia Mathias

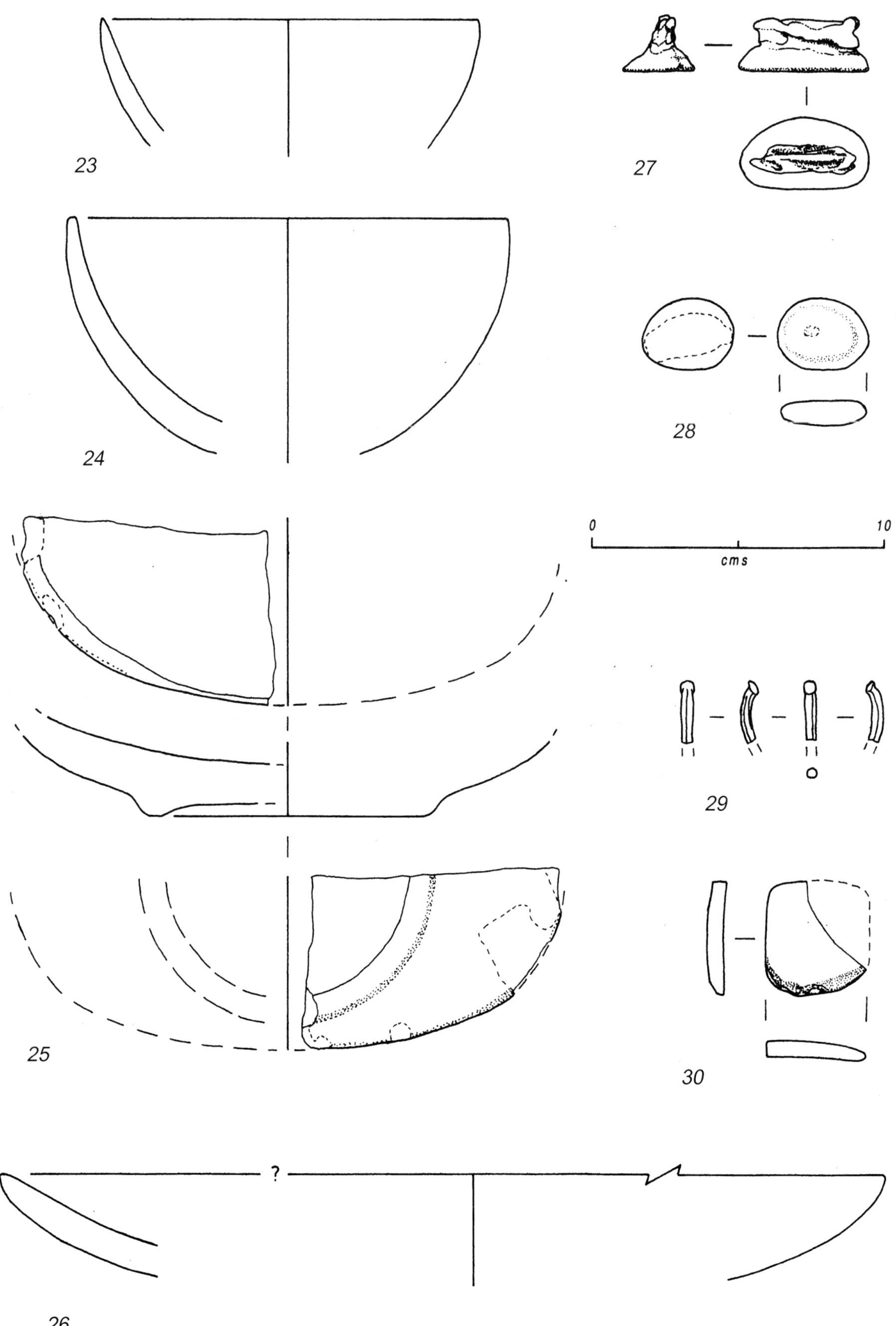

Fig. 6.3. Stone (vessels and small objects).

	Reg. No.	*Provenance*	*Phase*	
23	5299	602.34	4	Bowl fragment with very short length of rim; fine limestone or marl, brownish; outside and inside surfaces matt-polished.
24	5327	706.40	?4	Bowl rim/profile (large fragment); deposited limestone (calcite); fine, cream; surfaces finely ground but not polished.
–	5323	650.14	5	Bowl fragment; limestone (oolite, soft, no particular grain, easily worked); fine, pinkish cream; 10–13 mm thick. (Not illustrated.)
–	5324	654.9	5	Bowl fragment; mudstone; fine, mid-grey (may be discoloured); 10–13 mm thick. (Not illustrated.)
–	5353	706.42	2	Bowl fragment; fine-grained limestone, pinkish cream, greyish discolouration; 7.5–8 mm thick. (Not illustrated.)
25	5344	710.9	4	Ring-base of bowl (one quarter of base, no rim); probably limestone; fine, pale grey; all surfaces polished; upper edges reground to oval shape, *i.e.* after breakage.
26	5326	706.7	4	Rim fragment of large shallow thin-walled bowl; basalt, black; outside surface well ground, inside surface exceptionally smooth, matt.
27	5328	706.41	?4	Natural stone 'astragalus' water-worn pebble showing alternate hard, soft and hard layers; may have been collected for use as a gaming piece.
28	5272	644.16	4 (?3)	Small pebble, highly polished including edges, slightly duller area on one flat surface, flat oval shape; dense, black; polish probably from use, e.g. burnishing fine pottery or stone bowls.
29	5329	735.7	4	Possible stud for ear, nose or lip? Very small curved rod-shape 3–4 mm thick, wider head, other end broken; fine stone, grey; polished faceted surfaces.
30	5091	680.42	5	Small plaque or pendant (corner broken off, two-thirds remaining); mudstone; fine, brownish grey; well ground and slightly polished; appears to have been partly shaped as a pendant, probably unfinished and broken during working.

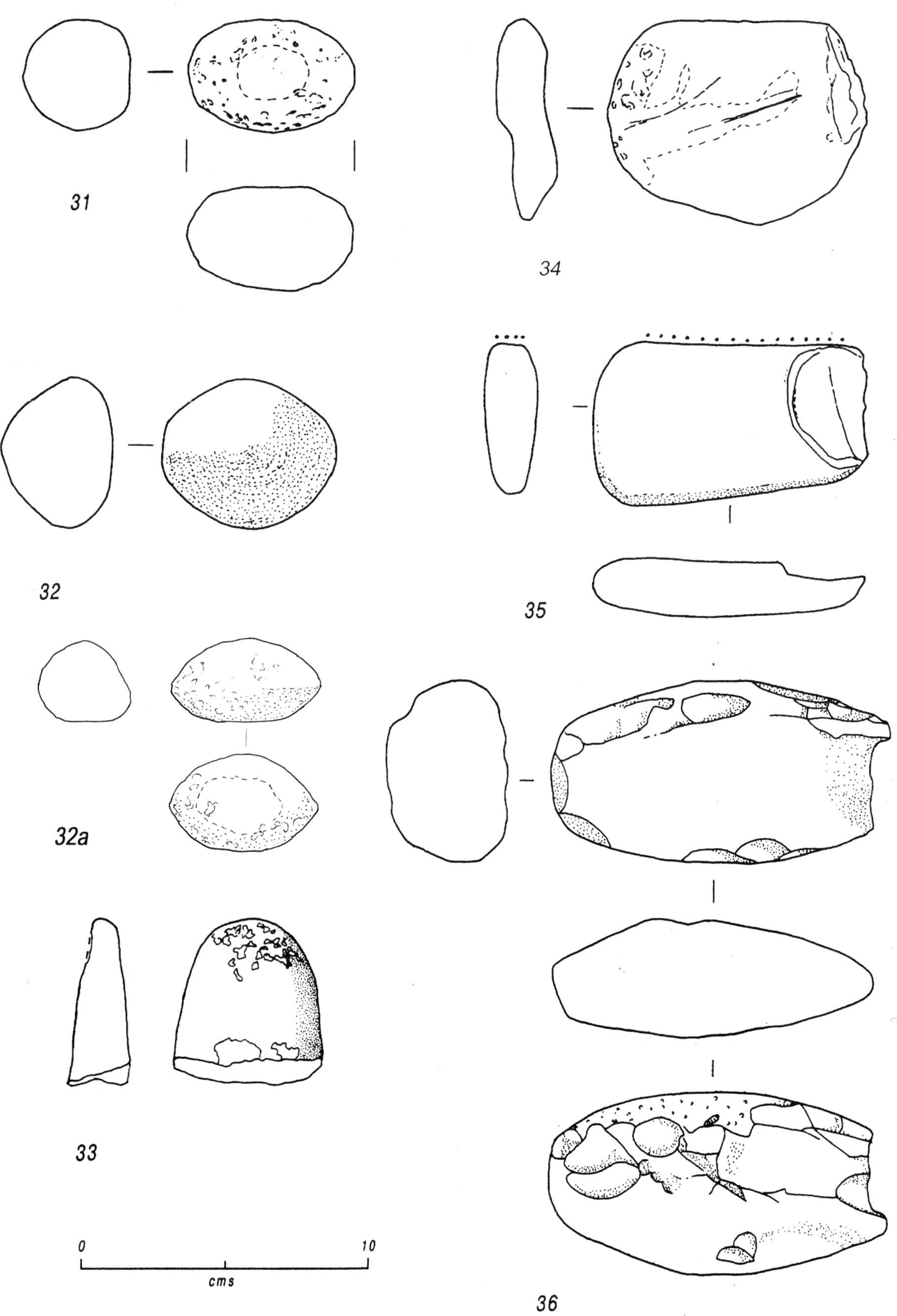

31

32

32a

33

34

35

36

0   10
cms

Fig. 6.4. Stone (shaped objects/tools).

	Reg. No.	*Provenance*	*Phase*	
31	5331	644.40	4	Rubbing stone(?), oval pebble, one flattened side (shaped or worn), some possible hammering on ends; basalt, greyish; pitted surfaces with reddish material or staining, also blackened.
--	5330	606.8	3	Natural pebble, oval, possible hammered ends; limestone, pale blue-grey. (Not illustrated.)
32	5108	680.42	5	Rubbing stone (slight wear); white; possible import.
32a	5293	705.63	?4	Slingshot (?). Oval pebble with both ends shaped to a rough point. Lower flattened surface slightly smoothed or worn (different or secondary use?). Greyish basalt, with naturally pitted surface.
33	5354	706.12	2	Basalt? Flat, smooth rounded sides, shaped/polished end? (appears battered in photo). Other end broken across; may be pebble.
34	5290	644.14	5	Rubbing stone/hammerstone, battered around all edges, especially ends, one side partly broken off, other side has 'grimy' stain around diagonal groove with longitudinal and lateral abrasion; coarse grey fluvial sandstone.
35	5285	644.39	3	Rubbing stone, flat tapering oblong, natural chip from narrow end (worn); soft stone, yellowish with orange surfaces; unchipped flat surface is worn and battered, perhaps from crushing limestone plaster, one long edge worn, from burnishing plaster?
36	5355	706.18	4	Elongated oval stone, chipped/worked; white; probably rough-out for ground-stone tool.

Virginia Mathias

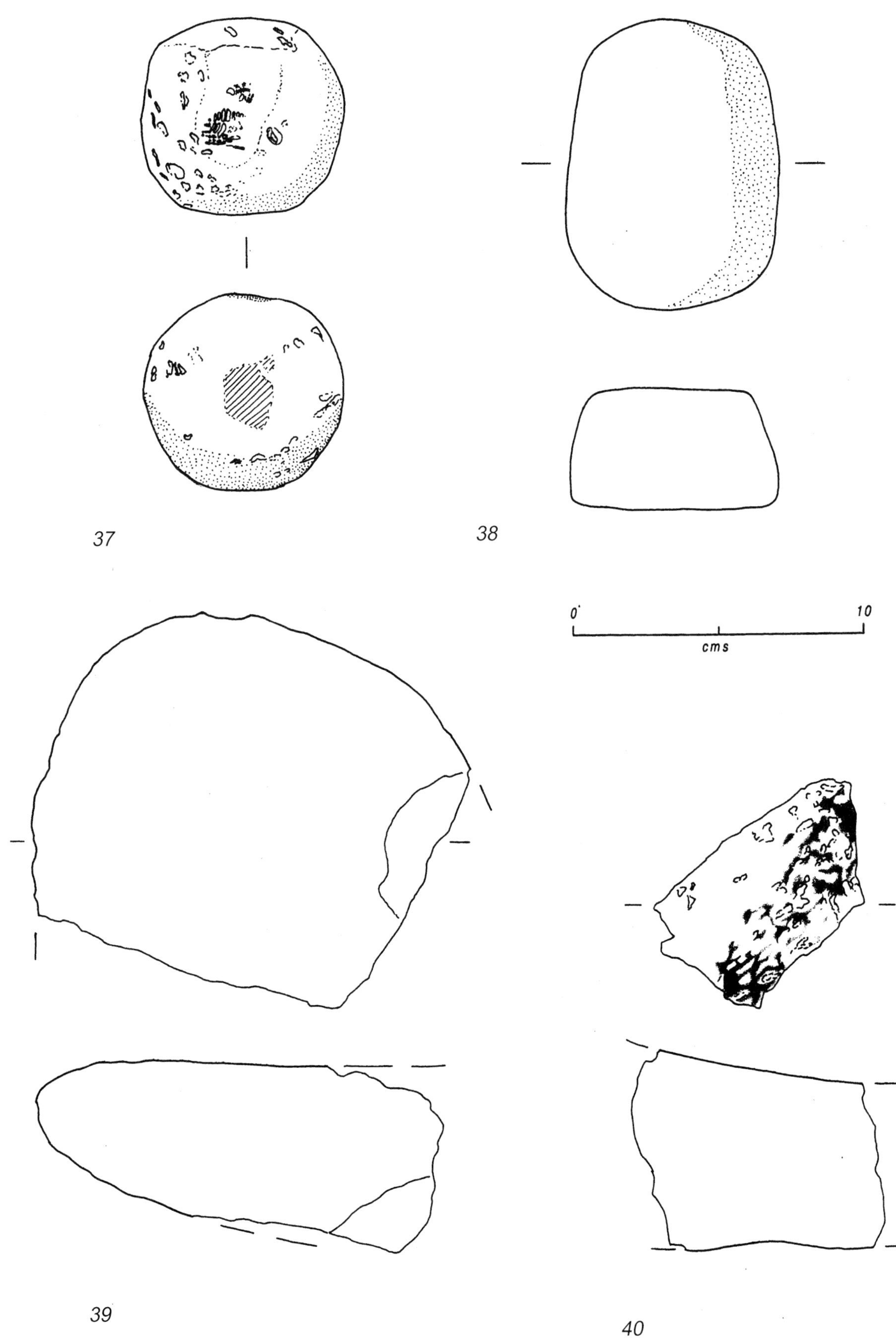

37

38

39

40

Fig. 6.5. Stone (shaped objects/tools, continued).

	Reg. No.	Provenance	Phase	
37	5107	680.42	5	Hammerstone, roughly spherical with small facets, battered; reef stone, fossilised coral? (large fossils visible); pink/whitish, 3 facets have reddish marks or staining.
38	5356	706.42	2	Rubbing stone (?) whole; oblong shape, rounded ends, upper and lower surfaces flat.
39	5357	710.2	5	Quern fragment (?) rounded end or corner, tapering to edge, flat upper surface, lower surface convex or natural curve; probably basalt.
40	5281	606.9	3	Quern fragment (?) upper surface slightly concave and sloping, underside natural, uneven but flattish (all edges broken); ground upper surface has fine polish in places, probably through use; dense black basalt.

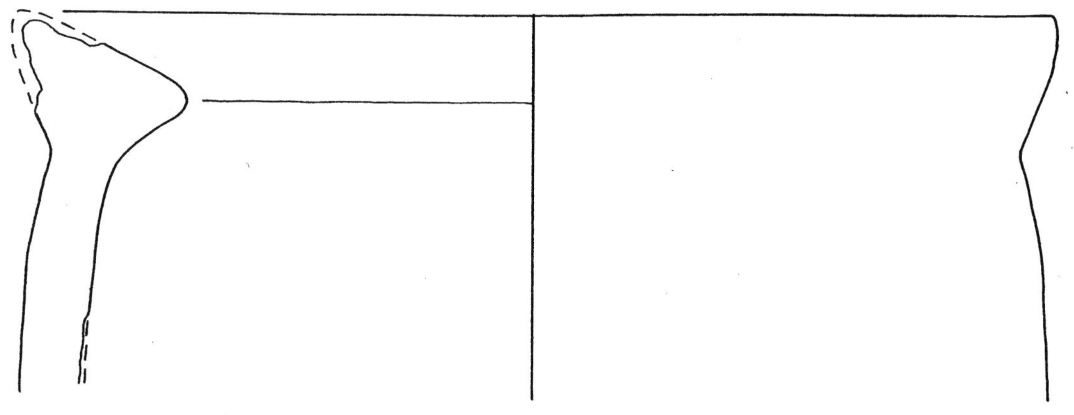

41

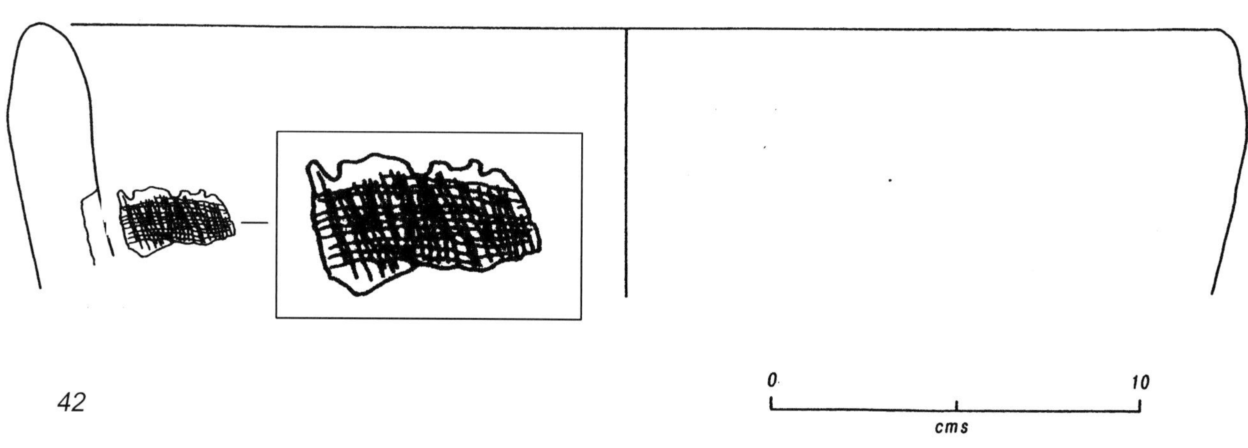

42

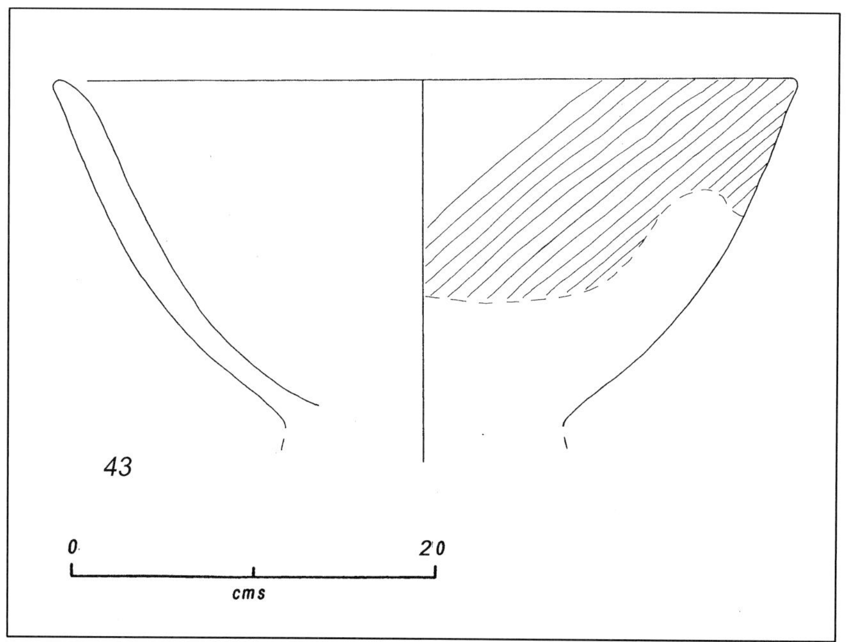

43

Fig. 6.6. White Ware.

	Reg. No.	*Provenance*	*Phase*	
41	5343	710.7	4	Rim, with double flange, deep basin or jar with sides slightly inverted towards rim; fairly fine white plaster, built up in two obvious stages: a much thinner core shape (already including the flanged rim, and possibly including old ground-up plaster) with a wiped or roughened surface, covered by a variable layer (2–5 mm) of fine plaster with a well smoothed surface; outside of vessel burnished, inside chipped and worn lower down.
42	5335	706.20	2 (?3)	Rim of open bowl with nearly upright sides; coarse pale-greyish plaster, with small brown and grey grits or burnt inclusions, also some small white, probably finely ground plaster; thick-walled, built up in layers, with cloth used as key or reinforcement, leaving a clear impression on internal surface of a fragment; all surfaces smoothed; orange-red traces on concave surface outside rim may be paint.
43	5333	706.18	4	Large flaring bowl with slightly everted rim, and high disc base or foot; fine white plaster, some fine grits or burnt inclusions; relatively thin-walled, with a thin (1–2 mm) outer layer of slightly finer plaster, with well-smoothed surfaces; possible blackish paint or wash on upper outside surface, pale brownish inside rim may be later staining.
–	5338	709.16	3	Body, very thick (40–45 mm); fine white plaster; one surface concave, one irregular; from vestigial plaster level/floor, and could be curve between floor and wall; however, both surfaces have a fine smoothed layer and may be White Ware.
–	5341	709.32	?4	Body, very thick (55 mm), both surfaces well smoothed (outer irregular); fine white plaster, small and large grey grits and stones, and possibly some pale buff. Massive White Ware vessel, or possibly part of a plaster installation.
–	5336	706.25	2	Body, thin (13–15 mm); fairly fine white plaster, fine dark grits or burnt inclusions; outside surface better smoothed and more curved than inside; concave outside near break, *i.e.* may be part of raised base, or flared rim, or neck/shoulder of jar shape.
–	5337	706.42	2	Body, thin (12 mm); very fine white plaster; outside surface well smoothed or burnished, inside slightly worn; possible shoulder/neck or raised base.
–	5339	709.19	4 (?2)	Body, thin (9–11 mm), very small piece; fine cream plaster; both surfaces well smoothed.
–	5342	710.4	5	Body, thin (12–14 mm); fine creamy-white plaster; both surfaces well smoothed or burnished, and well curved, *i.e.* relatively small vessel.

Plate 6.1. Selected objects.

7. Animal husbandry and domestication[1]

Caroline Grigson

The assessment of the fauna of the Early Pottery Neolithic levels at Tell Nebi Mend is important because the assemblage dates from the early part of the 7th millennium BC, when it is thought that cattle and pigs may have been in the process of domestication. In order to consider the fauna in diachronic and geographical context comparisons will be made with the results of the few faunal analyses of contemporary sites in the Levant that have been published, as well as with the nearby mid-6th- and early 5th-millennium site of Arjoune (Grigson 2003). Later periods are also represented at Tell Nebi Mend, but the present study is confined to the Neolithic levels excavated from 1982 to 1995. All the dates and periods mentioned in this paper are in calibrated years BC.

Criteria of domestication

Various stages in the domestication of animals have been postulated, most involving one or more intermediate stages of proto-domestication or incipient domestication. For example, Horwitz (1993) has proposed a four-step sequence of domestication from generalised hunting to selective hunting – that is, a new concentration on a particular species or on animals of a particular age or sex – followed by captivity and, finally, controlled breeding. Various criteria have been utilised to establish the presence of domestic rather than wild animals in archaeological assemblages, including a sudden introduction of a species outside its known geographical range, a reduction in size, differences in the representation of the sexes or ages of both, and, more recently, dental pathology (Ervynck *et al.* 2001; Dobney *et al.* 2007).

A reduction in size is one of the main effects of domestication in goats, sheep and other artiodactyls (see, for example, Zeuner 1963; Grigson 1969; 1978; 1989; Davis 1982; Uerpmann 1979; 1982; Clutton-Brock 1981;

Peters *et al.* 1999), and there is an increasing amount of published data on artiodactyl size in Middle Eastern archaeological sites. In many cases, however, only the basic statistical parameters, such as range, mean and standard deviation, are given and, although these are much better than nothing, they are not really adequate because it is necessary to know the *pattern* of the distribution of individual measurements within each size range. This is because the main factor known to affect size is sexual dimorphism, so the distribution of size within a range will vary if there is a preponderance of females or males, a pattern which is totally obscured when only the statistical parameters are given.

Uerpmann (1979) compared the measurements of sheep and goats from various sites of various periods in the Middle East with a 'standard animal' and showed that there was a significant size change in both goats and sheep between what he called the Proto-Neolithic (8th millennium) and the Early Neolithic (PPNB) at about 7000 BC. The diminution was really quite small, but definite enough to show that the sheep and goats in the Pre-pottery Neolithic B sites had already undergone morphological changes associated with domestication. I made a similar analysis of cattle bones (Grigson 1989) from a wide range of sites and showed that in the western part of the Middle East cattle appeared to have undergone a marked diminution in size in the 6th millennium (roughly 7th millennium if calibrated) – that is, during the early Pottery Neolithic. Since then Peters *et al.* (1999), on rather limited size data from sites along the Euphrates, have postulated that the domestication of cattle had already started during the middle PPNB. More recently, many more measurements of sheep, goats, cattle and pigs have been published and, when relevant, these have been incorporated within the present work in the comparisons of the size of the Tell Nebi Mend bones during the Neolithic.

Caroline Grigson

Age distributions are sometimes used to demonstrate demographic changes that might be attributable to one or other of the stages of domestication. Both the state of fusion of postcranial elements and tooth wear and eruption have been utilised by means of survivorship curves. It is claimed that people would have killed hunted and domesticated animals at different ages, the theory being that in domestic populations more young animals would be killed, but that wild animals would be hunted randomly, so that their kill-off patterns would reflect the natural demographic structure of the population in the wild (Hole *et al.* 1969; Hesse 1978; 1982; Hecker 1975; Zeder and Hesse 2000). However, there are problems with ageing as a criterion, as it has not been convincingly demonstrated that hunters do kill randomly; indeed, some hunters are definitely selective (Binford 1978). Other difficulties more relevant here are that the criteria used for ageing bones and teeth are still not universally agreed upon, particularly the degree of variation in times of epiphysial fusion (see, for example, Bullock and Rackham 1982); in addition, survivorship curves should theoretically fall with age, whereas sometimes they rise at 2 years (data based on the fusion of the distal tibia of sheep and goats). Other difficulties include the facts that the less dense younger bone may have been differentially destroyed, and most survivorship curves based on long bones span only the ages from birth to about 3.5 years.

Methods

The quantification of the various taxa at Tell Nebi Mend has been made on the basis of the number of bone finds – that is, the number of identified specimens (NISP in the American literature) – modified when it is clear that any one bone came from the same individual animal as another, as, for example, when bones of the same ankle were found together or when a collection of teeth obviously derive from the same jaw. Numbers were used rather than weight because of the varying amount of calcium carbonate coating and penetration.

Although calculations of the minimum number of individuals (MNI) may be useful in small closed features such as pits, both Gautier (1984) and Ducos (1983) have shown that the statistical chance that any one bone found on an open archaeological site belonged to the same individual as another is minute, particularly on sites which were occupied for several hundred years. Therefore I have used MNI counts only in the bone element analyses (as a basis for estimating which elements are under-represented in the assemblage), and I have *not* used them to quantify the relative contributions of the various taxa.

All measurements are in millimetres and are based on those defined by von den Driesch (1976). The measurements of the bones and teeth of each taxon are listed in Appendices 7.1 and 7.2.

The sample

Five stratigraphic phases were recognised within the Neolithic period, but as the deposits had been extensively disturbed by pits, both Neolithic and post-Neolithic, areas of continuous unbroken layers – floors, occupation material, destruction debris – were fragmentary and restricted in size. In consequence it often proved difficult if not impossible to assign every layer to a particular phase with absolute certainty. Moreover, Phase 4 comprised almost entirely pits, while Phase 5 is best understood as a period of abandonment of this part of the site following the Neolithic occupation; both are therefore likely to include a significant amount of material derived from earlier phases. In view of these considerations, the animal bone sample (as also the charred plant sample: see Chapter 8) has been analysed as a single Neolithic entity. As only a few deposits were sieved in excavation it is possible that very small bones may be under-represented.

Apart from a concentration of burnt equid bones in one layer, consisting of 'ashy/burnt soil' (706.33), there was no spatial patterning of burnt and unburnt bones, nor were any burnt bones particularly associated with hearths, which suggests considerable post-depositional mixing of what were essentially midden deposits.

The remains of 784 mammals were identified, as well as seven crab claws, four tortoise scutes and two bird bones, not identified to taxon. The numbers are set out in Table 7.1. A few of the pig and cattle bones are so large that they are thought to have been from wild animals.

Sheep (*Ovis aries*) and goats (*Capra hircus*)

The numbers of sheep and goats

The difficulties inherent in the separation of goat from sheep bones are well known and are further compounded at Tell Nebi Mend, as on most Middle Eastern sites, by the presence of gazelle. However, the number of definite gazelles is so small that it is statistically probable that those bones that could be identified only as sheep/goat/gazelle were of sheep or goats. The bones in the sheep/goat category have been allocated to the two species on the basis of the relative numbers of specifically identified bones (Table 7.2), and it seems that sheep outnumber goats by about 2.6:1. These figures have to be regarded as tentative, however; complicating factors include difficulties over the separation of sheep and goat, as some of the criteria used are not always as obvious as they seem to be in the standard works (Boessneck 1969; Lawrence 1980; Clutton-Brock *et al.* 1990), and the fact that goat and gazelle horncores seem to survive better than sheep horncores. It is possible that there were hornless female sheep at Tell Nebi Mend, so the absence of their horncores would bias the counts against them.

Goat horncore morphology

The morphology of goat horncores was discussed at length in the paper on Arjoune (Grigson 2003), which showed that wild and early domestic goats had scimitar-shaped cores and that, although screwed horns may have appeared as early as the 7th millennium, they did not become common until the 5th. Two of the 37 goat horncores at Arjoune in the mid-6th and early 5th millennia were screwed, the remainder being scimitar-shaped. Only four sheep or goat horncores were found at Tell Nebi Mend; all were fragmentary and only two could be definitely attributed to taxon, including the base of a horncore of a female goat, apparently not screwed.

Goat size

The size of the goat bones from Tell Nebi Mend has been compared with Uerpmann's (1979) standard animal (Table 7.3) and with his graphs of size change in different periods, updated with the addition of more recently published data but using the same formula for calculation, the index $= 1/9*(1250*n/st-800)$, where st = standard and n = measurement. The resulting histograms (Fig. 7.1 a1–a4) show that there was a steady decrease in size from the wild goats of the Epi-Palaeolithic and PPNA to the pre-Halaf of Sabi Abyad and Halula, with an increasing emphasis on females. Although some of the goat bones from Tell Nebi Mend and the other contemporary sites fall within the area of overlap between the wild goats and the domestic goats of the pre-Halaf (Fig. 7.1 b1), they are concentrated towards the left, and there is little doubt that they represent domestic animals, with one wild goat at Tell Aray.

There are no complete long bones of goats at Tell Nebi Mend, and the withers height cannot be calculated.

Sheep horncores

Hornlessness occurs in some female domestic female sheep from the Early Bronze Age onwards, but there was nothing at Tell Nebi Mend to indicate whether the ewes were hornless or not. A fragment of skull from which the horncore had been removed, leaving the base intact, was identified as from a ram.

Table 7.1. The animals represented at Tell Nebi Mend.

	Taxon	Neolithic	Neo/EB? 644.035
cattle	*Bos taurus*	77	6
cattle	*Bos primigenius*	6	
cattle?	*Bos?* sp.	9	1
pig	*Sus scrofa* (dom)	102	
wild boar	*Sus scrofa*	2	
sheep/goat	*Ovis/Capra*	397	23
sheep	*Ovis aries*	26	
goat	*Capra hircus*	10	
gazelle	*Gazella* sp	27	
deer *	*Cervus* sp.	12	
equid	*Equus* sp.	33	42
	total large mammals	701	72
dog	*Canis familiaris*	6	
fox	*Vulpes* sp.	3	
cat	*Felis* sp.	1	
hare?	*Lepus sp*	1	
bird		2	
tortoise		4	
crab		7	
	total others	24	0
	Total	725	72

* one antler tine was also found

Table 7.3. Standard wild goat.

Means of recent female goat (BMNH 653M) and male goat (BMNH 653L) from the Taurus Mountains, taken from Uerpmann (1979); those used in present study are:

humerus, breadth of trochlea (Bt)	34.2
radius, proximal breadth (Bp)	35.5
radius, distal breadth (Bd)	33.2
metacarpal, proximal breadth (Bp)	27.3
metacarpal, distal breadth (Bd)	30.5
astragalus, greatest length (GLl)	32.0
calcaneum, greatest length (GL)	65.5
metatarsal, proximal breadth (Bp)	23.0
metatarsal, distal breadth (Bd)	28.5

Abbreviations from von den Driesch (1976)

Table 7.2. The numbers of sheep and goats at Tell Nebi Mend.

	Taxon		allocated		
		raw data	proportionately	totals	%
sheep/goat	*Ovis/Capra*	420			
sheep	*Ovis aries*	26	303	329	72.2
goat	*Capra hircus*	10	117	127	27.8
	totals	456	420	456	100.0

Sheep size

As with goats, the size of the sheep bones from Tell Nebi Mend has been compared with Uerpmann's (1979) standard animal (Table 7.4) and with his graphs of size change in different periods, updated with the addition of more recently published data (Fig. 7.2 a1–a4). As with goats, there was a steady decrease in size, and the Tell Nebi Mend sheep are again concentrated on the left (Fig. 7.2 b1).

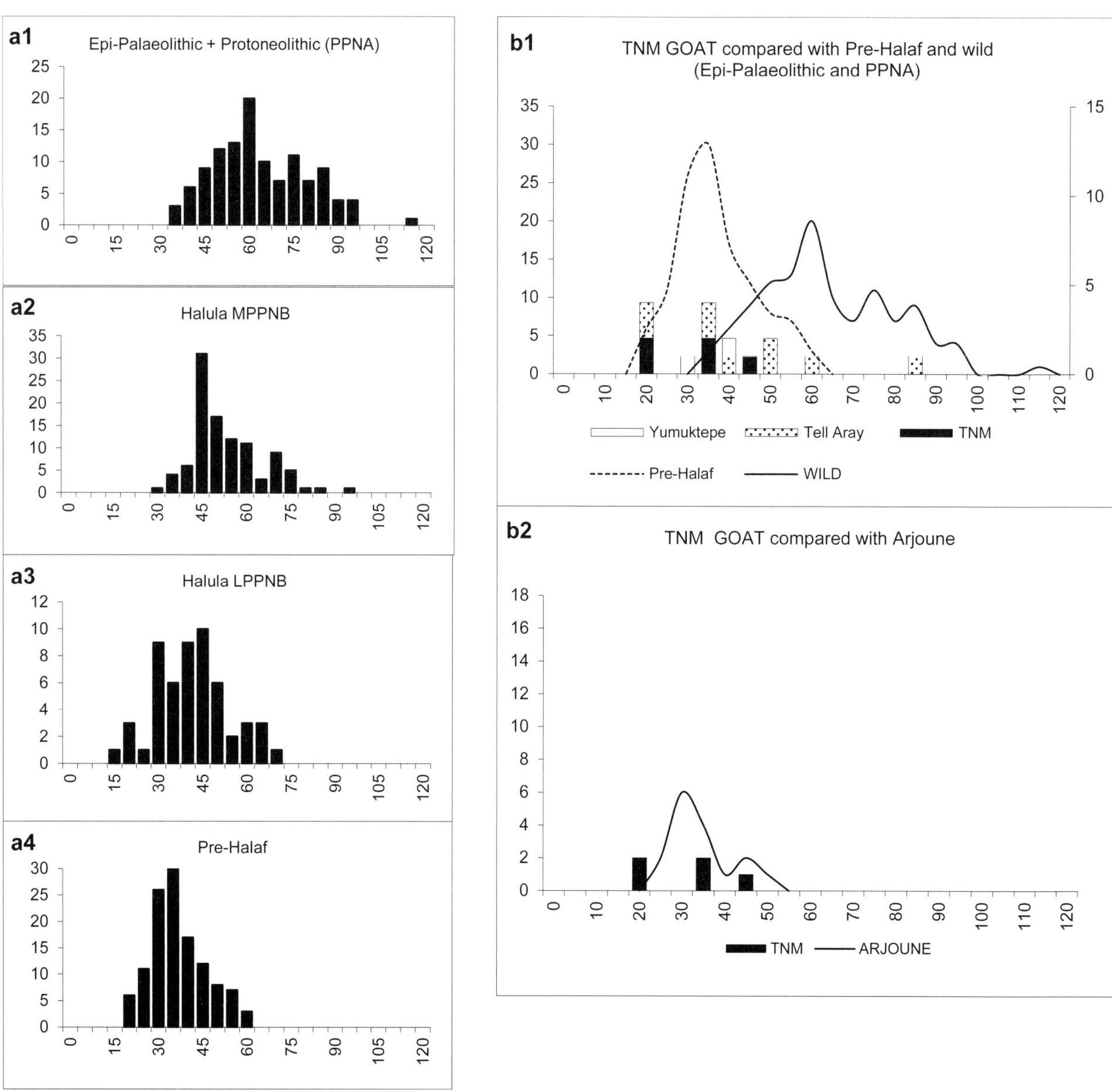

Fig. 7.1. The size of goats compared with Uerpmann's (1979) standard animal and with his graphs of size change in different periods, updated with the addition of more recently published data.
(a1) 'Wild'. Epipalaeolithic and PPNA (Protoneolithic). (a2) Middle PPNB. (a3) Late PPNB. (a4) Pre-Halafian.
Showing a steady decrease in size from the wild goats of the Epi-Palaeolithic and PPNA to the Pre-Halaf of Sabi Abyad and Halula, with an increasing emphasis on females. (b1) The size of goats at Tell Nebi Mend and other roughly contemporary sites compared with that of wild goats and domestic goats from the Pre-Halafian (see 1a4). Although some of the goat bones from Tell Nebi Mend and the other contemporary sites (Tell Aray and Yumuktepe) fall within the area of overlap between the wild goats and the domestic goats of the Pre-Halaf (Fig. 1b), they are concentrated towards the left and there is little doubt that they represent domestic animals, with one wild goat at Tell Aray. (b2) The size of goats at Tell Nebi Mend compared with Arjoune (see section on Arjoune).
For sources of data see Appendix 7.3.

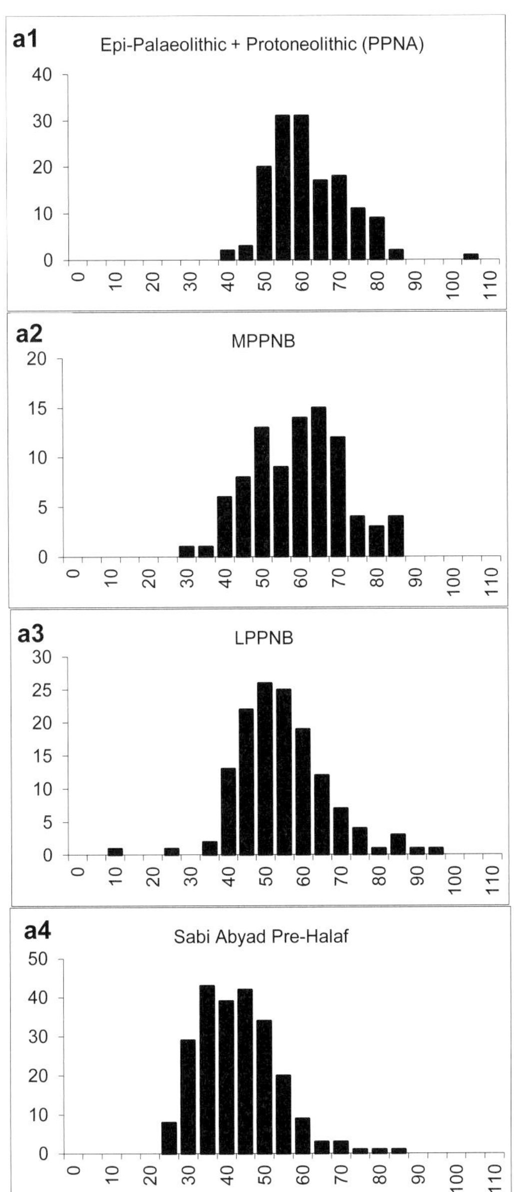

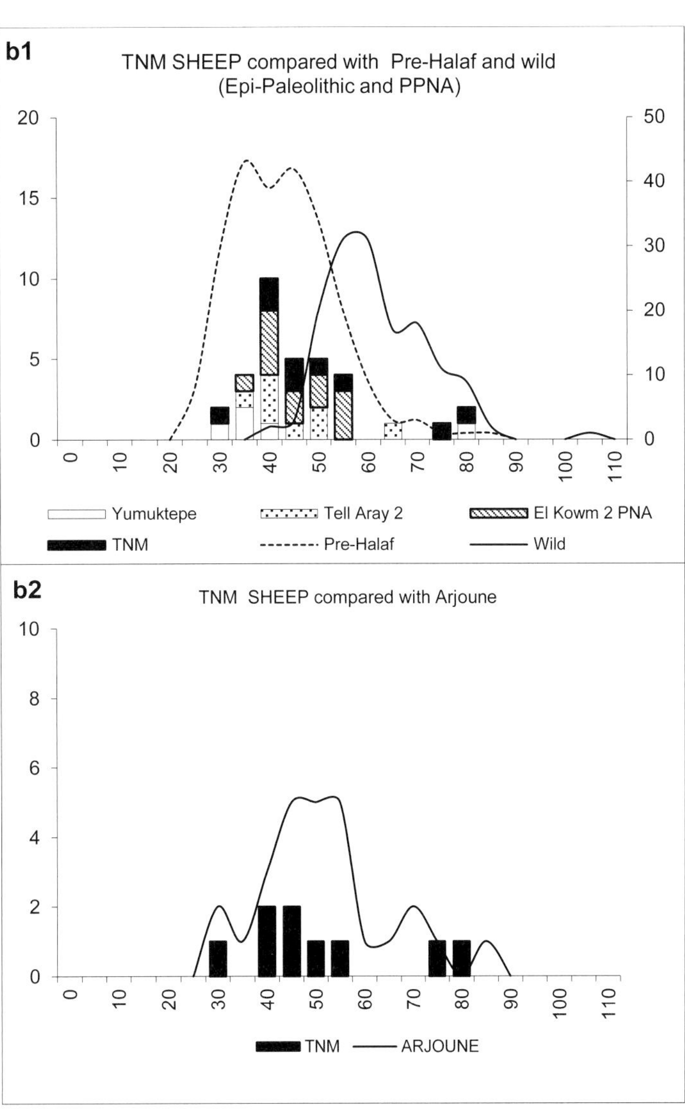

Fig. 7.2. The size of sheep compared with Uerpmann's (1979) standard animal and with his graphs of size change in different periods, updated with the addition of more recently published data. (a1) 'Wild'. Epipalaeolithic and PPNA (Protoneolithic). (a2) Middle PPNB. (a3) Late PPNB. (a4) Pre-Halafian.
There is a steady decrease in size over time. (b1) The size of sheep at Tell Nebi Mend and other roughly contemporary sites compared with that of wild sheep and domestic sheep from the Pre-Halafian (see a4). The Tell Nebi Mend sheep, along with those from Tell Aray and Yumultepe, are concentrated on the left. (b2) The size of sheep at Tell Nebi Mend compared with Arjoune (see section on Arjoune).
For sources of data see Appendix 7.3.

Table 7.4. Standard wild sheep.

Dimensions of recent female sheep (Field Museum of Natural History, Chicago, no. 57, 951) from western Iran, from Uerpmann (1979); those used in present study are:	
scapula, least length of neck (SLC)	19.5
humerus, breadth of trochlea (Bt)	29.5
radius, proximal breadth (Bp)	33.5
radius, distal breadth (Bd)	31.0
metacarpal, proximal breadth (Bp)	25.0
metacarpal, distal breadth (Bd)	26.5
astragalus, greatest length (GLl)	31.3
calcaneum, greatest length (GL)	64.0
metatarsal, proximal breadth (Bp)	22.5
metatarsal, distal breadth (Bd)	26.0

Abbreviations from von den Driesch (1976)

Fig. 7.3. Sheep/Goat ageing at Tell Nebi Mend. (a) Longbone fusion. Approximately 70% of the sheep and goats survived beyond the age of 3–3½ years. (b) Mandibular ageing (histogram) indicating roughly 53% survival beyond 3 years (age group E). (c) Mandibular ageing survival curves, compared with Payne's (1973) theoretical curves for meat, milk and wool production. The curve for Tell Nebi Mend shows a marked resemblance to the meat curve, but when adjusted for differential destruction the curve moves towards Payne's milk curve, suggesting that sheep and goat husbandry was generalised, though with meat as the main product.

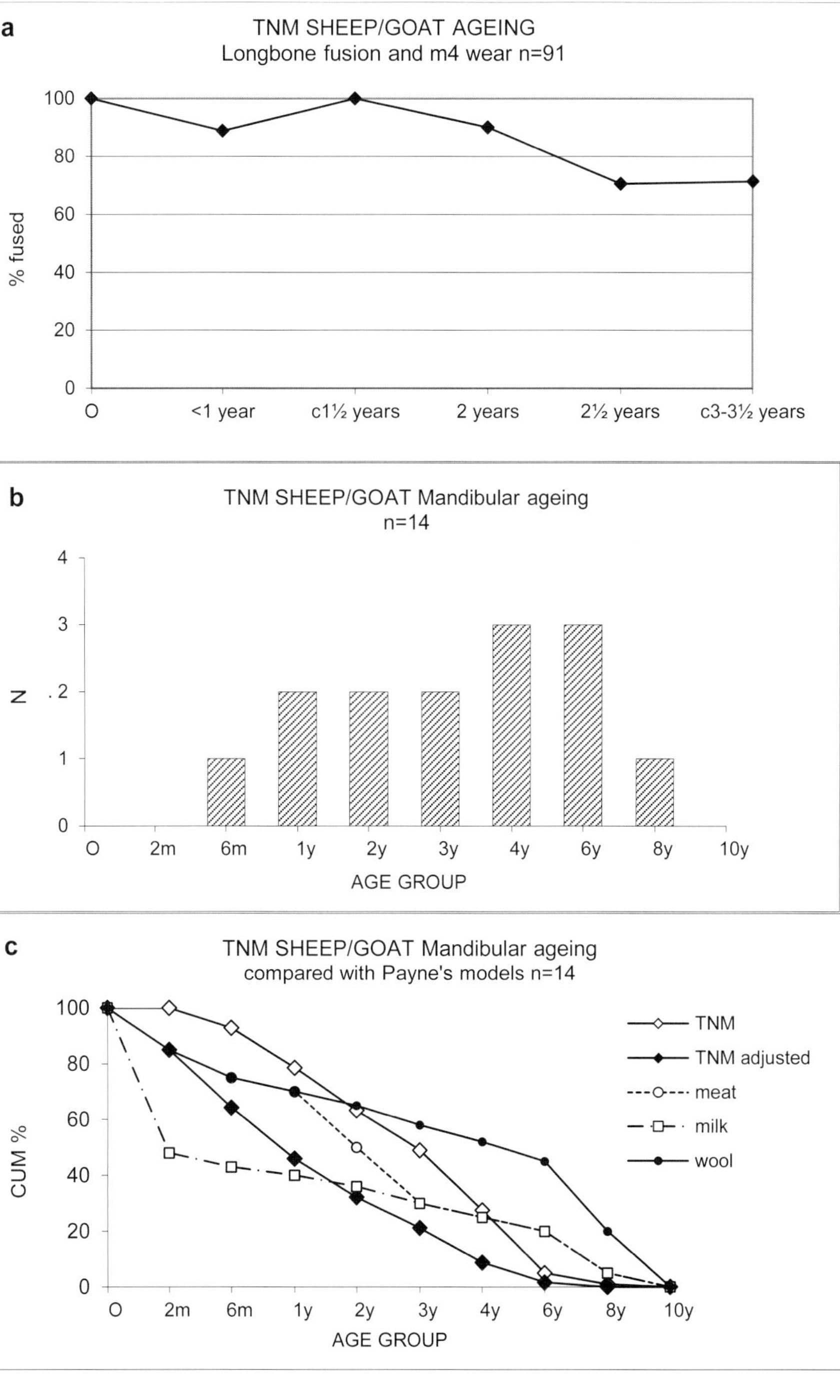

There are no complete long bones of sheep at Tell Nebi Mend, so the withers height cannot be calculated.

Sheep and goats: sexual attributes

Too few bones could be sexed for any meaningful statement to be made.

Sheep and goats: age distributions

An indication of the ages of the animals at death can be gauged from the state of fusion of the epiphyses of the long bones, with the addition of the state of wear of the lower deciduous fourth molar, following the method pioneered by Flannery and his colleagues (Hole *et al.* 1969). Although the sample is rather small, especially for the phalanges at about 1.5 years, the plot of the percentages of unfused to fused bones (Fig. 7.3 a) suggests that roughly 70% of the sheep and goats survived beyond the age of 3–3.5 years.

Only 14 sheep/goat mandibular toothrows and loose teeth could be aged according to the criteria of Payne (1973) and Deniz and Payne (1982). Of these, only seven could be assigned to a single age group; the remainder spanned two or three groups and were assigned to individual age

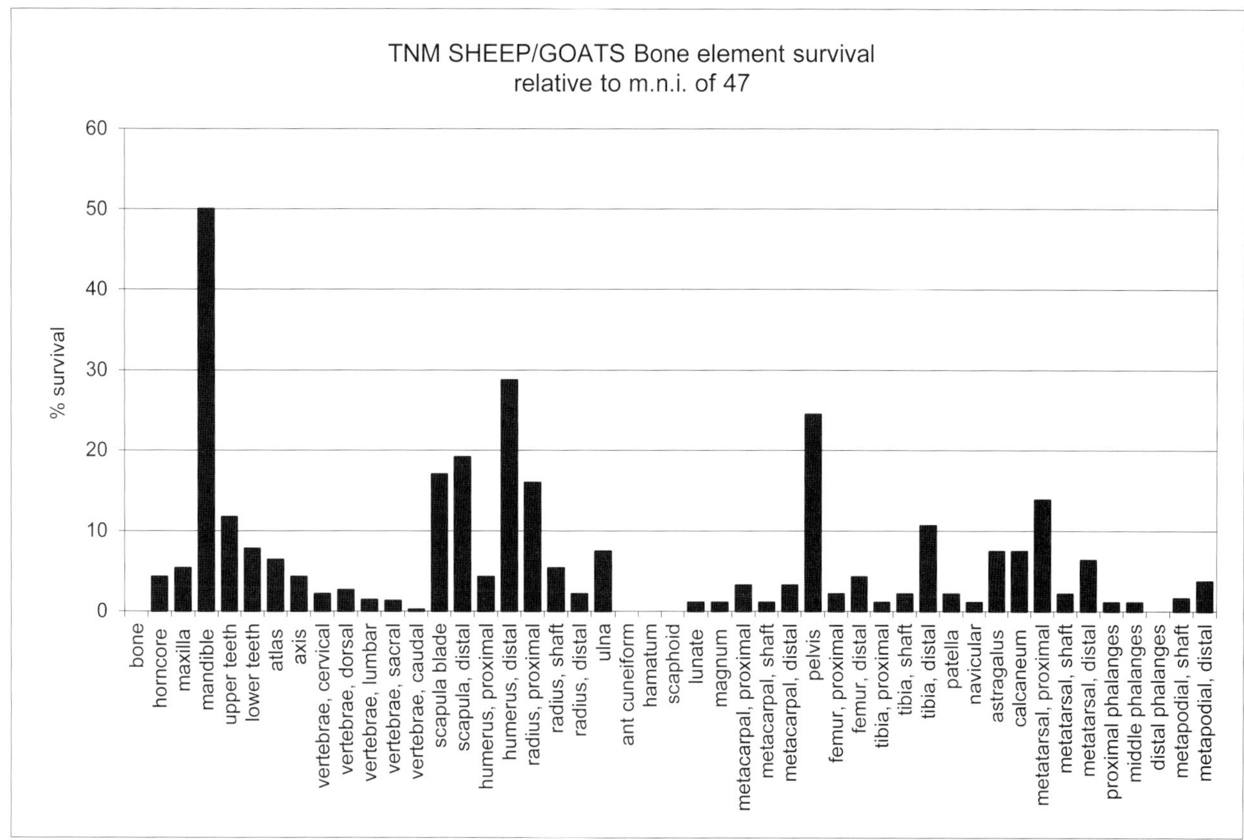

Fig. 7.4. Sheep/Goat bone element survival at Tell Nebi Mend: 1. Histogram showing the percentages of each element.

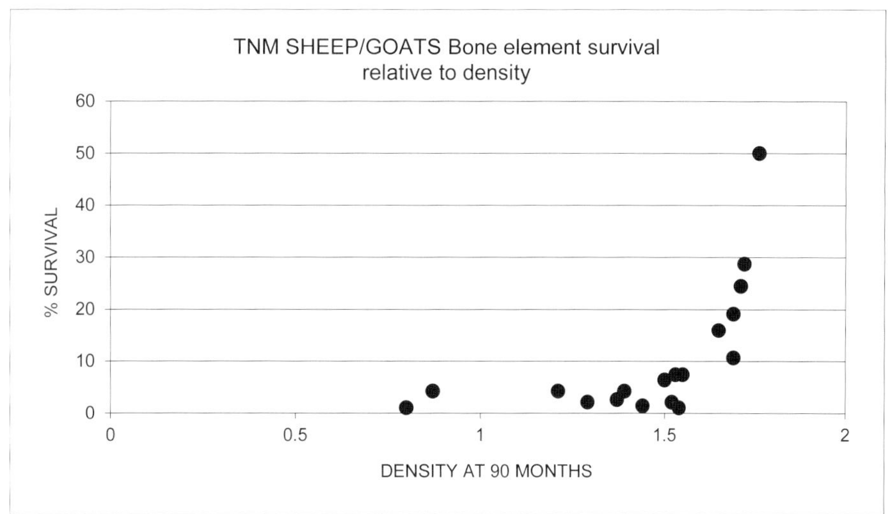

Fig. 7.5. Sheep/Goat bone element survival at Tell Nebi Mend: 2. Scattergram showing the close relationship between bone element survival and bone density. R = 0.58.

groups proportionately on the basis of the distribution of the more accurately aged mandibles. The results are shown in the form of a histogram (Fig. 7.3 b) and a survivorship curve (Fig. 7.3 c).

Theoretical curves for survivorship under three different specialised production regimes, for meat, milk and wool, have been modelled by Payne (1973) and these have been added to the graph (Fig. 7.3 c). The curve for the raw data from Tell Nebi Mend shows a marked resemblance to Payne's meat curve. However, the bone element analysis (see below) suggests that there has been a great deal of destruction of the less dense bone at Tell Nebi Mend. According to Binford and Bertram (1977) sheep mandibles have a relative density of 1.4 at the age of 6 months and 1.51

Table 7.5. Sheep and goat body parts at Tell Nebi Mend.

mni=47 bone	no. in skeleton	no. expected	no. found	max % survival	density at 90 m
horncore	2	94	4	4.3	
maxilla	2	94	5	5.3	
mandible	2	94	47	50.0	1.76
upper teeth	12	564	66	11.7	
lower teeth	20	940	73	7.8	
atlas	1	47	3	6.4	1.50
axis	1	47	2	4.3	1.39
vertebrae, cervical	5	235	5	2.1	1.29
vertebrae, dorsal	13	611	16	2.6	1.37
vertebrae, lumbar	6	282	4	1.4	1.44
vertebrae, sacral	5	235	3	1.3	
vertebrae, caudal	20	940	2	0.2	
scapula blade	2	94	16	17.0	
scapula, distal	2	94	18	19.1	1.69
humerus, proximal	2	94	4	4.3	0.87
humerus, distal	2	94	27	28.7	1.72
radius, proximal	2	94	15	16.0	1.65
radius, shaft	2	94	5	5.3	
radius, distal	2	94	2	2.1	1.52
ulna	2	94	7	7.4	
ant cuneiform	2	94	0	0	
hamatum	2	94	0	0	
scaphoid	2	94	0	0	
lunate	2	94	1	1.1	
magnum	2	94	1	1.1	
metacarpal, proximal	2	94	3	3.2	
metacarpal, shaft	2	94	1	1.1	
metacarpal, distal	2	94	3	3.2	
pelvis	2	94	23	24.5	1.71
femur, proximal	2	94	2	2.1	1.52
femur, distal	2	94	4	4.3	1.21
tibia, proximal	2	94	1	1.1	1.54
tibia, shaft	2	94	2	2.1	
tibia, distal	2	94	10	10.6	1.69
patella	2	94	2	2.1	
navicular	2	94	1	1.1	
astragalus	2	94	7	7.4	1.53
calcaneum	2	94	7	7.4	1.55
metatarsal, proximal	2	94	13	13.8	
metatarsal, shaft	2	94	2	2.1	
metatarsal, distal	2	94	6	6.4	
proximal phalanges	8	376	4	1.1	0.80
middle phalanges	8	376	4	1.1	0.80
distal phalanges	8	376	0	0	0.78
metapodial, shaft	4	188	3	1.6	
metapodial, distal	4	188	7	3.7	1.35

at 1 year 7 months. When these figures are compared on the bone element survival graph (Fig. 7.4) they imply a rate of destruction of the mandibles aged 6 months of about 95%, and of about 92% at the age of 1 year 7 months, compared with the mandibles of adults aged 90 months. When allowance is made for these differences, and if, like Payne, one assumes a 15% peri-natal mortality, the curve moves a little nearer to Payne's milk curve. So, despite the small sample size and the problems of differential destruction, it is probably safe to say that sheep and goat husbandry was rather generalised, with meat as the main product; one certain conclusion is that the Tell Nebi Mend strategy bears no resemblance to Payne's model for wool production.

Sheep and goat bone element analysis

Table 7.5 and Fig. 7.4 show that there is a wide discrepancy in the numbers of the different elements surviving. For example, there are 47 mandibular fragments, but two proximal femurs four proximal humeri and no distal phalanges. It is tempting to consider cultural reasons for this, such as butchery patterns and differential transport, but there are two much simpler explanations. The first is that as the deposits were not sieved the smaller bones are under-represented. The second is that Fig. 7.5 shows that there is a statistically significant correlation (r = 0.58) between the numbers of each element surviving and the density of that element, as calculated by Binford and Bertram (1977) for bones of sheep aged 90 months, which is significant at the 1% level, and this suggests *in situ* destruction of the less dense elements. Various factors can be surmised to favour the destruction of less dense bone: chewing by carnivores, especially dogs (Binford 1981), trampling by people, destruction by humic acids, crushing by overburden, alternate drying and wetting, alternate heating and cooling. All these factors probably contributed to the destruction of bone at Tell Nebi Mend. Dogs were certainly present, as two dog bones were found and a few sheep and goat bones had gnaw marks on them.

Cattle (*Bos primigenius/taurus*)

The numbers of cattle

A total of 99 cattle bones and teeth was identified at Tell Nebi Mend (including 10 bones less certainly from cattle); it is suggested below that very approximately six of these bones derived from wild animals, the aurochs *Bos primigenius*.

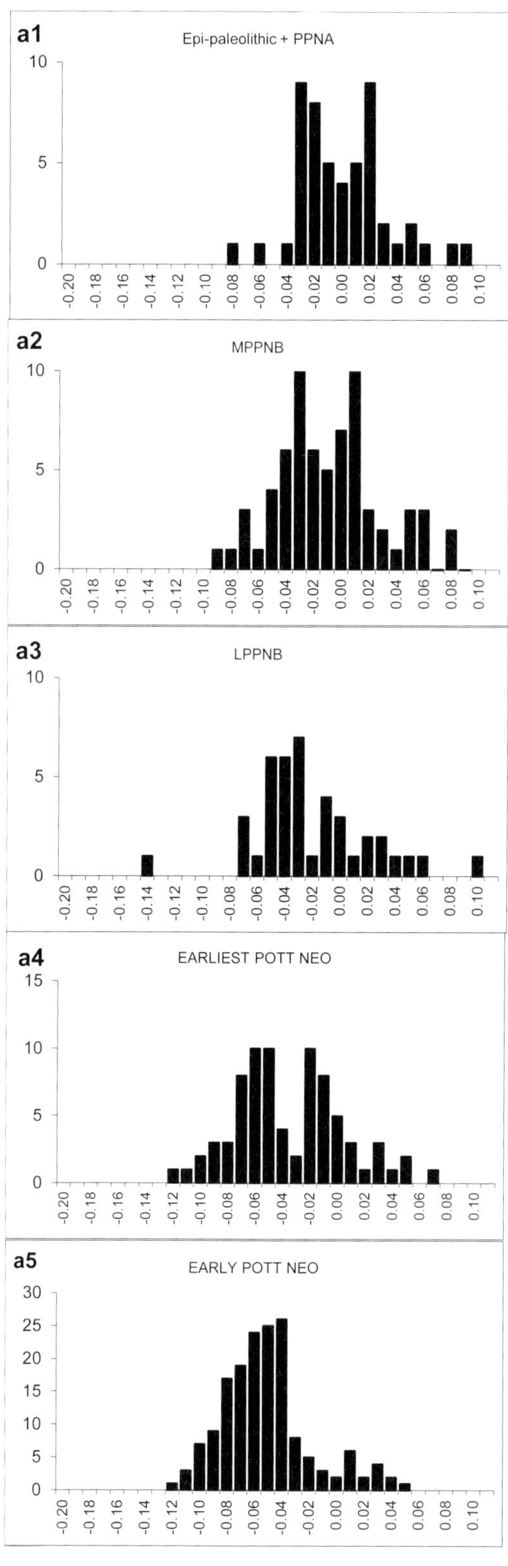
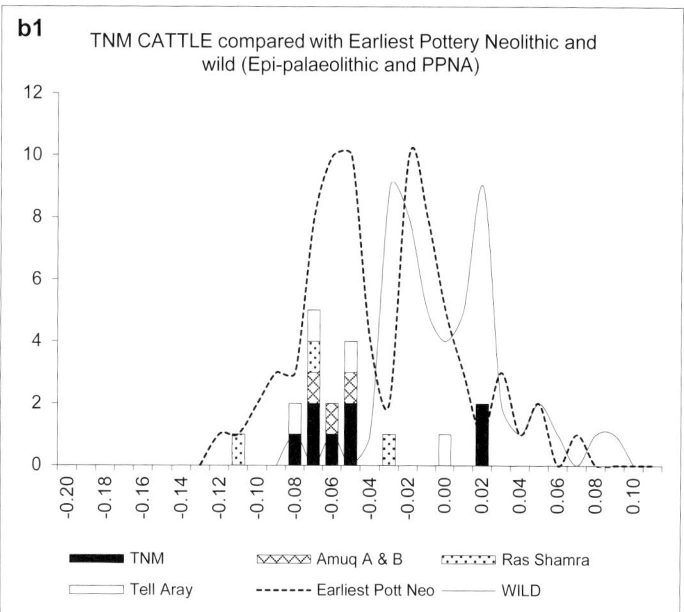
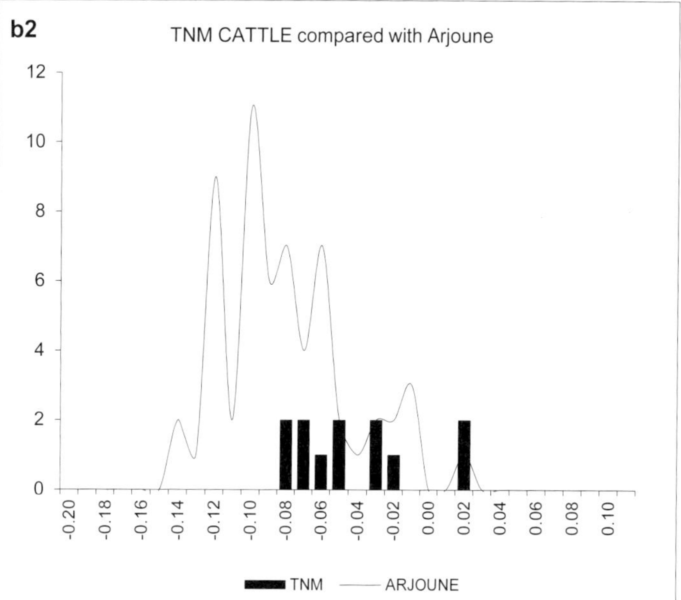

Fig. 7.6. The size of cattle compared with a standard animal and with graphs of size change in different periods, from Grigson (1989), updated with the addition of more recently published data.

(a1) Epipalaeolithic and PPNA. (a2) Middle PPNB. (a3) Late PPNB. (a4) Earliest Pottery Neolithic. (a5) Early Pottery Neolithic.

There is a reduction in size from the Middle PPNB onwards, with a concentration on females from the Late PPNB onwards, which becomes marked in the early Pottery Neolithic. (b1) The size of cattle at Tell Nebi Mend and other roughly contemporary sites compared with that of wild cattle and domestic cattle from the earliest Pottery Neolithic sites. Although most of the cattle bones from Tell Nebi Mend and contemporary sites are within the area of overlap between wild and domestic cattle, their concentration to the left suggests that most were domestic. (b2) The size of cattle at Tell Nebi Mend compared with Arjoune (see section on Arjoune).

For sources of data see Appendix 7.3.

Table 7.6. Cattle age at Tell Nebi Mend. Long bone fusion.

bone	part	age of fusion (months)	fused?	no.	% fused
pelvis	acetabulum	7–10	no	1	
scapula	distal	7–10	no	0	
pelvis	acetabulum	7–10	yes	0	
scapula	distal	7–10	yes	0	0
radius	proximal	12–18	no	0	
humerus	distal	12–18	no	0	
radius	proximal	12–18	yes	2	
humerus	distal	12–18	yes	1	100
prox phalanx	proximal	*c.* 18	no	2	
mid phalanx	proximal	*c.* 18	no	0	
prox phalanx	proximal	*c.* 18	yes	5	
mid phalanx	proximal	*c.* 18	yes	6	85
tibia	distal	24–30	no	0	
mcarpal	distal	24–30	no	0	
mpodial	distal	24–36	no	2	
mtarsal	distal	27–36	no	1	
tibia	distal	24–30	yes	0	
mcarpal	distal	24–30	yes	1	
mpodial	distal	24–36	yes	1	
mtarsal	distal	27–36	yes	0	40
calcaneum	tuber	*c.* 36	no	0	
calcaneum	tuber	*c.* 36	yes	1	100
femur	proximal	42	no	0	
radius	distal	42–48	no	0	
femur	distal	42–48	no	1	
tibia	proximal	42–48	no	0	
humerus	proximal	42–48	no	0	
femur	proximal	42	yes	0	
radius	distal	42–48	yes	0	
femur	distal	42–48	yes	1	
tibia	proximal	42–48	yes	1	
humerus	proximal	42–48	yes	0	67

Ages from Silver 1963

Cattle: domestic status and size

The standard animal used first by Buitenhuis (1985) and then by me (Grigson 1989) is the complete skeleton of an aurochs cow as published by Degerbøl (Degerbøl and Fredskild 1970), but with a different figure for the dimension of the distal humerus (Bd). In my study of the size of cattle in the Middle East (Grigson 1989) I concluded that cattle were domesticated in the western half of the area by or during the 6th millennium. At the time of publication radiocarbon dates were not calibrated; with calibration that period would now be roughly equivalent to the 7th millennium. With the publication of new data since then it is now possible to add to and refine the plots published in that paper. Fig. 7.6 a1–a5 shows a slight reduction in size over time, beginning in the middle PPNB, and with a concentration on females from the late PPNB onwards, which does not become really marked until the early Pottery Neolithic. These findings are in keeping with the results found by Peters *et al.* (1999) along the Middle Euphrates. Although most of the cattle bones from Tell Nebi Mend and other sites of the earliest Pottery Neolithic (Fig. 7.6 b1) are within the area of overlap between wild and domestic cattle, their concentration to the left suggests that most were domestic and only a few wild. With so few measurable bones it is not possible to say what proportion was definitely wild, although since in the process of identification only six bones were noted as being particularly large it is probable that the remainder were domestic animals.

Cattle: sexual attributes

There were too few cattle bones at Tell Nebi Mend to draw any conclusions about sex, except on the basis of size as shown above.

Cattle: ageing and sexing

There are too few bones or teeth that can be aged for any definite statement to be made as to a kill-off pattern. However, the results set out in Table 7.6 show that a large proportion survived into adulthood. The two bones of aurochs that can be aged are the calcaneum of an extremely old individual and a proximal phalanx with a fused proximal epiphysis indicating an age of at least 18 months.

Cattle: bone element analysis

Analysis of the cattle bone elements (Table 7.7 and Fig. 7.7) shows that there must have been much destruction of bones softer than fragments of mandible and pelvis. The proximal humerus and

Table 7.7. Cattle body parts at Tell Nebi Mend.

mni=5

bone	no. in skeleton	no. expected	no. found	max % survival
horncore	2	10	0	0.0
maxilla	2	10	0	0.0
mandible fragment	2	10	5	50.0
upper teeth	12	60	9	15.0
lower teeth	20	100	4	4.0
hyoid	2	10	0	0.0
atlas	1	5	0	0.0
axis	1	5	0	0.0
cervical vertebrae	5	25	4	16.0
dorsal vertebrae	13	65	5	7.7
lumbar vertebrae	6	30	4	13.3
sacral vertebrae	5	25	0	0.0
caudal vertebrae	28	140	1	0.7
scapula	2	10	3	30.0
humerus, proximal	2	10	0	0.0
humerus, distal	2	10	3	30.0
radius, proximal	2	10	2	20.0
radius, distal	2	10	0	0.0
ulna	2	10	1	10.0
anterior cuneiform	2	10	0	0.0
hamatum	2	10	0	0.0
scaphoid	2	10	3	30.0
metacarpal, proximal	2	10	2	20.0
metacarpal, distal	2	10	1	10.0
pelvis	2	10	6	60.0
femur, proximal	2	10	0	0.0
femur, distal	2	10	5	50.0
tibia, proximal	2	10	1	10.0
tibia, distal	2	10	0	0.0
navicular	2	10	1	10.0
posterior cuneiform	2	10	1	10.0
astragalus	2	10	2	20.0
calcaneum	2	10	7	70.0
fibula	2	10	0	0.0
metatarsal, proximal	2	10	4	40.0
metatarsal, distal	2	10	1	10.0
proximal phalanges	8	40	9	22.5
middle phalanges	8	40	6	15.0
distal phalanges	8	40	0	0.0
metapodial, distal	4	20	4	20.0
rib	26	130	1	0.8

proximal femur are completely absent, suggesting that there has been differential destruction of the less dense bone elements of cattle as well as of sheep and goats. In general all parts of the body are represented, so it is unlikely that there was any differential transport.

Pigs (*Sus scrofa*)

The numbers of pigs

There were 104 pig bones in the assemblage.

Pig: domestic status and size

It is particularly important to decide on the domestic status of the pigs at Tell Nebi Mend, as it is thought that it may have been during the 7th millennium that pigs were first domesticated in the Middle East. Criteria for the separation of wild and domestic pigs on the basis of size, particularly third molar length, have been much discussed (Flannery 1983, pers. comm.; Stampfli 1983; McArdle 1974). The sharp size division used by these authors is unsatisfactory, as there is a real possibility that pigs were in the course of domestication in the Neolithic sites discussed by these authors, resulting in overlapping rather than discrete size ranges, so the comparison of size *distributions* within the ranges is of greater value. One point which needs to be borne in mind is that modern wild pigs of the Near East (see Flannery 1983 and especially Payne and Bull 1988) are smaller than early Holocene wild pigs, even though the ranges overlap. This is often forgotten when modern data are used as a basis for the comparison of the actual size of prehistoric wild and domestic pigs.

The late Berin Kusutman measured a large number of pig bones from many Near Eastern sites stored in various museums in Britain, the United States, Israel and Turkey, and the data she published in her PhD thesis form an invaluable resource in the study of pig domestication (Kusutman 1991).

It has been stated that the pigs at Hallan Çemi, a 9th-millennium site in eastern Anatolia, were domesticated. Redding and Rosenberg (1998) reached this conclusion on a variety of grounds, including body-part distribution and age and sex profiles. Without any published details these cannot be assessed and are, in any case, rather dubious as criteria for domestication (Peters *et al.* 1999). However, they have published measurements of a few of the molars, which, when compared with the standard animal (see below), are rather smaller than those at contemporary sites, although there is much overlap. The problem here is that we do not know the state of wear of the teeth, since cheek tooth length tends to reduce with wear as animals age. At Çayönü, where nearly 50% of the bones from the PPNC were of pigs, it has been shown that there was a gradual intensification of the relationship between people and pigs during the late PPNB, culminating in the early Pottery Neolithic with full domestication (Hongo and Meadow 2000; Ervynck *et al.* 2001). At Hagoshrim in the Jordan Valley where 42% of the bones from the PPNC were of pigs, and Haber and Dayan (2004), using sophisticated statistical methods, have shown

                    Caroline Grigson

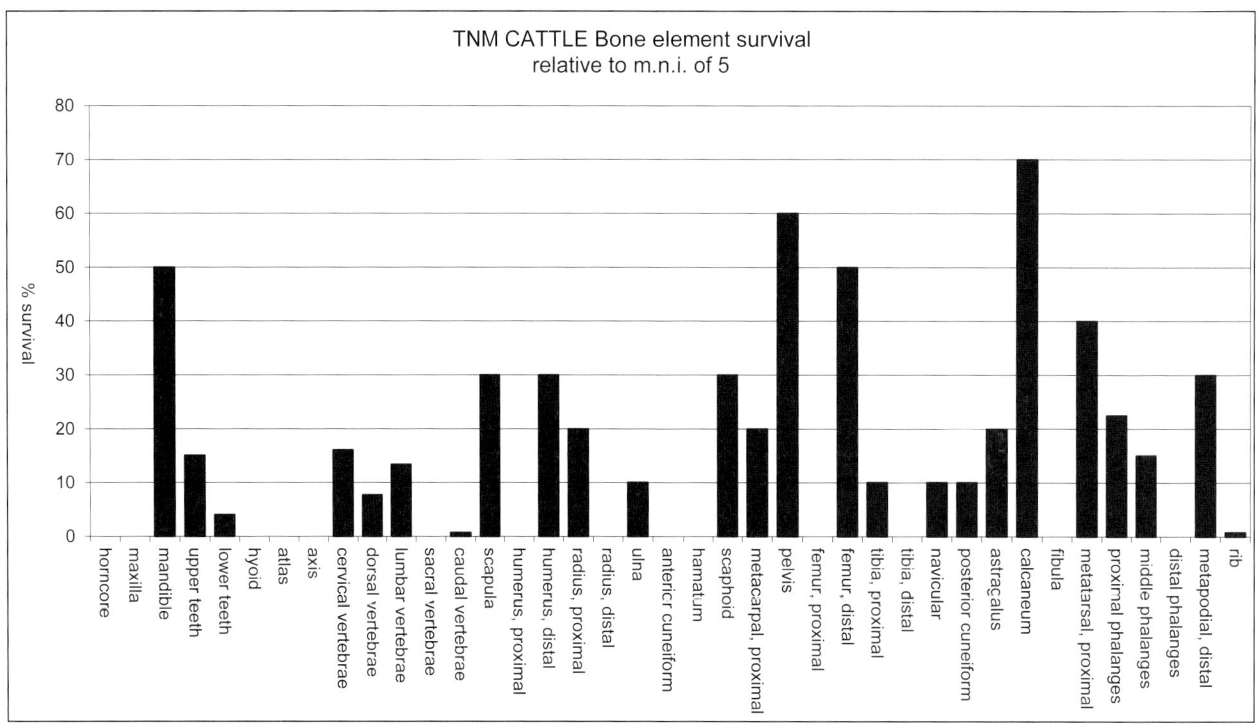

Fig. 7.7. Cattle bone element survival at Tell Nebi Mend. Histogram showing the percentages of each element. Distal metapodials have been grouped together.

that here too there was a similar intensification, although they believe the pigs in the PPNC to have been wild and that the domestication process started in an early phase of the Pottery Neolithic (Jericho IX), contining through the succeeding Wadi Rabah phase.

As with sheep, goats and cattle, size comparisons of size with a standard animal can be done for pigs, the standard used here being that produced by Payne and Bull (1988) and derived not from an individual animal but from a group of modern wild boar in Turkey (Table 7.8). Plots of size change (Fig. 7.8 a1–a4) show a slight diminution over time as early as the middle PPNB, as at Çayönü, but it is not until the earliest pottery Neolithic – using the example of the upper levels from Jarmo – that the shift to the left is more marked, and even then the size change is relatively small. Fig. 7.8 b1–b2 shows that the distribution of the pig dimensions from Tell Nebi Mend and other very early Pottery Neolithic sites is very similar to that from Jarmo, where it is thought that, while domestic pigs predominated, there were some wild animals as well (Stampfli 1983; Flannery 1983). At Tell Nebi Mend itself none of the bones on the graph was particularly large, but two unmeasurable bones were noted as exceptionally large and probably represent a minimum of two wild boar.

Pigs: sexual attributes

Pigs' jaws are easy to sex, provided that the sexually dimorphic canine or its alveolus are present, as was the case in three mandibles from Tell Nebi Mend – one male and three females (with another less certainly female skull fragment). But no conclusions can be drawn from such a small sample except to state that both sexes are represented.

Pigs: age distribution

The survival curve for pigs (Fig. 7.9) is based on only 22 bones, but suggests that less than a fifth of the animals survived beyond the age of 3.5 years, a younger profile than that of the sheep and goats. However, the body-part analysis of the sheep and goat bones demonstrated that there has been a significant degree of destruction of the softer bone, which may explain the rather small numbers of bones of young pigs.

Pig bone element analysis

At Tell Nebi Mend, as in many archaeological assemblages, the bones of the skulls of pigs survive to a much greater degree than the postcranials. Although the relative density of the various parts of the pig's skeleton has not been established, the skull bones seem to be denser than the rest of the skeleton. Table 7.9 and Fig. 7.10 show that the high degree of destruction implied by this pattern is reflected by the very small numbers of other bones that survived, apart from the scapula and astragalus.

Dogs (*Canis familiaris*)

Only six rather nondescript dog bones were found, enough only to indicate their presence, which is also attested by gnaw marks on some of the bones of other animals.

Equids (*Equus hemionus/africanus/asinus*)

The numbers of equids

A total of 75 remains was identified as equid, but, as we shall see, these were concentrated in two main areas of the excavation, one of which (layer 644.35 and adjacent layers) was a single pit containing 44 equid remains and only a few of other species.

The identification of equids

Three species of equid were present in the Middle East in the Holocene; the problem lies in their identification beyond genus. On the basis of size and dental morphology it is clear that the Tell Nebi Mend equids are not from horses (*Equus caballus*), so they must be from the other equid species known in the Holocene in the Middle East – onagers (*E. hemionus*) or wild or domestic asses (*E. africanus* or *E. asinus*). The difficulties of the separation of these species on bones and teeth are well known and have received much discussion in the various papers edited by Meadow and Uerpmann (1986 and 1991); and although various criteria for distinction have been established they are very variable and not always applicable to the material to hand. The problem is exacerbated by the likely presence, at least when domestic equids are present, of horse/ass hybrids (*i.e.* mules and jennies) and even ass/onager crosses (Zarins 1986; Clutton-Brock 1986; Buitenhuis 1991).

Ducos (1978) published a large and invaluable set of measurements of the equids from the PPNB of Tell Mureybet in northern Syria in the 8th millennium, which has been used a baseline for comparison with many other sites. On the basis of standard deviations calculated by Uerpmann (1982; 1986) they appear to come from a single population. As he has identified the one complete metapodial on the basis of its shape as asinine, Ducos (1975; 1978; 1986) has asserted that all the Mureybet equids were *E. africanus*, not *E. hemionus*. However, as discussed below, there are good reasons to suppose that the majority were actually *hemionus*.

The long bones of asses, both wild and domestic, tend to be rather short and robust compared with those of onagers, but complete long bones are rare, the most complete having been excavated from burials of domestic asses in both Egypt and the Middle East. These are particularly useful because it is also possible to demonstrate differences between the relative *lengths* of the long bones, such as the length of the radius compared with that of the metacarpal (Clutton-Brock 1986).

The most commonly occurring equid 'long' bone in archaeological assemblages is the proximal phalanx,

Table 7.8. Standard wild pig.

Means of measurements from a group of modern wild boar in Turkey (Payne and Bull 1989); those used in present study are:

M3 low L	41.5
Scapula SLC	29.8
humerus Bd	50.0
humerus, breadth of trochlea (Bt)	35.0
radius, proximal breadth (Bp)	34.2
radius, distal breadth (Bd)	41.3
pelvis LAR	36.3
tibia Bd	34.6
calcaneum, greatest length (GL)	95.2
astragalus, greatest length (GLl)	48.7
m4 up L	17.2
M1 up L	20.3
M2 up L	25.2
M3 up L	38.8
m4 low L	22.7
M1 low L	20.4
M2 low L	25.4

Abbreviations from von den Driesch (1976)

and its presence allows comparisons be made between a large number of specimens from many archaeological sites. The main problem is that the anterior and posterior phalanges are not exactly the same size and shape, and the Mureybet baseline usually used for comparison is unreliable. On first sight one can see that those listed as anterior actually seem to be posterior (as confirmed by Uerpmann 1986), but there is an additional difficulty, which is that they appear to have been arbitrarily assigned into two discrete clusters (anterior and posterior) on the basis of their width, implying a very large difference between these phalanges. Comparisons of phalanges known to be from the same individual show that this is *not* the case; the differences are there, but they are quite small. It is therefore necessary to treat the cluster from Mureybet as a single continuous distribution, and not to use the 'posterior' or the 'anterior' clusters alone, as done at ᶜAin Ghazal in Jordan (von den Driesch and Wodtke 1997).

It seems to be generally accepted that in many Middle Eastern sites onagers and wild asses were both present. Helmer (2000) believes that both species were present at El Kowm 2 in the PPNB and were sympatric throughout the region of the Middle Euphrates from at least the beginning of the Holocene. At Shams ed-Din, a Halafian site in the same area, although most of the equids were *E. hemionus* at least two bones, a proximal phalanx and an astragalus, have been identified as *E. asinus* (Uerpmann 1982; 1986; 1991). Uerpmann identified this phalanx

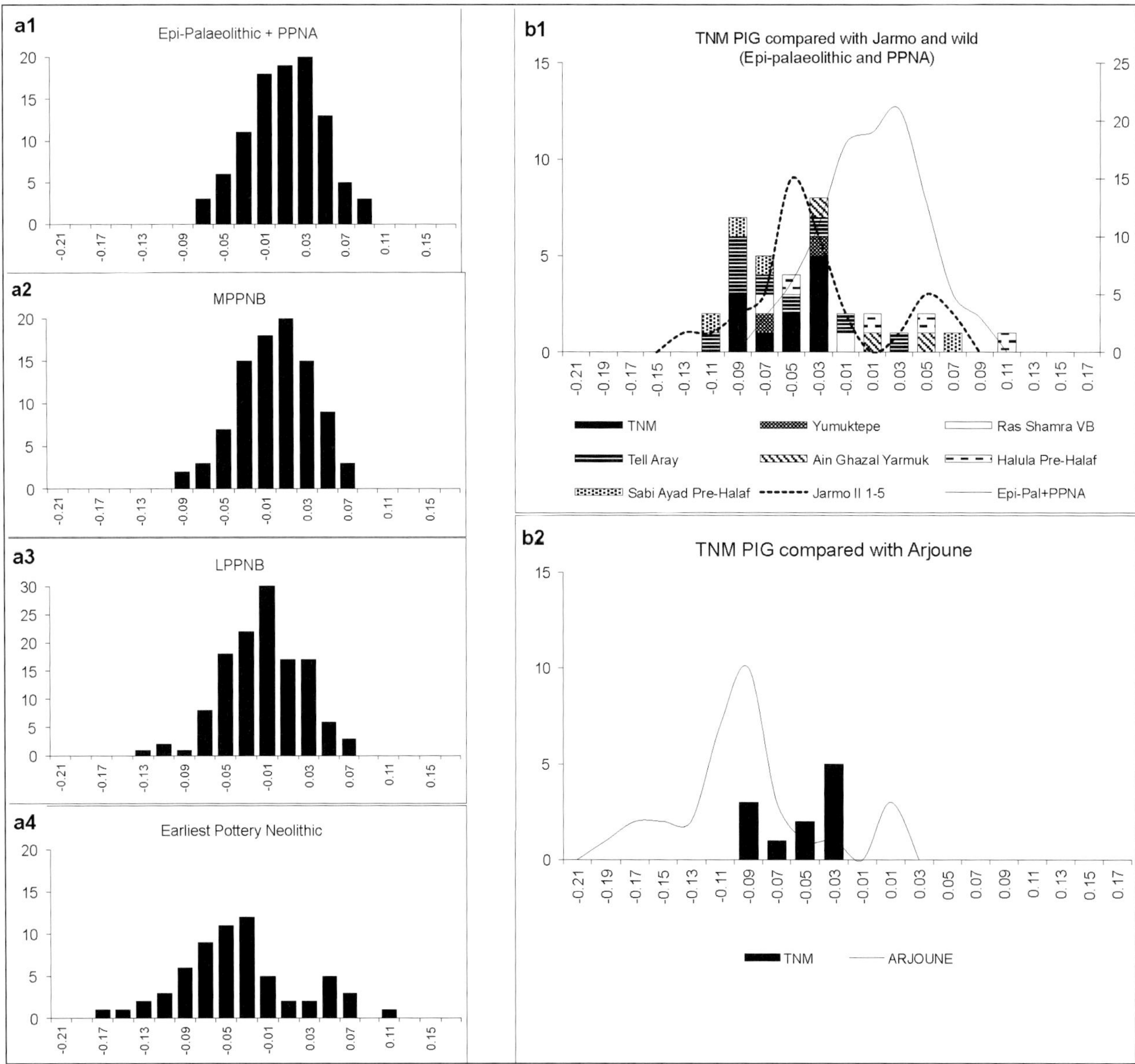

Fig. 7.8. The size of pigs compared with a modern standard for wild boar in Turkey (Payne and Bull 1988).
(a1) Epipalaeolithic and PPNA. (a2) Middle PPNB (Çayönü) (a3) Late PPNB (a4) Earliest Pottery Neolithic (Upper levels Jarmo) Showing a slight diminution over time from the Middle PPNB; in the earliest pottery Neolithic the shift to the left is slightly more marked. (b1) The size of pigs at Tell Nebi Mend and other roughly contemporary sites compared with that of wild pigs and domestic pigs from the earliest Pottery Neolithic at Jarmo. Although overlapping almost entirely with the size range of wild pigs the distribution of size of the bones at Tell Nebi Mend and contemporary sites is similar to that from Jarmo, suggesting that most were domestic, with a few wild boar as well. (b2) The size of pigs at Tell Nebi Mend compared with Arjoune (see section on Arjoune).
For sources of data see Appendix 7.3.

as *asinus*, as well as several from Arabia, on the basis of their robustness – all are more robust than those in the general scatter of Tell Mureybet phalanges, which seem to imply a difference and throws into question the identification of the majority of the Mureybet equids as *asinus*, a doubt also expressed by Meadow (1986), who found only *hemionus* at Çayönü, and by Uerpmann (1991, figs 3 and 4) who plotted the measurements of the Mureybet phalanges as *hemionus*. Measurements of the undoubted asses from Maadi in Egypt (Boessneck *et al.* 1989) are even more robust than those from Arabia, supporting the *asinus* identification. However, it should be

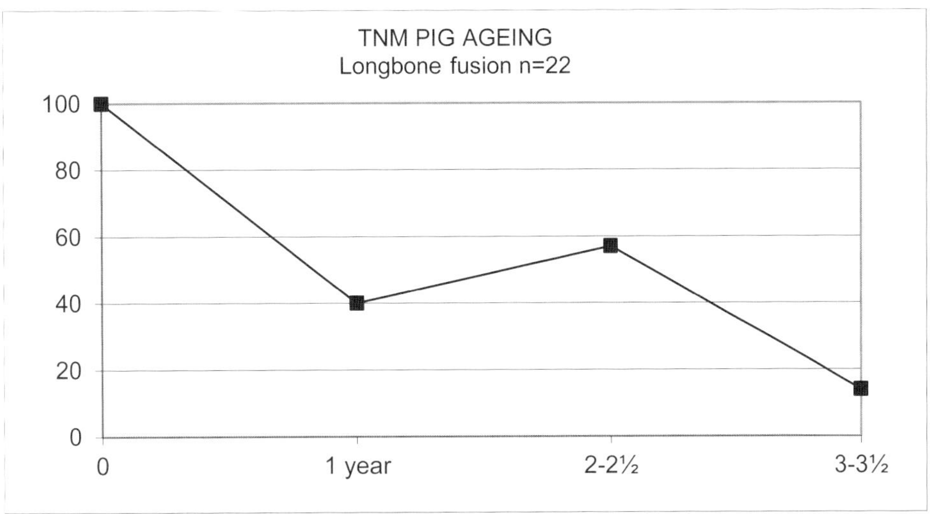

Fig. 7.9. Pig ageing at Tell Nebi Mend. Showing that about a third of the animals survived beyond the age of 3½ (n = 17).

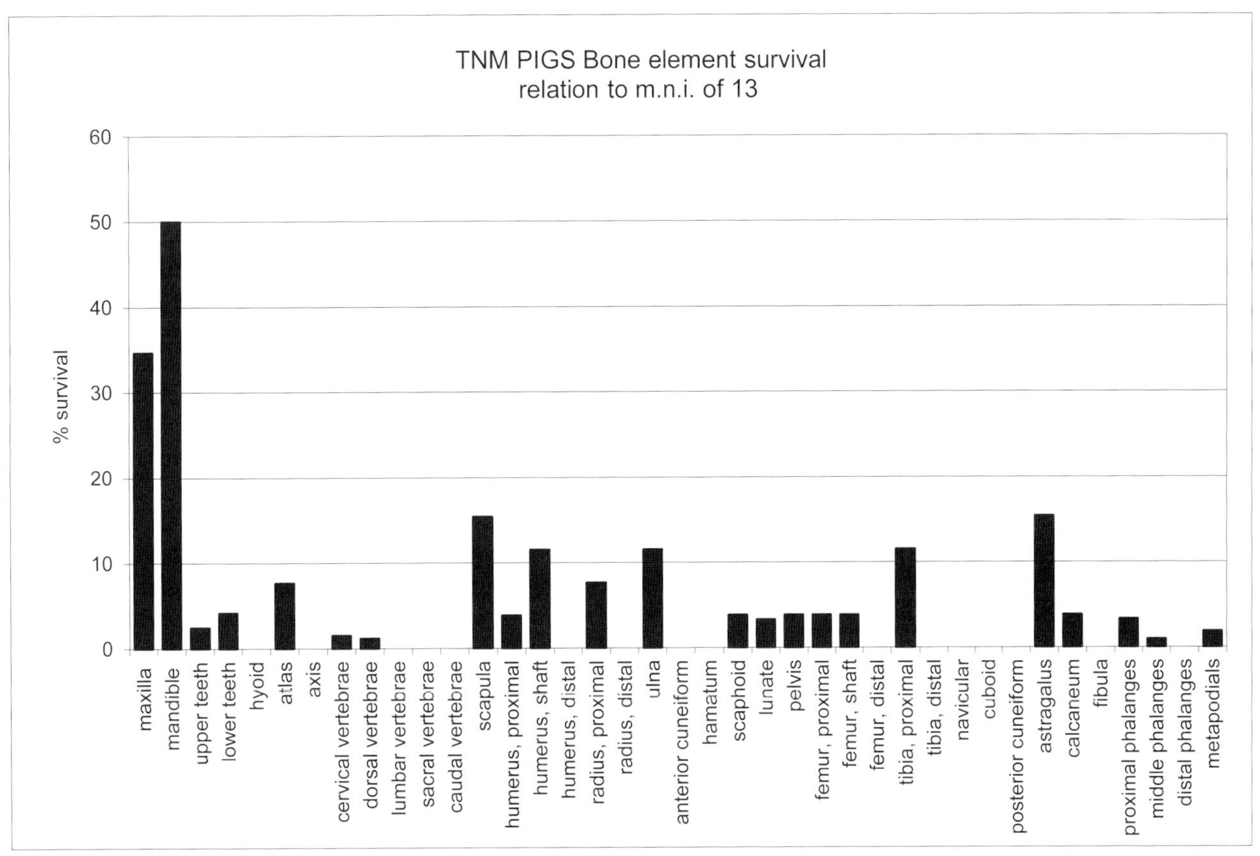

Fig. 7.10. Pig bone element survival at Tell Nebi Mend. Histogram showing the percentages of each element.

noted that von den Driesch and Wodtke (1997) asserted that, on the contrary, the larger, more robust bones from various periods at ᶜAin Ghazal in Jordan were *hemionus*, and the same was claimed by Boessneck (1987) for the larger equids from 3rd-millennium Uch Tepe in Iraq, a view which must surely be incorrect.

Close examination of the scattergram (Fig. 7.11) shows that while the phalanges of the larger asses are distinct from the presumed *hemionus* phalanges from Mureybet in both shape and size, those of the smaller (and domestic) asses fall within much the same range as the smaller phalanges from Mureybet and cannot be distinguished on that basis.

Table 7.9. Pig body parts at Tell Nebi Mend.

mni = 13

bone	no. in skeleton	no. expected	no. found	max % survival
maxilla	2	26	9	34.6
mandible	2	26	13	50.0
upper teeth	22	286	7	2.4
lower teeth	22	286	12	4.2
hyoid	2	26	0	0.0
atlas	1	13	1	7.7
axis	1	13	0	0.0
cervical vertebrae	5	65	1	1.5
dorsal vertebrae	13	169	2	1.2
lumbar vertebrae	6	78	0	0.0
sacral vertebrae	4	52	0	0.0
caudal vertebrae	23	299	0	0.0
scapula	2	26	4	15.4
humerus, proximal	2	26	1	3.8
humerus, shaft	2	26	3	11.5
humerus, distal	2	26	0	0.0
radius, proximal	2	26	2	7.7
radius, distal	2	26	0	0.0
ulna	2	26	3	11.5
anterior cuneiform	2	26	0	0.0
hamatum	2	26	0	0.0
scaphoid	2	26	1	3.8
lunate	2	30	1	3.3
pelvis	2	26	1	3.8
femur, proximal	2	26	1	3.8
femur, shaft	2	26	1	3.8
femur, distal	2	26	0	0.0
tibia, proximal	2	26	3	11.5
tibia, distal	2	26	0	0.0
navicular	2	26	0	0.0
cuboid	2	26	0	0.0
posterior cuneiform	2	26	0	0.0
astragalus	2	26	4	15.4
calcaneum	2	26	1	3.8
fibula	2	26	0	0.0
proximal phalanges	16	208	7	3.4
middle phalanges	16	208	2	1.0
distal phalanges	16	208	0	0.0
metapodials	16	208	4	1.9

My conclusion from this is that, in larger animals, the trend towards robustness is steeper in asses than in the Mureybet equids and that most of the latter were probably onagers.

Turning finally to the three proximal phalanges from Tell Nebi Mend, it can be seen from the scattergram that one seems to be of an ass and the other two from an onager,

but for all the reasons outlined above this conclusion has to remain tentative.

Some criteria have been established for the distinction between asinine and hemione teeth. In the mandibular cheekteeth the lingual sulcus is said to be V-shaped in asses and U-shaped in hemiones. At Tell Nebi Mend three teeth (P3, M1 and M2) from the same mandible have the V-shaped sulcus, so may be from an ass; however, this seems to be a rather variable character and is not a definite indication of taxon.

Equids: domestic status

Although it is not certain that the size of asses did initially diminish with domestication, their small size in the 3rd millennium in the Middle East shows that this did eventually happen. So if the equids at Tell Nebi Mend were smaller than those considered to be wild, it would be likely that they were domesticated. On the other hand, absence of a size change would prove nothing.

The method utilised for size comparisons of the equids from Arjoune is that devised by Uerpmann (1982; 1986). He used the cumulative frequency of various indices to compare the sizes of the equid bones from Shams ed-Din with those from Mureybet, where the equids were undoubtedly wild. This method takes advantage of the fact that, as the Mureybet equid sample was large, the variability of the various dimensions can be utilised. The standard measurements (means and standard deviations) are listed in Table 7.10.

The formula used for calculating the size of any particular dimension in an assemblage is: SI = (a − x̄) × 100/4s, where a is the dimension of a particular element, x̄ is the mean of that dimension at Mureybet and s is the standard deviation of that dimension at Mureybet. The indices are set out in ascending order of magnitude and plotted on the X axis against the percentages of their cumulative frequency on the Y axis. In such plots the mean of the standard is at 0 on the index scale, the standard deviation s is 25 and its theoretical range (x̄ ± 2s) is −50 to +50. The mean of each sample being compared with the standard can be read off from where the line connecting its points crosses the 50% level; s will be 25 and the range (x̄ ± 2s). If the dimensions of the sample are larger than those of the standard the mean will be to the right of the standard (*i.e.* +) and if smaller to the left (*i.e.* −). Using this method Uerpmann showed that the mean size of the equids in his sample was close to that at Mureybet; his results are set out in Fig. 7.12, with the addition of the size indices calculated for Tell Nebi Mend. Only nine measurements from Tell Nebi Mend are available, but they seem to indicate animals at least as large as those from Shams ed-Din, thus probably but not definitely wild.

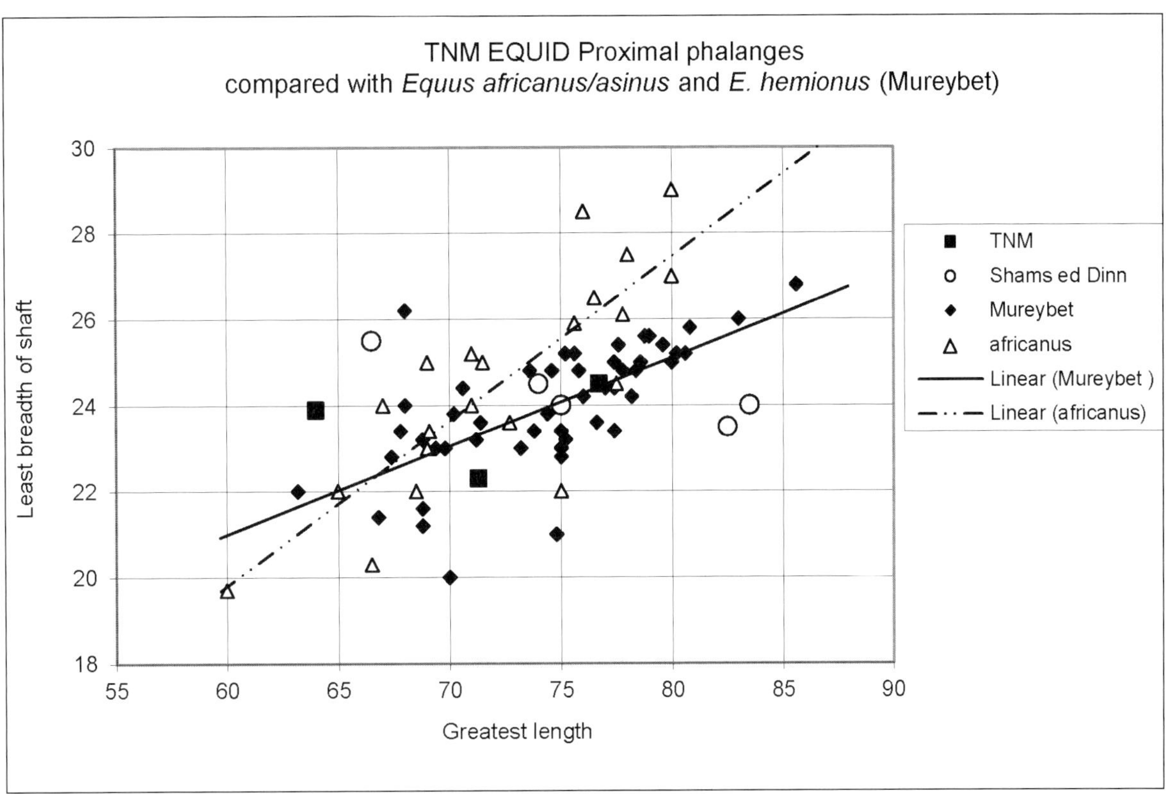

Fig. 7.11. Equid size 1. Scattergram of greatest length/least breadth (mm) of the proximal phalanges of known Equus asinus/ africanus and supposed E. hemionus. The hemionus trend line is derived from the Mureybet sample, and the africanus trend line from known asses in Egypt, Arabia and various sites in the Middle East. The graph suggests that only the larger bones can be distinguished on the basis of size or shape. As with Shams ed-Din the identification of the three phalanges from Tell Nebi Mend is uncertain. For sources of data see Appendix 7.3.

Equids: numbers

With 75 bones identified as equids, the number seems relatively high. However, 42 of these bones came from the same Phase 4 pit (Pit 10: layer 644.35) and the adjacent levels. Almost all the bones are carpals, tarsals, metapodials or phalanges. While a few could be shown to articulate with one another and none appeared to be pairs, there are suspicions that they represent the burial of the heads and feet of as few as two individual equids, tentatively identified on the basis of the shape of two proximal phalanges as hemiones (Fig. 7.13).

Gazelle (*Gazella gazella or subgutturosa?*)

Gazelles: numbers

A total of 27 bones of gazelle was retrieved from Tell Nebi Mend, including a female horncore, a skull fragment of a male with both horncore bases and a male horncore that had been damaged in excavation but was otherwise almost complete. A second nearly complete male horncore was unstratified and therefore not certainly Neolithic.

Gazelles: identification

There are three main species in the Middle East today, the mountain gazelle *Gazella gazella* in the Levant, the dorcas gazelle *G. dorcas* in the desert areas of the southern Levant and the goitered gazelle *G. subgutturosa* in the rest of the area, including the Syrian desert (Uerpmann 1987). The main criteria for the distinction between the gazelle species are the size and morphology of the male horncores and the fact that the females of *G. subgutturosa* are sometimes hornless (Groves and Harrison 1967; Tchernov *et al.* 1986–87). In addition, *G. dorcas* is definitely smaller than *G. gazella* and *G. subgutturosa*.

The few measurements of the gazelles from Tell Nebi Mend are all fairly large, so they are certainly not of *G. dorcas*. Helmer (2000) has suggested that *G. gazella* was (and is) larger than *G. subgutturosa*; this was on the basis of a comparison between the gazelles of El Kowm 2 in the Syrian desert, which were smaller than those identified as *G. gazella* from Hatoula in the southern Levant (Davis 1985 and 1994). Although he was not comparing like with like – since El Kowm 2 dates from the late PPNB and Hatoula from the Natufian and PPNA – if the Hatoula sample and another from the Natufian at Mallaha in the Jordan

Valley (Bouchud 1987) are compared with those from the contemporary site of Mureybet (Ducos 1978) in the Syrian desert this size difference still holds good, although there is a considerable degree of overlap. However, the sizes of the few postcranial bones from Tell Nebi Mend fall within the area of overlap, so their size is not diagnostic. The main osteological criterion for the distinction between *G. gazella* and *G. subgutturosa* is the fact that in *G. subgutturosa* the horns of the males originate close to the mid-line (less than 16 mm apart), while those of *G. gazella* are farther apart (*c*.25 mm) (Harrison and Bates 1991). The gap between the pedicel of the horncore and the frontal suture was 6 mm in one of the Tell Nebi Mend specimens and 7.1 mm in the other, each measurement, of course, being half the distance between the horncores. Helmer (2000), quantifying the same feature on a horncore from El Kowm 2, used a different measurement, the distance from the most anterior point of the horncore base to the mid-frontal suture – about 8 mm – a distance which he considered to be slight and so he identified the horncore as *G. subgutturosa*. The equivalent dimension in the Tell Nebi Mend horncore is about 12 mm. However, Harrison and Bates were noting the distance between the horns, not the underlying core, so this feature would be affected by the thickness of the horn sheath. If this criterion is correct, it is probable that the Tell Nebi Mend horncores represent *G. subgutturosa* rather than *G. gazella*.

A plot of the very few published data of the dimensions of the base of the horncore of presumed *G. gazella* from Mallaha (Bouchud 1987) and presumed *G. subgutturosa* from Tell Asmar and Rubeidheh in Mesopotamia (Hilzheimer 1941; Payne 1988) shows a wide range of variation, although those of *G. subgutturosa* tend to be more elliptical. When the dimensions of the male horncore bases from Tell Nebi Mend are added to the graph (Fig. 7.14) it can be seen that they appear closer to *G. subgutturosa*, but with such a wide range of variation in the Mallaha sample this can be only a very tentative conclusion.

Females of the *G. subgutturosa* are often, but not always, hornless, so the female horncore at Tell Nebi Mend could be from either species.

One gazelle horncore which was definitely Neolithic was clearly from an old male, with many quite deep longitudinal grooves all around. The patterning and depth of the grooves are said to be characteristic of the different species, but I have found them to be too variable to be utilised in this way. The second unstratified horncore had rather shallow grooves on the anterior and posterior faces, but was otherwise remarkably smooth. Two male and one female horncore are illustrated in Fig. 7.15.

Deer (*Cervus* sp.)

A total of 13 fragments was identified as deer, including a small piece of an antler tine. In general it is not possible to say whether both red deer (*Cervus elaphus*) and fallow deer

Table 7.10. Standard parameters of size for Equus hemionus/ africanus *at Mureybet (Ducos 1986), taken from Uerpmann (1986).*

dimension (A)	mean ($\bar{x}$)	s.d.
astragalus GLm	47.1	2.06
humerus Bt	60.0	1.77
metacarpal Bp	39.9	2.21
metapodial Bd	37.1	1.50
mid phalanx Bp	38.4	1.90
prox phalanx Bp	39.1	1.89
radius Bd	57.6	1.86
scapula LG	44.1	1.98
tibia Bd	55.3	1.84

Abbreviations from von den Driesch (1976)

(*C. mesopotamica*) are represented, but the small size of the only measurable bone suggests at least one fallow deer.

Pathology

Three lower first or second molars of sheep/goats had swollen roots. This condition is almost certainly a symptom of infection (Baker and Brothwell 1980), and is common in early domestic sheep, goats and cattle, but probably not in modern stock, as there seem to be no descriptions of it in the literature (Miles and Grigson 1990). One sheep/goat mandible had signs of an abscess in the premolar region. One set of mandibular teeth and a lower premolar were polished on the lingual side. Only one postcranial bone showed any pathological lesion, this being on the anterior face of a sheep/goat lunate, indicating a problem with the wrist joint.

Obviously the majority of animal diseases have no osteological manifestations, but nevertheless the almost total lack of pathological changes in the bones suggests a good level of nutrition for the animals, both wild and domestic, at Tell Nebi Mend in the Neolithic.

Bone modification

Burning

Table 7.11 shows that quite a high proportion of the identified bones had been burnt – about 15%. There was a particularly high proportion among the equid bones, especially in layer 706.33 (see below), but in general burnt and unburnt bones were found together in the same levels, which suggests considerable post-depositional mixing. The fact that three of the five crab claws and one tortoise scute had been burnt indicates that they were contemporary with the deposits and not intrusive. One gazelle tibia was burnt at the distal end, the proximal end probably having been protected by meat – suggesting that it had been roasted on a fire.

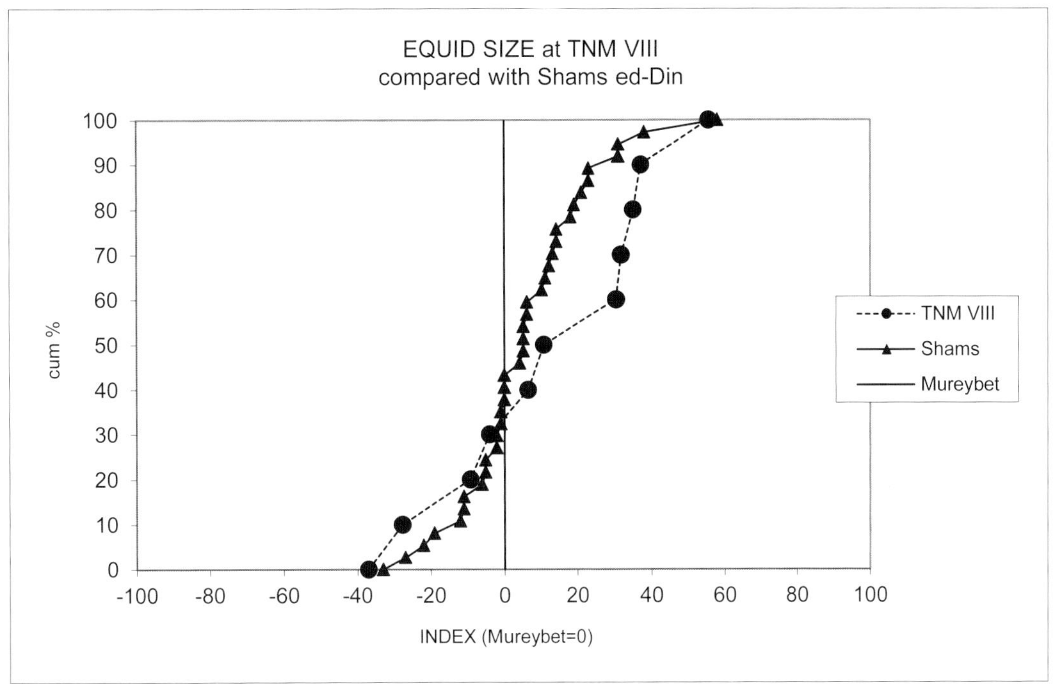

Fig. 7.12. Equid size 2. Cumulative frequency graph. The size of the equid bones from Tell Nebi Mend compared with those of Shams ed-Din and Mureybet (Uerpmann 1982; 1986). Like Shams ed-Din the mean size of the Tell Nebi Mend equids appears to be slightly larger than at the standard population at Mureybet (= 0).

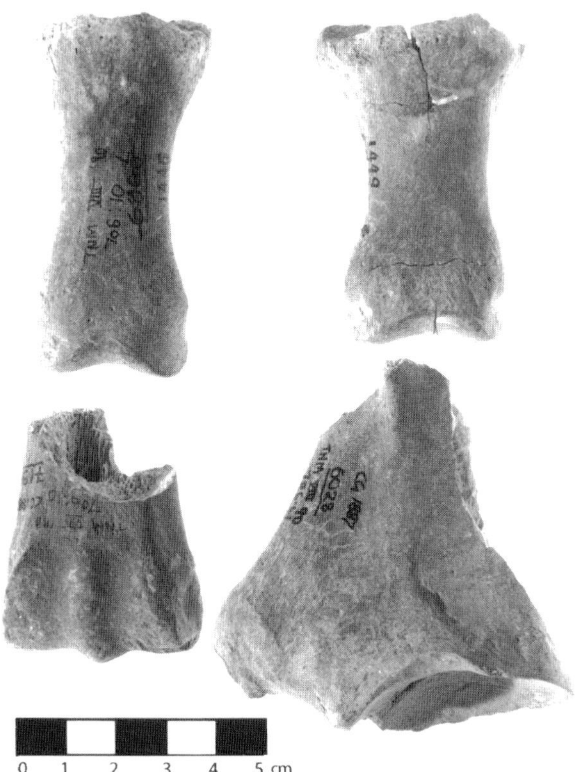

Fig. 7.13. Equid bones from Tell Nebi Mend. Above. Two proximal phalanges, the more slender one (left) is probably E. hemionus, the stouter one (right) which is from a mixed Neolithic/Early Bronze Age level may be asinus/africanus. Although respectively anterior and posterior this is not enough to account for the difference in shape. Below. Left: a distal metapodial which has been gnawed. Right: a distal scapula.

Horncores

One sheep horncore had been chopped off near the base, suggesting that some unknown use was made of the horns. The Neolithic gazelle horncore has a deep groove around the lateral and anterior faces of its base, clearly resulting from the removal of the horn.

Long bones

Almost all the long bones had been broken. Although in most cases it is impossible to tell from the type of fracture whether this was deliberate, the very high frequency suggests breakage for the extraction of marrow. Human activity is unequivocally suggested by the breaking of some of the long bones (including one gazelle, two ox and seven sheep/goat metapodials, and one ox, one deer, one pig and two sheep/goat radii) vertically through the epiphyses. This may have been for the manufacture of bone tools or the result of marrow extraction, or both.

No cut marks were recorded but these may have been obscured by the mineral deposits on many of the bones.

Although only five bones had tooth marks attributable to carnivores, probably dogs, the bone element analysis indicated that much of the softer bone is missing, suggesting that the whole assemblage owes much of its character to depredations by dogs.

Special deposits

No animal burials were detected at Tell Nebi Mend, but there were a few concentrations of particular groups of

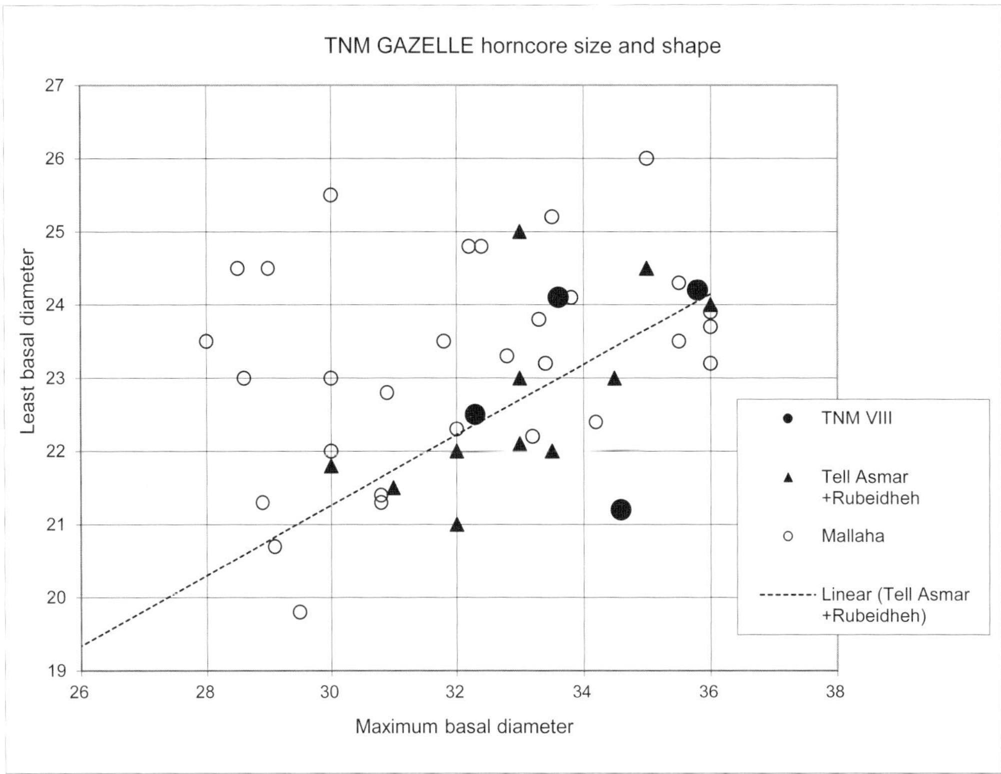

Fig. 7.14. Gazelle horncore shape. Scattergram of horncore dimensions at Tell Nebi Mend compared with presumed Gazella gazella *(from Mallaha in the Jordan Valley) and presumed* G. subgutturosa *(Tell Asmar and Rubeidheh in Mesopotamia). Despite a great deal of overlap, the distribution of measurements suggests that the horncores of* G. subgutturosa *tendeded to be rather more elliptical than those of* G. gazella; *those from Tell Nebi Mend seem more like* G. subgutturosa.

bones in particular levels. Layer 706.33, an ashy deposit probably of Phase 1, contained an unusually high number of equid remains, mostly mandibular fragments and teeth, several of which were burnt and some of which clearly came from the same individual. Two more equid lower teeth in 706.22 might be related. A Phase 4 pit (layer 606.27) had a high proportion of pig bones (11 out of a total of 32). In another small pit, 709.11, almost certainly associated with a human burial (Burial B), the navicular of a wild ox articulated on the proximal end of a metatarsal (bone nos 2012 and 2013) were set vertically in the centre of a ring of four small stones and a large shell; this is described in greater detail in Chapter 3.

Animal exploitation at Tell Nebi Mend

Hunting and husbandry

The uncertainties in the distinction between wild and domestic animals at Tell Nebi Mend make it difficult to assess the overall animal economy in terms of hunting and husbandry. However, domestic sheep and goat certainly predominated, and it is likely that most of the pigs and cattle were also domesticated, at least to some degree, with adult cows outnumbering adult bulls. The wild fauna included a

few of the cattle and pigs and the equids, deer and gazelles, and amounted to about 13% of the total (Table 7.12).

Artiodactyl proportions

Artiodactyl proportions are usually discussed in terms of the relative numbers of domestic sheep, goats, cattle and pigs; however, given the ambiguity of the wild/domestic status of an uncertain proportion of pigs and cattle at Tell Nebi Mend and most of the contemporary sites in the area, it has been necessary to include all bones of these taxa. The results are shown in Fig. 7.16. The proportion of pig bones varies from 0 to just over 50%; Tell Nebi Mend and Gürcütepe have 20% each.

The significance of the presence and absence of domestic pigs in later sites – that is, from the 5th to the 4th millennium (uncalibrated – roughly 6th to 5th calibrated) – has been discussed by me in various conference presentations and has recently been published (Grigson 2007). I found a direct correlation between pig numbers and the environment, with few if any pigs in the drier areas except when there was an exotic water supply or large-scale irrigation, as in Mesopotamia in the 3rd millennium. One would not expect wild pigs to be completely absent in dry areas since, to this day, they inhabit many of the wadi systems, venturing out

Fig. 7.15. Gazelle horncores, probably all Gazella subgutturosa. *Left: horncore of a male with many longitudinal grooves (damaged in excavation). Centre: horncore of a male with shallow grooves on the anterior and posterior surfaces (not certainly Neolithic). Right: horncore of a female.*

at dusk into the desert; however, raising pigs as domestic animals would be feasible only if they were present in significant numbers and in areas with ample food, water, shade and wallow.

It is noteworthy that all the sites where pigs make up more than about 20% of the sample are situated in areas where one would expect the rainfall to be high: that is, north-western Syria near the Mediterranean coast and marshy areas such as the El Rouj basin on the river Orontes in north-western Syria and the ⁣ᶜAmuq valley across the border in Turkey (Fig. 7.17). These sites are also characterised by the presence of dark-burnished ware (*i.e.* Tell Sukas and Ras Shamra near the coast, ᶜAmuq A and B, Tell Aray 2, Tell el Kerkh (Riis 1974; Poulain 1978; Stampfli 1983) and Tell Nebi Mend on the Orontes [indicated by the oval in Fig. 7.17]). It is possible that conditions were equally favourable in sites in the Jordan Valley (the rectangle in Fig. 7.17) such as Hagoshrim, Tel Te'o and Tell Ali (Haber and Dayan 2004; Horwitz 2001; Lev-Tov 2000), and at Yiftah'el in the Lower Galilee, which is situated in a swampy valley bordered by hills where the indigenous oak *Quercus ithaburensis* is still present (Horwitz 2003) – acorns, of course, being a particular food of pigs, though domestication may have occurred later here than in north-west Syria.

Table 7.11. *The numbers of burnt bones at Tell Nebi Mend.*

		total	burnt	
	taxon	*no.*	*no.*	*%*
cattle	*Bos* sp.	99	11	11.1
pig	*Sus scrofa*	104	7	6.7
sheep/goat	*Ovis/Capra*	456	62	13.6
gazelle	*Gazella* sp	27	5	18.5
deer *	*Cervus* sp.	12	4	33.3
equid	*Equus* sp.	75	12	16.0
	total large mammals	773	103	13.3
dog	*Canis familiaris*	6	0	0
fox	*Vulpes* sp.	3	0	0
hare	*Lepus* sp.	1	0	0
cat	*Felis* sp.	1		
bird		2	0	0
tortoise		4	1	25.0
crab		6	3	50.0
	Total	796	107	13.4

In contrast, the sites situated in the Syrian desert – El Kowm 2, Abu Hureyra and Bouqras – had no pigs and the sites on or near the fringes very few (Helmer 2000; Legge and Rowley-Conwy 2000; Buitenhuis and Caneva 1988).

Ungulate proportions

Given that some of the analysis of artiodactyl proportions included wild animal remains as well as domestic ones, it is necessary to look at the complete ungulate picture by including gazelles and equids (Fig. 7.18). None of the sites had significant numbers of equids and most, including Tell Nebi Mend, had only a few gazelles. The exceptions were Azraq, El Kowm 2, Abu Hureyra and Tell Halula (Garrard *et al.* 1988; Helmer 2000; Legge and Rowley-Conwy 2000; Saña Segui 1999), which are all situated well out in the desert. Azraq was omitted from the analysis of 'artiodactyl proportions' because over 75% of the bones were from gazelles. Surprisingly, the other desert site, Bouqras, had very few (Buitenhuis 1988), and Tell Aswad in the Jezirah had 20% (Helmer 1985b). However, in general it is sheep and goats that predominate, with significant numbers of cattle at most sites and of pigs at many.

Comparison: Tell Nebi Mend and Arjoune in the mid-6th and early 5th millennia

Because the site of Arjoune is situated so near to Tell Nebi Mend and in a similar situation near the Orontes it is worthwhile looking at their similarities and differences in terms of changing strategies of animal management. Arjoune was occupied apparently during two separate periods, first in the mid-6th and then in the early 5th

Table 7.12. Wild and domestic ungulates at Tell Nebi Mend (excluding level 644.035).

large mammals	taxon	Domestic	Wild	Uncertain	Domestic %	Wild %	Uncertain %
cattle	*Bos taurus*	86			12.1		
cattle	*Bos primigenius*		6			0.8	
pig	*Sus scrofa* (dom)	102			14.3		
wild boar	*Sus scrofa*		2			0.3	
sheep/goat	*Ovis/Capra*	397			55.8		
sheep	*Ovis aries*	26			3.7		
goat	*Capra hircus*	10			1.4		
gazelle	*Gazella* sp.		27			3.8	
deer	*Cervus* sp.		12			1.7	
equid	*Equus* sp.			33			4.6
dog	*Canis familiaris*	6			0.8		
fox	*Vulpes* sp.		3			0.4	
cat	*Felis* sp.		1			0.1	
hare?	*Lepus* sp.		1			0.1	
	totals	627	52	33	88.1	7.3	4.6

millennium (calibrated dates); for details of the fauna see Grigson (2003), but note that the dates quoted in that report are not calibrated.

Figs 7.1 b2 and 7.2 b2 show that the sizes of the sheep and goat bones at both Arjoune and Tell Nebi Mend indicate full domestication, with little if any difference in size, although the number of measurable goat bones at Tell Nebi Mend is very small. At Arjoune there was a significant difference in the proportion of sheep to goats in the two millennia, with sheep forming about 40% of the sheep/goat sample in the 6th millennium and rising in the early 5th to 82%. The interpretation was that the production of sheep's wool was increasing in importance over time. However, at 71% the proportion of sheep at Tell Nebi Mend was also high, surprisingly so. There was also a marked difference in the ageing pattern of the sheep and goats at Arjoune, suggesting an increased reliance on older animals in the early 5th millennium after a more generalised pattern in the sixth. This is consistent with the results from Tell Nebi Mend, where the age profile resembled that of the 6th millennium at Arjoune, but with a slightly wider age range, suggesting an even more generalised pattern.

The pattern of element destruction of sheep and goat bones was remarkably similar at both sites, with a definite correlation between percentage survival and bone density. At Tell Nebi Mend the coefficient of correlation was 0.58 and at Arjoune 0.64, both results being statistically significant.

Although the size range of the cattle at Arjoune overlaps with that of Tell Nebi Mend (Fig. 7.6 b2) and other sites of the early Pottery Neolithic, they are distinctly smaller, indicating full domestication at Arjoune but not necessarily at Tell Nebi Mend.

The Tell Nebi Mend pig measurements fall within the large range of variation of the pigs at Arjoune, but are distributed at the larger end of the range (Fig. 7.8 b2). The age distributions of pigs at the two sites is not directly comparable as it was calculated on limb bone fusion at Tell Nebi Mend and on dental criteria at Arjoune. Nevertheless, the results suggest that at Tell Nebi Mend about a third of the animals survived beyond the age of 3.5 years, an unusually high proportion, whereas at Arjoune the percentage survival beyond about 3 years was only 3%, suggesting a different management strategy.

There were very few measurable equid bones at either site, but those from Arjoune are within the range of the equids from Tell Nebi Mend (Fig. 7.12).

Although there were difficulties in establishing the domestic status of the cattle and pigs at Tell Nebi Mend, it is possible to say that the wild fauna included a few of the cattle and pigs, the equids, the deer and the gazelles, amounting to roughly 13% of the total. At Arjoune in the 6th millennium wild animals amounted to only 2%, although the proportion rose in the early 5th millennium to 6–11%, depending on whether the equids are considered to be domestic or wild.

The relative proportions of the artiodactyls seem to alter in a consistent manner, with an increase in the percentages of cattle, and to a lesser extent of pigs, at the expense of sheep and goats, from the early 7th millennium at Tell Nebi Mend and through the 6th to the early 5th millennium at Arjoune. This is perhaps indicative of a gradually more sedentary lifestyle in the vicinity over time.

When all the ungulates are compared a similar picture emerges, with cattle and pigs increasing over time at the expense of sheep and goats. Although the sample sizes of equids are small it is notable that they are present as 5–6% of the assemblage at Tell Nebi Mend and in the early 5th millennium at Arjoune, but in the 6th millennium at Arjoune they comprise only 0.6%. One possible explanation is that this reflects the introduction of domestic donkeys in the

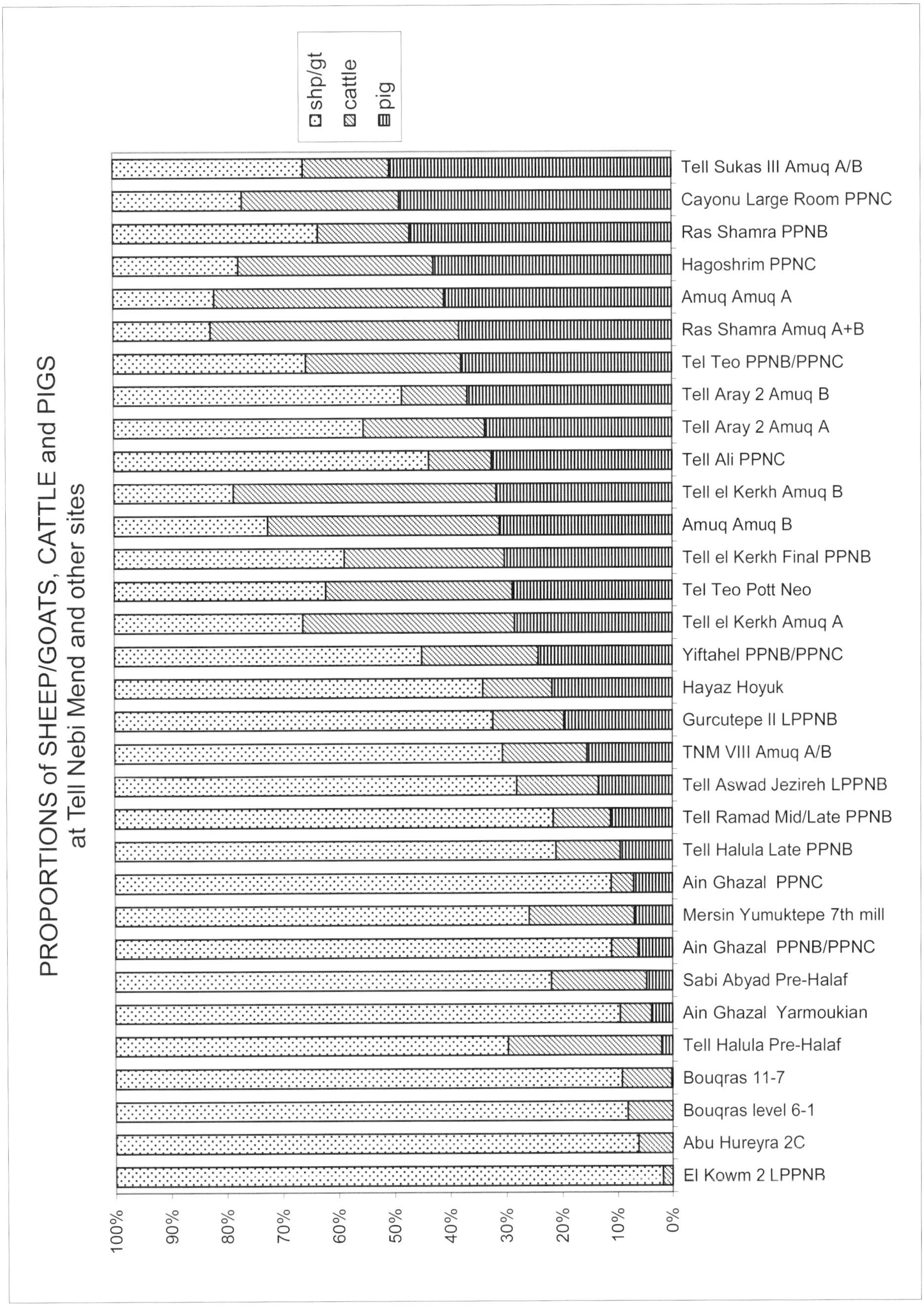

Fig. 7.16. Artiodactyl proportions. Showing the widely varying proportions of the three main taxa in various sites in the Levant.

  Caroline Grigson

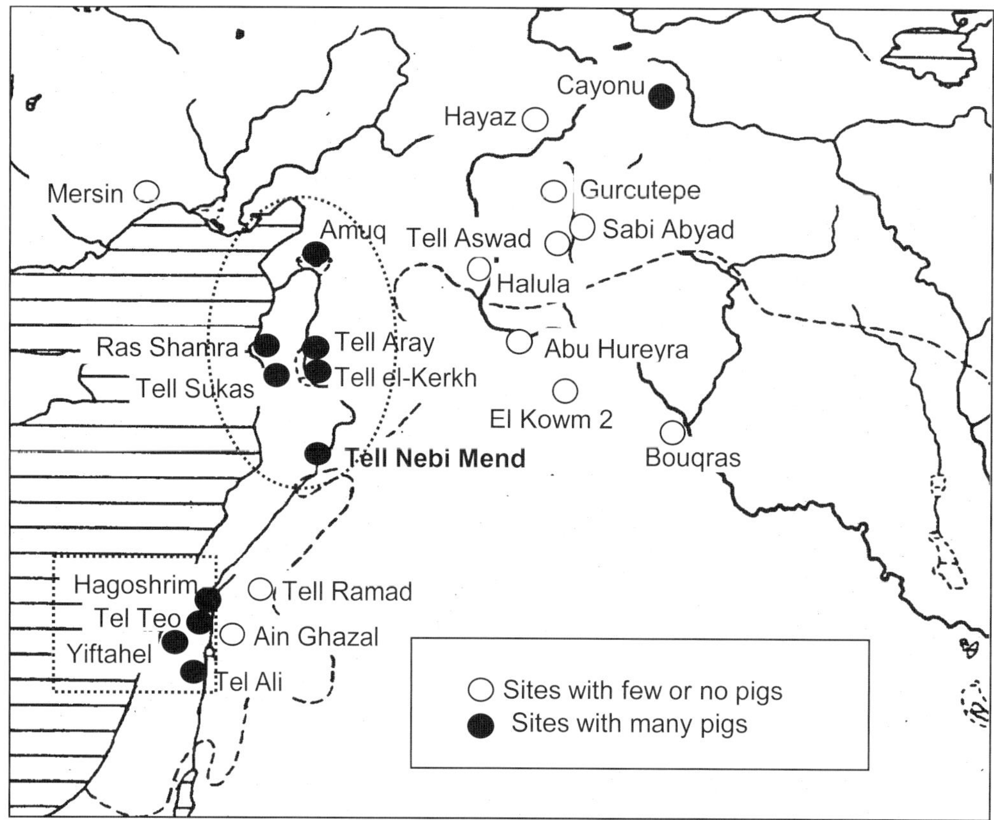

Fig. 7.17. Map of the Levant showing the distribution of sites with greater and lesser proportions of pigs. The sites within the rectangle and oval, including Tell Nebi Mend, have more than 15% of pigs. Those within the oval are characterised by the presence of Dark Burnished Ware.

early 5th millennium, which would be consistent with evidence from Chalcolithic sites in the southern Levant (Epstein 1985; Grigson 1987; 1993).

Conclusions

The rather scanty data seem to indicate that while the size of many of the cattle and pigs at Tell Nebi Mend and at other comparable sites fell in the areas of overlap between wild and domestic animals, there was nevertheless a tendency towards a reduction in size. In addition, the analysis of artiodactyl and ungulate proportions shows not only a dominance of domestic sheep and goats, as one would expect, but also, where conditions were suitable, of other potential and actual domesticates: that is, pigs and cattle may already have been in the process of domestication in the early 7th millennium BC at Tell Nebi Mend and other contemporary sites.

Note

1   Text completed 2009; referee's comments incorporated 2014.

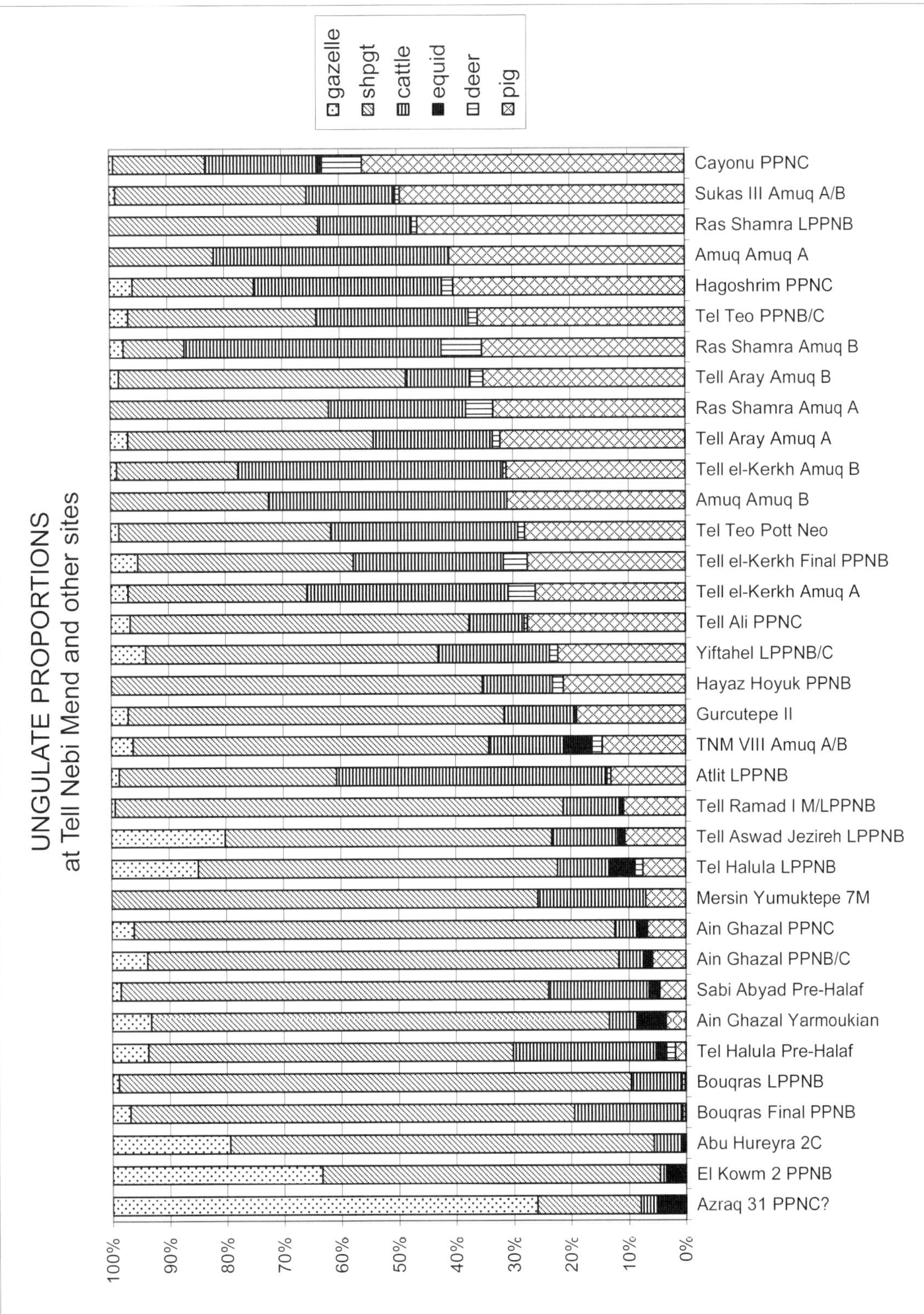

Fig. 7.18. *Ungulate proportions. Showing the varying proportions of the three main taxa (as in Fig. 7.14, with the addition of gazelles and equids. Most of the sites including Tell Nebi Mend had only a few gazelles, apart from four desert sites, Azraq, El Kowm 2. Abu Hureyra and Tell Halula (Garrard et al. 1988; Helmer 2000; Legge & Rowley-Conwy 2000; Saña Segui 1999), which had many. Tell Nebi Mend has a higher proportion of equids than the other sites, though the numbers are still low. In general sheep and goats predominated, with significant numbers of cattle in most sites and of pigs in many.*

APPENDIX 7.1 MEASUREMENTS OF CATTLE, SHEEP, GOATS, PIGS, GAZELLES and DEER

Measurement abbreviations from von den Driesch (1978)

taxon	bone no.	element	measurement	proximal epiphysis	distal epiphysis	age	sex	remarks
CATTLE								
bos	1314	humerus	Bt 78.8		fused			
bos	1734	astragalus	GL 70.5; Bd 45.6					v big
bos prim	437	calcaneum	l front tuber 88.7	fused		v old	male	
bos prim	2012	metatarsal	Bp 64.5					
bos prim	2013	navicular	GB 70.0					
bos prim?	1469	proximal phalanx ant outer	Glpe 65.2; Bp 34.4	fused				
bos	1486	proximal phalanx ant inner	GL 59.3; Bp 32.5	fused				
bos	283	proximal phalanx	Bp 34.4	fused				
bos	286	proximal phalanx	Glpe 64.2; Bp 29.2	fused				
bos	1473	proximal phalanx	Bp 34.3	fused				
bos	1520	middle phalanx	Bp 31.8	fused				
bos	1417	middle phalanx post inner	GLpe 40.2; Bp 28.0	fused				
bos	1943	middle phalanx	Bp 29.9	fused				
bos	2340	mandible	l toothrow 146; LM3 38.3					
SHEEP & GOAT								
goat	615	horncore	basal diameters 28.9 × 18.9			old?	female?	
goat	1785	horncore	max. basal diameter 29.8				female?	
goat	1571	scapula	LG 31.4, BG 24; SLC 19.8		fused			
goat	1335	humerus	Bt 27.5					
goat	1347	humerus	Bt 27.1					
goat?	1894	humerus	Bt 25.0					
goat	887	femur	Bd 34		fused			
goat?	2169	astragalus	GL 28.7; Bd 17.8					
goat	2166	metatarsal	Bd 25.8					
sheep	1373	horncore	basal diameters 54.8 × 34.4			young	male	sutures unfused
sheep	1566	scapula	LG 34; BG 26.6; SLC 22.2		fused			
sheep	1227	scapula	GLP 40.0; LG 31.0; BG 26.9		fused		male?	
sheep	518	humerus	Bd 28.2; Bt 26.8		fused			
sheep	2055	humerus	Bd 29.3; Bt 28.7		fused			
sheep	10154	humerus	Bd 34.7		fused			
sheep	10174	humerus	Bt 27.6		fused			
sheep	10149	humerus	Bt e35		fused			
sheep	39	radius	Bp 31.0		fused			
sheep	1451	astragalus	GL 30.3; Bd 21.3				male?	
sheep	963	metatarsal	Bd 24.3		fused	old		
sheep	1019	metatarsal	Bd 22.4		fused			
sheep	1361	proximal phalanx	Glpe 35.2; Bp 11.8					
sheep	2283	middle phalanx	Glpe 21.2; Bp 11.7	fused				
sheep	584	middle phalanx	Glpe 23.9; Bp 14.6	fused				

taxon	bone no.	element	measurement	proximal epiphysis	distal epiphysis	age	sex	remarks
SHEEP & GOAT cont.								
shpgt	96	humerus	Bt e36.3					
shpgt	53	radius	Bp 33.0	fused				
shpgt	1857	radius	Bp 32.6					
shpgt	633	tibia	Bd 24.4					
shpgt	631	tibia	Bd 24.1					
shpgt	628	tibia	Bd 23.5					
shpgt	1530	tibia distal	Bd 23.9		fused			
shpgt	311	astragalus	GL 28.3; Bd 18.4					
shpgt	2333	astragalus	GL 29.6; Bd 20.9				M?	
shpgt	949	metatarsal	Bp 18.3					
shpgt	940	metatarsal	Bp 21.1			old		
PIG								
pig	1194	M1 low	L M1 low 18.7					
pig	403	M2 up	L M2 up 23.5					
pig	808	M1-M2 up	L M1 up 18.2; L M2 up 22.5					P4 unw; M1 slw; M2 vslw; M3 open crypt
pig	623	skull	L M2 up 20.3					M3 up in crypt
pig	1196	skull	L M1 up 17.8					M2 up in crypt
pig	10143	scapula	SLC 26.8		fused			large
pig	1545	tibia	Bp 41.3	unfused		young		
pig	1521	tibia	Bd 27.6		fused			
pig	1443	astragalus	GL 38.1					burnt
pig	2341	astragalus	GL 39.9					
pig	2180	astragalus	GL 45.1					
pig	2163	proximal phalanx	GL 34.1	fused				
pig	396	proximal phalanx	GL 35.3; Bp 18.9	fused				
GAZELLE								
gazelle	1378	horncore	basal diameters 35.8×24.2			adult	M	pedicel base to frontal suture 6 mm
gazelle	1699	horncore	basal diameters e32.3×22.5			adult	M	pedicel base to frontal suture 6 mm
gazelle	1379	horncores L & R	basal diameters 34.6×21.2			adult	M	pedicel base to frontal suture 7 mm
gazelle	1464	horncore	basal diameters 33.6×24.1					not certainly Neolithic
gazelle	486	tibia	Bd 24.2		fused			
gazelle?	630	tibia	Bd 26.3		fused			?roe deer
DEER								
deer	10179	M3 low	LM3 23.8					
deer	1226	scapula	GLP 38.9; LG 28.4; BG 28.4					
deer	1600	tibia	Bd e38.5					

APPENDIX 7.2. EQUID MEASUREMENTS

LOWER TEETH						
tooth	P3	M3	M3	P3	M1	M2
bone no	329	57	2207	50*	51*	52*
occusal length	25.0	32.1	25.4	25.6	22.6	22.8
occusal breadth	15.6	9.5	—	13.7	13.7	12.8
ant crown height	45	34.5	—	76.7	75.5	
L post flexid	12.1	—	—	11.1	8.9	8.5
beadth silla	3.5	—	—	3.6	2.3	2.5
penetration	slight	—	—	not quite	not quite	not quite
shape lingual sulcus @	V			V	V	V
@ V shape indicates Equus asinus				* 50, 51 and 52 same mandible		

UPPER TEETH		
tooth	P3/P4/M1/M2*	P3/P4/M1/M2*
bone no	60	63
occusal length	26.1	—
occusal breadth	23.2	—
ant crown ht	58	58
length protocone	9.4	—
* uncertain which tooth		

SCAPULA	
bone no	1887
GLP	71.7
LG	44.6
BG	40.7
distal epiphysis	fused

ASTRAGALUS		
bone no	173	1732
LmT	49.6	52.5
GH	47.0	50.5

METAPODIAL			
bone no	1882	1002	1003
Bd	39.3	36.8	37.5
distal epiphysis	fused	fused	fused

PROXIMAL PHALANGES	anterior	posterior				
bone no	1445	1449	295	296	298	341
GL	71.3	e64.0	71.1	—	—	67.8
Bp	36.3	41.4	—	—	—	37
BFp	—	—	—	—	—	—
Dp	30.0	29.4	—	27.4	—	—
SD	22.3	23.9	—	—	—	—
Bd	31.1	32.3	34	37.2	35.2	32.3
Dd	17.7	18.2	—	—	—	—
proximal epiphysis	fused	fused	fused			fused

PROXIMAL PHALANGES cont					
bone no	470	471	1446	1447	1448
GL	71.0	81.0	76.7	—	—
Bp	43.3	41.5	38.4	39.9	41.9
BFp	—	—	—	38.5	40.2
Dp	30.7	31.3	29.8	30.5	29.7
SD	—	—	24.5	24.6	—
Bd	34.8	36.7	35.0	—	—
Dd	—	—	19.6	—	—
proximal epiphysis	fused	fused	fused	fused	fused

MIDDLE PHALANGES		
bone no	299	1884
GL	—	40.4
Bp	—	38.1
SD	—	32.5
Bd	30.8	35.1
proximal epiphysis	fused	fused

DISTAL PHALANGES		
bone no	194	10184
GL	—	37.2
GB	51.0	—
HP	e 37.0	—
Ld	37.6	—

APPENDIX 7.3

Sources of data used in Figures 7.1, 7.2, 7.6, 7.8, 7.11 and 7.17

Figure 7.1. The size of goats

(a1) Epipalaeolithic and PPNA (Protoneolithic) – Jiita, Palegawra, Jericho (Sultanian), Zawi Chemi Shanidar, Asiab (Uerpmann 1979).
(a2) Middle PPNB – Halula (Saña Segui 1999).
(a3) Late PPNB – Halula (Saña Segui 1999).
(a4) Pre-Halafian – Sabi Abyad (Cavallo 2000); Halula (Saña Segui 1999).
(b1) Tell Nebi Mend; Tell Aray (Hongo 1996); Yumuktepe (Buitenhuis and Caneva 1998).
(b2) Tell Nebi Mend; Arjoune (Grigson 2003).

Figure 7.2. The size of sheep

(a1) Epipalaeolithic and PPNA (Protoneolithic) – Palegawra, Mureybet, Zawi Chemi Shanidar, Asiab (Uerpmann 1979).
(a2) Middle PPNB – Ganj Dareh (Hesse 1978); Can Hasan III; Asikli (Uerpmann 1979); Jericho PPNB (Grigson, n.d.); Cafer Hoyuk (Helmer 1985a).
(a3) Late PPNB – ᶜAin Ghazal LPPNB (Von den Driesch and Wodtke 1997); Bouqras 11–7; Hayaz Hüyük (Buitenhuis 1988); Tell es-Sinn (Clason 1979/80).
(a4) Pre-Halaf – Sabi Abyad (Cavallo 2000).
(b1) Tell Nebi Mend; Tell Aray (Hongo 1996); Yumuktepe (Buitenhuis and Caneva 1998); El Kowm (Helmer 2000).
(b2) Tell Nebi Mend; Arjoune (Grigson 2003).

Figure 7.6. The size of cattle

(a1) Epipalaeolithic and PPNA – Hatoula 1980–82, El Wad B, Hayonim Cave B, Jericho PPNA, Kebara 1931 B, Shukbah B, Mureybet II and III (Grigson 1989, figs 3A and C); Hatoula 1983–88 (Davis 1994); Nemrik 9 (Lasota-Moskalewska 1990).
(a2) Middle PPNB – Ali Kosh, Asikli Hüyük, Beidha, Çafer Hüyük, Jericho PPNB, Suberde, Tel Eli IV (after Grigson 1989 figs 3D and E); Ganj Dareh (Grigson 1989, fig. 3B – redated); ᾽Ain Ghazal M/LPPNB (Von den Driesch and Wodtke 1997); Yiftah'el MPPNB (Horwitz 1987; 2003).
(a3) Late PPNB – Abu Ghosh (Ducos 1978); ᾽Ain Ghazal LPPNB; Bouqras 11–7 (Buitenhuis 1988); Halula 10–19 (Saña Segui 1999); Ras Shamra VC (Poulain 1978); Tell Molla Assad (Clutton-Brock 1985); Tell es-Sinn (Clason 1979–80).
(a4) Earliest Pottery Neolithic – Halula Pre-Halaf (Saña Segui 1999); Çatal Hüyük (Russell, Martin and Buitenhuis 2005), Sabi Abyad (Cavallo 2000), Bouqras VI–I (Buitenhuis 1988).
(a5) Early Pottery Neolithic – Ashkelon, Qalcat el-Mudiq, Fikirtepe (Grigson 1989, fig. 3G).
(b1) Tell Nebi Mend; Tell Aray (Hongo 1996); Amuq A and B (Stampfli 1983).
(b2) Tell Nebi Mend; Arjoune (Grigson 2003).

Figure 7.8. The size of pigs

(a1) Epipalaeolithic and PPNA – Ein Gev I and IV, Hatoula Late Natuf, Hayonim Terrace Natufian, Palegawra, Karim Shahir, M'lefaat, Netiv Hagdud (Kusutman 1991); Mallaha (Bouchud 1987); Ein Gev III (Davis 1991); Hatoula (Davis 1985; 1991; 1994); Asiab (Bokonyi 1977); Jericho PPNA (Grigson n.d.); Mureybet II and III (Ducos 1978); Nemrik 9 (Lasota-Moskalewska 1990).
(a2) Middle PPNB – ᾽Ain Ghazal MPPN (Von den Driesch and Wodtke 1997); Asikli Hüyük (Buitenhuis 1997; Payne 1985); Çafer Hüyük (Helmer 1985a, 1988); Ganj Dareh (Hesse 1978 and Kusutman 1991); Tell Aswad II (Damascene); Gritille Lower, Jericho PPNB (Kusutman 1991); Halula 1–9 (Saña Segui 1999); Yiftah'el PPNB (Horwitz 1987; 2003).
(a3) Late PPNB – Abu Ghosh (Ducos 1978; Kusutman 1991); ᾽Ain Ghazal LPPNB (Von den Driesch and Wodtke 1997); Ali Kosh (Hole, Flannery and Neely 1969); Beisamoun (Grigson n.d); Gritille Upper (Kusutman 1991); Halula 10–19 (Saña Segui 1999); Jarmo Aceramic (Stampfli 1983); Ramad I (Kusutman 1991); Ras Shamra VC (Poulain 1978); Tell Aswad (Djezireh) (Helmer 1985a); Hayaz Hüyük PPNB (Buitenhuis 1985; 1988).
(a4) Jarmo II 1–5 (Stampfli 1983; Flannery 1983).
(b1) Tell Nebi Mend; Tell Aray (Hongo 1996); Yumuktepe (Buitenhuis and Caneva 1998); Ras Shamra VB; Halula Pre-Halaf (Saña Segui 1999); Sabi Abyad Pre-Halaf (Cavallo 2000); Amuq A and B (Stampfli 1983); ᾽Ain Ghazal Yarmukian (Von den Driesch and Wodtke 1997).
(b2) Tell Nebi Mend; Arjoune (Grigson 2003).

Figure 7.11. Equid proximal phalanges

Equus hemionus – Mureybet (Ducos 1978).
Equus africanus/asinus – Maadi (Boessneck *et al.* 1989); Ra's en-Neqeb, Maysar 25 and modern E. africanus (Uerpmann 1991); Abusir (Boessneck *et al.* 1992); Timna (Grigson in press); Tell Ababra (von den Driesch and Amberger 1981).
Equus africanus/asinus/hemionus – Tell Nebi Mend; Shams ed-Din (Uerpmann 1982; 1986).

Figure 7.17. Map of the Levant

Abu Hureyra (Legge and Rowley-Conwy 2000); ᾽Ain Ghazal (Von den Driesch and Wodtke 1997); Amuq (Stampfli 1983); Bouqras (Buitenhuis 1988); Çayönü (Hongo and Meadow 2000; Ervynck *et al.* 2001); El Kowm 2 (Helmer 2000); Gürcütepe (von den Driesch and Peters 1999); Hagoshrim (Haber and Dayan 2004); Hayaz Höyuk (Buitenhuis 1988); Mersin Yumuktepe (Buitenhuis and Caneva 1998); Ras Shamra (Poulain 1978); Sabi Abyad (Cavallo 2000); Tel Te'o (Horwitz 2001); Tell Ali (Lev-Tov 2000); Tell Aray 2 (Hongo 1996); Tell Aswad (Jezireh) (Helmer 1985b); Tell el Kerkh (Anezaki and Yano 1998); Tell Halula (Saña Segui 1999); Tell Nebi Mend (present work); Tell Ramad (Ducos 1993; 2000); Tell Sukas (Riis 1974); Yiftah'el (Horwitz 1987; 2003).

8. The charred plant remains

Katherine Smith and Lisa Moffett

Introduction

Soil samples were collected at the excavators' discretion for the recovery of charred plant remains during the excavations. Seventeen samples were considered stratigraphically secure enough to merit further analysis and this report presents the results of the full analysis of eleven samples. They come from a variety of contexts: mudbrick debris, occupation debris, pits and a hearth. Full analysis of these samples allows us to examine:

1. what cereal crops were in use;
2. whether this assemblage provides information on crop-processing activities;
3. whether this assemblage provides information on cultivation conditions;
4. whether this assemblage provides information on patterns of rubbish disposal on site.

Method

Samples were collected from sealed deposits at the excavator's discretion and were processed on site either by bucket or machine flotation. Sample volumes range from 3 to 17 litres and are thus all smaller than the typical 20–30 litre sample collected for archaeobotanical analysis in the region today. The majority of the flots (the material which floats on the water's surface) were sieved over 1 mm and 250 µm mesh sieves and others (from contexts 655.3 and 655.7) were sieved over 1 mm and 500 µm mesh sieves. Heavy residues were collected and sieved over a 1 mm mesh sieve. Both the flots and heavy residues were air dried. Unfortunately, owing to time limitations, it was not possible to analyse the heavy residues as well and, therefore, this report is based only on the results from the flots.

The flots were initially sorted for charred plant remains in the field by Moffett, using a low-power binocular microscope at magnifications between ×6 and ×20. Final identifications were made by Smith at magnifications between ×6 and ×50 and in comparison with the authors' own modern seed collections. Nomenclature for the plant remains follows Moore (1982) for indigenous species and Zohary and Hopf (2000) for cultivated species. The traditional binomial system for the cereals has been maintained here, following Zohary and Hopf (2000, 28, table 3 and 65, table 5).

Results

Table 8.1 lists the taxa identified in all 11 samples and Table 8.2 provides a breakdown of the total identifications and the proportions of the various types of plant remains (*i.e.* cereal grain, cereal chaff, etc.). Fig. 8.1 provides a breakdown of the types of plants recovered in each sample. All of the samples contained mixtures of cereal grain, cereal chaff and weed/wild seeds.

The cereal crops recovered include hulled barley (*Hordeum* sp.), einkorn (*Triticum monococcum* L.) and emmer (*Triticum dicoccum* Schübl.). Emmer is the most dominant cereal recovered. Barley rachis and einkorn spikelets/glume bases were recovered only in small quantities. However, glume bases and complete spikelet forks of emmer were frequently abundant.

Other cultivated or possibly cultivated crops in these samples are limited. Small quantities of cultivated pulses, especially lentil (*Lens culinaris* L.), were recovered. A single olive stone (*Olea europaea* L.) was recovered from Phase 2 or 3 clay debris (706.20) and a fragment of a possible almond (*Amygdalus communis* L.) nutshell was recovered from the Phase 1 hearth (606.22). Whether these fruit and nut remains were accidentally incorporated in wood fuel or represent the remains of food is not clear. Certainly, non-cereal crops and/or collected wild foodstuffs are limited at Tell Nebi Mend. The overall dominance of cereal crops in the samples studied here is unlikely to be due to any particular scarcity of non-cereal crops but, instead, reflects the pattern of charring events on site, which appear to frequently involve cereal crops.

The weed/wild plants recovered from these samples most likely arrived in these deposits as weeds of the cereal crops, although it is possible that they could represent gardening waste or some other weeding debris (perhaps from field preparation). Modern agricultural practice, especially the use of herbicides, means that many of these taxa are rarely seen as weeds of cereal crops today; however, the weed/wild flora recovered from Tell Nebi Mend clearly contains species which are found frequently in association with ancient crop-processing waste at other sites in Syria (*e.g.* Moffett 2003; van Zeist and Bakker-Heeres 1985).

Discussion

The charred plant remains from Neolithic levels at Tell Nebi Mend provide evidence for cereal crops that were in use in this period, as well as crop-processing activities. Although only a limited flora of weed/wild plants was recovered, there is some information on cultivation conditions. Finally, there is limited evidence for the use, if not cultivation, of other plants (*i.e.* pulses, fruit and nuts) as well. Comparison of the results of Tell Nebi Mend with those from the neighbouring Halaf/Ubaid period site of Arjoune (Moffett 2003) reveal broad similarities.

Cereal crops cultivated

Glume wheats (emmer, *Triticum dicoccum* Schübl.; and/or einkorn, *Triticum monococcum* L.) dominate the assemblages studied here. The most commonly identified glume wheat in the assemblage was emmer (primarily glume bases and spikelets), which is also the dominant cereal recovered at the contemporary site of Tell Sukas, on the Syrian coast (Helbaek 1962). Of the 11 samples studied, 9 contained chaff remains of glume wheats accounting for more than 20% of the total identifications made. Owing to the poor state of preservation, it was not always possible to identify the glume wheat chaff to species level. However, when this was possible, the majority was identified as emmer. In addition to glume wheats, small quantities of hulled barley (*Hordeum* sp.) grain were recovered in 7 of the 11 samples studied. The sample from Layer 706.20 was the only one to contain barley chaff, which was identifiable as two-rowed barley (*Hordeum distichum* L.). Notably, two of the rachis nodes recovered were clearly pedicelled or lax (*sensu* Jacomet 1987).

Evidence for crop processing

Cereal chaff is less likely to survive charring than cereal grain (Boardman and Jones 1990). Glume bases and spikelet forks of hulled wheat, some of which were identified as emmer and einkorn, were dominant. Einkorn (*Triticum monococcum*) and emmer (*Triticum dicoccum*) are hulled wheats; which typically occur as single- or two-grain spikelets respectively; however, two grain einkorn and single grain emmer wheats are known and, of course, the terminal spikelet of many emmer wheats usually bears a single grain (Jacomet 1987). Although rarely grown today, hulled wheats do have a number of properties that would have been advantageous to past farmers. In particular, they can tolerate poor soil conditions and can resist a range of fungal diseases (Nesbitt and Samuel 1996, 42).

Ethnographic studies of crop processing of hulled wheats has resulted in the recognition of clear stages in the sequences involved in the separation of cereal grain (the product) from cereal chaff and weed seed contaminants (the by-products) (Hillman 1981; 1984a; 1984b; Jones 1981; 1984; 1987). During threshing, cereal ears of einkorn and emmer will break up into individual spikelets, which contain grains surrounded by tough chaff. At this point the ancient farmer could either store or further process the spikelets of hulled wheat. Storage of hulled wheat in spikelets is well known archaeobotanically and may serve to protect the grain from insect predation (Nesbitt and Samuel 1996, 52). In order to dehusk hulled wheat, the spikelets must be pounded and the resulting mixture of freed grain and chaff is then winnowed to separate light weed seeds and larger fragments of chaff from the grain, and then sieved, to remove any remaining weed seeds and smaller fragments of chaff from the grain.

All of the samples examined contained mixtures of cereal grain, cereal chaff and accompanying crop weeds (see Table 8.2 and Fig. 8.1). Three of the samples (706.10, 706.20 and 706.6) were clearly dominated by cereal chaff remains, which accounted for >50% of all identifications made. Small quantities of cereal grain and crop weeds were also recovered in these three samples. These assemblages most likely represent the remains from the final stage(s) of the crop-processing sequence; that is, they are either a winnowing or a fine-sieving by-product. One sample (from context 655.7) is clearly dominated by weed/wild seeds, which are most likely to be crop weeds. These were predominately large grass caryopses that were from a small sample (both in terms of sample volume and total number of identifications made from the flot) and, therefore, the results may not be reliable (see van der Veen and Fieller 1982 regarding the quantities of charred seeds that are reliably representative of an assemblage). The remaining seven samples contained fairly even mixtures of cereal grain, cereal chaff and weed seeds which clearly represent semi-processed crop remains and, possibly, mixed deposits.

At least two routes of arrival for this material into deposits at Tell Nebi Mend are possible:

1) It may be that winnowing or sieving by-products were intentionally destroyed or used as fuel. The combination of cereal chaff with small quantities of cereal grain and weed seeds may represent 'chob' or 'cavings' (extraction by hand of weed seeds, cereal chaff and tail grain during sieving: see Hillman 1984b, 2–3; Jones 1984, 46) which could be intentionally burned as fuel.

2) It could be that this material represents accidentally burned crop-processing material, perhaps in storage (as these by-products could be useful as feed for livestock) or even during small-scale crop processing (*i.e.* cleaning small amounts of grain prior to hand-milling). The presence of substantial quantities (*i.e.* > 20% of all identifications) of cereal grain, which is more likely to survive charring than cereal chaff (Boardman and Jones 1990), makes this interpretation fairly likely.

All of the samples are clearly secondary and, therefore, it is possible that much of the charred material has been reworked and/or represents a mixture of a series of dumping events. As a result, any precise identification of the route(s) of arrival of the mixture of cereal chaff, cereal grain and weed seeds recovered from these deposits is not possible. Use of cereal-processing waste as fuel is well attested (Hillman 1981; 1984a; 1984b) and disposal of spent fuel through dumping on site – into pits or abandoned buildings, for example – seems a likely explanation for the assemblages encountered.

Limited evidence for cultivation conditions

Several of the taxa identified, especially *Papaver cf. argemone* L. and *Buglossoides arvensis* (L.), are characteristic of arable and disturbed ground. The recovery of club rushes (*Scirpus* spp.), sedges (*Carex* spp.) and indeterminate Cyperaceae also provides limited evidence for cultivation in areas with wet soil conditions. However, it is unlikely that any of the deposits encountered are primary and, therefore, it is also possible that club rushes and sedges could have entered the deposit in other ways, perhaps as accidentally charred floor litter or basketry.

Evidence for other economic plants

In addition to cereals, small quantities of other crops have been identified in these samples. These include lentil (*Lens culinaris* L.) and olive (*Olea europaea* L.). Cultivated lentil is known from the 6th millennium BC; however, it is not certain whether the olive stone recovered is cultivated or wild. Zohary and Hopf (2000, 146) note that the stones of wild and cultivated varieties of olive can be indistinguishable. In addition, possible cultivated vetch/garden pea (*Vicia* sp./*Pisum sativum* L.) and a possible fragment of almond (*Amygdalus communis* L.) nutshell have also been identified. All of these crops are known from the Levant in the Neolithic period and, with the exception of olive, have been identified by Moffett (2003) in the later Neolithic at the neighbouring site of Arjoune.

Comparison of results with Arjoune

Seventeen samples from the neighbouring site of Arjoune, with calibrated dates ranging from the mid-6th to the mid-5th millennia BC, have been studied by Moffett (2003) and are directly comparable to the results presented here. Notably, the Arjoune assemblages were dominated by cereal chaff of glume wheats. Both emmer and einkorn were identified, but unfortunately, owing to poor preservation, the majority were classified as indeterminate glume wheat (Moffett 2003, 241). Although the sample sizes were considerably smaller than those from Arjoune, it is clear that the general character of the Tell Nebi Mend assemblages (*i.e.* a mixture of cereal grain, cereal chaff and accompanying crop weeds) appears to be quite similar to that from Arjoune. This suggests that a certain consistency in crop-processing activities and disposal of crop-processing debris existed at both sites.

Conclusions

The Tell Nebi Mend Neolithic archaeobotanical samples are dominated by cereal remains and consistently contain a mixture of cereal grain, cereal chaff and weed seeds regardless of the type of context sampled. Although sample volumes were smaller than desirable, the Neolithic samples studied from Tell Nebi Mend have produced assemblages that are extremely similar to those recovered from the later nearby site of Arjoune. This suggests that a fairly consistent pattern of activities in relation to the deposition of crop-processing waste existed at both sites. There is limited evidence from the weed flora to suggest that the cereal crops were grown as arable crops and not as small-scale garden crops. The recovery of club rushes and sedges suggests that cultivation occurred in areas of damp or wet ground. In addition to cereal crops, small quantities of other cultivars, such as lentil, olive, possible vetch/ garden pea and possible almond, also were encountered. The overall dominance of cereal crops appears to reflect a general pattern of charring events at Tell Nebi Mend, as well as Arjoune, that appear to frequently involve cereal grain.

Table 8.1. Charred plant remains from Trench VIII (Neolithic).

Sample number	606.22	706.22	706.26	706.42	706.20	706.6	606.16	655.3	655.7	706.10	706.21	
Phase	1(?2)	2	2	2	2(?3)	2(?3)	3	3	4	4	4	
Context type	Hearth	Mixed debris	Pit	Clay & ash	Clay debris	Grey ash	Pit/hearth	Plaster	Ashy pit	Pit	Pit 5	
Sample volume (L.)	10	8	8	17.00	8?[2]	9	7	3	5	11	5	
Seeds per litre	66.9	23.4	9.0	30.6	9.5	29.6	4.3	12.3	10.4	6.4	8.6	
Latin Binomial*												English Common Name
Cereal Grain												**Cereal Grain**
Triticum monococcum L./*dicoccum* Schübl.	8	2	–	–	2	–	1	–	2	2	1	einkorn/emmer
Triticum dicoccum Schübl.	2	–	–	–	1	3	–	–	–	–	–	emmer
Triticum cf. *dicoccum* Schübl.	–	–	–	–	–	2	–	1	–	–	1	possible emmer
Hordeum sp. – hulled	2	2	2	–	3	9[E]	1	–	–	–	1	hulled barley
cf. *Hordeum* sp. – hulled	–	1	3	1	–	–	–	–	–	–	1	possible hulled barley
Indeterminate Cereal	37[E]	7[E]	5	3	–	–	–	1	2	–	4[E]	indeterminate cereal
Indeterminate Cereal/Large GRAMINEAE	132[E]	15[E]	32	2[E]	58[E]	28[E]	7	–	10[e]	9[E]	6[E]	indet. cereal/large grass
Indeterminate Cereal/Large GRAMINEAE – detached embryo	–	–	–	–	–	–	–	–	1	–	–	indet. cereal/large grass
Cereal Chaff												**Cereal Chaff**
Triticum monococcum L. – spikelet	–	–	3 (=4gb)	–	–	–	–	–	–	–	–	einkorn
Triticum monococcum L. – glume base	–	–	–	–	–	–	–	–	–	–	–	einkorn
Triticum monococcum L./*dicoccum* Schübl. – spikelet	5[3] (=9 gb + 1r)	6 (=12 gb)	15[6] (=28 gb)	2 (=3gb)	27[4] (=46 gb)	15[7]= (26gb + 1r)	–	1 (=2 gb)	–	3[8] (= 6 gb)	–	einkorn/emmer
Triticum monococcum L./*dicoccum* Schübl. – glume base	23	4	5	10	123	10	–	6	–	13	3	einkorn/emmer
Triticum dicoccum Schübl. – spikelet	2 (= 4gb)	7 (=14 gb)	26 (=52 gb + 3r)	2 (=2gb + 1r)	32 (=50gb + 2r)	9 (16gb + 3r)	–	1 (= 2 gb)	–	4 (= 8gb)	2 (= 4gb)	emmer
Triticum dicoccum Schübl. – glume base	30	5	24	10	101	14	–	–	–	19	2	emmer
Triticum cf. *dicoccum* Schübl. – glume base	–	–	2	–	–	–	–	–	–	–	–	possible emmer
Triticum sp. – indeterminate awn	–	–	–	–	–	+[S]	–	–	–	–	–	indeterminate wheat
Triticum sp. – indeterminate glume/lemma	–	–	–	–	+++	–	–	1[e]	1[e]	–	–	indeterminate wheat
Triticum sp. – indeterminate rachis node	–	–	–	–	5	1	–	–	–	–	–	indeterminate wheat
Hordeum distichum L. – rachis node	–	–	–	–	115	–	–	–	–	–	–	two-rowed barley
Hordeum sp. – rachis node	–	–	–	–	2	+[S]	–	–	–	–	–	barley
Hordeum sp. – awn	–	–	–	–	–	3	–	–	–	–	–	barley
Indeterminate Cereal rachis node/internode	4[E]	–	5	2	–	1	–	1	–	1	1	indeterminate cereal

Table 8.1. Charred plant remains from Trench VIII (Neolithic) continued.

Sample number	606.22	706.22	706.26	706.42	706.20	706.6	606.16	655.3	655.7	706.10	706.21	
Phase	1(?2)	2	2	2	2(?3)	2(?3)	3	3	4	4	4	
Context type	Hearth	Mixed debris	Pit	Clay & ash	Clay debris	Grey ash	Pit/hearth	Plaster	Ashy pit	Pit?	Pit 5	
Sample volume (L.)	10	8	8	17.00	8?[2]	9	7	3	5	11	5	
Seeds per litre	66.9	23.4	9.0	30.6	9.5	29.6	4.3	12.3	10.4	6.4	8.6	
Latin Binomial*												**English Common Name**
Indeterminate Cereal/Large GRAMINEAE – culm node	–	–	–	–	–	–	–	–	–	1	1	indet. cereal/large grass
cf. Indeterminate Cereal/Large GRAMINEAE – culm base	–	–	1	–	–	–	–	–	–	–	–	possible indet. cereal/lg. grass
Pulses												**Pulses**
Vicia sp./*Pisum sativum* L.	–	–	–	–	–	–	–	–	–	–	–	vetch/garden pea
Vicia sp./*Lens culinaris* L./*Lathyrus* sp. – indet. fragment	–	–	–	–	1	–	–	–	–	–	–	vetch/lentil/vetchling
Lens culinaris Medik.	2	–	8	–	5	1	–	–	1	–	–	lentil
cf. *Lens culinaris* Medik.	–	–	–	–	–	–	1	–	–	–	–	possible lentil
LEGUMINOSAE – indeterminate large-sized (? cultivar)	4[E]	–	2	–	20[E]	–	–	–	2[c]	–	–	pea family
Fruit												**Fruit/Nuts**
cf. *Amygdalus communis* L. – fragment of nutshell	1[E]	–	–	–	–	–	–	–	–	–	–	possible almond
Olea europaea L. – (?cultivated/?wild)	–	–	–	–	1	–	–	–	–	–	–	olive
Weed/Wild Plants												**Weed/Wild Plants**
Rumex spp.	1	–	–	–	–	–	–	–	–	–	–	dock
Silene spp.	1	–	–	–	–	–	–	–	–	–	–	campion
Adonis sp.	–	–	–	–	1	–	–	–	–	–	–	pheasant's eye
cf. *Ranunculus ficaria* L.	4	–	–	–	–	1	1	–	–	–	1	lesser celandine
Papaver cf. *argemone* L.	2	–	–	–	–	–	–	–	–	–	1	prickly poppy
cf. PAPAVERACEAE – unidentified	1	–	–	–	–	–	–	–	–	–	–	possible poppy family
Vicia spp./*Lathyrus* spp.	3	–	–	–	3	–	–	1	–	–	–	vetch/vetchling
Melilotus spp./*Medicago* spp./*Trifolium* spp.	1	2	–	–	–	–	1	–	–	–	2	melilot/medick/clover
Melilotus spp./*Medicago* spp./*Trifolium* spp./*Lotus* spp.	–	–	–	–	–	–	1	–	–	–	1	melilot/medick/clover/bird's foot trefoil
LEGUMINOSAE – unidentified	–	1[IM]	–	–	–	–	1	–	–	–	–	pea family
cf. LEGUMINOSAE – unidentified	1	–	–	–	–	–	2	–	–	–	–	possible pea family
CUCURBITACEAE – unidentified	–	–	–	–	1	–	–	–	–	–	–	white bryony family
UMBELLIFERAE – unidentified	–	–	–	–	1	–	–	–	–	–	–	carrot family
Galium sp. – cf. *Galium mollugo* L. – type	1	–	–	–	–	–	–	–	–	–	–	hedge bedstraw type
Galium spp. – large-seeded	1	1	–	–	–	–	–	–	–	–	–	clever
Buglossoides arvensis (L.) I. M. Johnston	2[S]	2	1[S]	2[S]	5[S]	1	1[S]	1[S]	–	2 (1[S])	1[S]	field gromwell

Table 8.1. Charred plant remains from Trench VIII (Neolithic) continued.

Sample number	606.22	706.22	706.26	706.42	706.20	706.6	606.16	655.3	655.7	706.10	706.21	
Phase	1(?2)	2	2	2	2(?3)	2(?3)	3	3	4	4	4	
Context type	Hearth	Mixed debris	Pit	Clay & ash	Clay debris	Grey ash	Pit/hearth	Plaster	Ashy pit	Pit	Pit 5	
Sample volume (L.)	10	8	8	17.00	8?[2]	9	7	3	5	11	5	
Seeds per litre	66.9	23.4	9.0	30.6	9.5	29.6	4.3	12.3	10.4	6.4	8.6	
Latin Binomial*												English Common Name
COMPOSITAE – unidentified small, smooth-seeded	1	–	–	–	–	–	–	–	–	–	–	carrot family
Asphodelus spp.	2	–	–	–	–	–	1	–	–	–	–	asphodel
Lolium spp.	3	–	1	–	–	–	–	–	–	–	1	rye grass
GRAMINEAE – unidentified – small-sized caryopsis	16	9	3	10.00	6.00	–	1	15	5	–	2	small-seeded grass
GRAMINEAE – unidentified – medium-sized caryopsis	41	–	–	–	5.00	–	–	–	3	–	–	medium-seeded grass
GRAMINEAE – unidentified – large-sized caryopsis	4	–	44[E]	–	1.00	22[E]	1	–	22	10[E]	–	large-seeded grass
Scirpus spp.	4	–	–	–	25[E]	–	–	–	–	–	–	club rushes
Carex spp. – 2-sided	70	–	–	–	–	–	–	–	–	–	–	sedge
Carex spp. – 3-sided	2	–	–	–	–	–	–	–	–	–	–	sedge
cf. CYPERACEAE – indeterminate	–	–	–	–	–	1	–	–	–	–	–	sedge family
Unidentified – Type A (Spergula-like)	–	–	–	–	–	–	1	–	–	–	–	unidentified
Unidentified – Type B (Empetrum nigrum L. – like)	2	–	–	–	–	–	–	–	–	–	–	unidentified
Unidentified – bud	–	–	–	–	1.00	–	–	–	–	–	–	unidentified
Unidentified – capsule/nutshell fragment	–	–	1	–	1.00	–	–	–	–	–	–	unidentified
Unidentified – leaf	2	–	–	–	–	–	–	–	–	–	–	unidentified
Unidentified	57[E]	1	–	10.00	3.00	3	2	1	4	5	–	unidentified
Indeterminate	–	11	4	20.00	120[E]	–	7	50[c]	30[c]	1	11	indeterminate

*All eleven samples studied were pre-sorted by previous archaeobotanists on the Tell Nebi Mend project. Unfortunately there appears to be no record of the flot volumes. Nomenclature for cultivated taxa follows Zohary and Hopf (2000) and for indigenous taxa follows *Flora Europaea* (Moore 1982). The traditional binomial system for the cereals has been used here, following Zohary and Hopf (2000: 28, table 3 and 65, table 5). Overall taxonomic order within sections (i.e. Cereals, Pulses, Weed/Wild Plants, etc.) follows Moore (1982). N.B. *Flora Palaestina* may be ultimately adopted for nomenclature.
N[E] = estimate count of fragmentary seeds N[S] = seeds are possibly silicified and presumed ancient. N[IM] = possibly immature seed. Semi-quantitative scale used for items which cannot be quantified: + = 1 to 5 items, ++ = 6–10 items and +++ > 10 items.
[1] Context 706.20 was excavated in 1990, but unfortunately the sample processing notes do not include the volume for this context. Other deposits from the 706 contexts typically measured between 8 to 9 litres, and therefore an estimate of an 8 L volume for the sample seems reasonable.
[2] 2 of the spikelets are terminal.
[3] 2 of the spikelets are terminal.
[4] 2 of the two-row barley rachis nodes are clearly pedicelled (or lax).
[5] 2 of the spikelets are terminal.
[6] 2 of the spikelets are terminal
[7] 2 of the spikelets are terminal.

Table 8.2. Summary statistics for Tell Nebi Mend Neolithic samples from Trench VIII.

A: Total identifications by plant category

Sample number	606.22	706.22	706.26	706.42	706.20	706.6	606.16	655.3	655.7	706.10	706.21
Phase	1 (?2)	2	2	2	2 (?3)	2 (?3)	3	3	4	4	4
Context type	hearth	mixed debris	pit	clay & ash	clay debris	grey ashy	pit/ hearth	plaster	pit	pit	pit 5
Cereal grain	181	27	42	6	64	42	9	2	15	11	14
Cereal chaff	111	22	81	24	405	195	0	9	1	41	9
Pulses	6	0	10	0	26	1	1	0	3	0	0
Fruit/nut	1	0	0	0	1	0	0	0	0	0	0
Weed/wild plants	165	15	50	12	50	25	11	17	30	12	9
Unidentified	57	1	0	10	3	3	2	2	3	5	0
Indeterminate	0	11	4	20	120	0	7	7	0	1	11
Total	521	76	187	72	669	266	30	37	52	70	43

B: Proportion of plant remains by plant category (shading indicated dominate category)

(Shading indicates those samples where >50% of identifications are derived from a single plant category)

Sample number	606.22	706.22	706.26	706.42	706.20	706.6	606.16	655.3	655.7	706.10	706.21
Phase	1 (?2)	2	2	2	2 (?3)	2 (?3)	3	3	4	4	4
Context type	hearth	mixed debris	pit	clay & ash	clay debris	grey ashy	pit/ hearth	plaster	pit	pit	clay debris
Cereal grain	34.7%	35.5%	22.5%	8.3%	9.6%	15.8%	30.0%	5.4%	28.8%	15.7%	32.6%
Cereal chaff	21.3%	28.9%	43.3%	33.3%	60.5%	73.3%	0.0%	24.3%	1.9%	58.6%	20.9%
Pulses	1.2%	0.0%	5.3%	0.0%	3.9%	0.4%	3.3%	0.0%	5.8%	0.0%	0.0%
Fruit/nut	0.2%	0.0%	0.0%	0.0%	0.1%	0.0%	0.0%	0.0%	0.0%	0.0%	0.0%
Weed/wild plants	31.7%	19.7%	26.7%	16.7%	7.5%	9.4%	36.7%	45.9%	57.7%	17.1%	20.9%
Unidentified	10.9%	1.3%	0.0%	13.9%	0.4%	1.1%	6.7%	5.4%	5.8%	7.1%	0.0%
Indeterminate	0.0%	14.5%	2.1%	27.8%	17.9%	0.0%	23.3%	18.9%	0.0%	1.4%	25.6%

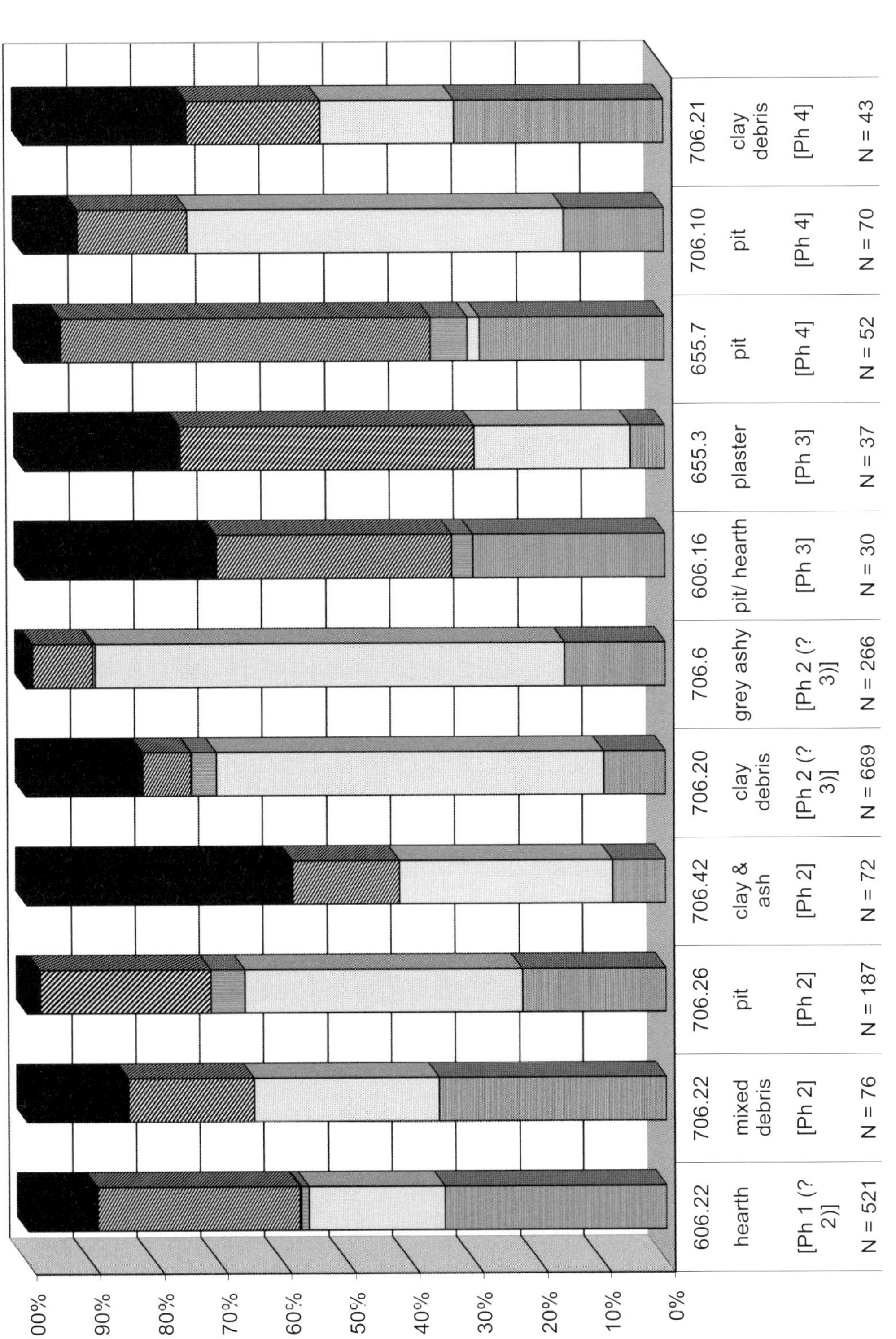

Fig. 8.1. Breakdown of plant remains recovered in Trench VIII Neolithic samples.

PART III:

THE ENCLOSURE

9. The Enclosure

Peter J. Parr

A description of the Enclosure has been given in Chapter 1 and need not be repeated. It will be remembered that the ditch which forms its southern boundary was already observed by the first visitor to publish an account of the site, W. M. Thomson (1848, 692), and that Burton and Drake, although not mentioning the ditch, reported 'earthwork embankments to the west of the Nahr Tannurin' (*i.e.* the Muqadiyah), presumably those forming the south-west corner of the Enclosure (Burton and Drake 1872, 222). Conder apparently did not see the ditch either, but he does mention it in his written account, having learned of its existence from reading Thomson (Conder 1881a, 166; 1881b, 142; 1885, 31). Conder's sketch plan does not show any features west of the Muqadiyah, and it thus seems probable that he did not investigate Burton and Drake's earthworks. His rather vague description of the topography of the site leaves it uncertain whether what he claimed to have identified on the ground as the 'double moat' shown in the Egyptian reliefs of the battle refers to these or to other, more ephemeral, features of the terrain, as Breasted thought likely (Breasted 1903, 16). It is also doubtful whether Koldewey (1898, 180 and fig. 81) ever investigated the terrain west of the Muqadiyah, since although his plan (see Fig. 1.10) clearly shows the southern ditch linking the two flood plains it gives no indication of a continuation beyond the tributary. It thus seems that it was Pézard who was the first to describe both the southern and the western ditches and the embankment associated with the latter and to note their correct relationship, a discovery which he justly claimed to have been one of the most important results of his work. His words deserve to be cited in full (Pézard 1922, 111–12; 1931, 23–4).

> Ses limites au Sud et à l'Ouest semblent bien constituées par un grand canal d'une vingtaine de mètres de large, coudé à angle droit, dont la trace se discerne parfaitement au milieu des plantations de blé et de seigle qu'il traverse; ses berges actuelles sont encore hautes de 2 à 5 mètres et dans le fond humide les herbes et les céréales poussent plus drues que sur les pentes et dans la plaine.
>
> Cette découverte apparaît comme l'une des plus importantes de la campagne de 1921; on se rappelle en effet, que le tell, bordé à l'Est et dans une partie de la face Nord par le Nahr-el-Asi, à l'Ouest et au Nord par le Aïn-Tannour, n'était pas fermé au Sud par un cours d'eau; c'était là l'une des principales objections soulevées contre l'identification de Tell Nebi Mend avec Kadesh, la Kadesh hittite étant complètement entourée d'eaux. La branche de ce canal, perpendiculaire au cours de l'Oronte, ferme le Tell au Sud et lève donc la difficulté; quant à la branche Ouest elle devait être parcourue dans l'antiquité par le Aïn-Tannour actuel, trop étroit aujourd'hui pour avoir jamais opposé à l'envahisseur une barrière quelconque; quand, pour des causes inconnues, le canal fut abandonné, cette petite rivière changea de lit, tout en suivant la même direction. Au Nord, la branche Ouest du canal, si elle n'aboutissait pas directement à l'Oronte, conduisait sans doute aux marécages de ce fleuve, comme cela ressort de l'examen du terrain.

It was also Pézard who first drew attention to the resemblance of the plan of these features at Tell Nebi Mend to the enclosure at Sefinet en-Nuh about 3 km further north, a site initially reported by Porter ('a very singular rectangular mound, hollow in the centre, and surrounded by a dyke of earth of uniform height along the sides, but elevated at the corners': Porter 1854, 675), mentioned briefly by Burton and Drake (1872, 224) and by Conder (1881a, 169; 1881b, 146; 1885, 36), and discussed in greater detail by Ronzevalle, who visited it during his pioneering examination of the fortifications at Mishrifeh/ Qatna in 1906 and 1912 (Ronzevalle 1911–21, 109–26). In this paper Ronzevalle not only noted the similarities between Mishrifeh and Sefinet en-Nuh (but not Tell Nebi Mend, which he apparently did not visit) but also drew attention to resemblances between these enclosures and

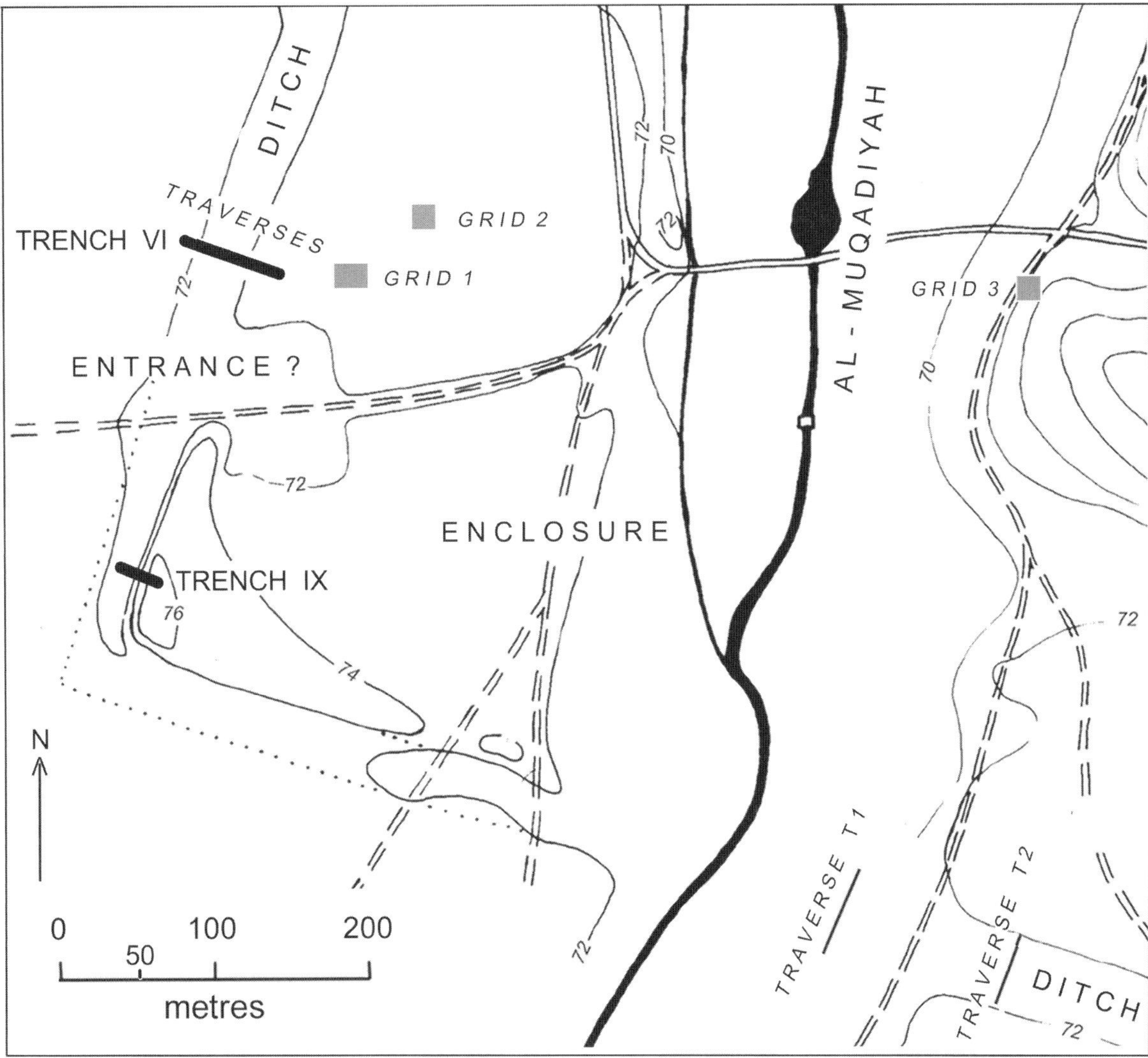

Fig. 9.1. Plan of the south-west corner of the Enclosure.

the 'fortified camp' at Tell el-Yahudieh in the Egyptian Delta, a structure attributed by Petrie to the Hyksos. This attribution was, however, rejected for the Syrian sites by the French scholar, who preferred to interpret them as the initial encampments of the Sea Peoples following their invasion of the Levantine coast at the close of the 13th century (Ronzevalle 1911–21, 119–22). Ronzevalle's analogy, though not his interpretation, was immediately accepted by Albright (1922, 122–3) and also by Mesnil du Buissson, who, for the first time, added Tell Nebi Mend to the list of 'villes carrées' in the Levant, dating them, with Petrie, to the early 2nd millennium (Mesnil du Buisson 1929, 175).

Despite a continuing debate during the following decades (for example, Yadin 1955; 1963; Parr 1968; Wright 1968; summarised and discussed by Burke 2008, 3–15), this was the generally accepted understanding in 1975, when the London expedition to Tell Nebi Mend began. As regards the northern Levantine sites, however,

it was an understanding based – as so often – on a very limited amount of excavated evidence, and during the second season of the project it was decided to attempt to establish the date and purpose of the Enclosure before the ever increasing threat from building and farming activities destroyed the surviving remains, even though this meant diverting scarce resources from the primary focus of the research on the main mound. Following a surface survey (admittedly rather cursory) of the flat area between the Main and Lower Tells and the western ditch – during which very little pottery was found and of this nothing earlier than Roman/Byzantine – a narrow trench, Trench VI, was dug in 1977 across the embankment and ditch just north of the possible entrance near the south-west corner, and another, Trench IX, in 1979, across the embankment only at its highest preserved point at the corner. These trenches were supplemented by a small-scale geophysical survey in the same region (Fig. 9.1).

Fig. 9.2. View of Trench VI across ditch, from the south-west.

Trench VI

This began as a 4.5 m × 2 m sounding (Area VI.100) on top of the low remains of the embankment, to which was later added a trench 1 m wide – just wide enough to enable a section to be drawn – stretching for 62 m between the crests of the two slopes defining the ditch. In fact, only 26 m at the eastern end (Areas 101 and 102) and 18 m at the western end (Area 103) were actually excavated, the middle 18 m being left for the convenience of agricultural traffic, since cultivation was in progress during the course of the excavation (Fig. 9.2). The section on the north face of the Trench was recorded, and is here published in two parts, the eastern part being Section 1A (Fig. 9.3) and the western part Section 1B (Fig. 9.4). The section of the western face of Area 100 (Section 2) is shown in Fig. 9.5. Of these Section 1A is most informative in terms of giving a clear picture of the original size and character of the embankment and the method of its construction.

Section 1A (Fig. 9.3)

Here – as over the entire site – the natural lacustine marlstone has an irregular indurated crust frequently penetrated by solution holes and root channels filled with reddish-brown soil, clay and gravel (Section 1A, Layer VI.102.6). (For a good description of the natural marl

deposits around Tell Nebi Mend see Bridgland *et al.* 2003.) In this part of the trench it is topped by a thin level surface on which, in places, there are traces of a very dark fossil soil, just a few centimetres thick even when best preserved, and clearly visible in the section (see Fig. 9.3). It was on this level surface that the first stage in the construction of the embankment took place, namely the collecting and piling up of the nearby reddish soil to form a low mound about 4 m to 5 m wide at its base and 1 m high (Section 1A, Layer VI.102.4; Fig. 9.6). The construction of this mound was clearly done with some care, since the material forming it is fairly fine and regular, and there are indications within it of horizontal surfaces, suggesting deliberate tamping to consolidate it as much as possible. It would thus have formed a stable core over which the next stage in the construction of the embankment, the depositing of a stony fill interspersed with yellow clayey layers, could take place (Section 1A, Layers VI.102.2, 102.7). This fill stretches westwards for approximately 8 m from the centre of the earth core and presumably for about the same distance eastwards, although the full extent in this direction was not excavated. On the west the base of the bank coincides exactly with the top of the eastern scarp of the ditch, quarried from the natural marl for another 5 m or so at an angle of about 24° from the horizontal (Fig. 9.7). If this angle were maintained for the slope of the embankment, which is likely, and the crest of the bank were not flattened, which is possible, the original height of the bank above the ground surface to the east would have been about 4 m, while to the west the combined height of ditch scarp and bank would have been about 7 m (Fig. 9.8). The ditch, however, continues further and increases this height: below the scarp, and after a narrrow ledge, it falls away vertically, but unfortunately to an unknown depth, since the water table was reached after 2 m and lack of resources prevented further excavation.

The only cultural material found in any layer securely associated with the construction of the embankment comprised about 50 storage jar body sherds (some of which fitted one another) which were all so similar in fabric and surface finish that they almost certainly represent one or two vessels at most. They are all of finely levigated clay with many small and medium white (lime), grey (chert) and black (basalt) grits, and are fired, with a greyish core and pale reddish-brown or greenish surfaces; in some examples a thin friable slip or wash is preserved. One sherd has a horizontal band of 14 finely incised comb incisions around the upper body, while another has two small vertical oblique 'slash' incisions (Fig. 9.9, no. 1). There can be little doubt that they belong to the earlier part of the Middle Bronze Age, although the absence of rim sherds makes it fruitless to seek closer analogies with the Tell Nebi Mend ceramic typology published by Bourke (1993). Although they are recorded as coming from several different layers – the dark red stony layer immediately overlying the natural marl (VI. 101.3 and VI.102.6), the fill of a small depression or pit in the marl (VI.102.5), and the hard red stony core of the bank itself (VI.102.4) – these red stony deposits are all very similar and distinguishing between them was often difficult, and it is possible that the sherds in fact form a single group. In any case, they can only be attributed to the phase either prior to or contemporary with the construction of the embankment, and they thus provide a *terminus post quem* of the early 2nd millennium BC for that event. A few more sherds of Middle Bronze Age fabric and form, including the bowl rims illustrated in Fig. 9.9 (nos 2 and 3), were also found, and even though these all came from later levels or from the topsoil, they confirm the presence of some measure of early 2nd millennium activity in the vicinity of Trench VI.

The rest of the diagnostic pottery recovered from Trench VI is illustrated on Fig. 9.9, (nos 4–16). It all comes from the topsoil, from deposits in the ditch or from disturbances associated with the use of this part of the site as a cemetery. Although no detailed typological study of this material has been made, it is reasonably homogeneous and the more distinctive specimens, such as nos 5, 6, 15 and 16, would indicate a central date of the 4th century AD, when is is known that the nearby Lower Mound was closely settled. Evidence for the cemetery can be seen at the eastern end of Section 1A (see Fig. 9.3) and in Section 2 (see Fig. 9.5). In the former a burial is situated at the base of a shaft 3 m deep (Layers 102.8 and 102.9) dug through the eastern slope of the embankment (Layer 102.7)

and into the underlying marl; since the top of the shaft has been destroyed and is now covered by plough soil it cannot be said whether the embankment was preserved to a greater height when the burial took place than it was in 1977. Two-thirds of the way down the shaft a slight ledge was cut into its northern and southern sides, and on these ledges four thick basalt slabs were laid, forming a closely fitting cover for the actual grave, which was another metre deep and measured 2.0 m × 0.6 m. Beneath the slabs an empty cavity was followed by a deposit of stiff yellow clay covering the undisturbed but very badly decayed remains of a wooden coffin, compressed to never more that about a centimetre in thickness and often represented by only a dark stain on the floor of the grave (Figs 9.10 and 9.11). Three of the iron nails used in the construction of the coffin were still preserved *in situ*, but of the body only a few bone fragments survived. The only artefactual evidence for the date of this inhumation consists of three body sherds, one of a Roman/Late Roman ribbed cooking pot and two from undiagnostic storage jars, and a fragment of a cylindrical glass bead, all from the fill of the shaft (Layer VI.102.8).

Section 2 (Fig. 9.5)

A few metres away, Area 200 of Trench VI provided evidence for three more burials. This area proved difficult to excavate and the various disturbances were not always distinguished or recorded accurately; nor, unfortunately, was a field plan made. However, the burials are clear in the section (see Fig. 9.5). Two are shaft graves similar to that described above, both dug through yellow and reddish stony deposits (Layers VI.100.23, 33 and 35), presumably part of the embankment fill, and penetrating into the natural clay and marl; the buried soil to which attention has already been drawn is visible as a thin black streak at the far northern end of the section. The third burial consists of a limestone sarcophagus, broken probably in antiquity, of which only part was excavated. This was certainly later than one, and probably both, of the shaft graves. No human or coffin remains were found directly associated with any of the graves, although the presence of several iron nails in disturbed contexts presumably testifies to the original existence of the latter. Owing to the complexity of the stratigraphy in the restricted area dug the attribution of the pottery – all Roman/Late Roman – to individual layers is not always certain, but mention should be made of the complete jar, reconstructed from sherds in Fig. 9.9 (no. 16), which came from the shaft of the southernmost burial, Layer 100.21.

Section 1B (see Fig. 9.4)

Little need be said about this except to draw attention to a degree of uncertainty over the first 14 m at the western end in distinguishing between what is obviously the undisturbed natural marl and the very similar but less homogeneous lacustine deposits lying between this and

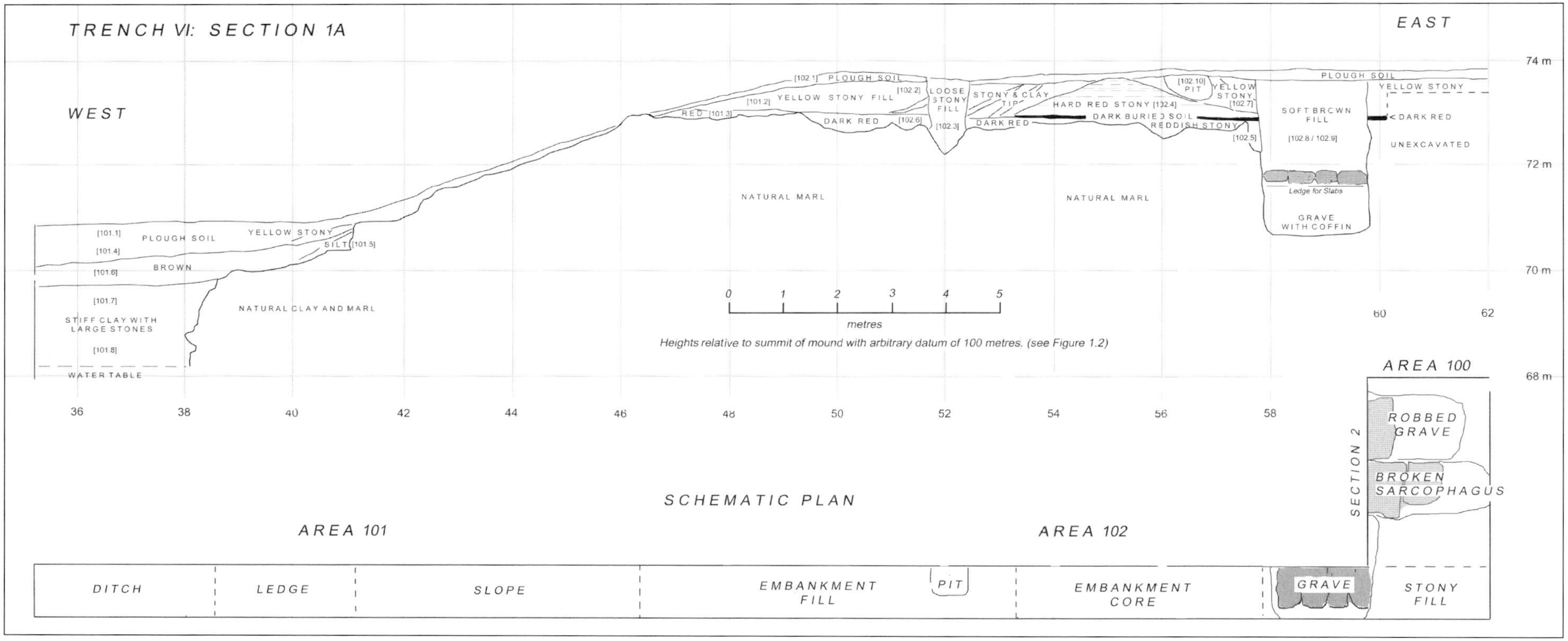

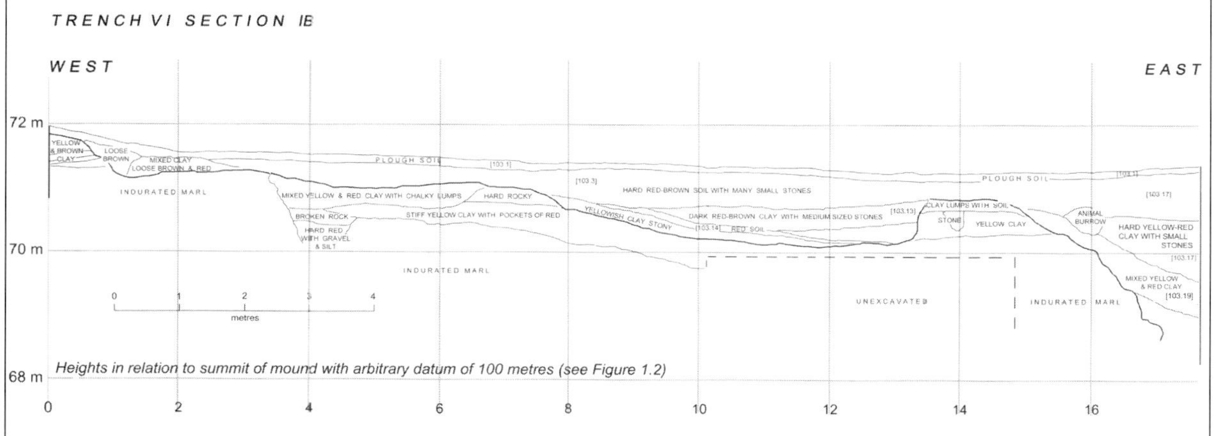

Fig. 9.3. Trench VI Section 1A.

Fig. 9.4. Trench VI Section 1B.

the present topsoil.[1] The relationship of this western end of the ditch with the ditch and embankment to the east is shown schematically in Fig. 9.8.

Trench IX

Like Trench VI, this is also between 1 m and 2 m wide (Figs 9.12, 9.13). It stretches for 36 m across the embankment to the edge of the ditch (Fig. 9.12); the drawing of its southern face is shown in Fig. 9.13. The interpretation of the section is more complicated than is that of Trench VI, owing again to the difficulty of not always being able to distinguish natural from man-made deposits in the almost total absence of artefacts. At the eastern end, between a horizontal distance of *c.*6 and 11 m, and in the centre, between *c.*19 and 22 m, what appears to be the indurated natural marl is sealed by a thin horizontal layer of red-brown soil sometimes mixed with pieces of marl (Layer IX.200.5), and on the analogy of Trench VI (see Fig. 9.3), where a similar soil line occured at approximately the same absolute elevation of *c.*83 m (in relation to the arbitrary datum of 100 m on the summit of the *tell*), it is reasonable to suppose that this is the surface of the natural terrain prior to the construction of the fortifications. However, unlike in Trench VI, the soil is covered here by about a metre of solid marl at the eastern end of the section (Layer IX.200.4) and of stiff stony yellow clay nearer the centre. If this deposit is man-made – and if it is not the red-brown soil beneath it must obviously be an earlier geological feature – it must be a fill designed to raise the natural land surface approximately to the level of the 'peak' in the natural marl visible a little further west. Whether natural or man-made, it was on this marl base that, just east of the 'peak', a low mound of stiff yellow clay and stones was placed, apparently the equivalent of the mound of reddish soil forming the core of the embankment in Trench VI. Against this and resting also on the horizontal marl base (IX.200.4) the inner slope of the embankment was then constructed, in the same manner as in Trench VI, with a succession of marl/clay, gravel and occasional red soil layers lying at an angle of about 30° (Layer IX.200.3). The uppermost of these tip layers (IX.200.2) is thicker and more compact than those lower down, and may represent the original reinforced surface of the embankment.

However, the western part of the section reflects a different situation. West of the 'peak' the surface of the natural marl begins to slope down rapidly, forming the upper part of the scarp of the ditch, as in Trench VI, though whether the scarp here is natural or man-made – as it was in Trench VI – could not be determined in the small area excavated. After this the marl levels out to form a ledge, similar again to that in Trench VI, before (presumably) the lower part of the ditch is reached (although this was not excavated). But the similarities with Trench VI now end. Instead of the regular alternating thin layers of marl, clay and gravel which constitute the eastern part of the bank, the

western part consists of a number of mixed, irregular and seemingly haphazardly placed deposits of marl, soil and gravel, together with a few large stones (Layers IX.300. 3 and 4), resting on the ledge and against the scarp in the natural marl. The junction of these deposits with the uniform layers of fill further east has unfortunately been destroyed by a later pit, making it impossible to be certain of the exact stratigraphic sequence and thus to understand fully the implications of the structural differences. It may be that the two parts of the embankment are contempoary, despite the differences, and are both part of the original design, though in this case it is difficult to understand why the scarp in the natural marl – if it is artificial, which seems most likely – was buried and not used as part of the defensive system, as it was in Trench VI. It is perhaps more likely that the western part of the embankment is a repair and strengthening of this vulnerable corner of the Enclosure following the collapse of the original structure.

Artefacts were very rare in Trench IX, comprising only a few Roman/Late Roman body sherds and glass fragments, a stone spindle-whorl or button (Reg. No. 0368), a fragment of bronze sheeting (Reg. No. 0431) and two Late Roman coins, one (Reg. No. 0432) illegible and the other (Reg. No. 0510) of Honorius/Arcadius. With the exception of this latter coin all came from the surface or the topsoil, and thus have no bearing on the date of origin of the fortification. But the Honorius/Arcadius coin is important, since it is noted in the field record as having come from Layer 100.3, the marl and gravel fill of the bank at about the centre of the trench (*c.*18–21 m horizontal distance). In an early preliminary report on the Tell Nebi Mend excavations it was stated that it provided 'a clear *terminus post quem*' of the late 4th century for the construction of the embankment (Parr 1983, 108), and – although this was not mentioned in that report – the presence of rectilinear fortified enclosures of Late Roman or Byzantine date at the sites of Jusiyeh el-ᶜAmar and Jusiyeh el-Harab, a few kilometres further south along the Orontes (Mouterde and Poidebard 1945, 31–6), probably unduly influenced this conclusion, which has since been cited at least twice in the secondary literature (Healy 1993, 52; Burke 2008, 21). However, further consideration of the evidence strongly suggests that this conclusion was incorrect. Reference to the section (see Fig. 9.13) shows that the layer in question, 100.3, has been partly destroyed by the large pit already mentioned, the pebbly fill of which is very similar in composition and appearance to the gravel and marl deposits through which it is cut. Presumably for this reason the pit was not recorded, and therefore not excavated, as a separate deposit, and it was only when the section was drawn and studied that it was recognised as a later disturbance. In view of the evidence from Trench VI, discussed above, showing that part of the embankment was being used as a cemetery in the Late Roman period, it seems highly probable that the pottery and coin recorded as coming from the fill of the embankment in Trench IX came, in fact, from the later pit and were incorrectly recorded in the field. They

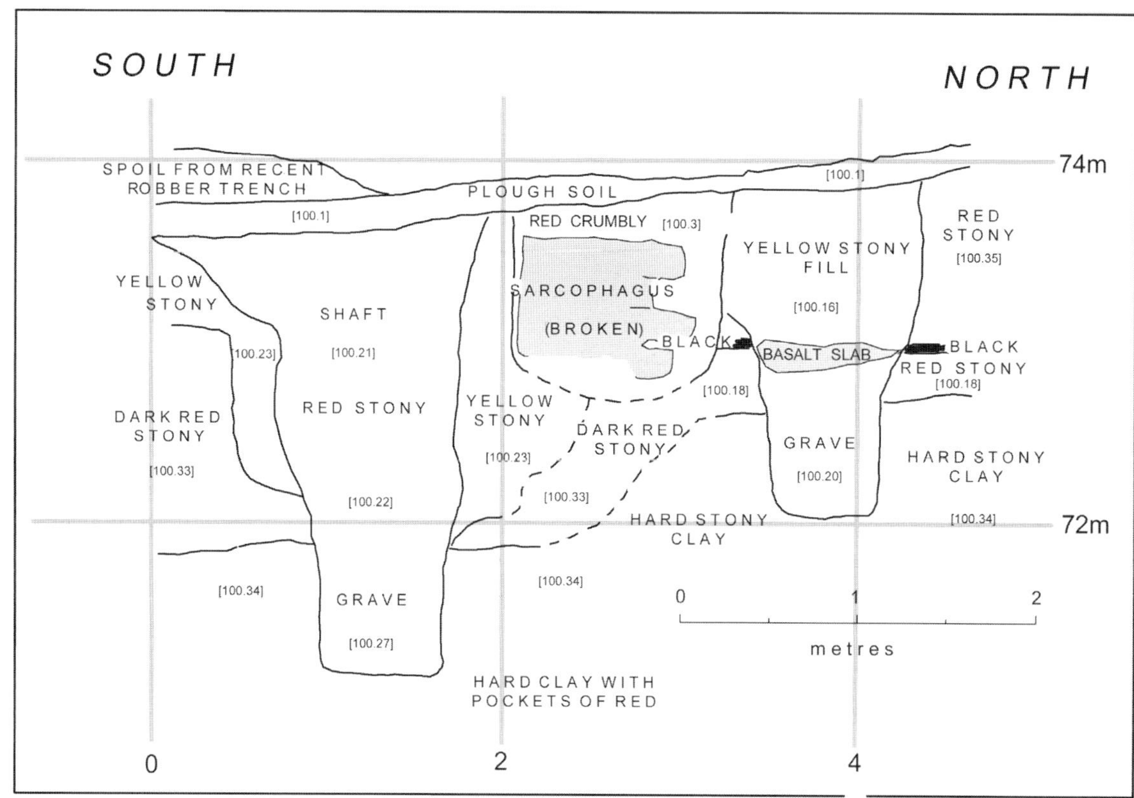

Fig. 9.5. Trench VI Section 2.

Fig. 9.6. Trench VI. Low earth mound forming the core of the embankment.

therefore no longer provide a *terminus post quem* for the construction of the embankment. It is regrettable that this was not appreciated when the comment quoted above was written; the error provides an excellent example of the dangers inherent in premature interim reports.

Fig. 9.7. Trench VI. Eastern scarp of ditch.

Geophysical survey

In 1978 a limited geophysical survey, using a combination of resistivity, magnetic susceptibility and very low frequency electromagnetic procedures, was conducted in the Enclosure (see Fig. 9.1). Two small grids, 20 m × 30 m and 20 m × 20 m respectively, were laid out close to Trench VI and a third (20 m × 10 m) further east, next to the modern track on the western edge of the Lower Tell, where lines of stone walling were visible on the surface and where excavation later revealed Hellenistic and Roman remains (Trench X, reported elsewhere). In addition, a number of traverses across the western embankment and ditch were made, some near and parallel to Trench VI and others further north, just beyond the point where surface indications of the western ditch disappeared. Three traverses were made across the line of the southern ditch on either side of the point where it joins the flood plain of the Muqadiyah. Since a brief report on similar geophysical work at the neighbouring prehistoric site of Arjoune, with a discussion of the methodology, instrumentation and problems encountered, has already been published (Hackmann 2003), these technical details are not repeated here. Suffice it to say that although much useful information concerning the use and value of these

methodologies in arid environments was obtained, the actual archaeological results of the work at Tell Nebi Mend were, except in one respect, limited. Anomalies in the data recorded from the grids near Trench VI revealed no coherent patterns and were clearly no more than a reflection of the underlying natural morphology. As for the traverses, those near Trench VI added no significant information to that already retrieved from the excavations, while those further north merely confirmed the continuation of the ditch in that direction, as already suspected. However, the traverses across the southern ditch do provide information which, although incomplete and inconclusive, is valuable in that it permits tentative speculation regarding the question of how the builders of the fortification managed its crossing of the Muqadiyah flood plain and whether the ditch was intended to be a water-filled 'moat' or a dry 'fosse' (to use the terminology suggested by Burke 2008, 56–9). The information comes from the resistivity readings from these traverses, T1 and T2, shown in Fig. 9.14. Traverse T2 crossed the ditch where it was (at least in 1977) clearly visible on the ground, with its moist fill represented on the graph by low readings and the drier, harder land on either side represented by higher readings. (It should be stressed that these higher readings are not in themselves evidence for an embankment, for which there are no surface indications along this stretch of the southern ditch, but only for the greater resistivity of the underlying material.) In Traverse T1, which is sited on the flood plain on the projected axis of the ditch about 120 m further west, although the low resistivity readings representing the soft moist soil near the river are longer bounded on the south by high readings, they are on the north, presumably indicating the presence here of some underlying feature of high resistivity, invisible on the surface. Whether this is a natural feature or an artificial barrier of some sort, either to prevent the use of the flood plain as an entry to the Enclosure from the south or to divert water from the ditch – if this were a real 'moat' – into the Muqadiyah, or for some other purpose, is not likely to be known without further investigation in the field.

Commentary

The Tell Nebi Mend Enclosure comprises, in its present form, a flattish area of about 40 ha situated to the south and west of the ancient city (or cities) represented today by the Main and Lower Mounds (see Fig. 1.1). It is protected by a ditch some 40 m wide but of unknown depth with, immediately adjacent to it on its inner side, an earthen embankment about 18 m wide and 4 m high, though perhaps higher at the corner, as at Sefinet en-Nuh. There is no berm between ditch and embankment, which are connected by a continuous slope, and there is no evidence of any wall or palisade which might once have existed. Similar artificial barriers to the north and east of the Main Mound are not known, either because they never existed, the Orontes and its flood plain being considered sufficient

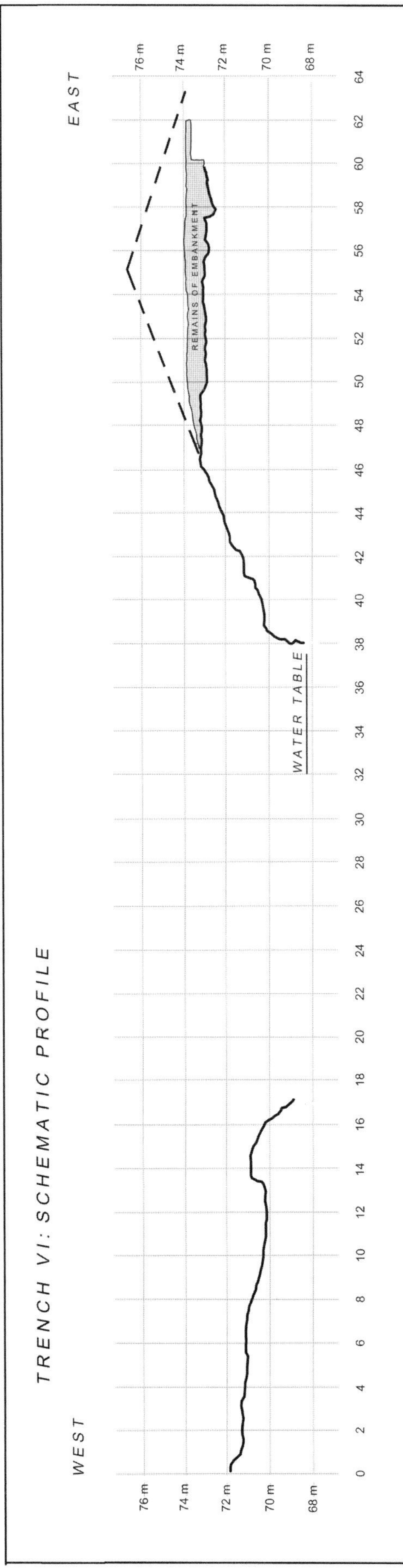

Fig. 9.8. Trench VI. Schematic profile across ditch and bank.

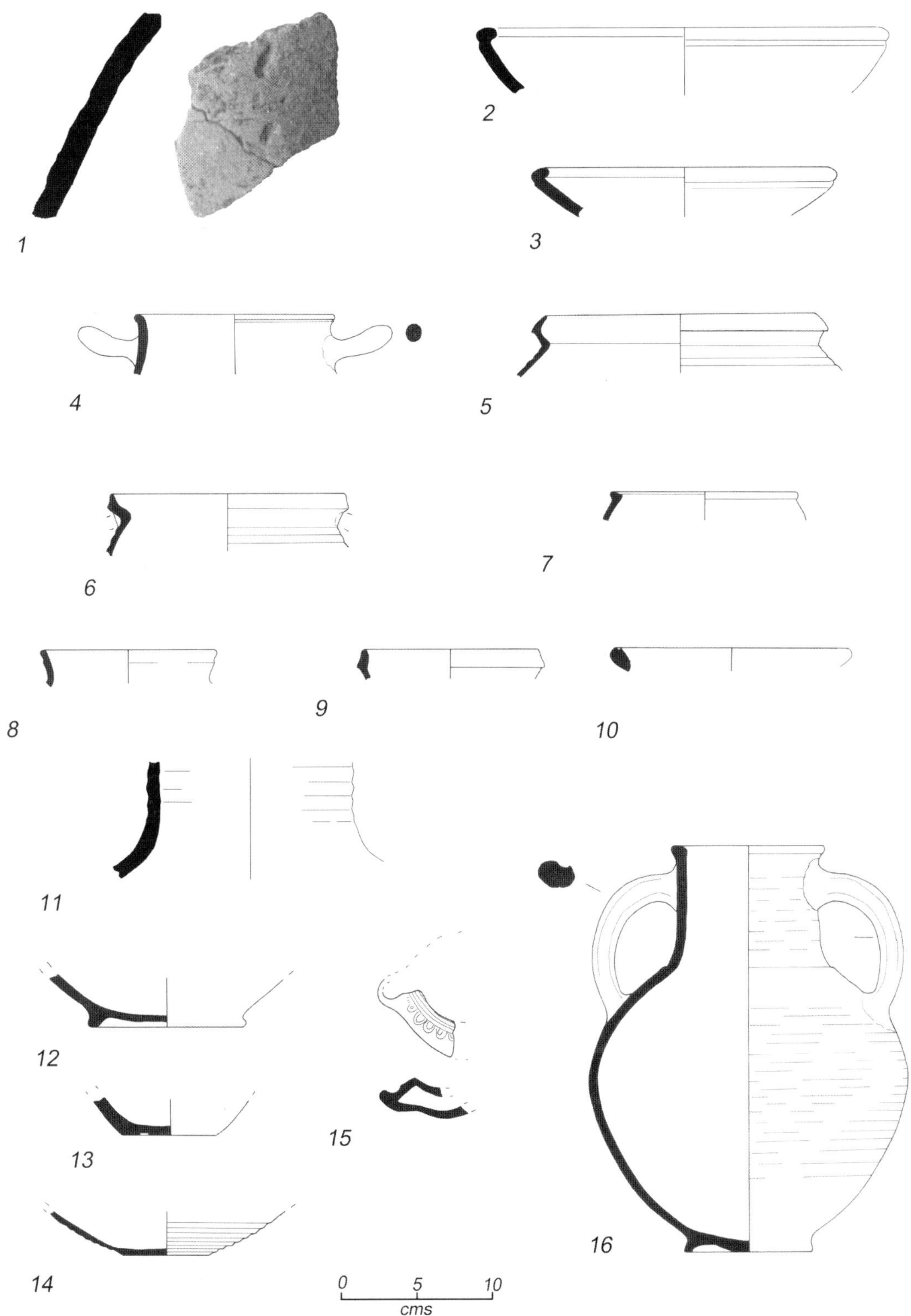

Fig. 9.9. Trench VI. Pottery. (See opposite page)

to fulfil the same functions, or because they did once exist but have been destroyed by human or natural activity. The presence today of standing water in the small part of the ditch excavated in Trench VI should not be taken as proof that it was originally intended to be filled with water, since the height of the water table will almost certainly have changed over the millennia. As for flowing water, Thomson's assumption that the southern ditch was dug to 'convey the water from one branch of the Orontes to the other' (Thomson 1848, 692) has been generally accepted,

1	Storage jar	Moderately to fairly finely levigated clay with many small brown grog (?), some white lime, and a few dark grey chert grits. Fired greenish buff throughout. Friable red-brown slip exterior only (but sherd is heavily eroded)	VI.102.4/4
2	Bowl	Fairly finely levigated clay with many small black basalt, small and medium white lime, and a few dark grey chert grits. Fired very dark grey to black at core and orangey brown at surfaces. Self slipped exterior and rim interior. Deep shallow groove below rim exterior	VI.100.21/1 and 100.25/4
3	Bowl	Very dark grey/black core, firing orange-brown; finely levigated with many small black basalt and small white lime grits; self slipped exterior rim interior	VI. 100.1a/1 and 100.25/1
4	Bowl	Terra Sigillata. Buff ware, well fired, hard; brick-red slip, highly burnished	VI.100.19/1
5	Small jar	No description	VI.100.5/3
6	Small jar	Thin, fairly hard, well fired, brick red	VI.100.22/1
7	Small jar	Thin, hard ware, brick-red, well fired, fine white grit. Ribbed outside	VI.100.27/1
8	Jar	Thin, fairly soft, grey ware, yellowish slip outside	VI.101.6/4
9	Jar	Thin buff ware	VI.101.6/3
10	Bowl?	Fairly thick, very soft cream ware	VI.101.6/5
11	Storage jar	Fairly thick, very hard ware, buff firing light red.fine grey and white grits; ribbed outside	VI.100.1a/2 and 100.4/2
12	Small jar	No description	VI.102.5/1
13	Small jar	No description	VI.101.6/6
14	Small jar	Thin, hard, red ware, with fine grey and white grits. Fine regular ribbing	VI.100.8/2
15	Lamp	Cream ware	VI.100.25/5
16	Jar	Buff ware, fairly soft, body and neck slightly ribbed	VI.100.21 [Reg. No. 0134]

and Mesnil du Buisson (1935–38, 911) also felt confident in asserting that the western part of the ditch was 'très certainement' filled with water by the Muqadiyah, despite Pézard's sensible observation that the right-angled junction of the ditches at the south-western corner might indicate that it was not a 'canal proprement dit' (Pézard 1922, 112; 1931, 24). But for the sake of accuracy it should be said that there is no actual evidence on the ground that the ditch did in fact reach the Orontes and thus directly connect the two rivers; it may simply have been intended to provide a barrier of marshy land, similar to the natural flood plains, to the south of the city. If the two water courses were ever actually connected (as the Egyptian reliefs certainly suggest and all commentators assume) an equally – perhaps more – suitable route for the link would have been the narrow constriction between the two halves of the Lower Mound about 250 m north of the existing ditch.

Excluding the Main and Lower Mounds and any land north of the Main Mound which may possibly also have been enclosed, the approximate area of the Enclosure is 40 ha – that is, about four times the size of the Main Mound. Over this area there are no surface indications of settled occupation, apart from an occasional scatter of Roman and Byzantine sherds, some of them clearly associated with disturbed burials but others, on slight rises in the terrain, possibly marking small isolated buildings. There is, however, evidence for ancient occupation on both the northern and southern parts of the Lower Mound, and this has to be considered before the date and purpose of

Fig. 9.10. Trench VI. Remains of wooden coffin.

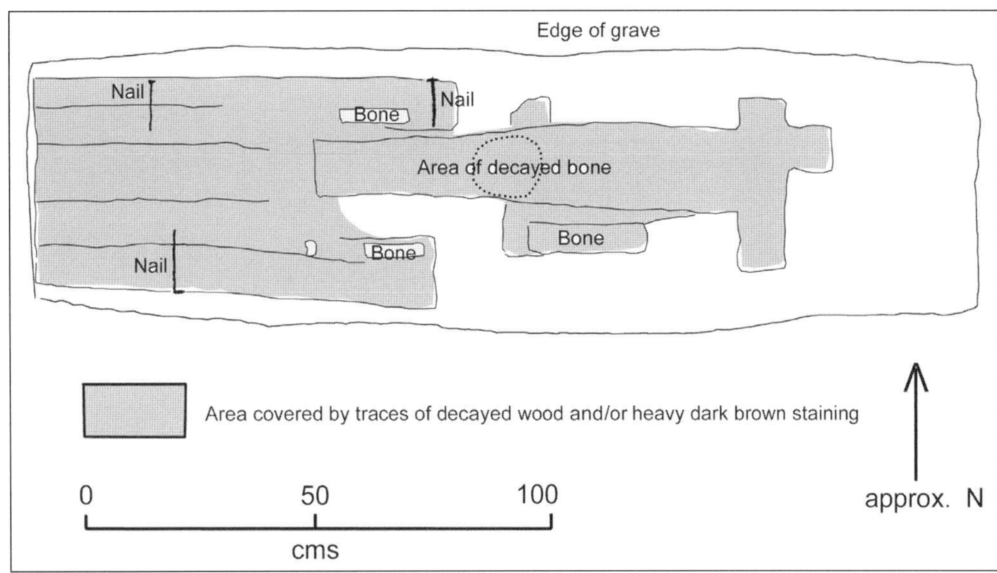

Fig. 9.11. Trench VI. Plan of grave with coffin.

Fig. 9.12. Trench IX from west.

the Enclosure itself are discussed. The northern, higher, part is covered today with the detritus of Hellenistic and Roman Laodicea – architectural fragments, roofing and building tiles, potsherds and so on – and nothing earlier, even where the surface has been considerably disturbed by recent agricultural and animal activities, although the presence of earlier structures beneath the classical remains obviously cannot be ruled out. Only in the basal levels on natural rock in a small sounding (Trench X; see Fig. 1.18) were a few prehistoric (Neolithic/ Chalcolithic) sherds retrieved (this Trench will be published elsewhere). As for the southern, less elevated, part of the Lower Mound, it was here that, during the course of the London excavations, the construction of the modern village provided ample opportunity to observe the natural marlstone at no great depth beneath the modern surface, with the foundations and lower walls of Late Roman/Byzantine buildings directly upon it; there was no evidence of earlier occupation. (An attempt made to excavate one of these buildings had to be abandoned, as noted in Chapter 1.)

What was its date and purpose? Much has been written about the function of such large 'fortified' areas adjacent to settlements, in the Levant and elsewhere, with suggestions including camps of the Hyksos (or, as was mentioned above, the Sea Peoples), depots, instruments of social cohesion, demonstrations of urban or tribal superiority, royal vanity or simply new living space to relieve the pressure on an overcrowded acropolis. In the book already cited Burke presents an extensive review of these theories which will not be repeated here, where the purpose is simply to comment on the structure at Tell Nebi Mend. In doing so we must emphasise, first, that we may be dealing with only the surviving part of a structure and that this does not necessarily accurately reflect its original purpose or purposes; and, secondly, that the date of the structure is still not known, the evidence from the excavations presented above showing only that it could not have been erected before the early 2nd millennium BC and that the embankments were being used as a cemetery in the 4th century AD, thus indicating that it had fallen or was falling into disuse as a fortification. Although it is tempting to see the Enclosure as a Middle or Late Bronze Age monument, as are, undoubtedly, many similar structures in the Levant, this cannot simply be assumed. It is relevant to note that there are other periods in the history of Tell Nebi Mend when works additional to conventional town walls may well have been thought necessary, as, for example, in the 1st

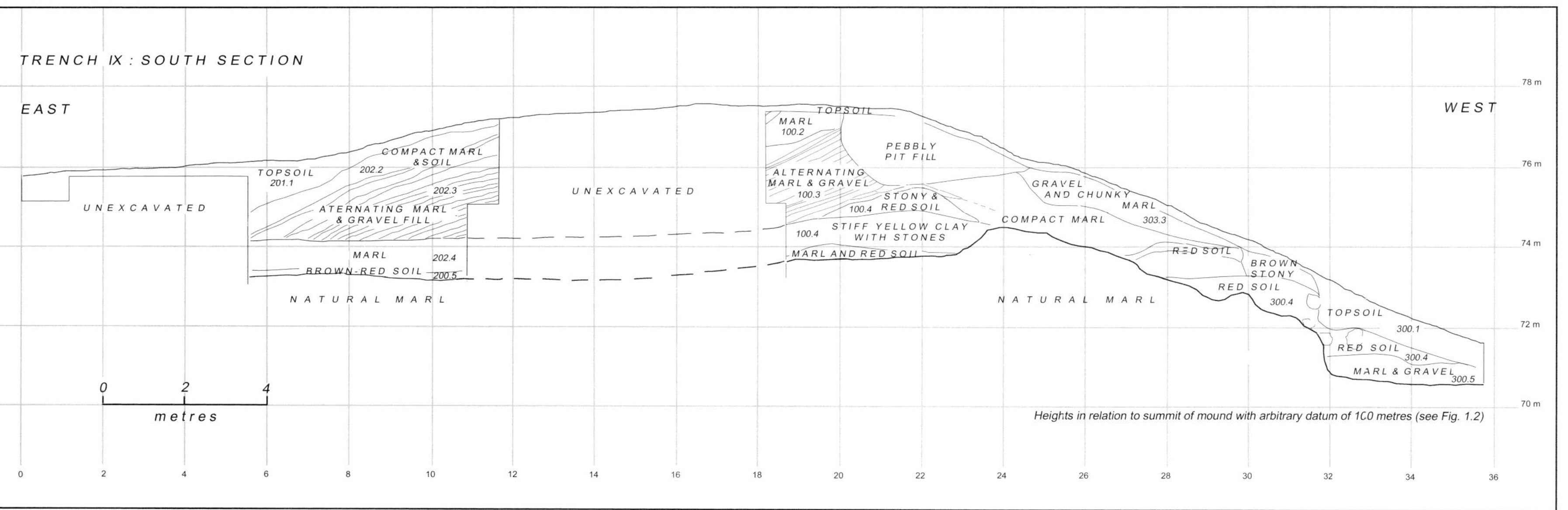

Fig. 9.13. Trench IX South Section.

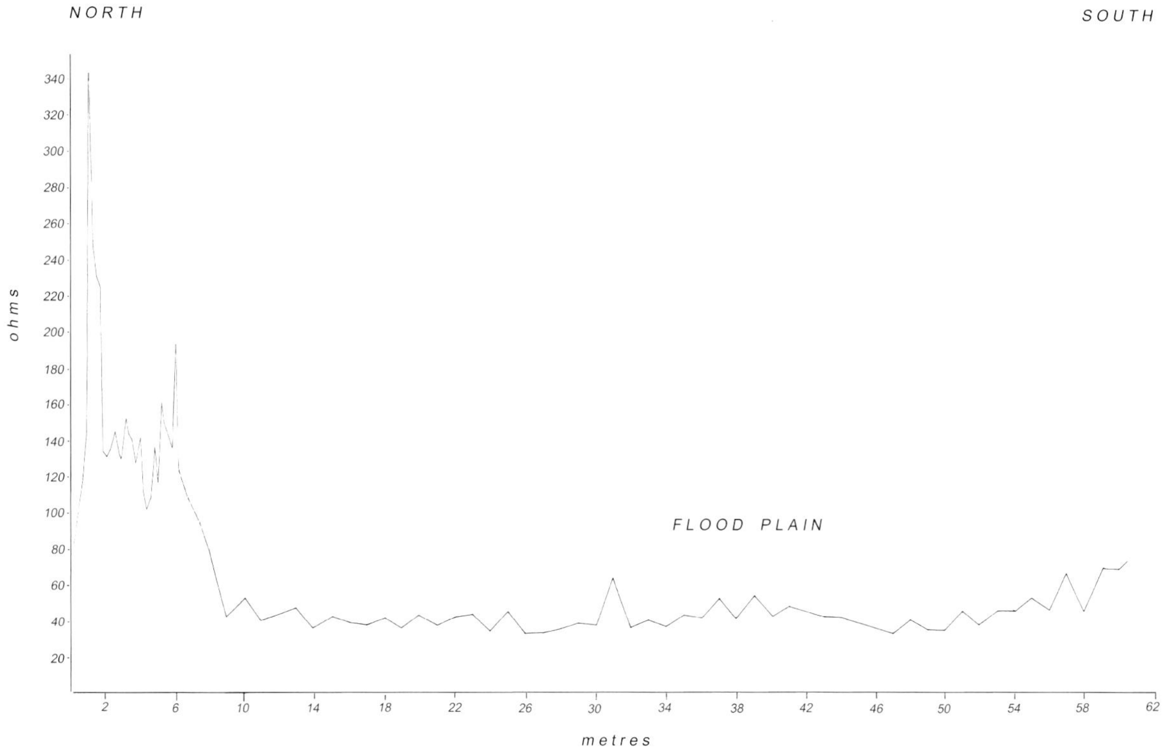

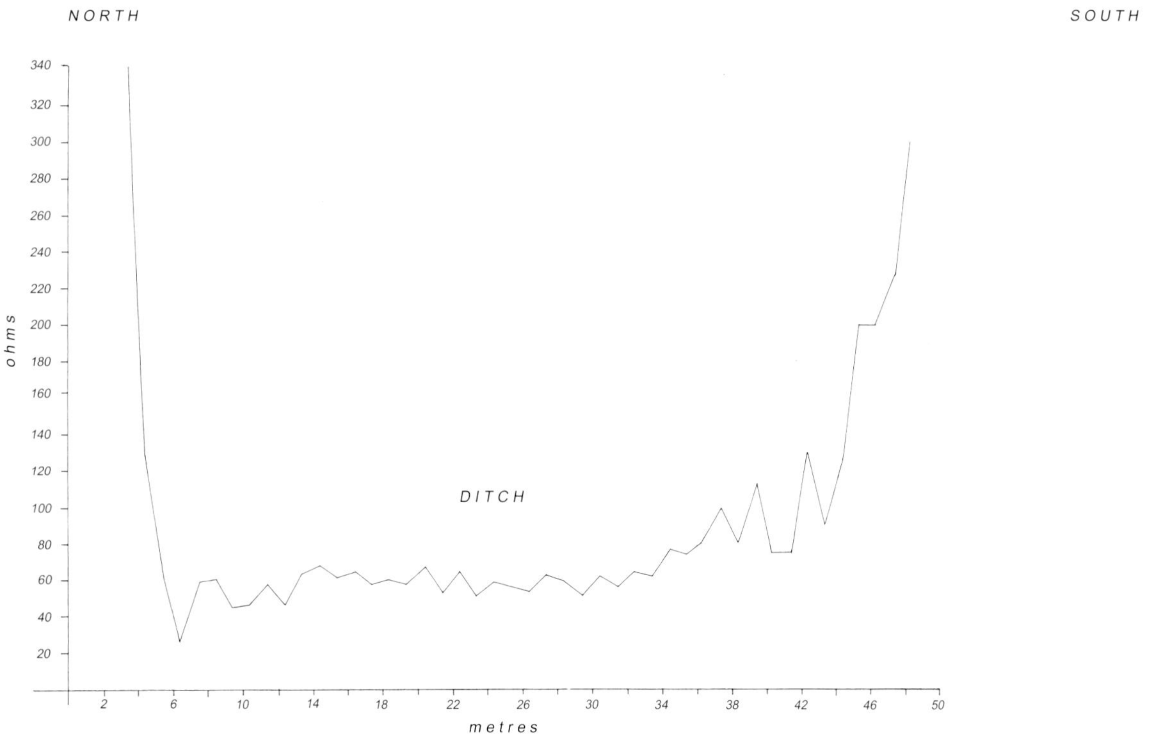

Fig. 9.14. Traverses T1 and T2. Resistivity readings.

millennium, when the site was an Assyrian military base, in the Hellenistic period, when it was the chief town of the strategic Seleucid district of Laodicene, or even later.

The prominence given in the Egyptian battle reliefs (see Fig. 1.5 b–c) to the aquatic encirclement of the city has understandably encouraged commentators to think of the Tell Nebi Mend ditch – and with it, necessarily, the accompanying embankment – regardless of date as, primarily, a military feature. But it has to be remembered that from at least as early as the first quarter of the 2nd millennium the town was also provided with conventional town walls, high on the crest of its mound and separate from any water, which are clearly shown not only in the scenes of Ramesses' battle but also in the representation of the capture of the city by Seti I a generation earlier – where, incidentally, there are no indications of a river or ditch (see Fig. 1.5 a). Furthermore, the texts accompanying the reliefs of the battle do not suggest that water obstacles, natural or artificial, played much of a role in the proceedings: they are not reported as having prevented or seriously hindered the movement of the Hittite army from the east to the west of the city, and feature in the story only when the Hittites are in retreat.

There is, of course, ample evidence that natural river courses were often utilised in the fortification systems of Bronze and Iron Age towns throughout the Near East, both to augment or, where the terrain was suitable, to replace conventional defences. There are also many examples of fortified extensions, circular or rectilinear, being added to earlier settlements. But although the inhabitants of Tell Nebi Mend were therefore not remarkable in following these practices, those who were responsible for constructing the Enclosure do seem to have been unusual, if not unique, in including within it at least one – we do not know about the other – of the natural watercourses, the Muqadiyah. We must remember that we are not at present fully cognisant of the flow regime of the Orontes

in antiquity but it is possible that a time came when although it continued to provide adequate protection to the eastern side of the city, the Muqadiyah did not to the western, and that the Enclosure ditch was built to replace it, an interpretation at which Pézard seemed to be hinting in his words quoted above. The opportunity could then have been taken to strengthen the southern defences of the city by digging the southern ditch as well. Moreover, it is surely not irrelevant that when the Muqadiyah was incorporated into the Enclosure so also was a considerable area of its flood plain: about half the area enclosed falls below the local 70 m contour, less than 2 m above the level of the river. Although this low land would probably have provided an additional barrier to hostile forces in times of war, it is possible that the protection of this nearby valuable agricultural resource would also have been a factor in the decision to extend the outskirts of the city. Foreign armies were not the only things from which settled communities needed protection: in peace time also bands of marauding humans and predatory wild beasts (which in the vicinity of Tell Nebi Mend would have included bears and possibly elephants) would have been a constant threat, and would have to be deterred from ravaging crops and stealing herds.

Although a firm date for the construction of the Tell Nebi Mend Enclosure has yet to be established, the work carried out here has thrown new light on its structure and its relationship to pre-existing natural features, and has thus provided important material for the continuing discussion concerning the purpose, or purposes, of similar structures throughout the Levant.

Note

1. I am indebted to Dr David Bridgland of the Department of Geography, University of Durham, for helpful advice on this problem.

Bibliography

Abdul-Hak, S. (1950) Les fouilles de la Direction Générale des Antiquités dans la Nécropole de Tell Nebi Mind. *Les Annales Archéologiques de Syrie* 1, 121–6.

Ahlström, G. W. (1993) *The History of Ancient Palestine*. Sheffield, Academic Press.

Akkermans, P. M. M. G. (1984) Archäologische Geländebegehung im Balik-Tal. *Archiv für Orientforschung* 31, 187–91.

Akkermans, P. M. M. G. (1990) *Villages in the Steppe: Later Neolithic Settlement and Subsistence in the Balikh Valley, Northern Syria*. Amsterdam, University of Amsterdam Press.

Akkermans, P. M. M. G. and Schwartz, G. M. (2003) *The Archaeology of Syria: From Complex Hunter-Gatherers to Early Urban Societies (ca. 16,000–300 BC)*. Cambridge, Cambridge University Press.

Albright, W. F. (1922) Palestine in the Earliest Historical Period. *Journal of the Palestine Oriental Society* 2, 110–38.

Albright, W. F. and Dougherty, R. D. (1926) From Jerusalem to Baghdad. *Bulletin of the American Schools of Oriental Research* 21, 1–21.

Anezaki, T. and Yano, S. (1998) The faunal remains. In Tsuneki, A., Hydar, J., Miyake, Y., Akahane, S., Akimura, M., Nishiyama, S., Sha'baan, H., Anezaki, T. and Yano, S. Second preliminary report of the excavations at Tell el-Kerkh, Northwestern Syria. *Bulletin of the Ancient Orient Museum* 29, 26–8.

Arnaud, D. (1985–87) *Emar VI: Textes sumériens et accadiens*. Paris.

Aurenche, O. and Kozlowski, K. (1999) *La Naissance du Néolithique au Proche Orient ou le paradis perdu*. Paris, Éditions Errance.

Aurenche, O. and Kozlowski, K. (2005) *Territories, Boundaries and Cultures in the Neolithic Near East*. British Archaeological Reports International Series 1362. Oxford, BAR.

Azoury, I. and Bergman, C. (1980) The Halafian lithic assemblage of Shams ed-Din Tanira. *Berytus* 27, 127–43.

Baker, J. and Brothwell, D. (1980) *Animal Diseases in Archaeology*. London, Academic Press.

Balty, J. and Zakzouk, A. (1970) Un chantier de recherches archéologiques Belges en Syrie: Apamée sur l'Oronte. *Textes et Documents* 255, 18–24.

Barnett, R. D. (1982) *Ancient Ivories in the Middle East and Adjacent Countries*. (*Qedem* 14). Jerusalem, Hebrew University.

Bartl, K. and Nieuwenhuyse, O. (2008) Reliefverzierte Keramik des Neolithikums aus Shir, West Syrien. *Fundstellen: Gesamte Schriften zur Archäologie und Geschichte Altvorderasiens,ad honorem Hartmut Kühne*. 9–16. Wiesbaden, Harassowitz.

Bartl, K., Haidar, A. and Nieuwenhuyse, O. (2006a) Shir: a Neolithic site in the Middle Orontes Region, Syria. *Neo-Lithics* 1/06, 23–7.

Bartl, K., Hijazi, A. and Haidar, A. (2006b) The Late Neolithic site of Shir; Preliminary Report of the German/Syrian Cooperation Project 2006. *Neo-Lithics* 2/06, 15–18.

Bell, G. (1907) *Syria. The Desert and the Sown*. London, Heinemann.

Bergman, C. and Newcomer, M. (1983) Flint Arrowhead Breakage: Examples from Ksar Akil, Lebanon. *Journal of Field Archaeology* 10, 231–43.

Bettles, E. A. (1994) Neolithic Pottery from the Syrian Sites of Tell Nebi Mend and Arjoune – A Comparative Analysis. MA dissertation, Institute of Archaeology, University College London.

Binford, L. R. (1978) *Nunamiut Ethnoarchaeology*. New York, Academic Press.

Binford, L. R. (1981) *Bones: Ancient Men and Modern Myths*. London, Academic Press.

Binford, L. R. and Bertram, J. B. (1977) Bone frequencies and attritional processes. In Binford, L. R. (ed.), *For Theory Building in Archaeology*. 77–153. London, Academic Press.

Boardman, S. and Jones, G. (1990) Experiments on the effects of charring on cereal plant components. *Journal of Archaeological Science* 17, 1–11.

Boessneck, J. (1969) Osteological differences between sheep (*Ovis aries* Linné) and goats (*Capra hircus* Linné). In Brothwell, D. and Higgs, E. S. (eds), *Science in Archaeology*, 2nd edn. 331–58. London, Thames and Hudson.

Boessneck, J. (1987) Tierknochenfunde vom Uch Tepe. *Acta Praehistorica et Archaeologica* 19, 131–63.

Boessneck, J., von den Driesch, A. and Ziegler, R. (1989) Die Tierreste von Maadi und Wadi Digla. In Rizkana, I. and Seeher, J. (eds.) *Maadi III*, 87–128. Mainz, Philipp von Zabern.

Bökönyi, S. (1977) *Animal Remains from the Kermanshah Valley, Iran*. British Archaeological Reports International Series 34. Oxford, BAR.

Bouchud, J. (1987) La faune du gisement Natoufien de Mallaha (Eynan) Israel. *Mémoires et Travaux du Centre de Recherche Français de Jérusalem* 4, 157–78.

Bourke, S. J. (1993) The Transition from the Middle to the Late Bronze Age in Syria: the Evidence from Tell Nebi Mend. *Levant* 25, 155–95.

Bradbury, J. N. (2011) Landscapes of Burial? The Homs Basalt, Syria in the 4th–3rd millennia BC. PhD Durham University (available online at http://etheses.dur.ac.uk/725/ Accessed February 2014).

Braidwood, R. and Braidwood, L. (1940) Report on Two Sondages on the Coast of Syria South of Tartous. *Syria* 21, 183–336.

Braidwood, R. and Braidwood, L. (1960) *Excavations in the Plain of Antioch*. Chicago, Oriental Institute Publications 61.

Breasted, J. H. (1903) *The Battle of Kadesh*. Chicago, University of Chicago Press.

Bridgland, D. R. , Philip, G., Westaway, R. and White, M. (2003) A long Quarternary terrace sequence in the Orontes valley, Syria: a record of uplift and human occupation. *Current Science* 84/8, 1080–89.

Brossé, L. (1923) La digue du lac de Homs. *Syria* 4, 234–40.

Brothwell, D. R. (1981) *Digging up Bones*. London and Oxford, British Museum (Natural History) and Oxford University Press.

Broman Morales, V. (1983) Jarmo figurines and other clay objects. In Braidwood, L. S., Braidwood, R. J., Howe, B., Reed, C. A. and Watson, P. J. (eds), *Prehistoric Archaeology along the Zagros Flanks*. 349–423. Chicago, Oriental Institute Publications 105.

Broman Morales, V. (1990) *Figurines and Other Clay Objects from Sarab and Çayönü*. Chicago, Oriental Institute Communications 25.

Buckingham, J. S. (1825) *Travels Among the Arab tribes Inhabiting the Countries East of Syria and Palestine*. London.

Buitenhuis, H. (1985) Preliminary report on the faunal remains of Hayaz Hüyük from the 1979–1983 seasons. *Anatolica* 12, 61–74.

Buitenhuis, H. (1988) *Archeolozoölogisch Onderzoek Langs de Midden-Eufraat*. Groningen, Biologish-Archaeologisch Institut.

Buitenhuis, H. (1991) Some Equid remains from South Turkey, North Syria and Jordan. In Meadow, R. H. and Uerpmann, H.-P. (eds), *Equids in the Ancient World*. 34–74. Beihefte zum Tübinger Atlas des Vorderen Orients. Reihe A (Naturwissenschaften) 19/2. Wiesbaden, Reichert.

Buitenhuis, H. (1997) Asikli Höyük: a 'protodomestic' site. In Kokabi, M. and Wahl, J. (eds), Proceedings of the 7th International Council for Archaeozoology Conference, *Anthropozoologica* 25/6, 655–62.

Buitenhuis, H. and Caneva, I. (1998) Early animal breeding in South-Eastern Anatolia: Mersin-Yumuktepe. In Anreiter, P. *et al.* (eds), *Man and the Animal World: Studies In Archaeozoology, Archaeology, Anthropology and Palaeolinguistics, in Memoriam Sándor Bökönyi*. 121–30. Budapest, Archaeolingua.

Bullock, D. and Rackham, J. (1982) Epiphysial fusion and tooth eruption of feral goats from Moffatdale, Dumfries and Galloway, Scotland. In Wilson, B., Grigson, C. and Payne, S. (eds), *Ageing and Sexing Animal Bones from Archaeological Sites*. 73–80. British Archaeological Reports British Series 109. Oxford, BAR.

Burke, A. A. (2008) *Walled Up to Heaven: The Evolution of Middle Bronze Age Fortification Strategies in the Levant*. Studies in the Archaeology and History of the Levant 4. Winona Lake IN, Eisenbrauns.

Burnham, H. B. (1965) Çatal Hüyük – The Textiles and Twined Fabrics. *Anatolian Studies* 15, 169–74.

Burton, R. F. and Drake, C. F. T. (1872) *Unexplored Syria*. London, Tinsley.

Calley, S. (1988) Some questions concerning Upsilon blades. *Anatolica* 15, 87–92.

Calvet, Y. and Geyer, B. (1992) *Barrages Antiques de Syrie*. Paris, Collection de la Maison de l'Orient Méditerranéen 21.

Campbell, E. F. (2002) *Shechem III. The Stratigraphy and Architecture of Shechem/Tell Balâṭah. 1 Text*. Boston, American Schools of Oriental Research.

Cauvin, J. (1968) Les Outillages Néolithiques de Byblos et du Littoral Libanaise. In Dunand, M. (ed.) *Fouilles de Byblos IV*. Paris, Maisonneuve.

Cauvin, J. (1978) *Les premiers villages de Syrie-Palestine du IXe au VIIe millennaire av. JC*. Lyon, Collections de la Maison de l'Orient Méditerranéen Ancien 4, Série archéologique 3.

Cauvin, M.-C. (1973) Problems d'emmanchement des faucilles de Proche Orient: les documents de Tell Assouad (Djezireh, Syrie). *Paléorient* 1, 103–8.

Cavallo, C. (2000) Animals in the steppe. A zooarchaeological analysis of Later Neolithic Tel Sabi Abyad, Syria. Thesis University of Amsterdam.

Charpin, D. (1998) Toponymie amorrite et toponymie biblique: La ville de Sîbat/Sobah. *Revue d'Assyriologie et d'Archéologie Orientale* 92: 79–92.

Clason, A. T. (1979/80) The animal remains from Tell es-Sinn compared with those from Bouqras. *Anatolica* 7, 35–53.

Clutton-Brock, J. (1981) *Domesticated Animals from Early Times*. London, Heinemann and British Museum (Natural History).

Clutton-Brock, J. (1985) Mammalian remains from Tell Molla Asad, Syria. In Sanlaville, P. (ed.), *Holocene Settlement in North Syria*. 163–5. British Archaeological Reports International Series 238. Oxford, BAR.

Clutton-Brock, J. (1986) Osteology of the equids from Sumer. In Meadow, R. H. and Uerpmann, H-P. (eds), *Equids in the Ancient World*. 207–29. Beihefte zum Tübinger Atlas des Vorderen Orients. Reihe A (Naturwissenschaften) 19/1. Wiesbaden, Reichert.

Clutton-Brock, J., Dennis-Bryan, K., Armitage, P. L. and Jewell, P. A. (1990) Osteology of the Soay sheep. *Bulletin British Museum Natural History (Zoology)* 56/1, 1–56.

Clutton-Brock, J. *et al.* (2000) Faunal evidence. In Oates, D., Oates, J. and McDonald, H. (eds), *Excavations at Tell Brak. Volume 2. Report on the 3rd Millennium B.C. material*. 327–50. Cambridge, McDonald Institute.

Cohen, G. (2006) *The Hellenistic Settlements in Syria, the Red Sea Basin and North Africa*. Berkeley, University of California Press.

Collon, D., Otte, C., Otte, M. and Zaqzouq, A. (1975) *Sondages au flanc sud du tell de Qalat el-Mudiq 1970, 1972, 1973 – Fouilles d'Apamée de Syrie: Miscellanea*, Fasc 11. Brussels, Centre Belge de Recherches Archéologiques à Apamée de Syrie.

Conder, C. R. (1881a) Kadesh. *Palestine Exploration Fund Quarterly Statement*, 163–75.

Conder, C. R. (1881b) Kadesh of the Hittites. *Palestine Exploration Fund Survey of Western Palestine, Special Papers*, 135–48. (Identical with Conder 1881a except for the omission of a sketch plan of the area around the Lake of Homs.)

Conder, C. R. (1885) *Heth and Moab. Explorations in Syria in 1881 and 1882*. New edition. London, Richard Bentley.

Contenson, H. de (1971) Tell Ramad, a village of Syria of the 7th and 6th millennia BC. *Archaeology* 24, 278–85.

Contenson, H. de (1977) Le Néolithique de Ras Shamra V d'après les Campagnes de 1972–1976 dans le Sondage SH. *Syria* 54, 1–23.

Contenson, H. de (1992) *Préhistoire de Ras Shamra: Les Sondages Stratigraphiques, 1955–1976*. Paris, Éditions Recherche sur les Civilisations.

Contenson, H. de (2000) *Ramad, site néolithique en Damascène (Syrie) aux VIIIe et VIIe millénaires avant l'ère chrétienne*. Beyrouth, Institut Français de l'Archéologie du Proche-Orient.

Contenson, H. de and Courtois, C. C. (1979) Vases en chaux: à-propos des recherches sur leur fabrication et leur origine. *Paléorient* 5, 177–82.

Contenson, H. de and Van Lière, W. J. (1964) Sondages à Tell Ramad en 1963: rapport préliminaire. *Annales Archéologiques Arabes Syriennes* 14, 109–24.

Contenson, H. de and Van Lière, W. J. (1966) Sondages à Tell Ramad en 1965: rapport préliminaire. *Annales Archéologiques Arabes Syriennes* 16, 167–74.

Copeland, L. (1969) Neolithic Village Sites in the South Beqaᶜ, Lebanon. *Mélanges de l'Université Saint-Joseph de Beyrouth* 45, 83–114.

Copeland, L. (1996) The Flint and Obsidian Industries. In Akkermans, P. M. M. G. (ed.), *Tell Sabi Abyad I: The Late Neolithic Settlement*. 285–339. Istanbul, Nederlands Historisch-Archeologisch Instituut.

Copeland, L. (2000) The flint and obsidian industries. In Verhoeven, M. and Akkermans, P. M. M. G. (eds), *Tell Sabi Abyad II: the pre-pottery B settlement. Report on the Excavations of the National Museum of Antiquities, Leiden, in the Balikh Valley, Syria*. 51–90. Istambul, Nederlands Historisch-Archeologisch Instituut.

Copeland, L. (2003) The Lithic Industries. In Parr, P. J. (ed.), *Excavations at Arjoune, Syria*. 71–151. British Archaeological Reports International Series 1134. Oxford, BAR.

Copeland, L. and Verhoeven, M. (1997) Bitumen-coated sickle blade elements at Tell Sabi Abyad II, Northern Syria. In Kozlowski, S. K. and Gebel, H. G. (eds), *Neolithic Chipped Stone Industries of the Fertile Crescent and their contemporaries in adjacent regions*. 327–30. Warsaw, Studies in Early Near Eastern Production, Subsistence and Environment 3.

Copeland, L. and Wescombe, P. (1965) Inventory of Stone Age Sites in Lebanon, Part I. *Mélanges de l'Université Saint-Joseph de Beyrouth* 41 (fasc. 2).

Copeland, L. and Wescombe, P. (1966) Inventory of Stone Age Sites in Lebanon, Part II. *Mélanges de l'Université Saint-Joseph de Beyrouth* 42 (fasc. 1).

Courbin, P. (1988) *What is Archaeology?* trans. from the French by Paul Bahn. Chicago, Chicago University Press.

Courtois, L. (1992) Examen microscopique pétrographique de poteries néolithiques de Ras Shamra V et IV. In Contenson, H. de (1992), 209–22.

Davis, S. J. M. (1982) Climatic change and the advent of domestication: the succession of ruminant artiodactyls in the Late Pleistocene-Holocene in the Israel regions. *Paléorient* 8, 5–15.

Davis, S. J. M. (1985) A preliminary report of the fauna from Hatoula. In Lechevallier, M. and Ronen, A. (eds), *Le Site Natoufien-Khiamien de Hatoula, pres de Latroun, Israël*. Jerusalem, Centre de Recherche Français.

Davis, S. J. M. (1991) When and why did prehistoric people domesticate animals? Some evidence from Israel and Cyprus. In Bar-Yosef, O. and Valla, F. (eds), *The Natufian Culture in the Levant*. 381–90. Ann Arbor, International Monographs in Prehistory, Archaeology Series 1.

Davis, S. J. M. (1994) The animal remains: new light on the origin of animal husbandry. In Lechevallier, M. and Ronen, A. (eds), *Le Gisement de Hatoula en Judeé Occidentale, Israël*. 83–132. Paris: Association Paléorient.

Degerbøl, M. and Fredskild, J. (1970) The Urus (*Bos primigenius Bojanus*) and Neolithic Domesticated Cattle (*Bos taurus domesticus* Linné) in Denmark. *Kongelige Danske Videnskabernes Selskab Biologiske Skrifter* 17, 1–177.

Delehaye, H. (1923) *Les saints stylites*. Brussels, Picard.

Deniz, E. and Payne, S. (1982) Eruption and wear in the mandibular dentition as a guide to ageing in Turkish Angora goats. In Wilson, B., Grigson, C. and Payne, S. (eds), *Ageing and Sexing Animal Bones from Archaeological Sites*. 155–205. British Archaeological Reports British Series 109. Oxford, BAR.

Dobney, K., Ervynck, A., Albarell, U. and Rowley-Conwy, P. (2007) The transition from wild boar to domestic pig in Eurasia, illustrated by a tooth development defect and biometrical data. In Alabella, U., Dobney, K., Ervynck, A. and Rowley-Conwy, P. (eds), *Pigs and Humans 10,000 Years of Interaction*. 57–82. Oxford, Oxford University Press.

Dorrell, P. (2003) The Environmental Setting. In Parr, P. J. (ed.), *Excavations at Arjoune, Syria*. 5–10. British Archaeological Reports International Series 1134. Oxford, BAR.

Drower, M. S. (1971) Syria before 2200 B.C. *Cambridge Ancient History*, 3rd edn, Vol. I, Part 2, Chapter XVII. Cambridge, Cambridge University Press.

Ducos, P. (1975) A new find of an equid metatarsal bone from Tell Mureybet in Syria and its relevance to the identification of equids from the Early Holocene of the Levant. *Journal of Archaeological Science* 2, 71–3.

Ducos, P. (1978) *Tell-Mureybet (Syrie, IX–VII millénaires) étude archéozoologique et problèmes d'écologie humaine*. Lyon, Centre National de Recherche Scientifique.

Ducos, P. (1983) La contribution de l'archéozoologie à l'éstimation des quantités de nourriture: évaluation du nombre d'individus. In Clutton-Brock, J. and Grigson, C. (eds), *Animals and Archaeology: 3. Early Herders and their Flocks*. British Archaeological Reports International Series 202. Oxford, BAR.

Ducos, P. (1986) The equid of Tell Muraibit. In Meadow, R. H. and Uerpmann, H.-P. (eds), *Equids in the Ancient World*. 237–45. Beihefte zum Tübinger Atlas des Vorderen Orients. Reihe A (Naturwissenschaften) 19/1. Wiesbaden, Reichert.

Ducos, P. (1993) Proto-élevage et élevage au Levant Sud au VIIe millénaire B.C., les données de la Damascène. *Paléorient* 19, 153–73.

Ducos, P. (2000) Quelques donnés sur l'élevage à Ramad à partir d'une première etude du materiel archézoologique. In Contenson, H. de (ed.) *Ramad: site néolithique en Damascène (Syrie) aux VIIIe et VIIe millénaires avant l'ère chrétien*. 275–82. Beirut, Institut français d'archéologie du Proch-Orient.

Dunand, M. (1973) *Fouilles de Byblos V: L'Architecture, les tombes, le matériel domestique, dès les origines néolithiques à l'avènement urbain*. Paris, Adrien Maisonneuve.

Dussaud, R. (1927) *Topographie historique de la Syrie antique et médiéval*. Paris, Geuthner.

Epstein, C. (1963) That Wretched Enemy of Kadesh. *Journal of Near Eastern Studies* 22, 242–6.

Epstein, C. (1985) Laden animal figurines from the Chalcolithic period in Palestine. *Bulletin of the American Schools of Oriental Research* 258, 53–62.

Ervynck, A., Dobney, K., Hongo, H. and Meadow, R. (2001) Born free? New evidence for the status of *Sus scrofa* at Neolithic Çayönü Tepesi. *Paléorient* 27, 47–73.

Flannery, K. V. (1983) Early pig domestication in the fertile crescent: a retrospective look. In Young, T. C., Smith, P. L. E. and Mortensen, P. (eds), *The Hilly Flanks. Essays on the Prehistory of Southwestern Asia*. 163–87. Chicago, Studies in Oriental Civilization 36.

Fujii, S., Akazawa, T., Nishiaki, Y. and Wada, H. (1987) *Thaniyyet Wuker, a Pre-Pottery Neolithic B site on the lacustrine terrace of Paleo-Palmyra lake*. Tokyo, University Museum.

Garfinkel, Y. (1992) *The Pottery Assemblages of Sha'ar Hagolan and Rabat Stages from Munhata (Israel)*. Paris, Cahiers du Centre de Recherche Français de Jérusalem 6.

Garfinkel, Y. (1999a) *Neolithic and Chalcolithic Pottery of the Southern Levant. (Qedem 39)*. Jerusalem, Hebrew University Institute of Archaeology.

Garfinkel, Y. (1999b) Radiometric Dates from Eighth Millennium BP Israel. *Bulletin of the American Schools of Oriental Research* 315, 1–13.

Garfinkel, Y. and Miller, M. (2001) *Sha'ar Hagolan*. Oxford, Oxbow.

Garrard, A., Colledge, S., Hunt, C. and Montague, R. (1988) Environment and subsistence during the Late Pleistocene and Early Holocene in the Azraq Basin. *Paléorient* 14, 40–9.

Gautier, A. (1984) How do I count you, let me count the ways? Problems of archaeozoological quantification. In Grigson, C. and Clutton-Brock, J. (eds), *Animals and Archaeology: Husbandry in Europe*. 237–51. British Archaeological Reports International Series 227. Oxford, BAR.

Gautier, J.-E. (1895) Note sur les Fouilles Entreprises dans la Haute Vallée de l'Oronte. *Comptes Rendus de l'Académie des Inscriptions et Belles-Lettres* 39/5, 441–64.

Grainger, J. D. (1990) *The Cities of Seleukid Syria*. Oxford, Clarendon Press.

Grant, C. P. (1937) *The Syrian Desert*. London, A. & C. Black.

Green, J. (1736) *A Journey from Aleppo to Damascus, with a Description of those two Capital Cities and the Neighbouring Parts of Syria*. London, W. Mears.

Grigson, C. (1969) The uses and limitations of differences in absolute size in the distinctions between the bones of aurochs (*Bos primigenius*) and domestic cattle (*Bos taurus*). In Ucko, P. and Dimbleby, G. W. (eds), *The Domestication and Exploitation of Plants and Animals*. 227–94. London, Duckworth.

Grigson, C. (1978) The craniology and relationships of four species of *Bos* IV. The relationship between *Bos primigenius* Boj. and *Bos taurus* L. and its implications for the phylogeny of the domestic breeds. *Journal of Archaeological Science* 5, 123–52.

Grigson, C. (1987) Shiqmim: pastoralism and other aspects of animal management in the Chalcolithic of the Northern Negev.

In Levy, T. E. (ed.), *Shiqmim I*. 219–41 and 535–46. British Archaeological Reports International Series 356. Oxford, BAR.

Grigson, C. (1989) Size and sex – morphometric evidence for the domestication of cattle in the Near East. In Milles, A., Williams, D. and Gardner, N. (eds), *The Beginnings of Agriculture*. 77–109. British Archaeological Reports International Series, 496. Oxford, BAR.

Grigson, C. (1993) The earliest domestic horses in the Levant? New finds from the fourth millennium of the Negev. *Journal of Archaeological Science* 20, 645–55.

Grigson, C. (2003) Animal husbandry in the Late Neolithic and Chalcolithic at Arjoune: the secondary products revolution revisited. In Parr, P. J. (ed.), *Excavations at Arjoune, Syria*. 187–240. British Archaeological Reports International Series 1134. Oxford, BAR.

Grigson, C. (2007) Culture, ecology and pigs from the fifth to the third millennium around the fertile crescent. In Umberto Alella, U., Dobney, K., Ervynck, A. and Rowley-Conwy, P. (eds.) *Pigs and Humans: 10,000 Years of Interaction*. Oxford, Clarendon Press.

Groves, C. P. and Harrison, D. L. (1967) The taxonomy of the gazelles (genus Gazella) of Arabia. *Journal of Zoology, London* 152, 381–7.

Haber, A. and Dayan, T. (2004) Analyzing the process of domestication, Hagoshrim as a case study. *Journal of Archaeological Science* 11, 1587–601.

Hackmann, J. T. (2003) The Resistivity Survey. In Parr, P. J. (ed.), *Excavations at Arjoune, Syria*. 23–5. British Archaeological Reports International Series 1134. Oxford, Archaeopress.

Haïdar-Boustani, M., Ibáñez, J. J., Al-Maqdissi, M., Armendáriz, A., Urquijo, J. G. and Teira, L. (2003–04) Prospections Archéologiques à l'Ouest de la Ville de Homs: Rapport Préliminaire Campagne 2004. *Tempora. Annales d'Histoire et d'Archéologie. Université St.-Joseph, Beyrouth* 14–15, 59–90.

Haïdar-Boustani, M., Ibáñez, J. J., Al-Maqdissi, M., Armendáriz, A., Urquijo, J. G. and Teira, L. (2005–06) Prospections Archéologiques à l'Ouest de la Ville de Homs: Rapport Préliminaire Campagne 2005. *Tempora. Annales d'Histoire et d'Archéologie. Université St.-Joseph, Beyrouth* 16–17, 9–38.

Haidar-Boustani, M., Ibanez, J., al-Maqdissi, M., Armendariz, A., Oruijo, J. and Teira, L. (2007) New Data on the Epipalaeolithic and Neolithic of the Homs Gap: Three Campaigns of Archaeological Survey (2004–2006). *Neo-Lithics* 1/07, 3–9.

Healy, M. (1993) *Qadesh 1300BC. Clash of the Warrior Kings*. London, Osprey.

Hecker, H. (1975) *The Faunal Analysis of the Primary Food Animals from Pre-Pottery Neolithic Beidha (Jordan)*. Ann Arbor, MI and London, University Microfilms International.

Helbaek, H. (1962) Les graines carbonisés de la 48ème couche de fouilles de Tell Sukas. *Annales Archéologiques Arabes Syriennes* 11–12, 185–6.

Helbaek, H. (1963) Textiles from Çatal Hüyük. *Archaeology* 16, 39–46.

Helck, W. (1971) *Die Beziehungen Ägyptens zu Vorderasien im 3. u. 2 Jahrtausend v. Chr.* Wiesbaden, Harrassowitz.

Helmer, D. (1985a) Étude préliminaire de la faune de Cafer Hoyuk (Malatya, Turquie). *Cahiers de l'Euphrate* 4, 117–20.

Helmer, D. (1985b) Étude de la faune de Tell Assouad (Djézireh, Syrie). *Cahiers de l'Euphrate* 4, 275–86.

Helmer, D. (1988) Les animaux de Cafer et des sites preceramiques du Sud-Est de la Turquie. Essai de synthese. *Anatolica* 15, 37–48.

Helmer, D. (2000) Étude de la faune mammalienne d'El Kowm 2 (Syrie) In Stordeur, D. (ed.), *El Kowm 2. Une île dans le desert. La fin du Néolithique précéramique dans le steppe syrienne.* Paris, Centre National de la Recherche Scientifique.

Hesse, B. (1978) *Evidence for Husbandry from the Early Neolithic Site of Ganj Daereh in Western Iran.* Ann Arbor and London, University Microfilms International.

Hesse, B. (1982) Slaughter patterns and domestication: the beginnings of pastoralism in western Iran. *Man (N.S.)* 17, 403–17.

Hillman, G. (1981) Reconstructing crop husbandry practices from the charred remains of crops. In Mercer, R. J. (ed.), *Farming Practice in British Prehistory.* 123–62. Edinburgh, Edinburgh University Press.

Hillman, G. (1984a) Traditional husbandry and processing of archaic cereals in recent times: the operations, products and equipment which might feature in Sumerian texts. Part I: The glume wheats. *Bulletin on Sumerian Agriculture* 1, 114–52.

Hillman, G. (1984b) Interpretation of archaeological plant remains: the application of ethnographic models from Turkey. In van Zeist, W. and Casparie, W. A. (eds), *Plants and Ancient Man: Studies in Palaeoethnobotany.* 1–41. Rotterdam, Balkema.

Hilzheimer, M. (1941) *Animal Remains from Tell Asmar.* Oriental Institute of the University of Chicago, Studies in Ancient Oriental Civilization 20.

Hodges, H. (1981) *Artifacts: an introduction to early materials and technology.* Atlantic Highlands NJ and London, Humanities Press and John Baker.

Hole, F. (1959) A Reanalysis of Basal Tabbat el-Hammam, Syria. *Syria* 36, 149–83.

Hole, F. (1994) Khabur Basin PPN and Early PN Industries. In Gebel, H. G. and Koslowski, S. L. (eds), *Neolithic Chipped Stone Industries of the Fertile Crescent.* 341–7. Warsaw, Studies in Early Near Eastern Production, Subsistence and Environment 1.

Hole, F., Flannery, K. and Neely, J. (1969) *Prehistory and Human Ecology of the Deh Luran Plain.* Ann Arbor, Memoirs of the Museum of Anthropology 1.

Hongo, H. (1996) Faunal remains from Tell Aray 2, Northwestern Syria. *Paléorient* 22/1, 125–44.

Hongo, H. and Meadow, R. H. (2000) Faunal remains from prepottery Neolithic levels at Çayönü, Southeastern Turkey: a preliminary report focusing on pigs (*Sus* sp.). In Mashkour, M., Choyke, A. M., Buitenhius, H. and Poplin, F. (eds), *Archaeozoology of the Near East IVA.* 121–63. Groningen, Archaeological Research and Consultancy Publication 32.

Horwitz, L. K. (1987) Faunal remains. In Braun, E. (ed.), *Yiftah'el. Salvage and Rescue Excavations at a prehistoric village in Lower Galilee, Israel.* 155–72. Israel Antiquities Authority Report 2.

Horwitz, L. K. (1993) A reassessment of caprovine domestication in the Levantine Neolithic. In Hershkovitz, I. (ed.), *People and Culture in Change.* 53–181. British Archaeological Reports International Series 508. Oxford, BAR.

Horwitz, L. K. (2001) The mammalian fauna. In Eisenberg, E. *et al.* (eds), *Tel Te'o: a Neolithic, Chalcolithic and Early Bronze Age site in the Hula Valley I.* 171–94. Israel Archaeological Authority Report 13.

Horwitz, L. K. (2003) Temporal and spatial variation in Neolithic caprine exploitation strategies: a case study of fauna from Yiftah'el (Israel). *Paléorient* 29/1, 19–58.

Hours, F. (1969) Saayideh et le néolithique pré-poterie au Liban. *Mélanges de l'Université Saint-Joseph de Beyrouth* 45, 29–42.

Hours, F., Aurenche, O., Cauvin, J., Cauvin, M.-C., Copeland, L. and Sanlaville, P. (1994) *Atlas des Sites du Proche Orient (14000–5700 B.P.).* Travaux de la Maison de l'Orient Méditerranéen 24. Lyon and Paris, Boccard.

Iwasaki, T. and Tsuneki, A. (eds) (2003) *Archaeology of the Rouj Basin – A Regional Study of the Transition from Village to City in Northwest Syria. Vol. 1: Al-Shark 2.* Studies for West Asian Archaeology 2. University of Tsukuba.

Iwasaki, T., Nishino, H. and Tsuneki, A. (1995) The Prehistory of the Rouj Basin, Northwest Syria: a Preliminary Report. *Anatolica* 21, 143–87.

Jacomet, S. (1987) *Prähistorische Getreidefunde. Eine Anleitung zur Bestimmung prähistorischer Gersten- und Weizenfunde.* Basel.

Joanne, A. and Isambert, É. (1861) *Itinéraire descriptive, historique et archéologique de l'Orient.* Paris, Hachette.

Jones, A. H. M. (1937) *Cities of the Eastern Roman Provinces.* Oxford, Clarendon Press.

Jones, G. (1981) Crop processing at Assiros Toumba: a taphonomic study. *Zeitschrift für Archäologie* 15, 105–11.

Jones, G. (1984) Interpretation of archaeological plant remains: ethnographic models from Greece. In van Zeist, W. and Casparie, W. A. (eds), *Plants and Ancient Man: Studies in Palaeoethnobotany.* 43–61. Rotterdam, Balkema.

Jones, G. (1987) A statistical approach to the archaeological identification of crop processing. *Journal of Archaeological Science* 14, 311–23.

Kafafi, Z. (1988) A Pottery Neolithic Village in Jordan. In Garrard, H. and Gebel, H. (eds), *The Prehistory of Jordan* I. 451–71. British Archaeological Reports International Series 396. Oxford, BAR.

Kafafi, Z. (1989) Late Neolithic Pottery from ᶜAin er-Rahub, Jordan. *Zeitschrift des Deutschen Palästina-Vereins* 105, 1–17.

Kafafi, Z. (1993) The Yarmukian in Jordan. *Paléorient* 19/1, 101–14.

Kafafi, Z. (2001) *Jebel Abu Thawwab (Er-Rumman), Central Jordan: Late Neolithic and Early Bronze Age.* Berlin, Ex Oriente.

Kaplan, J. (1958a) Excavations at Teluliot Batashi in the Vale of Sorek. *Eretz Israel* 5, 9–24 (English summary 83*).

Kaplan, J. (1958b) Kefar Giladi. *Israel Exploration Journal* 8, 274.

Kaplan, J. (1966) Kefar Giladi. *Israel Exploration Journal* 16, 272–3.

Kaplan, J. (1977) Neolithic and Chalcolithic Remains at Lod. *Eretz Israel* 13, 57–75 (English summary 291 2*).

Kenyon, K. M. (1955) Preliminary Report on the Jericho Excavations. *Palestine Exploration Quarterly*, 81–96.

Kenyon, K. M. (1971a) Syria and Palestine c.2160–1780. The Archaeological Sites. *Cambridge Ancient History*, 3rd edn, Vol. I, Part 2, Chapter XXI. Cambridge, Cambridge University Press.

Kenyon, K. M. (1971b) An Essay on Archaeological Technique: The Publication of Results from the Excavation of a Tell. *Harvard Theological Review* 64, 271–9.

Kenyon, K. M. (1981) *Excavations at Jericho.* Vol. III, ed. T. A. Holland. London, British School of Archaeology in Jerusalem.

Kenyon, K. M. and Holland, T. A. (1982) *Excavations at Jericho Vol IV: The Pottery Type Series and Other Finds.* London, British School of Archaeology in Jerusalem and Oxford University Press.

Khalaily, H. and Kamaisky, E. (2002) The Use of Sickle Blades for Decorating Pottery in the Wadi Rabah Culture: The Case of Tel Dover. In van den Brink, E. C. M. and Yannai, E. (eds), *In Quest of Ancient Settlements and Landscapes: Archaeological Studies in Honour of Ram Gophna*. 57–64. Tel Aviv, Ramot Publishing.

Kirkbride, D. (1969) Early Byblos and the Beqaᶜ. *Mélanges de l'Université Saint- Joseph de Beyrouth* 45, 43–61.

Kirkbride, D. (1972) Umm Dabaghiyah, 1971 Preliminary Report. *Iraq* 34, 3–19.

Klengel, H. (1965–69) *Geschichte Syriens im 2. Jahrtausend v.u Z*. Vols 1 and 2. Berlin.

Koldewey, R. (1898) Die Arkitectur von Sendschirli. In *Ausgrabungen in Sendschirli II*. Berlin.

Kuhrt, A. (1995) *The Ancient Near East c.3000–330 BC*. London, Routledge.

Kuschke, A. (1979) Das Terrain der Schlacht bei Qadeš und die Anmarschwege Ramses' II. *Zeitschrift des Deutschen Palästina-Vereins* 95, 7–35.

Kuschke, A., Mittmann, S. and Müller, U. (1976) *Archäologischer Survey in der nördlichen Biqaᶜ. (Tübinger Atlas des Vorderen Orients Reihe B, 11)*. Wiesbaden, Reichert.

Kusutman, B. (1991) The Origins of Pig Domestication with Particular Reference to the Middle East. PhD dissertation University College London.

Lasota-Moskalewska, A. (1990) Preliminary archaeozoological investigation of animal remains from site Nemrik 9 in Iraq. In Kozlowski, S. K., *Nemrik 9 Pre-Pottery Neolithic site in Iraq*. 185–208. Warsaw, Uniwersyttetu Warszawskiego.

Lawrence, B. (1980) *Principal Food Animals at Çayönü*. British Archaeological Reports International Series 138. Oxford, BAR.

Le Mière, M. and Picon, M. (1999) Les débuts de la céramique au Proche-Orient. *Paléorient* 24/2, 5–26.

Le Quien, M. (1740) *Oriens christianus in quatuor patriarchatus digestus* II. Paris.

Legge, A. J. and Rowley-Conwy, P. A. (2000) The exploitation of animals. In Moore, A. M. T., Hillman, G. C. and Legge, A. J. (eds), *Village on the Euphrates: From Foraging to Farming at Abu Hureyra*. 423–71. Oxford, Oxford University Press.

Lempriere, J. (1827) *A Classical Dictionary*. 6th American edn. New York.

Lev-Tov, J. (2000) Late prehistoric faunal remains from new excavations at Tel Ali (northern Israel). In Mashkour, M., Choyke, A. M., Buitenhius, H. and Poplin, F. (eds), *Archaeozoology of the Near East IVA*. 208–15. Groningen, Archaeological Research and Consultancy Publication 32.

McArdle, J. E. (1974) A Numerical (Computerized) Method for Quantifying Zooarcheological Comparisons. MSc thesis University of Illinois.

Maréchal, C. (1982) Vaiselles blanches du Proche-Orient. *Cahiers de l'Euphrate* 3, 217–51.

Marfoe, L., Copeland, L. and Parr, P. J. (1981) Arjoune 1978: Preliminary investigations of a prehistoric site in the Homs Basin, Syria. *Levant* 13, 1–27.

Masuda, S. and Shu'ath, S. (1983) Qminas, the Neolithic site near Tell Deinit, Idlib (Preliminary report). *Annales Archéologiques Arabes Syriennes* 33, 199–230.

Mathias, V. T. and Parr, P. J. (1989) The Early Phases at Tell Nebi Mend: a preliminary account. *Levant* 21, 13–29.

Meadow, R. H. (1986) Some equid remains from Çayönü, Southeastern Turkey. In Meadow, R. H. and Uerpmann, H.- P. (eds), *Equids in the Ancient World*. 266–301.

Beihefte zum Tübinger Atlas des Vorderen Orients. Reihe A (Naturwissenschaften) 19/1. Wiesbaden, Reichert.

Meadow, R. H. and Uerpmann, H.- P. (eds) (1986) *Equids in the Ancient World*. Beihefte zum Tübinger Atlas des Vorderen Orients. Reihe A (Naturwissenschaften) 19/1. Wiesbaden, Reichert.

Meadow, R. H. and Uerpmann, H.-P. (eds) (1991) *Equids in the Ancient World*. Beihefte zum Tübinger Atlas des Vorderen Orients. Reihe A (Naturwissenschaften) 19/2. Wiesbaden, Reichert.

Mellaart, J. (1967) *Çatal Hüyük, A Neolithic Town in Anatolia*. London, Thames and Hudson.

Mellaart, J. (1981) The Prehistoric Pottery from the Neolithic to the Beginning of Early Bronze IV (c.7000–2500 BC). In Matthers, J. (ed.), *The River Qoueiq, Northern Syria, and Its Catchment*. British Archaeological Reports International Series 98. Oxford, BAR.

Mesnil du Buisson, R. (1929) Compte rendu sommaire d'une mission à Tell el-Yahoudié. *Bulletin du Institut Français d'Archéologie Orientale* 29, 155–78.

Mesnil du Buisson, R. (1935–38) Le site de Qadesh (Tell Nebi Mend). In *Mélanges Maspero. Mémoires Publiés par les Membres de l'Institut Français d'Archéologie Orientale du Caire* 66, 909–27.

Miles, A. E. W. and Grigson, C. (1990) *Colyer's Variations and Diseases of the Teeth of Animals*. Cambridge, Cambridge University Press.

Millard, A. (2010) The Cuneiform Tablets from Tell Nebi Mend. *Levant* 42, 226–36.

Moffett, L. (2003) Wild and cultivated food plants and the evidence for crop processing activities at Arjoune. In Parr, P. J. (ed.), *Excavations at Arjoune*. 241–9. British Archaeological Reports International Series 1134. Oxford, BAR.

Molist Montana, M. (1996) *Tell Halula (Siria): un yacimiento neolitico del valle medio del Eufrates: Campanas de 1992 y 1992*. Madrid, Ministero de Educacion y Cultura.

Molleson, T. (1989) Seed Preparation in the Mesolithic: the osteological evidence. *Antiquity* 63, 356–62.

Molleson, T. (1994) The eloquent bones of Abu Hureyra. *Scientific American* 271, 70–75.

Moore, A. M. T. (1981) North Syria in Neolithic 2. In Cauvin, J. and Sanlaville, P. (eds), *Préhistoire du Levant: chronologie et organisation de l'espace depuis les origines jusqu'au VIe millenaire*. 445–56. Paris, Éditions de CNRS.

Moore, A. M. T., Hillman, G. H. and Legge, A. J. (2000) *Village on the Euphrates: From Foraging to Farming at Abu Hureyra*. London, Oxford University Press.

Moore, D. M. (1982) *Flora Europaea Check-list and Chromosome Index*. Cambridge, Cambridge University Press.

Morandi Bonacossi, D. (ed.) (2007) *Urban and natural landscapes of an ancient Syrian capital. Settlement and environment at Tell Mishrifeh/Qatna and in central-western Syria*. Documents d'archéologie syrienne XII. Udine, Forum.

Mortensen, P. (n.d.) The chipped stone industries from Labweh and 'Ard Tlaili. Unpublished report.

Mouterde, R. and Poidebard, A. (1945) *Le Limes de Chalcis*. Paris, Geuthner.

Muheisen, M., Gebel, H. G., Hannss, G. and Neef, R. (1988) Excavations at 'Ain er-Rahub, a Final Natufian and Yarmoukian Site near Irbid, 1985. In Garrard, A. and Gebel, H. (eds), *The Prehistory of Jordan* I. 473–502. British Archaeological Reports International Series 396. Oxford, BAR.

Müller-Neuhof, B. (1998) A preliminary note on the Pottery Neolithic at Tell Hmaira, Lebanon. *Neo-Lithics* 3/98, 4–6.

Negahban, E. O. (1979) A Brief Report on the Painted Building of Zaghe. *Paléorient* 5, 239–50.

Nesbitt, M. and Samuel, D. (1996) From staple crop to extinction? The archaeology and history of the hulled wheats. In Padulosi, S., Hammer, K. and Heller, J. (eds), *Hulled wheats. Promoting the Conservation and Use of Underutilized and Neglected Crops 4. (Proceedings of the First International Workshop on Hulled Wheats, 21–22 July 1995, Castelvecchio Pascoli, Tuscany, Italy)*. 41–100. Rome, International Plant Genetic Resources Institute.

Nieuwenhuyse, O. P. (2009) The Late Neolithic Ceramics from Shir: A First Assessment. *Zeitschrift für Orientalische Archäologie* 2, 310–56.

Nieuwenhuyse, O. P., Akkermans, P. M. M. G. and Plicht, J. van der (2010) Not so coarse, nor always plain – the earliest pottery of Syria. *Antiquity* 84, 71–85.

Nieuwenhuyse, O. P., Bartl, K. and Berghuijs, K. (2012) The cord-impressed pottery from the late Neolithic Northern Levant: case-study Shir (Syria). *Paléorient* 38/1–2, 65–77.

Nishiaki, Y. (1992) Corner-thinned blades: a new obsidian tool-type from a Pottery Neolithic mound in the Khabur Basin, Syria. *Bulletin of the American Schools of Oriental Research* 328, 5–14.

Nishiaki, Y. (2000) *The Lithic Technology of Neolithic Syria*. British Archaeological Reports International Series 840. Oxford, BAR.

Oates, J. (1983) Review of Kenyon, K. M., Jericho III. *Antiquity* 57, 222–3.

Obeidat, D. (1995) *Die neolitische Keramik aus Abu Thawwab, Jordanien*. Studies in Early Near Eastern Production, Subsistence and Environment 2. Berlin, Ex Oriente.

Oded, B. (1964) Two Assyrian References to the Town of Qadesh on the Orontes. *Israel Exploration Journal* 14, 272–3.

Otte, M. (1976) Données nouvelles sur le néolithique d'Apamée (Sondage A4). *Annales Archéologiques Arabes Syriennes* 26, 101–18.

Parr, P. J. (1968) The Origin of the Rampart Fortifications of Middle Bronze Age Palestine and Syria. *Zeitschrift des deutschen Palästina-Vereins* 84, 18–45.

Parr, P. J. (1983) The Tell Nebi Mend Project. *Annales Archéologiques Arabes Syriennes* 33/2, 99–117.

Parr, P. J. (1991) The Investigation of Qadesh-on-the-Orontes. *Journal of the Ancient Chronology Forum* 4, 1–8.

Parr, P. J. (ed.) (2003) *Excavations at Arjoune, Syria*. British Archaeological Reports International Series 1134. Oxford, Archaeopress.

Parr, P. J. (ed.) (2009) *The Levant in Transition: Proceedings of a Conference held at the British Museum on 20–21 April 2004.(PEF Annual IX)*. Leeds, Maney Publishing.

Payne, S. (1973) Kill-off patterns in sheep and goats: the mandibles from Asvan Kale. *Anatolian Studies* 23, 281–303.

Payne, S. (1985) Animal remains from Asikli Höyük. *Anatolian Studies* 35, 109–22.

Payne, S. (1988) Animal bones from Tell Rubeidheh. In Killick, R. G. (ed.), *Tell Rubeidheh, an Uruk Village in the Jebel Hamrin*. 98–135. Iraq Archaeological Reports 2. Warminster, Aris & Phillips.

Payne, S. and Bull, G. (1988) Components of variation in measurements of pig bones and teeth, and the use of measurements to distinguish wild from domestic pig remains. *Archaeozoologia* 2, 27–66.

Peña, I., Castellana, P. and Fernandez, R. (1975) *Les Stylites Syriennes*. Milan, Publications du 'Studium Biblicum Fransciscanum' Collection Minor.

Peters, J., Helmer, D., von den Driesch, A. and Saña Segui, M. (1999) Early animal husbandry in the Northern Levant. *Paléorient* 25/2, 27–47.

Pézard, M. (1922) Mission archéologique à Tell Nebi Mend (1921): Rapport Sommaire. *Syria* 3, 89–115.

Pézard, M. (1931) *Qadesh. Mission Archéologique à Tell Nebi Mend 1921–1922*. Paris, Geuthner.

Philip, G. (2007) Natural and cultural aspects of the development of the marl landscape east of Lake Qatina during the Bronze and Iron Ages. In Morandi Bonacossi, D. (ed.), *Urban and Natural Landscapes of an Ancient Syrian Capital*. 218–26. Udine, Forum Editrice.

Philip, G. and Bradbury, J. (2010) Pre-Classical Activity in the Basalt Landscape of the Homs Region, Syria. *Levant* 42, 136–69.

Philip, G., Jabour, F., Beck, A., Bshesh, M., Grove, J., Kirk, A. and Millard, A. (2002) Settlement and Landscape Development in the Homs Region, Syria. Research Questions, Preliminary Results 1999–2000 and Future Potential. *Levant* 34, 1–23.

Philip, G., Abdulkarim, M., Newson, P., Beck, A., Bridgland, D., Bshesh, M., Shaw, A., Westaway, R. and Wilkinson, K. (2005) Settlement and Landscape Development in the Homs region, Syria: Report on Work Undertaken during 2001–2003. *Levant* 37, 21–42.

Pococke, R. (1745) *A Description of the East and Some other Countries*. London.

Ponikarov, V. P. (ed.) (1966) *The Geological Map of Syria. Sheets I-36-XVIII, I-37-XIII (Trablus, Homs)*. Damascus, Ministry of Industry.

Porter, J. L. (1854) Notes of a Tour from Damascus to Ba'albek and Hums. *Bibliotheca Sacra* 11, 649–93.

Porter, J. L. (1855) *Five Years in Damascus*. Vol. II. London, John Murray.

Porter, J. L. (1868) *A Handbook for Travellers in Syria and Palestine, Part II*. London, John Murray.

Pough, F. H. (1953) *A Field Guide to Rocks and Minerals*. Boston, Houghton Mifflin.

Poulain, T. (1978) Étude de la faune, de quelques restes humains et de coquillages provenant to Ras Shamra (sondages 1955 à 1960). In Schaeffer, C. F. A. (ed.), *Ugaritica VII*. 161–80. Paris, Geuthner.

Pritchard, J. B. (1955) *Ancient Near Eastern Texts*. Princeton, Princeton University Press.

Redding, R. W. and Rosenberg, M. (1998) Ancestral pigs: a New (Guinea) model for pig domestication in the Middle East. *Museum Applied Science Center for Archaeology Research Papers in Science and Archaeology* 15, 65–76.

Redford, D. B. (1992) *Egypt, Canaan, and Israel in Ancient Times*. Princeton, Princeton University Press.

Riis, P. J. and Thrane, H. (1974) *Sukas III: The Neolithic Periods*. Copenhagen, Publications of the Carlsberg Expedition to Phoenicia 3.

Robinson, E. (1847) Notes on Biblical Geography. *Bibliotheca Sacra* 4, 404 and 408.

Robinson, E., Smith, E. *et al.* (1856) *Later Biblical Researches in Palestine and the Adjacent Regions. A Journal of Travels in the Year 1852*. Boston, Crocker and Brewster.

Rollefson, G. (1993) Origins of the Yarmukian at ᶜAin Ghazal. *Paléorient* 19/1, 91–100.

Rollefson, G., Kafafi, Z. and Simmons, A. H. (1993) The Neolithic Village of ᶜAin Ghazal, Jordan: Preliminary Report on the 1989 Season. *Annual of the American Schools of Oriental Research* 51, 107–26.

Ronzevalle, S. (1911–21) Le camp retranché d'El-Mišrifé. *Mélanges de la Faculté Orientale, Université Saint-Joseph, Beyrouth* 7, 109–26.

Rowton, M. R. (1951) Jeremiah and the Death of Josiah. *Journal of Near Eastern Studies* 10, 128–9.

Russell, N., Martin, L. and Buitenhuis, H. (2005) Cattle domestication at Catalhöyük revisited. *Current Anthropology* 46 (Supplement), 101–8.

Ryder, M. L. (1965) Report of Textiles from Çatal Hüyük. *Anatolian Studies* 15, 175–6.

Sachau, E. (1883) *Reise in Syrien und Mesopotamien.* Leipzig.

Saña Segui, M. (1999) *Arqueología de la domesticación animal. La gestation de los recursos animals en Tell Halula (Valle del Éufrates-Siria) del 8800 al 7000 BP.* Treball d'Arqueologia del Próxim Orient, 1. Barcelona, Universidad Autonóma.

Sauvaget, J. (1940) Caravansérails Syriens du Moyen-Âge: II. Caravansérails Mamelouks. *Ars Islamica* 7, 1–19.

Schaeffer, C. F. A. (1948) *Stratigraphie Comparée et Chronologie de l'Asie Occidentale.* London, Oxford University Press.

Simmons, A., Kafafi, Z., Rollefson, G. O. and Moyer, K. (1989) Test Excavations at Wadi Shu'eib. *Annual of the Department of Antiquities of Jordan* 33, 27–42.

Simmons, A., Rollefson, G. O., Kafafi, Z., Mandel, R. D., al-Nahar, M., Cooper, J., Köhler-Rollefson, I. and Durand, K. R. (2001) Wadi Shu'eib, A Large Neolithic Community in Central Jordan: Final Report of Test Investigations. *Bulletin of the American School of Oriental Research* 321, 1–39.

Smith, J. G. (1952) The Matarrah Assemblage. *Journal of Near Eastern Studies* 11, 5–75.

Sofaer Derevenski, J. (2000) Sex Differences in Activity Related Osseous Change in the Spine and the Gendered Division of Labour at Ensay and Wharram Percy, UK. *American Journal of Physical Anthropology* 111/3, 333–54.

Stampfli, H. R. (1983) The fauna of Jarmo, with notes on animal bones from Matarrah, the ᶜAmuq and Karim Shahir. In Braidwood, L. S., Braidwood, R., Howe, B., Reed, C. A. and Watson, P. J. (eds), *Prehistoric Archaeology along the Zagros Flanks.* 629–47. Chicago, Oriental Institute Publication 105.

Stekelis, K. (1972) *The Yarmukian Culture of the Neolithic Period.* Jerusalem, Magness Press.

Tchernov, E., Dayan, T. and Yom-Tov, Y. (1986–87) The paleogeography of *Gazella gazella* and *Gazella dorcas* during the Holocene of the southern Levant. *Israel Journal of Zoology* 34, 51–9.

Theusen, I. and Riis, P. (1988) *Hama: Fouilles et Recherches I, 1931–1938. The Prehistoric and Proto-historic Periods.* Copenhagen, Carlsberg.

Thomson, W. M. (1848) Journey from Aleppo to Mount Lebanon. *Bibliotheca Sacra and Theological Review* 5, 663–700.

Thuesen, I. and Gwozdz, R. (1982) Lime Plaster in Neolithic Syria. A preliminary report. *Paléorient* 8/2, 99–104.

Thuesen, I. and Riis, P. (1988) *Hama: Fouilles et Recherches I, 1931–1938. The Prehistoric and Protohistoric Periods.* Copenhagen, Carlsberg.

Tomkins, H. G. (1888) The Campaign of Rameses II in his Fifth Year against Kadesh on Orontes. *Transactions of the Society for Biblical Archaeology* 7, 390–406.

Tsuneki, A., Hydar, J., Miyake, Y., Akahane, S., Nakamura, T., Akimura, S. and Sekine, S. (1997) First Preliminary Report of the Excavations at Tell el-Kerkh. *Bulletin of the Ancient Oriental Museum (Tokyo)* 18, 1–40.

Tsuneki, A., Hydar, J., Miyake, Y., Akahane, S., Akimura, M., Nishiyama, S., Sha'baan, H., Anezaki, T., and Yano, S. (1998) Second Preliminary Report of the Excavations at Tell el-Kerkh. *Bulletin of the Ancient Oriental Museum (Tokyo)* 19, 1–40.

Tsuneki, A., Arimura, M., Maeda, O., Tanno, K. and Anezaki, T. (2006) The Early PPNB in the North Levant: a new perspective from Tell Ain el-Kerkh. *Paléorient* 32/1, 47–72.

Tubb, J. N. and Dorrell, P. G. (forthcoming) Survey of the Area around Tell en-Nebi Mend.

Uerpmann, H.-P. (1979) *Probleme der Neolithisierung des Mittelmeeraums.* Wiesbaden, Reichert.

Uerpmann, H.-P. (1982) Faunal remains from Shams ed-Din Tanira, a Halafian site in northern Syria. *Berytus* 31, 3–52.

Uerpmann, H.-P. (1986) Halafian equid remains from Shams ed-Din Tannira in northern Syria. In Meadow, R. H. and Uerpmann, H.-P. (eds), *Equids in the Ancient World.* 246–65. Beihefte zum Tübinger Atlas des Vorderen Orients. Reihe A (Naturwissenschaften) 19/1. Wiesbaden, Reichert.

Uerpmann, H.-P. (1987) *The Ancient Distribution of Ungulate Mammals in the Middle East.* Beihefte zum Tübinger Atlas des Vorderen Orients. Reihe A (Naturwissenschaften) 27. Wiesbaden, Reichert.

Uerpmann, H.-P. (1991) *Equus africanus* in Arabia. In Meadow, R. H. and Uerpmann, H.-P. (eds), *Equids in the Ancient World.* 12–33. Beihefte zum Tübinger Atlas des Vorderen Orients. Reihe A (Naturwissenschaften) 19/2. Wiesbaden, Reichert.

Unger-Hamilton, R. (1988) *Method in Microwear Analysis: Prehistoric Sickles and other stone tools from Arjoune, Syria.* British Archaeological Reports International Series 435. Oxford, BAR.

Van der Veen, M. and Fieller, N. (1982) Sampling seeds. *Journal of Archaeological Science* 9, 287–98.

Van Zeist, W. and Bakker-Heeres, J. A. H. (1985) Archaeobotanical studies in the Levant 1: Neolithic sites in the Damascus Basin: Aswad, Ghoraifé, Ramad. *Palaeohistoria* 24, 165–256.

Verhoeven, M. (1997) The 1996 Excavations at Tell Sabi Abyad II, a later PPNB site in the Balikh Valley, Northern Syria. *Neolithics* 1/97, 1–3.

Von den Driesch, A. (1976) *A Guide to the Measurement of Animal Bones from Archaeological Sites.* Peabody Museum Bulletin 1.

Von den Driesch, A. and Amberger, G. (1981) Ein altbabylonisches Eselskelett vom Tell Ababra/Iraq. *Bonner Zoologische Beitrage* 32/1–2, 67–74.

Von den Driesch, A. and Peters, J. (1999) Vorläufer Bericht über die archäologischen Untersuchungen am Göbekli Tepe und am Gürcütepe bei Urfa, Turkei. *Istanbuler Mitteilungen* 49, 23–39.

Von den Driesch, A. and Wodtke, U. (1997) The fauna of 'Ain Ghazal, a major PPN and early PN settlement in central Jordan. In Gebel, H., Kafafi, Z. and Rollefson, G. O. (eds), *The Prehistory of Jordan II: Perspectives from 1997.* 511–56. Berlin, Ex Oriente.

von der Osten, H. H. (1956) *Die Grabung von Tell-es-Salihiyeh.* Skrifter Utgivna av Svenska Institutet I Athen 4°, IV. Lund: Gleerup.

Walpole, R. (1820) *Travels in Various Countries of the East.* London, Longman.

Weulersse, J. (1940) *L'Oronte; Étude de Fleuve.* Tours, Arrault.

Wirth, E. (1971) *Syrien. Eine Geographische Landeskunde.* Darmstadt, Wissenschaftliche Buchgesellschaft.

Wiseman, D. J. (1956) *Chronicles of Chaldean Kings.* London, British Museum.

Wright, G. R. H. (1968) Tell el-Yehudiyah and the Glacis. *Zeitschrift des deutschen Palästina-Vereins* 84, 1–17.

Yadin, Y. (1955) Hyksos Fortifications and the Battering Ram. *Bulletin of the American Schools of Oriental Research* 137, 23–32.

Yadin, Y. (1963) *The Art of Warfare in Biblical Lands in the Light of Archaeological Study*. Jerusalem.

Zarins, J. (1986) Equids associated with human burials in third millennium B.C. Mesopotamia: two complementary facets. In Meadow, R. H. and Uerpmann, H.-P. (eds), *Equids in the Ancient World*. 164–93. Beihefte zum Tübinger Atlas des Vorderen Orients. Reihe A (Naturwissenschaften) 19/1. Wiesbaden, Reichert.

Zeder, M. and Hesse, B. (2000) The initial domestication of goats (*Capra hircus*) in the Zagros Mountains 10,000 years ago. *Science* 287, 2254–7.

Zeuner, F. E. (1963) *A History of Domesticated Animals*. London, Hutchinson.

Zohary, D. and Hopf, M. (2000) *Domestication of Plants in the Old World: The Origin and Spread of Cultivated Plants in West Asia, Europe, and the Nile Valley*. 3rd edn. Oxford, Oxford University Press.

COLOUR PLATES

Plate 1.1. The tell from the north-east.

Plate 1.2. The tell from the west.

Plate 4.1. Selected sherds, to show range of surface treatments.

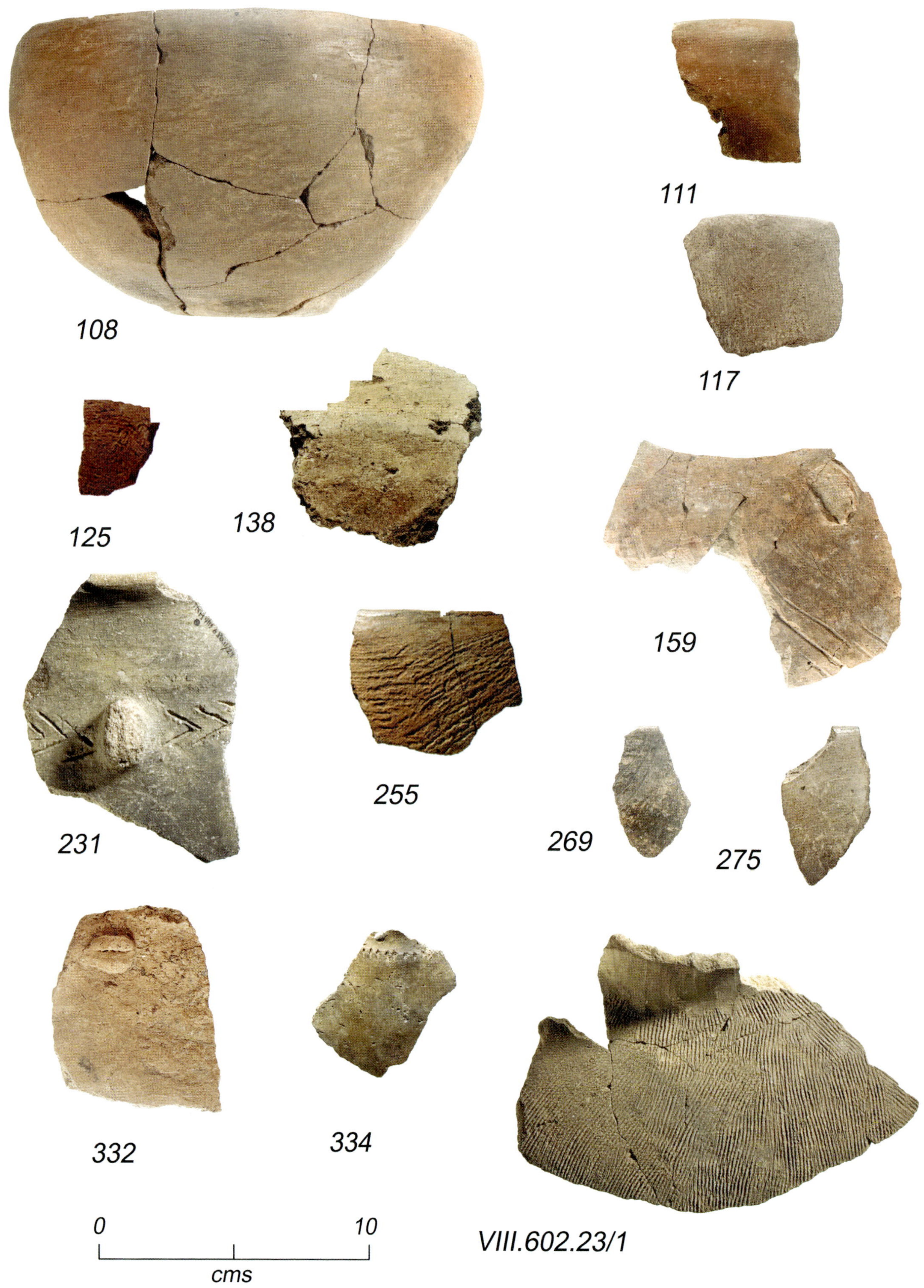

Plate 4.2. Selected sherds, to show range of surface treatments.